Goldie

Michigan Outlines

Subject-Matter Outlines for
the Non-MBE Essay Subjects Tested on
the Michigan Bar Examination

AmeriBar
Phone (800) 529-2651 • Fax (800) 529-2652

Michigan Outlines

Copyright 2011 AmeriBar

ISBN 1-44049-241-7

Table of Contents

- Complete outlines for MBE Subjects, which may also be tested on the essay exam, are not contained in this book.

STAR LEGEND

★★★★	4 Stars – Excellent chance of appearing on bar exam
★★★	3 Stars – Substantial chance of appearing on bar exam
★★	2 Stars – Very Good chance of appearing on bar exam
★	1 Star – Good chance of appearing on bar exam
	Everything Else – Fair Chance of appearing on bar exam

The outlines contained in this book are condensed outlines of legal issues that may appear on your examination. The star system is provided only to highlight important concepts.

INTRODUCTION

This book contains outlines designed to cover the substantive law that is likely to be tested on the essay portion of the Michigan Bar Examination. It does not include complete outlines for the subjects tested on the Multistate Bar Examination ("MBE"). It does include supplemental Michigan outlines for subjects tested on the MBE (Constitutional Law; Contracts; Criminal Law and Procedure; Evidence; Real Property; and Torts).

On the MBE, questions are to be answered according to general legal principles. With respect to preparing for the MBE, and answering MBE questions, you should use and rely on only your MBE outlines. On the essay portion of the Michigan Bar Exam, you should answer questions according to general legal principles and Michigan law (although note that Michigan law has not always been focused on in answers provided by the examiners). With respect to preparing for, and answering essay questions testing the MBE subjects, you should use and rely on your MBE outlines and the supplemental MBE-subject outlines covered herein. To the extent that Michigan law differs from traditional legal principles contained in your MBE outlines, distinctions likely to be tested will be set forth herein.

Utilize the outlines in this book, the lectures, and all of the materials provided in the other volumes. Do not rely on only one aspect of preparation. Instead, strike a balance in your studying between learning strategies, studying the law, and practicing questions. During your study period, to effectively prepare, you must learn, study and practice.

LEARN STRATEGIES

STUDY LAW

PRACTICE QUESTIONS

ESSAY QUESTION DESCRIPTIONS

The essay questions of the Michigan Bar Exam, which of course are testing your knowledge and understanding of the pertinent law and its application to the relevant facts, are presented in a variety of ways. The call of the question may:

- simply request a discussion of the issues raised by the question, the law, and the facts;
- ask for a description of the claims and defenses that could be made by certain parties in actions between them;
- involve describing the relative strengths and weaknesses of the case of a party or the arguments that could be made.
- ask you to analyze the situation as a lawyer for a client, such as an associate in a firm writing a memo.
- request that an answer be provided as a judge's clerk would when making recommendations to a judge regarding a case (for example, the question may require analysis that results in a conclusion with respect to what type of ruling should be made upon a motion made in a case.

AmeriBar
Action Plan

The two components of the bar exam are: 1) the MBE; and 2) the Essay Exam. In order to maximize your chances of passing the exam, you must develop an action plan for each portion of the exam. In addition to using this action plan, select a sample schedule that best reflects the time remaining until the exam. Follow the study instruction in the schedule and alter it, if necessary, to take into account your unique circumstances.

MBE – MULTISTATE BAR EXAMINATION		
Lectures	**Outline**	**Questions**
• Listen to lectures covering MBE subjects. • Follow along with outline TOC/handout. • Be interactive. Take notes in outline table of contents.	• Read outlines slowly and carefully. • Be interactive. Tear out the table of contents and use it as a skeleton for an outline you will create as you listen to lectures and read the outline text.	• Practice questions after you have outlined the subject. Complete 17-34 questions at a time (30-60 minutes). • Use questions to **refine** your knowledge of the law. Understand why you made mistakes and update your table of contents outline with the correct law.

MBE SUBJECTS: Contracts & Sales; Constitutional Law; Criminal Law and Procedure; Evidence; Torts; Property.

ESSAY EXAMINATION		
Lectures	**Outline**	**Questions**
• Listen to the essay-writing strategy lectures. They detail how your answers should be presented to the examiners. • Listen to the substantive law audio lectures. • The lectures are designed to introduce you to the legal concepts that are covered in the outline.	• Never rely only on lectures. • Read the outlines slowly and carefully. • Be interactive. Tear out the table of contents and use it as a skeleton for an outline you will create as you listen to lectures and read the outline text.	• When you are finished outlining, answer past essay questions. • When you no longer have time to write answers to past essay questions, read the questions and outline your answer. • When you no longer have time to outline answers, just read the past questions and analyses carefully to see how the subject has been tested in the past.

ESSAY SUBJECTS: Business Associations (Agency, Partnerships, Corporations, LLPs, and LLCs); Civil Procedure; Conflict of Laws; Creditors Rights; Domestic Relations; Equity; Ethics; No-Fault; Personal Property; Trusts, Wills & Estates; Uniform Commercial Code (Commercial Paper & Secured Transactions); Workers Compensation; and all MBE Subjects.

This course is a home study course. There are no set start or end dates for the program. Every student begins and progresses through the program at a personal pace.

* We do not recommend that you only spend 37 days studying for the exam. However, this schedule has been provided because former students have indicated that it would be useful.

Written Portion of Exam

The process for studying an essay subject is detailed in the strategy lecture lesson covering study efficiency. In accordance with those instructions, a review of an essay subject typically consists of doing the following things in order:

1) Create a photocopy of the Table of Contents (hereafter called "Your TOC") for the subject contained in AmeriBar's Outline Book (students are provided with a limited license to photocopy each table of contents);

2) Listen to the Lectures for the Subject while following along with Your TOC. The lectures are designed to introduce you to the subject;

3) Read the outline of the subject in the Outline Book slowly and carefully. Be sure to write the key elements and legal rules in Your TOC;

4) Practice answering several essay questions. The more essays you practice, the better;

5) When you finish reviewing the subject, periodically review Your TOC when studying other subjects in order to keep the material fresh.

Day	Topic	Alternate Timing	Breakdown
	You should take at least 1 day off per week. This schedule is designed to account only for study days. Remember to factor in days off.		
Pre	Strategy/Intro	2 Hours	1) Listen to Introductory Lectures including Study Efficiency
Day 1	Partnership	1 Day	1) Listen to Lectures 2) Read outline slowly and carefully. Write key elements in Your TOC Outline. 3) Complete & Review Practice Essays.
Day 2	Agency	1 Day	1) Listen to Lectures 2) Read outline slowly and carefully. Write key elements in Your TOC Outline. 3) Complete & Review Practice Essays.
Day 3 Day 4	Corporations	2 Days	1) Listen to Lectures 2) Read Outline and Carefully. Write key elements in Your TOC. 3) Complete & Review Practice Essays
Day 5	Conflict of Laws	1 Day	1) Listen to Lectures 2) Read outline slowly and carefully. Write key elements in Your TOC Outline. 3) Complete & Review Practice Essays.
Extra Time	Essay Writing	2-3 Hours	1) Listen to Strategy Lectures on Essay Writing, and IRAC, and take notes.
Day 6	Creditors' Rights	1 Day	1) Listen to Lectures 2) Read outline slowly and carefully. Write key elements in Your TOC Outline. 3) Complete & Review Practice Essays.
Day 7	Equity	1 Day	1) Listen to Lectures 2) Read outline slowly and carefully. Write key elements in Your TOC Outline. 3) Complete & Review Practice Essays.
Day 8	No-Fault	1 Day	1) Listen to Lectures 2) Read outline slowly and carefully. Write key elements in Your TOC Outline. 3) Complete & Review Practice Essays.
Day 9	Personal Property	1 Day	1) Listen to Lectures 2) Read outline slowly and carefully. Write key elements in Your TOC Outline. 3) Complete & Review Practice Essays.
Day 10	Workers Compensation	1 Day	1) Listen to Lectures 2) Read outline slowly and carefully. Write key elements in Your TOC Outline. 3) Complete & Review Practice Essays.
Day 11	Ethics	1 Day	1) Listen to Lectures 2) Read outline slowly and carefully. Write key elements in Your TOC Outline. 3) Complete & Review Practice Essays.
Day 12 Day 13	Civil Procedure	2-3 Day	1) Listen to Lectures 2) Read outline slowly and carefully. Write key elements in Your TOC Outline. 3) Complete & Review Practice Essays.
Day 14 Day 15 Day 16	UCC - Commercial Paper & Secured Transactions	3-4 Day	1) Listen to Lectures 2) Read Outline and Carefully. Write key elements in Your TOC. 3) Complete & Review Practice Essays (limited number)

Day 17 Day 18	Domestic Relations	2-3 Days	1) Listen to Lectures 2) Read Outline and Carefully. Write key elements in Your TOC. 3) Complete & Review Practice Essays
Day 19	Trusts	1-2 Days	1) Listen to Lectures 2) Read Outline and Carefully. Write key elements in Your TOC. 3) Complete & Review Practice Essays
Day 20 Day 21	Wills	2-3 Days	1) Listen to Lectures 2) Read Outline and Carefully. Write key elements in Your TOC. 3) Complete & Review Practice Essays

MBE Portion of Exam

The process for studying an MBE subject is detailed in the strategy lecture lesson covering study efficiency. In accordance with those instructions, a review of a subject typically consists of doing the following things in order:

1) Create a photocopy of the Table of Contents ("Your TOC") for the subject contained in your Outline Book;
2) Listen to the Online Lectures for the Subject while following along with Your TOC;
3) Read the outline of the subject in the Outline Book slowly and carefully. Be sure to write the key elements and legal rules in Your TOC;
4) Answer 100-200 MBE questions per topic.
   - Answer 17-34 questions (30-60 minutes) at a time. When you get a question wrong, review it.
   - When you review a question, determine why you answered incorrectly. Was it because you did not read carefully or because you did not know the law?
   - If you did not read carefully, understand what you misread. If you did not know the law, supplement Your TOC with the law to solidify your knowledge;
5) When you finish reviewing the subject, periodically review Your TOC when studying other subjects in order to keep the material fresh.

Day 22 Day 23	Criminal Law/Pro.	2-3 Days	1) Listen to Lectures 2) Read Outline Slowly and Carefully. Write key elements in Your TOC Outline. 3) Refine knowledge of general MBE principles by completing 100-200 Questions. 4) Review MBE Supplement for Subject (if applicable) 5) Complete and review past essay questions.
Day 24 Day 25	Evidence	2-3 Days	1) Listen to Lectures 2) Read General MBE Evidence Outline Slowly and Carefully. Write key elements in Your TOC Outline. 3) Refine Knowledge of general principles by completing 100-200 MBE Questions. 4) Review MBE Supplement for Subject (if applicable) 5) Complete and review past essay questions.
Day 26 Day 27	Torts	2-3 Days	1) Listen to Lectures 2) Read Outline Slowly and Carefully. Write key elements in Your TOC Outline. 3) Refine Knowledge of general MBE principle by completing 100-200 Questions. 4) Review MBE Supplement for Subject (if applicable) 5) Complete and review past essay questions.
Day 28 Day 29	Constitutional Law	2-4 Days	1) Listen to Lectures 2) Read Outline Slowly and Carefully. Write key elements in Your TOC Outline. 3) Refine knowledge of general MBE principles by completing 100-200 Questions. 4) Review MBE Supplement for Subject (if applicable) 5) Complete and review past essay questions.
Day 30 Day 31	Contracts/Sales	2-4 Days	1) Listen to Lectures 2) Read Outline Slowly and Carefully. Write key elements in Your TOC Outline. 3) Refine knowledge of general MBE principles by completing 100-200 Questions. 4) Review MBE Supplement for Subject (if applicable) 5) Complete and review past essay questions.
Day 32 Day 33 Day 34	Property	2-4 Days	1) Listen to Lectures 2) Read Outline Slowly and Carefully. Write key elements in Your TOC Outline. 3) Refine knowledge of general MBE principles by completing 100-200 Questions. 4) Review MBE Supplement for Subject (if applicable) 5) Complete and review past essay questions.

Day 35 Day 36	Review	2 Days	Review Your TOCs for Non-MBE Subjects – 1 Day. Read remaining essay questions and analyses and outline text for topics you feel uncomfortable with. Review Your TOCs for MBE Subjects – 1 Day. Read outline text for topics you feel uncomfortable with. Complete some practice questions and review incorrect answers. Determine why you answered incorrectly. Supplement Your TOC with correct law. Complete and review remaining essays for MBE subjects.
Day 37	Final Review	1 Day	Review Your TOCs for all Subjects. Refine knowledge of weak areas by reading outline text. Read any remaining essay questions and analyses. Get some rest before the exam!

AmeriBar – Sample 58 Day Schedule

This course is a home study course. There are no set start or end dates for the program. Every student begins and progresses through the program at a personal pace.

Written Portion of Exam

The process for studying an essay subject is detailed in the strategy lecture lesson covering study efficiency. In accordance with those instructions, a review of an essay subject typically consists of doing the following things in order:

1) Create a photocopy of the Table of Contents (hereafter called "Your TOC") for the subject contained in AmeriBar's Outline Book (students are provided with a limited license to photocopy each table of contents);
2) Listen to the Lectures for the Subject while following along with Your TOC. The lectures are designed to introduce you to the subject;
3) Read the outline of the subject in the Outline Book slowly and carefully. Be sure to write the key elements and legal rules in Your TOC;
4) Practice answering several essay questions. The more essays you practice, the better;
5) When you finish reviewing the subject, periodically review Your TOC when studying other subjects in order to keep the material fresh.

Day	Topic	Alternate Timing	Breakdown
	You should take at least 1 day off per week. This schedule is designed to account only for study days. Remember to factor in days off.		
Pre	Strategy/Intro	2 Hours	1) Listen to Introductory Lectures including Study Efficiency
Day 1	Partnership	1-2 Day	1) Listen to Lectures 2) Read outline slowly and carefully. Write key elements in Your TOC Outline. 3) Complete & Review Practice Essays.
Day 2	Agency	1 Day	1) Listen to Lectures 2) Read outline slowly and carefully. Write key elements in Your TOC Outline. 3) Complete & Review Practice Essays.
Day 3 Day 4	Corporations	2-3 Days	1) Listen to Lectures 2) Read Outline and Carefully. Write key elements in Your TOC. 3) Complete & Review Practice Essays
Day 5	Conflict of Laws	1 Day	1) Listen to Lectures 2) Read outline slowly and carefully. Write key elements in Your TOC Outline. 3) Complete & Review Practice Essays.
Extra Time	Essay Writing	2-3 Hours	1) Listen to Strategy Lectures on Essay Writing, and IRAC, and take notes.
Day 6	Creditors' Rights	1 Day	1) Listen to Lectures 2) Read outline slowly and carefully. Write key elements in Your TOC Outline. 3) Complete & Review Practice Essays.
Day 7	Equity	1 Day	1) Listen to Lectures 2) Read outline slowly and carefully. Write key elements in Your TOC Outline. 3) Complete & Review Practice Essays.
Day 8	No-Fault	1 Day	1) Listen to Lectures 2) Read outline slowly and carefully. Write key elements in Your TOC Outline. 3) Complete & Review Practice Essays.
Day 9	Personal Property	1 Day	1) Listen to Lectures 2) Read outline slowly and carefully. Write key elements in Your TOC Outline. 3) Complete & Review Practice Essays.
Day 10	Workers Compensation	1 Day	1) Listen to Lectures 2) Read outline slowly and carefully. Write key elements in Your TOC Outline. 3) Complete & Review Practice Essays.

Day 11	Ethics	1 Day	1) Listen to Lectures 2) Read outline slowly and carefully. Write key elements in Your TOC Outline. 3) Complete & Review Practice Essays.
Day 12 Day 13 Day 14	Civil Procedure	2-4 Day	1) Listen to Lectures 2) Read outline slowly and carefully. Write key elements in Your TOC Outline. 3) Complete & Review Practice Essays.
Day 15 Day 16 Day 17 Day 18	UCC - Commercial Paper & Secured Transactions	2-4 Day	1) Listen to Lectures 2) Read Outline and Carefully. Write key elements in Your TOC. 3) Complete & Review Practice Essays (limited number)
Day 19 Day 20 Day 21 Day 22	Domestic Relations	2-4 Days	1) Listen to Lectures 2) Read Outline and Carefully. Write key elements in Your TOC. 3) Complete & Review Practice Essays
Day 23 Day 24	Trusts	2-3 Days	1) Listen to Lectures 2) Read Outline and Carefully. Write key elements in Your TOC. 3) Complete & Review Practice Essays
Day 25 Day 26 Day 27	Wills	2-3 Days	1) Listen to Lectures 2) Read Outline and Carefully. Write key elements in Your TOC. 3) Complete & Review Practice Essays

MBE Portion of Exam

The process for studying an MBE subject is detailed in the strategy lecture lesson covering study efficiency. In accordance with those instructions, a review of a subject typically consists of doing the following things in order:

1) Create a photocopy of the Table of Contents ("Your TOC") for the subject contained in your Outline Book;
2) Listen to the Online Lectures for the Subject while following along with Your TOC;
3) Read the outline of the subject in the Outline Book slowly and carefully. Be sure to write the key elements and legal rules in Your TOC;
4) Answer 100-200 MBE questions per topic.
   a. Answer 17-34 questions (30-60 minutes) at a time. When you get a question wrong, review it.
   b. When you review a question, determine why you answered incorrectly. Was it because you did not read carefully or because you did not know the law?
   c. If you did not read carefully, understand what you misread. If you did not know the law, supplement Your TOC with the law to solidify your knowledge;
5) Complete and review past essay questions testing MBE subjects.
6) When you finish reviewing the subject, periodically review Your TOC when studying other subjects in order to keep the material fresh.

Day 28 Day 29 Day 30	Criminal Law/Pro.	3-4 Days	1) Listen to Lectures 2) Read Outline Slowly and Carefully. Write key elements in Your TOC Outline. 3) Refine knowledge of general MBE principles by completing 100-200 Questions. 4) Review MBE Supplement for Subject (if applicable) 5) Complete and review past essay questions.
Day 31 Day 32 Day 33	Evidence	3-4 Days	1) Listen to Lectures 2) Read General MBE Evidence Outline Slowly and Carefully. Write key elements in Your TOC Outline. 3) Refine Knowledge of general principles by completing 100-200 MBE Questions. 4) Review MBE Supplement for Subject (if applicable) 5) Complete and review past essay questions.
Day 34 Day 35 Day 36	Torts	3-4 Days	1) Listen to Lectures 2) Read Outline Slowly and Carefully. Write key elements in Your TOC Outline. 3) Refine Knowledge of general MBE principle by completing 100-200 Questions. 4) Review MBE Supplement for Subject (if applicable) 5) Complete and review past essay questions.
Day 37 Day 38 Day 39	Constitutional Law	3-4 Days	1) Listen to Lectures 2) Read Outline Slowly and Carefully. Write key elements in Your TOC Outline. 3) Refine knowledge of general MBE principles by completing 100-200 Questions. 4) Review MBE Supplement for Subject (if applicable) 5) Complete and review past essay questions.

Day 40 **Day 41** **Day 42** **Day 43**	Contracts/Sales	3-4 Days	1) Listen to Lectures 2) Read Outline Slowly and Carefully. Write key elements in Your TOC Outline. 3) Refine knowledge of general MBE principles by completing 100-200 Questions. 4) Review MBE Supplement for Subject (if applicable) 5) Complete and review past essay questions.
Day 44 **Day 45** **Day 46** **Day 47**	Property	3-5 Days	1) Listen to Lectures 2) Read Outline Slowly and Carefully. Write key elements in Your TOC Outline. 3) Refine knowledge of general MBE principles by completing 100-200 Questions. 4) Review MBE Supplement for Subject (if applicable) 5) Complete and review past essay questions.
Day 48- **Day 57**	Review	10 Days	Review Your TOCs for Non-MBE Subjects – 5 Days. Read remaining essay questions and analyses and outline text for topics you feel uncomfortable with. Review Your TOCs for MBE Subjects – 5 Days. Read outline text for topics you feel uncomfortable with. Complete some practice questions and review incorrect answers. Determine why you answered incorrectly. Supplement Your TOC with correct law. Complete and review remaining essays for MBE subjects.
Day 58	Final Review	1 Day	Review Your TOCs for all Subjects. Refine knowledge of weak areas by reading outline text. Read any remaining essay questions and analyses. Get some rest before the exam!

AmeriBar - Sample 71 Day Schedule

This course is a home study course. There are no set start or end dates for the program. Every student begins and progresses through the program at a personal pace.

Written Portion of Exam

The process for studying an essay subject is detailed in the strategy lecture lesson covering study efficiency. In accordance with those instructions, a review of an essay subject typically consists of doing the following things in order:

1) Create a photocopy of the Table of Contents (hereafter called "Your TOC") for the subject contained in AmeriBar's Outline Book (students are provided with a limited license to photocopy each table of contents);
2) Listen to the Lectures for the Subject while following along with Your TOC. The lectures are designed to introduce you to the subject;
3) Read the outline of the subject in the Outline Book slowly and carefully. Be sure to write the key elements and legal rules in Your TOC;
4) Practice answering several essay questions. The more essays you practice, the better;
5) When you finish reviewing the subject, periodically review Your TOC when studying other subjects in order to keep the material fresh.

Day	Topic	Alternate Timing	Breakdown
	You should take at least 1 day off per week. This schedule is designed to account only for study days. Remember to factor in days off.		
Pre	Strategy/Intro	2 Hours	1) Listen to Introductory Lectures including Study Efficiency
Day 1	Partnership	1-2 Day	1) Listen to Lectures 2) Read outline slowly and carefully. Write key elements in Your TOC Outline. 3) Complete & Review Practice Essays.
Day 2	Agency	1 Day	1) Listen to Lectures 2) Read outline slowly and carefully. Write key elements in Your TOC Outline. 3) Complete & Review Practice Essays.
Day 3 Day 4	Corporations	2-3 Days	1) Listen to Lectures 2) Read Outline and Carefully. Write key elements in Your TOC. 3) Complete & Review Practice Essays
Day 5	Conflict of Laws	1 Day	1) Listen to Lectures 2) Read outline slowly and carefully. Write key elements in Your TOC Outline. 3) Complete & Review Practice Essays.
Extra Time	Essay Writing	2-3 Hours	1) Listen to Strategy Lectures on Essay Writing, and IRAC, and take notes.
Day 6	Creditors' Rights	1 Day	1) Listen to Lectures 2) Read outline slowly and carefully. Write key elements in Your TOC Outline. 3) Complete & Review Practice Essays.
Day 7	Equity	1 Day	1) Listen to Lectures 2) Read outline slowly and carefully. Write key elements in Your TOC Outline. 3) Complete & Review Practice Essays.
Day 8	No-Fault	1 Day	1) Listen to Lectures 2) Read outline slowly and carefully. Write key elements in Your TOC Outline. 3) Complete & Review Practice Essays.
Day 9	Personal Property	1 Day	1) Listen to Lectures 2) Read outline slowly and carefully. Write key elements in Your TOC Outline. 3) Complete & Review Practice Essays.
Day 10	Workers Compensation	1 Day	1) Listen to Lectures 2) Read outline slowly and carefully. Write key elements in Your TOC Outline. 3) Complete & Review Practice Essays.

Day 11	Ethics	1 Day	1) Listen to Lectures 2) Read outline slowly and carefully. Write key elements in Your TOC Outline. 3) Complete & Review Practice Essays.
Day 12 Day 13 Day 14 Day 15	Civil Procedure	2-4 Day	1) Listen to Lectures 2) Read outline slowly and carefully. Write key elements in Your TOC Outline. 3) Complete & Review Practice Essays.
Day 16 Day 17 Day 18 Day 19	UCC - Commercial Paper & Secured Transactions	2-4 Day	1) Listen to Lectures 2) Read Outline and Carefully. Write key elements in Your TOC. 3) Complete & Review Practice Essays (limited number)
Day 20 Day 21 Day 22 Day 23	Domestic Relations	2-4 Days	1) Listen to Lectures 2) Read Outline and Carefully. Write key elements in Your TOC. 3) Complete & Review Practice Essays
Day 24 Day 25	Trusts	2-3 Days	1) Listen to Lectures 2) Read Outline and Carefully. Write key elements in Your TOC. 3) Complete & Review Practice Essays
Day 26 Day 27 Day 28	Wills	2-3 Days	1) Listen to Lectures 2) Read Outline and Carefully. Write key elements in Your TOC. 3) Complete & Review Practice Essays

MBE Portion of Exam

The process for studying an MBE subject is detailed in the strategy lecture lesson covering study efficiency. In accordance with those instructions, a review of a subject typically consists of doing the following things in order:
1) Create a photocopy of the Table of Contents ("Your TOC") for the subject contained in your Outline Book;
2) Listen to the Online Lectures for the Subject while following along with Your TOC;
3) Read the outline of the subject in the Outline Book slowly and carefully. Be sure to write the key elements and legal rules in Your TOC;
4) Answer 100-200 MBE questions per topic.
   a. Answer 17-34 questions (30-60 minutes) at a time. When you get a question wrong, review it.
   b. When you review a question, determine why you answered incorrectly. Was it because you did not read carefully or because you did not know the law?
   c. If you did not read carefully, understand what you misread. If you did not know the law, supplement Your TOC with the law to solidify your knowledge;
5) Complete and review past essay questions testing MBE subjects.
6) When you finish reviewing the subject, periodically review Your TOC when studying other subjects in order to keep the material fresh.

Day 29 Day 30 Day 31 Day 32	Criminal Law/Pro.	3-4 Days	1) Listen to Lectures 2) Read Outline Slowly and Carefully. Write key elements in Your TOC Outline. 3) Refine knowledge of general MBE principles by completing 100-200 Questions. 4) Review MBE Supplement for Subject (if applicable) 5) Complete and review past essay questions.
Day 33 Day 34 Day 35 Day 36	Evidence	3-4 Days	1) Listen to Lectures 2) Read General MBE Evidence Outline Slowly and Carefully. Write key elements in Your TOC Outline. 3) Refine Knowledge of general principles by completing 100-200 MBE Questions. 4) Review MBE Supplement for Subject (if applicable) 5) Complete and review past essay questions.
Day 37 Day 38 Day 39 Day 40	Torts	3-4 Days	1) Listen to Lectures 2) Read Outline Slowly and Carefully. Write key elements in Your TOC Outline. 3) Refine Knowledge of general MBE principle by completing 100-200 Questions. 4) Review MBE Supplement for Subject (if applicable) 5) Complete and review past essay questions.
Day 41 Day 42 Day 43 Day 44	Constitutional Law	3-4 Days	1) Listen to Lectures 2) Read Outline Slowly and Carefully. Write key elements in Your TOC Outline. 3) Refine knowledge of general MBE principles by completing 100-200 Questions. 4) Review MBE Supplement for Subject (if applicable) 5) Complete and review past essay questions.

Day 45 **Day 46** **Day 47** **Day 48**	Contracts/Sales	3-4 Days	1) Listen to Lectures 2) Read Outline Slowly and Carefully. Write key elements in Your TOC Outline. 3) Refine knowledge of general MBE principles by completing 100-200 Questions. 4) Review MBE Supplement for Subject (if applicable) 5) Complete and review past essay questions.
Day 49 **Day 50** **Day 51** **Day 52**	Property	3-5 Days	1) Listen to Lectures 2) Read Outline Slowly and Carefully. Write key elements in Your TOC Outline. 3) Refine knowledge of general MBE principles by completing 100-200 Questions. 4) Review MBE Supplement for Subject (if applicable) 5) Complete and review past essay questions.
Day 53- **Day 62**	First Review	10 Days	Review Your TOCs for Non-MBE Subjects – 5 Days. Read remaining essay questions and analyses and outline text for topics you feel uncomfortable with. Review essay questions you have already covered to solidify knowledge of tested issues. Review Your TOCs for MBE Subjects – 5 Days. Read outline text for topics you feel uncomfortable with. Complete several hundred practice questions and review incorrect answers. Determine why you answered incorrectly. Supplement Your TOC with correct law. Complete and review remaining essays for MBE subjects.
Day 63- **Day 70**	Second Review	8 Days	Review Your TOCs for Non-MBE Subjects – 4 Day. Read remaining essay questions and analyses and outline text for topics you feel uncomfortable with. Review Your TOCs for MBE Subjects – 4 Day. Read outline text for topics you feel uncomfortable with. Complete remaining practice questions and review incorrect answers. Determine why you answered incorrectly. Supplement Your TOC with correct law. Complete and review remaining essays for MBE subjects.
Day 71	Final Review	1 Day	Review Your TOCs for all Subjects. Refine knowledge of weak areas by reading outline text. Read any remaining essay questions and analyses. Get some rest before the exam!

AMERIBAR BAR REVIEW

Michigan Bar Review

BUSINESS
ASSOCIATIONS

(AGENCY, PARTNERSHIP, & CORPORATIONS)

AGENCY

AGENCY

Although Agency has not traditionally been directly tested in essay questions testing Business Associations, these three topics (Corporations, Partnership, and Agency) are treated as one subject on the examination. As such, an essay question may contain corporation, partnership, or agency issues, or elements of some or all of them. Therefore, be prepared to identify agency issues that are included as sub-parts of questions primarily testing the business association subjects.

For decades, the *Second Restatement of Agency* ("*Second Restatement*") provided definitive guidance regarding agency issues. In 2006, the American Law Institute published the *Third Restatement of Agency* ("*Third Restatement*"). While the *Third Restatement* minimally alters substantive agency law, it does modify the organization and presentation of the legal topics. Additionally, it expressly adds several topics which were not addressed in the *Second Restatement*, but have been developed in modern case law.

I.   AGENCY RELATIONSHIPS

"Agency is the fiduciary relation that arises when one person (a "principal") manifests assent to another person (an "agent") that the agent shall act on the principal's behalf and subject to the principal's control, and the agent manifests assent or otherwise consents so to act." *Third Restatement* § 1.

The agent must act primarily on behalf of the principal; merely benefiting another by one's conduct is insufficient. A person cannot become the agent of another by simply offering to help or by making a suggestion. The agency relationship is created when a principal provides authority to another to act on the principal's behalf and the agent consents.

A.   Creation

The two main elements required to create an agency relationship are consent and control.

1)   CONSENT

The parties must voluntarily consent to enter into an agency relationship. The parties manifest assent through written or spoken words or other conduct. Consent may be express or implied under the circumstances.

a)   Capacity

The principal must possess the capacity to contract. No capacity is required for the agent.

2)   CONTROL

The key element of the agency relationship is control of the agent; however, the realm of control may be limited. The element of subservience is critical.

B.   Types of Agents

1)   GENERAL AGENT

An agent is a general agent if authorized to act in place of the principal in any business capacity that the principal could act.

2)   SPECIAL AGENT

An agent is a special agent if authorized to perform specific acts as authorized by specific instructions.

3)   GRATUITOUS AGENT

An agent is a gratuitous agent if the agent is acting without any right to compensation.

4)   EMPLOYEE

An employee is an agent whose actions are under the direct control of the principal. Employees are traditionally known as a "servants." Employers are traditionally known as "masters."

5)   INDEPENDENT CONTRACTOR

An independent contractor is a type of quasi-agent who is only liable for delivering a finished product to the principal. Unlike employees, independent contractors are not directly supervised by the principal. They generally provide their own place of work, tools, supplies, and pay their own expenses. The independent contractor's business usually requires specialized or professional skills.

6)   SUB-AGENT

A sub-agent is "a person appointed by an agent to perform functions that the agent has consented to perform on behalf of the agent's principal and for whose conduct the appointing agent is responsible to the principal. The relationship between an appointing agent and a sub-agent is one of agency. . . ." *Third Restatement* § 3.15(1).

7)   CO-AGENT

Co-agents share the same principal. The principal or another agent actually or apparently authorized by the principal may appoint co-agents.

C.   Termination of Agency

Either the will of the parties or operation of law may terminate an agency relationship.

1)   TERMINATION BY WILL

     a)   Methods of Termination by Will

         (1)   Intent to Terminate

Agency authority, however created, terminates when either party manifests the desire to cease the relationship. Termination is effective when the other party receives notice of the termination.

            (a)   Power Distinguished from Right

The principal has the power to terminate an agent's authority at any time; however, the principal may not possess the legal right to do so. Thus, termination of an agency relationship may breach a contract between the agent and principal, leaving the principal liable for damages.

         (2)   Expiration of the Term of the Agency

An agency relationship may be terminated if the express term of the agency expires. For example, if a principal hires an agent for one year, once the year elapses, the agency relationship is terminated.

         (3)   Fulfillment of the Purpose of the Agency

An agency relationship may be terminated if the purpose of the agency is fulfilled. For example, if a principal hires an agent to purchase a building on its behalf, the agency relationship terminates once the building is purchased.

     b)   Notice to Third Parties

For general agents, a principal must provide notice of termination of the authority of the agent in order to protect himself against those who previously relied on the agent's authority or who may rely on an appearance of continuing authority.

         (1)   Actual Notice

The principal must provide actual notice to those persons who have previously dealt with the agent.

         (2)   Constructive Notice

The principal must provide constructive notice (e.g., publication, etc.) to third persons who have not actually relied on a manifestation made by the principal.

         (3)   Apparent Authority

Apparent authority is terminated when a third party knows or has reason to know that the principal no longer consents to the agent's authority.

2) TERMINATION BY OPERATION OF LAW

a) Death

An agency relationship is destroyed upon the death of either party. Termination as a result of the death of a principal is effective as soon as the agent receives notice of the principal's death. When an agent deals with a third party, notice to the third party is necessary for the termination of the agent's actual authority to become effective as against this third party.

b) Loss of Capacity

Loss of capacity of either the agent or the principal will terminate the agency relationship. When the principal loses his capacity, the agent's actual authority terminates and the termination is effective only when the agent has notice that: the principal's loss of capacity is permanent; or the principal has been adjudicated to lack capacity.

For the termination to become effective against third parties with whom the agent deals, the third parties must have notice that the principal's loss of capacity is permanent or that the principal has been adjudicated to lack capacity.

Note however that "[a] written instrument may make an agent's actual authority effective upon a principal's loss of capacity, or confer it irrevocably regardless of such loss."

c) Bankruptcy of the Principal

If a principal declares bankruptcy, the agency relationship terminates.

d) Breach of Fiduciary Duty

If an agent materially breaches a fiduciary duty owed to the principal, the agency relationship may terminate.

e) Cessation of Existence

Actual authority terminates when either the principal or agent, that is not an individual (e.g., a corporation), ceases to exist or begins a process that will lead to cessation of its existence, or when its powers are suspended.

f) No Notice for Termination by Law

Death or lack of capacity of either party to an agency relationship automatically terminates the relationship. Accordingly, under these circumstances, no notice to third parties relying in good faith on apparent authority of an agent is required.

II.   POWER OF AGENT TO BIND PRINCIPAL
★★
There are two main types of authority under which an act of an agent may bind a principal. An agent may bind a principal to a contract if the agent is acting within his 1) actual or 2) apparent authority or some substitute (e.g., estoppel, inherent authority).

★★   ### A.   Actual Authority

1)   CREATION OF ACTUAL AUTHORITY

"An agent acts with actual authority when, at the time of taking action that has legal consequences for the principal, the agent reasonably believes, in accordance with the principal's manifestations to the agent, that the principal wishes the agent so to act." *Third Restatement* § 2.01. It can be created by "written or spoken words or other conduct of the principal which, reasonably interpreted, causes the agent to believe that the principal desires him to so act on the principal's account. *Sea Lion Corp. v. Air Logistics of Alaska, Inc.,* 787 P.2d 109, 117, n.3 (Alaska 1990).

a)   Reasonable Interpretation of Principal's Manifestation

An agent is deemed to have reasonably interpreted the principal's manifestation if the interpretation reflects any meaning known by the agent to be recognized by the principal and, in the absence of any meaning known to the agent, as a reasonable person in the agent's position would interpret the manifestation in light of the context, including circumstances of which the agent has notice and the agent's fiduciary duty to the principal.

b)   Reasonable Understanding of Principal's Objectives

"An agent's understanding of the principal's objectives is reasonable if it accords with the principal's manifestations and the inferences that a reasonable person in the agent's position would draw from the circumstances creating the agency." *Third Restatement,* § 2.02 (3).

2)   TYPES OF ACTUAL AUTHORITY

a)   Express and Implied

Actual authority may be express or implied. If the principal directs the precise task, then the authority is said to be express. On most occasions, however, authority is created by implication. For example, the authority to "sell my house," implies an agent is authorized to take steps such as placing advertisements for the purpose of selling the principal's house. A common class of implied actual authority is called incidental authority. The *Restatement* provides that the "authority to conduct a transaction includes authority to do acts which are incidental to it, usually accompany it, or are reasonably necessary to accomplish it."

b)   Ratification

A principal may become liable to a third party if the agent purported to act on the principal's behalf, and the principal, with knowledge of the material facts, either: 1) affirmed the agent's conduct by manifesting the intent to treat the conduct as authorized; or 2) engaged in conduct that is only justifiable if he had such an intention (such as accepting the benefits of the agent's originally unauthorized action).

3)   LIABILITY OF PURPORTED AGENT

An agent purporting to act on behalf of a principal, but lacking the authority, becomes liable on the contract for breaching his implied authority. *Second Restatement* § 329.

★★ **B.   Apparent Authority**

1)   GENERAL

"Apparent authority is the power held by an agent or other actor to affect a principal's legal relations with third parties when a third party reasonably believes that actor has authority to act on behalf of the principal and that belief is traceable to the principal's manifestations." *Third Restatement* § 2.03. Apparent authority exists if the conduct *of the principal* leads the third party reasonably to believe that the agent has the authority. Apparent authority is created "by written or spoken words or any other conduct of the principal which, reasonably interpreted, causes the third person to believe that the principal consents to have the act done on his behalf by the person purporting to act for him." *Second Restatement* § 27. The principal must "be responsible for the information which comes to the mind of the third person," but this can occur if the principal provides "documents or other indicia of authority" to the agent that are subsequently shown to the third party. *Id.*, comment a.

a)   Third Party's Duty to Inquire

If the facts suggest that it may be unreasonable for a third party to believe that a purported agent has authority, then the third party has the duty to make further inquiry.

2)   AGENCY BY ESTOPPEL

If a principal silently stands by and permits an agent to act on his behalf, the principal is estopped from denying the agent's apparent authority. For example, suppose that Peter and Al are in a meeting with Tara. Al tells Tara that he is authorized to sell Peter's boat. Al is lying, and although hearing Al, Peter says nothing to contradict Al's statement. Peter will be bound by any contract Al enters into with Tara to sell Peter's boat. Although Al is not actually Peter's agent, Peter will be bound by the doctrine of agency by estoppel.

C.   Inherent Agency Power

1)   GENERAL

An agent may possess "inherent agency power" whereby, under limited circumstances, her principal may be held liable for damages even when the agent acted without actual or apparent authority or when there is estoppel. This occurs when the totality of the circumstances weighs against forcing the third party to absorb the damages. Pursuant to equitable considerations, the principal and the agent will be held liable for damages caused, even if the agent, acting alone, exceeded the scope of his actual authority and failed to inform the third party of such circumstance.

This power is defined as "the power of an agent which is derived not from authority, apparent authority or estoppel, but solely from the agency relation and exists for the protection of persons harmed by or dealing with a servant or other agent." If an agent has acted improperly in entering into a contract, the inherent agency power is not based either upon the consent of the principal or upon his manifestations. *Second Restatement* § 8A.

2)   SCOPE

The scope of the principal's liability under inherent agency power is set forth in the *Second Restatement*:

> "A general agent for a disclosed or partially disclosed principal subjects his principal to liability for acts done on his account which usually accompany or are incidental to transactions which the agent is authorized to conduct if, although they are forbidden by the principal, the other party reasonably believes that the agent is authorized to do them and has no notice that he is not so authorized." *Second Restatement* § 161, p. 378 (1958).

3)   RATIONALE FOR THE RULE

The *Second Restatement* justifies the rule because the principal's "liability exists solely because of his relation to the agent. It is based primarily upon the theory that, if one appoints an agent to conduct a series of transactions over a period of time, it is fair that he should bear losses which are incurred when such an agent, although without authority to do so, does something which is usually done in connection with the transactions he is employed to conduct. Such agents can properly be regarded as part of the principal's organization in much the same way as a servant is normally part of the master's business enterprise." *Second Restatement* § 161, p. 379.

4)   *THIRD RESTATEMENT* OMITS INHERENT AGENCY POWER

The *Third Restatement*, published in 2006, eliminates the inherent agency power. Nonetheless, the underlying concepts still apply. The rationale for the elimination is that the doctrine of apparent authority has been expanded to include situations under which the *Second Restatement* would have applied the inherent agency power. Thus, the result of any issue implicating the inherent agency power should be the same under the *Third Restatement*, but the result would be reached by analyzing apparent authority principles.

a)   Undisclosed Principal

Apparent authority would not apply in the case of an undisclosed principal. The *Third Restatement* has rectified this problem caused by the elimination of the inherent agency power by providing that an undisclosed principal is liable for the actions of an agent, acting without actual authority, if a third party detrimentally relies on the agent and the principal does not take reasonable steps to notify the third party of the misplaced reliance.

III. VICARIOUS LIABILITY OF PRINCIPAL FOR ACTS OF AGENT

A. Contractual Liability of Principal to Third Party

Generally, a principal becomes liable to a third party for transactions entered into by: a) a person acting on the principal's behalf if this person possesses actual or apparent authority; b) an agent by estoppel; c) a person who possesses inherent agency power; or d) a purported agent if the principal ratifies the actions of the purported agent.

1) EXTENT OF LIABILITY

The extent of liability depends upon the extent to which the principal is known to the third party.

a) Disclosed Principal

A principal is disclosed if the third party knows that the agent is acting for a principal and knows who the principal is. A disclosed principal is liable for authorized contracts the agent makes on his behalf. The agent is *not* personally liable for these types of contracts.

b) Partially Disclosed Principal

A principal is partially disclosed if the third party knows that the agent is acting on behalf of a principal, but does not know the identity of the principal. A partially disclosed principal is liable for authorized contracts the agent makes on his behalf. The agent is also liable for these types of contracts.

c) Undisclosed Principal

A principal is undisclosed if the third party does not know that the agent is acting on behalf of a principal. An undisclosed principal is liable for authorized contracts made by the agent. The principal may also liable for unauthorized contracts made by the agent. Liability for unauthorized contracts will depend upon whether an agent is a general or specific agent.

(1) General Agent

A general agent for an undisclosed principal subjects the principal to liability for acts done on his account, if the acts are usual or necessary under the circumstances, even if the agent is not expressly authorized.

(2) Special Agent

A special agent for an undisclosed principal subjects the principal to liability for acts done on his account only if the actions are done with actual or apparent authority, inherent agency power, ratification, or estoppel. The actions of a special agent not conducted under these circumstances may bind the principal if the agent's only departure from authority (actual or apparent) is:

- in naming or disclosing the principal;
- having an improper motive;
- being negligent in determining the facts on which his authority is based; or
- in making misrepresentations.

B.   Liability of a Third Party to an Undisclosed Principal

1)   GENERAL

A person who enters into an agreement with the agent of an undisclosed principal, on account of his principal and within the authority of the agent to bind his principal, is liable to the principal as if the principal had personally made the contract with him unless the undisclosed principal is excluded by the form or terms of the contract.

A third person cannot, however, be made liable to the principal if the principal's existence is fraudulently concealed or there is a set-off or a similar defense against the agent.

2)   AGENT CANNOT AVOID LIABILITY

An agent who contracts in his own name for an undisclosed principal does not avoid becoming a party to the agreement because of his status as an agent. Such an agent, if personally liable, may enforce the agreement even if the principal has renounced it

C.   Tort Liability of Principal

A principal is liable for his own torts and may be liable for the torts of an agent acting with authority.

1)   DIRECT LIABILITY

The personal liability of the principal may arise from his own misconduct. This claim for personal liability may, for example, take the form of a negligence action.

a)   Negligent Employment

A principal may be liable for failing to exercise due care in hiring an agent.

b)   Negligent Supervision

A principal may be liable for failing to exercise due care in supervising an agent by:

- failing to supervise,
- failing to provide proper orders, or
- condoning misconduct.

2)   VICARIOUS LIABILITY

Vicarious liability is a form of indirect liability. Under the doctrine of vicarious liability, one party may be held liable for the acts or omissions of another party. A principal may be held liable for the acts or omissions of the agent that arise from the agency relationship under limited circumstances.

a)   General

A principal may be liable for the torts of an agent if two requirements are satisfied: 1) a master-servant relationship exists between the parties; and 2) the agent's act or omission occurs within the scope of employment. *Second Restatement* § 219(1). A principal is also liable if the principal expressly authorizes the wrongful act of the agent.

(1)   Master-Servant Relationship

"A master is a principal who employs an agent to perform services and who controls or has a right to control the physical conduct" of the agent's performance. *Second Restatement* § 2(1). Determining whether a master-servant relationship exists requires a fact-based analysis of the agency relationship. The most important consideration is the extent of control that a principal exercises over the details of the agent's work. The *Third Restatement* uses the language "employer-employee" instead of "master-servant."

(2)   Scope of Employment

An act is done in the scope of employment if it is done to further the interest of the principal. The scope of employment "includes only acts of the kind authorized, done within limits of time and space which approximate those created by the authorization." *Id.*, at comment a. Moreover, activity is "within the scope of employment" when this conduct is "of the same general nature as that authorized, or incidental to the conduct authorized." *Second Restatement* § 229(1). The factors used in evaluating whether employee conduct is within the scope of the employee's employment include: 1) it is of the type and nature for which the employee was hired to perform; 2) it occurs substantially within the authorized time and space limits; 3) it is conducted to serve the employer; and 4) where force is intentionally used by an employee against another, the use of force is not unexpected by the employer. *Second Restatement* § 228.

b)   Independent Contractor

A principal is generally not liable for unauthorized acts of an independent contractor. According to the *Second Restatement*, "[a]n independent contractor is a person who contracts with another to do something for him but who is not controlled by the other nor subject to the other's right to control with respect to his physical conduct in the performance of the undertaking. He may or may not be an agent." *Second Restatement* § 2(3).

The principal's lack of control is the key factor in determining whether an agent is an independent contractor. Under the *Second Restatement*, several additional relevant factors include: 1) whether the one employed is engaged in a distinct occupation or business; 2) the skill required in the particular occupation; 3) who supplies the materials to perform and the place to perform the service; 4) method of payment; and 5) how the parties characterize the transaction. *Second Restatement* § 220 (2).

(1)   Exceptions

(a)   Misrepresentations

A principal is liable for misrepresentations of an independent contractor that are made for the benefit of the principal.

(b)   Ultra-Hazardous Acts

A principal is liable for ultra-hazardous or inherently dangerous acts of an independent contractor.

(c)   Apparent Authority

A principal will be liable for the torts of any agent or independent contractor if the principal is responsible for holding out the person as authorized to act on his behalf (under the theory of apparent authority).

D.   **Miscellaneous Concepts**

1)   <u>AGENT NOT SERVING INTERESTS OF PRINCIPAL</u>

A disclosed principal is "subject to liability upon a contract purported to be made on his account by an agent authorized to make it for the principal's benefit, although the agent acts for his own or another's improper purposes, unless the [third] party has notice that the agent is not acting for the principal's benefit." *Second Restatement* § 165; *U.S. Fid. & Guar. Co. v. Anderson Constr. Co.*, 260 F.2d 172 (9th Cir. 1958).

2)   <u>SECRET LIMITING INSTRUCTIONS</u>

"A disclosed or partially disclosed principal authorizing an agent to make a contract, but imposing upon him limitations as to incidental terms intended not to be revealed is subject to liability upon a contract made in violation of such limitations with a third person who has no notice of them." *Second Restatement* § 160; *Hunt v. Davis*, 387 So. 2d 209 (Ala. Civ. App. 1980) (holding that secret limitations on an agent's authority do not bind third parties); *Wittlin v. Giacalone*, 171 F.2d 147 (D.C. Cir. 1948).

IV.   **FIDUCIARY DUTIES BETWEEN PRINCIPAL AND AGENT**

An agent owes certain fiduciary duties to the principal. The agent is liable for actions occurring within the scope of his agency.

A.   Duties of Agent

1)   DUTY OF CARE

a)   General

An agent owes a duty to the principal to act with reasonable care and skill. An agent should make reasonable efforts to accomplish the intended result. The degree of skill that is required from the agent is the degree of skill common among those engaged in like businesses or pursuits. A paid agent is under a duty to act with the ordinary skill of persons performing similar work.

b)   Gratuitous Agent

A gratuitous agent is held to a lower standard. Gratuitous agents are liable if they commit gross negligence, but not ordinary negligence.

c)   *Third Restatement*'s Duty of Performance

The *Third Restatement* has reorganized the agent's duties and categorized the duty of care under a duty of performance. Also expressly included under the duty of performance are the duties of competence and diligence, although these would also implicitly apply under the *Second Restatement's* duty of care. The *Third Restatement's* duty of performance also expressly includes a duty of good conduct, a duty to provide information to the principal, and several duties regarding the safeguarding of the principal's property including segregation, record-keeping, and accounting.

2)   DUTY OF LOYALTY

a)   General

An agent cannot place his interests above the interests of the principal. As a fiduciary, the agent is bound to make a full and prompt disclosure of all facts that threaten to affect the principal's interests. The agent is liable for any profits gained from violating the duty of loyalty. The duty of loyalty includes a duty not to use any confidential information in competition with or to the injury of the principal.

The *Second Restatement* provides that an agent possesses a duty to act solely for the benefit of the principal in all matters connected with the agency. An agent possesses a duty not to act on behalf of an adverse party in a transaction connected with the agency without the principal's knowledge. An agent possesses a duty not to compete with the principal concerning the subject matter of his agency. An agent possesses a duty not to act or to agree to act during the period of his agency for persons whose interests conflict with those of the principal in matters which the agent is employed.

      b)   Post-Termination Competition

      (1)   Trade Secrets

A former agent cannot use the trade secrets of a former principal. A trade secret includes any formula, pattern, device, or compilation of information which is used in business and which gives a party an opportunity to obtain an advantage over competitors.

      (2)   Covenant Not to Compete

Non-competition covenants are enforceable if narrowly drawn to protect only the legitimate interest of the employer and so long as they are reasonable and not primarily designed to limit competition or restrain the right to engage in a common calling. Courts will sometimes reform a broad covenant if enforceable language is severable. This is called "blue-penciling" the covenant.

      c)   *Third Restatement* Modifications

      (1)   Express Additions to Duty of Loyalty

The *Third Restatement* expressly addresses several situations under the duty of loyalty. Despite these express additions, the treatment of the duty of loyalty is almost identical under the *Third Restatement*. Examples of the express additions include:

- An agent must act for the principal's benefit in all matters connected to the relationship.
- An agent must not acquire a material benefit for his own personal gain.
- An agent must not act on behalf of a party adverse to the principal or as if he were adverse to the principal.
- An agent may not use the principal's property or confidential information for personal gain.
- An agent may not compete with, or assist anyone in competing with, the principal.

      (2)   Consent of Principal

An agent will not be liable for a breach of the duty of loyalty if the agent obtains the principal's consent to do an act and in doing so:

- acts in good faith;
- discloses to the principal all materials facts that the agent knows, has reason to know, or should know as facts that would reasonably affect the principal's judgment unless the principal has manifested that such facts are already known to him or that he wishes not to know them; and
- deals fairly with the principal.

The principal's consent must relate to specific acts or transactions that are reasonably expected to occur in the ordinary course of the agency relationship.

(3)   Multiple Principals

An agent who acts for more than one principal, in a transaction between or among them, has the duty, to each principal, to deal with them in good faith and to deal with them fairly. The agent must also disclose to each principal: 1) the fact that the agent is acting for other principals, and 2) all other facts that the agent knows, has reason to know, or should know as facts that would reasonably affect the principal's judgment unless the principal has manifested that such facts are already known to him or that he wishes not to know them.

★   3)   DUTY OF OBEDIENCE

An agent acts for and on behalf of his principal and subject to his control. As such, an agent owes a duty to the principal to act within her actual authority and to follow the principal's instructions. An agent is liable for damages stemming from the violation of the duty of obedience.

a)   *Third Restatement* Incorporates Obedience in Duty of Performance

The *Third Restatement* has incorporated the duty of obedience into the duty of performance. Under the *Third Restatement*, the agent must act only within the scope of his actual authority in the agency relationship. He must comply with all lawful instructions given by: 1) the principal, and 2) any person(s) designated by the principal.

4)   DUTY TO ACCOUNT

As a corollary to the three main duties owed by an agent to a principal, an agent owes the principal a duty to account for any violations of a fiduciary duty. For example, if an agent violates the duty of obedience, resulting in financial damages to the principal, the agent will be liable to the principal for the damage.

With regard to the duty of loyalty, an agent may be "disgorged" of any profits made as a violation of the duty of loyalty. The principal is entitled to the "disgorged" profits.

B.   Duties of Principal

The principal has the duty to act in accordance with the express and implied terms of any contact between the principal and the agent.

1)   DUTY TO INDEMNIFY

The principal has a duty to indemnify an agent in accordance with the terms of any contract between them. Unless otherwise agreed, the principal must comply with the duty of indemnification when:

- the agent makes a payment within the scope of the agent's actual authority; or
- the agent makes a payment that is beneficial to the principal, unless the agent acts officiously in making the payment; or
- the agent suffers a loss that fairly should be borne by the principal in light of their relationship.

2) DUTY TO DEAL FAIRLY AND IN GOOD FAITH

The principal's duty to deal with the agent fairly and in good faith includes the duty to provide the agent with information:

- that the principal knows, has reason to know, or should know;
- in relation to the presence of risks of physical harm or pecuniary loss in connection with the agent's work; and
- that the agent does not know.

PARTNERSHIPS

PARTNERSHIPS

Past essay questions on the Michigan Bar Exam ("Exam") regarding Corporations, Partnership, and Agency ("CPA") usually tested issues arising in the context of small businesses like corporations. However, such questions can involve issues concerning corporations, partnerships, or agency. Some testable issues regarding partnerships include, but are not limited to, their formation and the fiduciary duties of partners pursuant to Michigan's Uniform Partnership Act, Mich. Comp. Laws §§ 449.1-449.49 (Act 72 of 1917). Traditionally, each Exam has contained one CPA question.

I.   CREATION OF PARTNERSHIPS

The relations among the partners and, between the partners and the partnership, are generally governed by a partnership agreement. To the extent that the partners fail to agree upon a contrary rule, state statutes mirroring the Uniform Partnership Act ("UPA") or the Revised Uniform Partnership Act ("RUPA") generally provide the default rules governing the relations between the parties.

It is important to understand the distinctions between both the UPA and RUPA approaches because exam questions often test the distinctions of these widely adopted statutes.

A.   Aggregate vs. Entity Theories of Partnership

The UPA and RUPA treat partnerships differently. Under the UPA, partnerships are merely an aggregate of their partners. The partnership itself is not considered a legal "entity." Under RUPA, the partnership is considered a legal entity separate and distinct from its members.

1)   AGGREGATE THEORY (UPA) -- MICHIGAN

The UPA employs the "aggregate" theory of partnership law. Under the UPA, a partnership is an aggregate of individuals acting with a common goal. They share profits and losses. They hold partnership assets in joint ownership

Under the UPA, partners act as joint principals. Thus, a partnership is in business for only so long as its exact aggregate of partners exists. This rule has the following, seemingly harsh, consequences:

- If one partner leaves or dies, or a new partner is admitted, the partnership is automatically dissolved.

- If the remaining partners continue the business in the partnership form, they do so in a "new" partnership that is wholly distinct from the prior partnership the aggregate has changed.

- The remaining partners may continue to operate under the prior agreement to the extent it is applicable.

2)   ENTITY THEORY (RUPA) – OTHER JURISDICTIONS

RUPA rejects the aggregate approach and adopts the entity theory. Under the entity theory, a partnership is a legal entity (like a corporation) that is separate and distinct from its partners. As an entity, the partnership can hold title to partnership property and is capable of suing and being sued.

A key distinction under RUPA is that partners function as agents of the partnership entity, not joint principals.

B.   General Partnerships

★★★★
A general partnership is defined as "the association of two or more persons to carry on as co-owners a business for profit forms a partnership, whether or not the persons intend to form a partnership." Memorize this definition.

The Michigan Uniform Partnership Act, Mich. Comp. Laws § 449.1 *et seq.,* similarly defines a partnership as an association of two or more persons to carry on as co-owners a business for profit. Mich. Comp. Laws § 449.6(1). Although Michigan law does not include the last phrase of the above definition from the model UPA of 1994 regarding the persons' intent, Michigan law is consistent with that definition. *Byker v. Mannes,* 465 Mich. 637 (2002). In Michigan, the intent to form a partnership generally is not required if the parties' conduct and acts otherwise indicate that they carried on as co-owners a business for profit. *Id.*

In Michigan, a partnership exists where the parties agree and intend to enter into a relation "in which the elements of partnership may be found." *Miller v. City Bank & Trust Co.,* 82 Mich. App. 120, 124 (1978). The elements of a partnership are generally considered to include:

> "a voluntary association of two or more people with legal capacity in order to carry on, via co-ownership, a business for profit. Co-ownership of the business requires more than merely joint ownership of the property and is usually evidenced by joint control and the sharing of profits and losses." *Id.*

There is no requirement that an agreement to form a partnership must be in writing. Rather, the creation of a partnership is a function of the intent of the partners to establish an association of two or more persons to carry on as co-owners a business for profit for a partnership. A key issue in determining whether parties have formed a general partnership is whether the parties agree to share profits and control.

No specific form of agreement is necessary to constitute a partnership. Nor need there be subjective intent to form a partnership, only that the parties intend to run a business as co-owners. RUPA § 202(a). The parties' intent may be implied from their conduct. *Yoder v.*

Hooper, 695 P.2d 1182, (Colo. App. 1984), *aff'd* 737 P.2d 852 (Colo. 1987). *Nelson v. Seaboard Sur. Co.,* C.A. Minn., 269 F.2d 882. (Conduct alone may be sufficient to form a partnership.).

★ It has been held in Michigan that absent an express agreement, the test to be applied in determining whether a partnership existed is to examine the acts, declarations , and conduct of the parties, in relation to the business and from the nature and scope of the business in which the acts are committed. *Western Shoe Co. v. Neumeister,* 258 Mich. 662, 667 (1932). *Also, Van Stee v. Ransford,* 346 Mich. 116 (1956).

The Michigan Supreme Court has held that the question of intent to form a partnership is not solely determinative of whether a partnership actually existed. *Byker v. Mannes,* 465 Mich. 637, 653 (2002). "Pursuant to MCL 449.6(1), in ascertaining the existence of a partnership, the proper focus is on whether the parties intended to, and in fact did, 'carry on as co-owners a business for profit' and not whether the parties subjectively intended to form a partnership" *Id.* The Court further stated that it is unimportant whether the parties would have labeled themselves as "partners," as partners need not be aware of their status as "partners" in order to have a legal partnership. *Id.* "The gist of the partnership relation is mutual agency and joint liability." *Lobato v. Paulino,* 304 Mich. 668 (1943). It has also been held that important indicia of a partnership include the filing of certificate of partnership, common authority in the administration and control of the business, a common interest in the capital employed a sharing in the profits and losses of the business. *Barnes v. Barnes,* 355 Mich. 458 (1959).

Some steps to formalize a partnership include, for example, filing a certificate of partnership (as required by Mich. Comp. Laws § 449.101) or signing a partnership agreement.

The party alleging the partnership has the burden of proving that it exists. *Grosberg v. Michigan Nat'l Bank Oakland,* 113 Mich. App. 610 (1982), *aff'd,* 420 Mich. 707 (1984).

In *Harper v. Warju,* an unpublished opinion per curiam of the Court of Appeals, issued December 17, 1999 (Docket No. 211650); 1999 Mich. App. LEXIS 2204, the Court of Appeals found a partnership did exist where both parties contributed a portion of a down payment on a residence, purchasing the property together, with the agreement to split expenses equally with the goal of building quick equity.

In determining whether a partnership is formed, the following guidelines may apply:

1) JOINT OWNERSHIP

Joint ownership of property may by itself, but does not necessarily, establish partnership. RUPA § 202(c)(1).

2) SHARING OF PROFITS

The most important factor evidencing co-ownership is the sharing of profits, which is "prima facie evidence that a person is a partner in the business." RUPA § 202(c)(3). A person who receives a share of the profits of a business is presumed to be a partner in the business. This non-conclusive presumption may, of course, be overcome with sufficiently clear contrary evidence.

This presumption does not apply if a partner receives profits in payment of a debt or as services, or as wages, rent, retirement or health benefits, interest on a loan, or sale of goodwill of a business. RUPA § 202(c)(3).

3)   SHARING OF CONTROL

The sharing of control, capital investment, labor, and losses tend to show co-ownership.

4)   SHARING OF GROSS RETURNS

The sharing of gross returns does not by itself establish a partnership, even if the persons sharing them have a joint or common right or interest in property from which the returns are derived. RUPA § 202(c)(2), and *Yoder v. Hooper,* 695 P.2d 1182, (Colo. App. 1984), Aff'd 737 P.2d 852 (Colo. 1987).

5)   MISCELLANEOUS POINTS

An entity (such as a corporation) can be a partner in a general partnership.

Additionally, absent an agreement to the contrary, no individual or entity can become a partner without the consent of all of the other partners.

C.   Limited Partnerships

In order to form a limited partnership, a written certificate of limited partnership must be executed and filed with the Secretary of State. RULPA §201. The subjective belief of the parties that they had formed a limited partnership is irrelevant if they have not filed a certificate of limited partnership.

A certificate of limited partnership must contain the following elements:

(1)   the name of the limited partnership, which must contain the letters "L.P." or the words "Limited Partnership";

(2)   the street and mailing address of the initial designated office and the name and street and mailing address of the initial agent for service of process;

(3)   the name and the street and mailing address of each general partner; and

(4)   the signature of all general partners.

The certificate of limited partnership must be in "substantial compliance" with these requirements. The "substantial compliance" test is a ripe ground for potential essay questions because it requires a case-by-case factual analysis.

D.   Limited Liability Partnerships

1)   GENERAL

A limited liability partnership is a business entity that limits a partner's liability for professional malpractice not involving that particular partner.

In general, a partner in a registered limited liability partnership is jointly and severally liable for the acts and obligations of the partnership. However, a partner's liability for professional malpractice is limited to three circumstances:

- The liability arises from the malpractice of the partner.

- The partner supervised or directed the person who committed the malpractice.

- The partner was directly involved in the specific activity which resulted in the malpractice.

Although not nearly a majority rule, a modern trend is to limit an LLP partner's liability for contractual debts of the LLP to the amount the partner invested in the LLP.

2)   CREATION

A partnership may elect to become a limited liability partnership by a vote of the partners. After approval, a partnership may become a limited liability partnership by filing a "Statement of Qualification." The statement must contain the following information:

- the name of the partnership;
- the street address of the partnership's chief executive office and, if different, the street address of an office in this State, if any;
- if the partnership does not have an office in the state, the name and street address of the partnership's agent for service of process. The agent must be a resident of the state or otherwise authorized to do business in the state;
- a statement that the partnership elects to be a limited liability partnership; and
- a deferred effective date, if any.

The status of a partnership as a limited liability partnership and the liability of its partners is not affected by any errors or subsequent changes in the information required to be contained in the Statement of Qualification. The filing of a statement of qualification alone establishes that a partnership has satisfied all conditions precedent to the qualification of the partnership as a limited liability partnership.

The name of a limited liability partnership must end with "Registered Limited Liability Partnership," "Limited Liability Partnership." "R.L.L.P.," "L.L.P.," "RLLP," or "LLP."

3)   ANNUAL REPORT

A limited liability partnership must file an annual report in the appropriate state office (usually the Secretary of State) which contains:

- the name of the limited liability partnership and the State or other jurisdiction under whose laws the foreign limited liability partnership is formed;
- the street address of the partnership's chief executive office and, if different, the street address of an office of the partnership in the State, if any; and
- if the partnership does not have an office in the State, the name and street address of the partnership's current agent for service of process.

A state may revoke the statement of qualification of a partnership that fails to file an annual report when due or pay the required filing fee. To do so, the state must provide the partnership at least 60 days' written notice of intent to revoke the statement. The notice must be mailed to the partnership at its chief executive office set forth in the last filed statement of qualification or annual report. The notice must specify the annual report that has not been filed, the fee that has not been paid, and the effective date of the revocation. The revocation is not effective if the annual report is filed and the fee is paid before the effective date of the revocation.

A partnership whose statement of qualification has been revoked may apply to the state for reinstatement within two years after the effective date of the revocation. The application must state:

- the name of the partnership and the effective date of the revocation; and
- that the ground for revocation either did not exist or has been corrected.

A reinstatement relates back to and takes effect as of the effective date of the revocation, and the partnership's status as a limited liability partnership continues as if the revocation had never occurred.

II.   POWER AND LIABILITY OF PARTNERS

The general rules detailed in this outline regarding partner and partnership liability are the rules for general partnerships. Rules for limited partnerships and limited liability partnerships will be specifically identified as such.

★   **A.   Tort Liability**

1)   LIABILITY OF THE PARTNERSHIP

A general partnership, limited partnership, or limited liability partnership, is liable for the wrongful acts or omissions of any partner acting in the ordinary course of the partnership's business or with the authority of the other partners to the same extent as the partner so acting or omitting to act.

2)   LIABILITY OF THE PARTNERS

Like the partnership, individual partners in a general partnership are jointly and severally liable for all obligations of the partnership arising from any wrongful act or omission of any partner acting in the ordinary course of the business of the partnership, or with the authority of the co-partners, to the same extent as the partner so acting or omitting to act.

★   **B.   Contract Liability**

1)   LIABILITY OF THE PARTNERSHIP

Every partner is an agent of the partnership for the purpose of its business, and the act of every partner, including the execution of an instrument in the partnership name, for apparently carrying on in the usual way the business of the partnership of which he is a member binds the partnership, unless the partner so acting:

- Has in fact no authority to act for the partnership in the particular matter; and

- The person with whom he is dealing has knowledge or notice of the fact that he has no such authority. No act of a partner in contravention of a restriction on his authority will bind the partnership to persons having actual knowledge of the restriction.

An act of a partner, which is not apparently for the carrying on of the business of the partnership in the usual way, does not bind the partnership unless authorized by the other partners. For example, a law firm partner's act of purchasing a steel mill, if the law firm does not carry on the business of purchasing steel mills, will not bind the partnership unless authorized by the partners (by actual or apparent authority).

2)   LIABILITY OF THE PARTNERS FOR CONTRACTS

Under the UPA, all partners are jointly liable for all other debts and obligations of the partnership. Under RUPA, all partners are jointly and severally liable for all other debts and obligations of the partnership. The chief distinction between the two kinds of shared liability is procedural. If liability is joint, the plaintiff must usually proceed against all who share liability in the same proceeding. If liability is joint and several, the plaintiff may elect to proceed against defendants separately.

Common law concepts of agency are also relevant. When analyzing a claim regarding the liability of partners, always remember to include a discussion on the agency concepts of apparent and actual authority. Under RUPA, each partner is an agent of the partnership.

C.   Incoming/Outgoing Partners

1)   LIABILITY OF INCOMING PARTNERS

a)   Liability for Acts and Obligations Before Admission as Partner

A person admitted as a partner into an existing partnership is not generally personally liable for any partnership obligation incurred before the person's admission as a partner. In effect, a new partner has no personal liability to existing creditors of the partnership.

b)   Investment in Partnership is at Risk

An incoming partner's investment in the firm (as opposed to unlimited personal liability) is at risk for the satisfaction of existing partnership debts.

c)   Personal Liability for New Obligations

A new partner's personal assets are at risk, of course, with respect to partnership liabilities incurred after his admission as a partner.

2)   LIABILITY OF OUTGOING PARTNERS

As a general rule, absent a settlement or some other release given by the third party, a partner leaving a partnership will remain liable for all debts and obligations created while the individual was a partner in the partnership. Furthermore, the partner will be liable for future debts and obligations until the outside party is given notice that the partner is no longer a partner in the partnership.

D.   **Miscellaneous Concepts**

1)   EXHAUSTION OF PARTNERSHIP ASSETS

The Uniform Partnership Act and the Revised Uniform Partnership Act treat the exhaustion of partnership assets issue differently. The issue of the exhaustion of partnership assets arises the partnership is subject to a civil judgment. If relevant, both approaches should be discussed on your exam.

a)   UPA

The UPA does not require that a plaintiff exhaust the partnership assets before making a claim against one or more partners individually. Thus, a plaintiff can seek to satisfy a judgment from the assets of any partner or the partnership, in any sequence.

b)   RUPA

Under RUPA, a judgment against a partnership can be satisfied from the personal assets of a partner only if the partnership has failed to satisfy the judgment or is in bankruptcy or if the liability would have been imposed on the partner regardless of the existence of the partnership.

2)   LIABILITY DURING DISSOLUTION

Dissolution of a partnership does not immediately terminate the partnership. Rather, the partnership enters the winding up phase, which continues until the winding up of the partnership's affairs is completed. Winding up generally includes completion of old business of the partnership, collection of any funds owed to the partnership, payment of partnership debts, and distribution of the assets to the partners.

Dissolution does not immediately terminate the partner's authority to bind the partnership or the other partners. As between the partners, the authority of a partner to act for the partnership terminates when the partner has knowledge of the dissolution of the partnership by another partner except for actions that are necessary to wind up the partnership or to complete transactions that have begun but are not yet completed. Accordingly, partners may be liable for any acts, omissions, or obligations created in furtherance of the winding up. Additionally, a person winding up a partnership's business may continue its business in order to enhance its liquidation value as a going concern.

3)   CONTRIBUTION

Under the principles of contribution, a partner personally paying a debt or judgment of the partnership would be entitled to payment from the other partners for their proportional share of the damages.

4)   INDEMNIFICATION

Under the principles of indemnification, a partner personally paying a debt or judgment of the partnership would be entitled to be indemnified by the partnership for any payments made and for liabilities incurred by the partner in the ordinary course of the business of the partnership or for the preservation of its business or property.

III.   RIGHTS OF PARTNERS AMONG THEMSELVES

A.   Profits and Losses

1)   PROFITS AND LOSSES SHARED EQUALLY

As a general rule, absent agreement to the contrary, each partner is entitled to an equal share of the partnership profits and is chargeable with a share of the partnership losses in proportion to the partner's share of the profits.

Under the default rule, partners share profits *per capita* and not in proportion to capital contribution, as do corporate shareholders or partners in limited partnerships. For example, suppose that Bill and Ted form a partnership to sell time machines. Bill contributes $100,000 but Ted only contributes $1,000. If the parties do not agree to split the profits in a certain proportion, then Bill and Ted will each be entitled to one-half of the profits. They will also split losses in the same proportion as profits – 50/50. However, if Bill and Ted signed a partnership agreement under which Bill would be entitled to 75 percent of the profits, Bill would also be subject to 75 percent of the losses (the same split as profits), unless the agreement allocated losses in a different manner. Of course, as with most partnership rules, the partners can agree to a different arrangement.

2)   PARTNER'S RIGHT TO COMPENSATION FOR SERVICES

As a general rule, a partner is not entitled to separate remuneration for services. The reasoning behind the rule is that a partner's compensation for the partner's services is the partner's share of profits, not a separate salary. The two exceptions to the rule are as follows:

- In the case of wind up, a surviving partner is entitled to reasonable compensation for services rendered in connection with winding up the business of the partnership.

- A partner is entitled to compensation for her efforts if the partners agree to such an arrangement. If the partners desire to pay salaries, then they must agree to do so.

Some courts have permitted remuneration based on an implied agreement to compensate a partner under limited circumstances.

3)   PARTNER'S RIGHT TO REIMBURSEMENT

a)   Contributions

A partner is entitled to be repaid by the partnership for contributions to partnership property made by the partner. A partner is not entitled to interest on a contribution unless the partnership has not paid back the contribution by an agreed upon date. At that time, if the partnership does not repay the partner, the partnership may be liable for interest on a going forward basis.

b)   Advance

A partnership must reimburse a partner for an advance to the partnership beyond the amount of capital the partner agreed to contribute. Regardless of whether the partnership has sufficient funds, a partner may possess such a right. With regard to an advance, as opposed to a contribution, the partner is entitled to interest on the advance.

B.   Management and Control

1)   EQUAL RIGHTS TO MANAGEMENT AND CONTROL

As a general rule, subject to any agreement between the parties, all partners have equal rights in the management and control of the partnership business. Disagreements relating to the ordinary matters connected with the partnership business may be decided by a majority of the partners.

2)   MATTERS NOT IN ORDINARY COURSE OF BUSINESS

Matters outside the ordinary course of a partnership's business must be unanimously approved by the partners. Moreover, no act in contravention of the partnership agreement may rightfully be accomplished without the consent of all of the partners.

Some matters outside the ordinary course of a partnership's business include:

- Assigning of the partnership property in trust for creditors or on the assignee's promise to pay the debts of the partnership;

- Disposing of the goodwill of the business;

- Doing any other act which would make it impossible to carry on the ordinary business of the partnership;

- Confessing a judgment;

- Submitting a partnership claim or liability to arbitration or reference.

3)   PARTNERSHIP BOOKS AND RECORDS

a)   General

Subject to any contrary agreement by the partners, the partnership books are to be kept at the principal place of business of the partnership and every partner must, at all times, have access to and the right to inspect them. On demand, the partnership must render true and full information of all things affecting the partnership to any partner or the legal representative of any deceased partner or partner under disability.

b)   Reasonable Limitations Permitted

The right of access is limited to ordinary business hours. Moreover, the partnership may charge a reasonable fee for providing copies of the documents.

c)   Motive of Partner is Irrelevant

A partner's right to inspect the partnership's records is not conditioned on the partner's purpose or motive. The reasoning behind the rule is that the partner's unlimited personal liability justifies an unqualified right to access the partnership books and records. However, an abuse of the right may constitute a violation of the obligation of good faith and fair dealing for which the other partners would have a remedy.

d)   Agreement Cannot Unreasonably Limit Right to Inspect

The partner's right to access partnership books and records may not be unreasonably restricted by the partnership agreement. To preserve a partner's core information rights despite unequal bargaining power, an agreement limiting a partner's right to inspect and copy partnership books and records is subject to judicial review. Nevertheless, reasonable restrictions regarding access to partnership records by agreement are authorized. For example, a provision in a partnership agreement denying partners access to the compensation information of other partners may be upheld.

4)   USE OF PARTNERSHIP PROPERTY

Absent an agreement to the contrary, a partner may only use or possess partnership property on behalf of the partnership or for partnership purposes.

5)   PARTNER'S RIGHT TO SUE THE PARTNERSHIP

a)   UPA

Under the UPA, a partner may not sue the partnership at law because the partner would be liable for any potential debts of the partnership. This rule is a rigid rule that makes dissolution an almost absolute prerequisite to any action against other partners.

b)   RUPA

(1)   Partner Can Sue Partnership

Under RUPA, a partner may sue the partnership on a tort or other theory during the term of the partnership, rather than being limited to the remedies of dissolution and an accounting.

(2)   Rationale for RUPA Rule

The new rule reflects a new policy choice that partners should have access to the courts during the term of the partnership to resolve claims against the partnership and the other partners, leaving broad judicial discretion to fashion appropriate remedies. It reflects the increased willingness courts have shown to grant relief without the requirement of an accounting, in stark contrast to the rigid UPA rule.

Accordingly, under RUPA, a partner may bring a direct suit against the partnership or another partner for almost any cause of action arising out of the conduct of the partnership business. RULPA makes it clear that a partner may recover against the partnership and the other partners for personal injuries or damage to the property of the partner caused by any other partner. Moreover, a partner's negligence is not imputed to bar another partner's legal action.

★   **C.   Duty of Care**

Each partner is an agent of the partnership. Accordingly, a partner must refrain from engaging in grossly negligent or reckless conduct, intentional misconduct, or a knowing violation of the law.

Moreover, a general partner of a limited partnership has a fiduciary duty to the limited partners of the partnership similar to that which a partner of a general partnership has to the other general partners. RULPA § 403(b).

★   **D.   Duty of Loyalty**

1)   GENERAL PARTNERSHIP

a)   Good Faith

The partners are in a fiduciary relationship with each other and with regard to the partnership as a whole. UPA § 21. An important fiduciary duty owed by a partner to the partnership is the duty of loyalty. The duty of loyalty is a very demanding duty.

In general, the duty of loyalty requires a partner to act in good faith and to act fairly toward the other partners. When a partner has a conflict of interest, he is obligated to resolve the conflict in favor of the partnership or to fully disclose the conflict and get the consent of the other partners. Among other things, two main activities can violate a partner's duty of loyalty:

- Competing with the partnership within the scope of the business and even during dissolution. For example, a partner must refrain from dealing with the partnership during winding up of the partnership business on behalf of a party having any interest adverse to the partnership; and

- Usurping a business opportunity that properly belongs to the partnership.

A strained relationship between the partners does not excuse a violation of fiduciary duties.

b)   Damages

A partner who breaches his fiduciary duty of loyalty must account to the partnership for any profits earned because of the breach. This is called "disgorging" the profit.

c)   Burden on Partner

When an act by a partner is challenged as a violation of the duty of loyalty, the accused partner will have the burden of proving that the terms of the transaction are fair, such as would be negotiated by the parties to an arms-length transaction, unless it has obtained prior consent of the other partners.

2)   LIMITED PARTNERSHIP

A general partner of a limited partnership has a fiduciary duty to the limited partners of the limited partnership similar to that which a partner of a general partnership has to the other general partners. RULPA § 403(b).

★   E.   Fiduciary Duties

1)   MICHIGAN LAW

In Michigan, a fiduciary relationship arises from "the reposing of faith, confidence, trust and the reliance of one upon the judgment and advice of another." *First Pub. Corp. v. Parfet*, 246 Mich. App. 182, 189 (2001); citing *Vicencic v. Jaime Ramirez, M.D., P.C.*, 211 Mich. App. 501, 508 (1995). Partners stand in a fiduciary relationship to one another, and are charged with the duty of honesty, good faith, and full and frank disclosure of all relevant information. *Van Stee, supra* at 133; *also, Johnson v. Ironside*, 249 Mich. 35 (1929).

Further, Mich. Comp. Laws § 449.21(1) provides that:

> Every partner must account to the partnership for any benefit, and hold as trustee for it any profits derived by him without the consent of the other partners from any transaction connected with the formation, conduct, or liquidation of the partnership or from any use by him of its property.

An argument can be made that a fiduciary duty arises "from any transaction connected with the formation . . . of the partnership." Mich. Comp. Laws § 449.21(1).

IV.   DISSOLUTION

★   ### A.   Dissolution under the UPA

Under the UPA, the dissolution of a partnership is the change in relation of the partners caused by any partner ceasing to be associated in the carrying on as distinguished from the winding up of the business. Dissolution triggers windup and termination of the partnership business. As a general rule, every partner possesses the power to dissolve the partnership at any time. However, if the dissolution is wrongful, the dissolving partner may be held liable in damages to the remaining partners.

The UPA approach is known as the "Aggregate Theory" of partnership because any change in membership always results in automatic dissolution unless a contrary agreement has been reached. Under the UPA, dissolution sets the stage for termination of the business.

Nonetheless, under the UPA, there is still a statutory right for the remaining partners to continue the business when a partner wrongfully dissolves the partnership.

B.   Dissolution under RUPA

RUPA dramatically alters the law governing partnership dissolution. An entirely new concept called "dissociation" replaces the UPA term "dissolution." Dissociation denotes the change in the relationship caused by a partner ceasing to be associated in the carrying on of the partnership business. The term "dissolution" remains, however, under RUPA, it possesses a different meaning. The entity theory adopted by RUPA to replace the aggregate theory of partnership under the UPA, provides a basis for continuing the partnership despite a partner's withdrawal from the partnership.

1)   DISSOLUTION

Under RUPA, unlike under the UPA, the dissociation of a partner does not automatically trigger a dissolution and winding up of the business of the partnership. RUPA does contain a recital of the situations in which the dissociation of a partner would cause a winding up of the business. They are as follows:

a)   Partner Forces Liquidation

In a partnership at will, a partner who is not dissociated may notify the partnership of the intent to withdraw as a partner. Such a partner may require dissolution. Accordingly, under RUPA, a partner in a partnership at will can force liquidation under these circumstances.

b)   Termination by Will or Upon Expiration of Term

In a partnership for a definite term or particular undertaking, the express will of all of the partners to wind up the partnership business will result in dissolution of the partnership. Additionally, in a partnership created for a specific term or undertaking, the expiration of the term or the completion of the undertaking can result in dissolution. Moreover, if the partners agreed that the happening of a specific event would lead to dissolution, then the occurrence of that event will result in the winding up of the partnership business.

2)   DISSOCIATION

In all other situations, the remaining partners may buy out the dissociated partner's interest in the partnership in lieu of a windup of the partnership business. In those other situations, the partnership entity continues, unaffected by the partner's dissociation. RUPA sets forth events that may trigger dissociation of a partner and classifies them as "wrongful" and "not wrongful."

a)   Wrongful Dissociation

(1)   Breach of Partnership Agreement

A partner's dissociation is wrongful if it breaches an express provision of the partnership agreement; or

(2)   Partnership for a Term or Particular Undertaking

In a partnership for a definite term or particular undertaking, a partner's dissociation is wrongful if:
- The partner withdraws before the expiration of the term or the completion of the undertaking; or
- generally if the partner withdraws by express will; or
- the partner is expelled by judicial order; or
- the partner is dissociated by becoming a bankruptcy debtor.

(3)   Liability for Damages

A partner who wrongfully dissociates is liable to the partnership and to the other partners for damages caused by the dissociation. The liability is in addition to any other obligation of the partner to the partnership or to the other partners.

b)   Dissociation that is not "wrongful"

Under all other circumstances, dissociation is not "wrongful." Remember, these are not mutually exclusive from the events triggering dissolution. For example, a partner in a partnership at will may be dissociated or force the liquidation of the partnership. The circumstances triggering dissociation are set forth as follows:

(1)   by will of a partner to withdraw as a partner;

(2)   an event agreed to in the partnership agreement as causing dissociation;

(3)   expulsion of a partner pursuant to the partnership agreement;

(4)   expulsion of a partner by unanimous vote of the other partners under certain circumstances;

(5)   expulsion of a partner by judicial determination because:

    (i)   wrongful conduct - the partner engaged in wrongful conduct that adversely and materially affected the partnership business;

    (ii)   breach - the partner willfully or persistently materially breached the partnership agreement or a duty owed to the partnership or the other partners; or

    (iii)   catch-all - the partner engaged in conduct relating to the partnership business, which makes it not reasonably practicable to carry on the business in partnership with the partner.

(6)   a partner became a debtor in bankruptcy; or

(7)   death or incapacity of a partner.

C.   Distinguished from Winding up and Termination

Dissolution does not immediately terminate the partnership. Rather, the partnership enters winding up phase, which continues until the winding up of the partnership's affairs is finished. Winding up generally includes completion of old business of the partnership, collection of monies owed to the partnership, payment of partnership debts, and distribution of the assets to the partners. Therefore, as between the partners, the authority of a partner to act for the partnership terminates when the partner has knowledge of the dissolution of the partnership by another partner except for actions that are necessary to wind up the partnership or to complete transactions which have begun but are not yet completed. Accordingly, partners will be liable for any acts, omissions, or obligations created in furtherance of the winding up. Additionally, a person winding up a partnership's business may continue its business in order to enhance its liquidation value as a going concern.

D.   Rightful Versus Wrongful

1)   POWER VS. RIGHT

A partner always possesses the power to dissolve a partnership. A partner's act of dissolution may be either a wrongful dissolution (without right) or a permitted action (with right). If the partnership agreement does not specify a definite term or a specified objective for the partnership to achieve during its operations, then dissolution does not contravene the partnership agreement. A partnership has been established for a particular undertaking if it has a stated purpose that can be achieved at a recognizable time, even if that time could not have been predicted when the partnership was established.

The UPA sets forth the following standards for determining whether dissolution is rightful or wrongful.

> a)   Rightful (Partner has the power and right)

Under the UPA, dissolution is rightful under the following four circumstances:

- at expiration of definite term or particular undertaking specified in the partnership agreement; or

- by the express will of any partner when no definite term or particular undertaking is specified because, absent agreement to the contrary, a partnership is an at will entity; or

- by the express will of all the partners who have not assigned their interests or allowed them to be charged for their separate debts, either before or after the termination of any specified term or particular undertaking; or

- by the expulsion of any partner from the business in accordance with such a power conferred by the agreement between the partners.

> b)   Wrongful (Partner has the power, but not the legal right)

Under the UPA, dissolution is wrongful if the circumstances do not permit rightful dissolution. The partner who has caused a wrongful dissolution may be liable to the remaining partners for damages (but of course, the partnership will still be dissolved).

> 2)   DISSOLUTION BY OPERATION OF LAW

Under the UPA, a partnership is dissolved by operation of law if:

1. any event occurs which makes it unlawful for business to be carried on; or

2. by the death of any partner; or

3. by the bankruptcy of any partner; or

4. by decree of court.

V.   SPECIAL RULES CONCERNING LIMITED PARTNERSHIPS

Limited Partnerships are partnerships that have general partner and limited partners. Generally, a general partner is subject to unlimited personal liability for the debts of a partnership to the same extent as if he was a partner in a general partnership. The general partner(s) typically manages the day-to-day operations of the limited partnership. The limited partner(s) of a limited partnership generally are only liable for the partnership obligations, to the extent of their investment in the limited partnership. Limited partners are generally not subject to unlimited personal liability for the obligations of the partnership.

A.   Disclosure Requirements of LPs

1)   GENERAL PARTNER'S RIGHTS

General Partners possess a right to copy and inspect the limited partnership's records. Regardless of a partner's purpose, a general partner may inspect and copy, in the limited partnership's designated office, the limited partnerships "required information." The "required information" is detailed below. A general partner is also entitled to inspect, at a reasonable location specified by the limited partnership, any other records maintained by the limited partnership regarding the limited partnership's activities and financial condition.

2)   DISSOCIATED GENERAL PARTNER'S RIGHTS

Upon 10 days' demand, a person dissociated as a general partner may have access to the information and records if the information or record pertains to the period during which the person was a general partner, and the dissociated general partner seeks the information or record in good faith.

3)   DUTIES TO DISCLOSE TO GENERAL PARTNER

By law, every general partner and the partnership must furnish certain information to a general partner. The information must be disclosed either upon demand of the general partner, or even without demand.

a)   Without Demand

Any information concerning the limited partnership's activities and activities reasonably required for the proper exercise of the general partner's rights and duties under the partnership agreement or the law must be available to a general partner even without a demand for the information.

If material information is apparent in the records of the limited partnership, whether a general partner is obliged to disseminate that information to fellow general partners depends upon an examination of the facts. With regard to information required to be disclosed without demand, the issue is whether the disclosure by one general partner is reasonably required for the other general partner to properly exercise her rights and duties.

b)   Upon Demand

Any other information concerning the limited partnership's activities, except to the extent the demand or the information demanded is unreasonable or otherwise improper under the circumstances, must also be made available to a general partner upon demand by the general partner.

c)   Specific Examples

(1)   Example 1

A limited partnership has two general partners who are regularly engaged in conducting the activities of the limited partnership. Both general partners are aware of, and have regular access to, all limited partnership records. Neither general partner has a special responsibility for, or knowledge about, 1) any particular aspect of business, or 2) the records pertaining to any particular aspect of the business. Under these circumstances, neither general partner will likely be obliged to draw the other general partner's attention to information reasonably apparent in the limited partnership's records.

(2) Example 2

A limited partnership has three general partners. Partner A is the managing partner with day-to-day responsibility for running the limited partnership's activities. The other two general partners - B and C - meet occasionally with Partner A. Together, the three function in a manner similar to that of a corporate board of directors. Under these circumstances, the managing general partner will likely possess a duty to draw the attention of Partners B and C to important information, regardless of whether that information would be apparent from a review of the limited partnership's books and records.

d) Reasonable Restrictions on Use of Information

The limited partnership may impose reasonable restrictions on the use of disclosed information. However, in any judicial action involving the restriction, the limited partnership must carry the burden of proving reasonableness.

e) Copy Fees

A limited partnership may charge a dissociated partner that makes a demand for copying and inspection, the reasonable costs of copying. No charge is permitted for current general partners because they would be entitled to reimbursement under RULPA. RULPA, however, authorizes charges to current limited partners.

★ **B. The Control Limitation**

1) LIABILITY IN A LIMITED PARTNERSHIP

a) General Partner

A general partner is subject to unlimited personal liability for the obligations of a limited partnership.

b) Limited Partner

Generally, a limited partner will not be personally liable unless one of the following exceptions apply.

(1) Limited Partner's Name used in LP Name

A limited partner may be personally liable for the debts of a limited partnership if the name of the limited partner is used in the name of the limited partnership

(2)   Limited Partner is really a General Partner

A limited partner is personally liable if he is, in reality, a general partner. The actions of a limited partner must be measured against the duties and responsibilities of a general partner. If he is acting as a general partner, he will be treated as a general partner for liability purposes.

(3)   Limited Partner Participation

The doctrines governing liability of a limited partner have evolved dramatically over time. At first, a limited partner could take no active role in the management and control of the entity. Slowly, the doctrine evolved to the point in which today, under RULPA, a limited partner will not be held liable, even if she takes an active role in the control and management of the entity. The reasoning for the shift is clear – the advent and evolution of other liability-limiting entities has made the old rule unnecessarily harsh.

(a)   Original Uniform Limited Partnership Act (ULPA)

Under the original ULPA, "a limited partner shall not become liable as a general partner unless . . . he takes part in the control of the business." The Michigan Revised Uniform Limited Partnership Act is similar. Mich. Comp. Laws § 449.1303(a) (Act 213 of 1982).

(b)   1986 Version of ULPA (Majority Rule)

The control rule was only applicable in cases involving "persons who transact business with the limited partnership reasonably believing, based upon the limited partner's conduct, that the limited partner is a general partner."

(c)   Current RULPA (Minority Rule)

An obligation of a limited partnership is not the obligation of a limited partner. A limited partner is not personally liable, directly or indirectly, for an obligation of the limited partnership solely by reason of being a limited partner, even if the limited partner participates in the management and control of the limited partnership.

(i)   Evolution of the Rule

Modern RULPA eliminates the so-called "control rule" with respect to personal liability for entity obligations and brings limited partners into parity with LLC members and corporate shareholders. The shield established by RULPA protects only against liability for the limited partnership's obligations and only to the extent that the limited partner is claimed to be liable because of being a limited partner. Therefore, a person that is both a general and limited partner will be liable as a general partner for the limited partnership's obligations. Be sure to analyze the actions of the limited partner and compare them to the duties of the general partners.

Moreover, no rule prevents a limited partner from being liable because of the limited partner's own conduct. Therefore, any limitation rule is inapplicable when a third party asserts that a limited partner's own wrongful conduct has injured the third party.

This rule is also inapplicable to claims by the limited partnership or another partner that a limited partner has breached a duty under this Act or the partnership agreement.

C.   Economic Rights of Limited Partners

1)   REQUIRED INFORMATION

A limited partnership must maintain at its designated office the following information, which is called the "Required Information" of the limited partnership:

- a current list showing the full name and last known street and mailing address of each partner, separately identifying the general partners, in alphabetical order, and the limited partners, in alphabetical order;

- a copy of the initial certificate of limited partnership and all amendments to and restatements of the certificate, together with signed copies of any powers of attorney under which any certificate, amendment, or restatement has been signed;

- a copy of any filed articles of conversion or merger;

- a copy of the limited partnership's federal, state, and local income tax returns and reports, if any, for the three most recent years;

- a copy of any partnership agreement made in a record and any amendment made in a record to any partnership agreement;

- a copy of any financial statement of the limited partnership for the three most recent years;

- a copy of the three most recent annual reports delivered by the limited partnership to the Secretary of State pursuant to Section 210;

- a copy of any record made by the limited partnership during the past three years of any consent given by or vote taken of any partner pursuant to this Act or the partnership agreement; and

- unless contained in a partnership agreement made in a record, a record stating:

    (A)   the amount of cash, and a description and statement of the agreed value of the other benefits, contributed and agreed to be contributed by each partner;

    (B)   the times at which, or events on the happening of which, any additional contributions agreed to be made by each partner are to be made;

(C)   for any person that is both a general partner and a limited partner, a specification of what transferable interest the person owns in each capacity; and

(D)   any events upon the happening of which the limited partnership is to be dissolved and its activities wound up.

RULPA § 111.

2)   RIGHT TO INSPECT BOOKS AND RECORDS

Upon ten days demand, a limited partner may inspect and copy "Required Information" in the limited partnership's office. The limited partner does not need to have a particular purpose for seeking the information. However, the right to such information and its use can be limited by the partnership agreement.

3)   RIGHT TO INFORMATION REGARDING STATE OF ACTIVITIES

A limited partner may inspect and copy true and full information regarding the state of the activities and financial condition of the limited partnership and other information regarding the activities of the limited partnership as is just and reasonable. However, the information is only available if:

*   The limited partner seeks the information for a purpose reasonably related to the limited partner's interest as a limited partner in the limited partnership;

*   The limited partner makes a demand describing the information sought and the purpose for seeking the information with reasonable particularity; and

*   The information sought is directly related to the limited partner's purpose.

If such a requested is made, within 10 days, the limited partnership must document the request and inform the limited partner of:

*   The information that the limited partnership will provide in response to the demand;

*   When and where the limited partnership will provide the information; and

*   If the limited partnership denies any part of the request, it must state the reason for such denial.

4)   DISSOCIATED LIMITED PARTNER'S RIGHT TO RECORDS

A person who is a dissociated limited partner may inspect and copy required information in the limited partnership's designated office if:

1.   The information pertains to the period during which the person was a limited partner;

2.   The person seeks the information in good faith;

3.   The limited partner seeks the information for a purpose reasonably related to the limited partner's interest as a limited partner in the limited partnership;

4.   The limited partner makes a demand describing the information sought and the purpose for seeking the information with reasonable particularity; and

5.   The information sought is directly related to the limited partner's purpose.

a)   Example 1

A limited partner who was dissociated seeks data compiled by the limited partnership, which relates to the period when the person was a limited partner, but which is not within the definition of "Required Information." It is, therefore, beyond the scope of the information required by RULPA. Consequently, no matter how reasonable the person's purpose and how well drafted the person's demand, the limited partnership is not obligated to provide the information.

b)   Example 2

A limited partner who was dissociated seeks access to "Required Information" pertaining to the time when the person was a limited partner. The person makes a demand, merely stating a desire to review the "Required Information" at the limited partnership's office. In particular, the demand does not describe with reasonable particularity, the information sought and the purpose for seeking the information. The limited partnership is not obligated to permit access because the dissociated limited partner failed to meet requirements of three, four, and five.

5)   REASONABLE RESTRICTIONS ON USE OF INFORMATION

The limited partnership may impose reasonable restrictions on the use of disclosed information. Moreover, in any judicial action interpreting the restriction, the limited partnership has the burden of proving reasonableness. A limited partnership may also charge a dissociated limited partner that makes a demand for copying and inspection, the reasonable costs of copying.

6)   LP'S DUTY TO DISCLOSE INFORMATION TO LIMITED PARTNER

When a partnership agreement or the law provides for a limited partner to give or withhold consent to a matter, before the limited partner acts, the limited partnership must, without demand, provide the limited partner with all information material to the limited partner's decision that the limited partnership "knows."

The law imposes an affirmative duty to volunteer information, but that obligation is limited to information that is both material and known by the limited partnership. This duty applies to known and material information, even if the limited partnership does not know that the information is material. A limited partnership "knows" what its general partners know.

CORPORATIONS

CORPORATIONS

Past essay questions on the Michigan Bar Exam ("Exam") regarding Corporations, Partnership, and Agency ("CPA") usually tested issues arising in the context of small businesses such as corporations. However, these questions can examine issues concerning corporations, partnerships, and agency. Traditionally, each Exam has included a CPA question.

Facts and rules derived from cases decided by the Michigan Court of Appeals and/or the Michigan Supreme Court have provided the basis for some past CPA questions and answers. Michigan's Business Corporation Act ("BCA"), Mich. Comp. Laws §§ 450.1101-450.2099, is the source for tested rules as well. Although the sample answers for some past questions indicate that Michigan statutes and court cases should be the basis for answering those questions, future questions could be answerable using controlling general legal principles of CPA contained in the outlines for Corporations, Partnership, and Agency. A CPA question could include the text of the controlling statute for purposes of analysis and answering the question. Of course, answering such a question may be easier to do if one is already familiar with the rule beforehand, even if it is stated within the question. Such a question, as with other questions in which the rule is not stated, still requires thorough analysis in terms of applying the rule to the facts.

Among other issues, certain prior CPA questions have tested the issues of a lawsuit alleging breach of fiduciary duty, notice of a special meeting, objections to meetings, interested directors, tendering return of payment and a lawsuit to rescind a stock purchase agreement, a shareholder's derivative action, dissenter's rights and fair value, piercing the corporate veil, a request for corporate records, and illegal, oppressive, fraudulent conduct.

If a question testing corporations and limited liability companies appears on the exam, it will likely be testing the business entity of a corporation. However, although not traditionally tested often, certain aspects of limited liability company ("LLC") law also may be tested. An LLC is a business entity that offers the advantage of limited liability (similar to corporations), while also offering partnership-like taxation benefits, in which profits are "passed through" to the owners of the LLC and taxed on personal income tax returns. To the extent that you should know about LLC law, the pertinent provisions are provided herein.

I.   FORMATION OF ORGANIZATIONS

Generally, one or more people may act as the incorporator or incorporators of a corporation by delivering articles of incorporation to the appropriate state official for filing. A corporation takes on an independent existence as its own legal entity separate and distinct from its incorporators.

A.   Articles of Incorporation

A corporation's articles of incorporation (sometimes called certificate of incorporation) are the basic charter of the corporation. Generally, they spell out the name, purpose, amount and types of stock that may be issued, and any special characteristics of the corporation such as it being a non-profit or a professional corporation.

1)   REQUIRED PROVISIONS

Usually, the articles of incorporation ("articles") must set forth the following information:

a)   Name

The articles must set forth the name of the corporation. Mich. Comp. Laws § 450.1202(a). The name of a corporation must contain some indication that the entity is not a natural person. Satisfactory phrases include "Incorporated," "Inc.," "Corporation," "Corp.," or another word which clearly identifies it as not being a natural person. Mich. Comp. Laws § 450.1211.

b)   Purpose

The articles must set forth the corporation's purpose for existence, which may be specifically described and/or generally stated in the articles as "that the corporation may engage in any activity within the purposes for which corporations may be formed under" Michigan's BCA. Mich. Comp. Laws § 450.1202(b).

c)   Authorized Shares

The articles must set forth the number of shares the corporation is authorized to issue. Mich. Comp. Laws § 450.1202(c). The articles must state which shares are, or will be, "divided into classes, or into classes and series, the designation of each class and series, the number of shares in each class and series, and a statement of the relative rights, preferences and limitations of the shares of each class and series." Mich. Comp. Laws § 450.1202(d). The articles must state any "authority vested in the board to divide the class of shares into series, and to determine or change for any series its designation, number of shares, relative rights, preferences and limitations." Mich. Comp. Laws § 450.1202(e).

d)   Registered Office and Resident Agent

The articles must set forth (1) the mailing address and street address of the corporation's initial registered office and (2) the name of the person designated as the corporation's resident agent. Mich. Comp. Laws § 450.1202(f).

e)   Incorporators

The articles must set forth the name and address of each of the incorporators. Mich. Comp. Laws § 450.1202(g).

f)   Duration

The articles must set forth the corporation's duration if the corporation's duration is not perpetual. Mich. Comp. Laws § 450.1202(h).

2)   OPTIONAL PROVISIONS

Certain information may be set forth in the articles. Optional provisions include:

a)   Management

The articles may set forth provisions for the management of the business and for the conduct of the affairs of the corporation. Mich. Comp. Laws § 450.1209(1)(a).

b)   Powers

The articles may set forth provisions "creating, defining, limiting, or regulating the powers of the corporation, its directors," stockholders, or any class of the stockholders. *Id.*

c)   Bylaws

The articles may set forth a provision that Michigan's BCA requires or permits to be set forth in the bylaws. Mich. Comp. Laws § 450.1209(1)(b).

d)   Director's Liability

The articles may set forth provisions limiting or eliminating a director's liability to the corporation or its stockholders for money damages for failing to take action or taking action as a director, with the exceptions of liability for: a) intentional criminal acts; b) intentional infliction of harm upon the stockholders or the corporation; c) the amount of a financial benefit that the director received and to which the director is not entitled; or d) the authorization of distributions or dividends or the making of loans. Mich. Comp. Laws § 450.1209(1)(c).

e)   Miscellaneous

The articles may include any other lawful provision. Mich. Comp. Laws § 450.1209(1).

3)   CORPORATE EXISTENCE BEGINS WHEN ARTICLES ARE FILED

Unless a delayed effective date is specified in the articles themselves, the corporate existence begins when the articles of incorporation are filed. Mich. Comp. Laws §§ 450.1221, 450.1131. The articles must specify the duration of the corporation's existence as being perpetual or for a specified term. Mich. Comp. Laws § 450.1202(h).

4)   AUTHORITY LIMITED BY ARTICLES OF INCORPORATION

Historically, the articles of incorporation contained limitations on the corporation's authority. A shareholder could challenge corporate action as beyond its scope of authority, or *ultra vires.*

Today, the articles of most corporations authorize the conduct of "any and all lawful business." Michigan's BCA generally governs what constitutes lawful business. Mich. Comp. Laws § 450.1202(b).

MBCA sec. 3.04, 3rd Ed., states that "ULTRA VIRES (a) Except as provided in subsection (b), the validity of corporate action may not be challenged on the ground that the corporation lacks or lacked power to act. (b) A corporation's power to act may be challenged: (1) in a proceeding by a shareholder against the corporation to enjoin the act; (2) in a proceeding by the corporation, directly, derivatively, or through a receiver, trustee, or other legal representative, against an incumbent or former director, officer, employee, or agent of the corporation; or (3) in a proceeding by the attorney general under section 14.30."

B.   Bylaws

Bylaws are the written rules for conduct of a corporation. They should not be confused with the articles of incorporation, which only state the corporation's general charter. Bylaws, by contrast, generally provide for meetings, elections of a board of directors and officers, filling vacancies, notices, types and duties of officers, committees, assessments, and other ordinary business conduct. Corporate bylaws are, in essence, a contract that must be formally adopted and/or amended.

- The incorporators or board of directors of a corporation adopts the initial bylaws for the corporation.

- The bylaws of a corporation may contain any provision for managing the business and regulating the affairs of the corporation that is not inconsistent with law or the articles of incorporation.

1)   OPERATING AGREEMENTS

Limited liability companies, and in some jurisdictions, close corporations, may possess operating agreements. Operating agreements fulfill the same function as bylaws.

C.   Articles of Organization; Certificates of Formation

A limited liability company is governed by its articles of organization, which are sometimes called a certificate of formation. The Michigan Limited Liability Company Act, Mich. Comp. Laws § 450.4101 *et seq.*, refers to them as articles of organization. *E.g.,* Mich. Comp. Laws § 450.4102(1)(b). They serve as an LLC's basic charter. Generally, it spells out the name, purpose, amount and types of stock that may be issued, and any of the LLC's special characteristics.

1)   REQUIRED PROVISIONS

In Michigan, the articles of organization ("articles") must provide certain information.

a)   Name

The articles must contain the LLC's name. Mich. Comp. Laws § 450.4203(1)(a).

b)   Purpose

The articles must contain the purpose for which the LLC is organized. Mich. Comp. Laws § 450.4203(1)(b).

c)   Address

The articles must contain the street address of the LLC's initial registered office, its mailing address if different, and the name of its registered agent at that address. Mich. Comp. Laws § 450.4203(1)(c).

d)   Managers

If the LLC is to be managed by managers, the articles must state that its business will be managed by, or under the authority of, managers. Mich. Comp. Laws § 450.4203(1)(d).

e)   Duration

The articles must contain the period of the duration of the LLC, which may be perpetual or for a certain period. If the LLC's duration is not perpetual, its maximum duration must be stated. Mich. Comp. Laws § 450.4203(1)(e).

2)   PERMISSIVE PROVISIONS

a) Any Lawful Provision

The LLC's articles may also contain any other provisions not inconsistent with the law. Mich. Comp. Laws § 450.4203(2).

D.   Defective Incorporation

Defective incorporation occurs when a corporation has failed to come into a valid statutory existence because of a defect in the formation process.

1)   "DE FACTO" CORPORATION

A de facto corporation is a company that operates as if it were a corporation although it has not completed the legal steps to become incorporated. For example, it 1) failed to file its articles; or 2) filed defective articles; or 3) has been dissolved or suspended but continues to function. Sometimes, a court may temporarily treat the corporation as if it were valid in order to avoid unfairness to people who thought the corporation was legal. In that event, it is critical that they acted in good faith reliance on that fact.

2)   CORPORATION BY ESTOPPEL

Corporation by estoppel prevents an entity that had prior dealings with a defective corporation from denying that corporation's existence in a later suit that is brought against the entity.

II.   PROMOTER LIABILITY

A promoter is the party who assists in the planning and formation of a new business. Hamilton, *Corporations* § IILA (3d ed. 1992).

A.   Contractual Liability

1)   CONTRACTS

A promoter who enters into a contract with a third party on behalf of a corporation that both parties to the transaction know is not yet formed is personally liable on the contract unless the other party to the transaction agrees to look solely to the corporation for performance. Where a person knowingly enters into an agreement with a promoter of a nonexistent corporation, there is an inference that the person intends to make a present contract with the promoter. As a result, there is a rebuttable inference that the parties intend the promoter to be a party to that agreement. An exception to that rule applies when it is clear that the person agreed to look solely to the to-be-formed corporation for payment.

a)   Novation Required to Release Promoter

Subsequent adoption of a pre-incorporation contract by the corporation after it is formed generally will not release a promoter from liability unless there is a novation by which the other contracting party agrees to release the promoter from liability and look solely to the corporation. *E.g., Decker v. Juzwik,* 255 Iowa 358, 121 N.W.2d 652, 659 (1953) (finding a novation).

b)   Indemnification by Corporation

A promoter who has not violated any fiduciary duties to a corporation but is held liable on a pre-incorporation contract will often be able to obtain indemnity from the corporation. Hamilton, *Corporations* 176 (3rd ed. 1992). In addition, indemnification of the promoter may be provided for in the organizational documents signed by the initial board of directors in connection with incorporation of the corporation.

c)   Liability of Corporation

Upon incorporation, a corporation is not automatically bound by the contracts that were previously entered into by its promoters. Henn & Alexander, *Laws of Corporations* § 107 (3d ed. 1983). However, after a corporation is formed, the corporation may adopt a pre-incorporation contract and become liable under that contract. A corporation may adopt a contract in the same manner that will render an original contract effective. Thus, in an appropriate case the adoption need not be express. Rather, it may be inferred from the actions of the corporation or its agents who accept the benefits of that contract.

B.   Subscription for Shares

A subscription for shares is an offer to purchase shares made to the corporation by a person or entity seeking to become a shareholder. In Michigan, the subscription agreement, to be enforceable, must be in writing and signed by the subscriber. Mich. Comp. Laws § 450.1305(1). The testable question that recurs regarding subscriptions is whether they are revocable.

1)   IRREVOCABLE FOR SIX MONTHS

A subscription to purchase shares that is made before a corporation is formed is generally irrevocable for six months, unless otherwise provided by the terms of the subscription or if the parties consent to the revocation. Mich. Comp. Laws § 450.1305(2).

2)   PAYMENT

Unless the subscription agreement provides otherwise, payment for a subscription must be made as determined by the board in terms of when payment is made, in full or by installments. Mich. Comp. Laws § 450.1306(1)(a). Any call made by the board of directors for payment on subscriptions must be uniform as to all shares of the same class or series. Mich. Comp. Laws § 450.1306(1)(b).

C.   Financing the Organization

Organizations are financed either by loans from creditors or investments that are made in response to the issuance of securities. The loans may either be unsecured or secured by collateral such as real or personal property. The investments that are made typically are evidenced by securities or stocks.

The legal standard for determining the sufficiency of a corporate entity's financing is adequate capital. An adequate amount of capital will meet both a company's future needs and pay its debts when they are due. To meet that standard, a subsidiary should possess enough capital to be financially independent of the parent corporation.

D.   Sources of Finance

Securities or stocks may be issued by both private and public corporations. The issuance of private corporation stock is usually governed by state law. The issuance of public corporation stock is generally governed by federal law that is enforced by the Securities and Exchange Commission (SEC). There are two types of securities, both of which are issued at a value that corresponds to the investment's dollar amount.

1)   EQUITY SECURITIES

Equity securities reflect a corporation's capital that is at risk in conducting business. Their holders are not entitled to either a return on their investment or repayment of their investment. If, however, the corporation is liquidated and its creditors are paid, then these shareholders own the company's remaining assets. These shareholders possess the following rights:

- right to a residual share of the corporation's assets after its liquidation;
- right to vote regarding the corporation's management; and
- right to a present return on their investment.

2)   DEBT SECURITIES

Debt securities reflect those funds that are loaned to a corporation by a creditor. There are three main types of debt securities:

Notes represent long-term debt that may or may not be secured by collateral. Unlike bonds and debentures, they are usually not transferred or traded and involve institutional lenders.

Debentures are a corporation's unsecured financial obligations that are possessed by general creditors.

Bonds are corporate obligations involving mortgages or security interests upon the corporation's property. Their holder has a right of priority over holders of equity securities in the event of a corporate liquidation. Registered bonds are owned by a specific individual. Bearer bonds are owned by their present holder.

★ III.   PIERCING THE CORPORATE VEIL

A.   General Rule – Shareholders Not Personally Liable

The law treats a corporation as an entirely separate entity from its stockholders, even where one person owns all of the corporation's stock. Generally, shareholders of a corporation are not personally liable for the debts of a corporation. Harry G. Henn & John R. Alexander, *Laws of Corporations,* § 146 at 344-347 (1983). The major exception to this rule is the doctrine of piercing the corporate veil.

B.   Standard Required to Pierce the Corporate Veil

1)   GENERAL CONSIDERATIONS

Sometimes, a court will permit a creditor to "pierce the corporate veil" and hold a shareholder personally liable. The traditional basis for piercing the corporate veil has been to protect a corporation's creditors where there is a unity of interest of the stockholders and the corporation, and where the stockholders have used the corporate structure in an attempt to avoid legal obligations.

In determining whether to hold a shareholder personally liable for the debts of a corporation, courts will generally examine whether the corporation has been so dominated by an individual or another corporation that it may be considered as the other's "alter ego." Robert W. Hamilton, *The Law of Corporations*, § 6.2 at 829-831 (1987). Courts will additionally examine any evidence of 1) fraud, illegality, or estoppel; 2) undercapitalization; or 3) disregard of corporate formalities.

★★   2)   MICHIGAN LAW OF PIERCING CORPORATE VEIL

          a)   Personal Liability for Injustice or Fraud

The doctrine of piercing the corporate veil imposes liability on an individual who uses a corporation as an instrumentality to transact the individual's own personal business with personal liability arising when an injustice or fraud is committed against third parties dealing with the corporation. *In re RCS Engineered Prods. Co., Inc.*, 102 F.3d 223 (CA 6, 1996).

          b)   Factors for Analysis of Relevant Facts

In Michigan, there is no single rule for when the corporate entity may be disregarded. The courts consider all relevant facts in light of the corporation, its economic justification, and its operation to determine if the corporate form (i.e., structure) has been abused. *Klager v. Robert Meyer Co.*, 415 Mich. 402 (1982). The Michigan Court of Appeals has used the following standard for piercing the corporate veil: (1) the corporate entity is merely an agent or instrumentality of another individual, its shareholders, or another entity; (2) the corporate entity was used to commit an injustice, fraud, or wrong; and (3) the plaintiff suffered an unjust loss or injury. *SCD Chem. Distribs., Inc. v. Medley,* 203 Mich. App. 374 (1994); also *Foodland Distribs. v. Al-Naimi,* 220 Mich. App. 453 (1996); *Rymal v. Baergen*, 262 Mich. App. 274 (2004).

          (1)   Showing of Fraud Not Always Necessary

In a more modern decision of the Court of Appeals, the trial court was reversed when it required plaintiff to prove fraud to pierce the corporate veil. Instead, the Court of Appeals held that plaintiff could pierce the corporate veil if it showed that the corporate defendant was "defendants' 'agent,' 'mere instrumentality', or device to avoid legal obligations." *L & R Homes Inc v. Jack Christenson Rochester, Inc.,* 475 Mich. 853 (2006) and *Foodland Distrib. v. Al-Naimi,* 220 Mich. App. 453 (1996). So, arguably a showing of fraud may not necessarily be required in order to pierce the corporate veil if the facts fit the other elements of the three part-test set forth earlier in this outline.

          3)   WHO IS LIABLE?

As a general rule, when courts pierce the corporate veil, all of the shareholders of that corporation are liable. Some courts, however, have not extended liability to passive investors. There "is some authority, for example, for piercing the corporate veil to hold shareholders active in the business personally liable, but recognizing the same corporation's separate existence to protect passive investors from the same liability." Hamilton § 6.9 at 99. *Musco Corp. v. Qualite, Inc.,* 1994 U.S. Dist. Lexis 9799 at n.6. Protecting passive investors seems particularly appropriate if the corporate shield is being pierced because the corporation is the alter ego or agent of dominant shareholders.

4)   RELATED CORPORATIONS (PARENT/SUBSIDIARY/AFFILIATE)

When analyzing whether a parent corporation is liable for the obligations of its subsidiary, courts have looked for the existence of the following circumstances:

- "The formalities of separate corporate procedures for each corporation are not observed." Henn & Alexander, § 148 at 356 (1983).

- "The corporation is inadequately financed as a separate unit." *Id.* The courts analyze whether the corporation is adequately capitalized to meet "its normal obligations foreseeable in a business of its size and character..." *Id.*

- "The policies of the corporation are not directed to its own interests primarily but rather to those of the other corporation." *Id.*

Courts will not usually disregard the corporate entity if only one of the above criteria is met. Courts normally require, for example, that both the corporate formalities are lacking and that the corporation is inadequately capitalized.

5)   SHAREHOLDER AS TORTFEASOR

The general rule is that if "the shareholder personally commits a tort while acting as an agent for his or her corporation, he or she is personally liable for the tort because of the general rule that tortfeasors are personally liable even though they are acting as agents." Hamilton, § 6.3, at 83. *Also* Henn & Alexander, § 146 at 347. Likewise, an "agent who does an act otherwise a tort is not relieved from liability by the fact that he acted at the command of the principal or on account of the principal." *Restatement (Second) of Agency* § 343 (1957).

IV.   CAPITAL STOCK STRUCTURE

A.   Classes of Stock

A corporation may attach different rights to different classes of equity securities or stock, including rights regarding 1) voting, 2) dividends, and 3) liquidation preferences. The number of issued shares can never exceed the number of authorized shares that are set forth in the articles of incorporation.

1)   COMMON STOCK

Common stock is a security that represents ownership in a corporation. Holders of common stock exercise control by electing a board of directors and voting on corporate policy. Common stockholders are on the bottom of the priority ladder for ownership structure. In the event of liquidation, common shareholders have rights to a company's assets only after bondholders, preferred shareholders, and other debt holders have been paid in full.

2)   PREFERRED STOCK

Preferred stock is a class of ownership in a corporation with a stated dividend that must be paid before dividends are payable to common stockholders. Preferred stock does not always have voting rights. Shares are "preferred" if: their holders are 1) entitled to receive payment of dividends before any payment of dividends on some other class or series of shares; or 2) entitled in the event of any voluntary liquidation, dissolution. or winding up of the corporation to receive payment or distribution of a preferential amount before any payments or distributions are received by some other class or series of shares.

3)   AUTHORIZED SHARES

Authorized shares are the maximum number of shares that a corporation is legally permitted to issue under its articles of incorporation.

4)   OUTSTANDING SHARES

Outstanding shares are the number of shares that are currently owned by investors. They include restricted shares, which are owned by a company's officers and insiders, and shares that are held by the public. Shares that the company has repurchased are not considered outstanding stock.

5)   TREASURY STOCK

Treasury stock consists of shares that a company issued and that the company subsequently reacquired.

6)   OPTIONS

A corporation may issue options for the purchase of its shares on terms and conditions that are determined by its board of directors. Shares may be issued, and options extended, for different types of consideration, including both "services performed" and "contracts for services to be performed." Revised Model Business Corporation Act ("RMBCA") § 6.21(b).

a)   Limited to Authorized Shares

A corporation must have a sufficient number of authorized shares to cover all of its issued and outstanding shares, as well as all shares that are subject to options that have been issued. Articles of incorporation are required to state the number of authorized shares of the corporation.

B.   Stock Characteristics

1)   SHARES WITHIN CLASS MUST POSSESS IDENTICAL RIGHTS

All shares within a class of stock must have identical rights and preferences unless the shares within a class are divided into separate series. RMBCA § 6.02(c); Hamilton, *Corporations,* V.CA, at 243 (1992). In addition, shares that have a preferred right to receive dividends or distributions on liquidation should not be called "common" shares. Henn and Alexander, *Laws of Corporations* § 160, at 403 (1983). *McKinney's N. Y. Business Corporation Law* § 501(b).

2)   PREEMPTIVE RIGHTS

A preemptive right is the right of a current shareholder to maintain her fractional ownership of a company by buying a proportional number of shares of any future issue of common stock. Under the RMBCA and many state statutes including the Michigan's BCA, a corporation must "opt in" to create preemptive rights by expressly including that right in its articles of incorporation. Mich. Comp. Laws § 450.1343(1). In other states, preemptive rights are presumed to exist unless the corporation "opts out" and expressly excludes such rights in its articles. In Michigan, an agreement between at least one shareholder and the corporation can provide for preemptive rights. *Id.*

Holders of common shares have no preemptive rights to preferential shares unless those shares are convertible to common shares. RMBCA § 6.30(b)(5); Mich. Comp. Laws § 450.1343(2)(e). So long as the preferred shares, which are entitled to preferential rights, are not convertible into common shares and carry no rights to acquire common shares, common shares have no preemptive rights with regard to preferential shares.

a)   Exceptions

Unless otherwise set forth in the articles or an agreement, preemptive rights never exist for:

- shares that the articles authorize which are issued within six months of incorporation;
- shares issued as compensation to directors, officers, agents, or employees;
- shares issued to satisfy option or conversion rights providing compensation to directors, officers, agents, or employees; or
- shares issued for a consideration other than cash.

Mich. Comp. Laws § 450.1343(2)(c).

C.   Dividends and Distributions

★   ### 1)   GENERAL

Dividends and distributions are usually to be paid at the discretion of the board of directors, unless the articles of incorporation provide otherwise. Only the board of directors has the discretion to authorize dividends. However, the board may not authorize a distribution if, after giving effect to the distribution: 1) The corporation would be unable to pay its debts as they become due in usual course of business; or 2) The corporate assets would be less than the sum of its liabilities plus--unless the articles of incorporation provide otherwise--the amount needed if the corporation was dissolved (at the time of the distribution) to satisfy preferential rights on dissolution of those shareholders whose preferential rights are superior to those receiving distribution. Mich. Comp. Laws § 450.1345(3). The first of both those main restrictions upon the ability to make distributions is known as the "equity insolvency test," while the second one is known as the "balance sheet test."

a)   Types of Dividends

A company may issue cash, other property, or additional stocks to a stockholder as dividends.

2)   BAD-FAITH EXCEPTION

If the board of directors refuses to issue dividends in bad faith, but not necessarily in bad judgment, the shareholder may be able to compel distribution.

★   ### 3)   DIRECTOR LIABILITY

a)   Improper Distribution

In the event the board approves an improper dividend, those directors who voted to approve it may be liable for paying it back to the corporation. Such directors will be jointly and severally liable when concurring in or voting to declare a distribution contrary to the BCA or restrictions in a corporation's articles of incorporation. Mich. Comp. Laws § 450.1551(1)(a).

(1)   Shelter Rule

An exception to this liability applies to shelter a director otherwise subject to this liability when the director acts in good faith, with due care, and reasonably believed that he acted in the corporation's best interest. Mich. Comp. Laws § 450.1541a(1).

D.   Consideration for Shares

1)   GENERAL

The board of directors may authorize shares to be issued for consideration consisting of any tangible or intangible property or benefit to the corporation, including, but not limited to: cash, promissory notes, services performed, contracts for services to be performed, or other securities of the corporation. Mich. Comp. Laws § 450.1314(1).

a)   Judgment of Board Conclusive

The judgment of the board of directors as to the consideration received for the shares issued is conclusive in the absence of actual fraud in the transaction. Mich. Comp. Laws § 450.1314(3).

2)   WATERED STOCK

This is stock issued gratuitously, or by agreement under which its holder pays less than its par value. This type of stock issuance is binding upon the corporation and any of the stockholders that agree or acquiesce to the transaction. Any dissenting stockholders have the right to sue for cancellation of the stock. When watered stock is part of the original stock issued, it technically represents fraud on future creditors of the corporation who deal in the good faith that the stock has been fully paid. So, if the corporation becomes insolvent, the holders of watered stock may be held liable for its par value to pay to creditors. By using no par value stock, the problems of dealing with watered stock can be decreased or avoided.

E.   Redemption and Repurchases

1)   REDEMPTION

Usually only a corporation's articles of incorporation may provide it with the right to require that a shareholder sell back the corporation's stock to the corporation. Mich. Comp. Laws § 450.1304a. This corporate right generally only applies to preferred stock and should be ratably made among all of those shares.

2)   REPURCHASE

A corporation may enter into an agreement to buy back its own shares of stock. The articles of incorporation do not need to authorize such an agreement. An insolvent corporation cannot repurchase shares. A solvent corporation cannot make a repurchase if doing that would impair preferred stockholder's rights. Repurchased stock may become treasury stock or be retired.

V.   MANAGEMENT AND CONTROL

A.   Shareholders

1)   MEETINGS

a)   Annual Meetings

A corporation must hold a meeting of shareholders annually at a time that is stated or fixed in accordance with the bylaws. Mich. Comp. Laws § 450.1402.

★   (1)   When Shareholder May Compel Shareholders' Meeting

A corporation's shareholder may compel a shareholders' meeting by filing an application with the Michigan circuit court of the county in which the corporation's registered office or principal place of business is located when either of these circumstances exist: 1) no meeting date is designated for 15 months after organization of the corporation or after its last annual meeting; or 2) the annual meeting is not held for 90 days after the date designated for the meeting. *Id.*

b)   Special Meetings

"Special meetings" can generally be called by a demand of 10 percent of the shareholders. Mich. Comp. Laws § 450.1403.

c) Action Without Meeting

An action by the shareholders may be taken without a meeting if the action is taken by all of the shareholders of outstanding shares who are entitled to vote on the action. Mich. Comp. Laws § 450.1407. The action must be evidenced by written consents that are signed by all the shareholders who are entitled to vote. *Id.*

★ d) Notice to Shareholder

As a general matter, shareholders entitled to vote must be provided with notice of all annual and special meetings. For special meetings, in addition to notice of the meeting itself, shareholders must also be provided with notice of the purpose of the meeting. Mich. Comp. Laws § 450.1403. In many states including Michigan, the notice must be provided 10-60 days before the meeting. Mich. Comp. Laws § 450.1404. The purpose of the time notice requirement is to permit the shareholders the opportunity to attend the meeting. Another purpose of the time notice is to allow the shareholder the opportunity to prepare and to study a proposal related to the meeting's purpose. If there is a deficiency in the time notice requirement, but the shareholder attends the meeting, he has not been harmed by inadequate notice of the time of the meeting.

e) Quorum

Quorum refers to the number of shareholders who must be present in order for the shareholders to take an action. General quorum requirements mandate that at least a majority of shareholders who are entitled to vote must be present. Mich. Comp. Laws § 450.1415(1). In most states including Michigan, the articles of incorporation may provide for a greater quorum requirement. *Id.*

2) VOTING

Voting rights of shareholders are generally determined by statute or the articles of incorporation. In general, unless provided otherwise by law, all shareholders' votes are counted equally regardless of class. The shareholders who are entitled to vote at a meeting are not the shareholders as of the date of the meeting. Instead, only the shareholder as of the designated record date before the meeting are entitled to vote at a meeting.

a) Cumulative Voting

Shareholders elect directors either directly (one share-one vote) or cumulatively. In cumulative voting, voters cast as many votes as there are seats, but voters are not limited to giving only one vote to a candidate. Instead, they can put multiple votes on one or more candidates. Cumulative voting is considered a means to provide fair representation of the minority shareholder's interests.

b)   Proxies

A proxy vote occurs when a person authorizes another person to vote her shares. Oral proxies are generally revocable. Written proxies are revocable unless they are coupled with an interest. A proxy is coupled with an interest when the recipient of the proxy possesses an economic interest in the shares.

c)   Voting Trusts (for a term)

Voting trust agreements among shareholders confer upon a trustee a right to vote their shares a certain way. Voting trust agreements only confer that right for a limited time of up to 10 years. Mich. Comp. Laws § 450.1466. Any such agreement must be in writing and filed in the corporation's registered office. *Id.*

★   d)   Shareholders' Voting Agreements

By signing a shareholders' voting agreement, shareholders may agree that stock must be voted:

- pursuant to the provisions of the agreement;
- as they may subsequently agree; or
- in accordance with an agreed upon procedure.

A voting agreement is specifically enforceable. Mich. Comp. Laws § 450.1461.

★   e)   Effect of Voting

The assent of a shareholder to a corporate transaction generally means that the shareholder cannot later challenge the validity of the transaction in court. This rule does not apply if the now-dissenting shareholder can prove that any complaint or objection to the transaction would have been futile. A court would probably hold that the lack of a vote against the proposal would have the same effect as an affirmative vote.

★★   3)   <u>RIGHT TO INSPECT RECORDS</u>

In Michigan, a shareholder's right to inspect corporate records is set forth at section 450.1487 of the Michigan Compiled Laws, which provide in part:

(2)   Any shareholder of record . . . shall have the right during the usual hours of business to inspect for any proper purpose the corporation's stock ledger, a list of its shareholders, and its other books and records, if the shareholder gives the corporation written demand describing with reasonable particularity his or her purpose and the records he or she desires to inspect, and the records sought are directly connected with the purpose. A proper purpose shall mean a purpose reasonably related to such person's interest as a shareholder. The demand shall be delivered to the corporation at its registered office in this state or at its principal place

of business. In every instance where an attorney or other agent shall be the person who seeks to inspect, the demand shall be accompanied by a power of attorney or other writing which authorizes the attorney or other agent to act on behalf of the shareholder.

(3)   If the corporation does not permit an inspection within five business days after a demand has been received in compliance with subsection (2), or imposes unreasonable conditions upon the inspection, the shareholder may apply to the circuit court of the county in which the principal place of business or registered office of the corporation is located for an order to compel the Inspection. If the shareholder seeks to inspect the corporation's books and records other than its stock ledger or 'List of shareholders, he or she shall first establish that he or she has complied with this section respecting the form and manner of making demand for inspection of the documents, that the inspection he or she seeks is for a proper purpose, and that the documents sought are directly connected with the purpose. If the shareholder seeks to inspect the corporation's stock ledger or list of shareholders and has established compliance with this section respecting the form and manner of making demand for the inspection of the documents, the burden of proof shall be upon the corporation to establish that the inspection that is sought is for an improper purpose or that the records sought are not directly connected with the person's purpose. The court may, in its discretion, order the corporation to permit the shareholder to inspect the corporation's stock ledger, a list of shareholders, and its other books and records on conditions and with limitations as the court may prescribe and may award other or further relief as the court may consider just and proper. . . .

(5)   If the court orders inspection of the records demanded under subsection (3) . . ., it shall also order the corporation to pay the shareholder's or director's costs, including reasonable attorney fees, incurred to obtain the order unless the corporation proves that it failed to permit the inspection in good faith because it had a reasonable basis to doubt the right of the shareholder or director to inspect the records demanded.

a)   Proper Purpose for Inspection of Records

A "proper purpose" is one that is reasonably related to the person's interest as a shareholder. Under the common law, a shareholder stated a proper purpose for an inspection by raising doubts whether corporate affairs had been properly conducted by idle directors or management. The courts have held that curiosity or mere speculation of mismanagement is insufficient to justify an inspection, but the Michigan Legislature did not intend to erect a formidable obstacle for shareholders. Under Michigan's BCA statute, a proper purpose for inspection is one that in good faith seeks information bearing upon protection of the shareholder's interest and that of other shareholders of the corporation, and is not contrary to the corporation's interests. If a corporation's shareholder does not make a demand in good faith for the protection of the interests of the corporation or its shareholders, then the stockholder has no right to an order compelling the inspection of corporate documents. *Slay v. Polonia Pub. Co.*, 249 Mich. 609 (1930). It is a proper purpose to seek a shareholder list for purposes of getting elected to the board of directors. *George v. Int'l Breweries, Inc.*, 1 Mich. App. 129 (1965).

By statute, the corporation must either approve or reject the request within the five-day period if the shareholder's request complied with the statute. In the absence of a request that complies with the statute, the corporation's response, or lack thereof, does not provide a basis for the relief requested. The statute does not contemplate a shareholder's request for the corporate officer's income tax returns, which would not be permitted. *North Oakland County Bd. of Realtors v. Realcomp, Inc.*, 226 Mich. App. 54 (1910).

B.   Directors

The business of every corporation must be managed by a board of directors. Mich. Comp. Laws § 450.1501. All directors must be natural persons who are generally at least 18 years of age (19 in some states). In Michigan, the bylaws or articles of incorporation can prescribe the qualifications of directors. *Id.*

1)   COMPOSITION OF THE BOARD

a)   One Minimum

A corporation must have at least one director. Mich. Comp. Laws § 450.1505(1). The corporation's bylaws may fix the number of directors, or provide the manner for fixing their number, unless the articles of incorporation fix that number. *Id.* Generally, those documents can provide for a variable number of directors within a fixed minimum and maximum, and for the manner in which the number of directors may be increased or decreased.

b)   Need not be Shareholder

Unless otherwise provided in the articles of incorporation, directors need not be stockholders.

c)   Voting Agreements

Voting agreements between board members are void and unenforceable.

d)   Elections

Directors are elected at each annual meeting unless otherwise agreed.

2)   AUTHORITY OF DIRECTORS

Subject to any limitations by law, or the articles of incorporation of the corporation, the board of directors has full control over the affairs of the corporation and to:

a)   Make Bylaws

Subject to the bylaws, if any, adopted by the stockholders, the directors may make the bylaws of the corporation.

b)   Fill Vacancies

Generally, a vacancy in the board of directors may be filled by the remaining directors, unless otherwise required by articles. Mich. Comp. Laws § 450.1515a(1)(b).

★   3)   EXERCISE OF AUTHORITY

General quorum requirements mandate that at least a majority of directors must be present at a meeting for a valid vote to occur. Mich. Comp. Laws § 450.1523(1). For the board to take an action, generally it must have the support of a majority of the directors present. *Id.* Moreover, the directors must have notice of special, not regular, meetings. It is presumed that directors should have knowledge of regular meetings. A director of a corporation is not to be trapped into the attendance of a meeting against his will. Generally, the board cannot meet except at a regular consensual meeting.

a)   Informal Action

Informal action by the board may be taken with unanimous consent of the board members in writing or by electronic transmission. Mich. Comp. Laws § 450.1525. Such a consent resolution is the effective equivalent of a unanimous vote. *Id.*

b)   Action by Committee

Action by committee occurs when a board delegates the daily operations of a corporation to an executive committee of its officers. The board may not avoid any legal responsibility or liability by means of delegation. Action by committee is not permissible with respect to:

- amending the articles of incorporation;
- approving a merger or share exchange;
- recommending the following types of proposed action to the shareholders: (A) dissolution of, or revocation of dissolution of, the corporation; or (B) "sale, lease, or exchange of all or substantially all of the corporation's property and assets";
- amending the corporation's bylaws;
- filling vacant seats on the board; or
- authorizing the issuance stock or declaring a dividend or distribution to shareholders -- unless a board resolution, the bylaws, or the articles of incorporation expressly provide a committee the authority or power to take those two types of action.

Mich. Comp. Laws § 450.1528.

c)   Subject to Articles and Bylaws

Action by the board is subject to the provisions of the corporation's articles of incorporation and its bylaws. Within those limitations, the board is free to determine how to lawfully carry out its functions.

★   4)   OBJECTIONS TO ACTIONS

A director who votes for a course of corporate conduct may not subsequently dissent from that vote. A director who opposes such a course must, by affirmative conduct, dissent when a vote on that conduct is taken. If a director fails to raise an objection during a board meeting is considered to approve of the decisions that were made at that meeting.

Michigan's BCA states that:

> A director who is present at a meeting of the board . . . at which action on a corporate matter . . . [for which a director may be liable] is taken is presumed to have concurred in that action unless his dissent is entered in the minutes of the meeting or unless he files his written dissent to the action with the person acting as secretary of the meeting before or promptly after the adjournment thereof. The right to dissent does not apply to a director who voted in favor of the action. A director who is absent from a meeting of the board . . . at which any such action is taken is presumed to have concurred in the action unless he files his dissent with the secretary of the corporation within a reasonable time after he has knowledge of the action.

Mich. Comp. Laws § 450.1553.

As a general matter, a director who attends a special meeting and refuses to participate in the vote at the meeting on an issue that the notice of the meeting failed to state does not thereby waive the director's objection to the issue. *Darvin v. Belmont Indus., Inc.*, 40 Mich. App. 672 (1972).

C.   **Officers**

The board of directors generally delegates day-to-day management of the corporation's business to officers. Traditionally, officers had only those powers conferred on them by the bylaws or resolutions of the board of directors. *Black v. Harrison Home Co.*, 99 P. 494 (Cal. 1909); *Daniel Webster Council, Inc. v. St. James Assoc., Inc.*, 533 A.2d 329 (N.H. 1987). Today, most states presume that the president has the inherent power to act for the corporation so long as the matter is within the scope of its ordinary business.

Officers are generally appointed by the board of directors. Mich. Comp. Laws § 450.1531. In Michigan, every corporation must have a president, a secretary and a treasurer (can be same person). *Id.* The board may remove officers with or without cause, however, such action may possibly subject the corporation to a breach of contract action. Mich. Comp. Laws § 450.1535.

1)   LIABILITY ON CORPORATE OBLIGATIONS

One of the purposes of incorporation is to protect the individual officers who are involved with a corporation from exposure to personal liability. To minimize an officer's exposure to liability, under MBCA sec. 8.42(a), 3rd Ed., STANDARDS OF CONDUCT FOR OFFICER, "An officer, when performing in such capacity, shall act: (1) in good faith; (2) with the care that a person in a like position would reasonably exercise under similar circumstances; and (3) in a manner the officer reasonably believes to be in the best interests of the corporation."

MBCA sec. 8.42(c), 3rd Ed., further provides in part that: "An officer shall not be liable to a corporation or its shareholders for any decision to take or not to take action, or any failure to take any action, as an officer, if the duties of the office are performed in compliance with this section. Whether an officer who does not comply with this section shall have liability will depend in such instances on applicable law."

2)   LIABILITY OF CORPORATION FOR ACTS OF PRESIDENT

The president of a corporation possesses the authority to bind a corporation by acts that are conducted in the ordinary course of business. However, the president does not have the authority to bind the corporation by extraordinary acts. In many cases, there is no bright line test for determining whether an act is "ordinary." Any attempt at precision in drawing this line would almost certainly be futile, because the issue is highly dependent on the context in which it arises, and the types of business transactions that may arise are endlessly variable. Factors that a court may consider in determining whether a transaction is extraordinary include the economic magnitude of the action in relation to corporate earnings and assets, the extent of the risk involved, the time span of the action's effect, and the cost of reversing the action. *Id. Also Joseph Greenspon's Sons Iron & Steel Co. v. Pecos Valley Gas Co.*, 156 A. 350, 352-53 (Del. Super. 1931).

D.   Members and Managers (LLC)

An LLC's articles of organization may designate between one of two types of management structures. An LLC can be either manager-managed, or member-managed. If an LLC is manager-managed, the power and authority of the company's management lies within its board of managers, which is similar to the board of directors of a corporation. If an LLC is member-managed, there is no board of managers, and the LLC is directly managed by its members as the owners.

Either type of management (members or board of managers) can delegate power and authority to the company's officers. If the management does delegate authority, it will retain the responsibility to oversee the affairs and activities of the company.

1)   LIABILITY

An LLC provides legal and financial liability protections to its members if their business conduct is not irresponsible, unethical, or illegal. The financial liability protection is that a member generally is not personally liable for certain valid business-related debts of an insolvent LLC. Only the LLC's business assets are subject to claims of a financial or legal nature. Thus, the creditors of an LLC usually cannot attach a member's personal assets to recover the LLC's debts. The legal liability protections include reduced exposure from lawsuit judgments for damages that are not based on claims such as willful misconduct or professional malpractice.

2)   POWERS

Generally, an LLC may be authorized to conduct any and all lawful business, unless its articles of organization more narrowly define and describe the type and extent of business activities that the LLC will conduct. For example, the LLC's articles may specify that it will provide certain services.

VI.   FIDUCIARY DUTIES

Directors, officers, and employees of a corporation owe fiduciary duties to its shareholders. Those general fiduciary duties owed to shareholders include the duty of care and the duty of loyalty.

- Time Limit for Commencing Breach of Fiduciary Duty Action

A party must commence an action against a director or officer for breach for fiduciary duty within the earlier of three years after the cause of action accrued, or two years after discovery of the action or when the party reasonably should have discovered it. Mich. Comp. Laws § 450.1541a(4).

★★★ A.   Duty of Care

Directors and officers owe the corporation a duty of care. This duty includes the duty to take reasonable steps to monitor the corporation's management; the duty to remain informed about the corporation's business; and the duty to be satisfied that any proposals are in the corporation's best interests. In essence, duty of care requires fiduciaries to act carefully when acting on behalf of the corporation.

★★★   1)   GOOD-FAITH

This duty has been interpreted to require that the fiduciary discharge his duties in good faith, with "the care an ordinarily prudent person in a like position would exercise under similar circumstances" and in a manner the officer reasonably believes to be in the corporation's best interests. Mich. Comp. Laws § 450.1541a(1).

a)   Reliance upon Information

A fiduciary is entitled to rely on information from officers or employees whom she believes to be reliable. Mich. Comp. Laws § 450.1541a(2)(a). However, a fiduciary is not acting in good faith if the fiduciary has knowledge of the matter at issue which makes the fiduciary's reliance unwarranted. Mich. Comp. Laws § 450.1541a(3).

(1)   Reasonableness of Reliance upon Information

An allegation of good faith reliance by a fiduciary must be evaluated by the reasonableness of the fiduciary's belief in: (a) the accuracy and completeness of information provided to the fiduciary by another individual; (b) this individual's competency and reliability; or (c) the performance of a committee within its allocated authority and in a manner the fiduciary considers as warranting confidence.

In general, the duty of care requires that a director take steps to become informed about facts before taking any action. Henn at § 234.

★★★   2)   BUSINESS JUDGMENT RULE

The business judgment rule is a doctrine that protects officers and directors of a corporation from personal liability so long as the actors acted in good faith, with due care, and within their authority.

a)   Presumption

This doctrine provides a presumption to that affect -- absent evidence of bad faith, fraud, or self-dealing (as further described later). The presumption of the business rule considers business decisions to be made by independent, disinterested, and informed directors of a corporation who believe in good faith that these decisions will be in the best interest of the corporation and its shareholders.

(1)   Judicial Evaluation

Upon the filing of a lawsuit against the directors, a trial court will initially consider the decision to the degree required to conclude if the evidence presented by the complaining party has overcome this presumption. If not, then the trial court may not consider the merits of the business decision at issue. Accordingly, the directors will be shielded by this doctrine from liability for their decision regardless of its outcome.

★★   3)   LIMITATION ON LIABILITY

A corporation's articles may reasonably limit the liability of officers and directors for bad judgment, but not for bad faith misconduct in, or relative to, the discharge of their duties.

★★★ B.   Duty of Loyalty

Directors and officers have a duty to avoid implicating her personal interests. Such interests may not conflict with the interests of the corporation. The classic breach of the duty of loyalty involves insider trading. Examination questions may involve interested transactions. The following rules, which may only refer to directors, generally also apply as a matter of principle to officers of a corporation.

1)   INTERESTED TRANSACTIONS

a)   Does a Conflicting Interest Exist?

Under the RMBCA, a director has a "conflicting interest" in a transaction if the director either is a "party to the transaction," or "has a beneficial financial interest in ... the transaction... of such financial significance to the director...that the interest would reasonably be expected to exert an influence on the director's judgment if...called upon to vote on the transaction..." RMBCA § 8.60(1)(i).

b)   Required Disclosure Regarding Conflicting Interests

The board cannot vote to authorize a transaction unless the interested directors have made certain required disclosures to the entire board of directors. RMBCA § 8.62(a). The required disclosures include all "facts known to him respecting the subject matter of the transaction that an ordinarily prudent person would reasonably believe to be material to a judgment about whether or not to proceed with the transaction." RMBCA § 8.60(4)(ii).

c)   Authorization of Interested Transactions

If the interested directors make the required disclosure, the "qualified" (non-interested) members of a board of directors can ordinarily act to authorize a director's conflicting interest transaction. RMBCA § 8.62(a). A "qualified" director is a director who does not have a conflicting interest with respect to the transaction and does not have a familial or other relationship with a director that has a conflicting interest. RMBCA § 8.62(d). Such approval requires "the affirmative vote of a majority (but no fewer than two) of those qualified directors on the board of directors." RMBCA § 8.62(a). If only one director is "qualified," the board of directors cannot properly authorize the transaction. RMBCA § 8.62(a). Note that some states (including Delaware) require the vote of a majority of disinterested directors, but such majority may be only one director. In Michigan, a majority of the directors who had no interest in the transaction can authorize it even though they are less than a quorum. Mich. Comp. Laws § 450.1107(2). If the transaction is authorized without compliance with these requirements, the action of the board may still be valid if the director can demonstrate that it was fair to the corporation.

★   (1)   Fairness of Transaction to Corporation

A "transaction involving an interested officer or director shall not be set aside or give rise to an award in damages if the person interested in the transaction establishes that the transaction was fair, the transaction was approved by independent directors upon disclosure of all material facts, or the transaction was approved by the shareholders upon disclosure of all material facts." *Camden v. Kaufman*, 240 Mich. App. 389 (2000). For example, if a transaction is fair to a corporation when entered into, and the material facts of the transaction and the majority shareholders'/directors' interest were disclosed to the board and to the other shareholders entitled to vote on a transaction, and they ratified the transaction, then the courts will not set aside the transaction.

2)   USURPING CORPORATE OPPORTUNITIES

The corporate opportunity doctrine prohibits directors or officers from appropriating to themselves business opportunities that rightfully belong to the corporation. Whether a particular business opportunity belongs to the corporation or is personal to an individual depends upon the facts and circumstances of each particular case. Otherwise, the director or officer may be liable for "disgorgement of profits."

C.   Majority Shareholder

Majority shareholders may owe a fiduciary duty to minority shareholders including the duty to act in good faith and inherent fairness. This is especially applicable in close corporations where shareholders will be held to a higher standard that is akin to the standard for partners in a partnership.

D.   Creditors and Shareholders

Directors usually lack any fiduciary duties to the creditors of their corporation. Actually, directors may be liable for preferring the creditors more than the corporation's shareholders.

1)   CREDITORS

Ordinarily, courts will decide that instruments of credit or debt establish duties of contract by the corporation and entitle the creditors to performance of the contract by the corporation, rather than providing the creditors with an equitable interest in the corporation that affords them more rights. Accordingly, the creditors will not need more protection from the corporation's board when they have negotiated particular remedies and rights in the event of non-payment within a contract, purchase agreement, loan instrument, or other course of conduct.

2)   SHAREHOLDERS

In the event of the corporation's insolvency, a question arises as to the whether its directors' duty runs to the creditors or shareholders of the corporation. Within this "zone of insolvency," courts will determine whether the insolvency: 1) results from the corporation's value being less than its debts to creditors; or 2) means that the corporation cannot pay its debts upon their due date.

The latter type of insolvency might result from inadequate capitalization or a short-duration cash shortage. This type of insolvency could exist even while the corporation possesses an unrealized value greater than its debts to creditors. Such unrealized value might be from an asset, which could substantially perform in the future, such as some existing franchise, product, or proprietary right. When these distinguishable types of insolvency coexist, the duty of the directors remains to the corporation and its shareholders. In accordance with the circumstances, this duty may shift to some extent to the creditors when the enterprise's value falls below the sum of corporate debt to them.

E.   Members and Managers (LLC)

The Uniform Limited Liability Company Act ("ULLCA") imposes the duties of care and loyalty upon managers of an LLC. Members of a manager-managed LLC owe no fiduciary duties because of being members. However, when they exercise managerial powers, they are bound by the same fiduciary duties as managers with respect to those powers. If the LLC is member-managed, the members have fiduciary duties to the LLC and the other members. The ULLCA does not permit members to eliminate the duty of loyalty, but they may modify it as long as not "manifestly unreasonable." Similarly, the duty of care may not be unreasonably reduced and reasonable standards may be set for the good faith and fair dealing obligation.

VII.   ORGANIZATIONAL STRUCTURE

A.   Amendments

1)   ARTICLES OF INCORPORATION

A corporation may change its articles of incorporation at any time. Mich. Comp. Laws § 450.1601(1). Directors have the right to make some minor changes in the articles of incorporation (such as address of agent) without the approval of the shareholders. Mich. Comp. Laws § 450.1611(2). However, most changes can only be made by the directors acting in concert with the shareholders. Mich. Comp. Laws § 450.1611(3). In Michigan, such an amendment generally requires its proposal by the board of directors and an affirmative vote of the majority of the outstanding shares entitled to vote. Mich. Comp. Laws § 450.1611(5).

Making this type of a change is a two-step process. First, the board of directors must pass a resolution declaring such amendment advisable and either calling a meeting of the stockholders entitled to vote on the amendment or directing that the proposed amendment be considered at the next annual meeting of shareholders. *Generally* Mich. Comp. Laws § 450.1611(3)-(4).

Second, an affirmative vote of a majority (unless otherwise provided by the articles) of all outstanding shares entitled to vote will result in passage of the proposed change in Michigan. Some states other than Michigan require two-thirds approval of shareholders.

a)   Class Rights

If a potential amendment would adversely modify any preference or right of one or more classes or series of stock, then holders of such affected class are, unless articles provide otherwise, entitled to vote as a class on the amendment. Generally, a majority vote of the outstanding shares of that class is necessary to pass the amendment. Mich. Comp. Laws § 450.1611(5).

b)   Before First Board Meeting

Before the board of director's first meeting, a majority of the incorporators may amend the articles of incorporation by signing and filing a certificate of amendment certifying the amendment's adoption by the incorporator's unanimous consent prior to the board's initial meeting. Mich. Comp. Laws §§ 450.1611(1), 450.1631(1).

★★   **B.   Mergers and Consolidations**

1)   GENERAL CONSIDERATIONS

A potential merger, consolidation, or share exchange of two corporations requires approval of their boards of directors, stockholders, and the provision of appraisal rights to dissenting shareholders of those corporations. A merger occurs when one of two existing corporations is absorbed into another corporation. If, however, two existing corporations combine into one new corporation, the result is a consolidation. A share exchange can have this result. Generally, a merger or consolidation requires the recommendation of an absolute majority of the board of directors and the agreement of each corporation (by an absolute majority of shareholders) to a plan of merger or consolidation. Some states instead require a two-thirds vote of shareholders.

2)   MERGER -- MICHIGAN LAW

Several former provisions of Michigan's BCA regarding consolidation were repealed. *E.g.,* Mich. Comp. Laws §§ 450.1703, 450.1721-1723, 450.1731-1734. In Michigan, a merger generally requires the recommendation of a majority of the board of directors and the agreement of each corporation (by a majority of outstanding shares entitled to vote) to a plan of merger. Mich. Comp. Laws §§ 450.1523(1), 450.1703a. Once the plan of merger is approved, a certificate of merger must be filed with the state. Mich. Comp. Laws § 450.1707(1). Generally, the certificate becomes effective when it is filed with the state, unless the parties abandon the merger before that filing occurs. Mich. Comp. Laws §§ 450.1707(2), 450.1741.

★   ### 3)   DISSENTERS' RIGHTS – FAIR VALUE

Generally, a merger or share exchange would trigger the dissenters' rights as the minority. The price paid to the dissenters is "fair value." *E.g.,* Mich. Comp. Laws § 450.1762(1). That is defined as "the value of the shares immediately before the effectuation of the corporate action to which the dissenter objects, excluding any appreciation or depreciation in anticipation of the corporate action unless exclusion would be inequitable." RMBCA § 13.01(3). However, obtaining fair value, a dissenting shareholder will lose the right to challenge the action (absent fraud). Accordingly, the dissenter has the option to either challenge the action or receive fair value. Fair value is determined immediately before the effectuation of the corporate action.

4)   SHORT-FORM MERGER

Under many state statutes including Michigan's BCA, if a parent corporation owns at least 90 percent of the stock of a subsidiary, the subsidiary may be merged into the parent absent voting approval by the shareholders of either company. Mich. Comp. Laws § 450.1711(1).

5)   SHARE EXCHANGE--MICHIGAN LAW

Michigan's BCA provides that the board of directors of two corporations may adopt a plan of share exchange. Mich. Comp. Laws § 450.1702(2). This plan results in a first corporation's acquisition of all of at least one series or class of a second corporation's outstanding shares of stock. Mich. Comp. Laws § 450.1702(1). That plan indicates what the second corporation receives in return for those shares, such as property, cash, or other obligations and securities. *Id.* A plan of share exchange generally requires the recommendation of a majority of the board of directors and the agreement of each corporation (by a majority of outstanding shares entitled to vote) to the plan of share exchange. Mich. Comp. Laws §§ 450.1523(1), 450.1703a. Once the plan of share exchange is approved, a certificate of share exchange must be filed with the state. Mich. Comp. Laws § 450.1707(1). Generally, the plan becomes effective when it is filed with the state, unless the parties abandon it before that filing occurs. Mich. Comp. Laws §§ 450.1707(2), 450.1741.

★★ **C.   Sales of Substantially All Corporate Assets**

1)   GENERAL--SHAREHOLDER APPROVAL REQUIRED

Under Michigan's BCA, shareholder approval is required only for the corporation to "sell, lease, exchange, or otherwise dispose of all, or substantially all, of its property" otherwise than in "the usual and regular course of business." Mich. Comp. Laws § 450.1753(1). Michigan's BCA differentiates between sales of all or substantially all of the assets of a corporation made in the usual and regular course of business and such sales that are not made in the usual and regular course of business. Compare Mich. Comp. Laws § 450.1753(1) with Mich. Comp. Laws § 450.1751(1).

2)   ORDINARY COURSE OF BUSINESS EXCEPTION

If a sale of corporate property occurs in the usual and regular course corporate business, it may be accomplished without the approval of the shareholders, unless otherwise required by the articles of incorporation. Mich. Comp. Laws § 450.1751(1)(a), (2). If not, the sale of all or substantially all of the assets must be approved by a majority of all the shares voting together.

★ ### 3)   DISSENTERS' RIGHTS

A sale of corporate property not in the usual and regular course of corporate business would also trigger the dissenters' rights of the minority shareholders. A sale that occurs outside of the course of business would give rise to dissenters' rights even if this were not provided for in the articles of incorporation and the corporate bylaws. However, in order for a shareholder to properly exercise dissenter's rights, the shareholder needs to follow the requirements found in Michigan's BCA. Mich. Stat. §§ 450.1761-450.1772.

First, the corporation must provide the appropriate notices. Mich. Stat. § 450.1764. Once the shareholder receives the notice of the proposed action, the shareholder is required to provide to the corporation, before the vote of shareholders, written notice of his demand for payment for his shares. Mich. Stat. § 450.1765. If the shareholder does this and then the vote of the shareholders approves the sale, the corporation will be required to send the shareholder a notice no later than 10 days thereafter advising the shareholder of the action of the corporation and advising the shareholder where the demand for payment must be sent and where the shareholder's shares must be deposited. Mich. Stat. § 450.1766. The shareholder would then be required to demand payment and deposit these shares where directed. Mich. Stat. § 450.1767. The corporation would then be required to pay the dissenter with the amount the corporation estimates to be the fair value of the shares, plus interest. Mich. Stat. § 450.1769(1).

D.   Recapitalizations

A recapitalization is a change in the corporation's stock structure in order to achieve a particular goal. A typical goal is to change the rights of a class of stock. For example, if a corporation owes back dividends to preferred shares, the shareholders may attempt to alter the preference rights of those shares to eliminate the payment. Essentially, a recapitalization may result in the majority hindering the rights of the minority. Those who are adversely affected can challenge a recapitalization. They must demonstrate the unfairness and lack of legitimate purpose for the recapitalization.

E.   Dissolution of Organization

1)   MAJORITY OF BOARD AND SHAREHOLDERS

The voluntary dissolution of a corporation generally must be recommended by a majority of the board of directors and approved by a majority of the shareholders of outstanding shares entitled to vote. Mich. Stat. § 450.1804. Some states other than Michigan require a two-thirds vote of shareholders instead of a majority vote in order for dissolution to be effective.

2)   DISSOLUTION DOES NOT TRIGGER DISSENTERS' RIGHTS

Dissolution does not trigger dissenters' rights, since the dissolution process contemplates a liquidation of the corporate assets and distributions of their proceeds to the shareholders. RMBCA § 14.05(a).

★   3)   INVOLUNTARY DISSOLUTION (CLOSE CORPORATIONS)

a)   General Considerations

Courts may intervene in the affairs of closely-held corporations under limited circumstances. A court may dissolve a corporation in a shareholder-initiated proceeding if it is established that the directors or those in control of the corporation have acted, are acting, or will act in a manner that is illegal, oppressive, or fraudulent.

The legal standard for oppressive conduct is not clearly established in some jurisdictions other than Michigan. Some courts define oppression as violating the reasonable expectations of shareholders. Many courts have taken an alternative approach, finding that in closely held corporations, controlling shareholders have a higher fiduciary duty to minority shareholders than in publicly held corporations. Whether the standard is reasonable expectations of shareholders or the duty of good faith and loyalty from majority to minority shareholders, it is clear that attempts to freeze out minority shareholders are oppressive if the majority shareholders profit from the corporation to the detriment of minority shareholders.

★   b)   Michigan Law – Oppressive Conduct

Actions of a closely-held corporation create special problems for a minority shareholder and are closely scrutinized by the courts.

Employment and board membership are not generally listed among rights that automatically accrue to shareholders. Some states have enacted statutes that specifically protect the interest of minority shareholders in their capacities as employees and directors and some states without such statutes have protected these interests through court decisions. Michigan's BCA specifically addresses this issue and is clear in its terms that a suit for oppression of a shareholder's interest can only be sustained for conduct that substantially interferes with the interest of the shareholder as a shareholder, rather than in the capacity of an employee and director. *Franchino v. Franchino,* 263 Mich. App. 172 (2004).

Michigan's BCA specifically provides that minority shareholders can bring suit for oppression only for conduct that "substantially interferes with the interest of the shareholder as a shareholder." Mich. Comp. Laws § 450.1489. The pertinent portions of Michigan's BCA regarding illegal, illegal, fraudulent, or oppressive conduct provide that: "A shareholder may bring an action . . . to establish that the acts of the directors or those in control of the corporation are illegal, fraudulent, or willfully unfair and oppressive to the corporation or to the shareholder." *Id.* Michigan's BCA further states that: "'willfully unfair and oppressive conduct' means a continuing course of conduct or a significant action or series of actions that substantially interferes with the interests of the shareholder as a shareholder." *Id.*

★   c)   Buyout Option

The RMBCA provides that if a proceeding is started to dissolve a corporation, the corporation may terminate the action if it, or a shareholder, purchases the complaining shareholders' shares for fair value. RMBCA § 14.34(a).

VIII.   CLOSE CORPORATIONS AND SPECIAL CONTROL DEVICES

Under Michigan law, a corporation is considered closely held (i.e., a close corporation) when its shareholders participate in its management and family members control the majority of its stock. *Estes v. Idea Engineering and Fabricating, Inc.,* 250 Mich. App. 270 (2002).

★   **A.   Share Transfer Restrictions**

A share transfer restriction is a restriction in the articles of incorporation, which provides that shares cannot be transferred by a shareholder without the prior consent of a majority or all of the board of directors and/or shareholders.

              1)   GENERALLY VALID IF REASONABLE

As a general rule, share transfer restrictions are invalid if they are unreasonable restraints on alienation of stock. Thus, an absolute restraint on alienation of stock is *per se* unreasonable and void. Usually, however, courts will permit share transfer restrictions if they are adopted for a lawful purpose and they are not manifestly unreasonable. Lawful purposes include keeping a corporation closely held or keeping a corporation in the family. H. Henn & J. Alexander, *Laws of Corporations* § 281, at 756-58 (3d ed. 1983).

a)   Restrictions Requiring Consent for Sale of Shares

Some transfer restrictions require the consent of all other shareholders and the approval by such shareholders of a proposed transferee in order for a shareholder to sell her stock. Consent restraints are among the most restrictive stock transfer restraints because they make stock unassignable if one shareholder refuses to vote to approve the transfer. The courts are split on the enforceability of consent restrictions. Some jurisdictions have considered such a restriction to be tantamount to an absolute restraint on alienation, manifestly unreasonable and void. *Hill v. Warner, Berman & Spitz P.A.,* 197 N.J. Super. 152, 484 A.2d 344 (1984); *Rae v. Hindin,* 29 A.D.2d 481, 288 N.Y.S.2d 662 (Sup. Ct. N.Y. 1968), *aff'd,* 23 N.Y.2d 759, 296 N.Y.S.2d 955 (1968). Other jurisdictions, however, have enforced transfer restrictions of this type. *Gray v. Harris Land & Cattle Co.,* 227 Mont. 51, 737 P.2d 475 (1987); *Benson v. RMJ Secs. Corp.* 683 F. Supp. 359 (S.D.N.Y. 1988); Henn & Alexander, *Laws of Corporations* at 759; Del. Gen. Corp. Law § 202(c)(3).

2)   ENFORCEABILITY AGAINST TRANSFEREE

Assuming that a share transfer restriction is enforceable against a selling shareholder, it must be determined whether the restriction is binding on the transferee as well. Such a restriction will only be enforceable against the transferee if: 1) he had actual notice of the restriction; or 2) the restriction is conspicuously noted on the stock certificate.

B.   **Special Agreements Allocating Authority**

1)   DIRECTORS UNNECESSARY

The articles of incorporation of a close corporation may provide that the business of the corporation shall be managed by the shareholders of the corporation rather than by a board of directors.

2)   CLOSE CORPORATION MANAGED AS PARTNERSHIP

The parties to a shareholder agreement of a close corporation may agree to treat the corporation as if it were a partnership. Such an agreement may arrange relations among the shareholders or between the shareholders and the corporation in a manner that would be appropriate only among partners.

C.   **Resolution of Disputes and Deadlocks**

1)   VOLUNTARY MEANS

Articles of incorporation of close corporations may provide means to resolve shareholder disputes and voting deadlocks. Such means may include alternative dispute resolution or a potential buy-out agreement to end an irreconcilable conflict. The articles may also allow for dissolution of the corporation based on some contingency or a certain percentage of the shares. Those means should be conspicuously noted on the shares.

2) INVOLUNTARY MEANS

A court may appoint custodians to operate a corporation whose managing shareholders are deadlocked in a dispute that threatens the corporation with irreparable injury.

A court may appoint an independent provisional director to assist the board of a corporation that is subject to an irreconcilable deadlock.

A court may appoint a receiver to manage a corporation in the event of its insolvency.

D. Option or Buy/Sell Agreement

1) OPTION AGREEMENT

A first option agreement obligates a stockholder to initially offer her shares to other stockholders or the corporation before the stockholder may sell them to outsiders. The agreement may provide an order of priority for making that offer. Occurrence of the following specified conditions may cause the option to apply: the corporation's bankruptcy, termination of the stockholder's employment, the stockholder's death, a proposed transfer or sale of the stock. The agreement needs to state if the seller may vote her stock on the issue of if the corporation may repurchase her shares. In order for the agreement to be sufficiently definite to be enforceable, it should specify the price at which the option may be exercised. An option agreement provides a voluntary allowance of the stockholders or the corporation to acquire the shares

2) BUY/SELL AGREEMENT

A buy/sell agreement is very similar to an option agreement except that it requires the other stockholders or the corporation to purchase the stock upon the specified condition's occurrence. This type of agreement provides assurance to the corporation. The stock price must be specified in order to establish the stock's value.

★★   a)   Rescission of Agreement

Former shareholders of a closely-held corporation who voluntarily sell their stock pursuant to a stock purchase agreement must tender to its purchasers a return of the payment received for the stock before filing a lawsuit to rescind the agreement. Otherwise, the former shareholders will be unable to prevail in their lawsuit. The lawsuit can seek rescission based on, for example, allegations that the purchasers obtained the former shareholders' consent to this sale through breach of fiduciary duty, fraud, innocent or negligent misrepresentation, if the facts support these claims. *McCarthy v. Miller*, Unpublished Opinion Court of Appeals No. 231829, 02/21/03.

Leave denied, 469 Mich. 976 (2003).

IX.   FEDERAL SECURITIES LAWS (SEC)

A.   Rule 10(b)5

Any person is liable under Rule 10(b)5 for the 1) intentional use of 2) any means of interstate commerce (i.e., telephone) 3) a) to defraud, b) make material omissions or misrepresentations or c) acts which tend to defraud another in the purchase or sale of securities in close or public corporations.

1)   INTENTIONAL

There must be some *scienter* whether intentional or reckless.

2)   INTERSTATE COMMERCE

"Means of interstate commerce" is broadly defined. Use of telephones or the mail is sufficient.

3)   DEFRAUD – INSIDER TRADING

a)   General

An insider (officer, shareholder, director) may not use inside corporate information for private gain.

b)   Tipping

An insider will be liable for "tipping" off another person about inside information regarding a stock if she does so with an improper purpose. Generally, a court will examine whether the tipper would receive any direct or indirect financial gain. Again, there must be *scienter*. Mistake or inadvertence, absent recklessness, is not enough. The tippee will be liable to the extent that the tipper is liable.

c)   Misappropriation

Courts have adopted the misappropriation theory as a way of grounding liability in non-insiders. Traditionally, if a non-insider was aware of insider information, he would not be liable under the rule for using it to his advantage. Today, courts hold that anybody, even a non-insider, is liable for purchasing a stock on insider information if he breached the trust of the source of the information. For example, if a director, in confidence, informed her friend that the approval of a new cancer treatment was to be announced the next day, and the friend purchased the stock in reliance on such information, the friend would be liable for misappropriation.

4)   MATERIALITY OF OMISSIONS OR REPRESENTATIONS

a)   General

Materiality is based on the reasonable person standard: whether a reasonable person would attach importance or significance to the information so as to influence the person's decision regarding the value of the stock and whether to buy or sell the person's shares.

b)   Affirmative Duty to Correct Statements

Directors have an affirmative duty to correct misleading information that may be attributed to the corporation if they have reason to know that people are trading based upon the information.

5)   <u>DAMAGES</u>

Generally, a person violating the rule is subject to general and out-of-pocket damages.

a)   General Damages

If the stock is resold, then general damages amount to the buyer's profit (price of stock bought minus price of stock sold).

b)   Out of Pocket Damages

Out-of-pocket damages amount to the difference between the price one bought or sold stock for and what stock is worth.

c)   Rescission

If the stock was not resold, the sale may be rescinded.

d)   No Punitive Damages

Punitive damages may be available by state statute, but not by federal law.

B.   Rule 16(b)

Section 16(b) imposes "strict liability" on any 10 percent shareholder, officer, or director of a public corporation from purchasing and selling stock of the company within six months of each transaction. Accordingly, there is no *scienter* requirement. Rule 16(b) also applies to any corporation with over $10,000,000 in assets and 500 shareholders. A person who violates Section 16(b) is liable to the corporation for the profits from such a transaction. Profits under section 16(b) amount to the difference between the lowest price in the six-month period and the highest price in the six-month period.

X.   SHAREHOLDER LITIGATION: DIRECT AND DERIVATIVE

★★   **A.   Derivative Claims**

When harm is done to a corporation, a shareholder may bring a derivative action on behalf of the corporation, with recovery going to the corporation. H. Henn & J. Alexander, *Laws of Corporations* §§ 358-360 (3rd ed. 1986, 1983).

A breach of the directors' fiduciary duties that depletes or diverts corporate assets and injures the corporation, including all of the shareholders, gives rise to a derivative claim. Henn, *supra* §§ 358-360.

1)   DEMAND

Shareholders who bring a derivative action are suing to enforce the corporation's rights when the corporation has failed to do so itself. Therefore, the shareholders must allege that they have made a demand on the corporation to file the suit. Henn, *supra* §§ 364-366.

a)   Michigan's BCA – Demand and Waiting Period

Michigan's BCA requires that a shareholder make a written demand on the board in all circumstances before commencing a derivative action. Mich. Comp. Laws § 450.1493a. The shareholder must then wait 90 days after making the demand to file the derivative action, unless: 1) the board rejects the demand during the 90-day period; or 2) irreparable injury would result to the corporation by waiting for the 90-day period's expiration. *Id.*

b)   Common Law – Demand Unless Futile

Under the common law, a demand need not be made when it would be futile to do so. Henn, *supra* § 365. To establish demand futility, it is insufficient for the shareholder to allege in a conclusory manner that the suit names all of the directors as defendants and that, therefore, they are incapable of considering the demand in a disinterested manner. However, if the shareholder can allege facts in its complaint that demonstrate a reasonable basis for the belief that the members of the board are interested in the transaction being challenged, or that they failed to exercise their duty of care in approving the matter at issue, that will be enough to show demand futility. *Id.*

2)   SHAREHOLDER STANDING

a)   Real Party in Interest

In Michigan, one must prosecute an action in the name of the real party in interest. MCR 2.201(B). Under this standing doctrine, a real party in interest has the right of action on a claim, although another may have the beneficial interest on the claim. *Michigan Nat'l Bank v. Mudgett*, 178 Mich. App. 677 (1989). Therefore, the shareholder must bring a derivative action in the corporation's name as the real party in interest. *Id.*

b)   Statutory Requirements for Maintaining Derivative Action

In Michigan, only current shareholders, not former shareholders, can possess standing to commence a shareholder derivative action. Michigan's BCA provides that a shareholder derivative action requires that (a) the shareholder was a shareholder of the corporation at the time of the act or omission complained of, (b) the shareholder fairly and adequately represents the interest of the corporation in enforcing the right of the corporation, and (c) the shareholder continues to be a shareholder until the time of judgment, unless the failure to continue to be a shareholder is the result of corporate action in which the former shareholder did not acquiesce. Mich. Comp. Laws § 450.1492a.

★   **B.   Direct Claim**

By comparison, a wrongful act that does not deplete the corporate treasury or divert corporate assets but instead deprives a shareholder of a right to which his shares entitle him, or which is personal to the shareholder and not shared by other shareholders, gives rise to a direct claim. Henn, *supra* § 360. For example, a claim for a violation of a shareholders' agreement implicates individual rights. Therefore, such a claim should be brought against the other shareholders in their capacities as shareholders, that is, as a direct claim.

MICHIGAN

AMERIBAR BAR REVIEW

Michigan Bar Review

CIVIL PROCEDURE

CIVIL PROCEDURE

CIVIL PROCEDURE

Sample answers for some past Civil Procedure questions indicate that federal law and/or Michigan law, such as that which this outline contains, should be the basis for answering Civil Procedure questions. Facts and rules derived from cases decided by Michigan appellate courts and federal courts have provided the basis for certain past Civil Procedure questions and answers. The Federal Rules of Civil Procedure ("FRCP" or "Federal Rules") and the Michigan Rules of Court ("Michigan Court Rules" or "MCR") also are other sources of testable law.

Traditionally, one issue tested more often than others in certain past questions is a motion for summary disposition, although generally different grounds for this motion were tested each time, along with some related issues such as supporting evidence. Some other issues that were examined a few times include Michigan state court jurisdiction, removal of a case from Michigan state court to federal court, federal subject matter jurisdiction, federal question jurisdiction, diversity jurisdiction and a lack thereof, determining a corporation's citizenship, personal jurisdiction, Michigan's long-arm statutes, constitutional due process including sufficient minimum contacts and notice. Some other previously tested issues include Michigan state court subject matter jurisdiction, Michigan's general venue statute, class actions, affirmative defenses, compulsory counterclaims in federal court versus Michigan state court, Michigan's corporate survival statute, physical examinations, motion for sanctions, *res judicata*, case evaluation and a related ethical issue, discovery, the hearsay rule with its business record exception, and evidence initially submitted on appeal.

I.   JURISDICTION

Jurisdiction refers to the court's power to hear a case and render a binding judgment.

A.   Subject Matter Jurisdiction

For a court to undertake a civil case, it must possess the authority to adjudicate the type of dispute before it. In other words, the court must have jurisdiction over the subject matter of the dispute. Accordingly, subject-matter jurisdiction, in contrast to personal jurisdiction, refers to whether a court has the power or competence to decide the kind of controversy involved. Subject matter jurisdiction is not an alternative to personal jurisdiction. Rather it is an additional requirement that must be met.

Subject-matter jurisdiction cannot be consented to or waived by the parties. Accordingly, a party can challenge the existence of subject-matter jurisdiction at any time in the case, even on appeal.

★★   1)   <u>FEDERAL COURTS</u>

Article III of the *United States Constitution* creates the Supreme Court of the United States. Articles I and III give the United States Congress the authority to establish lower federal tribunals as it sees fit. Congress has created a number of lower federal courts, including 13 "circuit" courts, and 91 "district" courts. The lower federal courts are tribunals of "limited" jurisdiction. Consequently, for a controversy to come within the subject-matter jurisdiction of a federal court, it must comport with one of several alternative requirements.

★★   a)   Federal Question Jurisdiction

Federal district courts possess limited original jurisdiction over cases arising under the United States Constitution, federal statutory or common law, and federal treaties. Congress has conferred upon federal courts the jurisdiction to decide those "federal questions." 28 U.S.C. § 1331. Article III of the U.S. Constitution requires that an actual "case or controversy" exist between the parties. A "case or controversy" involves a federal question only when a plaintiff's complaint states a claim or cause of action that involves federal law. A state common law breach of contract claim does not arise under the Constitution, laws, or treaties of the United States. 28 U.S.C. § 1331. Therefore, no federal question is raised by such a claim.

(1)   Well-Pleaded Complaint Rule

Federal question analysis is governed by the well-pleaded complaint rule. Under this rule, federal jurisdiction exists when a federal question is presented on the face of a plaintiff's properly pleaded complaint. A federal question is "presented" when the complaint invokes any type of federal law as the primary basis for relief.

(a)   Plaintiff is Master of Claim

The rule makes a plaintiff the "master" of the claim. The plaintiff must affirmatively invoke federal subject matter jurisdiction by pleading a federal-law claim within the complaint. Conversely, the plaintiff may avoid such jurisdiction by relying exclusively on state law to present claims. It is insufficient to obtain federal question jurisdiction by alleging facts in support of an asserted state-law claim that could also support a federal-law claim.

(b)   Federal Defense Insufficient

Under the Well-Pleaded Complaint Rule, a federal court lacks original jurisdiction over a case in which a plaintiff's complaint presents a state-law cause of action, but also asserts that:

- Federal law deprives a defendant of a defense that the defendant might raise (e.g., federal immunity); or
- A federal defense that a defendant may raise is not sufficient to defeat a claim of the complaint.

★★   b)   Diversity of Citizenship Jurisdiction

In addition to jurisdiction over federal questions, federal district courts possess original jurisdiction over cases between parties of diverse state citizenship if the claims of a complaint satisfy the jurisdictional "amount in controversy" requirement. With respect to diversity jurisdiction cases, the jurisdiction of the court is defined by who the parties to the litigation are, rather than the topic of the underlying controversy. Diversity subject-matter jurisdiction exists if 1) the opposing parties are citizens of different states and 2) the amount in controversy exceeds $75,000, exclusive of interests and costs.

Complete diversity of citizenship must exist between the parties on each side of a case. Accordingly, all of the plaintiffs must be citizens of different states than all of the defendants. Complete diversity means that there is no diversity jurisdiction when any party on one side of a dispute is a citizen of the same state as any party on the opposing side of the dispute. In other words, when a federal question is not present, an action is removable only if none of the parties in interest--properly joined and served as defendants--is a citizen of the state in which the action is brought. 28 U.S.C. § 1441(b).

★★   (1)   Determination of Citizenship

Citizenship is determined as of the time that the action is commenced.

                                (a)   Individuals

Citizenship, in the context of diversity jurisdiction, means domicile. See the discussion of domicile in the section on personal jurisdiction for a detailed analysis.

                                (b)   Corporations

Corporations can potentially possess two citizenships.

- Corporations are "citizens" of their state of incorporation.

- Corporations are citizens of the state in which they have their principal place of business and the state in which it is incorporated. Moreover, a corporation generally has only one principal place of business for purposes of diversity jurisdiction.

★★   (2)   Amount in Controversy

Diversity jurisdiction can be invoked only if the amount in controversy exceeds $75,000, exclusive of interest and costs. If the matter in controversy is $75,000 or less, diversity jurisdiction does not exist. In determining whether the amount in controversy requirement is satisfied, courts will examine the sum that is demanded by a plaintiff in the complaint.

- Aggregation of Claims

If a plaintiff possesses two unrelated claims, which total over $75,000, against a single defendant, a plaintiff may sue in federal court since the aggregate exceeds $75,000. However, if two different plaintiffs each possess a $50,000 claim against one defendant, they cannot aggregate the claims, regardless of how similar the claims are. Additionally, a plaintiff may aggregate claims against multiple defendants if they are joint tortfeasors under one claim.

- Counterclaims

A counterclaim is a claim made by a defendant against a plaintiff. It may or may not arise from the same transaction or occurrence giving rise to the plaintiff's claim.

If a counterclaim is compulsory (i.e., arising from same transaction or occurrence), it will fall within the jurisdiction of the court and may be heard regardless of the amount in controversy. Accordingly, if a defendant's counterclaim from the same transaction or occurrence as a plaintiff's claim is in the amount of $15,000, the defendant may assert it if the plaintiff's claim exceeds $75,000.

If a counterclaim is permissive (i.e., not arising from the same transaction or occurrence), it must possess an independent jurisdictional basis for federal jurisdiction. Therefore, a permissive counterclaim must independently fulfill the jurisdictional amount requirement. Thus, in order to assert a counterclaim that is unrelated to the same transaction or occurrence, the amount of the defendant's claim must be in excess of $75,000.

- Injunctive Relief

For making a counterclaim, the amount of a claim of injunction may be valued either by the amount that it will benefit a plaintiff or by the cost that a defendant will incur to comply with it. The topic of injunctions is separately discussed later in this outline.

c)   Supplemental Jurisdiction

As previously elaborated, subject-matter jurisdiction in federal district courts is generally limited to those types of controversies that are specifically enumerated in the United States Constitution and that Congress has authorized those courts to exercise. Additionally, federal courts may exercise jurisdiction over certain claims (not "cases or controversies") that fall outside of those three categories when such claims are properly joined in a single lawsuit with a distinct cause of action that is jurisdictionally sufficient.

At common law, those concepts were included under the doctrines of "pendent" and "ancillary" jurisdiction, which need no further discussion in this outline. Congress codified those concepts under the doctrine of "supplemental jurisdiction." 28 U.S.C. § 1367. Accordingly, under that statutory doctrine, certain new parties and new claims may be added to a case without needing to satisfy the independent subject-matter jurisdiction tests. Thus, certain claims can, in effect, be added to the heart of a controversy under specific circumstances.

(1)   General Rule

Pursuant to statute, in any civil action of which the district courts have original jurisdiction, the district courts will have supplemental jurisdiction over all other claims that are so related to claims in the action within such original jurisdiction that they form part of the same case or controversy. 28 U.S.C. § 1367(a). The Supreme Court has held that two claims have the requisite connection if they "derive from a common nucleus of operative fact."

(2)   Rule 14 Exception

Congress created a notable statutory exception to the general rule of supplemental jurisdiction. Supplemental jurisdiction will not extend to "claims by plaintiffs against persons made parties under Rule 14." 28 U.S.C. § 1367(b). Rule 14 permits a party to bring a third-party complaint. When a party brings a third-party complaint against another entity, supplemental jurisdiction is unavailable. Under these circumstances, the claim must possess a satisfactory independent basis for subject matter jurisdiction.

★   2)   MICHIGAN COURTS

Subject-matter jurisdiction is the authority of "the court to exercise judicial power over that class of case . . . of the kind or character of the one pending." *Joy v. Two-Bit Corp.*, 287 Mich. 244, 253 (1938).

a)   General Jurisdiction

In the aggregate, the Michigan court system is one of general jurisdiction. This means that absent a specific federal law preserving exclusive federal jurisdiction over a claim, any action can be brought in some Michigan court.

For example, because general Michigan tort law is not reserved exclusively for federal courts by federal jurisdiction law, there may be a Michigan state trial court in which to file a plaintiff's tort action. In this situation, the relevant inquiry is which one.

b)   Michigan Trial Court Jurisdiction

The Michigan court system offers several types of state trial courts: district courts, circuit courts, probate courts, and the court of claims.

★★   (1)   Circuit Court Jurisdiction

The Michigan Constitution provides that the state "circuit court shall have original jurisdiction in all matters not prohibited by law." Mich. Const. 1963, art. VI, § 13. Michigan circuit courts possess general original jurisdiction in cases involving more than $25,000. Mich. Comp. Laws § 600.8301.

(a)   Other Trial Courts' Jurisdiction

If the amount involved in a case exceeds $25,000, then a Michigan state district court (or any municipal court) will lack subject matter jurisdiction. *Id.* The probate court lacks subject matter jurisdiction over a tort matter, for example. If the defendant is a private entity, not the State of Michigan, then the Court of Claims lacks subject-matter jurisdiction. In other words, the Court of Claims could exercise subject-matter jurisdiction over certain claims against the State of Michigan.

★

(i)   The Court of Claims

The Court of Claims possesses exclusive jurisdiction regarding claims and demands, unliquidated and liquidated, *ex delicto* and *ex contractu*, against the State of Michigan "and any of its departments, commissions, boards, institutions, arms or agencies." Mich. Comp. Laws § 600.6419(1)(a). For example, the Department of Corrections constitutes a department of this State. Mich. Comp. Laws § 791.201. An example of a claim over which the Court of Claims will exercise exclusive jurisdiction would be a breach of contract action by a contractor that entered into an agreement the Department of Corrections. *Parkwood v. State Housing Dev. Auth.*, 468 Mich. 763 (2003).

★★   c)   Lack of Subject Matter Jurisdiction

The parties cannot agree to confer subject matter jurisdiction over a case. *Hastings v. Hastings*, 154 Mich. App. 96 (1986). At any time, a party may assert that a court lacks subject-matter jurisdiction. MCR 2.116(D)(3); *Nat'l Wildlife Fed'n v. Cleveland Cliffs Iron Co.*, 471 Mich. 608 (2004). A motion for summary disposition can be made under MCR 2.116(C)(4) alleging that a court lacks subject matter jurisdiction. Thus, a party may file such a motion at any time during the lawsuit, even on appeal. Motions for summary disposition are discussed later in this outline.

★★★ **B.   In Personam Jurisdiction – Jurisdiction "Over the Person"**

In personam means "over the person." Personal jurisdiction must exist in order for a court to adjudicate a case, even if subject matter jurisdiction already independently exists. In other words, without personal jurisdiction over a party, the existence of subject matter alone cannot confer jurisdiction upon a court to adjudicate a case against the party.

1)   BASES OF PERSONAL JURISDICTION

Generally, a person may be subject to a court's personal jurisdiction under the following circumstances:

- Transient Presence: The person is physically in the forum state when served there;
- Domicile: The person is domiciled in the state where the court is located. The state where the court is located will be referred to as the "forum state."
- Consent: The person provides valid consent to the court's personal jurisdiction.
- Appearance: The person appears in the court regarding the case against the person; or
- Minimum Contacts: A person who is not domiciled in the forum state may possess sufficient minimum contacts with the forum state to authorize personal jurisdiction.

a)   Transient (Presence)

Even before domicile began to be used as a basis for personal jurisdiction, a person's presence within the forum state and service of process therein provided a general basis for jurisdiction. A state is presumed to possess limited legal authority over all of the people who are found within its borders. If a person is served while present in a state, any length of stay therein, no matter how brief, will be sufficient to establish transient jurisdiction. In one case, personal jurisdiction was found to exist over a defendant after service of process upon the defendant occurred in an airplane while it was flying over the forum state. *Grace v. MacArthur*, 170 F. Supp 442 (E.D. Ark. 1959). Note that service, which is procured by fraudulently luring a defendant into the forum state, will not be upheld as valid to provide personal jurisdiction.

★★   b)   Domicile

Domicile did not always provide a proper basis for the exercise of personal jurisdiction. In fact, the issue of its propriety did not become settled until the United States Supreme Court decided *Milliken v. Meyer. Milliken v. Meyer*, 311 U.S. 457 (1940). In *Milliken*, the Supreme Court held that a person who possesses a domicile in a state is subject to a lawsuit in that forum state regarding a dispute that originated anywhere in the world. A corporation can establish minimum contacts with Michigan by domiciling itself in Michigan by incorporating in this state.

A person can have many residences, but only one domicile. A state is a person's domicile if the person:

- resides in the state; and

- possesses an intent to reside there indefinitely (*First Restatement*) or to make it his home for the time at least (*Second Restatement*).

An objective test is used to determine a person's domicile. Courts will examine property records, tax records, registrations, etc., to determine if a state is a person's domicile. Accordingly, a change of domicile may be accomplished when a person changes the person's place of residency to a new location with an intention to remain there, and while regarding it as the person's home. Friedenthal, Kane & Miller, *Civil Procedure* 31 (1996).

(1)   Forum State Rule Governs Domicile Determinations

Due to the relative uniformity with which the issue of domicile is treated throughout most jurisdictions in the United States, the question of which rule applies to determine domicile is usually insignificant. Occasionally, however, local rules of construction regarding the rule may alter the analysis of which domicile is proper. Generally, each jurisdiction will apply its own rules regarding domicile when that issue arises in a case.

c)   Consent

A person may be subject to the jurisdiction of a court if the person expressly consented to the court's jurisdiction. Consent, in that context, usually takes the form of a clause in a contract between the parties to a dispute. Such a clause usually states that the parties agree in advance of any dispute to be subject to, or submit to, a particular court's jurisdiction. Traditionally, courts would not enforce such a clause if the parties to the contract possessed a disparate level of bargaining power. Although such a clause could potentially be inherently unfair to a party, it would probably be enforceable in the absence of fraud or duress, even if it were contained in a standard form agreement. *Carnival Cruise Lines, Inc. v. Shute*, 499 U.S. 585 (1991). This subtopic is further discussed later under the subtopic of Limitations on Personal Jurisdiction.

d)   Appearance

Traditionally, a party to a lawsuit who voluntarily appeared in a court (in which a plaintiff filed a lawsuit)--without making an objection to the court's personal jurisdiction over the party--was considered to have voluntarily submitted to the court's jurisdiction. Centuries ago, that rule had the effect of eliminating a party's right to directly attack the court's jurisdiction. If a party appeared in a court to attack its jurisdiction, then the party would have been considered to have submitted to the court's jurisdiction. As a result, a party that neither attacked nor submitted to the court's jurisdiction would have been subject to the entry of a default judgment. The defaulting party could only collaterally attack that judgment when a prevailing party sought to enforce it in the defaulting party's home state.

Today, that harsh result has almost been entirely removed from the jurisprudence in the United States. In almost all jurisdictions, a party may object to and directly attack the jurisdiction of a court at the outset of the case. However, if the objecting party also seeks affirmative relief from the court, the objection to jurisdiction is waived and the attack will fail.

★★   e)   Minimum Contacts

For taking exams, the most important type of personal jurisdiction determination will be to analyze the extent of a person's minimum contacts with a forum state. In other words, the most commonly tested basis for personal jurisdiction is if a person's contacts with a forum state are sufficient to reasonably require the person to defend a lawsuit that is filed in the forum state.

International Shoe Co. v. Washington provides the general rule that a person who has never been present in a state may be subject to personal jurisdiction that would require the person to defend against a lawsuit in the state if the person possesses:

- "sufficient minimum contacts" with that forum state;
- such that requiring the person to appear and defend in a court there would not;
- "offend traditional notions of fair play and substantial justice."

It is recommended that this rule be committed to memory.

For example, if a plaintiff's injuries, which occurred in Michigan, were the foreseeable and conceivable result of a defendant's tortious conduct in Ohio, sufficient minimum contacts may exist to assert personal jurisdiction in Michigan. *James v. HRP, Inc.*, 852 F.Supp. 620, 625 (W.D. Mich., 1994); *Cole v. Doe*, 77 Mich. App. 138, 143 (1977).

(1)   General and Specific Jurisdiction

- Continuous and Systematic Contacts (General Jurisdiction)

If the defendant's contacts with the forum state are continuous and systematic, then personal jurisdiction over the defendant is appropriate in a case involving the defendant's activity in the state or any activity unrelated to the defendant's activity in the forum state (general jurisdiction).

- Sporadic Activity (Specific Jurisdiction)

Sporadic activity of the defendant in the forum would not justify the exercise of jurisdiction over a defendant if the cause of action were unrelated to that forum activity. If the defendant's activity in the forum is sporadic, instead of continuous and systematic, the defendant may be subject to personal jurisdiction if the cause of action arises out of that state activity (specific jurisdiction). Consequently, the threshold for satisfying minimum contacts in the general jurisdiction case is higher than in specific jurisdiction cases.

(2)   Purposeful Availment

The exercise of personal jurisdiction is more likely if a party "purposefully availed" itself of the forum state. For example, if the party advertised to a market in the state, the court would be more likely to exercise jurisdiction over the person. In *Hanson v. Denckla*, the United States Supreme Court stated that: "It is essential in each case that there be some act by which the defendant purposefully avails itself of the privilege of conducting activities within the forum state, thus invoking the benefits and protections of its laws."

(3)   Reasonableness

The overall question that one must keep in mind when conducting any minimum contacts analysis is whether the assertion of jurisdiction is reasonable under the circumstances. Accordingly, courts will examine whether the defendant have reasonably anticipated being haled into court in the jurisdiction.

In *World-Wide Volkswagen Corporation v. Woodson*, plaintiffs were New York citizens who filed a tort action in an Oklahoma court to recover damages for the injuries that they suffered in an automobile accident in that forum state. Two defendants, a New York car dealer and a New York car distributor, challenged the forum court's personal jurisdiction over them. The United States Supreme Court determined that the fact that those defendants' placed the automobile into the "stream of commerce" did not alone warrant personal jurisdiction over them. Rather, the Supreme Court concluded that:

> The foreseeability that is critical to due process analysis is not the mere likelihood that a product will find its way into the forum State. Rather, it is that the defendant's conduct and connection with the forum State are such that he should reasonably anticipate being haled into court there…It is foreseeable that purchasers of automobiles sold by [defendants]   may take them to Oklahoma. But the mere unilateral activity of those who claim some relationship with a non-resident defendant cannot satisfy the requirement of contact with the forum State'.

In *Asahi Metal Industry Company v. Superior Court*, a Japanese manufacturer served as a primary supplier of tire valves to a tire-tube manufacturer in Taiwan. The Japanese manufacturer knew that some of the tire-tubes would be sold in California. The United States Supreme Court determined that a California court lacked personal jurisdiction over the Japanese manufacturer in an indemnification action by the other manufacturer. The Supreme Court concluded that minimum contacts do not result simply by placing a product in the "stream of commerce," even if that placement occurred knowing that the forum state was the product's ultimate market The Supreme Court decided that an exercise of personal jurisdiction in that case would offend the notions of fair play and substantial justice because:

 (1)   The "alien defendant" did not purposefully direct its product to the forum;

 (2)   A forum-state court would have to adjudicate an international case;

 (3)   The "alien defendant" would suffer a heavy burden to defend the case; and

 (4)   The state had a weak interest in providing a forum for non-citizens.

★★   f)   Long-Arm Statute – Authorizes Jurisdiction and Out of State Service

A personal jurisdiction analysis is a two-fold inquiry: (1) do the defendant's acts fall within the applicable long-arm statute, and (2) does the exercise of jurisdiction over the defendant comport with due process? *Starbrite Distrib., Inc. v. Excelda Mfg. Co.*, 454 Mich. 302 (1997).

Accordingly, testing the existence of personal jurisdiction is generally a two-step approach. First, one must examine whether personal jurisdiction exists under the jurisdiction's long-arm statute. Second, one must examine whether jurisdiction satisfies constitutional requirements (most often minimum contacts).

               (1)   General

There are two types of long-arm statutes: unlimited statutes, which give courts the maximum jurisdiction permissible under the Due Process Clause of the *United States Constitution*, and limited long-arm statutes, which specify in detail when courts may exercise jurisdiction.

               (a)   Maximum Scope

In many states, long-arm statutes generally authorize personal jurisdiction over, and service of process upon, out of state parties in a civil action on any basis that is consistent with the limits of the Due Process Clause of the *United States Constitution*. The scope of that basis is usually determined by relevant precedent. Those long-arm statutes are the most liberal in terms of their scope of reach outside of the forum state.

★★   (i)   Michigan's General Long-Arm Statutes

Michigan's general long-arm statutes permit a court to hear any action against a defendant (1) who is present in Michigan at the time process is served, (2) who is domiciled in Michigan at the time process is served, (3) who consents to the exercise of personal jurisdiction, (4) which is a corporation, partnership, or association that is incorporated or formed under Michigan law, or (5) which is a corporation, partnership, or association that carries on a "continuous and systematic part of its general business" within Michigan. Mich. Comp. Laws §§ 600.701, 600.722, 600.721, and 600.731.

(b)   Specified Scope

The long-arm statutes in other states, however, are more limited in their extent of certain enumerated permissible grounds for obtaining personal jurisdiction over, and service of process upon, out of state parties in a civil action. Those long-arm statutes provide that only specified types of activity constitute a contact with the forum state that would empower a court's exercise of personal jurisdiction. Usually the occurrence of only one contact with the forum state as a result of those activities will provide a basis for jurisdiction. Those long-arm statutes are more conservative in terms of their scope of reach outside of the forum state.

The types of activities that may subject a party to personal jurisdiction include, but are not necessarily limited to:

- the transaction of any business within the state;
- the commission of a tort within the state;
- the ownership, use, or possession of real estate in the state; and
- the making of, or the performance of, any contract in the state.

For example, the United States Supreme Court held in *Burger King v. Rudzewicz* that Florida courts possessed personal jurisdiction over a Michigan franchisee based on a contract that indicated that the parties' relationship was established in Florida and that Florida Law governed their contractual relationship. The Supreme Court ruled, however, that the existence of such a contract cannot, of itself, give rise to a non-forum state party's sufficient minimum contacts with the forum state. Rather, the Supreme Court sustained the personal jurisdiction on the following grounds that may be relevant to analyzing an exam issue:

- The parties engaged in a substantial and continuous business relationship;
- The non-forum state party received fair notice that it could be subject to personal jurisdiction in the forum state. That notice resulted from the contract's terms and the parties' course of dealings; and
- The non-forum state party was sophisticated and experienced in business and did not enter into the contract due to duress or economic disadvantage.

★★   (i)   Michigan's Limited Long-Arm Statutes

Michigan's limited long-arm statutes permit a court to hear an action against a defendant arising out of (1) the transaction of any business within Michigan, (2) the doing or causing an act to be done, or consequences to occur, in Michigan resulting in an action for tort, (3) the ownership, use, or possession of real or tangible personal property situated within Michigan, (4) a contract to insure a person, property, or risk located within Michigan, (5) a contract for services to be rendered or for materials to be furnished in Michigan by the defendant, (6) the defendant's service as an officer of a corporation incorporated under the laws of Michigan or having its principal place of business within Michigan, or (7) the maintenance of a domicile in Michigan while subject to a marital or family relationship that is the basis of a claim for divorce, alimony, separate maintenance, property settlement, child support, or child custody. Mich. Comp. Laws §§ 600.705, 600.715, 600.725 and 600.735.

★   (2)   Federal Courts

Although no general federal long-arm statute exists, Federal Rule 4(k)(1)(A) authorizes the federal courts to utilize the long-arm statute of the forum state in which they are located. Pursuant to this Rule, each federal court must analyze personal jurisdiction as if it were a court of the state in which it is located. For example, whether a federal district court in Michigan has personal jurisdiction over an Ohio resident is dependent upon Michigan's long-arm statutes. Consequently, the federal courts possess the same scope of personal jurisdiction as the state courts of the forum state.

★★   (3)   Michigan Courts – Jurisdiction over Person or Corporation

In Michigan, a state court has jurisdiction over a person if two prongs are satisfied: (1) Michigan's long-arm statutes and (2) federal constitutional due process. By statute, Michigan has general personal jurisdiction over a corporation incorporated under Michigan law. Mich. Comp. Laws § 600.711. Michigan also has limited personal jurisdiction over a corporation that, among other things, transacts business within the state or enters into a contract for materials to be furnished in the state by the defendant. Mich. Comp. Laws § 600.715.

★   2)   <u>NOTICE AND OPPORTUNITY TO BE HEARD</u>

Beyond the requirement that a court possess jurisdiction over a case, constitutional due process requires that a party to a lawsuit receive notice of the case and an opportunity to be heard in a court. A judgment that is entered in an action in which a party did not receive notice or have an opportunity to be heard is invalid and will not be enforceable against the party.

                  a)   Notice

Notice may be given by serving (i.e., delivering) the requisite legal papers upon a party in person, even if the service occurs outside of the court's scope of personal jurisdiction. The papers served on a party must be reasonably calculated to adequately inform a defending party of the nature of a cause of action that is asserted by a claiming party. Additionally, the defending party must be provided with a reasonable time to respond and prepare a defense to the cause of action. Remember that notice, as a legal issue, is distinct from the issue of a court's jurisdiction. The subject of notice is discussed further under the section regarding service of process.

                  b)   Opportunity to Be Heard

The concept of an "opportunity to be heard" arises from the common law notion that a person with a legitimate dispute is entitled to a have a proverbial "day in court." The concept is now included under the constitutional principal of due process. An "opportunity to be heard" means that the parties to a dispute are entitled to receive an impartial hearing in a court of their claims and defenses.

3)   LIMITS ON EXERCISE OF PERSONAL JURISDICTION

a)   Traditional Limitations

(1)   Choice of Forum by Agreement

The existence of a forum-selection clause in a contract will be a significant factor that figures centrally in a court's decision of whether to exercise jurisdiction over a party. The court must evaluate the fairness of the proposed exercise of jurisdiction in light of the forum-selection clause. Although that clause must be treated as a "significant factor" when a court evaluates jurisdiction, the United States Supreme Court has held that the existence of a forum-selection clause is not "dispositive" of the issue of jurisdiction.

As mentioned earlier under the subtopic of "Consent" to personal jurisdiction, an inequality of bargaining power between the parties may warrant giving less effect to their contract's forum-selection clause. Similarly, litigating in its preordained forum may impose significant and unusual hardships on one of the parties. The questions for evaluating a forum-selection clause are:

- Does the forum selected in the clause have some connection to the contract? and
- Has a party overreached by attempting to include the clause in the contract?

(2)   Fraud, Force, and Privilege

Jurisdiction that is obtained by fraud or force is invalid. For example, if a plaintiff tricks or lures a defendant into coming into a forum state and serves the defendant with process while the defendant is in that state, a court will lack jurisdiction over the defendant. Additionally, representatives of foreign sovereigns who are in a forum state on business are generally immune from service. Moreover, people who are present in a forum state to address the needs of litigation there may not be subject to personal jurisdiction as a result of service of process upon them in that state.

b)   Constitutional Limitations (due process)

Regardless of which type of long-arm statute is controlling in a particular case, a court's exercise of personal jurisdiction that exceeds the scope of personal jurisdiction, which is allowed under the Due Process Clause, would be unconstitutional and could result in an invalid and unenforceable judgment.

C.   In Rem Jurisdiction

In rem jurisdiction is a court's jurisdiction over property that is located within the forum state. In a usual dispute that gives rise to *in personam* jurisdiction, two or more people attempt to adjudicate their rights *vis-à-vis* each other. Conversely, when *in rem* jurisdiction is invoked, a court adjudicates the entire world's rights *vis-à-vis* a piece of property. The property can be real property, such as a building or land. The property can be personal property such as a decedent's estate. In an *in rem* proceeding, the court may exercise its power to determine the ownership of the property. That judicial determination is binding with respect to all possible interest holders if reasonable notice of the proceeding was given.

D.   Quasi In Rem Jurisdiction

A *quasi in rem* action is different from an *in personam* action that determines the rights of parties to certain property that is at issue. A *quasi in rem* action is initiated when a plaintiff seizes property within a forum state by means of attachment or garnishment. Traditionally, the property seized is used as a pretext for a court to decide a case without possessing personal jurisdiction over a defendant. Although the court may decide issues in a case that are unrelated to the property, the amount of the judgment is limited to the value of the property that is seized. The judgment cannot be sued upon in any other court. The United States Supreme Court has severely limited, if not eliminated, classic *quasi in rem* jurisdiction.

E.   Appeals

1)   FINAL JUDGMENT RULE

As a general matter, appeals can only be taken from a final judgment. An appeal from most pretrial orders is typically considered interlocutory, and, therefore, not appealable as a final decision. It may, however, instead be subject to a collateral attack.

a)   Collateral Order Exception

The United States Supreme Court has held that sometimes the determination of questions that are collateral to other rights, which are asserted in an action, may be too important to be deferred for appellate review until after the whole case is adjudicated. That small category of questions consists of interlocutory orders that satisfy three criteria:

- The court's order must finally dispose of a disputed question;
- The question must be completely collateral to the cause of action; and
- The order that relates to the question must involve an important right that;
- would be "lost, probably irreparably," if review of the question had to wait until after a final judgment occurred.

F.   Removal to Federal Court from State Court

★★

1)   CONDITIONS OF REMOVAL

Federal courts are courts of limited jurisdiction. Pursuant to a federal statute, a defendant may remove any action brought in a state court of which the district courts of the United States have original jurisdiction. 28 U.S.C. § 1441(a). A federal court will have original jurisdiction in a case when there is either a federal question or diversity jurisdiction exists.

A case that is originally filed in a state court may be removed to a federal court for adjudication on the merits if:

- The case could have been originally filed in a federal court (i.e., federal subject matter jurisdiction must exist);
- A federal statute provides for removal;
- Only a defendant may remove a case;
- All defendants must agree to remove a case;
- The grounds for removal are included in at least one claim of a plaintiff. Thus, the grounds cannot be based on an Affirmative Defense or a Counterclaim; and
- In diversity cases, a defendant cannot be a resident (i.e., citizen) of the forum state.

Accordingly, when a federal question is not present, an action is removable only if none of the parties in interest, properly joined and served as defendants, is a citizen of the state in which the action is brought. 28 U.S.C. § 1441(b).

If the plaintiff fraudulently joins a party in order to destroy diversity in order to prevent removal, the defendant may remove the case if he would have been able to remove the case absent the fraudulent joinder. In order to determine whether joinder is fraudulent for removal purposes, the federal court will inquire whether there is absolutely no chance that the cause of action against the purported defendant will succeed. If no chance exists, the court may find fraudulent joinder.

Under a statute, it is appropriate to remove only to a district court "embracing the place where such action is pending." 28 U.S.C. § 1441(a). Suppose, for example, that a case is pending in Wayne Circuit Court in Michigan. Were defendant to request removal of the case, that court could only do so to a federal district court in Michigan, the Eastern District of Michigan.

2)   PROCEDURES FOR REMOVAL

A defendant files a notice of removal containing a short and plain statement of the grounds for removal, together with a copy of all process, pleadings, and orders served upon the defendant(s) in the action.

A defendant must seek removal within 30 days from when a plaintiff served a complaint or the case otherwise becomes removable. However, a case that would be grounded in diversity is not removable more than one year from the date of the commencement of the action. However, note, if the plaintiff manipulates the timing of the case to avoid removal on this ground, the defendant(s) will be permitted to remove the case after this deadline.

* The determination of which federal district court is proper is discussed later in this outline under the topic of Venue.

3)   MOTION TO REMAND

A federal court to which a case is removed possesses discretion to retain the entire case or remand to the state court certain claims that would not be within its original jurisdiction or if the procedural requirements set forth above are not satisfied. A party must move for remand within 30 days from being served with a removal notice.

Note: A plaintiff may prevent a defendant from removing a case by:

- not raising a federal claim; or
- not joining a party of diverse citizenship, and
- requesting a lesser amount of damages than the amount in controversy.

If a federal court grants a motion for remand on the basis that the court lacks jurisdiction, the party who sought removal cannot appeal.

4)   EFFECT ON TIMING

a)   Time to Answer

In a removed action in which the defendant has not answered, the defendant must answer and/or present defenses within 1) 21 days after the receipt of a copy of the complaint or summons or 2) within 7 days after the filing of the notice for removal, whichever period is longest. Receipt of a copy of the complaint need not be through service. If the defendant received a copy through another method, the time will run from such receipt, despite the fact that plaintiff has not served the complaint.

b)   Jury Demand

A party entitled to trial by jury must serve a demand within 14 days after the notice of removal is filed if the party is the removing party, or if not the moving party, within 14 days after service on the party of the notice of removal. A party who, prior to removal, made an express demand for trial by jury in accordance with state law, need not make a demand after removal.

II.   SERVICE OF PROCESS

A.   Issuance

Upon or after filing the complaint, the plaintiff may present a summons to the clerk for its signature. If the summons is in proper form, the clerk must sign, seal, and issue it to the plaintiff for service on the defendant. The plaintiff is responsible for service of the summons and a copy of the complaint.

B.   Personal Service on Individual

1)   FRCP

An individual may be served in any federal judicial district pursuant to the state law of the jurisdiction in which the defendant is found. Alternatively, an individual defendant may be served in the following three manners:

1.   delivery in person;

2.   copy at residence or usual place of abode with person of suitable age and discretion residing thereon; or

3.   delivery to authorized agent.

An infant or incompetent person may be served only in a manner prescribed the state in which the defendant is to be served.

2)   MCR

a)   Service upon Individuals

(1)   Personal Service – Residents or Nonresidents

MCR 2.105(A) provides that a resident or nonresident can be served either by delivery in person to him or her or by certified or registered mail, return receipt requested with delivery restricted to the defendant.

(2)   Substituted Service

(a)   Nonresident

Under MCR 2.105(B)(1), a nonresident can be served by (1) delivery to this defendant's "agent, employee, representative, sales representative, or servant" and (2) sending a copy by registered mail to the defendant.

(b)   Minor

A minor may be served by delivery to a person possessing control and care of the minor and with whom the minor resides. MCR 2.105(B)(2).

(c)   Conservator or Guardian

Service may be made to the conservator or guardian of a defendant under MCR 2.105(B)(3).

b)   Service upon Agent

MCR 2.105(H)(1) authorizes service upon an agent authorized by law or written appointment to receive service.

C.   Service on Corporations

1)   FEDERAL RULES

Under the Federal Rules, a corporation may be served in any federal judicial district pursuant to the state law of the jurisdiction in which the defendant is found.

Alternatively, service may be made by delivering a copy of the summons and complaint to an officer, a managing or general agent, or to any other agent authorized by appointment or by law to receive service of process.

2)   MICHIGAN RULES

Service upon a corporation can be made to its (1) officer or resident agent; or (2) "a director, trustee, or person in charge of an office or business establishment of the corporation" and sending service to the corporation's principal office by registered mail. MCR 2.105(D)(1)-(2).

D.   Time for Service

1)   FEDERAL RULES – 120 DAYS

Pursuant to the Federal Rules, if summons and complaint are not served on the defendant within 120 days after filing of complaint and party seeking service cannot show good cause, the action should be dismissed as to that defendant without prejudice.

2)   MICHIGAN RULES – 91 DAYS

Pursuant to MCR 2.102(D)-(E), if summons and complaint is not served on defendant within 91 days after filing of complaint -- and party seeking service does not show due diligence in attempting to serve first summons in order to obtain a second summons for service after initial 91 days -- the action is deemed dismissed as to that defendant without prejudice.

E.   Who May Serve

Under the Federal Rules, the summons and complaint may be served by any citizen of the United States who is over 18 years of age and not a party. In addition, a party may request that service be made by a U.S. Marshal, Deputy Marshal or other appropriate official. Under MCR 2.103(A), a legally competent adult who is neither a party nor a corporate party's officer can generally serve process.

F.   Federal Waiver of Service

A person or entity subject to service that receives proper notice of an action has a duty to avoid unnecessary costs of serving the summons. To avoid costs, the plaintiff may notify a defendant of the commencement of the action and request that the defendant waive service of a summons. The notice and request must be in writing and addressed to the defendant. It must be dispatched by first class mail or other reliable means. It must contain a copy of the complaint and must inform the defendant of the consequences of compliance and of a failure to comply with the request.

The defendant possesses a reasonable time to return the waiver, which must be at least 30 days from the date on which the request is sent.

If a defendant located within the United States fails to comply with a proper request for waiver, the court will impose the costs subsequently incurred in effecting service on the defendant unless good cause for the failure is shown.

A defendant that timely returns a waiver so requested is not required to serve an answer to the complaint until 60 days after the date on which the request for waiver of service was sent.

G. Constitutional Requirements

In addition to meeting statutory requirements, service of process must meet constitutional requirements. In order for a method of service to satisfy constitutional requirements, the method must be reasonably calculated to provide notice to the defendant.

III. VENUE

★★★ A. General

Venue is the location of a court in which a judicial proceeding takes place. Unlike the concept of jurisdiction, venue usually does not implicate the constitutionality of a court's exercise of authority to adjudicate. Venue rules concern the propriety of the location of the court in which proceedings are conducted based on the parties' location and the legal questions that are at issue.

★★ 1) FEDERAL COURT

The propriety of venue in a federal district court is based on both the type of parties that are involved and a consideration of the parties' circumstances.

a) Individual Parties

There are four factors that must be analyzed in order to determine appropriate venue for actions involving individuals. The first two factors apply to cases in which the subject matter jurisdiction is based on either diversity of citizenship or a federal question. The third factor only applies to cases based on diversity of citizenship jurisdiction. The fourth factor only applies to cases based on federal question jurisdiction.

(1)   Residence

Venue is proper in a judicial district where any defendant resides, if all defendants reside in the same state; or

(2)   Act

Venue is proper in a judicial district in which a substantial part of the events or omissions giving rise to the claim occurred; or most the property that is subject to the action is located.

(3)   Diversity Only

Venue is proper in a judicial district in which the defendants are subject to personal jurisdiction at the time the action is commenced, if there is no district in which the action may otherwise be brought.

(4)   Federal Question Only

Venue is proper in a judicial district in which any defendant may be found, if there is no district in which the action may otherwise be brought.

• **Waiver**

As with personal jurisdiction objections, venue objections may be waived if not timely asserted.

b)   Corporate Parties

Different circumstances need to be considered when determining venue for corporations. 28 U.S.C. § 1391(c). For venue purposes, a defendant corporation is deemed to reside in any judicial district in which it is subject to personal jurisdiction at the time the action is commenced. In a state which has more than one judicial district and in which a defendant that is a corporation is subject to personal jurisdiction at the time an action is commenced, such corporation will be deemed to reside in any district in that State within which its contacts would be sufficient to subject it to personal jurisdiction if that district were a separate State, and, if there is no such district, the corporation will be deemed to reside in the district within which it has the most significant contacts.

c)   Local Action

A local action is one that must be filed where a *res*, or real property is located. Conversely, all other types of actions are deemed transitory. The common law rule is followed in a federal statute, which is captioned: "Defendants or property in different districts in the same State." 28 U.S.C. § 1392. It provides that: "Any civil action, of a local nature, involving property located in different districts in the same State, may be brought in any of such districts." *Id.*

2)   <u>REMOVAL VENUE</u>

In cases removed to a federal court from a state court, venue is proper in the federal district in which the state court sits. This special rule under a federal statute produces an anomalous result because it makes venue proper in a federal district in which the action could not have originally been brought if a plaintiff had initially filed a lawsuit in that improper venue. 28 U.S.C. § 1441(a).

3)   IMPROPER VENUE DISMISSAL

A defendant may make a motion to dismiss a plaintiff's lawsuit on the basis that it was filed in the improper venue. This motion may be made pursuant to Federal Rule 12(b)(6), which is further discussed later in this outline.

4)   OPTIONS OTHER THAN DISMISSAL FOR IMPROPER VENUE

Instead of filing a motion to dismiss a plaintiff's lawsuit on the basis of improper venue, a defendant may make a motion to transfer venue or a motion that asserts the defense of *forum non conveniens*, both of which are described more later in this outline.

★★   ### 5)   STATE COURT

a)   General Michigan Venue Statute

The general Michigan venue statute provides that an action may be brought in the "county in which a defendant resides, has a place of business, or conducts business, or in which the registered office of a defendant corporation is located." Mich. Comp. Laws § 600.1621(a). If defendant does not meet the criteria of § 1621(a), the proper county is one in which plaintiff meets the same criteria of § 1621(a). Mich. Comp. Laws § 600.1621(b).

(1)   Exception for Tort Actions

However, this general venue statute is subject to several exceptions, one of which pertains to tort actions. Section 600.1629(1) of the Michigan Compiled Laws provides in pertinent part that in an action based in tort, proper venue is:

(a)   the county in which the original injury occurred and in which either of the following applies is a county in which to file and try the action:

(i)   the defendant resides, has a place of business, or conducts business in that county; or

(ii)   the corporate registered office of a defendant is located in that county.

(b)   If a county does not satisfy the criteria under the foregoing subdivision (a), the county in which the original injury occurred and in which either of the following applies is a county in which to file and try the action:

(i)   The plaintiff resides, has a place of business, or conducts business in that county.

(ii)   The corporate registered office of a plaintiff is located in that county.

(c)   If a county does not satisfy the criteria under subdivision (a) or (b), a county in which both of the following apply is a county in which to file and try the action:

(i)   The plaintiff resides, has a place of business, or conducts business in that county, or has its corporate registered office located in that county.

(ii)   The defendant resides, has a place of business, or conducts business in that county, or has its corporate registered office located in that county.

Under the venue statutes, one meets the "conducting business" element where there is "some real presence such as might be shown by systematic or continuous business dealings inside the county." *Coleman v. Gurwin*, 443 Mich. 59, 62 (1993).

B.   Venue Transfer

1)   GENERAL GROUNDS FOR CHANGE OF VENUE

In many cases, more than one venue may be appropriate for the adjudication of a case. In that event, a defendant in the case may wish to change the initial venue that the plaintiff selected to a subsequent venue that the defendant prefers. A defendant may be entitled to a change or transfer of venue if the initial venue is improper or if a subsequent venue would be more convenient to the parties and the witnesses.

2)   MOTIONS FOR CHANGE OF VENUE

A defendant may file a motion to transfer venue on the basis that the existing venue is inappropriate and another venue would be more appropriate. Alternatively, a federal court may, *sua sponte*, make its own motion to transfer venue.

a)   Improper Venue

Generally, if a court orders a change of venue to remedy a plaintiff's improper selection of venue, then the case should be transferred to another court within that judicial system that possesses proper venue.

b)   More Convenient Venue

(1)   General Considerations

Even if a plaintiff filed a lawsuit in a proper venue, that initial court possesses discretion to order a change of venue to a subsequent court in a location that is more appropriate for the case. In that event, if a defendant files a motion to transfer venue to a subsequent court in the same state, the initial court may grant it if the result would increase the convenience of the parties and the witnesses and promote the interests of justice. Some of the other factors that an initial court will examine when ruling on the defendant's motion include the location of the evidence and judicial efficiency.

(a) Federal District Court Authority

In *Hoffman v. Blaski*, the United States Supreme Court interpreted the phrase "might have been brought" in section 1404(a) as limiting a federal district court's discretionary power to transfer a case to those other venues wherein a plaintiff could have originally filed the lawsuit. Thus, both personal jurisdiction and venue must exist then and cannot have been waived.

(2) Michigan Grounds for Motion for Change in Venue

In Michigan courts, a party can file a motion to change venue based on the grounds of inconvenience or hardship. Mich. Comp. Laws § 600.1629(2).

C. Forum Non Conveniens

The doctrine of *forum non conveniens* allows for the dismissal of a case despite the existence of proper venue, personal jurisdiction, and subject matter jurisdiction if another forum is more convenient and the interests of justice would be served by litigating the case elsewhere.

Federal district courts now primarily analyze a *forum non conveniens* issue under a federal statute, rather than applying that doctrine. 28 U.S.C. § 1404(a). A federal district court may, however, grant a dismissal of a case based on the doctrine if the only permissible alternative forums would be either a state court or a court of a foreign nation.

IV. PRE-TRIAL PROCEDURES

A. Pleadings

Pleadings include, but are not limited to, the Complaint, Answer, Cross-Claim, Counterclaim, Answer to Counterclaim (FRCP), Reply to Answer, Third-party Complaint, and Third-party Answer.

★ • Notice Pleading in Federal and Michigan Courts

Under the FRCP and MCR, "notice" pleading is required. A Complaint must provide the opposing party with "notice" of the nature of the claim. Pleadings must be simple, concise and direct. They may also be inconsistent, alternative, short and plain statements. Special matters must be pleaded with particularity including: fraud/mistake; judgments; and special damages.

Verification (e.g., by oath or notarization) is generally unnecessary unless required by statute, rule (MCR), or unless requesting equitable relief (FRCP). Generally, once a pleading is verified, responsive pleadings must also be under oath.

1)   COMPLAINT

A Complaint is the legal pleading filed with a court clerk by the plaintiff to initiate a lawsuit. The Complaint sets out facts and legal claims (usually called causes of action). To complete the initial stage of a lawsuit, the Complaint (and summons) must be served on the defendant, who then has the opportunity to respond.

★   2)   ANSWER

An Answer is a pleading that challenges a plaintiff's right to the relief that is requested in the Complaint. The Answer must admit or deny the allegations that are set forth in the Complaint. A failure to deny an allegation may result in an admission. The Answer may also assert a defendant's lack of sufficient knowledge to admit or deny an allegation. A failure to respond to an allegation may result in an admission of the allegation.

a)   Time for Service

An Answer must be served within 21 days (FRCP and MCR) after the service of the Complaint occurred.

b)   Affirmative Defenses

(1)   FRCP

Pursuant to the Federal Rules, Affirmative Defenses may be served concurrently with the Answer. They must be short and specific. Any omitted defenses may be asserted in an amended pleading either as of right or pursuant to the granting of a motion to amend the pleading.

★   (2)   MCR

Pursuant to MCR 2.117(F)(2)(a) and MCR 2.116(D)(2), generally an affirmative defense must be pled no later than the party's first responsive pleading. This can be accomplished by motion or the assertion of the affirmative defense in the answer as the first responsive pleading. Failure to assert an affirmative defense in one of these two ways results in a waiver of that defense.

★   3)   COUNTERCLAIMS

A Counterclaim is a claim that is made by a defendant in a civil lawsuit against a plaintiff. It is generally served with the Answer and the Affirmative Defenses within 21 days (FRCP and MCR) from the receipt of process. In essence, it is a counter suit within a lawsuit. Counterclaims are either compulsory or permissive. See the section on joinder later in this outline for a discussion of the significance of those classifications of a Counterclaim.

4)   ANSWER TO COUNTERCLAIM; REPLY TO ANSWER

In federal court, a plaintiff files an Answer to a Counterclaim designated within 21 days of service. It is similar to an Answer. In Michigan state court, a party files a Reply to an Answer within 21 days after service. A federal court may order a Reply to an Answer.

      5)   <u>CROSS-CLAIM</u>

A Cross-Claim is a claim by one party against a co-party (e.g., Defendant 1 v. Defendant 2).

      6)   <u>AMENDMENT OF PLEADINGS</u>

      a)   Federal Rules

Pursuant to Federal Rule 15(a), a party may amend the party's pleading once as of right within 21 days after serving it. Or, if the pleading is one to which a responsive pleading is required, the party may amend within the earlier of 21 days after service of a responsive pleading or a motion under Rule 12(b), (e), or (f). Otherwise a party may amend the party's pleading only by leave of court or by written consent of the adverse party; and leave must be freely given when justice so requires. A party must plead in response to an amended pleading within the time remaining for response to the original pleading or within 14 days after service of the amended pleading, whichever period may be the longer, unless the court otherwise orders. Further amendments are permitted at the discretion of a court. Leave to amend is liberally granted.

      b)   Michigan Rules

Pursuant to MCR 2.118(A)(1), a party can amend the party's pleading once as of right within 14 days after a responsive pleading is served. Or, if the pleading is one to which no responsive pleading is required, the party may amend its pleading at any time within 14 days after it is served. Otherwise a party may amend the party's pleading only by leave of court or by written consent of the adverse party; and leave must be freely given when justice so requires. MCR 2.118(A)(2). A party must plead in response to an amended pleading within the time remaining for response to the original pleading or within 21 days after service of the amended pleading, whichever period may be the longer, unless the court otherwise orders. For example, a party may seek to amend a pleading in order to assert a defense that otherwise the party would waive by failing to assert the defense. *Harris v. Lapeer Pub. Sch. Sys.*, 114 Mich. App. 107 (1982).

      c)   Relation Back Doctrine

      (1)   Same Conduct, Transaction, or Occurrence

Whenever the claim or defense asserted in the amended pleading arose out of the conduct, transaction, or occurrence set forth or attempted to be set forth in the original pleading, the amendment will be treated as if it was filed on the date of the original pleading.

      (2)   New Party

A common issue involves the addition of a new party after the statute of limitations has expired. As a general rule, such an amendment will only be permitted if the new party had notice and a mistake was made.

- Notice

The new party must have had notice of the suit such that it would not be prejudiced in being required to respond.

- Mistake

The new party knew or should have known that, but for a mistake in the identification of the proper party, the new party would have been served earlier.

7)   SUPPLEMENTAL PLEADINGS

Supplemental pleadings are used to set forth events that have happened since the filing date of a prior pleading that is sought to be supplemented. Leave of court, after giving notice to all other parties and making a motion to file supplemental pleadings, must be obtained to serve such a supplemental pleading. The courts' practice is usually liberal in allowing the filing of supplemental pleadings.

B.   Federal Abstention

An abstention doctrine is any one of several alternative doctrines that a federal court may invoke to refuse to hear a case otherwise properly before it when hearing the case would potentially intrude upon the powers of state courts. In general, parties may proceed to judgment in a federal district court action without regard to the pendency of state proceedings that seek similar relief. *Kline v. Burke Constr. Co.*, 260 U.S. 226 (1922). Indeed, a federal district court has a "duty . . . to adjudicate a controversy properly before it," and it may abstain "only in the exceptional circumstances where the order to the parties to repair to the State court would clearly serve an important countervailing interest." *Colorado River Water Conservation Dist. v. United States*, 424 U.S. 800, 813 (1976).

There are four alternative abstention doctrines.

1)   *PULLMAN* ABSTENTION

Pullman abstention is an equitable doctrine that operates only when the state court's resolution of unsettled state law issues may eliminate the need of resolving a difficult federal law issue. Like all abstention doctrines, *Pullman* abstention is an extraordinary and narrow exception to the duty of a district court to adjudicate a controversy properly before it.

Two elements must be met for *Pullman* abstention to apply:

- The case must present an unsettled question of state law; and

- The question of state law must be dispositive of the case or would materially alter a question presented.

If a court invokes *Pullman* abstention, it should stay the federal constitutional question until the matter has been sent to state court for a determination of the uncertain state law issue.

2)   *BURFORD* ABSTENTION

Abstention under the *Burford* doctrine is appropriate only if federal adjudication would interfere with a state's administration of a complex regulatory scheme. The most commonly cited example of a complex regulatory scheme is state insurance regulation. The reason for abstaining under *Burford* is that the state courts would likely possess a greater expertise in a particularly complex area of law such as a complex state regulatory scheme. The *Burford* case, for example, dealt with the regulation of oil drilling operations in Texas.

3)   *YOUNGER* ABSTENTION

Younger abstention may apply when the state's interest in the smooth functioning of its criminal justice system or its civil enforcement machinery is threatened by a federal court action that would interfere with those types of pending state proceedings.

There are three requirements for *Younger* abstention to apply:

- Pending or on-going state proceedings which are judicial in nature;
- The state proceedings must implicate an important state interest; and
- The state proceedings must afford an adequate opportunity to raise any constitutional issues.

4)   *COLORADO RIVER* ABSTENTION

Colorado River abstention comes into play when both federal and state court proceedings are simultaneously being carried on to determine the rights of parties with respect to the same issues of law. Under these circumstances, it would waste judicial resources for both courts to carry on. Application of the doctrine is not governed by a rigid rule, but by the application of an elaborate balancing test. *Moses H. Cone Mem. Hosp. v. Mercury Constr. Corp.*, 460 U.S. 1, 16 (1983).

There must be evidence of factors that disfavor proceeding with the federal litigation, such as the risk of inconsistent rulings with respect to a particular piece of property or clear evidence of a federal policy favoring unitary adjudication of the claims at issue. In conducting the balancing inquiry, the balance is heavily weighted in favor of the exercise of jurisdiction.

C.   Pre-Trial Conference and Order

1)   PRE-TRIAL CONFERENCE

a)   Objectives of Conference

Pursuant to Federal Rule 16, the court may direct the attorneys for the parties and any unrepresented parties to appear before it for a conference before trial for such purposes as:

- expediting the disposition of the action;
- establishing early and continuing control so that the case will not be protracted because of lack of management;
- discouraging wasteful pretrial activities;
- Improving the quality of the trial through more thorough preparation; and
- facilitating the settlement of the case.

b)   Authority of Counsel at Pre-Trial Conference

(1)   FRCP

Pursuant to part of Federal Rule 16(c), at least one of the attorneys for each party participating in any conference before trial must possess the authority to enter into stipulations and to make admissions regarding all matters that the participants may reasonably anticipate may be discussed. If appropriate, the federal district court may require that a party or its representatives be present or reasonably available by telephone in order to consider possible settlement of the dispute.

(2)   MCR

Pursuant to MCR 2.401(E), the lawyers attending the conference must be familiar with the case and possess the authority necessary to participate in the conference. Also, the court can require attendance at the conference by the lawyers who intend to try the case.

c)   Final Pre-Trial Conference

If the federal district court holds a final pre-trial conference pursuant to Federal Rule 16(e), it must be held as close to the time of trial as reasonable under the circumstances. The participants at any such conference must formulate a plan for trial, including a program for facilitating the admission of evidence. The conference must be attended by at least one of the attorneys who will conduct the trial for each of the parties and by any unrepresented parties.

d)   Pre-Trial Orders

Under Federal Rule 16(e), after any pre-trial conferences an order must be entered reciting the action taken. This order controls the subsequent course of the action unless it is modified by a subsequent order. The order following a final pre-trial conference will be modified only to prevent manifest injustice.

Under MCR 2.401(C)(2), as appropriate the court must enter an order including agreements reached and decisions made at the conference.

e)   Sanctions

(1)   FRCP

Under Federal Rule 16(f), a federal district court may issue such orders that are just, and among other options, may impose discovery sanctions:

- if a party or the party's attorney fails to obey a scheduling or pretrial order;
- if no appearance is made on behalf of a party at a scheduling or pretrial conference;
- if a party or party's attorney is substantially unprepared to participate in the conference; or
- if a party or party's attorney fails to participate in good faith.

In lieu of or in addition to any other sanction, the judge can require the party or the attorney or both to pay the reasonable expenses incurred because of any noncompliance.

(2)   MCR

Under MCR 2.401(G), if a party, the party's lawyer, or its representative fails to attend a pretrial conference or possess adequate authority or information to participate in the conference, this failure may be a basis for a default or dismissal. The court can, however, excuse such failures and enter a just order if the court finds that:

- "Entry of an order of default or dismissal would cause manifest injustice; or
- "The failure was not due to the culpable negligence of the party or the party's attorney."

The court can condition the order upon the payment of reasonable expenses by the offending attorney or party. Also, under MCR 2.401(H), an order requiring the payment of reasonable expenses, including attorney fees, can be entered following a post-discovery pre-trial conference upon a finding that a party's lack of reasonable diligence resulted in an action not being ready for trial.

2)   SCHEDULING ORDERS

a)   FRCP

Pursuant to Federal Rule 16(b), after receiving the parties' discovery reports, a federal district court must enter a scheduling order that limits the time to:

- join other parties and to amend the pleadings;
- file motions; and
- complete discovery.

The scheduling order may also include:

- modifications of deadlines for required Federal Rule 26 disclosures (which are discussed later in this outline in the section about Discovery);
- the dates for any pre-trial conferences and trial; and
- any other appropriate matter given the circumstances of the case.

The order should be issued as soon as practicable. A schedule may not be modified except upon a showing of good cause and by leave of the court.

b) MCR

Pursuant to MCR 2.401(B)(2)(a), after any pre-trial conference or whenever a scheduling order would facilitate the case's progress, a Michigan state court can enter a scheduling order to set times for appropriate events including, but not limited to:

- starting or ending alternative dispute resolution;
- amending pleadings;
- adding parties;
- filing motions;
- completing discovery;
- exchanging witness lists; and
- scheduling a pretrial conference, settlement conference, or trial.
-

V. MOTIONS

Unlike the pleading, a motion is an application to a court in order to obtain some rule or order of court, which the party thinks becomes necessary in the progress of the cause, or to get relieved in a summary manner, from some matter that would work injustice.

Whether either the FRCP or MCR or both of them provide for any of the following types of motions is indicated by citations and/or textual references. The absence of citations and/or textual references indicates that the motion exists under the FRCP and MCR.

A.   Motion to Dismiss

★   1)   FEDERAL RULE 12(B) MOTIONS

A Federal Rule 12(b) motion to dismiss may be served upon a plaintiff in lieu of a defendant's Answer. A Rule 12(b) motion usually should be made prior to a trial in a case and before the close of the pleadings. A Rule 12(b) motion attacks the sufficiency of the pleadings, usually a Complaint. The granting of a Rule 12(b) motion may result in a dismissal of a case. Usually, that dismissal is made without prejudice, which means that a plaintiff may re-file its Complaint within a limited time period after making changes to the pleading in order to avoid another dismissal on the same grounds. Sometimes, however, that dismissal may be made with prejudice, meaning that the plaintiff is entirely precluded from re-filing a revised Complaint against the defendant.

a)   Defenses Appropriate for Rule 12(b) Motions

(1)   Lack of Subject-Matter Jurisdiction

Lack of subject-matter jurisdiction may never be waived as a defense. That defense may be asserted at any time.

The following four defenses may be waived. These defenses may be asserted either in a defendant's answer or in a Rule 12(b) motion. If the defendant fails to raise any of these defenses in either the answer or that motion, the defense is waived pursuant to Rule 12(h)(1).

(2)   Lack of Personal Jurisdiction

(3)   Improper Venue

(4)   Insufficiency of Process

(5)   Insufficiency of Service of Process

(6)   Failure to State a Claim

This defense is generally not waived if not asserted in a Rule 12 motion or the Answer. The relevant inquiry for such a motion is whether, on the face of the complaint, a defendant is entitled to judgment. For example, the motion will be granted if a plaintiff has failed to allege an element of a cause of action. However, the complaint is construed in the light most favorable to the non-moving party. In other words, it is not easy to dismiss a complaint for failure to state a claim, especially in notice pleading jurisdictions, such as the federal courts, where factual allegations need be minimal.

(7)   Failure to Join an Indispensable Party

Failure to join an indispensable party is not waived if it is not asserted in a Rule 12 motion or in the Answer.

b)   Waiver of Defenses

Some of the above defenses will be waived if they are neither asserted in a responsive pleading (such as the answer) nor raised in a Rule 12(b) motion. The defenses that are listed in Rule 12(b) are not waived, however, if they were not raised in a responsive pleading but they were instead raised in a Rule 12(b) motion. None of the defenses that are enumerated in Rule 12(b) are waived by raising them in conjunction with, or independently of, any of those other defenses. Rule 12(b) provides that:

> Every defense, in law or fact, to a claim for relief in any pleading, whether a claim, counterclaim, cross-claim, or third-party claim, shall be asserted in the responsive pleading thereto if one is required, except that the following defenses

may at the option of the pleader be made by motion: (1) lack of jurisdiction over the subject matter, (2) lack of jurisdiction over the person, (3) improper venue, (4) insufficiency of process, (5) insufficiency of service of process, (6) failure to state a claim upon which relief can be granted, (7) failure to join a party under Rule 19. A motion making any of these defenses shall be made before pleading if a further pleading is permitted. No defense or objection is waived by being joined with one or more other defenses or objections in a responsive pleading or motion.

2)   MCR 2.504 MOTION

a)   Grounds for Involuntary Dismissal

(1)   Non-Compliance

Under MCR 2.504(B)(1), a defendant can make a motion for involuntary dismissal if the plaintiff does not comply with a court order or the MCR.

(2)   Bench Trial -- No Right to Relief

Pursuant to MCR 2.504(B)(2), in a non-jury action tried before the court, after plaintiff presents its evidence, defendant can make a motion for involuntary dismissal on the basis that plaintiff has shown "no right to relief" under the law and facts. The court can then render judgment against plaintiff or can wait to do that until after the close of all the evidence.

b)   Effect of Involuntary Dismissal

According to MCR 2.504(B)(3), usually an order of involuntary dismissal that is not for "for lack of jurisdiction or for failure to join a party" is an adjudication on the merits unless the order indicates otherwise.

B.   Motion for a More Definite Statement

Sometimes, a party's pleading is so unclear that a responding party cannot understand or respond to it. In other words, the pleading is vague or ambiguous. A Motion for a More Definite Statement seeks to require the filing of a revised pleading that is sufficiently clear and definitive.

C.   Motion to Strike

Under Federal Rule 12(f) and MCR 2.115(B), a party may move to strike redundant, immaterial, impertinent, scandalous, or indecent matter in a pleading. If a court grants the motion, any such matter will be excluded from the record.

D.   Motion for Judgment on the Pleadings

This pre-trial motion under Federal Rule 12(c) is similar to a Federal Rule 12(b) Motion to Dismiss. What distinguishes a Rule 12(c) motion from a Rule 12(b) motion is that the former motion must be filed after the pleadings are closed. The relevant inquiry for the former motion is whether, on the face of all pleadings, the movant is entitled to judgment. Rule 12(c) provides that:

> After the pleadings are closed but within such time as not to delay the trial, any party may move for judgment on the pleadings. If, on a motion for judgment on the pleadings, matters outside the pleadings are presented to and not excluded by the court, the motion shall be treated as one for summary judgment and disposed of as provided in Rule 56, and all parties shall be given reasonable opportunity to present all material made pertinent to such a motion by Rule 56.

If a Motion to Dismiss (Rule 12(b)) or a Motion for Judgment on the Pleadings (Rule 12(c)) includes new or additional matters that are outside of the existing pleadings' contents, a court will usually treat those motions the same as it treats Motions for Summary Judgment.

★   **E.   Motion for Summary Judgment**

A Motion for Summary Judgment will be granted when no genuine issue of material fact exists and the movant is entitled to a judgment as a matter of law. Federal Rule 56 provides that this motion may be supported by an affidavit and may be met by contradicting affidavits which raise issues of fact that are required to be resolved at a trial and by a finder of fact. An affidavit should set forth with particularity the facts upon which each claim or defense is based. A summary judgment may be only partial with respect to certain issues in a particular case. It may also be rendered on the issue of liability alone, although a genuine issue as to the amount of damages remains to be determined.

1)   TIMING OF MOTION

A party may move for summary judgment until 30 days after the close of discovery. A party opposing the motion must file a response within the later of either within 21 days after the motion is served or a responsive pleading is due. The party moving for summary judgment may file a reply within 14 days after the response to the motion for summary judgment is served.

F.   Motion for Judgment as a Matter of Law (formerly Directed Verdict)

At any time after the close of the opponent's evidence and before the case is submitted to the trier of fact, either party may move for judgment as a matter of law on the basis that the evidence is insufficient to support their adversary's position. The motion should be granted if there is no legally sufficient evidentiary basis for the jury to find in favor of the non-moving party.

A party must move for a motion for judgment as a matter of law to preserve a Renewed Motion for Judgment as a Matter of Law (formerly JNOV motion - same grounds after judgment is entered) in federal court. The purpose of requiring that a motion for judgment as a matter of law be made prior to the submission of the case to the jury "is to assure the responding party an opportunity to cure any deficiency in that party's proof that may have been overlooked until called to the party's attention by a late motion for judgment." The renewed motion must be made within 28 days of the judgment.

G.   Motion for Directed Verdict

At the close of the opponent's evidence, either party may move for a directed verdict under MCR 2.515. This motion must state the specific grounds in support of it. The moving party can offer evidence if the motion is not granted. Generally, the motion may be granted if the evidence is insufficient to support the other opponent's position.

H.   Motion for a Default Judgment

It is important to explain the terms "entry of default" and "default judgment" including what actions the judge takes and what actions the clerk takes to effect them. The plaintiff makes an application to the clerk to file an entry of default in the case. The plaintiff must attach affidavits and any other proof relevant to the question of the defendant's response to the suit to this application for entry of default. The entry of default is a preliminary step where the clerk examines the docket and papers the plaintiff files to determine if there has been an answer or responsive pleading. If not, the clerk enters the default, which is not a judgment. The plaintiff then applies to for a default judgment. There is no default judgment until the judge orders it.

1)   ENTRY OF DEFAULT

FRCP 55 and MCR 2.603 apply when a party against whom a judgment for affirmative relief is sought has failed to timely plead or otherwise defend a lawsuit. In that event, the party is considered to have committed a default that will be entered by the court's clerk.

2)   JUDGMENT

Once entry of default is entered by the clerk, the plaintiff may be able to obtain a judgment of default. It the claim is for a sum certain (a definite identifiable amount of money damages), the plaintiff may present an affidavit to that effect to the clerk, and the clerk will enter a default judgment. If the amount demanded is not a sum certain, the plaintiff must apply to the court for a default judgment.

3)   DAMAGES

If damages are not liquidated, there must be a hearing where evidence on damages is offered. This hearing can be accomplished in some cases on documentary evidence such as affidavits. A hearing may also be required if the court needs evidence to establish the truth of other averments.

4)   SETTING ASIDE DEFAULT

a)   Good Cause and Meritorious Defense

A defaulting party may move for relief from the entry of a default and/or a default judgment. To persuade a court to grant a motion to set aside a default or a default judgment, the movant must: 1) demonstrate good cause or a reasonable excuse for failure to timely plead or otherwise defend the lawsuit; and 2) state ultimate facts in support of a meritorious defense to a default. The judgment may also be set aside if the grounds for a motion for relief from judgment under Rule 60 or MCR 2.612 are satisfied. The commonly tested ground is that the judgment is void. A judgment may be void if the court lacks jurisdiction.

I.   Voluntary Dismissal of Claim

An action may be dismissed without court order 1) by the plaintiff alone by filing a notice of dismissal at any time before the adverse party serves an answer or a motion for summary judgment (FRCP) or summary disposition (MCR) (whichever comes first); or 2) by stipulation of dismissal signed by all parties who have appeared in the action. Otherwise, the parties seeking dismissal must obtain a court order.

Unless otherwise stated, the first such dismissal is without prejudice. The second dismissal of an action based on or including the same claim may act as a judgment on the merits.

★★ J.   Motion for Summary Disposition – MCR 2.116

A motion for summary disposition applies to both claims and defenses and can be compared to federal motions. A party can make a motion for summary disposition seeking a dismissal of, or a judgment upon, a claim. MCR 2.116(B)(1). A party against can move for summary disposition of a defense asserted against the party. *Id.* The motion can be based on at least one of several enumerated grounds and must specify the grounds it is based upon. MCR 2.116(C).

★★

1)   GROUNDS FOR MOTION

a)   Lack of Jurisdiction (over person or property)

This (C)(1) ground will be waived if it is not raised in the first filed of a party's (A) first motion for summary disposition or (B) responsive pleading. MCR 2.116(D)(1).

b)   Insufficient Process or Insufficient Service of Process

These (C)(2) or (C)(3) grounds will be waived if they are not raised in the first filed of a party's (A) first motion for summary disposition or (B) responsive pleading. *Id.*

★★★

c)   Lack of Subject Matter Jurisdiction

A motion for summary disposition can be made under MCR 2.116(C)(4) alleging that a court lacks subject matter jurisdiction. A (C)(4) motion may be made at any time during the proceedings. MCR 2.116(D)(3). For example, a party may file this motion after the expiration of the time in which to file dispositive motions as provided by a scheduling order. *Id.* at cmt. This defense neither needs to be preserved nor may it be waived by the parties.

★   d)   Lack of Capacity to Sue

This (C)(5) ground must be raised in a party's responsive pleading unless this ground is stated in a motion for summary disposition filed before the party's first responsive pleading. MCR 2.116(D)(2). For example, a competent, adult individual generally has the capacity to sue or be sued in the individual's own name. MCR 2.201(C)(1). In contrast, an incompetent, minor child usually lacks the capacity to sue or be sued in the child's own name.

              e)   Another Action (between same parties with same claim)

This (C)(6) ground must be raised in a party's responsive pleading unless this ground is stated in a motion for summary disposition filed before the party's first responsive pleading. MCR 2.116(D)(2).

              f)   Claim Barred for Specific Reasons (i.e., Defenses)

The reasons in MCR 2.116(C)(7) include: "release, payment, prior judgment, immunity granted by law, statute of limitations, statute of frauds, an agreement to arbitrate, infancy or other disability of the moving party, or assignment or other disposition of the claim before commencement of the action." These grounds must be raised in a party's responsive pleading unless this ground is stated in a motion for summary disposition filed before the party's first responsive pleading. MCR 2.116(D)(2).

★   (1)   Prior Judgment

A motion for summary disposition can raise one of the foregoing enumerated MCR 2.116(C)(7) defenses, such as *res judicata* (i.e., prior judgment). *Res judicata* is an affirmative defense. *E & G Fin. Co. v. Simms,* 362 Mich. 592 (1961). Michigan law regarding *res judicata* is described later in Section XI of this outline, titled "Res Judicata."

★   (2)   Statute of Limitations

A motion for summary disposition can be made under MCR 2.116(C)(7) alleging that a lawsuit is time barred under the applicable limitations period. A (C)(7) motion "must be raised in a party's responsive pleading." MCR 2.116(D)(2). If a party fails to file a (C)(7) motion in its responsive pleading, this (C)(7) defense will be deemed waived. *Huntington Woods v. Ajax Paving Industries, Inc.,* 179 Mich. App. 600 (1989).

              (3)   Other Defenses

Other defenses include statute of frauds, arbitration agreement, the moving party's disability (i.e., infancy), release, payment, legal immunity, and assignment or other disposition of the claim. MCR 2.116(D)(7).

★   g)   Failure to State a Claim

When deciding a motion for summary disposition under MCR 2.116(C)(8), the trial court must determine whether the opposing party has failed to state a claim on which relief can be granted. In doing so, the trial court may only consider the pleadings. MCR 2.116(G)(5). To that end, a defendant can prevail only if the defendant is able to show that the plaintiff's complaint failed to state a claim. If the plaintiff's complaint sets forth a *prima facie* case, the defendant's (C)(8) motion would therefore fail. Generally, the ground for this motion can be raised at any time, unless a scheduling order establishes the period in which to file dispositive motions. In that event, a trial court has discretion to allow consideration of a motion filed after such period. MCR 2.116(D)(4).

h)   Failure to State a Defense

That the opposing party has failed to state valid defense to the claim asserted against that party is another basis for this motion. MCR 2.116(C)(9). Generally, this ground for the motion can be raised at any time, unless a scheduling order establishes the period in which to file dispositive motions. In that event, a trial court has discretion to allow consideration of a motion filed after such period. MCR 2.116(D)(4).

★★   i)   No Genuine Issue of Material Fact (other than amount of damages)

A motion for summary disposition can be made under MCR 2.116(C)(10) testing the factual sufficiency of the complaint. In evaluating a motion for summary disposition brought under (C)(10), a trial court must consider the affidavits, pleadings, depositions, admissions, and other documentary evidence submitted by the parties (including all inferences that can be drawn from that evidence), in the light most favorable to the party opposing the motion. MCR 2.116(G)(5); *Maiden v. Rozwood,* 461 Mich. 109, 119-120 (1999). If the proffered evidence fails to establish a genuine issue regarding any material fact, the movant is entitled to judgment as a matter of law. MCR 2.116(C)(10); MCR 2.116(G)(4); *Maiden, supra* at 120. Only substantively admissible evidence that is actually proffered in opposition to the motion may be considered. *Maiden, supra* at 121. The evidence offered in support must be admissible as evidence to support a genuine issue of material fact in favor of the non-moving party. MCR 2.116(G)(6). Generally, the grounds for this motion can be raised at any time, unless a scheduling order establishes the period in which to file dispositive motions. In that event, a trial court has discretion to allow consideration of a motion filed after such period. MCR 2.116(D)(4).

★   (1)   Sufficiency of Evidence

"A litigant's mere pledge to establish an issue of fact at trial cannot survive summary disposition under MCR 2.116(C)(10)." *Maiden, supra* at 120. A legal conclusion does not create a question of fact regarding a party's negligence. *Maiden, supra* at 129, n 11; *also Downie v. Kent Products,* 420 Mich. 197, 205 (1984).

★   (2)   Hearsay Evidence

"When the document to be admitted contains a second level of hearsay, it also must qualify under an exception to the hearsay rule." *Maiden, supra* at 124; *also Merrow v. Bofferding,* 458

Mich. 617 (1998).

★   (3)   Evidence on Appeal

In reviewing the propriety of a grant of summary disposition, the appellate court is governed only by the evidence that was before the trial court at the time the motion was granted. *Maiden, supra* at 126; *also Quinto v. Cross & Peters,* 451 Mich. 358, 366 (1996). If evidence is submitted for the first time on appeal, it is irrelevant to the Michigan Court of Appeals' analysis.

                         j)   Governmental Immunity

A motion for summary disposition may raise the ground of governmental immunity at any time, regardless of whether the motion is filed after the expiration of the time in which to file dispositive motions as provided by a scheduling order. MCR 2.116(D)(3), cmt.

★   2)   FILING, SERVING, AND TIMING OF MOTION

Generally, a party must file in the court and serve the other parties with a motion for summary disposition at least 21 days before the motion's hearing. MCR 2.116(G)(1)(a)(i). Generally, a party must file and serve a response to the motion at least seven days before the hearing. MCR 2.116(G)(1)(a)(ii).

★   K.   **Motion to Adjourn**

              1)   GOOD CAUSE BASIS REQUIRED FOR ADJOURNMENT

Generally, a Michigan trial court may adjourn pre-trial conferences, motion hearings, and trials. MCR 2.503(A). A party may make a motion requesting an adjournment based on good cause. For example, a party could make a motion for an adjournment of a trial on the basis that good cause exists for the adjournment because the party's lawyer is seriously ill and, as a sole practitioner, lacks a substitute counsel prepared to represent the client at the trial. Alternatively, parties may make a stipulation requesting an adjournment based on good cause. MCR 2.503(B)(1). For example, the respective counsel for a plaintiff and a defendant could execute a stipulation seeking to adjourn a motion hearing on the basis that they each are involved in separate trials of other cases on the date of the motion hearing. A request for an adjournment by a motion or a stipulation may be made in writing or orally in open court. *Id.*

VI.   JOINDER

Joinder refers to the addition of claims or parties to a case that are beyond the scope of the initial pleadings such as a Complaint and an Answer.

A.   **Joinder of Claims**

In federal courts, the requirements of subject-matter jurisdiction and personal jurisdiction must be satisfied with respect to each claim that is joined in an existing case.

1) COMPULSORY JOINDER OF CLAIMS

Due to the claim preclusion doctrine of *res judicata*, a party must essentially present a complete "claim" to a court. Although the party is not "required" to present the entire claim, if the party fails to do that, the party will be barred from bringing any other portions of the claim in a later suit. Courts generally conduct a "transaction" test to determine whether two separate requests for relief arise from the same "claim" for *res judicata* purposes.

★   ### 2) COMPULSORY COUNTERCLAIMS

a) Rule 13

Rule 13 requires a defending party to put forward any claim that the defending party possesses "against any opposing party, if it arises out of the transaction or occurrence that is the subject matter of the opposing party's claim." The failure to assert such a counterclaim precludes its assertion in a subsequent action.

b) MCR 2.203(A)

According to MCR 2.203(A), a "pleading that states a claim" against an opposing party must include all other claims arising out of the transaction or occurrence that is the subject matter of the action, assuming that those additional claims do not require the presence of parties over whom the court cannot acquire jurisdiction. *Id.* If defendant files an answer to a complaint that includes a counterclaim -- which is a "pleading that states a claim" -- MCR 2.203(A) requires that defendant join any claim arising out of the transaction or occurrence underlying the complaint or the counterclaim. Suppose, for example, that defendant's breach of contract claim arises out of the same contract that is the basis for plaintiff's contract claim in plaintiff's complaint. If defendant fails to raise the breach of contract claim along with another unrelated claim in defendant's counterclaim, defendant may be barred from litigating the breach of contract claim in the future under the principles of claim preclusion and compulsory joinder. In order for defendant to avoid waiving its breach of contract claim, defendant should raise it as a counterclaim to plaintiff's lawsuit.

Michigan's rule of compulsory joinder differs from the comparable Federal Rule 13. Rule 13(a) states that "a pleading shall state as a counterclaim any claim which at the time of serving the pleading the pleader has against any opposing party, if it arises out of the transaction or occurrence that is the subject matter of the opposing party's claim." Thus, compulsory joinder applies under Rule 13 regardless of whether a responsive pleading "states a claim." If Rule 13 applied to the foregoing example, defendant would be required to raise its breach of contract claim in a responsive pleading regardless of whether defendant also filed an unrelated claim. Under the MCR, however, defendant is required to file a breach of contract claim only because defendant is also raising an unrelated claim and is therefore filing a "Pleading that states a claim."

3) PERMISSIVE JOINDER OF CLAIMS

Parties generally enjoy great discretion regarding which claims may be joined in the parties" pleadings. The Federal Rules and MCR 2.203(B) generally allow for liberal joinder of different and alternative claims in a cause of action provided that the requirements of subject-matter jurisdiction and personal jurisdiction are satisfied with respect to each claim.

4) PERMISSIVE COUNTERCLAIMS

A defending party may assert against an opposing party any counterclaim that the defending party possesses.

The failure to assert a permissive counterclaim does not preclude its assertion in a subsequent action.

5) CROSS-CLAIMS

A defendant may assert a claim regarding the same transaction against a third party, rather than the plaintiff, that is already involved in the litigation (i.e., co-defendant).

B. Joinder of Parties

Rule 13(h) states that:

> Persons other than those made parties to the original action may be made parties to a counterclaim or cross-claim in accordance with the provisions of Federal Rules 19 and 20.

1) COMPULSORY JOINDER OF PARTIES

Federal Rule 19 and MCR 2.205 govern which persons must be joined in an action. There are two general types of parties subject to compulsory joinder – necessary and indispensable parties.

a) Necessary Parties

A party is a "necessary" party if in the person's absence complete relief cannot be accorded among those parties who are already litigating a case. A necessary party must be joined if feasible. Joinder may not be possible in certain circumstances. For example, in federal courts, joinder may destroy diversity of citizenship for the purposes of subject-matter jurisdiction. Under those circumstances, the federal court must then determine if the party that is sought to be joined in the case is "indispensable."

b) Indispensable Parties

An indispensable party is a party without which a case cannot proceed if that party cannot be joined. When determining whether a party is indispensable, a court will generally examine the following factors:

- the extent to which a judgment rendered without the party might prejudice an absentee or existing parties;
- whether the prejudice can be lessened or avoided by appropriately shaping the relief granted;
- whether adequate relief can be granted without the absentee; and
- whether the plaintiff has an adequate remedy if the action is dismissed for non-joinder.

Several decided cases have held that causes of actions seeking the rescission of a contract must be dismissed unless all parties to the contract, and any others having a substantial interest in it, can be joined. Moreover, when ownership of real property is involved in litigation, any and all people who possess an interest in that property are usually considered indispensable parties.

2)   PERMISSIVE JOINDER OF PLAINTIFFS

Federal Rule 20(a) and MCR 2.206(A)(1) permit plaintiffs to join their claims in a single action when those claims arise out of a single event and share at least one common issue of law or fact. Rule 20(a) and MCR 2.206(A)(1) state in part that:

> All persons may join in one action as plaintiffs if they assert any right to relief jointly, severally, or in the alternative in respect of or arising out of the same transaction, occurrence, or series of transactions or occurrences and if any question of law or fact common to all these persons will arise in the action.

Rule 20(a) does not independently confer subject matter jurisdiction on the U.S. district court to hear the respective claims of the plaintiffs. It simply provides the mechanism for joining claims over which the U.S. Constitution and the Congress have given it subject matter jurisdiction.

3)   PERMISSIVE JOINDER OF DEFENDANTS

Just as Federal Rule 20(a) and MCR 2.206(A)(1) permits plaintiffs to join in an action, they permit a plaintiff or plaintiffs to join defendants in the action when the plaintiffs' claims against each defendant arise from a single transaction and share a common issue of fact or law. The permissive joinder rule allows a plaintiff to choose and name the defendants but does not require that a plaintiff name all defendants who might be joined. Rule 20(a) and MCR 2.206(A)(2) provides in part that:

> All persons (and only per Rule 20(a) any vessel, cargo or other property subject to admiralty process in rem) may be joined in one action as defendants if there is asserted against them jointly, severally, or in the alternative, any right to relief in respect of or arising out of the same transaction, occurrence, or series of transactions or occurrences and if any question of law or fact common to all defendants will arise in the action.

Note: The entire Rule 20(a) does not independently confer subject-matter jurisdiction on a federal district court to either hear a claim against a joined defendant or a joined plaintiff. It simply provides the mechanism for joining claims over which that court may exercise subject matter jurisdiction. Thus, joinder may be defeated when the court lacks subject-matter jurisdiction over a joined claim.

C.   Miscellaneous Joinder Concepts

1)   INTERVENTION

Intervention is a procedure that permits a nonparty applicant to participate in ongoing litigation between parties in order to protect the applicant's interests that may be affected by the litigation's results.

a)   Intervention of Right

Intervention is of right when a federal statute or Michigan statute confers an unconditional right upon a nonparty applicant to intervene in ongoing litigation. For example, the United States can always intervene in any action challenging the constitutionality of a federal statute. Moreover, intervention is of right when, under certain circumstances, the applicant asserts an interest that relates to the property or transaction that is the subject of the litigation.

b)   Permissive Intervention

Intervention is permitted when a court determines that the interests of the original parties would not be prejudiced by allowing a nonparty applicant to participate in the ongoing litigation. Also under MCR 2.209(B), an applicant may intervene when a common question of law or fact exists in the main action and the applicant's claim or defense.

A nonparty applicant is generally entitled to intervene when the applicant's position is similar to that of a "necessary" party as discussed earlier. Accordingly, if the applicant would be substantially affected by a determination that is made in the litigation, the applicant would usually be entitled to intervene.

2)   IMPLEADER

a)   Definition

Impleader is a form of third-party practice that gives rise to derivative liability. Third-party practice is not a general device for bringing in additional parties to the action. It is appropriate only when a defending party, as a third-party plaintiff, makes a claim for some kind of derivative or secondary liability against a third-party defendant. It can be used for claims of indemnity, suretyship, subrogation, or contribution and warranty from parties other than joint tortfeasors.

b)   Impleader by Motion

A defending party may file a motion asking a court for authorization to join a nonparty as a third-party defendant. Such a motion should state the defending party's reasons for joining the nonparty in a case. If the motion is granted, the defending party becomes a third-party plaintiff and the nonparty becomes a third-party defendant.

c)   Purpose

Impleader allows a third-party plaintiff to bring a claim against a third-party defendant who may be liable to the third-party plaintiff for all or part of a claim that was made against the third-party plaintiff in a case. The third-party plaintiff may seek and/or recover derivative relief in the case for all or part of the claim if a judgment is entered against the third-party plaintiff.

3)   <u>INTERPLEADER</u>

Interpleader permits a party (as a "stakeholder") to avoid the risk of potential multiple liability by requiring two or more other claimants with actual or potential claims against the stakeholder to assert their respective claims in one suit. Interpleader can be brought as either a separate action or a cross-claim or a counterclaim. Interpleader is a somewhat infrequently used, but significant, joinder device whose core function is to save stakeholders, such as bailees and insurance companies, from logically inconsistent liability to claimants with respect to a single thing or asset.

Interpleader stems from a basic proposition of justice that the law should not require a stakeholder to give the same thing to two or more different claimants. For example, if a first bailee checks a coat at a cloakroom and a second bailee comes along claiming to be the owner of the coat and that the first bailee stole the coat from the second bailee, then the bailor should have a way to avoid the threat of two independent actions with the possibility of orders in each to give the same coat to a different bailee. Similarly and more realistically, a life insurance company ought to have some way to protect itself against inconsistent claims to a single benefit. That might occur if an insured designates a first spouse as a beneficiary but has purportedly become remarried to a second spouse. In that instance the first spouse might challenge the validity of the divorce proceeding, and consequently claim an entitlement to the proceeds of the policy in contravention of the second spouse's claim.

4)   <u>CONSOLIDATION</u>

The consolidation of cases is governed by Federal Rule 42(a) and MCR 2.505(A). When actions involving a common question of law or fact are pending before a court, the court may order a joint hearing or trial of any or all of the matters that are in issue in those actions. Moreover, the court may order that all of those actions be consolidated into once case. Further, the court may make any orders concerning proceedings in that case, which would tend to avoid unnecessary costs or delay. The interests sought to be promoted through consolidation of the actions are judicial expediency and efficiency.

5)   <u>SEVERANCE</u>

The severance of claims is controlled by Federal Rule 42(b) and MCR 2.505(B). A court, in furtherance of convenience or to avoid prejudice, may order a separate trial of any claim, cross-claim, counterclaim, third-party claim, or issue. The court may also order a separate trial of any separate issue or of any number of claims, cross-claims, counterclaims, third-party claims, or issues. The court must always preserve inviolate the right of trial by jury.

VII. CLASS ACTIONS

★★ **A. Certification**

Federal Rule 23(a) and MCR 3.501(1) identify the similar prerequisites that must be satisfied before any class may be certified. Rule 23(a) and MCR 3.501(1) include, in part, the following requirements:

1) NUMEROSITY

The numerous members of a class render impracticable joinder of them all.

2) COMMONALITY

Common question of law and fact exist among the members of the class.

3) TYPICALITY

The claims of the representatives and the members of the class must be typical. The claims will be considered typical if all they arise from a single event or if they all are based on common legal theories. *Rall v. Medtronic*, 1986 WL 22271 (D. Nev. 1986).

4) ADEQUACY OF REPRESENTATION

The adequacy of representation requirement involves a two-part inquiry. First, a court must ask whether the representative's interests are aligned closely enough with other class members to ensure fair representation of the absentee class members. Second, the court must ensure that the counsel for the class are experienced and qualified to carry out the litigation in order to fairly and adequately protect the interests of the class. Under Rule 23(a) and MCR 3.501(1)(d), the representative parties must fairly and adequately assert and protect the interests of the class.

5) SUPERIORITY

Under Rule 23(b)(3) and MCR 3.501(1)(e), the maintenance of the class action must be superior to other available methods of adjudication in promoting the convenient administration of justice. In determining whether a class action is superior, a court considers the factors listed in Rule 23(b) and MCR 3.501(A)(2) to maintain a class action.

★★ **B. Maintenance**

A lawsuit may be maintained as a class action if the prerequisites of Rule 23(a) and MCR 3.501(A)(1) are satisfied and in addition, either of the following factors is fulfilled:

- Risk of Inconsistency

The prosecution of separate actions by or against the members of the class would create a risk of inconsistency or varying adjudications that would present the party-opponent with incompatible standards of conduct; or "adjudication with respect to individual members of the class that would as a practical matter be dispositive of the interests of other members not parties to the adjudications or substantially impair or impede their ability to protect their interests."

- Class Questions Predominate

Questions of law or fact common to the members of the class predominate over any questions that only affect individual members. Again, a class action must be superior to all other available methods for the fair and efficient adjudication of the controversy.

Additional factors for the court to consider regarding whether a lawsuit can be maintained as a class action under MCR 3.501(2) are:

"(b)   whether final equitable or declaratory relief might be appropriate with respect to the class;"

"(c)   whether the action will be manageable as a class action;"

"(d)   whether in view of the complexity of the issues or the expense of litigation the separate claims of individual class members are insufficient in amount to support separate actions;"

"(e)   whether it is probable that the amount which may be recovered by individual class members will be large enough in relation to the expense and effort of administering the action to justify a class action; and"

"(f)   whether members of the class have a significant interest in controlling the prosecution or defense of separate actions."

C.   **Adequate Notice Must Be Given to the Class**

In order to maintain a class action, adequate notice of the lawsuit must be given to the class. Sometimes, the provision of actual notice to every class member may be impossible. In that event, a court, in its discretion, may order the provision of such notice that it deems necessary to protect the interests of the class and the parties.

VIII.   **TRIALS**

A.   **Right to a Jury Trial**

1)   GENERAL – ACTIONS AT LAW

      a)   FRCP

In federal court, pursuant to the Seventh Amendment to the United States Constitution and Federal Rule 38(a), parties possess a right to a jury trial in all actions at law (for damages) for claims exceeding a claim amount of $20. Pursuant to the Rules, any legal claims should be tried before any equitable claims are tried.

Rule 38(a) states that:

> The right of trial by jury as declared by the Seventh Amendment to the Constitution or as given by a statute of the United States shall be preserved to the parties inviolate.

      b)   MCR

MCR 2.508(A) states that the right to a jury trial as provided in the Michigan Constitution is preserved to the parties inviolate. The right of trial by jury must remain, but will be waived in all civil cases unless one of the parties demands it. Mich. Const. art. I, § 14.

2)   EQUITABLE CLAIMS

A party asserting equitable claims or remedies does not have a right to a jury trial. A party may possess both legal and equitable claims in one action.

3)   WAIVER OF THE RIGHT TO A JURY TRIAL

      a)   FRCP

Rule 38(b) requires that a party file and serve a jury trial demand within 14 days of the filing of the last pleading that is directed to the issue for which the basis for a right to a jury trial exists. Otherwise, the right to a trial by jury will be waived.

      b)   MCR

MCR 2.508(B) provides that a party may file a written jury trial demand within 28 days of the filing of the answer or a timely reply. Otherwise, the right to a trial by jury will be waived under MCR 2.508(D)(1).

B.   Number of Jurors and Verdict

1)   FRCP

A minimum of 6 and a maximum of 12 jurors must participate in the verdict. Unless the parties otherwise stipulate: 1) the verdict must be unanimous; and 2) no verdict may be taken from a jury that is reduced in size to fewer than six members.

2)   MCR

Michigan's legislature can authorize a trial by a jury of fewer than 12 jurors. Mich. Const. art. IV, § 44. In cases tried by 12 jurors, a verdict must be received once 10 jurors agree. Mich. Const. art. I, § 14.

C.   Judicial Findings and Conclusions

In a bench trial, the judge is the finder of fact and decides the questions of law. In a jury trial, the jury is the finder of fact and the judge decides the questions of law.

D.   Jury Instructions

1)   GENERAL

a)   FRCP

Federal Rule 51(a) provides in part that after the close of the evidence any party may serve written requests that the court instruct the jury on the law as it is set forth in the requests. The court must inform the counsel of its proposed action upon the requests before they present their arguments to the jury. The court may instruct the jury after the counsel finish making their arguments.

b)   MCR

MCR 2.516(A)(1) provides in part that "at or before the close of the evidence," the parties may file written requests for jury instructions. The court may instruct the jury before and/or after the counsel finish making their arguments pursuant to MCR 2.516(B)(3).

2)   OBJECTIONS (PRESERVATION OF ERROR IN JURY CHARGE)

Under Federal Rule 51(b)-(c) and MCR 2.516(C), no party may assign as error the court's giving or failure to give a written instruction to the jury unless:

(1)   the party objects with particularity to that giving or failure to give the written instruction
(2)   before the jury retires to consider its verdict.

The court must afford the objecting counsel an opportunity to object outside of the jury's presence.

3)   JUDGE CANNOT EXPRESS OPINION

In charging the jury, the court may not express its opinion regarding the evidence.

★★ **IX.   DISCOVERY**

Discovery is the process of gathering information (potential evidence) in preparation for a trial. There are several different discovery vehicles for parties to utilize. The scope of discovery is broad and is to be construed liberally. Discovery is permitted under Federal Rule 26(b)(1) and MCR 2.302(B)(1) regarding any evidence that is relevant to the controversy, provided that the evidence is neither privileged nor an attorney's work product. Thus, the Federal and Michigan Rules of Evidence do not generally apply during the discovery process. Rather, they apply to the admissibility at trial of the evidence that is obtained through discovery.

Note that discoverable evidence need not be admissible itself. It must only be reasonably calculated to lead to the discovery of admissible evidence. However, items that were prepared in anticipation of litigation are protected from discovery unless the party seeking discovery can show that the party is unable without undue hardship to obtain the substantial equivalent of the materials by other means.

Parties may engage in discovery after a civil action commences in Michigan circuit courts. MCR 2.302(A)(1). The filing of a complaint commences a civil action. MCR 2.101(B).

A.   Federal Rule 26 Disclosures

1)   INITIAL DISCLOSURES

Under Rule 26(a)(1), the parties in a case must make initial disclosures to an opponent even without being requested to do so. Each party must provide all relevant materials to each opposing party's counsel. Among other items of information, disclosures may include: 1) names and contact information of all witnesses; 2) lists, categories, and descriptions of relevant documents; and 3) lists and computations for damages that are sought.

In federal court actions, the parties must hold an initial conference to plan the process of discovery under Federal Rule 16(a). Rule 26(a)(1) disclosures must be made at or within 14 days after that conference occurs unless a different time is set by a stipulation of the parties or by a court order.

Under Rule 26(a)(2) a party must disclose the identity of any expert who may be used at trial. That disclosure must be made before, and included in, a scheduling order that the court must issue at least 90 days before the trial begins unless the court directs otherwise.

2)   PRE-TRIAL DISCLOSURES

Rule 26(a)(3) provides that a party must provide to another party the following information that may be presented at trial for purposes other than the impeachment of a witness:

- The identity of each witness who may be called to testify.

- A designation of those witnesses whose testimony is to be presented by deposition, along with a transcript of relevant portions of each deposition.
- An identification of each document or exhibit that may be offered as evidence at the trial.

B.   Depositions

A deposition is a process whereby the parties to litigation may present questions to an opposing party and/or any witnesses. The Rules refer to such a person who is subject to a deposition as a deponent. A deposition usually occurs before a trial and generally takes place outside of a courtroom. The counsels who represent the parties formulate and ask the questions for the purposes of fact-finding and preparation for a trial.

1)   ORAL EXAMINATION

A party desiring to take an oral deposition under Federal Rule 30 and MCR 2.306(B)(1) must give reasonable notice to every other party, stating the time and place and names and addresses of all persons to deposed. A subpoena may be served on the person to be examined. The subpoena directs the person to appear for questioning at a certain place on a specific date and at a particular time. A subpoena *duces tecum* includes that same information, as well as requests that the person produce certain materials, such as documents, regarding the subject-matter of the parties' dispute. The party that issues the subpoena may review those materials in advance of the deposition and then question the witness about them during the deposition.

2)   CORPORATE DEPOSITION

Under Federal Rule 30(b) and MCR 2.306(B)(5), a party may notice a corporation or other organization and designate matters on which examination is requested. The organization must designate a person or people to testify as to matters known or reasonably available to the organization. If a subpoena *duces tecum* is used, the person or people who are deposed may be questioned about certain documents such as business records.

3)   ON WRITTEN QUESTIONS

A party may take a deposition upon written questions pursuant to Federal Rule 31 and MCR 2.307.

★   C.   Interrogatories

Interrogatories under Federal Rule 33 and MCR 2.309 may be only served on a party. They are written questions asked by one party of an opposing party, who must answer them in writing under oath. The answers often can be used as evidence in the trial. Absent court permission to ask more questions, Rule 33(a) imposes a presumptive limit of 25 total questions including subparts. By its terms, MCR 2.309 does not expressly address the number of questions. The general rule under Rule 33(b)(3) is that a party must serve its answers to the interrogatories within 30 days of being served with those questions. The general rule under MCR 2.309(B)(4) is that a party must serve its answers to the interrogatories within 28 days of being served with those questions. In Michigan, a party may serve interrogatories on a civil defendant with service of the summons and complaint. MCR 2.309(A)(2).

D.   Requests for Admission

A request for admission under Federal Rule 36 and MCR 2.312 is a written statement served by one party on another party requesting that the responding party admit or deny the truth of the statement. A party may serve a request for admission on any other party regarding any issue of fact. A party cannot request an admission regarding an issue of law. Under Rule 36, a party must serve a response to a request within 30 days of being served. Under MCR 2.312(B)(1), a party must serve a response to a request within 28 days of being served. Any failure to respond may be construed as an admission of that issue of fact.

★   **E.   Request for Production**

Under Federal Rule 34(a) and MCR 2.310 party may request any other party to produce and/or permit inspection or copying of designated documents or other tangible things. Under Rule 34(b), a party must permit inspection or otherwise serve a response to such a request within 30 days of being served. Under MCR 2.310(C)(2), a party must serve a response to such a request within 28 days of being served stating whether the request is granted or the reasons for objecting to the request. A party may also seek the production of discoverable documents from a non-party by the use of a subpoena duces tecum. In Michigan, a party may serve requests for the production of documents on a civil defendant when serving the summons and complaint. MCR 2.310(C)(1).

F.   Physical or Mental Examination

★   **1)   GENERAL CONSIDERATIONS**

The mental or physical condition of a party under Federal Rule 35(a) and MCR 2.311(A) can be made the focus of an examination by a physician only upon a motion and good cause shown. Further, the physical or mental condition must be an issue in controversy. Specifically, MCR 2.311(A) provides that when the mental or physical condition of a party is in controversy, "the court in which the action is pending may order the party to submit to a physical or mental or blood examination by a physician (or other appropriate professional)." This court order "may be entered only on motion for good cause with notice to the person to be examined and to all parties." In addition to the order specifying the time, place, manner, conditions, and scope of the examination, it "may provide that the attorney for the person to be examined may be present at the examination."

a)   Good Cause

"What may be good cause for one type of examination may not be so for another. The ability of the movant to obtain the desired information by other means is also relevant." *Brewster v.*

Martin Marietta Aluminum Sales, Inc., 107 Mich. App. 639, 644 (1981) quoting *Schlagenhauf v. Holder,* 379 U.S. 104, 118 (1964).

b)   Prior Examinations

Under Federal Rule 35(b) and MCR 2.311(A)(1), the party causing the examination must furnish the examined party with all earlier examinations to which the party may have access, including test results. The examined party must then make similar disclosure in return.

★   c)   Presence of Attorney

Under MCR 2.311(A), the court order may provide that the person to be examined may have his attorney present at the examination. Note that, in the absence of a court order allowing the person's attorney to be present, this rule provides no guidance on whether the person being examined has a right to demand the attorney's presence at the physical examination the person volunteered to attend.

★   d)   Physician-Patient Privilege

While medical records are usually privileged under Michigan's statutory physician-patient privilege, the patient holds the privilege, not the physician. Mich. Comp. Laws § 600.2157. Thus, a patient can voluntarily and intentionally waive the patient's physician-patient privilege. *Kelly v. Allegan Circuit Judge,* 382 Mich. 425 (1969). A patient's physician is a "custodian" of the patient's medical records. MCR 2.314(D)(1). Thus, the physician must "comply with a properly authorized request for the medical information within 28 days after the receipt of the request" for a patient's medical information. *Id.*

A physician may assert the physician-patient privilege to prevent discovery of the medical records of the physician's other (non-party) patients. The physician-patient privilege protects the names and records of nonparty patients. *Dorris v. Detroit Osteopathic Hosp.,* 460 Mich. 26 (1999).

(1)   Medical Malpractice Insurance Policy

A party may discover the terms and existence of a physician's medical malpractice insurance policy. MCR 2.302(B)(2). Although any reference to liability insurance during trial is precluded, the extent or amount of insurance coverage is a matter that affects the way a case is defended or prosecuted, and so is relevant to the case. Mich. Comp. Laws § 500.3030. Thus, a party may obtain discovery "of the existence and contents of an insurance agreement under which a person carrying on an insurance business may be liable to satisfy part or all of a judgment." MCR 2.302(B)(2).

(2)   Physician's Personal Finances

A physician's personal finances are not discoverable. A defendant physician's financial status, beyond insurance coverage, is irrelevant in a medical malpractice action. *Bauroth v. Hammoud,* 465 Mich. 375 (2001).

(3)   Other Medical Malpractice Lawsuits

The existence of other medical malpractice lawsuits against a physician is subject to discovery in a civil action against the physician. This information is relevant because it may prove that a physician has a habit of being negligent in certain relevant ways. For example, this could occur when the physician practices medicine without wearing glasses needed to see clearly. Moreover, the existence of other medical malpractice lawsuits is not subject to a privilege under Michigan law. Michigan's statutory physician-patient privilege only applies to "information that [a] person has acquired in attending a patient in a professional character." Mich. Comp. Laws § 600.2157. Therefore, Michigan's statutory physician-patient privilege does not pertain to the existence of other medical malpractice lawsuits.

G.   Miscellaneous Discovery Issues

1)   DISCOVERY BEFORE ACTION IS FILED

A petitioner may attempt under Federal Rule 27(a) and MCR 2.303(A)(1) to obtain discovery before an actual case is filed in the court. A person or entity seeking to obtain such discovery may file a verified petition in the federal district court or the Michigan circuit court in the county of the residence of any expected adverse party.

2)   USE OF DEPOSITIONS AT TRIAL

a)   FRCP

Federal Rule 32 provides that, so far as otherwise admissible under the Federal Rules of Evidence, any part or all of a deposition (if necessary to be fair), may be submitted at a trial:

- to impeach a deponent as a witness;
- for any purpose if the deponent was a corporate representative and the evidence is used against the corporation; or
- for any purpose if the deponent is dead or unavailable because the deponent is outside of a court's subpoena power.

b)   MCR

MCR 2.308(A) provides that, as far as otherwise admissible under the Michigan Rules of Evidence, any part or all of a deposition may be submitted at a trial, an interlocutory proceeding, or in a hearing on a motion.

3)   EXPERT TESTIMONY

When knowledge of a technical subject matter might be helpful to a trier of fact, a person having special training or experience in that technical field, one who is called an expert witness, is permitted to state the person's opinion concerning those technical matters even though the person was not present at an event that relates to a disputed issue. For example, an arson expert could testify about the probable cause of a suspicious fire. The information that an expert relies on to testify, or to prepare a report that the expert relies upon when testifying, is discoverable.

4)   PROTECTIVE ORDER

A party or person from whom discovery is being sought may file a motion for a protective order under Federal Rule 26(c) or MCR 2.302(C) upon a showing of good cause. The order may serve to limit the scope and nature of discovery methods or to preclude the discovery of certain information. The court may make any order that justice requires in order to protect a party or person from annoyance, embarrassment, oppression, undue burden, or expense. A protective order may cut off or limit the scope, manner, and time of discovery, as well as the persons who may be present then. A protective order may serve to seal depositions from public access. A protective order may require that certain discoverable materials be submitted to discovery under seal to the court in order to protect confidential information such as trade secrets.

★   ### 5)   SANCTIONS

a)   General Considerations

A trial court plays an integral role as the supervisor of discovery. Under Federal Rule 37 and MCR 2.313(B), that court may sanction parties or attorneys for unreasonable, groundless, abusive, or obstructionist conduct during the discovery process. Also, the court may require the parties to meet for discovery conferences to expedite the discovery process.

b)   When Appropriate

Pursuant to MCR 2.313(B)(2), sanctions are appropriate only if a party "fails to obey an order to provide or permit discovery, including an order entered . . . [under MCR 2.313(A)] or under MCR 2.311." Thus, sanctions can be imposed where there is a failure to comply with a court order compelling discovery entered pursuant to MCR 2.313(A) or MCR 2.311. MCR 2.313(B)(2). Note, however, that MCR 2.313 nowhere suggests that violations of informal discovery agreements are sanctionable.

c)   Order Taking Facts as Established

Under MCR 2.313(B)(2)(a), a court may order as a sanction for a failure to comply with an order to provide or permit discovery "that the matters regarding which the order was entered or other designated facts may be taken to be established for the purposes of the action in accordance with the claim of the party obtaining the order."

d)   Who is Subject to Order

MCR 2.313(B)(2) refers to "a party or an officer, director, or managing agent of a party, or a person designated under MCR 2.306(B)(5) or 2.307(A)(1) to testify on behalf of a party" that fails to obey an order to provide or permit discovery.

6)   DEFERENCE TO TRIAL COURT

A trial court is afforded significant discretion in making discovery decisions. Accordingly, an appellate court would only overturn a trial court decision regarding discovery if the court abused its discretion. Thus, such trial court's decisions are entitled to significant deference on appeal.

7)   MOTION TO COMPEL DISCOVERY

A motion to compel discovery under Federal Rule 37(a)(2) or MCR 2.313(A) is a motion requesting that a trial court require a person to make disclosures, to respond to a discovery request, or to make more detailed disclosures or responses to a discovery request. A party may also request that the court impose sanctions on a person that fails to comply with the court's order to compel discovery or otherwise obstructs discovery.

8)   DUTY TO SUPPLEMENT DISCOVERY

a)   Federal Rules

Under Federal Rule 26(e), a party is under a duty to supplement its discovery disclosures when the party learns of new information. A party is also under a duty to amend its answers to Interrogatories, Requests for Production, and Admissions if new information comes to light that impacts its previous disclosures that are contained in those types of discovery responses. However, this rule does not apply to depositions.

b)   Michigan Rules

Under MCR 2.302(E)(1), a party who has made a complete response to a discovery request generally is not obligated to supplement the response to include subsequently obtained information, except that:

(1)   Supplement Response

A party is obligated to seasonably supplement its response to a question directly addressed to:

- "the identity and location of persons having knowledge of discoverable matters; and
- the identity of each person expected to be called as an expert witness at trial, the subject matter on which the expert is expected to testify, and the substance of the expert's testimony."

MCR 2.302(E)(1)(a).

(2)   Amend Response

A party is obligated to amend a response if the party obtains information from which the party knows that:

- "the response was incorrect when made; or
- the response, though correct when made, is no longer true and the circumstances are such that a failure to amend the response is in substance a knowing concealment."

MCR 2.302(E)(1)(b).

(3)   Source of Duty

A duty to supplement responses can be imposed by a court order, the parties' agreement, or at any time prior to trial by requests for supplementation of prior responses. MCR 2.302(E)(1)(c).

X.   POST-JUDGMENT OR APPELLATE PROCEEDINGS

A.   Post-Trial Motions

A party has certain general motion options to obtain relief from an unfavorable judgment.

1)   <u>RENEWED MOTION FOR A JUDGMENT AS A MATTER OF LAW</u>

Under the Federal Rules, a party must move for a motion for judgment as a matter of law, formerly called a directed verdict, to preserve a Renewed Motion for Judgment as a Matter of Law, formerly called a JNOV motion. The standard is the same as for a motion for judgment as a matter of law, set forth earlier, except it is made after the judgment is entered. The purpose of requiring that a motion for judgment as a matter of law be made prior to the submission of the case to the jury "is to assure the responding party an opportunity to cure any deficiency in that party's proof that may have been overlooked until called to the party's attention by a late motion for judgment." The renewed motion must be made within 28 days of the judgment.

2)   <u>MOTION FOR JUDGMENT NOTWITHSTANDING THE VERDICT</u>

Within 21 days from entry of judgment, a party can make a motion to set aside the verdict and judgment and for entry of a judgment in favor of the moving party, pursuant to MCR 2.610(A)(1).

Under MCR 2.610(A)(2), if the jury does not return a verdict, a party can move for a judgment within 21 days from when the jury is discharged.

"A motion to set aside or otherwise nullify a verdict or a motion for a new trial is deemed to include a motion for judgment notwithstanding the verdict as an alternative." MCR 2.610(A)(3).

3)   <u>MOTION FOR A NEW TRIAL</u>

a)   When to Make

A motion for a new trial must be made within 28 days of the judgment under the FRCP or 21 days of the judgment under MCR 2.611(B). As a general matter, the party must move for a new trial to preserve appeal right. A motion for a new trial usually suspends the time for appeal.

b) Grounds for Motion

In order for a motion for a new trial to be granted, there must be a fundamental error affecting the trial outcome such as irregularity, misconduct, new evidence, inadmissible evidence, instruction error, etc. A court should grant a new trial motion if it is convinced that the jury has reached a seriously erroneous result or that the verdict is a miscarriage of justice.

c) Distinguished from FRCP Motion for Judgment as a Matter of Law

Unlike a motion for judgment as a matter of law, a motion for a new trial may be granted even if there is substantial evidence to support the jury's verdict. Also unlike a motion for judgment as a matter of law, a trial judge considering a motion for a new trial is free to weigh the evidence herself and need not view it in the light most favorable to the verdict winner.

4) MOTION FOR RELIEF FROM JUDGMENT

A party may make a motion pursuant to Federal Rule 60 and MCR 2.612 to obtain relief from a judgment. Relief will be available if the judgment is a result of a mistake or even excusable fault.

a) Clerical Mistakes

Clerical mistakes in judgments arising from oversight or omission may be corrected by the court at any time of its own initiative or on the motion of any party.

b) Other Grounds

On motion, the court may relieve a party from a final judgment pursuant to Rule 60 and MCR 2.612 for, among other things, the following reasons:

- mistake, inadvertence, surprise, or excusable neglect;
- newly discovered evidence which by due diligence could not have been discovered in time to move for a new trial;
- fraud, misrepresentation, or other misconduct of an adverse party; or
- any other reason justifying relief from the operation of the judgment.

c) Timing

Generally, a Rule 60 motion and a MCR 2.612 motion must be made within a reasonable time from judgment. Although no firm rule exists in federal court, four months has been considered a reasonable time. A motion regarding the first three of the four types of reasons described above must be made within one year from judgment pursuant to MCR 2.612(C)(2).

B.   Preservation of Error

1)   GENERAL

Generally, a party must object to a ruling of a court that the objecting party considers erroneous in order to preserve the matter for appeal. The objection must be made 1) contemporaneously to the ruling; and 2) with particularity regarding the grounds for the objection. If an objection to the admissibility of evidence is sustained, the non-objecting party is prevented from introducing that evidence at trial. Consequently, in order to challenge the ruling on appeal, the non-objecting party must make an offer of proof that demonstrates what the purported evidence was intended to prove. That party may present appellate arguments in support of the admissibility of the purported evidence.

a)   Plain Error Exception – Contemporaneous Objection not Required

Plain error is a flaw in the trial process that is so obvious that a failure of the parties or the court to notice and rectify it would seriously affect the fairness or integrity of the judicial proceedings. To rise to the level of plain error, an asserted error must not only seriously affect a party's substantial rights, but it must also have an unfair prejudicial impact on the jury's deliberations. The plain error exception to the contemporaneous objection rule is to be used sparingly, in only those circumstances in which a miscarriage of justice would otherwise result.

b)   Harmless Error Rule

The harmless error rule provides that any error that does not affect the substantive rights of the parties cannot be the grounds for an appeal. Generally, the standard in a civil case is whether an erroneous charge of the jury or ruling of the court would likely have affected a trial's result.

XI.   RES JUDICATA

Res Judicata is a general term that refers to all of the different ways in which a prior judgment or determination could have a binding effect on subsequent litigants. It includes both the concepts of claim preclusion and issue preclusion. Claim preclusion prevents a party from litigating an entire claim or any issue which could have been litigated in the prior adjudication of any claim. In contrast, issue preclusion only precludes the re-litigation of a single issue that was actually litigated and determined.

★   A.   Claim Preclusion

The doctrine of claim preclusion forbids re-litigating entire claims, which were, or could have been, litigated in prior actions. The modern view regarding the scope of a "claim" is that it includes all of the party's rights to remedies against the other party with respect to the same transaction from which the action arose.

For claim preclusion to apply, the following requirements must be met:

- Identical parties must exist in both lawsuits;

- • The prior judgment must have been rendered by a court of competent jurisdiction;

- • A final judgment on the merits must exist; and

- • The same cause of action must be involved in both cases.

The most easily tested prong of the claim preclusion test is the fourth one. In order to determine whether the same cause of action is involved in both lawsuits, courts generally use the same transaction test. The test provides that if a claim arose from the same transaction, it is deemed a part of the same cause of action. Michigan law generally follows this approach.

Specifically, in order for *res judicata* to apply to a plaintiff's second action, (1) the first action must have been decided on the merits, (2) the matter contested in the second action must have been (or could have been) resolved in the first action, and (3) both actions involve the same parties or their privies. *Sewell v. Clean Cut Management,* 463 Mich. 569, 575 (2001). Michigan courts apply *res judicata* broadly to bar not only claims already litigated, but also every claim arising from the same transaction that the parties, exercising reasonable diligence, could have raised but did not. *Id.*

B.   Issue Preclusion (Collateral Estoppel)

The doctrine of collateral estoppel, or issue preclusion, generally prevents a party from re-litigating issues (as opposed to entire claims), that have been previously litigated and determined in a prior action.

1)   TRADITIONAL APPROACH

The traditional requirements for asserting collateral estoppel were:

- • A valid and final judgment was rendered in a prior action;
- • An issue of fact was actually litigated, determined, and essential to the judgment in the prior action;
- • The same issue arises in a subsequent action; and
- • The same parties are litigants in both actions.

2)   MODERN APPROACH -- MICHIGAN

The modern approach to issue preclusion eliminated the fourth element that the same parties are litigants in both actions. Pursuant to the modern approach, a party who is precluded from re-litigating an issue with an opposing party, is also precluded from doing so with another person unless he lacked a full and fair opportunity to litigate the issue in the first action, or other circumstances justify affording him on opportunity to re-litigate the issue. Accordingly, when the modern approach is followed, there is a new fourth element in place of the "same parties" requirement that is set forth above. The new fourth element is that the party to be precluded had a full and fair opportunity to litigate the same issue in the prior action.

Michigan's version of the modern approach to collateral estoppel provides that:

"(1)   '[A] question of fact essential to the judgment must have been actually
        litigated and determined by a valid and final judgment';
(2)   '[T]he same parties must have had a full [and fair] opportunity to litigate
        the issue'; and
(3)   '[T]here must be mutuality of estoppel.'"

Monat v. State Farm Ins. Co., 469 Mich. 679, 683-684; (2004), quoting *Storey v. Meijer, Inc.*, 431 Mich. 368, 373 n 3; (1988).

XII.   EQUITABLE REMEDIES

Both this outline and the Equity outline discuss the equitable remedies of injunctions, restraining orders, and declaratory judgments because those topics are testable in either an Equity question or a Civil Procedure question. As a general rule, a prerequisite for a party to obtain equitable remedies such as injunctions is that the party lacks an adequate remedy at law. *E.g., O'Melia v. Berghoff Brewing Corp.*, 304 Mich. 471 (1943). A court exercises it discretion regarding whether to grant injunctive relief.

A.   Injunctions

Courts use injunctions to order litigants to engage in, or refrain from engaging in, an act. Sometimes injunctions are classified as being either mandatory or prohibitory: an injunction, which compels an act, is referred to as mandatory, while one, which forbids an act, is a prohibitory injunction.

1)   PERMANENT INJUNCTION

A party may seek a permanent injunction as the ultimate relief in a case. In other words, a party may make a prayer for relief requesting a permanent injunction. For example, if a plaintiff alleges that the defendant is violating a non-competition agreement, the plaintiff may seek an injunction prohibiting the defendant's wrongful actions. The entry of the permanent junction, as opposed to temporary injunctions, would only be permissible after a full trial. By contrast, temporary injunctions may be ordered after only a hearing.

In order to obtain a permanent injunction, the plaintiff must establish that (1) he will suffer irreparable injury unless an injunction is issued, (2) his threatened injury outweighs any harm the proposed injunction may cause to the opposing party, and (3) an injunction would not be adverse to the public interest.

2)   TYPES OF NON-PERMANENT INJUNCTIONS

Usually, a party cannot wait until a final determination for entry of a permanent injunction. Such a process may take months or even years. Therefore, a litigant may seek a temporary injunction for the time up until the final determination. There are two types of non-permanent injunctions –

temporary restraining orders (TROs) and preliminary injunctions. Practically speaking, the difference between the two is timing. A TRO is sought in emergency situations when notice to the other party is unfeasible. A preliminary injunction is often sought after a TRO is set to expire.

a)   Temporary Restraining Order

Pursuant to Federal Rule 65(b) and MCR 3.310(B), a court may issue a temporary restraining order on an *ex-parte* basis (without the other party present) when that is necessary to prevent irreparable injury. Because notice to the other party may not be required, a TRO is an extraordinary remedy.

To obtain an *ex-parte* temporary restraining order, the moving party must meet three conditions:

(1)   Irreparable Injury

The moving party must set out "specific facts" in the verified complaint or by affidavit that show that immediate and irreparable injury will result to the applicant before the adverse party can be heard in opposition; and

(2)   Efforts Made

The moving party's attorney must certify to the court in writing the efforts, if any, which have been made to give the notice and the reasons supporting the claim that notice should not be required; and

(3)   Security (FRCP) or Record (MCR)

(a)   Security (FRCP)

The moving party must provide a bond to the court in such a sum as the court deems proper to compensate the defendant in the event that the TRO is wrongfully entered.

The Federal Rules limit temporary restraining orders to 14 days absent good cause.

(b)   Record (MCR)

MCR 3.310(B)(1)(c) requires that permanent record be made of any non-written argument, evidence, or other representations made in support of the application for a TRO.

MCR 3.310(B)(3) limits TROs to 14 days absent good cause, except in domestic relations cases.

Remember, the key characteristic of a TRO is that notice to the other party may not be required.

★   b)   Preliminary Injunction

The only practical difference between a TRO and a preliminary injunction under Rule 65(a) and MCR 3.310(A) is that a preliminary injunction is issued: 1) after a moving party provides notice to a non-moving party; and 2) after the non-moving party has an opportunity to be heard. The purpose of a preliminary injunction is to maintain the *status quo* until the parties' claims can be investigated and adjudicated.

(1)   Notice

Unlike for TROs, reasonable notice is required for preliminary injunctions.

(2)   Factors Courts Generally Examine

(a)   Likelihood of Success on Merits

Has the petitioner made a strong showing that it is likely to prevail on the merits?

(b)   Irreparable Injury

Has the petitioner shown that without such relief it will suffer irreparable injury?

(c)   Harm to Others

Would the issuance of the injunction substantially harm other interested parties?

(d)   Public Interest

The court must conduct an examination of the public interest under the circumstances.

(3)   Trial on the Merits

Unless the parties stipulate otherwise or good cause is shown, after a Michigan trial court grants a preliminary injunction, a trial of the matter on the merits must occur within six months from when the court granted the injunction. MCR 3.310(A)(5).

B.   Declaratory Judgments

An action seeking a declaratory judgment may be instituted to seek the court's opinion regarding the parties' rights under the law or an instrument such as a contract. Essentially, the parties ask the court whether a certain action is prohibited before a contract is breached or a law is violated.

1)   SCOPE OF DECLARATORY JUDGMENTS

Any person interested under a deed, contract or other writings or whose rights are affected by a law may have the court determine any question of construction or validity arising under the instrument or law and obtain a declaration of rights thereunder. The declaration may be either affirmative or negative in form and effect, and such declarations will have the force and effect of a final judgment.

XIII. ACCOUNTABILITY OF COUNSEL

A.   FRCP 11 and MCR 2.114

Although the following discussion regarding accountability of counsel mainly describes the provisions of Federal Rule 11, they are similar to some comparable provisions of MCR 2.114.

1)   SIGNATURE REQUIREMENT

Every pleading, motion, or other paper of a party represented by an attorney must be signed by at least one attorney of record. For a willful violation of Rule 11, an attorney may be subjected to disciplinary action. Similar action may be taken if scandalous or indecent matter is inserted.

2)   REPRESENTATIONS

By presenting the filing to the court, the party or attorney represents the following:

a)   No Improper Purpose

The attorney or party represents that the claim, defense, request, demand, objection, contention, or argument is not presented or maintained for any improper purpose, such as to harass or to cause unnecessary delay or needless increase in the cost of litigation.

b)   Legal Grounding

The attorney or party represents that the claims, defenses, and other legal contentions therein are warranted by existing law or by a non-frivolous argument for the extension, modification, or reversal of existing law or the establishment of new law.

c)   Evidentiary Support

The attorney or party represents that the allegations and other factual contentions have evidentiary support or, if specifically so identified, are likely to have evidentiary support after a reasonable opportunity for further investigation or discovery.

d)   Denials

The attorney or party represents that the denials of factual contentions are warranted on the evidence or, if specifically so identified, are reasonably based on a lack of information or belief.

3)   PROCESS FOR SANCTIONS

If after notice and a reasonable opportunity to respond, the court finds that the rules have been violated, the court may impose an appropriate sanction upon the lawyers, law firms, or parties that have committed or are responsible for the violation.

Sanctions may be imposed either by motion or on the court's own initiative under the following circumstances.

a) By Motion

A motion for sanctions must describe the specific conduct alleged to violate Rule 11. The motion should not be filed with or presented to the court unless within 21 days after service of the motion the challenged claim, defense, request, demand, objection, contention, or argument is not withdrawn or appropriately corrected. If warranted, the court may award to the party prevailing on the motion the reasonable expenses and attorney's fees incurred in presenting or opposing the motion.

b) On Court's Initiative

On its own initiative, the court may enter an order describing the specific conduct that appears to violate the Rule and directing a lawyer, law firm or party to withdraw or correct the questioned claim, defense, request, demand, objection, contention or argument or to show cause why it has not violated the rule with respect thereto.

4) NATURE OF SANCTIONS

A sanction imposed for violation of the rule is limited to that which is sufficient to deter repetition of the conduct or comparable conduct by others similarly situated. The sanction may consist of or include directives of a nonmonetary nature, an order to pay a penalty into court, or, if imposed on motion and warranted for effective deterrence, an order directing payment to the movant of some or all of the reasonable attorney's fees and other expenses incurred as a direct result of the violation.

XIV. LIMITATIONS PERIODS

★ **A. Statute of Limitations**

The time period in which a party can prosecute a civil cause of action against another party may be restricted by a statute of limitations. In Michigan, the Revised Judicature Act of 1961 contains these types of time limits upon certain causes of action. *Generally*, Mich. Comp. Laws §§ 600.5801-600.5869. Usually, absent an applicable exception, a party cannot seek a legal remedy from the other party after the statutory time limit expires.

1) TYPES OF ACTIONS

a) Breach of Contract

There is a six-year statute of limitations for breach of contract actions in Michigan. Mich. Comp. Laws § 600.5807(8).

        b)   Fraud

The statute of limitations for fraud actions in Michigan is six years. Mich. Comp. Laws § 600.5813.

        c)   Defamation (Slander or Libel)

A one-year statute of limitations applies to defamation actions for slander or libel. Mich. Comp. Laws § 600.5805(9).

        d)   Certain Intentional Torts

A two-year statute of limitations applies to the intentional torts of battery, assault, malicious prosecution, or false imprisonment. Mich. Comp. Laws § 600.5805(2), (5).

        e)   Personal Injury or Death from Negligence

A three-year statute of limitation generally applies to negligence torts resulting in personal injury or death. Mich. Comp. Laws § 600.5805(10).

        f)   Personal Injury by Professional Malpractice

A medical malpractice action must be brought either within the later of two years of its occurrence or within six months from the discovery of its occurrence, to at most six years from the occurrence of the omission or act giving rise to the personal injury. Mich. Comp. Laws §§ 600.5805(6), 600.5838(2), 600.5838a(2).

        g)   Product Liability

A three-year statute of limitation usually applies to product liability actions. Mich. Comp. Laws § 600.5805(13).

        h)   Harm to Personal Property

A three-year statute of limitation applies to torts resulting injury to personal property. Mich. Comp. Laws § 600.5805(10).

        2)   RELATION TO MOTION FOR SUMMARY DISPOSITION

When a lawsuit is time barred under the applicable statute of limitations period, a defendant should file a motion for summary disposition under MCR 2.116(C)(7). Unlike a MCR 2.116(C)(4) motion for summary disposition alleging a lack of subject matter jurisdiction, which may be made at any time during the proceedings, a MCR 2.116(C)(7) motion for summary disposition -- alleging that a claim is barred due to certain reasons such as a statute of limitation -- "must be raised in a party's responsive pleading." MCR 2.116(D)(2). If a defendant fails to file a MCR 2.116(C)(7) motion for summary disposition in its responsive pleading, the defendant's MCR 2.116(C)(7) defense will be deemed waived. *Huntington Woods v. Ajax Paving Indus., Inc.,* 179 Mich. App. 600 (1989).

★ **B.   Corporate Survival Statute**

Michigan's Business Corporation Act provides that a dissolved corporation may publish notice of its dissolution (after the date its dissolution becomes effective) requesting that claims be made against the corporation pursuant to the notice. Mich. Comp. Laws § 450.1842a(1). This Act includes a corporate survival statute that provides a time period after a corporation's dissolution for a claimant to file a claim and this time period can be extended for good cause. All claims against a dissolved corporation are barred unless the claimant commences a proceeding to enforce the claim against the dissolved corporation within one year after the publication date. Mich. Comp. Laws § 450.1842a(3). The courts have determined that this is not a statute of limitation, but a "corporate survival statute." This one-year time period may be extended by the courts upon a showing of good cause and as long as the corporation has not made a complete distribution of its assets.

The purpose of the "survival statute" is to allow claims under certain conditions to be filed after the effective date of dissolution. The Michigan Legislature created a process whereby a dissolved corporation can bar future claims, thus cutting off the possibility that the corporation's potential liability could never be completely resolved. The issue of the discovery of the claim does not affect this time period. The claim has to be presented within this time period or it is barred. If the claim is barred, there is no liability for either the dissolved corporation or its insurance carrier. *Gilliam v. Hi-Temp Prods., Inc.,* 260 Mich. App. 98 (2003).

★ **XV.   CASE EVALUATIONS**

MCR 2.403 sets forth the rules governing case evaluation. In general, case evaluation is intended to force parties to make a serious evaluation of the merits of their respective cases and parties are aided in this assessment by a panel of independent lawyer/evaluators selected pursuant to MCR 2.404. The case evaluation rule imposes substantial sanctions for a party's improvident rejection of a case evaluation award.

★ **A.   Both Parties Accept the Case Evaluation**

A party may accept a case evaluation award. If the other party also accepts the case evaluation award, then a judgment will enter in accordance with the evaluation and the judgment will be deemed to dispose of all claims in the action. MCR 2.403(M)(1); *CAM Constr. v. Lake Edgewood Condo. Ass'n,* 465 Mich. 549, 555 (2002).

★ **B.   One Party Accepts and the Other Party Rejects the Case Evaluation**

On the other hand, if one party rejects a case evaluation award and the opposing party accepts the award, the rejecting party may be required to pay the opposing party's "actual costs." Actual costs are (1) costs taxable in any civil action, and (2) a reasonable attorney fee based on reasonable hourly or daily rate as determined by the trial judge for services necessitated by the rejection of the case evaluation. MCR 2.403(0)(6).

If one party has rejected the case evaluation award, and the action proceeds to a verdict, that party must pay the opposing party's actual costs "unless the verdict is more favorable to the rejecting party than the case evaluation." MCR 2.403(0)(1). The "verdict" is the jury verdict, the judgment of the court after a nonjury trial, or a judgment entered as a result of ruling on a motion after rejection of the case evaluation. MCR 2.403(0)(2). The verdict must be adjusted by adding assessable costs and interest on the amount of the verdict from the filing of the complaint to the date of the case evaluation, and, if applicable, by making an adjustment for future damages. MCR 2.403(0)(3).

Whether a verdict after adjustment is favorable is determined by comparing the verdict to the case evaluation award. A verdict is more favorable to the defendant if it is more than 10 percent below the evaluation, and it is more favorable to the plaintiff if it is more than 10 percent above the evaluation. *Id.* If the evaluation was zero, a verdict finding that a defendant is not liable to the plaintiff is deemed more favorable to the defendant. *Id.*

If only one party rejects the case evaluation award, this party is entitled to costs only if the verdict is more favorable to that party than the case evaluation award. MCR 2.403(0)(1). The same definition of "verdict" and the same determination of favorability apply where both parties reject the case evaluation. If both parties reject the case evaluation award, the verdict must be more favorable to either rejecting party for that party to be entitled to actual costs.

Note that an attorney is obligated to advise a client of the pitfalls of accepting and rejecting a case evaluation award. MRPC 1.2(a), 1.4(a)-(b). Certain Michigan Rules of Professional Conduct are also discussed in the Ethics Outline.

MICHIGAN

AMERIBAR BAR REVIEW

Michigan Bar Review

CONFLICT OF LAWS

TABLE OF CONTENTS

CONFLICT OF LAWS

The Michigan Board of Law Examiners indicated that Conflict of Laws may be one of the subjects of the 15 essay questions on the essay portion of the Michigan Bar Exam. If tested, Conflict of Laws will probably make up the main issue of this essay question. Although Michigan case law provided the basis for a past question and its sample answer, a question could be answered using controlling general legal principles detailed in this outline.

I.   CHOICE OF LAW

A.   Basic Concepts

1)   LEGAL CHARACTERIZATION

The problem of legal characterization was a by-product of the *First Restatement*'s approach to conflicts issues. Under that framework, the choice-of-law rule that applied was wholly dependent upon what type of case the action was characterized as. For example, contract cases possessed different choice-of-law approaches than did workers' compensation or property cases. Under the old rules, courts could and often did, manipulate the characterization of cases to reach favored results. Under the modern framework, because the same general approaches exist regardless of the characterization of the claim, such problems have largely disappeared.

2)   RENVOI

Usually, a state applies its own choice of law rules. Through a choice-of-law analysis, the court may conclude, however, to use the substantive law of another jurisdiction. On some occasions, however, a court may apply the choice-of-law rules of the other jurisdiction. Specifically, if the other jurisdiction would not have used its own substantive law had the case been filed in the other jurisdiction, the local court may use the substantive law that the other forum would have used. This is called "renvoi." A local court may "accept" or "reject" the "remission" from the foreign law.

Example: P sues D in State A, on a mortgage guarantee for property that is located in State B. The contract was negotiated in State A. State A law would apply the law of the state of the situs of the property under such circumstances. Assume, however, that State B itself would have used the law of the state in which the contract was negotiated (State A). Under these circumstances, because State B would not have applied its own law, State A would not apply State B's law either.

3)   DEPEÇAGE

Depeçage refers to the situation when a court will treat individual issues in a case differently under choice-of-law analysis. For example, a court may use the law of the place the contract was executed to determine formation issues. On the other hand, it may apply the law of the state in which performance is due to decide issues concerning performance.

The modern trend favors depeçage because it takes into account the multi-jurisdictional nature of today's business world.

4)   PROOF OF FOREIGN LAW

The proof of foreign law method is the procedure that the local forum will employ to determine the substantive law of the foreign jurisdiction.

a)   Judicial Notice

A court may take judicial notice of foreign law. Counsel generally presents the position to the court in a motion for judicial notice.

b)   Failure of Counsel to Prove Law

Sometimes, counsel will fail to prove the substantive law of the foreign jurisdiction. Courts take varied approaches under these circumstances. Some courts will dismiss the case altogether. Other courts will apply the law of the forum state on fundamental legal principles. Still other courts may make a *sua sponte* inquiry into the law.

c)   Certification

Many states have adopted the Uniform Certification of Questions of Law Act (the "Act"). Under the Act, a federal court or state appellate court may certify a 1) question of unsettled state law that is 2) determinative of a case to the highest court in another state.

B.   Choice of Law Theories

1)   TRADITIONAL "VESTED RIGHTS" APPROACH

The traditional vested rights approach to choice of law was prevalent in the first half of the twentieth century. The rule was set forth in commentary as follows: "A right having been created by the appropriate law, the recognition of its existence should follow everywhere. Thus an act valid where done cannot be called into question anywhere." J. Beale, *3 Cases on the Conflict of Laws* 517 (1901). The rule was set forth in the *First Restatement of Conflict of Laws*. As a practical matter, it generally provides that 1) if an action is a tort at the place of the wrong, it can be enforced in any other state, and 2) if an action is not a tort at the place of the wrong, it can be enforced in no other state. Accordingly, the primary consideration in the vested rights analysis is, in which jurisdiction did the injury occur? If such a jurisdiction exists, its law will be enforced.

2)   CONTEMPORARY POLICY APPROACHES

a)   Governmental Interest Test

Governmental interest analysis requires a step-by-step consideration. In these jurisdictions, the governmental interest analysis would even be used to determine which jurisdiction's statute of limitations should apply. Although many states have adopted variations of this approach, the basic scheme is as follows:

When a court addresses whether to apply another state's law, it should inquire into the policies expressed in the respective laws (the forum state's and the other state's). Moreover, it should also examine whether it is reasonable for the respective states to assert an interest in the application of those policies under the circumstances.

Three results may follow:

1.   If the court finds that one state has an interest in the application of its policy in the circumstances of the case and the other has none, it should apply the law of the only interested state.

2.   If the court finds an apparent conflict between the interests of the two states, it should reconsider. A more moderate and restrained interpretation of the policy or interest of one state or the other may avoid conflict.

3.   If, upon reconsideration, the court finds that a conflict between the legitimate interests of the two states is unavoidable, it should apply the law of the forum.

b)   Most Significant Relationship Test (*Second Restatement*)

The rigid rules of the traditional choice-of-law approaches slowly gave way to the flexible approach adopted in the *Second Restatement*. The *Second Restatement* possesses a two-step approach to choice-of-law issues. First, the court must inquire whether the forum jurisdiction has adopted a choice-of-law statute governing disposition of the choice-of-law issue. If it has, then the court must implement the provisions of the statute. If the jurisdiction does not have such a statute, the court must examine a number of enumerated considerations in order to determine which jurisdiction has the most significant relationship to the problem at issue.

The considerations set forth in the *Restatement* include:

- needs of interstate and international system
- relevant policies of the forum
- relevant policies of any other states and their interests in resolution of instant issue
- protection of justified expectations
- policies underlying field of law
- uniformity of result
- ease in application of law to be utilized

The court is afforded great discretion in how much weight to give each consideration. Critics of this approach believe that its widespread judicial acceptance stemmed from the fact that jurists could justify almost any conclusion by weighing factors to their liking for each particular case.

C.   **Application in Specific Areas**

1)   <u>TORTS</u>

Choice-of–law issues arising in the tort context are the most unsettled of all subject areas. There is a true split in jurisdictions among several different approaches.

★★   a)   Vested Rights Approach

Some states (over a dozen), still utilize the vested rights approach set forth in the First *Restatement*. As set forth above, it generally provides that 1) if an action is a tort at the place of the wrong, it can be enforced in any other state, and 2) if an action is not a tort at the place of the wrong, it can be enforced in no other state. Under this principle, a court will determine the substantive rights of an injured party according to the law of the state where the injury occurred.

★★   b)   Government Interest Analysis

Other jurisdictions have rejected the vested rights approach and adopted the government interests analysis. Under this approach, set forth above, the court will conduct a step-by-step approach to determine which state has a true interest in enforcing its laws under the particular circumstances of the case.

★★   c)   Significant Relationship Test

Other courts will examine the factors set forth in the *Second Restatement* (most significant relationship test) to determine which law to apply under the circumstances. In addition to the factors set forth above in Section III(B)(2)(b), courts will examine:

- the place of the injury;
- the place where conduct causing injury occurred;
- the connection of the parties to the relevant fora; and
- the place where the relationship between the parties (if any exists) is centered.

The parties' connection to the relevant fora involves contacts such as their residence, domicile, nationality, place of business, and place of incorporation.

Although choice-of-law in the tort context is in a relative state of disarray, the underlying theme apparent in analyzing recent cases is that courts tend to enforce the rights of forum resident plaintiffs. As such, results tend to generally disfavor the forum-shopping plaintiffs.

★★   d)   Michigan Law

"In tort cases, Michigan courts use a choice of law analysis called "interest analysis" to determine which state's law governs a suit where more than one state's law may be implicated." *Hall v. Gen. Motors Corp.*, 229 Mich. App. 580, 582 N.W.2d 866 (1998). "Although this balancing approach most frequently favors using the forum's (Michigan's) law, Michigan courts nonetheless use another state's law where the other state has a significant interest and Michigan has only a minimal interest in the matter." *Id.*

(1)   Presumption

A presumption exists that Michigan law will be applied by Michigan courts in tort cases. *Sutherland v. Kennington Truck Svc., Ltd.,* 562 N.W.2d 466, 454 Mich. 274 (1997). These courts:

> will apply Michigan law unless a "rational reason" to do otherwise exists. In determining whether a rational reason to displace Michigan law exists, we undertake a two-step analysis. First, we must determine if any foreign state has an interest in having its law applied. If no state has such an interest, the presumption that Michigan law will apply cannot be overcome. If a foreign state does have an interest in having its law applied, we must then determine if Michigan's interests mandate that Michigan law be applied, despite the foreign interests. *Id.*

(2)   Residency of a Plaintiff

Under a "Michigan choice-of-law analysis, a plaintiff's residency is determined as of the date of the injury." *Hall v. Gen. Motors Corp.*, 229 Mich. App. 580 (1998). However, "plaintiff's residence, with nothing more, is insufficient to support the choice of a state's law." *Home Ins. Co. v. Dick*, 281 U.S. 397, 408; 50 S.Ct. 338, 74 L. Ed. 926 (1930).

(a)   Example

Suppose, for example, that a plaintiff who resides in Indiana sues a defendant who resides in Michigan in a Michigan state trial court for an alleged tort by the defendant against the plaintiff that occurred in Ohio. Although Ohio, the state where the injury occurred, has an interest in conduct within its borders, the interest in the litigation is minimal when none of the parties to litigation is an Ohio resident. *Olmstead v. Anderson*, 428 Mich. 1, 28 (1987). "This rationale holds true whether the parties are from the same state . . . or, as here, from different states. The operative fact is that neither party is a citizen of the state in which the wrong occurred." *Id.* Moreover, although "[t]he injury state always has an interest in conduct within its borders, whether or not its citizens are involved . . . the issue in this case does not involve conduct, but, instead, damages or limitation thereof." *Id.*

2)   CONTRACTS

a)   General Approaches Absent Clause Governing Choice-of-Law

If a contract does not possess a valid choice-of-law provision, courts will employ one of several tests to determine which forum's law to apply

(1)   *First Restatement* (Place of Making Rule)

Under the *First Restatement*, a court will employ the law of the place where the contract was "made." Accordingly, a court would examine where the contract was entered into (not necessarily negotiated), and enforce the law of that state with regard to most contract issues. Consequently, contracts made at a business meeting in a distant location with no connection to the parties were governed by the laws of the distant location.

(a)   Exception - Performance Issues

When examining issues of performance of the contract, the court will examine the law of the jurisdiction in which performance was due.

★★   (2)   *Second Restatement*

The *Second Restatement* rejected the "place of making" approach of the *First Restatement*. Under the *Second Restatement*, a court must determine which court possesses the most significant relationship with the contract under the circumstances. Courts will examine the general considerations set forth above. Additionally courts will examine the following factors:

- the place where the contract was made;
- the place where the contract was negotiated;
- the place of performance;
- location of the subject of contract (if applicable); and
- the connection of the parties to the forums.

This last factor can include consideration of the domicile, residence, nationality, place of incorporation and the place of business of the parties.

(a)   Michigan Law

Michigan no longer follows the *First Restatement* rule that a contract dispute is to be resolved by the law of the state in which the contract was entered into. Michigan now favors a more "policy" center approach of the *Second Restatement* rule, "where the rights and duties of the parties with respect to an issue in contract are determined by the local law of the state, which, with respect to that issue, has the most significant relationship to the transaction and to the parties." This approach involves a consideration of the foregoing five factors with respect to a contract dispute. *Chrysler Corp. v. Skyline Indus. Services, Inc.*, 448 Mich. 113, 223 (1995).

(i)   Contract Law Objectives

The "[p]rime objectives of contract law are to protect the justified expectations of the parties and to make it possible for them to foretell with accuracy what will be their rights and liabilities under the contract." *Chrysler*, *supra* at 126 citing comments to § 187 of the *Restatement (Second) Conflicts of Law*. However, "[f]ulfillment of the parties' expectations is not the only value in contract law; regard must also be had for state interests and for state regulation." *Id.*

(ii)   Public Policy

There is no public policy argument that would require Michigan courts to enforce Michigan law in interpreting a contract between Ohio corporations involving an Ohio resident. *Mitchell v. Travelers* (unpublished Court of Appeals #234941) decided 12/13/02. For example, a question could test which of two states' similar and opposite legal provisions apply to a contract dispute involving an insurance policy.

b)   Party Autonomy (Contractual Choice-of-Law Clauses)

Courts generally favor contracting parties' right to dictate which law will govern the interpretation of contracts. Therefore, as a general rule, choice-of-law clauses in a contract will be enforced. However, if a party overreaches or enforcing the choice-of-law provision would offend public policy, it will not be enforced.

(1)   Overreaching – "Substantial Relationship" Requirement

Courts will examine whether the jurisdiction selected to govern contract interpretation possesses a substantial relationship with the parties and the subject-matter of the contract. If no apparent connection exists, or the jurisdiction was selected for some arbitrary reason, the provision may not be enforced.

(2)   Public Policy

Any provision that would be contrary to public policy of the forum may not be enforced. For example, a non-compete provision prohibited by the forum state, but permitted by the state selected in the contractual choice-of-law provision, may not be enforceable.

3)   <u>PROPERTY</u>

a)   Traditional Approach – Law of Situs of Land

The traditional choice of law rule is that all issues affecting title to land are determined by the law of the situs of the land. Occasionally, however, a court will characterize a case involving property as a contract case and apply the law of the place where the contract was made. However, generally, situs law governs the validity of contracts to convey land. *Restatement 2nd Conflict of Laws* § 189.

b)   Modern Approach – More Significant Relationship

Modern approaches to choice of law, however, would permit departure from this traditional rule if a state other than the situs state had a "more significant relationship" to the facts of the case or a greater interest in the outcome." Courts may examine factors such as: where the contract at issue was negotiated; where the parties entered the contract; and where the parties to the contract are domiciled. Courts will also examine any state policy of protecting the expectations of land purchasers or a general interest in securing the integrity of transactions that occur within a state borders.

Although attractive, the modern approach is not likely to be adopted by most courts. It is likely that most courts would adhere to the traditional rule that the situs state's law determines the validity of contracts to convey land in the state. The simple explanation for this is that the situs state always has a strong, perhaps dominant, interest in any action that will affect title to its land. The situs state is the only state that can, in the end, award title to anyone.

4)   CORPORATIONS

Choice-of-law issues concerning corporations involve two variations.

a)   Internal Affairs

A corporation's internal affairs (such as director duties, shareholder power, etc.), are governed by the law of the state of incorporation.

b)   External Relations

Any issue involving the law to be applied when a corporation is involved in a dispute with another person or entity, the other subject areas choice-of-law rules will apply. For example, in a contract dispute, the court may apply the most significant relationship test to decide which law will apply.

5)   WORKER'S COMPENSATION

a)   Introduction

Workers' compensation issues focus on the Full Faith and Credit Clause of the United States Constitution. In one case, an employer in Massachusetts sent an employee to a branch office in California for an assignment. While in California, the employee was injured. He applied for, and was awarded, workers' compensation benefits in California. The employer alleged that Massachusetts law, however, applied, because the company and, originally the employee, were located there. If Massachusetts law applied, the award would not have been made because the employee did not send notice as required under Massachusetts law. The Supreme Court inquired as to whether California possessed a significant interest in the dispute. It concluded that it did. Consequently, the Court held that Massachusetts could not enforce its laws to prevent a right bestowed by another state (the state in which such injury occurred). *Pacific Employers Ins. Co. v. Indus. Accident Comm'n*, 306 U.S. 493 (1939).

b)   Traditional Rule (Minority)

The general rule in a minority of jurisdictions follows the approach in tort cases. The law of the place of the injury generally applies.

      c)   Significant Interest Test

In other states, if a state concludes that it possesses a significant interest in the dispute, it may apply its own workers' compensation law.

      6)   FAMILY LAW

      a)   Marriage

The law of the place where the marriage was entered into governs formation of marriage. This rule is called *lex celebrationis.* The rule is applied almost uniformly. For example, even where the parties leave their home jurisdiction to get married because their jurisdiction would not permit them to be married, their home jurisdiction will recognize their marriage as legally entered into. The two exceptions to this rule are as follows: 1) When the state clearly states, through legislation, that the general rule must not be followed; or 2) The marriage offends public policy (bigamy, polygamy, etc.).

      b)   Divorce

So long as the court possesses jurisdiction (see Domestic Relations Outline), as a general rule, it will apply its own law regarding divorce. Courts justify this result because jurisdiction requires that at least one of the parties be domiciled in the state. If one party is domiciled in the state, then the marriage is deemed "located" within the state.

      7)   SUBSTANCE VS. PROCEDURE

As a general rule, courts use their own laws for procedural issues and the law of another jurisdiction (if applicable) to substantive matters. Therefore, classification of an issue as procedural or substantive is critical.

In diversity actions, federal courts use state law to determine the limitation period applicable to state causes of action. In determining which state's limitation period to use, federal courts must look to the choice of law rules of the state in which they sit. *Klaxon Co. v. Stentor Elec. Mfg. Co.,* 313 U.S. 487 (1941).

      a)   Statute of Limitations – Substantive Law or Procedure?

Most states treat statute of limitations as procedural for choice of law purposes. If a state treats statutes of limitations as procedural, it would ordinarily apply its own statute of limitations in the absence of a borrowing statute indicating that some other state's statute of limitations should be used.

      (1)   Exception - Right vs. Remedy Approach

Where a statute of limitations is specific to a particular kind of claim and was created by the law that created the cause of action to which it applies, courts will often characterize the statute of limitations as substantive. In such cases, a court may disregard its own statute of limitations and apply the foreign "substantive" statute of limitations, at least if the foreign law creating the cause of action will be used to determine other substantive rights in the case. This old doctrine (that statutes of limitations are substantive when they go to the right and not just the remedy) was preserved in the *Second Restatement of Conflict of Laws*. *Restatement (Second) Conflict of Laws*, § 143, and *Restatement (Second) Conflict of Laws*, § 142 (1988 revision). *Also* Uniform Conflict of Laws Limitations Act, 12 U.L.A. 61 (Supp 1992) (adopted in six states, this uniform act provides that the applicable limitations period should be that set by the state whose substantive law will be used to decide the case). However, this traditional rule may not lead to application of the other states statute of limitations unless it will apply to *bar* the action otherwise timely under forum law, not when the foreign statute *extends* the period for bringing the action.

D.   Defenses against Application of Foreign Law

1)   LOCAL PUBLIC POLICY

A court may refuse to enforce the laws of another jurisdiction if those laws offend the public policy of the local jurisdiction. For example, assume an action is filed attempting to validate a foreign contract dealing with indentured servants. If a party alleges that a foreign jurisdiction's law permitting such agreements applies, the local court will refuse to enforce it on policy grounds. A tougher question is presented when the other jurisdiction is a sister state, as opposed to a foreign nation. Courts will be less likely to find that a sister state's laws, as opposed to those of a "less civilized" jurisdiction, offend public policy.

2)   PENAL LAWS

No court may enforce the penal laws of another jurisdiction. The problem that may arise is which laws are "penal laws?" A court must analyze whether the law to be enforced is criminal or civil in nature. If criminal, it cannot be enforced by the other jurisdiction.

3)   REVENUE LAWS

Under the traditional approach, a court could not enforce the tax laws of a sister jurisdiction. Although the rule's existence is traced back to the prohibition against enforcing penal laws, no similar justification (i.e., respecting sovereignty) exists. On the contrary, the only result of the traditional approach was to provide tax shelters for tax evaders.

Under the modern approach, most courts would not hesitate to enforce the tax laws of other jurisdictions. In fact, many jurisdictions possess reciprocal agreements to do exactly that.

E.   Constitutional Limitations

States cannot merely apply any law they wish to resolve a dispute. They are limited by several constitutional provisions.

1) DUE PROCESS

In order to satisfy the Due Process, a state may only select to apply the substantive law of a forum which has "a significant contact or significant aggregation of contacts, creating state interests such that choice of its law is neither arbitrary nor fundamentally unfair." Essentially, any due process inquiry will focus on the territorial reach of state power and fairness in application of that power to individuals.

2) FULL FAITH AND CREDIT

Under due process, discussed above, a court is concerned with whether the parties possess enough of a connection to some jurisdiction, that it would be justified in enforcing such jurisdiction's law. Under a Full Faith and Credit Clause analysis, however, the court is required to determine whether another state possesses such a connection with the dispute, that the state must recognize its laws. In the past, states were under an obligation to impose the law of another jurisdiction if analysis of the interests involved weighed in favor of the other jurisdiction (unless the other law was "obnoxious" to the forum). Such a test, however, proved extremely unpopular (because it often required the forum to defer to foreign law) and unworkable. Today, a forum court has the discretion to apply whatever law it deems appropriate under the circumstances subject to a standard almost identical to that set forth for due process.

The Supreme Court has stated the test as follows:

> Where more than one State has sufficiently substantial contact with the activity in question, the forum State, by analysis of the interests possessed by the states involved, could constitutionally apply to the decision of the case the law of one or another state having interest in the multistate activity.

Richards v. United States, 369 U.S. 1, 15 (1962)

3) PRIVILEGES AND IMMUNITIES

The Privileges and Immunities Clause of the United States Constitution provides that every citizen is entitled to "the Privileges and Immunities of Citizens in the several states." Accordingly, some commentators argue that the clause provides a basis for invalidating a choice-of-law determination or standard made solely on the basis of the domicile of the parties. However, this result is rare given the flexibility and comprehensiveness of modern choice-of-law analysis. Moreover, even if government implicates the clause, it must only be rationally related to a legitimate governmental interest to be sustained. Consequently, little, if any, governmental action will be invalidated on this ground especially if any other basis existed or the determination.

F. Federal-State Conflicts

1)   FEDERAL SUPREMACY

    a)   Derivation of Federal Supremacy

The preemption doctrine derives its existence from the Supremacy Clause of the United States Constitution. The Supremacy Clause states that the "Constitution and the laws of the United States . . . shall be the supreme law of the land . . . anything in the constitutions or laws of any State to the contrary notwithstanding." Consequently, any federal law -- even a regulation of a federal agency -- trumps any conflicting state law.

    b)   Types of Preemption

Preemption is either express or implied.

    (1)   Express Preemption

If Congress chooses to expressly preempt a subject matter, the only question for courts becomes determining whether the challenged state law is one that the federal law is intended to preempt.

    (2)   Implied Preemption

Implied preemption presents issues that are more complex. The court must determine whether: 1) Congress has "occupied the field" in which the state is attempting to regulate; or 2) a state law directly conflicts with federal law; or 3) enforcement of the state law would frustrate federal purposes.

2)   *ERIE* DOCTRINE

    a)   General: Apply choice-of-law rules of forum state

The *Erie* doctrine, set forth in *Erie R.R. Co. v. Tompkins*, 304 U.S. 64 (1938), applies to choice--of--law rules. *Klaxon Co. v. Stentor Elec. Mfg. Co. Inc.*, 313 U.S. 487 (1941). Under *Klaxon*, in diversity cases, the choice-of-law rules of the state in which the federal court sits would be used to determine which state's substantive law governs. The principal reason for this application of *Erie* is to deter forum-shopping as between federal and state courts in the same state and thereby to protect the integrity and uniformity of state law within its territory.

    (1)   Effect of Venue Transfer

Van Dusen v. Barrack, 376 U.S. 612 (1964), established that a transfer of a civil action initiated by a defendant in a federal case, under 28 U.S.C. § 1404(a), does not alter the choice-of-law rule that was or would have been adopted by the transferor court. *Ferens v. John Deere Co.*, 110 S.Ct. 1274 (1990), carries the *Erie*-based, anti--forum--shopping rule of *Van Dusen* one step further. *Ferens* held that even where the plaintiff institutes the transfer, the transferor court's rules generally would govern in the transferee court.

b)   No Federal Common Law in Diversity Cases - Apply State Law

Separate and apart from the issue of which state's law to apply, a federal court must not avoid state law when it does not agree with a state court's conclusion on a particular issue. As a general rule, there is no federal common law for diversity cases. Consequently, when a federal court is hearing a case under its diversity jurisdiction, it must apply the same substantive law that would have been applied if the suit had been filed in a court of the state where the federal court is located. *Erie R.R. Co. v. Tompkins*, 304 U.S. 64 (1938). The federal court is not free to make its own independent judgment, from a policy standpoint, of the better construction of an ambiguous statute. *Id.* Instead, the federal court must try to predict from available state case law how the state's highest court would be likely to interpret the statute.

II.   RECOGNITION AND ENFORCEMENT OF OTHER STATES' AND FOREIGN JUDGMENTS

★   **A.   Full Faith and Credit**

The United States Constitution provides:

> Full faith and credit shall be given in each state to the public acts, records, and judicial proceedings of every other state. And the Congress may by general laws prescribe the manner in which such acts, records, and proceedings shall be proved, and the effect thereof.

By statute, the Congress has required that full faith and credit be given to judgments between and among: 1) state courts; 2) federal courts; and 3) courts of the U.S. territories. Consequently, assuming no "defense" set forth below applies, "[t]he full faith and credit clause of the United States Constitution requires that a final judgment entered in a sister state must be respected by the courts" of another state. *Karow v. Mitchell*, 110 Nev. 958 (1994).

B.   Defenses to Recognition or Enforcement

1)   OTHER STATE'S JUDGMENT

a)   Lack of Jurisdiction

A court is not required to enforce the judgment of another court if 1) the other court lacked jurisdiction and 2) the party challenging the judgment did not litigate the jurisdictional issue (or have the opportunity to) in the other court.

b)   Fraud; Equitable Defenses

A judgment obtained by fraud is not entitled to full faith and credit. There are two types of fraud.

(1)   Extrinsic Fraud

Fraud in the judgment is categorized as extrinsic fraud if it was procured by outright fraudulent tactics going to the heart of the judgment itself such as bribery of judicial officers.

> (2)   Intrinsic Fraud

Intrinsic fraud occurs when a party uses fraudulent documents or commits perjury. Essentially, it is fraud committed regarding an element of the overall case.

> c)   Not on Merits

A judgment that is entered "not on the merits," is not entitled to full faith and credit. An elementary example should illustrate the point: If a case is dismissed in one state because of lack of subject-matter jurisdiction, the dismissal would not preclude the plaintiff from bringing the action in another forum with subject-matter jurisdiction.

> d)   Judgments Lacking Finality

Judgments that are on appeal, or otherwise not final, are not entitled to full faith and credit.

> 2)   INTERNATIONAL JUDGMENT

International judgments are not subject to full faith and credit. A court would examine the following factors in determining whether to enforce such a judgment:

> a)   Lack of Jurisdiction

An international judgment rendered by a court which did not have jurisdiction is not enforceable in the United States. The court will not look to the jurisdictional determination of the foreign court, but rather will attempt to decide whether due process requirements have been met. If the American court finds that due process was violated, it will not enforce the judgment. Accordingly, if a foreign judgment rests on suspect jurisdictional grounds, it will not likely be enforced. Examples include jurisdictions that recognize personal jurisdiction over people even if only limited personal assets are in the jurisdiction. Other countries may find that jurisdiction exists merely if the person was once a resident of the country.

> b)   Public Policy

If enforcement of a foreign judgment would offend the public policy of the forum court, the judgment will not be enforced. Examples may include judgments based on contracts involving involuntary servitude or other offensive subject-matter. Incidentally, public policy used to be a ground to invalidate sister state's judgments as well. Today, however, the United States Supreme Court has made it clear that the policy of one state cannot be so repugnant to another, such that the other would be justified in not giving full faith and credit to a money judgment.

CREDITOR'S RIGHTS

TABLE OF CONTENTS

CREDITOR'S RIGHTS

Creditor's Rights is one of the testable subjects on the essay portion of the Michigan Bar Exam. Traditionally, Creditor's Rights questions did not appear in every administration of the Michigan Bar Exam and sometimes appeared every other administration. Of course, this subject could be tested more or less frequently.

According to the Michigan Board of Law Examiners, testable issues regarding Creditor's Rights include mortgages, garnishments, and attachments. Some previously tested issues include whether the use of the money from the mortgage to pay a land contract constitutes a purchase money mortgage, the priority of a lien versus a mortgage on the same real property, and the priority of a mortgage versus mechanic's liens on the same real property. This Creditor's Rights Outline includes some Michigan specific law along with some other general legal principles regarding mortgages, liens, garnishment, and attachment. See the Property Outline provided for the Multistate Bar Exam for further discussion of mortgages and liens.

I.   MORTGAGES

★★ **A.   Purchase Money Mortgage**

Ordinarily, a purchase money mortgage is created when a mortgagor conveys title to real property to a mortgagee in exchange for a down payment, a mortgage on the property, and a promissory note or loan for the remaining balance due on the purchase price. Generally, purchase-money mortgages receive priority over every other type of interest attached to the property subject to the mortgage. A transaction that is not a purchase money mortgage will not receive such priority.

1)   DEFINITION

A purchase money mortgage is one "which takes effect immediately, as part of the 'same transaction by which seisin was acquired by the mortgagor.'" *Graves v. Am. Acceptance Mortgage Corp.,* 469 Mich. 608 (2004), quoting *Fecteau v. Fries,* 253 Mich. 51 (1931). A purchase money mortgage arises where the mortgagor purchases property and gives a mortgage for the purchase money as one transaction. *Graves, supra.*

2)   TRANSACTION NOT A PURCHASE MONEY MORTGAGE

The Michigan Supreme Court has held that the use of the money from a later mortgage on property to pay off an earlier land contract on the property does not constitute a purchase-money mortgage. A land contract vests equitable title in the vendee, while legal title remains vested in the vendor. *Graves, supra.* Therefore, as the vendee has equitable title to the property, the vendee also has seisin, which is defined as "Possession of real property under claim of freehold estate . . . Possession with an intent on the part of him who holds it to claim a freehold estate." *Graves, supra,* n. 3, quoting *Black's Law Dictionary* (6th ed.) Thus, when a vendee purchases real property on a land contract, the vendee takes equitable title, which the vendee may then sell, devise, or encumber, and has "in a real sense, purchased the relevant property." *Graves, supra,* at 616.

II.   LIENS

★   **A.   Construction Lien Act**

1)   PRIORITY OF LIENS

Under the Construction Lien Act ("Act") of Michigan, all liens date back to the date of the first improvement on the property. Section 570.1119(3) of the Michigan Compiled Laws provides:

> A construction lien arising under this act shall take priority over all other interests, liens, or encumbrances which may attach to the building, structure, or improvement, or upon the real property on which the building, structure, or improvement is erected when the other interests, liens, or encumbrances are recorded subsequent to the first actual physical improvement.

Thus, the effective date of a lien claimants' lien is the first date of improvement regardless of when the lien claimant files its own lien. When, for example, the first visible improvement to the real estate occurred before a mortgage was filed, the lien claimants would possess priority over a mortgage recorded by a lender after that first visible improvement occurred.

2)   ACTUAL PHYSICAL IMPROVEMENT

Once any lien has priority over a mortgage, then all subsequent liens enjoy that priority. An actual physical improvement, as defined under the Act, generally requires that visible, on-site construction work has begun on the property. Grading of the property, for example, would certainly be a visible on-site improvement. The Michigan Supreme Court has stated: "We believe MCL 570.1119(3) [quoted above] continues to reflect the longstanding tradition of affording priority in the payment of those laborers, contractors, and suppliers who provide the building blocks and whose physical efforts go into a construction project. The underlying intent and purpose of the act is to protect the right of lien claimants to payment for wages or materials when others have been provided with notice that there may be outstanding liens against the property because construction work is in progress." *Williams & Works, Inc. v. Springfield Corp.,* 408 Mich. 732 (1980).

3)   PROTECTION OF INSTITUTIONAL LENDERS

There is a recognized risk to institutional lenders regarding their priority under the Act. Section 570.1119(4) of the Michigan Compiled Laws does provide some protection with respect to advances that they make under certain circumstances. Specifically, it provides that advances made by mortgage lenders after the first actual physical improvement may still enjoy priority over construction liens if the mortgagee has:

- received a sworn statement from the contractor pursuant to section 570.1110 of the Michigan Compiled Laws,
- made disbursements pursuant to the contractor's sworn statement, and
- received waivers of lien from the contractor and all subcontractors, laborers, and suppliers who have provided notices.

III.   GARNISHMENT

A common type of garnishment is the procedure that allows a portion of the wages of a person to be withheld for payment of a debt. Through the garnishment process, a creditor, with the aid of the courts, may require a debtor's employer to hold back a portion of this debtor's wages and pay that amount to the court or to the creditor.

A.   General Considerations

Garnishment typically occurs after a judgment has been rendered for a creditor against a debtor. Garnishment basically involves petitioning for and getting a court order directing a garnishee (e.g., a person or entity) to withhold funds and pay them to the judgment creditor when these funds are otherwise payable from the garnishee to the judgment debtor. The purpose is to make assets of a judgment debtor available from the garnishee for application in payment of the judgment to the judgment creditor. As a general rule, in order for garnishment to lie, the indebtedness must be due without contingency.

1)   TIME OF GARNISHMENT

Garnishment generally occurs after a judgment has been entered.

2)   AFFIDAVIT

Usually, a party seeking the garnishment must swear to allegations supporting garnishment under oath.

IV.   ATTACHMENT

A party may also seek to attach funds currently owned or possessed by a party through the judicial attachment procedure. Attachment is the seizing of money or property in the state prior to obtaining a judgment in court, in contemplation that the plaintiff will win at trial.

A.   General Considerations

Generally, property may be attached in cases to enforce the collection of a debt or in cases seeking any ascertainable demand of money. Property also can be attached to recover for a breach of contract or when the action sounds in damages only. Additionally, property may be attached in any other case where the court finds that extraordinary circumstances exist which will make it improbable for the plaintiff to reach the property of the defendant by execution after the judgment has been entered.

B.   Requirement of a Judicial Hearing

The United States Supreme Court mandates that an attachment be made only after a hearing before a judge in which both sides can argue the likelihood that the party being sued will leave the area or otherwise avoid probable payment. The motion may be granted only if the court determines that the plaintiff has established the probable validity of the claim against the defendant upon which the attachment is based.

C.   Attachment Without Notice

Certain grounds exist for attachment without notice to the property's owner. The cases in which property may be attached include the following:

- when the defendant resides out of the state;
- when the defendant leaves the jurisdiction to evade authority;
- when the defendant avoids service;
- when the defendant is about to leave the state;
- when the defendant is about to remove his property from the state; and
- when the defendant has disposed of, or is fraudulently about to dispose of, property.

D.   Affidavit with Application for Attachment

An affidavit must be provided in support of an application for attachment without notice. The affidavit must describe in reasonable and clear detail all the facts that show the existence of one or more of the grounds for an attachment without notice. The affidavit must also describe the money or property sought to be attached.

MICHIGAN

AMERIBAR BAR REVIEW

Michigan Bar Review

DOMESTIC RELATIONS

TABLE OF CONTENTS

DOMESTIC RELATIONS

Traditionally, a Domestic Relations question appears on the essay portion of each Michigan Bar Exam ("Exam"). The majority of these past questions have arisen from the factual context of a divorce. The minority of them have involved other factual situations such as cohabitation and a purported common law marriage and/or attempted marriage. A couple of frequently tested issues that can contain sub-issues are the validity of marriage and the division or distribution of property of the parties either in divorce or after the end of their relationship that did not result in a formal marriage. Other issues that have often been tested include prenuptial agreements, spousal support, child support, common law marriage, marriage licenses and the solemnization of marriage. Somewhat less frequently tested issues involve child custody, capacity to marry, and consent to marry. Certain child support issues including termination, modification, and arrearage were tested sometimes. Other occasionally tested issues are jurisdiction for divorce, grounds for annulment, the "equitable parent" doctrine, palimony, relocation of a child, grandparents' visitation rights, termination of parental rights, and gifts in contemplation of marriage.

Facts and rules derived from cases decided by the Michigan Court of Appeals and/or the Michigan Supreme Court have provided the basis for some past Domestic Relations questions and answers. The Michigan Compiled Laws is another source for tested rules as well. Although the sample answers for certain past questions indicate that Michigan statutes and court cases should be the basis for answering questions, questions could be answerable using controlling general legal principles contained in this outline.

I.   GETTING MARRIED

A.   Controversies Arising in Anticipation of Marriage

1)   BREACH OF PROMISE TO MARRY

This cause of action finds its roots centuries ago in the common law. It has been treated as an action in both tort and contract. Because of the nature of the action, litigants often used circumstantial evidence as proof. As such, this cause of action was greatly abused and has been criticized throughout the twentieth century. Almost all jurisdictions including Michigan do not recognize this action any longer. *E.g.,* Mich. Comp. Laws § 600.2901(4). However, a minority, including Georgia, Hawaii, Kansas, Nebraska, Texas, and Washington, still recognize the action.

2)   FRAUDULENT INDUCEMENT TO MARRY

If the consent of either party to a marriage has been obtained by fraud, the marriage will be void from the time its nullity is declared by a court of competent jurisdiction. This cause of action has not been quite as limited as the breach of promise to marry, but does not, by any means, enjoy popular appeal. In Michigan, an independent tort action for fraudulent inducement to marry cannot be maintained in the context of a divorce action when the allegations of fraud relate to the marital relationship's existence. *Gubin v. Pavlovich*, 197 Mich. App. 84 (1992). The wronged spouse could instead seek and obtain relief in the divorce action when the other spouse's alleged misconduct is taken into consideration as a factor of property division. *Id.*

For example, suppose that A represents to B that he is single and would like to marry B. B accepts. The parties have a ceremonial marriage. If A was already married at the time of the ceremony with B, A may be liable for fraudulent inducement to marry.

3)   CONTRACTS RESTRAINING OR PROMOTING MARRIAGE

Contracts restraining or promoting marriage are disfavored because the right to marry is fundamental. General restraints on such right are invalid. Partial restraints may be valid if they are reasonable under the circumstances.

For example, suppose that A is wealthy and, for no practical reason, promises B $200,000 if he does not get married for twenty years. This is an unenforceable general restraint on the right to marry.

On the other hand, suppose that A, B's ill 75 year old grandparent, offers B, 45 years old, A's home if B lives with A, remains unmarried, and cares for A for five years. Under these circumstances, a court may find this restraint valid because the restraint appears to be reasonable under the circumstances.

★   ### 4)   PREMARITAL GIFTS

Disputes often arise regarding the disposition of premarital gifts conditioned on marriage (i.e., conditional prenuptial gifts). The most common, of course, is the engagement ring.

a)   Traditional Rule

Traditionally, such gifts were returned to the donor if the donor was not at fault for the break-up.

b)   Modern Trend -- Michigan

Under the modern trend, which applies in Michigan, the gifts should be returned to the donor regardless of fault. *Meyer v. Mitnick*, 244 Mich. App. 697 (2001). Courts justify this "no fault" rule because "fault" does not really exist in this context. One person merely changed her mind about the engagement.

★★
TEST
TIP Remember, these rules only apply if the gift was conditioned on marriage. If the gift was unconditional, such as a birthday gift, the person who received the gift is entitled to keep the property. The outlines for Personal Property and Wills & Estates further address gifts.

B.   Limitations on Who May Marry

For a marriage to be valid in Michigan, the following must be true: (1) the parties must not already be married, (2) the parties must not be of the same sex, (3) the parties must not be related within a prohibited degree of consanguinity, (4) the parties must be of marriageable age, (5) the parties must be mentally competent, and (6) the parties must be entering into the marriage without fraud or duress. Citizenship of the parties generally is irrelevant. The general rules relative to these requirements for the validity of a marriage in Michigan are further discussed later.

1)   VOID/VOIDABLE MARRIAGES

An invalid marriage is either void or voidable.

a)   Void

A void marriage is a legal nullity. It is treated as if it never existed. As a general rule, invalid marriages are "void" if they suffer a more serious defect. In most jurisdictions, incestuous and bigamous marriages are void.

b)   Voidable

A voidable marriage can be annulled by one of the parties. If not, it may become a valid marriage.

c)   Significance of Distinction

The distinction becomes important if, for example, a party dies believing she is married. If the marriage is declared void for some reason, the surviving spouse may not receive any interest in the property of the deceased. If, by contrast, the marriage is only voidable, the survivor may be treated as a surviving spouse.

2)   SAME SEX MARRIAGES

Almost every jurisdiction including Michigan does not statutorily permit homosexual couples to marry. Mich. Comp. Laws §§ 551.3-551.4.

3)   BIGAMY/POLYGAMY

a)   Generally Void

No state recognizes the validity of a bigamous marriage. A bigamous marriage is void. A number of states, however, have statutes providing that if a marriage is invalid because there is an impediment to it when contracted (for example, one party is still married to another spouse), it becomes a valid marriage when the impediment is removed. *E.g.,* Uniform Marriage and Divorce Act § 207(b) (UMDA). Some statutes require, in addition, that one of the parties have entered the marriage in the good-faith belief that the marriage was valid.

b)   Removal of "Impediment"

Other statutes, however, require that the parties to the initially invalid marriage continue to cohabit after the impediment is removed and that one party continue to believe in good faith that they were always validly married. *E.g.,* Wis. Stat. § 765.24.

4)   INCESTUOUS MARRIAGE

Marriages declared incestuous are treated as void. The problem on most exams is which marriages are to be treated as incestuous. Jurisdictions are fairly evenly split regarding whether cousins may marry. Michigan law prohibits marriage between cousins of the first degree. Mich. Comp. Laws §§ 551.3-551.4.

a)   The Uniform Marriage and Divorce Act (Cousins may marry)

Under the UMDA, there are three general types of prohibitions. They include the following:

- ancestors and descendants;
- siblings (regardless of whole/half blood or adoption); or
- uncles and nieces or aunts and nephews.

b)   Michigan Law (First cousins may not marry)

(1)   Man Prohibited from Marrying

In Michigan, a man may "not marry his mother, sister, grandmother, daughter, granddaughter, stepmother, grandfather's wife, son's wife, grandson's wife, wife's mother, wife's grandmother, wife's daughter, wife's granddaughter, brother's daughter, sister's daughter, father's sister, mother's sister, or cousin of the first degree, or another man." Mich. Comp. Laws § 551.3.

(2)   Woman Prohibited from Marrying

In Michigan, a woman may "not marry her father, brother, grandfather, son, grandson, stepfather, grandmother's husband, daughter's husband, granddaughter's husband, husband's father, husband's grandfather, husband's son, husband's grandson, brother's son, sister's son, father's brother, mother's brother, or cousin of the first degree, or another woman." Mich. Comp. Laws § 551.4.

5)   MINORS

In almost every state including Michigan, a person must be 18 years of age to be married. Mich. Comp. Laws § 555.103(1). However, many states including Michigan provide that people 16 or 17 years old may marry with parental consent. *Id.* In Michigan, a person under 16 years of age may not marry. Mich. Comp. Laws § 555.51.

a)   Void/Voidable

A majority of jurisdictions treat underage marriage as voidable, although some jurisdictions would still treat the marriage as void. In Michigan, the marriage of a person under 16 years of age is void. *Id.*

> b)   Estoppel

If a person who was a minor at the time of the marriage misrepresented himself as older than the age of majority, some courts may estop that person from annulling that marriage when the person reached the age of majority. A majority of jurisdictions treat underage marriages as voidable, although some jurisdictions such as Michigan still treat the marriage as void. *Id.*

> 6)   PHYSICAL INCAPACITY

A marriage is voidable if one party is unable to physically consummate the marriage and the other party was unaware of the problem at the time of the solemnization.

> 7)   FRAUDULENT MARRIAGE

A marriage is voidable if one party procured the marriage by fraud. The test for determining whether the marriage may be annulled is as follows:

- There was a material fraud; and
- The fraud affects the essentials of the marriage.

> a)   Material Fraud

The following has been held to be a material fraud:

- lying about an intent not to have sexual intercourse;
- concealing impotency;
- concealing pregnancy by another;
- lying about religious beliefs.

The following lies have been held not to be a material fraud. They include lying about:

- wealth;
- citizenship;
- chastity;
- age;
- number of prior marriages.

> b)   Annulment for Force or Fraud -- Michigan

In Michigan, a marriage may not be annulled for force or fraud if the parties voluntarily cohabited as wife and husband prior to their lawsuit for annulment. Mich. Comp. Laws § 552.37.

★★★ C.   Procedural Requirements

In order for a marriage to be valid, the parties must consent to the marriage. Additionally, the marriage must be solemnized. If solemnized in Michigan, a marriage that is prohibited by law because either party was not capable in law of contracting at the time of the solemnization is absolutely void. Mich. Comp. Laws § 552.1.

★★   1)   SOLEMNIZATION

             a)   Marriage License

The parties must obtain a marriage license prior to the solemnization of the marriage. In Michigan, as a general matter if two individuals who go through a purported marriage ceremony fail to obtain a marriage license, they are not legally married.

                   (1)   When Marriage License is Delivered

Generally, a marriage license must not be delivered by the county clerk to the applicant within three days, including the date of application. Mich. Comp. Laws § 551.103a. The county clerk may, however, deliver the license immediately after the application for good cause shown. *Id.*

                   (2)   Where to Use Marriage License

A license is defective if it was used in a county other than the one in which it was issued as required when the parties are both residents of another state (i.e., non-residents of Michigan). Mich. Comp. Laws § 551.101 (last sentence).

                   (3)   When to Use Marriage License

Formerly, a marriage license will be void if the marriage ceremony occurs more than 30 days after application for the license. Mich. Comp. Laws § 551.103a, last sentence (as effective in 1962). Presently, a marriage license will be void if the marriage ceremony occurs more than 33 days after the application. *Id.* (as effective since 2007).

             b)   Ceremony

                   (1)   Who May Conduct Ceremony

A ceremony may be conducted by either clergy (authorized religious official) or most judges. Mich. Comp. Laws § 551.7(1)(a)-(e), (h)-(i). A ceremony can be conducted by either a city's mayor within the county where the city is located or a county clerk in the county where the clerk serves that has over two million inhabitants. Mich. Comp. Laws § 551.7(1)(f)-(g). Generally, a ceremony conducted by an unauthorized person will not result in a valid marriage. In addition to religious considerations, the state's purposes for solemnization include instilling upon the parties the serious nature of the act and creating a public record.

(2)   Two Witness Requirement

In Michigan, for a statutory marriage to occur there must be two witnesses. Mich. Comp. Laws § 551.9.

★★   **D.   State of Mind Requirements**

1)   <u>CONSENT REQUIRED</u>

Consent of the parties is a prerequisite to a valid marriage. The parties must consent to many aspects of marriage – not just the wedding ceremony. A court will examine the parties' consent to emotional and sexual fidelity, economic interdependence, and commitment to the relationship. While it would be possible to interpret the consent requirement as applying only to participation in the wedding ceremony, courts do not take this approach. Instead, they consider what policies would be advanced or impeded by treating parties as married in a particular case.

a)   Extent of Consent - Traditional Approach

Some Benefits of Marriage - A court taking the traditional approach would treat parties as married if they participated in a valid ceremony and sought to obtain at least some of the benefits of marriage.

b)   Extent of Consent - Modern Approach

Usual Obligations of Marriage - The other major approach is to conclude that the parties are married only if they intended to take on the "usual obligations" of marriage. *E.g., Faustin v. Lewis*, 85 N.J. 507, 427 A.2d 1105 (1981) (granting an annulment on facts similar to question). The theory underlying this approach is that no good purpose is served by treating people as married if they have not taken on the commitments of marriage. Accordingly, this is a slightly heightened standard.

E.   Common-Law Marriage and Other Curative or Mitigative Doctrines

★★★   1)   <u>COMMON LAW MARRIAGE</u>

a)   Abolition of Common Law Marriage

In most states including Michigan, common law marriages have been abolished. In jurisdictions that recognize common law marriages, the party claiming that such a marriage exists must prove at a minimum (1) that the parties cohabited, (2) that they held themselves out as married, and (3) that they intended to be married. Homer H. Clark, Jr., *Domestic Relations* § 2.4 (student ed. 1988). Often, the emphasis in common law marriage cases is placed on the couple's "holding themselves out" as married, and sometimes, intent can be inferred from that fact.

b)   Limited Recognition of Common Law Marriages -- Michigan

Common law marriages were abolished in Michigan in 1957. Common law marriages are only recognized in Michigan (1) if the couple had a valid common law marriage prior to January 1, 1957, or (2) if the couple legally entered into such a marriage in a state permitting it. Mich. Comp. Laws §§ 551.2, 750.335.

The standard of a common-law marriage in Michigan for a relationship existing before January 1, 1957, is (1) a present agreement to live together as husband and wife by people who are free to marry and (2) the subsequent cohabitation as husband and wife. *In re Estate of Leonard*, 45 Mich. App. 679 (1973). For example, a pledge of fidelity and the giving of a ring do not constitute present intent to be husband and wife.

An unmarried male and female cohabitating by agreement who do not fall into one of the foregoing two categories for a valid common law marriage, violate Michigan law, which prohibits male and female "lewd and lascivious" cohabitation. Mich. Comp. Laws § 750.335.

★ 2) PUTATIVE SPOUSE DOCTRINE

   a) General Considerations

A person whose marriage was legally invalid, but who participated in a ceremony or solemnization in the reasonable and good-faith belief that the marriage was indeed valid, is a putative spouse. A putative spouse possesses the legal rights of a spouse in a valid marriage as long as the spouse does not lose the good-faith belief. The status of a putative spouse is not certain in many jurisdictions.

   b) Michigan Law

"In cases involving putative spouses, one or both of the parties mistakenly believe in good faith that they are legally married, only to discover at a subsequent date that they are not." *Carnes v. Sheldon*, 109 Mich. App. 204 (1981). In certain circumstances, Michigan courts have been willing to grant equitable relief to putative spouses. For example, "in the putative spouse situation a concealment of material facts by one spouse may constitute actionable fraud and permit the defrauded spouse to recover a portion of the property accumulated during the period of cohabitation." *Walker v. Walker*, 330 Mich. 332 (1951).

  3) PROXY MARRIAGES

A proxy marriage is a marriage in which another person stands in for one of the parties. Specifically, during the solemnization of the marriage, an agent acts on behalf of one of the parties through power of attorney. Very few jurisdictions recognize proxy marriage today.

  4) MARRIAGE BY ESTOPPEL

Marriage by estoppel, where recognized, occurs in very limited circumstances. If two parties marry each other, but one's divorce from another has not been finalized, the parties are married by estoppel, even though the second marriage is void as bigamous. The rationale is that a party should not be permitted to enter into an invalid marriage and simply exit at whim, on the ground of invalidity, without consequence.

5)   DE FACTO MARRIAGE

De facto marriage is a legal doctrine that has very little judicial support. Under this doctrine, unmarried cohabitants can obtain the legal rights of a spouse under extreme circumstances. For example, in one case, a couple that was married for over twenty years obtained a divorced. They began cohabiting again, but did not remarry when the husband was rendered impotent. The court found that parties entered into a de facto marriage. *Bullock v. United States*, 487 F. Supp. 1078 (D.N.J. 1980).

TEST TIP This doctrine has received very little support. If the facts of a question warrant it, you should bring it up. However, you should be very hesitant to conclude that a court would likely determine that a de facto marriage exists.

6)   LAST IN TIME PRESUMPTION

The last in time marriage presumption comes into play in very specific factual circumstances. If a person was married multiple times and passes away, a prior spouse cannot claim that his marriage with the deceased never validly terminated. Prior spouses may desire to make such a claim to collect on a wrongful death action or other potential benefits. Under the last in time presumption, the person who was last married to the deceased is deemed the final spouse and all prior marriages are declared terminated.

F.   Premarital Contracts

★★★

1)   GENERAL RULE

a)   General Considerations

Most states will enforce premarital (i.e., prenuptial) agreements if they are just and reasonable. The terms of a premarital agreement will be carefully scrutinized. A premarital contract is generally valid if it meets the following three conditions:

- It is in writing;
- It is voluntary; and
- It is executed after full disclosure.

Premarital contracts are covered by the Statute of Frauds and so must be in writing to be enforceable. Uniform Premarital Agreements Act § 2. Today, most courts and statutes also require either that the terms of the agreement not be unconscionable or that the spouses have made adequate disclosures to each other before entering into the agreement. *E.g.,* Uniform Premarital Agreements Act § 6. In many jurisdictions, if the provisions are disproportionately advantageous to one party, a presumption of concealment of assets exists which must be overcome by the other party.

b)   Michigan Law Considerations

A prenuptial agreement is a valid type of contract under Michigan law. Marriage is considered a sufficient consideration for the contract.

(1)   Void and Unenforceable

Upon divorce, the agreement can affect the division of property and spousal support. If the court finds the agreement was obtained through fraud, duress or mistake, misrepresentation, or nondisclosure of or withholding a material fact, the court may find the prenuptial agreement void and unenforceable. Other grounds for finding the prenuptial agreement void and unenforceable are that it was unconscionable when reached or the circumstances are so changed that enforcement of it would be unfair.

A prenuptial agreement is not void *ab initio* simply because it was reached before 1991, when it was first expressly held in Michigan that prenuptial agreements governing the division of property upon divorce could be enforced. *Reed v. Reed,* 265 Mich. App. 131, 141-142 (2005), *Rinvelt v. Rinvelt,* 190 Mich. App. 372 (1991). *Reed* held there was no clear authority supporting the conclusion that the parties' 1975 prenuptial agreement was void merely because it was entered into before *Rinvelt* was decided. The duration of the marriage, children, and accumulation of wealth are all changes that are anticipated when the agreement was reached. *Reed,* pp. 144-147. One spouse has the responsibility or "burden" to void the prenuptial agreement as the one who might challenge the claim by the other spouse under it. *Reed,* pp. 147-148.

2)   LIMITATIONS ON PREMARITAL CONTRACTS

However, there are limits on spouses' ability to enter into legally binding agreements to alter their marital obligations. Under the modern view, the spouses' ability to define the terms of their relationship is much greater than in earlier times, but courts frequently still do not enforce agreements to limit the spouses' support duties during marriage.

★★★   3)   SPECIFIC LIMITATIONS - SUBJECT-MATTER

a)   Divorce

Traditionally, agreements contemplating what would occur if the parties divorce, have been unenforceable based on the policy in favor of discouraging divorce. Today, many courts are more likely to uphold such agreements under certain circumstances. For example, a court is more likely to enforce the agreement if the marriage is the parties' second marriage or if the agreement divides marital property, rather than dictates support obligations.

b)   Marriage

Agreements dealing with everyday aspects of married life are generally unenforceable. For example, agreements dealing with sexual relations, family religion, and the upbringing of children are usually invalid.

c)   Child Custody

It is highly unlikely that provisions in a premarital agreement regarding child custody and child support would be enforceable. Although the ability to contract with respect to child custody is not entirely clear, most courts would hold that child custody should be determined by the court according to the best interests of the child at the time of the divorce or custody hearing, rather than by agreement of the parties prior to marriage. Therefore, a court could and probably would hold that it is not bound by a premarital custody provision.

★   In Michigan, a court is not bound to a parties' agreement regarding child custody. A court may take the parties' stipulation about custody into consideration, but the court must find that the arrangement is in the best interests of the child. *Koron v. Melendy,* 207 Mich. App. 188 (1994).

d)   Child Support

(1)   General Considerations

Finally, parents have an absolute obligation to support their children. A child's right to support cannot be adversely affected by a premarital agreement. Moreover, federal law requires that each state have child support guidelines, which set out a rebuttable presumption with respect to the amount of child support that will be ordered. Deviations from the guideline must be justified by the court through specific findings of fact.

★   ### (2)   Michigan Law

In Michigan, parents may enter into a prenuptial agreement to address marital property and spousal support, but parents may not bargain away a child's right to adequate support. Provisions that attempt to put a ceiling on support available in the future are unenforceable. Although a court may consider an agreement between the parties, the court is not bound by it. *Bowman v. Coleman,* 35 Mich. 390 (1959); *Carlston v. Carlston,* 182 Mich. App. 501 (1990); *Ballard v. Ballard,* 40 Mich. App. 37 (1972).

II.   BEING MARRIED

A.   Rights and Responsibilities of Spouses

Entering into a marriage bestows several rights and obligations upon the spouses.

1)   PROPERTY RIGHTS

There are two different approaches to the system of property rights during marriage. They are the common law property and community property approaches.

a)   Common Law Theory of Property Rights

Traditionally, the common law property rights system was wholly inequitable. Due to the unity theory of marriage, the legal identity of the wife disappeared and the husband controlled virtually all of the property. Under this system, title to property was the paramount consideration of determining right. Due to the male dominated society of prior centuries, title was almost always held in the husband's name. As a result, property held in the husband's name was deemed his alone.

(1)   Rights on Death

Several doctrines such as dower and curtesy, as well as the modern spousal elective share, were established to provide support for widows. According to the dower doctrine, a wife was entitled to a life estate in one-third of the real property owned by the husband. The husband was entitled to a curtesy share of the wife's estate including a life estate in all real property owned by the deceased wife. Curtesy was conditioned on the birth of a child by the spouses. Today, the doctrine of elective share has evolved to protect widowed spouses from disinheritance.

b)   Community Property Theory of Property Rights

A few jurisdictions adopted the civil law community property theory of marriage. Under the community property theory of marriage, the parties possess an equal share in all marital property. Most property obtained through the efforts of either spouse during the marriage is deemed marital property. A person entering into a marriage, however, does not lose property rights in separate property existing at the time of the marriage.

★   2)   SUPPORT

a)   The Necessaries Doctrine

At common law, husbands were legally responsible for supporting their wives. This duty could be enforced under the necessaries doctrine. Clark, *supra* § 6.3 at 265. This doctrine allows a wife to purchase goods or services on credit and charge them to her husband. The creditor who furnishes "necessaries" to a wife may recover the fair market value of the goods or services from the husband even if he did not enter into a contract to pay for them or otherwise authorize her to pledge his credit. A "necessary" item is something suitable to the parties' station in life. Medically necessary care generally is considered to be within the support duty. *E.g., Greenspan v. Slate,* 12 N.J. 426, 97 A.2d 390 (1953), (parent liable for a child's medical bills under the necessaries doctrine).

(1)   Common Law Approach

At common law, only husbands had spousal support duties; wives did not. Modern cases and statutes, however, generally recognize that spouses have mutual support duties. Clark, *supra* § 6.1 at 251. *But see Shands Teaching Hosp. and Clinics, Inc. v. Smith,* 497 So.2d 644 (Fla. 1986) (upholding the traditional necessaries doctrine against an equal protection attack).

(2)   Modern Approach

(a)   Abolishing Doctrine of Necessaries -- *MICHIGAN*

Those courts, which have held that the traditional necessaries doctrine cannot survive in the modem era of formal gender equality, differ about whether a creditor may seek payment for necessaries from either spouse. In a few states including Michigan, courts have abolished the necessaries doctrine by statute or in response to the equal protection challenge. *E.g., Condore v. Prince George's County*, 289 Md. 516, 425 A.2d 1011 (1981). The Michigan Supreme Court has stated that "the common-law necessaries doctrine violates equal protection principles, and we remedy this unconstitutionality by abrogating the doctrine, holding that neither a husband nor a wife is liable, absent express agreement, for necessaries supplied to the other." *North Ottawa Community Hosp. v. Kieft,* 457 Mich. 394 (1998) (reversing Michigan Court of Appeals case holding in part that married women's property act was unconstitutional). In many states, however, a parent is still liable for the necessaries of a child.

(b)   Modification of Doctrine of Necessities

Most states excluding Michigan, however, have retained the necessaries doctrine but modified it. In some states a creditor may sue either spouse or both, e.g., *North Carolina Baptist Hosps. v. Harris,* 319 N.C. 347, 354 S.E.2d 471 (1987). In other states, wives are only secondarily liable for necessaries supplied the other spouse, e.g., *Marshfield Clinic v. Discher*, 105 Wis. 2d 506, 314 N.W.2d 326 (1982), and in some states a creditor must first seek payment from the spouse who incurred the obligation, e.g., *Jersey Shore Med. Ctr.-Fitkin Hosp. v. Baum's Estate,* 84 N.J. 137, 417 A.2d 1003 (1980).

(c)   Family Expense Statutes

About 20 states have enacted family expense statutes making both spouses liable for the expenses of the family. Clark, *supra*, § 6.1 at 257.

b)   Separate Maintenance

Under the common law action for separate maintenance, a husband is obligated to provide for the support of his wife during a period of separation (not divorce). The wife would forfeit any entitlement to separate maintenance if she was at fault for the separation. This doctrine, like so many other traditional common law doctrines, has been criticized in several jurisdictions. In Michigan, a separate maintenance action is statutory and discussed later under the subheading of Separate Maintenance. In Michigan, spousal support (i.e., alimony) can be awarded in both actions for separate maintenance or divorce. Mich. Comp. Laws § 552.23(1).

B.   Family Privacy

1)   COMMON-LAW DOCTRINE

a)   General

The common law doctrine of family privacy protected the decision-making authority of the male head of household regarding all other members of the family from outside interference. Consequently, statutes challenging family privacy in contravention of common law were narrowly construed. Moreover, those reinforcing the common law by protecting morals throughout civil society were given considerable latitude.

b)   Purpose and Consequences

The reasoning behind the rule was that the state's purpose was to promote marriage as an institution, to support procreation, and to shield the family as a unit. Protecting marriage and the patriarchal order resulted in limiting privacy protection to the nuclear family. The elimination of the individuality of the married woman--her merging into the husband's legal identity--fit the common law model perfectly. As a result, states possessed considerable discretion to regulate nonmarital or extramarital relationships.

2)   CONSTITUTIONAL PRIVACY

The more modern constitutional privacy analysis completely alters the common law approach. The power of the state to regulate marriage and marital activities contains a significant constitutional limitation grounded in the elusive "right to privacy."

a)   Prohibition of Marriage

The right to marry is a fundamental right. If the state seeks to prevent a party from exercising this fundamental right, a law is subject to strict scrutiny. The state must possess a compelling state interest that is narrowly tailored.

For example, a statute prohibiting a person with an unpaid child support obligation from marrying is unconstitutional. The state can enforce child support orders in a less restrictive manner.

b)   Regulation of Marriage

If the state law merely regulates marriage, then the state must only provide a rational basis for the law.

For example, a law requiring a person under 18 to obtain parental consent is constitutionally valid. The state is merely delaying, not prohibiting, marriage. The purpose of protecting minors is considered paramount.

3)   REPRODUCTIVE CHOICES

a)   Fundamental Right

The right to reproductive choices and the use of contraceptives is a fundamental right. The United States Supreme Court extended that right to unmarried people as well. A law attempting to prohibit the use of contraceptives will be unconstitutional if not narrowly tailored to serve a compelling state interest. The right can be implicated by laws prohibiting use of contraceptives, limiting their advertising, and prohibiting their distribution.

      b)   Minors Possess Right

Even minor children possess a right, although not as expansive, in this context.

      4)   <u>EVIDENTIARY PRIVILEGES</u>

      a)   Spousal Incompetency

A person cannot be called to testify against his spouse in any criminal prosecution. In some jurisdictions, the privilege extends to civil actions. The privilege covers testimony regarding events occurring at any time, even before the marriage. The focus of the privilege is not on the content of the testimony, by rather on prohibiting testimony against the spouse.

      (1)   Who Holds the Privilege

      (a)   General Considerations

In federal courts, the witness, not the party spouse, holds the privilege. However, in most jurisdictions, the spouse who is a party in the case, not the testifying witness, holds the privilege. Therefore, even if the witness wishes to testify, she cannot unless the party spouse waives the privilege.

      (b)   Michigan Law

In civil actions in Michigan courts, the spouse who is not the witness holds the privilege. Mich. Comp. Laws § 600.2162(1). In criminal cases in Michigan courts, the spouse who is the witness holds the privilege. Mich. Comp. Laws § 600.2162(2).

      (2)   Terminates upon Divorce

The privilege only lasts so long as the parties are married. Once the marriage is terminated, the privilege is eliminated.

      (3)   Family Disputes Exempt

Such a privilege does not exist if the spouses are involved in litigation with each other.

      b)   Confidential Marital Communications Privilege

Unlike spousal incompetency, this privilege concerns itself with the content of the testimony. A spouse cannot testify regarding confidential communications between the spouses while married. Additionally, unlike spousal incompetency, this privilege can be asserted even if the parties get divorced. Moreover, either party can assert the privilege. Like spousal incompetency, this privilege is unavailable if the spouses are involved in litigation with each other.

C.   Remedies for Tortious Interference with the Marital Relationship

1)   GENERAL

The tort of alienation of affections is the "willful and malicious interference with the marriage relation by a third party, without justification or excuse." The marital interests protected by the tort "include the affections, society and companionship of the other spouse, sexual relations and the exclusive enjoyment thereof," and services in the home and support. *Donnell v. Donnell*, 220 Tenn. (24 McCanless) 169, 179-80, 415 S.W.2d 127, 132 (1967). Thus, the essence of the tort is an injury to the right of consortium. *Kelley v. Jones*, 675 S.W.2d 189, 190 (Tenn. Ct. App. 1984)." *Lentz v. Bakier*, 792 S.W.2d 71 (Tenn. Ct. App. 1989)

2)   WHO MAY BRING ACTION

Originally, the only the husband could bring the action. As the common law evolved, women were able to bring actions for alienation of affections. In few jurisdictions, the action is available to a child who has been deprived of the affections of a parent. Alienation of affections has been abolished and/or severely limited in a majority of jurisdictions including Michigan. *E.g.,* Mich. Comp. Laws § 600.2901(1).

3)   LACK OF AFFECTION AS DEFENSE

Lack of affections between the parties is not a complete defense. Rather, it is a doctrine of mitigation. Accordingly, a third person interferes with a marriage relationship at his peril. Even if the spouses have been estranged, there is the possibility of reconciliation, and a third person has the burden of justifying his actions when he encourages a divorce, or seeks to entice away even an estranged spouse, or to prevent reconciliation.

III.   SEPARATION, DIVORCE, DISSOLUTION, AND ANNULMENT

A.   Grounds and Defenses

★   1)   ANNULMENT

Annulment is the judicial declaration that a marriage never existed. A marriage can be annulled if it is void or voidable. In most states, generally incestuous and bigamous marriages are void. Generally, all other defects render a marriage voidable.

a)   Grounds for Annulment

Common grounds for annulment include the following:

(1)   Lack of Capacity to Consent

A party may lack capacity for consent at the time of the marriage either because of mental incapacity or infirmity or because of the influence of alcohol, drugs or other incapacitating substances, or a party was induced to enter into a marriage by force or duress or by fraud involving the essentials of marriage.

★The consent of the parties capable in law of contracting is essential to a valid marriage. In Michigan, the law of contracts dictates whether a person has the ability to enter into a marriage contract. A marriage can be deemed invalid and annulled for fraud, duress, mistake, lunacy, inability to contract due to age and intoxication. It must be shown that one of the parties did not have the ability to enter into a contract. Mich. Comp. Laws §§ 551.2, 551.4; *Chudnow v. Chudnow*, 2001 WL 672571 (April 27, 2001); *Castle ex rel Gulliver v. Deising*, 2001 WL 633702 (May 25, 2001).

(2)		Lack of Capacity to Consummate Marriage by Sexual Intercourse

This ground is available so long as at the time the marriage was solemnized, the other party did not know of the incapacity.

(3)		Minor

It is a ground for annulment if a party was underage and did not have the consent of his parents or guardian or judicial approval. This ground may be asserted until the party reaches the age of consent. In Michigan, in an action to annul the marriage of a minor, the marriage may not be annulled when the parties to the marriage freely cohabited as wife and husband after they attained the age of majority. Mich. Comp. Laws § 552.34.

(4)		Prohibited by Law

It is a ground for annulment if the marriage is otherwise prohibited (bigamy, incest, etc.).

b)		Defenses to Annulment

(1)		Ratification

Ratification may be a defense to an action for annulment. A void marriage (bigamy or incest) can never be ratified. A voidable marriage can be ratified under certain circumstances.

(a)		Time Limitation

In particular, some jurisdictions provide a statutory time limitation for annulment proceedings (generally one to two years from the date of the marriage or the date of discovery of the defect). For example, in Michigan an action by a plaintiff injured party to annul a marriage on the basis that the defendant lacks physical capacity must be brought within two years from the solemnization of their marriage. Mich. Comp. Laws § 552.39. If there is no statutory timeframe, the party must bring an annulment action within a reasonable of time from discovering the defect.

2)   LEGAL SEPARATION

     a)   General Considerations

A legal separation is where a married couple mutually agrees to live apart by judicial decree. It is one step short of a divorce. A party to a marriage may obtain a decree of legal separation by essentially showing that the party desires to live separately and apart from the other spouse. If the court possesses jurisdiction to enter a divorce decree, it will also have jurisdiction over a legal separation. The main effect of the decree of legal separation is that, after its entry, the spouses' earnings will be their separate property (for the purposes of subsequent dissolution proceedings), and a spouse may convey his or her real estate without the signature of the other party.

     b)   Michigan Law

Although legal separation does not exist in Michigan, an analogous type of action for separate maintenance does. Butler, Durham & Toweson, PLLC, *Michigan Separate Maintenance FAQ's*, July 17, 2004, at http://www.divorcenet.com/states/michigan/mifaq03.

3)   SEPARATE MAINTENANCE -- MICHIGAN

     a)   Judgment of Separate Maintenance / Judgment of Divorce

In Michigan, a plaintiff spouse can bring an action for separate maintenance in the same way and on the same grounds as for a divorce action. *Id*.: Mich. Comp. Laws § 552.7(1). In response to a plaintiff spouse's action for separate maintenance, a defendant spouse can bring a counterclaim for divorce. Mich. Comp. Laws § 552.7(2). If the evidence shows that a "breakdown in the marriage relationship" has occurred "to the extent that the objects of matrimony have been destroyed" and "no reasonable likelihood that the marriage can be preserved" remains, the court must enter a judgment: 1) of separate maintenance if no counterclaim for divorce was filed; or 2) of divorce if a counterclaim for divorce was filed. Mich. Comp. Laws § 552.7(4).

     (1)   Distinguishing Separate Maintenance from Divorce

If a judgment of separate maintenance is entered pursuant to Mich. Comp. Laws § 552.23, the parties remain technically married. Butler, Durham & Toweson, PLLC, *Michigan Separate Maintenance FAQ's*, July 17, 2004, at http://www.divorcenet.com/states/michigan/mifaq03. The judgment is from bed and board, but not from the bonds of matrimony. *Id.* The court will divide the property of the marriage and can order spousal support. *Id.*

If, however, a judgment of divorce is entered, then the parties' divorce is from both (1) bed and board and (2) the bonds of matrimony. Mich. Comp. Laws § 552.23. The court will divide the property of the marriage and can order spousal support. *Id.*

Accordingly, an action for separate maintenance, if it results in a judgment of separate maintenance, may be a preferred legal outcome than a judgment of divorce for an individual "whose religious beliefs do not permit divorce" because the judgment of separate maintenance does not terminate the bonds of matrimony. *Id.*

A separate maintenance action is not a bar to a subsequent divorce action. *Engemann v. Engemann*, 53 Mich. App. 588 (1974).

4)   DIVORCE

Traditionally, divorce was only permitted if one party was determined to be "at fault." Today, every state has adopted some form of no-fault divorce procedures, although they differ with regard to the precise process. Michigan is a no-fault divorce state.

Initially, the only grounds for a divorce were adultery and desertion by either party, although wives were also afforded divorce on the ground of cruelty. During the nineteenth and twentieth centuries, grounds for divorce were expanded to include incapacity, crimes against nature with man or beast, alcohol and drug addiction, and certain felony convictions.

a)   Traditional Fault Grounds

Under the common law, and in most jurisdictions today, a divorce may still be granted on fault grounds.

(1)   Cruelty

Cruelty is the most common fault ground for divorce. Cruelty consists of acts and conduct which destroy the peace of mind and happiness of one of the parties to the marriage and thereby render the marital relationship intolerable. The function for the court is "not to determine intent but, rather, the result of the conduct of defendant and whether or not it was such as to render it 'unsafe or improper for the plaintiff to cohabit with the defendant.'" *Wenzel v. Wenzel*, 472 N.Y.S.2d 830 (N.Y. Sup. Ct Suffolk County 1988). In most jurisdictions that retain this ground, a court may consider mental or physical cruelty.

(2)   Adultery

Adultery is a ground for divorce in a majority of jurisdictions. Adultery is sexual intercourse by a spouse with another. A minority of jurisdictions consider homosexual relations as adultery.

(3)   Desertion/Abandonment

(a)   General Rule

Desertion is the "'voluntary separation of one of the married parties from the other with the intent to desert.' . . . Two elements . . . must be affirmatively stated, namely, the cessation of cohabitation and the intent to desert." *Hosking v. Hosking*, 186 P.2d 503 (Mont. 1947). In addition to these elements, many statutes require desertion for a minimum time period, generally one or two years.

(b) Constructive Desertion

"[T]he willful withdrawal from sexual intercourse, when accompanied by willful breach and neglect of other marital duties, is considered a general withdrawal from the duties of the marital relationship, and, if without just cause or excuse, constitutes desertion." *Petachenko v. Petachenko*, 232 Va. 296, 299 n.*, 350 S.E.2d 600, 602 n.* (1986) (citations omitted). However, "a mere denial of sexual intercourse, where other marital duties are performed, does not constitute desertion." *Id.* The constructive desertion must last for a significant period of time.

b) Defenses to Fault Grounds

These defenses apply only to fault-based grounds for divorce. They do not affect no-fault divorce.

(1) Connivance

Connivance has been defined as the plaintiff's consent, express or implied, to the misconduct alleged as a ground for divorce. Connivance denotes direction, influence, personal exertion, or other action with knowledge and belief that such action would produce certain results and which results are produced. The defense of connivance is based on the premise that one is not legally injured if he has consented to the act complained of or was willing that it should occur.

(2) Condonation

Condonation is a one spouse's forgiveness of another spouse's adulterous misconduct. Usually, condonation is evidenced by the resumption and continuation of normal matrimonial relations. Knowledge of the adultery is required before condonation can occur. Condonation differs from connivance in when the act of consent occurs. While condonation occurs after the misconduct, connivance occurs before the misconduct.

(3) Recrimination

Recrimination is the defense that the divorce petitioner has also committed a fault ground for divorce. It bars the divorce suit founded on cause, regardless of whether the defendant is guilty.

(4) Collusion

Collusion is an attempt to defraud the court by obtaining a divorce where no ground for it exists. For example, it is committed by the parties agreeing to commit adultery to create a ground for divorce.

(5) Justification

Justification is a defense to desertion. Justification is a valid defense if a party can demonstrate that, under the circumstance, she was justified in deserting the other party. Usually, a court will require a showing that the other spouse committed another ground for divorce or there was a constructive desertion.

c) No-Fault Divorce

Slightly less than half the states have completely abolished fault as a ground for divorce. The remainder of states supplement fault grounds with no-fault statutes. Although the procedure varies greatly state-by-state, no-fault divorce has been universally adopted.

(1) General Standard

The wording of statutes varies by jurisdiction. Some common statutes provide for no-fault divorce upon showings of "irreconcilable differences," "incompatibility," or "living separate and apart."

(2) Mutual Consent

Some courts have held that both parties must consent to the no-fault divorce. Otherwise, the petitioner must satisfactorily demonstrate that the marriage cannot be salvaged.

(3) UMDA

Under UMDA, may be dissolved if it is "irretrievably broken." The court must find: 1) that the parties have lived separately for 180 days; or 2) serious marital discord adversely affecting the attitude of one or more parties towards the marriage exists. Additionally, consent of both parties is not required under UMDA.

★ #### (4) Michigan Standard for Divorce (or Separate Maintenance)

In Michigan, a spouse can assert as a basis for a divorce (or separate maintenance) that a "breakdown of the marriage relationship" has occurred "to the extent that the objects of matrimony have been destroyed and there remains no reasonable likelihood that the marriage can be preserved." Mich. Comp. Laws §§ 552.6(1), 552.7(4). A plaintiff spouse's divorce complaint must make no other explanation of the grounds for divorce than the foregoing statutory language. Mich. Comp. Laws § 552.6(1). If the evidence shows that a "breakdown in the marriage relationship" has occurred "to the extent that the objects of matrimony have been destroyed" and "no reasonable likelihood that the marriage can be preserved" remains, the court must enter a judgment of divorce. Mich. Comp. Laws § 552.6(3). The evidence could include, for example, the parties' conduct.

d) Procedural Requirements for Divorce

★ #### (1) Domicile

The court must possess jurisdiction to enter a divorce decree. Most states require residency for a certain period such as 90 days to six months prior to commencement of the action. In order to file a complaint for divorce in Michigan, a spouse must reside in Michigan for 180 days and in the county for 10 days. Mich. Comp. Laws § 552.9(1).

B.   Jurisdiction and Recognition of Decrees

1)   ANNULMENT

a)   Which jurisdiction

Under the traditional rule, the state in which the marriage was entered into had jurisdiction to enter an annulment. If the parties were domiciled in another state at the time of the marriage, the state of domicile possessed jurisdiction. Under the modern majority rule, a state where either party is domiciled has jurisdiction to enter the divorce.

b)   Ex Parte

Under the traditional rule, an annulment could not be entered *ex parte*. Under the modern majority rule, however, annulments can be entered *ex parte* in the state where either spouse is domiciled.

★★   #### 2)   DIVORCE

Jurisdiction over divorces is vested solely in the state courts. Federal courts have no such jurisdiction.

a)   Jurisdiction over Divorce

(1)   Domicile is Critical

Under the Full Faith and Credit Clause of the United States Constitution, states must recognize and enforce a divorce granted by a court of a state if that state was the domicile of the petitioning person, regardless of whether that court had personal jurisdiction over the other spouse. A person is domiciled in the state in which the person resides with the intent to remain indefinitely. If a divorce is collaterally attacked in another state, the only issue in that state will be whether the petitioner was in fact domiciled in the first state. If it does, then all other states must give the divorce full faith and credit, provided that the petitioner gave the other spouse constitutionally adequate notice of the divorce proceedings.

(2)   Adequate Notice

Due process requires that a divorce petitioner provide adequate notice of the proceeding to the other spouse. Depending upon the circumstances, notice need not be actual. The inquiry is whether the person was served in a manner reasonably calculated to provide notice.

b)   Jurisdiction over Marital Property

A state may not assert jurisdiction to divide property that is located in another state. This distinction between the marriage and the property is called the concept of "divisible divorce." However, it may assert jurisdiction to divide their personal property located within its borders. The United States Supreme Court has held that due process requires that a state have "minimum contacts" with a defendant in another state to impose a child support obligation on that person. It can reasonably be inferred that the same test must be satisfied before a state may assert jurisdiction to divide property not located in that state. While *Shaffer v. Heitner* held that the presence of property in a state alone is an insufficient basis for the exercise of general personal jurisdiction, the Court suggested that a state may constitutionally assert jurisdiction to determine the ownership of property located in that state on that basis alone.

C.   Preliminary Interlocutory and Final Orders

1)   GENERAL

Some states grant interlocutory divorce orders. These orders are not final divorce decrees. Depending upon the statute, some jurisdictions provide that when an interlocutory order is in effect for a certain period of time, it automatically becomes final. In other jurisdictions, the court must enter a separate final decree.

2)   COMMON ISSUES

An issue that may arise in this context is what occurs if a spouse dies or gets remarried during this period.

a)   Remarriage

First, if a spouse gets remarried, that marriage is void as bigamous.

b)   Death

It is well-settled that the death of either spouse to a divorce proceeding before final decree abates the action. However, in some jurisdictions, in an action which has been bifurcated (divided into two portions – entry of divorce and division of property), if a divorce decree has been entered, the court may continue to divide the property after the death of a spouse.

★★★ D.   Division of Property

1)   ANNULMENT

Under the traditional rule, which is the majority rule, because the marriage was treated as a nullity, no support obligation exists absent statutory authority. Some jurisdictions, however, recognize the impracticality of the traditional rule and recognize support obligations in annulled marriages.

2)   DIVORCE

a)   Different Approaches

(1)   Traditional Separate Property Approach

In separate property states, each spouse continues to own any property the spouse owned before the marriage. Additionally, the spouse was entitled to any property she acquired during the marriage, regardless of how it was acquired (i.e., occupation, gift, inheritance, etc.). Unfortunately, the non-earning spouse was virtually property-less upon divorce.

★   (2)   Modern Equitable Distribution Doctrine

Most states provide for an "equitable distribution" of property upon divorce. Michigan provides for an "equitable division" (i.e., "equitable distribution") of the marital assets. A court attempts to arrive at a fair distribution of marital property.

(a)   Fault Not Considered – Some States

Fault is generally not taken into account in modern property division.

★   (b)   Fault Considered -- Michigan

Although Michigan is a no-fault divorce state, fault can play a role in the court's division and award of marital assets. *Sparks v. Sparks*, 440 Mich. 141 (1992). In particular, the parties' conduct is one of several factors described later that the court can consider in dividing and awarding marital assets. *Id.*

(3)   Community Property States

Property acquired during marriage, other than by gift or inheritance, is generally marital property equally owned by both spouses. Pre-marital property and any property acquired by gift or inheritance remains separate property of each spouse. When divorced, the court must assign the separate property to the each spouse and divides marital property.

★★★   b)   Equitable Distribution Approach

The standard in Michigan is an "equitable division" (i.e., "equitable distribution") of the marital assets. The equitable distribution of property is a three-step process. First, a court must classify assets as marital or separate property. Second, the court must value the assets of the parties. Finally, the court must arrive at a distribution of the marital assets.

★★   (1)   Marital/Separate Property

(a)   Marital Property

Property, which spouses acquire during the marriage, is presumed to be marital property. Uniform Marital Property Act § 4(b)(1983); Uniform Marriage and Divorce Act (UMDA) § 307, 9 U.LA. 490 (1973); H. Clark, *The Law of Domestic Relations, Second* § 15.2 & nn.3,7 (1988). Unlike under the traditional rule, the fact that title to property is held in one spouse's name alone does not rebut this presumption.

(i)   Marital Property Definition and Exclusions

In Michigan, marital property (i.e., a marital asset) is defined as property accumulated during the marriage as a result of one or both parties' contributions or efforts during the marriage. This is generally interpreted to mean property acquired during the marriage, excluding gifted or inherited property or passive appreciation of premarital property. *Reeves v. Reeves,* 226 Mich. App. 490 (1997). Also, Michigan courts usually award "stay at home" mothers an equitable division of a husband's business when declaring the business a marital asset. *Id.* and *Hanaway v. Hanaway,* 208 Mich. App. 278 (1995).

★   (ii)   Retirement Accounts — Michigan

Retirement accounts opened and funded during marriage may be marital assets. Division of them upon divorce will depend on whether the accounts were established prior to the marriage. If most of the funds were accumulated during the marriage, the entire account will most likely be a marital asset. If the court awards one party's retirement account, or a portion thereof, to the other party, a Qualified Domestic Relations Order must be executed by the court as a part of the divorce judgment.

(iii)   Acquisition of Advanced Degree

Generally, one non-student spouse's contribution to the other student spouse's acquisition of an advance degree by means of "concerted family effort" may give rise to the non-student spouse's equitable claim for compensation in terms of the advance degree constituting marital property (i.e., asset) subject to distribution. *Postema v. Postema,* 189 Mich. App. 89 (1991). Basically, concerted family effort involves these spouses' "mutual sacrifice, effort, and contribution" towards acquisition of the advance degree. *Id.* Such a *Postema* claim for compensation is distinct and separate from an award of spousal support (i.e., alimony). *Id.* Note that a *Postema* claim for compensation in property distribution is not a factor in a determination of spousal support. *Id.*

(iv)   Causes of Action

Generally, causes of action are marital property. *Heilman v. Heilman,* 95 Mich. App. 728 (1980).

(b)   Separate Property

Separate property generally includes:

- All property of either spouse owned by the spouse before marriage;
- All property acquired during marriage by either by gift or inheritance (i.e., bequest, devise, or descent);
- All property either spouse acquires with the proceeds of the spouse's separate property.

Michigan law generally follows this rule. *Reeves v. Reeves,* 226 Mich. App. 490 (1997).

(i)   Personal Injury Awards

Personal injury awards for pain and suffering are personal to the injured party. *Bywater v. Bywater*, 128 Mich. App. 396 (1983).

★★   (ii)   Separate Property Awarded to Other Spouse

In some jurisdictions, some property acquired before a marriage can be distributed to both spouses. For example, if property is acquired in anticipation of a marriage, and for use by the married couple, it may be divided among the spouses.

In Michigan, a court may only award one party's separate property to the other party if the claimant meets one of two tests: 1) that the claimant contributed to the acquisition, improvement, or accumulation of the property, or 2) that the award to the claimant out of the marital assets is insufficient for the suitable support and maintenance of the claimant and any children in his or her care. Mich. Comp. Laws §§ 552.401, 552.23.

In other words, Michigan law allows separate assets to be invaded when one or another of two statutory exceptions occurs. One is when a party to divorce demonstrates added need. Mich. Comp. Laws § 552.23(1). The other is for "contribution to the acquisition, improvement, or accumulation of the property." Mich. Comp. Laws § 552.401. "When one significantly assists in the acquisition or growth of a spouse's separate asset, the court may consider the contribution as having a distinct value deserving of compensation." *Reeves v. Reeves,* 226 Mich. App. 490 (1997).

Separate estates may be invaded if necessary to provide suitable support and maintenance of the other party. *Id.* and Mich. Comp. Laws §§ 552.19, 552.23, 552.101.

In Michigan, the court must make a provision in lieu of dower of the wife in the property of the husband. Mich. Comp. Laws § 552.101.

★   (c)   Commingling

Commingling involves the mixture of separate property and marital property. For example, money from a trust (that was a separate asset before and during marriage), which was applied towards the purchase of a marital asset of the marital home during marriage, may be commingled with this marital asset during marriage.

In this situation, "the sharing and maintenance of a marital home affords both spouses an interest in any increase in its value (whether by equity payments or appreciation) over the term of a marriage. Such amount is clearly part of the marital estate. However, [in this case] the down payment, the equity built up before the parties' marriage, and any appreciation that occurred before the parties' marriage should have been considered defendant [spouse]'s separate estate." *Reeves v. Reeves,* 226 Mich. App. 490 (1997).

(d)   Judicial Classification Doctrines

(i)   Source of Funds

In some states, a court will examine whether marital or separate funds were used to acquire the property. This issue often arises in the context of encumbered real property. For example, assume a husband enters a marriage with title to Blackacre in his name. Blackacre, however, has a mortgage equivalent to its market value when the husband marries. During the marriage, mortgage payments are made using marital property. If a court employs the "source of funds" doctrine, it would classify Blackacre as marital property.

(ii)   Inception of Title

The inception of title rule is the alternative approach to "source of funds" doctrine. Under the inception of title rule, classification of property stems back to the first inception of title. In the above example regarding Blackacre, the real property would be classified as the husband's separate property under the inception of title rule.

(iii)   Transmutation

Transmutation is the process by which property changes classification as time passes.

(2)   Distribution

Courts are afforded significant discretion in determining the equitable distribution of property upon divorce. Several statutes enumerate factors that should be considered.

(a)   50/50 Presumption

A few jurisdictions possess a presumption that a 50/50 division is equitable. Other jurisdictions use 50/50 as a starting point. A number of jurisdictions, however, do not use either of these approaches. In Michigan, division of marital property need not be equal in order to be equitable.

(3)   Factors to Consider for Property Division

★

(a)   General Considerations

Courts are afforded significant discretion in determining the equitable distribution of property upon divorce. Several statutes enumerate factors that should be considered. General factors that courts consider include:

- Finances - The income, property, and liabilities of each party;
- Duration - The duration of the marriage;
- Prior Obligation - Any obligation for support arising out of a prior marriage;
- Contribution to Career - The contribution made by one spouse to help educate or develop the career potential of the other spouse;
- Contribution to Property Acquisition - Any direct or indirect contribution made to the acquisition of the marital property by a party not having title, including a contribution as a home-maker;
- Just and Proper - Any other factor which the court finds to be just and proper.

(b)   Michigan Considerations

In Michigan, all marital property is subject to equitable division by the family court. *Sparks v. Sparks,* 440 Mich. 141 (1992). The court must consider many factors in deciding what is equitable including: (1) the duration of the marriage; (2) contributions of the parties to the marital estate; (3) the age of the parties; (4) the health of the parties; (5) life status of the parties; (6) necessities and circumstances of the parties; (7) earning ability of the parties; (8) past relations and conduct of the parties, and (9) general principles of equity. *Id.*

With respect to the foregoing factor of the parties' relations and conduct, although tort claims that relate to their marital relationship's very existence cannot be maintained as separate actions in a divorce proceeding, a court can consider those tort damages when making an award of property. *Gubin v. Lodisev,* 197 Mich. App. 84 (1992).

c)   Hotchpot Approach (Minority)

A minority of states (about fourteen) authorize the courts to divide all the property held by the spouses at the time of divorce without regard to when, how, or by whom the property was acquired or how the title was held. This is known as the "hotchpot" approach. Uniform Marriage and Divorce Act (UMDA), Alternative A, 9 U.L.A. (Part I) 288 (1988).

E.   Maintenance or Alimony

In Michigan, spousal support is the legal term generally used to refer to support payments that may be awarded from one spouse to the other one in a separate maintenance or divorce case. These payments, which provide for an adverse party's suitable maintenance, are also known as alimony in Michigan. Mich. Comp. Laws § 552.13(1).

★★   1)   GENERAL FACTORS

Spousal support is to be awarded to either spouse if the spouse's separate property is insufficient for the maintenance of a spouse. The award must be based on a number of factors, including the payor's ability to pay, the recipient's need and ability to be self-supporting, the duration of the marriage, and the marital standard of living. Courts are afforded great discretion in making this determination. A court will usually examine a spouse's need under the totality of the circumstances.

a) Need and Contribution

In all equitable distribution states, spousal contribution and need are the primary factors in property division. Homemaking and parenting are recognized forms of spousal contribution. These same services, when they substitute for paid employment over a lengthy period, will also evidence a spouse's need. ALI PRINCIPLES. Some equitable distribution states have a presumption that a homemaker's contribution is equal to a breadwinner's and that an equal division is most just. *E.g., Brown v. Brown,* 914 P.2d 206, 209 (Alaska 1996); Or. Rev. Stat. Sec. 107.105(1)(f).

(1) Minority Rule

In a minority of states, a person is not considered to be in need if the person has sufficient income to support a modest standard of living, regardless of the marital standard of living. However, in most states, spouses are considered to be in need if their income is insufficient to maintain the marital standard of living, at least in some circumstances.

b) Michigan Rules and Factors

A Michigan divorce court possesses discretion to award alimony as it deems just and reasonable. Mich. Comp. Laws § 552.23; *Ianitelli v. Ianitelli,* 199 Mich. App. 641 (1993). The primary objective of alimony is to balance the parties' needs and incomes in a manner that will not impoverish either of them. *Hanaway v. Hanaway,* 208 Mich. App. 278 (1995).

In Michigan, when deciding whether to award spousal support, the court must make findings on each of the following relevant factors: (1) the parties' past relations and conduct; (2) the length of the marriage; (3) the parties' ability to work; (4) the source and amount of property awarded to the parties; (5) the parties' ages; (6) the ability to pay spousal support; (7) the parties' present situation; (8) the parties' needs; (9) the parties' health; (10) the prior standard of living of the parties and whether the parties support others; (11) the parties' contributions to their joint estate; (12) any party's fault in causing the divorce; (13) the effect of the parties' mutual, premarital cohabitation on a party's financial status; and (14) general principles of equity. *Sparks v. Sparks,* 440 Mich. 141 (1992); *Olson v. Olson,* 256 Mich. App. 619 (2003).

With respect to the foregoing factor of the parties' relations and conduct, although tort claims that relate to their marital relationship's very existence cannot be maintained as separate actions in a divorce proceeding, a court can consider those tort damages when making an award of alimony. *Gubin v. Lodisev,* 197 Mich. App. 84 (1992).

c) Fault as a Factor

In most states other than Michigan, marital fault cannot be taken into account in making alimony determinations. In Michigan, the court can consider fault when deciding whether to award spousal support. *E.g., Korth v. Korth*, 256 Mich. App. 286 (2003).

In virtually all states, "economic" fault, including dissipation of marital assets, is relevant to property distribution. Ellman, Kurtz & Scott, *supra*, at 414 (mentioning "general agreement that dissipation of assets is a relevant factor in the equitable distribution of property"). Dissipation is generally thought to be "the use of marital property for the sole benefit of one of the spouses for a purpose unrelated to the marriage at a time that the marriage is undergoing an irreconcilable breakdown." *In re Marriage of O'Neill*, 563 N.E.2d 494, 497 (Ill. 1990).

> 2)   TYPES OF SPOUSAL SUPPORT

> a)   Temporary/*Pendente Lite*

A court may award temporary alimony while a divorce action is pending in order to provide for the spouse until the final order is entered. *E.g.,* Mich. Comp. Laws § 552.13(1).

★   b)   Permanent Support

"Permanent" spousal maintenance awards were more common under the common law. Today, courts are less likely to award "permanent" alimony unless the spouse is older and lacks job skills. "Permanent" alimony lasts until a spouse dies or remarries. Permanent spousal support can be awarded in Michigan. *Id.*; *e.g., Gates v. Gates*, 256 Mich. App. 420 (2003). The court must consider a number of factors set forth earlier, including the length of the marriage, the respective incomes of the parties, past relations and conduct, ability to work, and need. A spousal support determination can also be affected by the property awarded to the parties in the case. Generally, the amount of spousal support awarded should be just and reasonable under the circumstances. *Id.*

> c)   Lump Sum Payments

A court may award a lump sum maintenance award.

★   d)   Rehabilitative Support

Today, because most parents are in the work force, courts no longer favor permanent support. Instead, provisions are made for "rehabilitative" support, which lasts for a finite period of time. Courts take the factors set forth above into account and set the time period for which support is required. Rehabilitative spousal support can be awarded in Michigan. *Id.* The court must consider a number of factors set forth earlier, including the length of the marriage, the respective incomes of the parties, past relations and conduct, ability to work, and need. A spousal support determination can also be affected by the property awarded to the parties in the case. Generally, the amount of spousal support awarded should be just and reasonable under the circumstances. *Id.*

3)   UMDA TWO-STEP APPROACH – ELIGIBILITY AND AMOUNT

Under the UMDA, spousal maintenance determinations are a two-step process. First, a court must determine that the spouse is eligible. Second, the court must determine what amount is proper.

a)   Eligibility

Under the UMDA, a spouse is eligible for spousal maintenance if:

1)   The spouse lacks property sufficient for the spouse's reasonable needs; and
2a)   The spouse is unable to support themselves through gainful employment; or
2b)   The spouse is the custodian of a child such that it would be inappropriate for the spouse to work.

b)   Amount

Once a court determines that a person is eligible for spousal maintenance, the court must determine the appropriate amount to award. Typical factors include:

- The financial resources of the party seeking maintenance;
- The time necessary to acquire sufficient education or training to enable the party to find appropriate employment;
- The standard of living established during the marriage;
- The duration of the marriage;
- The age, physical and emotional condition, and financial obligations of the spouse seeking maintenance; and
- The ability of the spouse from whom maintenance is sought to meet his needs and financial obligations while meeting those of the spouse seeking maintenance.

c)   Fault as a Factor

(1)   UMDA – Fault not a factor

Fault may not be considered under UMDA § 308(b) and under the laws of many states.

(2)   Minority Rule – Fault can be taken into account

In a few states, however, the commission of adultery or the existence of another basis of fault could preclude a spouse from being awarded spousal support. In others, it would diminish the amount she received. Clark, *supra,* § 16.4 & n.21.

★★   **F.   Child Support**

1)   GENERAL FACTORS

Child support awards are generally based on several factors including:

- finances - the parents' capacity to pay;
- income - the parents' income;
- standard of living - the standard of living the child would have had if the marriage were not dissolved; and
- needs - the needs (physical, emotional, educational, etc.) of the children.

2)   STATE CHILD SUPPORT GUIDELINES

All states possess child support guidelines, as required by federal law. Social Security Act, 42 U.S.C. § 667. The guidelines must consider the income of the non-custodial parent and must also provide for the child's health care needs. 45 C.F.R. § 302.56 (1996).

a)   Guideline Amount is Presumed Proper

In all states, the amount produced by the formula is presumed to be the proper amount of the award, although this presumption is rebuttable. Although you do not need to know what the guidelines are, you should generally be aware that they exist. Deviations from the guideline can be made only upon express findings of fact.

★★   (1)   Michigan's Child Support Formula

In Michigan, to determine whether a spouse will be required to pay child support, the court (through the Friend of the Court) will apply the Michigan Child Support Formula. The formula is based upon the needs of the child and the actual resources of the parent. The court may deviate from the formula if it determines that application would be unjust or inappropriate. Numerous factors are considered such as parental income, family size, the ages of the children, child care, dependent health care coverage costs, and other criteria. The Michigan Child Support Formula also takes into consideration the amount of time spent with the non-custodial parent and credit is allowed for consecutive time spent with the non-custodial parent.

b)   High Income Parents

Where the parents' combined income is very high, some state guidelines establish a presumptive amount that would be far more than any measure of the children's needs. Other guidelines would not address this situation at all. In either case, most courts probably would not apply the guidelines or extrapolate from them in a way that resulted in an extremely high award. Instead, the primary factor that a court would most likely consider is the children's needs, generously defined. Clark, *supra,* § 17.1. Another factor might be the degree of luxury established during the marriage. UMDA § 309. Lynn D. Wardle, Christopher L. Blakesley & Jacqueline Y. Parker, *Contemporary Family Law: Principles, Policy and Practice* § 38.02 (1988).

3)   *PENDENTE LITE* CHILD SUPPORT ORDERS

A court may enter a child support *pendente lite* (during the course of divorce proceedings), to provide for the children until the final support order is entered.

4) DURATION OF CHILD SUPPORT OBLIGATIONS

★★

a) Child Support Prior to Majority

In Michigan, parents are jointly obligated to support their minor child. Their child support obligations generally last until the child becomes emancipated by operation of law (i.e., emancipation). Mich. Comp. Laws § 722.4.

(1) Events Causing Emancipation

* minor child reaches the age of majority -- 18 years old;
* valid marriage; or
* active military duty.

★

b) Child Support Post-Majority

Michigan's child support laws allow courts to order post-majority support for the benefit of a child between the ages of 18 and 19 if the child: 1) is regularly attending high school full time; 2) has a reasonable expectation of completing sufficient credits to graduate from high school, and 3) *is* living full time with the payee of support or at an institution. *Rowley v. Garvin,* 221 Mich. App. 699 (1997).

✶

5) CHILD SUPPORT ARREARAGE

In Michigan, a parent owed unpaid child support can collect at any time. An income withholding order or a contempt order may be issued to enforce this obligation. Mich. Comp. Laws §§ 552.151, 552.607.

★

6) EQUITABLE PARENT DOCTRINE

Michigan law recognizes the "equitable parent" doctrine when a child is born and conceived during the marriage, and the parent and child acknowledge a relationship as parent and child, although the husband is not the biological father. The husband must desire the rights of paternity and must be willing to pay child support. *Atkinson v. Atkinson,* 160 Mich. App. 601 (1987). This doctrine essentially allows a third party to exercise parental rights, including custody and parenting time. The court has refused to extend this doctrine when the parties are not married and the child was born out of wedlock (i.e., illegitimate child).

★

7) CHILD BORN OUT OF WEDLOCK

In Michigan, responsibility for a child depends on the status as a parent, not marriage. A child born out of wedlock's parents are liable for the child's support. Mich. Comp. Laws § 722.712(1). A mother of such a child can claim support from the child's father upon proving his paternity. *Id.* Generally, a father is responsible for a child if (1) he admits paternity or (2) it is established by evidence of a DNA test if the father denies paternity.

G. Modification of Maintenance and Child Support

★   1)   SPOUSAL MAINTENANCE MODIFICATION

Modification of spousal support is allowed only upon a showing of a substantial and continuing change in circumstances making the prior order unreasonable. Under the UMDA, a modification of spousal support is allowed "only upon a showing of changed circumstances so substantial and continuing as to make the terms unconscionable." Unif. Marriage and Div. Act § 316(a), 9A D.L.A. 102 (1987). Most jurisdictions are not as stringent as UMDA, but most place a heavy burden on the party requesting the modification (e.g., requiring a substantial change in circumstances that rendered the original award unreasonable and unfair). *E.g., Gates v. Gates*, 256 Mich. App. 420 (2003) (must show new facts or changed circumstances). Courts consider whether the change in circumstances was anticipated at the time the original award was made and the good faith of the party asking for the modification. *E.g., Pope* v. *Pope,* 559 N.W.2d 192 (Neb. 1997). A change in the payor's ability to pay or in the recipient's needs may be taken into account.

★★   2)   CHILD SUPPORT MODIFICATION

Under the UMDA, modification of a child support order is allowed "only upon a showing of changed circumstances so substantial and continuing as to make the terms unconscionable." Unif. Marriage and Div. Act § 316(a), 9A U.LA. 102 (1987). However, modifications based on changed circumstances are allowed in most jurisdictions upon the less stringent showing of a material or substantial change of circumstances, although the burden on the party requesting the modification is still a heavy one. Donald T. Kramer, *Legal Rights of Children* § 4.07 (2d ed. 1994 and Supp. 1997). *E.g.,* generally Mich. Comp. Laws § 552.517b(8). Under any standard, however, the changes must be more or less permanent, rather than temporary. *Id.*

a)   No Retroactive Adjustments

Under UMDA, a modification of support can be made retroactive only from the date of service of the motion to modify on the other party. Unif. Marriage and Div. Act § 316(a), 9A U.L.A. 102 (1987). Therefore, if a court were able to modify the child support obligation, the modification could only be made retroactive to the date of service.

Federal law requires the same result with respect to retroactive modification of child support orders. Section IV-D of the Social Security Act requires a state, as a condition of participation in the federally funded child support programs, to have procedures that require that "any payment or installment of support under any child support order. . . [be] . . . not subject to retroactive modification by such State or by any other State." 42 U.S.C. § 666(a)(9).

b)   Jurisdiction to Modify Child Support Order

(1)   General

The interstate enforcement of child support orders is governed by the Uniform Interstate Family Support Act (UIFSA), which has been adopted by every state. Under the UIFSA, a registered child support order issued in another state is "enforceable in the same manner and is subject to the same procedures as an order issued by a tribunal of this State." Mich. Comp. Laws § 552.1603.

(2)   Continuing Jurisdiction

Under the UIFSA, the state that originally issued a child support order has continuing, exclusive jurisdiction to modify the order if that state remains the residence of the support obligee, the child, or the obligor. Therefore, no other court may attempt to modify such an order. *E.g.,* Mich. Comp. Laws § 552.1224(1)(a).

If all of the parties no longer reside in the forum, the court no longer possesses continuing exclusive jurisdiction. Additionally, the parties may consent to the jurisdiction of another forum.

H.   Enforcement of Awards

1)   FULL FAITH AND CREDIT

Under federal law, states are required to give full faith and credit to child support awards from other states. Under a federal statute, each state: "(1) shall enforce according to its terms a child support order made consistently with this section by a court of another State." 28 U.S.C. § 1738B(a). Section 1738B is known as the Full Faith and Credit for Child Support Orders Act.

2)   SOCIAL SECURITY ACT

Section IV-D of the Social Security Act also requires a state, as a condition of participation in the federally funded child support programs, to have procedures that require that "any payment or installment of support under any child support order. . . [be] . . . entitled as a judgment to full faith and credit in such State and in any other State." 42 U.S.C. § 666(a)(9). This amendment to the Social Security Act may also be called The Child Support Enforcement Act or the IV-D Program.

3)   UNIFORM INTERSTATE FAMILY SUPPORT ACT

The same result is mandated by the Uniform Interstate Family Support Act (UIFSA), legislation which states are required to adopt under federal law. Section IV-D of the Social Security Act requires that a state, as a condition of participation in the federally funded child support programs, have the UIFSA in effect. 42 U.S.C. § 666(f). The UIFSA provides a simple procedure for the registration of the child support order of another state. The order is then enforced in the same manner as an order issued by the registering state. UIFSA § 603.

I.   Mediation and Other Alternative Means of Dispute Resolution

Alternative dispute resolution (ADR) techniques in the context of divorce disputes have been gaining increased support. Due to the overwhelming adoption of no-fault bases for divorce actions, ADR has become an attractive alternative to protracted and expensive litigation – especially when children are involved. ADR takes many different forms, but the two most important for divorce purposes are mediation and arbitration.

1)   MEDIATION

In mediations regarding divorce disputes, a neutral mediator can assist the parties in achieving acceptable resolutions regarding custody and support agreements, as well as property division.

a)   Role of the Mediator

The role of the mediator is not to attempt to reconcile the parties. Rather, the mediator's goal is to seek a quick, inexpensive and mutually agreeable resolution of the issues.

b)   Voluntary

In contrast to child support mediation, which is mandated in some states, divorce mediation is generally a voluntary process.

2)   ARBITRATION

Arbitration is a process by which the parties to a dispute voluntarily submit the dispute to a third-party decision-maker whose opinion is binding. A few states use arbitration to settle divorce disputes. Arbitration is an attractive alternative because it avoids the time-delay and public nature of litigation proceedings.

a)   Finality of Decisions

Generally, the decision of an arbitrator is final unless: 1) it was procured fraudulently; or 2) the arbitrator did not act impartially.

J.   Separation Agreements

1)   GENERAL

Generally, in order to facilitate a swift and amicable settlement of marital disputes, separation agreements are generally upheld. If an agreement is entered into when divorce or separation is imminent and it is not unconscionable, then public policy weighs in favor of enforcement. Separation agreements usually govern the consequences of divorce including property division and spousal maintenance. "Absent fraud, coercion, or duress, the adults to the marriage have the right and the freedom to decide what is a fair and appropriate division of the marital assets, and our [Michigan state] courts should not rewrite such agreements." *Lentz v. Lentz*, 271 Mich. App. 465 (2006) (declining to analyze separation agreement in same manner as premarital contract).

2)   CONTRACT REQUIREMENTS GOVERN

A separation agreement must adhere to contract requirements in order to be enforceable. As long as the agreement is not unconscionable, it will be enforced.

3)   EFFECT OF RECONCILIATION

Reconciliation of the parties effectively voids all executory provisions of a separation agreement.

IV.   CHILD CUSTODY

There are two types of custody. They are legal and physical custody. Physical custody is actual possession of the child. Legal custody is the right to make decisions for the child (educational, medical, etc.).

A.   Standards for Decision

★★★   1)   BEST INTERESTS STANDARD

In all American jurisdictions including Michigan custody of the children would be determined by their "best interests." H. Clark, *The Law of Domestic Relations in the United States* § 19.4 (2nd 1988); Mich. Comp. Laws §§ 722.23, 722.25(1).

a)   Initial Consideration of Established Custodial Environment

A determination of whether an established custodial environment exists is the initial step in deciding any child custody dispute. *Stringer v. Vincent*, 161 Mich. App. 429 (1987). A Michigan court may not issue a new order that changes a child's established custodial environment unless clear and convincing evidence shows that this change is in the child's *best interest*. Mich. Comp. Laws § 722.27(1)(c). An established custodial environment exists if, "over an appreciable time, the child naturally looks to the custodian in that environment for guidance, discipline, the necessities of life, and parental comfort." *Id*. Also, the court must consider the child's age, the physical environment, and the inclination of the custodian and the child as to permanency of their relationship. *Id*. Next, the court will consider the substantive law of Michigan child custody factors.

b)   Michigan Child Custody Factors

Before making a child custody determination, a Michigan state court must consider and make findings on each of the following multiple statutory child custody factors (also known as the "best interests" factors), even if only to say that a factor is irrelevant, to determine what custody order will serve the children's best interests. *Overall v. Overall*, 203 Mich. App. 450 (1994).

A.   The love, affection, and other emotional ties existing between the parties involved and the child;

B.   The capacity and disposition of the parties involved to give the child love, affection, and guidance and to continue the education and raising of the child in the child's religion or creed, if any;

C.   The capacity and disposition of the parties involved to provide the child with food, clothing, medical care, or other remedial care recognized and permitted under the laws of Michigan in place of medical care, and other material needs;

D.   The length of time the child has lived in a stable, satisfactory environment, and the desirability of maintaining continuity;

E.   The permanence, as a family unit, of the existing or proposed custodial home or homes;

F.   The moral fitness of the parties involved;

The entire analysis of all these factors seeks to evaluate parents solely as to how the factor relates to how they will function as a parent; it does not seek to determine which parent is morally superior as a human being. *Fletcher v. Fletcher*, 447 Mich. 871 (1994).

G.   The mental and physical health of the parties involved;

H.   The home, school, and community record of the child;

I.   The recognizable preference of the child, if the court considers the child to be of sufficient age to express preference;

Although a Michigan state court must consider all these multiple factors to determine what custody order will serve the children's best interests, in some circumstances, one of the most important considerations could be the wishes of the children. In some states other than Michigan, if a child has reached sufficient age, the court must award custody consistently with the child's wishes. In Michigan, at no age is the preference of a child determinative of the custodial situation. *Id.*

More commonly courts consider a child's wishes, and as the age and maturity of the child increases, the wishes are given greater weight. In Michigan, the court may take into account the child's preference if the child is old enough to express a preference. Mich. Comp. Laws § 722.23. In that event, the Michigan state court is required, upon request of either parent, to interview the minor children. This interview is done privately by the court and the statements of the children are not revealed to either party or the attorneys. *Fletcher v. Fletcher*, 200 Mich. App. 505 (1993). The court has the discretion to attach whatever importance the court decides to the statements of the child. The court must limit its discussions with the child to a determination of the child's preference. *Molloy v. Molloy*, 243 Mich. App. 595 (2000).

J.   The willingness and ability of each of the parties to facilitate and encourage a close and continuing parent-child relationship between the child and the other parent or the child and the parents;

K.   Domestic violence, regardless of whether the violence was directed against or witnessed by the child;

L.   Any other factor considered by the court to be relevant to a particular child custody dispute.

Mich. Comp. Laws § 722.23.

With respect to that last statutory factor, for example, parental fitness and fault may also be an issue, even though Michigan is a no-fault divorce state. Such other factors must be considered along with all other factors to determine the child's best interest.

(1)   Relevancy of Factors

Not every factor is relevant to every case, but a Michigan state court must make a finding on each factor (even if only to say it is irrelevant). *Overall v. Overall*, 203 Mich. App. 450 (1994). The court makes its finding based on the best interest factors overall; there is no numerical "scoring."

An exam question focusing on the issue of child custody is an excellent opportunity to showcase your ability to discuss and analyze a complex fact pattern. Your answer should be thorough and contain plenty of analysis. If you answer the question (conclude) too quickly, then you are missing possible points.

★★   2)   TENDER YEARS PRESUMPTION

In very few states, if any, courts may utilize the "tender years presumption." The presumption is grounded in the belief that a young child should be in the custody of the mother unless she is unfit. Because this expressly gender-based rule is of doubtful constitutionality, most states have abandoned it. Michigan law uses the best interest standard instead. Mich. Comp. Laws § 722.23.

3)   PRIMARY CARETAKER

a)   General Considerations

In response to the declining favor of the tender years presumption, a number of states have created a statutory or case law preference or presumption in favor of custody in a child's primary caretaker, an approach that may have the same effect as the tender years presumption without being expressly gender-based.

★★   4)   SAME GENDER PREFERENCE

Some states traditionally expressed preference for granting custody to the parent of the same gender as the child. This rule is also of doubtful constitutionality because it is expressly gender-based. Michigan law does not follow this rule. *Id.* Some empirical evidence supports the claim that on average, children do better when placed with the parent of the same gender. Therefore, a court could reach the same result without relying on the express gender-based rule.

5)   ABANDONMENT

a)   Majority - Subjective Test

In some states, a parent cannot be found to have abandoned her child so long as she subjectively intends to maintain a relationship with the child. Under this traditional law, to establish "abandonment," courts required proof that the parent subjectively intended to abandon the relationship. Proof of behavior that objectively suggests a fixed loss of interest in the child is not sufficient. *E.g., In re Adoption of Walton,* 123 Utah 380, 259 P.2d 881 (1953).

b)   Minority – Objective Test

Some states utilize an objective test for abandonment. If a parent has failed to express substantial interest in her child, the parent may be found to have abandoned the child, regardless of subjective intent. The inquiry under this test is whether the parent has acted in ways that indicate a commitment to maintaining the parent-child relationship, and includes factors such as whether the parent paid support or visited the child. *E.g., In the Matter of the Appeal in Pima County Juvenile Severance Action No. S-II4487,* 179 Ariz. 86, 876 P.2d 1121 (1994) (en banc).

B.   Visitation

    1)   <u>GENERAL</u>

        a)   Right and Denial of Right

When one parent is granted custody of a child, the other parent is usually entitled to visitation rights. A parent's visitation right is a natural right. It should only be denied under extreme circumstances such as when visitation could harm the child. An example of a circumstance that may justify denying visitation rights is if a parent is addicted to narcotics or if a parent has been convicted of extremely violent offenses.

★   b)   Parenting Time

The Michigan Complied Laws refer to child visitation by a parent of the child as parenting time. The relevant statute lists several factors for a court to consider when making decisions about parenting time. Mich. Comp. Laws § 722.27a. Moreover, parenting time must be granted to a parent in a frequency, duration, and type reasonably calculated to promote a strong relationship between the child and the parent granted parented time. *Id.* Among the statutory factors are the inconvenience to, and burdensome impact or effect on, the child of traveling for the purpose of parenting time and whether a parent can reasonably be expected to exercise parenting time in accordance with the court order and any other relevant factors. *Id.*

    2)   <u>THIRD PARTIES</u>

In most states, a court cannot award visitation rights to a third party without statutory authority. In a minority of states, however, courts may make such an award if it is in the child's best interest -- at least to parties who have stood in *loco parentis* to the child.

In this minority of states, statutes authorize courts to order visitation for a nonparent who has a substantial relationship with a child if visitation is in the child's best interest. *E.g.,* Or. Rev. Stat. § 109.119; Cal. Fam. Code § 3100(a); Alaska Stat. § 25.24.150(a). In the absence of such a statute, courts may lack jurisdiction to enter such orders because they are inconsistent with the parents' custodial rights, which include determining with whom a child will associate. *Troxel v. Granville,* 530 U.S. 57 (2000). Some courts, however, have held that they have inherent authority to make visitation orders in a child's best interest. *E.g., Spells v. Spells,* 250 Pa. Super. 168, 378 A.2d 879 (1977) (awarding visitation to a former stepparent); *Simpson v. Simpson,* 586 S.W.2d 33 (Ky. 1979) (adopting the in loco parentis approach in holding that visitation with a surrogate parent may be in the child's best interest); *Gribble v. Gribble,* 583 P.2d 64 (Utah 1978); *Rhinehart v. Nowlin,* 111 N.M. 319, 323, 805 P.2d 88, 92 (1990) (holding that the trial courts are given "exclusive jurisdiction of all matters relating to the guardianship, care, custody, maintenance and education of the children," which includes "the granting of visitation rights to a person or persons who the trial court determines are significant and important to the welfare of the children"); *Looper v. McManus,* 581 P.2d 487 (Okla. App. 1978); *Wills* v. *Wills,* 399 So. 2d 1130 (Fla. App. 1981); *Evans v. Evans,* 302 Md. 334, 488 A.2d 157 (1985). Although the status of third party visitation is still somewhat unclear, one thing is certain -- in order for any order granting third party visitation rights to be constitutionally permissible, great weight must be given to the parent's wishes when determining the best interests of the child.

★   3)   GRANDPARENT VISITATION

           a)   General Considerations

In some states, grandparents possess a statutory right to visitation. This right has been challenged by parents in several states. Courts are split as to whether grandparent visitation rights are constitutional as violations of the parent's right to control the upbringing of the child by excluding visits with grandparents. As with third party visitation in general, in order for any order granting grandparent visitation rights to be constitutionally permissible, great weight must be given to the parent's wishes when determining the best interests of the child.

           b)   Michigan Law

On July 31, 2003, the Michigan Supreme Court declared that Michigan's then-existing Grandparenting Time statute was unconstitutional because it removed all deference from the parents. *DeRose v. DeRose,* 469 Mich. 320 (2003). Consequently, the right of grandparents to ask the court for visitation with their grandchildren then ceased to exist for some time. *Id.* Since that decision, however, the Michigan Legislature has amended this statute. Mich. Comp. Laws § 722.27b (History). The amended statute includes provisions designed to protect the constitutional rights of parents as required by the foregoing decision of the Supreme Court. Butler, Durham & Toweson, PLLC, *Michigan Grandparent Visitation Law,* February 05, 2005, at http://www.divorcenet.com/states/michigan/michigan_grandparent_visitation_law. The amended statute includes legal standards that apply with respect to grandparents who were not allowed to visit their grandchildren. *Id.* The amended statute affords grandparents access to the courts to prove that they should be entitled to visit their grandchildren when they believe that an unreasonable denial of their visitation request occurred. *Id.*

       C.   **Joint Custody**

1)   INTRODUCTION

In recent years, some courts have moved away from granting sole custody in one parent. Instead, the parents are granted joint custody and, in theory, each possesses equal custody rights. If it appears to the court that joint custody would be in the best interest of the child, the court may grant custody to the parties jointly.

2)   MECHANICS OF JOINT CUSTODY

When parents are awarded joint custody, they share in the legal custody of the children. In other words, the both participate in decision-making regarding the upbringing of the child. Additionally, either or both parents may be awarded physical custody. However, as a practical matter, equality in physical custody is virtually impossible to achieve.

3)   TREATMENT OF JOINT CUSTODY BY THE STATES

Some states contain statutory presumptions favoring joint custody. In other states, most states in which it is statutorily recognized, a court must determine that joint custody is in the best interests of the child in order to award the parents joint custody.

D.   Enforcement

If the parent with custody refuses to permit judicially ordered visitation, a parent may attempt to enforce the visitation order through statutory or judicial remedies.

1)   STATUTORY REMEDIES

Many jurisdictions have enacted statutes providing for a judicial procedure to enforce visitation orders. If a parent does not comply with an order, under some of these statutes, a court may order the custodial parent to pay a bond to guarantee future compliance. Moreover, the custodial parent may be found in contempt of court, fined, or even sentenced to jail.

2)   JUDICIAL REMEDIES

Courts have found that custodial parents possess a duty to deliver the child to the noncustodial parent for visitation. Courts possess great discretion to enforce visitation orders if a custodial parent attempts to evade the noncustodial parent or influence the child against the noncustodial parent in any manner. In extreme circumstances, a court has even reversed a custody determination.

E.   Procedural Issues

1)   JURISDICTION TO DECIDE CUSTODY

★   a)   General – Original Jurisdiction

Michigan law provides that, in matters regarding children (e.g., child support, parenting time, physical and legal custody), the divorce court has continuing jurisdiction to modify the judgment when there is a significant change in circumstances or proper cause which warrants that change. Mich. Comp. Laws §§ 552.17a, 722.27.

Pursuant to the Uniform Child Custody Jurisdiction and Enforcement Act (UCCJEA), adopted in most states, a court has exclusive continuing jurisdiction to make a child custody determination as follows:

★   (1)   Home State Test

A jurisdiction has "home state" jurisdiction if: 1) it is the home state of the child at the time of commencement of the proceeding; or 2) the state had been the child's home state within six months before commencement of the proceeding, and the child is absent from this State because of his removal or retention by a person claiming his custody or for other reasons, and a parent or person acting as parent continues to live in this State.

If a state possesses and exercises home state jurisdiction, then no other state can take jurisdiction.

(2)   Significant Connection Test

If no state possesses home state jurisdiction, or if the home state declines jurisdiction, then a court may exercise jurisdiction based on one of the following tests.

A jurisdiction has "Significant Connection Jurisdiction" if it would be in the best interest of the child that a court of the State assume jurisdiction because: 1) the child and his parents, or the child and at least one contestant, have a significant connection with this State; and 2) there is available in the State substantial evidence concerning the child's present or future care, protection, training, and personal relationships.

(3)   Other Court Defers to State

All courts having jurisdiction under the home state and significant connection tests have declined to exercise jurisdiction on the ground that a court of this state is the more appropriate forum to determine the custody of the child; or

(4)   No Other State Jurisdiction

No court of any other state would have jurisdiction under the first three provisions.

(5)   Temporary Emergency Jurisdiction

A court has temporary emergency jurisdiction if the child is present in the state and the child has been abandoned or it is necessary in an emergency to protect the child, a sibling or parent of the child.

(a)   Physical Presence

Physical presence, in a State, of the child and/or a contestant is not alone sufficient to confer jurisdiction on a court to make a child custody determination.

Additionally, physical presence of the child, although desirable, is not required for jurisdiction to determine custody.

b)   Jurisdiction to Modify Other State Order

A court will not modify a child custody determination made by a court of another state unless the court has jurisdiction to make an initial determination under either the home state or significant connection test.

Even if it does satisfy one of these prongs, however, 1) the other state's court must have determined it no longer has exclusive, continuing jurisdiction or that a court of this state would be a more convenient forum or 2) the court must determine that the child, the child's parents, and any person acting as a parent do not presently reside in the other state.

c)   Balancing Doctrines

Once a court determines that it has jurisdiction, it must then apply the following balancing doctrines to determine whether to retain jurisdiction.

(1)   Inconvenient Forum

A court may decline to exercise jurisdiction if it is an inconvenient forum and the court in another state is a more appropriate forum. A court must examine several factors in making such a determination.

(a)   Factors

The relevant factors that favor a finding that a state is an inconvenient forum are:

- whether domestic violence or mistreatment or abuse of a child or sibling has occurred and is likely to continue in the future and which state could best protect the parties and the child;

- the length of time the child has resided outside this state;

- the distance between the court in this state and the court in the state that would assume jurisdiction;

- the relative financial circumstances of the parties;

- any agreement of the parties as to which state should assume jurisdiction;

- the nature and location of the evidence required to resolve the pending litigation, including testimony of the child;

- the ability of the court of each state to decide the issue expeditiously and the procedures necessary to present the evidence; and
- the familiarity of the court of each state with the facts and issues in the pending litigation.

    (2)   Unclean Hands

        (a)   Common Law and UCCJEA (modification only)

Under this doctrine at common law, courts refused to assume jurisdiction to reexamine an out-of-state custody decree when the petitioner had abducted the child or had engaged in some other objectionable scheme to gain or retain physical custody of the child in violation of the decree. Fain, *Custody of Children*, The California Family Lawyer I, 539, 546 (1961); *Ex Parte Mullins*, 26 Wash.2d 419, 174 P.2d 790 (1946); *Crocker v. Crocker*, 122 Colo. 49, 219 P.2d 311 (1950); and *Leathers v. Leathers*, 162 Cal.App.2d 768, 328 P.2d 853 (1958). But if adherence to this rule would lead to punishment of the parent at the expense of the well being of the child, it will not be applied. *Smith v. Smith*, 135 Cal.App.2d 100, 286 P.2d 1009 (1955) and *In re Guardianship of Rodgers*, 100 Ariz. 269, 413 P.2d 744 (1966).

The most common violation is the removal of the child from the state by the parent who has the right to custody, thereby frustrating the exercise of visitation rights of the other parent. The refusal of jurisdiction is entirely discretionary because it depends on the circumstances whether non-compliance with the initial court order is serious enough to warrant the drastic sanction of denial of jurisdiction.

        (b)   Parental Kidnapping Prevention Act

If a State asserts jurisdiction under these circumstances, its custody order may not be entitled to full faith and credit under the Parental Kidnapping Prevention Act ("PKPA"). 28 U.S.C. § 1738A. The PKPA requires states to enforce custody orders from other states based on "significant connection" jurisdiction only if no other state would have jurisdiction as a child's home state at the time the order was issued.

    (3)   Simultaneous Proceedings

A court in one state must not exercise its jurisdiction if, at the time of filing the petition, a proceeding concerning the custody of the child was pending in a court of another state exercising jurisdiction substantially in conformity with the UCCJEA, unless the proceeding is stayed by the court of the other state because State A is a more appropriate forum or for other reasons.

    2)   CHILD'S PREFERENCE

Although a court should consider multiple factors to determine what custody order will serve the children's best interests, in some circumstances, one of the most important considerations is the wishes of the children. In some states, if a child has reached sufficient age, the court must award custody consistently with the child's wishes. More commonly courts consider a child's wishes, and as the age and maturity of the child increases, the wishes are given greater weight

> 3) COUNSEL FOR THE CHILD

In most states, courts are permitted to appoint counsel to represent a child in a divorce or custody proceeding. Courts are not, however, required to do so.

>> a) Standard

The issue that frequently arises regarding such an appointment is how the attorney should approach the representation.

>>> (1) Wishes of the Child

Some commentators believe that an attorney appointed to represent a child should be a zealous advocate of the child's wishes.

>>> (2) Independent Assessor

Other commentators contend that an attorney should conduct an independent assessment of the best wishes of the child, regardless of the child's wishes.

>>> (3) Hybrid

Still, others feel that the attorney must take a hybrid approach to the situation, which takes into account both the subjective wishes of the child and the child's best interests.

> **F. Modification**

★★   > 1) STANDARDS

>> a) Best Interests

In order for a party to obtain a judicial modification of a child custody decree, the parent must demonstrate that 1) circumstances have changed and 2) that the modification would be in the best interest of the child. Mich. Comp. Laws § 722.27(1)(c). The changed circumstances must always be balanced against the need for continuity and stability in the child's custody. There must always be new facts that have arisen since the prior decree was entered.

>> b) Significant Change or Proper Cause

In Michigan, a divorce court may modify a divorce judgment when there is a significant change in circumstances or proper cause that warrants that change. Mich. Comp. Laws §§ 552.17a, 722.27. Until a proper cause or a significant change in circumstances is shown, a court has no authority to reconsider the best interests of a child or the existence of an established custodial environment. *Vodvarka v. Grasmeyer*, 259 Mich. App. 499 (2003), *Dehring v. Dehring*, 220 Mich. App. 163 (1996). The alleged proper cause/change in circumstance may not be a normal life change, but must be something generally not anticipated or predictable at the time of the consent judgment, for example. *Vodvarka, supra*. Remarriage is a normal life event, thus foreseeable, and therefore not a proper change in circumstances to reconsider child custody. *Id.*

★★   2)   <u>EVIDENTIARY HEARING</u>

The court cannot change custody absent an evidentiary hearing; *Mann v. Mann*, 190 Mich. App. 526 (1991), which should not be scheduled unless the moving party can provide an offer of proof sufficient that, if proved, it would comprise a significant change of circumstances or proper cause.

          a)   Established Custodial Environment

In Michigan, the first threshold the court must address at the evidentiary hearing is whether an "established custodial environment" exists when modifying child custody. Mich. Comp. Laws § 722.27(1)(c). This is important because whether an established custodial environment exists is a necessary determination before the standard of proof can be determined. *Id.*

                 (1)   Definition

Michigan law discusses an established custodial environment as: "the custodial environment of a child is established if over an appreciable time, the child naturally looks to the custodian in that environment for guidance, discipline, the necessities of life, and parental comfort. The age of the child, the physical environment, and the inclination of the custodian and the child as to permanency of the relationship shall also be considered." Mich. Comp. Laws § 722.27(1)(c). An established custodial environment is not determined simply by a parent having 51% of the children's time. The court is required to make a finding on each of the child custody factors (also known as the "best interests" factors set forth earlier), even if only to say it is irrelevant. *Overall v. Overall*, 203 Mich. App. 450 (1994).

                 (2)   Burdens of Proof

If one "established custodial environment" exists, the court cannot enter an order to change this custodial environment unless clear and convincing evidence exists that the change would be in the best interests of the child. *Id.* If no established custodial environment exists or both parents have an established custodial environment, a preponderance of the evidence standard is sufficient to change custody. *Id.*

          b)   Who Conducts the Evidentiary Hearing

The evidentiary hearing can be heard in front of a referee or the family court judge; if done in front of a referee, either party is entitled to a de novo review prior to the change being made. A de novo hearing includes a review by the family court judge based on a review of the transcript and exhibits from the referee hearing and does not require a live hearing. MCR 3.215[F][2]. The post-judgment cases must go back in front of the same judge throughout the minority of the child, so that the judge remains familiar with the circumstances of the family. MCR 8.111[D].

G. Moving the Child

1) GENERAL CONSIDERATIONS

Relocation of a child may not be permitted under certain circumstances. In determining whether moving the child is permissible, a court may balance the impact on visitation by the noncustodial parent against the benefits of the move to the children and the custodial parent. The trend has been toward permitting the custodial parent leniency in moving the child. Some states permit the move unless the motives for moving are vindictive. *E.g., Aaby v. Strange*, 924 S.W.2d 623 (Tenn. 1996). Others require the parent wishing to relocate to demonstrate that the move would serve the child's best interests. *E.g., Pollock v. Pollock*, 889 P.2d 633 (Ariz. 1995). Still others permit the parent to relocate unless the evidence shows that the move is detrimental to the child. *E.g., Marriage of Pape*, 989 P.2d 1120 (Wash. 1999).

★★   #### 2) MICHIGAN'S 100-MILE RULE

Michigan's 100-mile rule generally applies to a change of the legal residence (i.e., domicile) of a child whose custody is with the child's parent(s). When a child's custody is governed by a court order, the child's legal residence is with each parent. Mich. Comp. Laws § 722.31(1). The rule applies when the parents share joint legal custody and live within 100 miles of each other when their case begins. The rule applies to interstate changes in the residence of the child and parent.

a) General Rules

Generally, the parent must not change the child's legal residence to a location over 100 miles from the child's legal residence existing at the time when the action in which the order was issued commenced. *Id.* Such a move can occur, however, if either (a) the other parent consents to it or (b) the court permits it. Mich. Comp. Laws § 722.31(2).

(1) Exceptions

This law does not apply if either, when the action in which the order was issued commenced: 1) both of the child's residences were over 100 miles apart; or 2) the move results in both of the child's residences being closer to each other than before the move. Mich. Comp. Laws § 722.31(3).

b) Evidentiary Hearing

Because Michigan law generally prohibits moving a child's domicile greater than 100 miles without either the other parent's consent or court permission, an evidentiary hearing may be held on a parent's motion to move the child over 100 miles away. Before the court permits the move, it must consider and address the following factors in the hearing, "with the child as the primary focus in the court's deliberations:"

- if the move may improve the quality of life for the child and the relocating parent;

- the extent to which each parent has complied with, and utilized her or his time under, a court order governing parenting time with the child, and whether the relocating parent's plan to move was inspired by that parent's desire to frustrate or defeat the parenting time schedule;

- the extent to which the court finds that by permitting the move, it is possible to modify the parenting time schedule and the child's schedule in a way that can foster and preserve the parental relationship, and if each parent is likely to comply with the modification;

- how much the parent opposing the move is motivated by the desire to obtain a financial advantage with respect to the support obligation; and

- domestic violence, either directed against the child or witnessed by the child.

Mich. Comp. Laws § 722.31(4).

If a parent proves the above factors, then the court would have to decide if the move changed the child's established custodial environment. Earlier this outline addresses that type of change.

An order modifying or determining custody or parenting time must state the parents' agreement regarding how a move will be handled. Mich. Comp. Laws § 722.31(5). If such a provision is included in the order and the move occurs pursuant to that provision, then the foregoing law does not apply. *Id.*

H.   Mediation and Other Alternative Means of Dispute Resolution

1)   STANDARD

There has been a modern trend towards encouraging alternative dispute resolution in child custody actions. In some states, a court has the authority to order mediation of custody disputes. In others, for example California, mediation is mandated by statute under certain circumstances.

2)   MEDIATOR'S ROLE

The mediator must attempt to reach a settlement that is in the best interests of the children. Under certain circumstances, the mediator may exclude counsel from the mediation proceedings.

Additionally, the mediator has the authority to interview the children in an effort to resolve the dispute.

V.   RIGHTS OF UNMARRIED COHABITANTS

★   A.   **Rights of Cohabitants Inter Se**

1)   ECONOMIC SHARING

a)   Express Contract

In the majority of jurisdictions, if unmarried cohabitants agree to share property or otherwise to engage in forms of economic sharing, their agreement is enforceable, so long as the economic sharing is not intended as payment for sexual services. Carol Bruch, *Cohabitation in the Common Law Countries a Decade After* Marvin: *Settled In or Moving Ahead?* 22 U.C. Davis L Rev. 717 (1989); *also* Clark, *supra*, § 1.2. Some jurisdictions continue to refuse to recognize such claims. *Hewitt v. Hewitt*, 394 N.E.2d 1204 (Ill. 1979) (rejecting claim by unmarried cohabitant to property because relationship contrary to state public policy in support of marriage).

b)   Quasi-Contract

Even without an express contract, however, a court might still consider dividing the property. Some courts, following the lead of the California Supreme Court, also allow unmarried cohabitants to seek remedies based on implied-in-fact contract, resulting trust, constructive trust, or *quantum meruit* theories. *Marvin v. Marvin*, 55 P.2d 106 (Cal. 1976). Courts' application of these theories varies substantially.

★★   (1)   Implied-in-Fact – Michigan Law

Michigan courts will recognize a contract implied in fact if the parties have an express agreement based upon independent consideration regarding their cohabitation. *In re Lewis Estate,* 168 Mich. App. 70 (1988). The court will enforce an agreement made during the relationship on proof of additional independent consideration. The agreement must be express or implied in fact because the court will not recognize a contract implied at law since this would, in effect, recognize common law marriages. *Featherstone v. Steinhoff,* 226 Mich. App. 584 (1997); *Whitson v. Kaltz,* (Unpublished opinion per curiam of the Court of Appeals, issued Sept 20, 2002 [Docket No. 229289]).

★★★   (a)   Property Ownership

As a general matter, determining the ownership of property of parties who cohabited involves a consideration of whether the property belonged to only one party or to both parties jointly (e.g., as joint tenants). One party will have a right to the assets purchased by the party with that party's funds during the relationship. A gift made by one party to the other during their cohabitation belongs to the other party. A gift involves donative intent, delivery, and acceptance.

One of the parties to the cohabitation may lack an interest in real property purchased by the other party unless the deed has been placed in both of their names. However, if the parties jointly held property during their cohabitation they each will possess a one-half interest in the property (e.g., a checking account). Courts may also examine factors such as the commingling of funds.

(2)   Resulting Trust

To make a claim to property titled in the name of another on a theory of resulting trust, traditionally a person must have contributed money to the purchase of the asset under circumstances indicating that the contributor intended to retain equitable ownership of an interest in the asset, rather than making a gift.

(3)   Constructive Trust

A constructive trust is imposed to prevent a party from being unjustly enriched by profiting from wrongful conduct.

(4)   Quantum Meruit

A *quantum meruit* claim requires that a person pay the fair market value of services rendered to avoid unjust enrichment.

★   c)   Palimony

Michigan courts have yet to recognize "palimony" as a legitimate award in cohabitation cases. Palimony is defined as having a "meaning similar to alimony except that the award, settlement or agreement arises out of a nonmarital relationship of the parties." *Black's Law Dictionary*. Although recognized by other states, Michigan courts have yet to recognize an award of support payments on the termination of a cohabitation relationship.

2)   DISTINGUISHED FROM RIGHTS OF MARRIED COUPLES

In many jurisdictions, when a bystander witnesses an accident, which kills or seriously injures a close family member, and the bystander suffers from severe emotional distress, there may be a cause of action against the tortfeasor for negligent infliction of emotional distress. W. Page Keeton & William L. Prosser, *Prosser & Keeton on Torts* § 54 (5th ed. 1984); *Dillon v. Legg*, 441 P.2d 912 (Cal. 1968).

A majority of jurisdictions would be unlikely to expand liability to a cohabiting fiancée, as opposed to a close family member. This reluctance is based on the difficulties of determining which cohabitants should be allowed to recover and problems of proving the importance of the relationship. *Elden v. Sheldon*, 758 P.2d 582 (Cal. 1988). Some courts might also take the position that recognition of cohabitants' rights in this cause of action would undermine the strong public policy in support of marriage. Harry D. Krause, *Family Law in a Nutshell* § 6.5 (3d ed. 1995).

On the other hand, some jurisdictions have allowed engaged cohabitants to recover in a tort suit of this type. *E.g., Dunphy v. Gregor,* 642 A.2d 372 (N.J. 1994); Krause, *supra,* § 6.3.

B.   Unmarried Parents and their Children: Illegitimacy

A child is "illegitimate" or a "nonmarital" under the law, if he is born to parents who are not married to each other.

1)   CONSTITUTIONAL LIMITS ON DISCRIMINATION

The Equal Protection Clause has been utilized to strike down several laws providing unequal treatment of nonmarital children.

a)   Unfavorable Treatment of Illegitimate Children

(1)   Traditional Treatment

Traditionally, illegitimate children were discriminated in almost every aspect of the law. They did not possess rights of inheritance or status as legal child for purposes of standing (i.e., wrongful death). In the last half of the twentieth-century, however, the law has been significantly altered to provide protections to illegitimate children.

(2)   Supreme Court Challenges

In a series of United States Supreme Court decisions in equal protection challenges, the Court:

- struck down a law creating a cause of action for wrongful death in favor of marital children (to the exclusion of nonmarital children);
- held that a nonmarital child was entitled to workers' compensation benefits to the same extent as was a marital child;
- held that, if paternity was proven, both parties had a constitutional duty to support the non-martial child (sounds elementary today);
- held that a nonmarital child could inherit just as a marital child.

b)   Unfavorable Treatment of Unmarried Parents

The unfavorable treatment of unmarried parents is the basis for perhaps the most apparent gender discrimination in the law. Traditionally, the mother would be awarded custody. Conversely, a father would have to demonstrate paternity before even attempting to seek custody of the child.

2)   PRESUMPTION OF LEGITIMACY

At common law and under the statutes or case law of most states, a child born to a married woman is presumed to be her husband's child. Homer H. Clark, Jr., *The Law of Domestic Relations in the United States* § 4.4 at 191 (2d ed. 1988); Uniform Parentage Act of 1973 § 4; Uniform Parentage Act of 2000 § 204(a)(1). A party challenging paternity must demonstrate either 1) impossibility of paternity in spouse-husband or 2) lack of access of spouse-husband to mother.

In some states, a biological father may still be denied the status of legal father if he has not attempted to assume his parental responsibilities. *Cf. In re Raquel Marie X*, 570 N.Y.S.2d 604 (App. Div. 1991) (finding father's consent to the adoption of his child was unnecessary because father's conduct did not demonstrate intent to pursue a meaningful relationship with child). Courts will take into account any offers to pay the expenses of the child's birth and to support the child. If a biological father can demonstrate that, on balance, he has attempted to exercise his parental responsibilities, it would arguably violate the father's due process rights to accord him fewer legal rights than other biological fathers. *Cf. John S. v. Kelsey S.*, 4 Cal. Rptr. 2d 615 (Cal. 1992) (invalidating California statute that allowed mother to unilaterally thwart father's efforts to become "presumed father," thereby allowing father's rights to be terminated on best interest grounds).

There is a very high burden on the party challenging paternity because society favors the family relationship. Indeed, in some jurisdictions, courts have authority to exclude evidence that would rebut the presumption favoring paternity in the wife's husband if rebutting the presumption would be contrary to the child's best interest. *E.g., Ban v. Quigley*, 812 P.2d 1014 (Ariz. Ct. App. 1990); *Turner v. Whisted*, 607 A.2d 935 (Md. 1992); *R.H. v. K.D.*, 506 N.W.2d 368 (N.D. 1993).

3)   ESTABLISHING PATERNITY

a)   Introduction

More often than not, the father is attempting to evade a determination of paternity in order to avoid financial support obligations. A mother or governmental entity may bring a paternity action to establish that a child was born to her father. Mothers are required to cooperate with governmental officials in these actions.

(1)   Burden of Proof

In a majority of states, the burden of proof is a preponderance of the evidence. A minority of jurisdictions use the clear and convincing evidence standard.

(2)   Defenses

Fraud is not a defense to a paternity action. The purpose of a paternity action is to provide protection for the child. Therefore, the court will not allow fraud as a defense for a male who alleges that the mother deceived him into believing that she could not have children.

b)   Uniform Parentage Act

Pursuant to the Uniform Parentage Act, the father-child relationship is established between a man and a child by 1) an effective acknowledgment of paternity by the man unless the acknowledgment has been rescinded or successfully challenged; 2) an adjudication of the man's paternity; 3) adoption of the child by the man.

(1)   Presumption of Parentage

Moreover, a man is presumed to be the father of a child if 1) he and the mother of the child are married to each other and the child is born during the marriage; 2) he and the mother of the child were married to each other and the child is born within 300 days after the marriage is terminated; 3) before the birth of the child, he and the mother of the child married each other in apparent compliance with law, even if the attempted marriage is or could be declared invalid, and the child is born during the invalid marriage or within 300 days after its termination.

4)   LEGITIMATION

Legitimation, by contrast to an action to establish paternity, is a legal action brought by a father to establish his legal rights concerning his child who was "born out of wedlock."

a)   Legitimation by Marriage

The marriage of the mother and reputed father of a nonmarital child renders the child "legitimate" if the child is recognized by the father as his child.

b)   Legitimation by Petition

Many states possess statutes governing the judicial procedure a father can utilize to establish paternity.

(1)   Role of Mother

Generally, the mother must have notice of the petition for legitimation. The mother of an illegitimate child is entitled to file objections to a petition brought by a putative father to legitimate such child. Moreover, the husband of a woman at the time of conception or birth is a party at interest when another man claims fatherhood of a child in a legitimation proceeding, and due process requires that he be served as well.

(2)   Rights of Father

Only the mother of a nonmarital child is entitled to custody, unless the father legitimates the child. Even though the mother of an illegitimate child is entitled to custody, the putative father has rights and duties regarding the child.

(3)   Purpose

The purpose of the legitimation procedure is to provide for the establishment, not the disestablishment of legitimacy and paternity. Therefore, a party cannot file a petition seeking to be determined not a parent of a marital child.

(4)   Effect of Legitimation Order

Upon successful legitimation, the father stands in the same position as any other parent regarding parental and custodial rights with respect to the child.

VI.   PARENT, CHILD, AND STATE

A.   Legal Disabilities of Childhood

1)   LIABILITY OF PARENT FOR ACTS OF CHILD

a)   Traditional and Majority Approach – No Liability

Paternity alone does not impose liability on parents for the torts of a minor child. Of course, if a parent is negligent in some way, liability may be grounded in negligence.

b)   Modern Statutes – Limited Liability

Some states have enacted statutes providing for parental liability if a child willfully causes injury to a person or property. Generally, liability is limited to a nominal amount.

★   2)   CONSENT FOR MEDICAL PROCEDURES

A doctor who performs surgery on a minor child without a parents' consent is liable in tort. Homer Clark, *The Law of Domestic Relations in the United States* § 9.3.

a)   Exceptions

There are several exceptions to this general rule.

(1)   Emergency

Consent is not necessary in emergency cases when there is no time to obtain parental consent.

(2)   Public Health Concerns

Moreover, by statute, most states do not require parental consent for particular types of medical care, usually related to public health concerns, such as treatment for venereal disease (although sometimes even these statutes exempt children whose parents object to treatment on religious grounds).

(3)   Age of Child Taken into Account

Some states, by statute or case law, make an exception to the parental consent requirement for older children, either specifying an age or indicating that the minor must be mature. Typically, however, the "mature minor" must be near the age of majority, and the medical procedure must be minor.

★   3)   *PARENS PATRIAE*

        a)   General

Under the *parens patriae* authority of the state, the state can intervene to protect children when parents deny them needed medical care. One child labor case is often cited to support the state's right to protect children. *Prince v. Massachusetts*, 321 U.S. 158 (1944). "Parents may be free to become martyrs themselves. But it does not follow that they are free . . . to make martyrs of their children." *Id.* at 170. Generally, if a parent fails to provide needed medical care, a child can be adjudicated neglected and the state can order the medical treatment. In addition, many states have exemptions to the abuse and neglect statutes that allow the state to order the medical care without a finding of parental fault if the parents object to the child's treatment on religious grounds. Homer Clark, *The Law of Domestic Relations in the United States* § 9.3 (2d ed. 1988).

        (1)   Need

When parents object to the medical care, however, the concept of "need" is interpreted narrowly. Courts will examine whether a condition is life threatening or whether it can be postponed until the child reaches the age of majority. In these medical treatment cases, the courts weigh the risks and benefits of treatment.

B.   Duty to Support

Parents are legally obligated to support their children, regardless of whether they are marital or nonmarital children. There is an overriding public policy in favor of children being supported, combined with the implicit or explicit conclusion that a man who has sexual relations with a woman necessarily takes the risk that she may become pregnant. *E.g., Matter of L. Pamela P. v. Frank S.*, 449 N.E.2d 713 (N.Y. 1983) (rejecting argument that mother had deprived father of his constitutional right to decide whether to be a parent); *Stephen K. v. Rona L.*, 164 Cal. Rptr. 618 (1980) (rejecting breach of contract, fraud and misrepresentation arguments); *Douglas R. v. Suzanne M.*, 487 N.Y.S.2d 244 (1985) (same); *Linda D. v. Fritz C.*, 687 P.2d 223 (Wash. 1984) (same).

C.   Intra-Family Immunities

        1)   INTER-SPOUSAL IMMUNITY

For many years, husbands and wives could not sue each other in tort. In the vast majority of jurisdictions including Michigan, however, inter-spousal immunity has been abolished. *E.g.,* Mich. Comp. Laws § 600.2001. The usual reasons for such immunity were that such suits would be destructive of marital harmony and would encourage fraud and collusion against insurance companies. Homer Harrison Clark, *The Law of Domestic Relations in the United States* § 11.1 (2d ed. 1987). In the vast majority of jurisdictions, however, inter-spousal immunity has been abolished as courts have dismissed fears of disrupting familial harmony and of collusion. John

DeWitt Gregory et al., *Understanding Family Law* § 6.02 (2d ed. 1993).

2)   PARENT-CHILD IMMUNITY

a)   General Considerations

Historically, just as husbands and wives could not sue each other, and for comparable concerns about family harmony, minor children could not sue their parents for personal injury torts. Many jurisdictions have abolished this absolute immunity. Even where it does still exist, there are exceptions for willful and wanton action as opposed to mere negligence.

b)   Michigan Law

In Michigan, parental immunity is generally abolished and general intra-family tort immunity is abrogated. *Spikes v. Banks*, 231 Mich. App. 341 (1998). Accordingly, a child can sue the child's parents for injuries resulting from their ordinary negligence except: "1) where the alleged negligent act involves an exercise of reasonable parental authority over the child; and (2) where the alleged negligent act involves an exercise of reasonable parental discretion with respect to the provision of food, clothing, housing, medical and dental services, and other care." *Plumley v. Klein*, 388 Mich. 1 (1972).

D.   Claims for Loss of Consortium

Loss of consortium, which is recognized in almost all U.S. jurisdictions, is intended to compensate a spouse for loss of such things as the other spouse's companionship, sexual relations, and affection. While originally only the husband could recover for loss of consortium, the right was extended to wives during the mid-twentieth century. Compensation for loss of consortium typically is available only to the legally recognized spouse of the injured party, not to a fiancée or cohabitant. *E.g., Ford v. Wagner*, 153 Mich. App. 466 (1986).

E.   Parental Right to Control Child's Upbringing

1)   RELIGIOUS EDUCATION

The right of parents to direct the upbringing of their child includes control over the child's religious education. Moreover, children generally have a duty to obey their parents.

Parents generally have a right to raise their children as they see fit. *Wisconsin v. Yoder,* 406 U.S. 205 (1972) (compulsory education case). A child who fails to follow parental commands is disobedient, and the state seeks to reinforce the parents' control over their child, not undermine it. Leslie Harris, Lee Teitelbaum, & Carol Weisbrod, *Family Law* 1484-85 (1996).

2)   PARENTAL DISCIPLINE OF A CHILD

a)   Generally Permitted

A parent has the legal authority to discipline the parent's child. However, the punishment must be within the bounds of moderation. If the parent exceeds due moderation, the parent may incur criminal liability.

        b)   Moderation is Question of Fact

The issue of whether the punishment exceeds the bounds of moderation is a question for a trier of the facts, who may take several factors into account including, but not limited to: the age of the child; the injuries inflicted; conduct of the child.

F.   Custodial Disputes between Parents and Third Parties

A child's fit legal parent is presumptively entitled to custody as against a nonparent. Homer H. Clark, Jr., *The Law of Domestic Relations in the United States* 811 (2d ed. 1988). In most jurisdictions, to rebut the presumption favoring custody in the legal parent, a third party must demonstrate that awarding custody to the legal parent will be detrimental to the child. *E.g., Painter v. Bannister,* 140 N.W.2d 152, 156 (Iowa 1966); *Guardianship of Phillip B.,* 188 Cal. Rptr. 781, 788 (Cal. App. 1983). This standard is clearly intended to be more favorable to the legal parent than is the best interest of the child test, which is used in custody disputes between parents and does not imply a preference in favor of either claimant. Some states, however, apply a best interest test to custody disputes between third parties and parents. This test typically applies only if the nonparent is living with the child and functioning as a parent. An application of the best interest standard in other situations arguably raises constitutional concerns. *Cf. Troxel v. Granville,* 530 U.S. 57, 69-70 (2000) (invalidating application of visitation statute where lower court gave no weight to the presumption that fit parents act in their children's best interest).

VII.   ADOPTION

Adoption is a two-part process. It includes the termination of rights of birth parents and the formation of legal bonds with adoptive parents. Adoption is a statutory procedure.

A.   Jurisdiction

        1)   UNIFORM ADOPTION ACT/COMMON LAW

Under traditional common-law principles and the Uniform Adoption Act as it existed before 1994, the domicile of the adoptive parents possesses jurisdiction. Uniform Adoption Act § 4 (1969).

        2)   UCCJEA

Under more current jurisdictional principles, expressed in the Uniform Child Custody Jurisdiction and Enforcement Act and the Uniform Adoption Act, the essential inquiry is whether a state possesses a sufficiently strong connection with the child and whether substantial evidence concerning the case is present there.

Many states have not adopted the Uniform Adoption Act and use the more general principles of the UCCJEA to determine jurisdiction for adoption.

B.   Agency versus Independent Placements

1)   AGENCY PLACEMENTS

Agencies are licensed by the states to place children for adoption. Agencies must conduct extremely thorough background checks of adoptive parents. They usually place the child after termination of the biological parents' rights. Additionally, they may place child in foster home until rights are terminated.

Traditionally, agencies do not convey identifying information about biological parents. They may still give non-identifying information including, but not limited to, the following:

- ages,
- circumstances, and
- medical background.

Agencies attempt to ensure that the adoptive parents are not adopting for improper reasons. For example, if the parents are adopting in an attempt to save their marriage, etc.

2)   PRIVATE/INDEPENDENT PLACEMENTS

Independent placements are completely prohibited in some states. In most jurisdictions, however, the majority of placements occur through independent placements. The growth of independent placements has been fostered by:

- the inflexibility of agencies,
- long waiting periods to adopt through agencies, and
- more privacy is available through independent placements.

Arrangement is usually made by an individual (such as a doctor/lawyer/pastor). Arrangement can even be made by the natural parents. In many states that permit private placements, there must be a pre-placement home study of the family. A licensed social worker conducts the evaluation. Upon completion, the social worker files results with the court.

A financial statement regarding the placement is required. Paying the medical expenses of the birth mother may be permitted. However, excessive fees or costs are prohibited. A court will examine the totality of the circumstances to determine whether a fee is excessive.

Benefits of independent placement include the following: 1) babies are usually placed for adoption quickly; and 2) independent placements allow for more open information.

Criticisms of independent placement include the following:

- Babies are usually placed for adoption quickly. As a consequence, the natural parents' legal rights are not usually terminated. Accordingly, there is a danger that the biological parents may change their minds.
- Independent placements do not generally investigate the adoptive parents as thoroughly as an agency would.
- There is a greater opportunity for questionable financial dealings.

3)   FACTORS AFFECTING PLACEMENT

   a)   Foster Parents

Traditionally, there was hostility in allowing foster parents to adopt their foster children unless the child is hard to place for adoption. The justification for this was because foster parents are often older and not as financially secure as potential adoptive parents. Additionally, traditional agency arguments for not permitting foster parents to adopt included that:

- Foster parents were aware that the child was not being placed permanently, but rather temporarily.
- Permitting foster parents to adopt would short-circuit the system.
- There is a dearth of foster parents, but an overabundance of adoptive parents.

Modern trend prefers foster parents. Many jurisdictions now provide foster parents with a preference for adoption if the child has been with them for a specific period of time. Generally, the period is eighteen months.

   b)   Native American

If the child has Native American blood, the Indian Child Welfare Act of 1978 (ICWA) may apply. The ICWA:

- provides great preference to native American families,
- provides limited jurisdiction for tribal courts,
- provides tribes with a right of intervention in adoption proceedings, and
- Native American biological parents can revoke consent until the final decree of adoption.

   c)   Religion

Biological parents can generally limit the religion of the adoptive parents in some states.

   d)   Homosexual Adoptive Parents

States take a few different approaches towards adoption of children by homosexuals. A few states have an absolute prohibition against it. Some states say expressly permit it. Some states have not taken an express position.

A prospective homosexual parent may have no relation to the child, or may be the homosexual partner of a child's biological parent. An issue that arises in the latter context is whether the adoption, if permitted, terminates the right of the biological parent.

- If the statute expressly permits the adoption, then the relationship with the other biological parent is terminated.
- In the absence of express authority, there is a split in jurisdictions.

e)   Race as a Factor

Race may be taken into account to evaluate a prospective parent's capacity to deal with the particular needs of a child. Nonetheless, race, national origin, or ethnicity, should not, by themselves, be the basis of a placement decision.

C.   Parental Consent Issues

Consent issues come in two varieties. Either the biological parent 1) has given consent and then claims it was invalidly given, or 2) the biological parent gives valid consent, which is later revoked.

1)   CHALLENGE TO VALIDITY OF CONSENT

a)   Duress or Coercion

A biological parent who consented to the adoption may challenge the consent on the ground that it was procured by duress or coercion. Mere stress is insufficient. There must be extreme duress. Among other things, courts will examine the following: 1) parent's state of mind at the time; and 2) the purported pressure exerted on parent (case-by-case).

b)   Minors

As a general rule, minor parents can give consent for adoption without the consent of parents.

c)   Failure to Comply with Formalities

Some states require two witnesses to the consent. Additionally, some states provide a waiting period after the birth. For example, a mother cannot give consent for an adoption under 72 hours after birth in some states. Most states declare pre-birth adoptions invalid.

2)   REVOCATION OF VALID CONSENT

a)   Statutory Approaches

There are generally three different statutory approaches to revocation including:

- Consent is revocable at any time until the final decree is entered (usually one year).

- Consent is permitted at the discretion of the court up to a particular period of time. Under this approach, the court is afforded great discretion. In most jurisdictions courts examine the best interests of the child. Adoptive parents will generally have a presumption in their favor. However, some states prefer biological parents.

- Absent fraud or duress, consent is not revocable.

        b)   Michigan Procedure

In Michigan, the person who granted consent may petition the court for a hearing on whether to grant revocation. Mich. Comp. Laws § 710.29(10). Consent may not be revoked if the child has been placed with an adoptive family unless an appeal of a termination of parental rights proceeding is pending and a petition has been filed for a rehearing within the time required. *Id.*

       3)   CONSENT OF UNWED FATHER–CONSTITUTIONAL CONCERNS

        a)   Fundamental Right

The United States Supreme Court has held that parental rights are fundamental rights protected by the United States Constitution. *Santosky v. Kramer,* 455 U.S. 745 (1982); *Lassiter v. Dept. of Soc. Serv., 452* U.S. 18 (1981). While the Supreme Court has never decided a case about the substantive showing that must be made to justify terminating parental rights, it can reasonably be inferred that heightened scrutiny would be used, since the Supreme Court has subjected actions limiting parental care and custody to heightened scrutiny. *Id.*

        b)   Generally, Notice is Required

In *Stanley v. Illinois,* the Supreme Court held that an unwed father who was denied notice of juvenile court proceedings to determine the custody of his child had a constitutionally protected interest and that due process entitled him to notice. 405 U.S. 645 (1972). In *Caban v. Mohammed,* the Supreme Court also found that an unwed father had such an interest and held that a statute which protected his relationship to his children less than it protected their relationship to their mother violated equal protection. 441 U.S. 380 (1979).

        c)   Limitation

          (1)   State Putative Father Registries

However, in *Lehr v. Robertson,* the Supreme Court held that a state may allow the adoption of a child born outside of marriage without actual notice to a known biological father who did not satisfy a limited set of criteria for receiving notice. 463 U.S. 248 (1983). In *Lehr,* the father had not established a relationship with his child and had not registered his claim to paternity with the state putative father registry. He was not, therefore, entitled to notice under the statute. In upholding the statute, the Supreme Court held, "[t]he possibility that he may have failed to [file with a putative father registry, which would have entitled him to notice under the statute] because of his ignorance of the law cannot be a sufficient reason for criticizing the law itself. The New York legislature concluded that a more open-ended notice requirement would merely complicate the adoption process, threaten the privacy interests of unwed mothers, create the risk of unnecessary controversy, and impair the desired finality of adoption decrees." The Supreme Court characterized the issue as whether the statute" adequately protected his opportunity to form such a relationship."

(2)   No Acknowledgment of Paternity

The Due Process Clause does not require that notice of an adoption be given to an unwed father who knew of the pending birth of his child but who neither acknowledged paternity nor took steps to establish legal paternity or an actual parent-child relationship with the child.

★   d)   Termination of Parental Rights – Michigan Law

Michigan law provides for termination of parental rights under certain circumstances, including when there is clear and convincing evidence that the child or a sibling of the child has suffered physical injury or physical or sexual abuse under certain circumstances, such as when:

> "The parent's act caused the physical injury or physical or sexual abuse and the court finds that there is a reasonable likelihood that the child will suffer from injury or abuse in the foreseeable future if placed in the parent's home."

> "A nonparent adult's act caused the physical injury or physical or sexual abuse and the court finds that there is a reasonable likelihood that the child will suffer from injury or abuse by the nonparent adult in the foreseeable future if placed in the parent's home."

Mich. Comp. Laws § 712A.19b(3)(b)(i), (iii).

Other grounds for termination of parental rights include desertion, abuse, or conviction for certain crimes. Mich. Comp. Laws § 712A.19b(a)(ii), (k), (1).

If the court finds that grounds for termination exist, the court must "order termination of parental rights and order that additional efforts for reunification of the child with the parent not be made, unless the court finds that termination of parental rights to the child is clearly not in the child's best interests." Mich. Comp. Laws § 712A.19b(5).

VIII. ALTERNATIVES TO ADOPTION

    A.   **Artificial Insemination by Donor**

Artificial insemination by a donor generally occurs when a male is infertile. The woman seeking to become pregnant is inseminated with semen from a donor male.

1)   PARENTAL RIGHTS

The key issue regarding this topic is whether the spouse of a woman having a child through artificial insemination possesses parental rights. Consent is key.

Many states have enacted statutes to clarify which party has paternal rights under these circumstances. Generally, if the mother is married, the mother's husband is the legal father of the child born from artificial insemination. In many jurisdictions, the husband is not even required to adopt the child. These states extinguish any parental rights of the sperm donor. Usually, the husband must consent in writing prior to the insemination. If no writing exists, courts generally find that implied oral consent is enough. If the wife fraudulently forged the husband's signature, the husband may be able to avoid paying child support.

In some states, no statute has been enacted. In these states, if the husband has consented (written or implied oral) to the insemination, he is generally obligated to support the child.

B.   Surrogacy Arrangements and

C.   In Vitro Fertilization, Gestational Surrogacy, and Embryo Transplantation

1)   SURROGACY ARRANGEMENTS

a)   Classic Surrogate Arrangement

In the classic surrogacy arrangement, in contrast to gestational surrogacy, the father's sperm is used to inseminate a surrogate mother. The surrogate mother, generally in return for financial remuneration, agrees to bear the child and permit the father and his partner to raise the child.

b)   Gestational Surrogacy

In a gestational surrogacy, the partner of the father is able to produce an ovum, but unable to carry a baby to term. In this situation, the father and his partner conceive through in vitro fertilization. Once that occurs, the fertilized ovum is placed in the surrogate mother. Generally, in return for financial remuneration, the surrogate agrees to bear the child and permit the father and his partner (both genetic parents) to raise the child.

c)   Contract for Services

Usually, the surrogacy agreement is framed as a contract for the provision of services by the surrogate mother in an effort to avoid the prohibition on selling babies. In fact, the father's partner is rarely even mentioned in the contract.

d)   Treatment by the Courts

(1)   Void

In one high-profile case, a court held that surrogacy contracts are unenforceable contracts because they are against public policy. Primarily, the court held, these contracts do not account, in any way, for the best interests of the child. In essence, they amount to baby selling. In fact, a few states consider it a crime to enter into such a contract. In other states, the surrogacy arrangement is treated as void, but there are no criminal consequences.

(2)   Permitted Conditionally

Some states permit surrogate contracts. However, the birth mother is provided with a window of time after the birth in which to change her mind. In fact, no state law provides that these contracts are enforceable to the extent that the surrogate mother is required to turn over the child.

2)   IN VITRO FERTILIZATION

In vitro fertilization is a process by which a female's egg is removed from her body and fertilized by the husband's sperm outside the body. Once fertilized, the pre-embryos are implanted in the wife's uterus. The rate of pregnancy after in vitro fertilization is directly related to the number of embryos implanted. Therefore, usually, several more pre-embryos are created than are finally utilized.

a)   Common Issues

This brings up several ethical issues such as: 1) Can the pre-embryos be given to another person? 2) Can they be sold without the couple's consent? 3) What occurs if the couple divorces?

(1)   Parental Disputes

Usually, one parent wants the pre-embryos destroyed, but the other wants them preserved. Under these circumstances, courts will examine whether any prior agreement of the parties existed and will typically enforce one. There is a strong policy concern against "forcing" someone to become a parent, therefore, if an agreement providing that the pre-embryos should be destroyed is almost always enforced. Additionally, if the party seeking to preserve the pre-embryos is physically able to conceive a child, but the party seeking destruction of the embryos is not, it is to be taken into account in any judicial determination.

(2)   Responsibility of Physician

Generally, destroying a pre-embryo may subject a physician to criminal prosecution. Therefore, a physician can choose from the following courses of action with regard to excess pre-embryos:

- implant all excess pre-embryos to increase likelihood of successful birth;
- freeze pre-embryos for future use; and
- make them available to other couples.

The third option is the most controversial. Certainly, a physician should receive consent from the genetic parents before making their pre-embryos available to others.

AMERIBAR BAR REVIEW

Michigan Bar Review

EQUITY

TABLE OF CONTENTS

EQUITY

The essay portion of the Michigan Bar Exam includes Equity as a separately testable subject, although questions regarding some other separately testable subjects such as Contracts and Real & Personal Property may also examine equity issues and rules that specifically pertain to that subject. Generally, such rules are addressed in the outlines for those subjects. Both this outline and the Civil Procedure outline address the equitable remedies of injunctions, restraining orders, and declaratory judgments because those topics are testable in either an Equity question or a Civil Procedure question. The Michigan Rules of Court are referred to herein as MCR.

I.   INTRODUCTION

Equity essentially means fairness. When a party seeks an equitable remedy, it requests that the court do what is fair. As such, equitable remedies are only available when "equity" and "conscience" demand them. Equitable relief is highly discretionary. A court may deny equitable relief even though plaintiff's legal remedy is inadequate. The following doctrines are common threads that run through all questions regarding equitable remedies.

★★   **A.   Inadequate Remedy at Law**

Equitable relief is only available when the plaintiff's legal remedy (i.e., money damages) is inadequate. This principle is also known as the "irreparable harm" requirement. Injunctions may not be granted for the retention of personal property unless it is found to be unique or otherwise peculiar. There is no general rule for determining when harm is or is not irreparable. The determination must be made on a case-by-case basis.

A court may not use its equity powers to avoid the application of a statute. *Stokes v. Millen Roofing Co.*, 466 Mich. 660 (2002). Moreover, equity follows the law.

B.   Equitable Defenses

★★   1)   BALANCING THE EQUITIES

Equity may deny relief if the damage to the plaintiff is small and the hardship to the defendant is great.

★★   2)   UNCLEAN HANDS

Does the plaintiff come into the court with clean hands? Court will refuse relief where the plaintiff, by prior conduct in relation to the matter in litigation, has acted in bad faith or violated some equitable principle. The doctrine of "unclean hands" generally includes all misconduct and wrongdoing that is sufficiently related to the plaintiff's claim. Almost any conduct considered to be unfair, unethical, improper, or illegal, can be raised as a bar against equitable relief.

★★

3)   LACHES

Has the plaintiff delayed so long in bringing the action that to grant relief would be inequitable? *Laches* is any unreasonable delay by the plaintiff in instituting or prosecuting an action under circumstances where the delay causes prejudice to the defendant.

4)   EQUITABLE ESTOPPEL

a)   General Considerations

The doctrine of equitable estoppel prevents a party from adopting a new position that contradicts a prior position maintained by words, silence, or actions when allowing the new position to be adopted would unfairly harm the other person who has relied on the previous position to the person's detriment.

★   b)   Michigan Rule

Equitable estoppel may arise where (1) a party, by representations, admissions, or silence intentionally or negligently induces another party to believe facts, (2) the other party justifiably relies and acts on that belief, and (3) the other party is prejudiced if the first party is allowed to deny the existence of those facts.

II.   COERCIVE REMEDIES

A.   Injunctions

1)   PERMANENT INJUNCTION

Courts use injunctions to order litigants to engage in, or refrain from engaging in, an act. Sometimes injunctions are classified as being either mandatory or prohibitory: an injunction, which compels an act, is referred to as mandatory, while one, which forbids an act, is a prohibitory injunction.

In order to obtain a permanent injunction, the plaintiff must establish that (1) he will suffer irreparable injury unless an injunction is issued, (2) his threatened injury outweighs any harm the proposed injunction may cause to the opposing party, and (3) an injunction would not be adverse to the public interest.

2)   SCOPE AND FORM OF INJUNCTIONS

Every order granting an injunction must set forth 1) the reasons for its issuance; 2) must be specific in terms; 3) must describe in reasonable detail the act or acts sought to be restrained; and 4) is binding only upon the parties to the action.

★★   3)   TYPES OF NON-PERMANENT INJUNCTIONS

★★   a)   Temporary Restraining Order ("TRO")

Pursuant to Rule 65(b) and MCR 3.310(B), a court may issue a temporary restraining order on an *ex-parte* basis (without the other party present) when that is necessary to prevent irreparable injury. Because notice to the other party may not be required, a TRO is an extraordinary remedy.

To obtain an *ex-parte* temporary restraining order, the moving party must meet three conditions:

(1)   Irreparable Injury

The moving party must set out "specific facts" in the verified complaint or by affidavit that show that immediate and irreparable injury will result to the applicant before the adverse party can be heard in opposition; and

(2)   Efforts Made

The moving party's attorney must certify to the court in writing the efforts, if any, which have been made to give the notice and the reasons supporting the claim that notice should not be required; and

(3)   Security (FRCP) or Record (MCR)

(a)   Security (FRCP)

The moving party must provide a bond to the court in such a sum as the court deems proper to compensate the defendant in the event that the TRO is wrongfully entered.

The Federal Rules limit temporary restraining orders to 10 days absent good cause.

(b)   Record (MCR)

MCR 3.310(B)(1)(c) requires that permanent record be made of any non-written argument, evidence, or other representations made in support of the application for a TRO.

MCR 3.310(B)(3) limits TROs to 14 days absent good cause, except in domestic relations cases.

Remember, the key characteristic of a TRO is that notice to the other party may not be required.

b)   Preliminary Injunction

Generally speaking, the only practical difference between a TRO and a preliminary injunction under Rule 65(a) and MCR 3.310(A) is that a preliminary injunction is issued: 1) after a moving party provides notice to a non-moving party; and 2) after the non-moving party has an opportunity to be heard. The purpose of a preliminary injunction is to maintain the *status quo* until the parties' claims can be investigated and adjudicated.

(1)   Notice

Unlike for TROs, reasonable notice is required for preliminary injunctions.

(2)   Factors Courts Generally Examine

(a)   Likelihood of Success on Merits

Has the petitioner made a strong showing that it is likely to prevail on the merits?

(b)   Irreparable Injury

Has the petitioner shown that without such relief it will suffer irreparable injury?

(c)   Harm to Others

Would the issuance of the injunction substantially harm other interested parties?

(d)   Public Interest

The court must conduct an examination of the public interest under the circumstances.

4)   VIOLATING INJUNCTIONS

Once a court enters an order on an injunction, the parties must obey the injunction or risk being held in contempt of court. There are two main defenses for contempt: (1) no notice of the injunction; and (2) lack of jurisdiction by the court entering the order.

★   B.   Specific Performance

Specific performance is a remedy in which the court requires a party to a contract to perform specifically what the party has agreed to do.

1)   ELEMENTS REQUIRED FOR SPECIFIC PERFORMANCE

a)   Certain Terms

A contract must exist. Contract terms must be sufficiently certain for judicial enforcement including: parties, price, time and manner of performance and payment, etc.

b)   Conditions Fulfilled

Conditions and contingencies for performance must be performed or otherwise satisfied. At a minimum, one party must have tendered performance or be willing to tender performance.

c)   Inadequate Remedy at Law

As with all equitable remedies, money damages must be an insufficient remedy. The thing bargained for must be "rare" or "unique." Generally, real property is always unique. Factors a court may consider in determining whether the subject matter of the contract is rare or unique include:

> (1)   uniqueness in kind or in short supply;
> (2)   chattel of personal significance to vendee; or
> (3)   UCC considers "unique" or other "proper circumstances."

d)   No Defenses

Because the form of an action for specific performance is essentially a breach of contract claim, breach of contract defenses, such as unconscionability, statute of limitations, *laches*, etc., are available and applicable.

2)   PERSONAL SERVICE CONTRACT BREACH

Equity will not generally order performance of a personal service contract because the court will not force someone to work against their will.

III.   DECLARATORY REMEDIES – DECLARATORY JUDGMENT

An action seeking a declaratory judgment may be instituted to seek the court's opinion regarding the parties' rights under the law or an instrument. Essentially, the parties ask the court whether a certain action is prohibited before a contract is breached or a law is violated.

A.   Scope of Declaratory Judgments

Any person interested under a deed, contract or other writings or whose rights are affected by a law may have the court determine any question of construction or validity arising under the instrument or law and obtain a declaration of rights thereunder.

★★IV.   RESTITUTIONARY REMEDIES

★★ A.   Equitable Rescission of Voidable Contracts

1)   INTRODUCTION

A contract may be rescinded under certain circumstances. Rescission returns the parties to the position they were in before the contract was entered into. Essentially, the contract is treated as if it never existed.

2)   CIRCUMSTANCES SUPPORTING RESCISSION

Mutual mistake or misrepresentation of material fact (fraud) is generally enough for rescission. Additionally, duress, undue influence, lack of capacity and failure of consideration is usually sufficient to support rescission. Unilateral mistake is generally insufficient to support rescission.

★★ **B.   Reformation of Valid Contracts**

Reformation is intended to give effect to the intentions of the parties to conform the writing to the agreement in order to accurately reflect the "meeting of the minds."

1)   MISTAKE

Mutual mistake or unilateral mistake, if both of the parties should have been aware of the mistake or misrepresentation, may be corrected by the equity court. For example, if the incorrect price was placed into contract by typographical mistake, the parties may reform the contract to the correct price by an action for reformation. Parol evidence is generally permitted to show error and correction.

2)   INCONSISTENT PROVISIONS

Inconsistent provisions may show no "meeting of the minds" or may reflect the mutual mistake to support the reformation.

C.   Constructive Trust

To prevent unjust enrichment when a defendant holds title to property, which the plaintiff is equitably entitled, and the plaintiff has no adequate remedy at law, the court will construe the property being held in trust for the plaintiff. The party entitled to the constructive trust may be awarded, not only the property taken, but all property derived therefrom (increases). The key for a constructive trust is that the party holding the property holds title to the property.

D.   Equitable Lien

An equitable lien is imposed on a defendant's personal property to secure debt owed to the plaintiff in order to prevent unjust enrichment. An equitable lien is not a debt or a property right. Rather, it is a remedy for a debt. The court must find: (1) a debt, duty, or obligation owing by one person to another, and (2) a res or property to which that obligation attaches.

1)   EXPRESS AGREEMENT OR FAIRNESS

An equitable lien may arise in two situations. First, the lien may arise where the parties express in writing their intention to make personal property, or some fund, the security for a debt, but for some reason, the writing fails. Second, equity recognizes such a lien without an express agreement between the parties, which arises wholly from general considerations of fairness and justice.

E.   Equitable Mortgage

An equitable mortgage of land is one where the mortgagor does not regularly convey the land, but does some act by which he manifests his determination to bind the same for the security of a debt he owes. There are many kinds of equitable mortgages, as there are a variety of ways in which parties may contract for security by pledging some interest in lands. Whatever the form of the contract may be, if it is intended thereby to create a security, it is an equitable mortgage, that is, of course, if it is not a legal mortgage.

"In order for an equitable mortgage to exist, it is essential that the mortgagor have a mortgageable interest in the property sought to be charged as security; that there be clear proof of the sum which it was to secure; that there be a definite debt, obligation or liability to be secured, due from the mortgagor to the mortgagee; and the intent of the parties to create a mortgage, lien or charge on property sufficiently described or identified to secure an obligation." *Barnett v. Waddell*, 248 Ala. 189.

F.   Subrogation

Subrogation is the substitution of one creditor for another, with the substituted person succeeding to the legal rights and claims of the original claimant. The right of subrogation may be based upon contract or equity. Equitable subrogation arises as a result of the equities between the parties, and is awarded as a matter of equity. The two elements required for equitable subrogation are that:

(1)   The party whose debt was discharged was primarily liable on the debt; and

(2)   The claimant paid the debt involuntarily.

★★   G.   Purchase Money Resulting Trust

Where one party has provided all or part of the consideration for purchase of property, but title to the property is taken in another party's name, a resulting trust will be imposed in favor of the party that has provided the consideration. Where the title holding party sells the property to a third party, the party providing consideration may impose a resulting trust on the consideration the title-holder received in exchange for the property.

MICHIGAN

ETHICS

TABLE OF CONTENTS

ETHICS

Traditionally, the essay portion of each Michigan Bar Exam includes one Professional Conduct question. Occasionally, an essay question from another subject, such as Civil Procedure, has also tested a Professional Conduct issue. This Ethics Outline covers general rules and concepts of Professional Conduct according to the Model Rules of the American Bar Association ("ABA") as well as Michigan specific rules and concepts based on the Michigan Rules of Professional Conduct ("MRPC") and other relevant law.

Some past Professional Conduct questions focused upon several aspects of one rule of the MRPC. More often, previous questions focused on how various MRPC applied to the facts. Although some MRPC have been fairly frequently tested, usually the questions raise different issues and involve a variety of MRPC. Types of previous calls of questions included, but were not limited to, asking: for a description of arguments that could be made, what ethical obligations an attorney had, how an attorney should proceed, the propriety of representing clients, or asked for a written memo discussing relevant issues.

Traditionally, some of the most frequently tested issues include the duty of confidentiality and the duty of loyalty. Some of the less frequently tested issues include direct conflicts of interest involving present clients and/or former clients, and fairness towards third parties and opposing counsel. Some other issues that sometimes have been tested involve the duty to communicate, the duty to safekeep client's property, candor towards the tribunal, inducement for testimony, having an organization as a client, dealing with represented people, financial assistance to a client, and withdrawal. Some occasionally tested issues include an agreement restricting the lawyer's right to practice, fiduciary duties to non-clients, imputed disqualification, attorney fees, dealing with unrepresented people, false statements or fraud, non-disclosure and disclosure, conduct prejudicial to the administration of justice, reporting professional misconduct, advertisement and solicitation, using threats of criminal charges in exchange for settling a civil matter, and supervisory and subordinate lawyers.

I.   THE CLIENT-LAWYER RELATIONSHIP

A.   Duties to Clients

1)   DUTY OF COMPETENCE

★★

The lawyer has a duty to act competently with regard to the legal representation. She must apply the 1) diligence, 2) learning and skill, and 3) mental, emotional, and physical ability reasonably necessary for the performance of the legal service requested. In an emergency (e.g., a person dying who wants to make a will), a lawyer may give advice or assistance in a matter in which the lawyer does not have the skill ordinarily.

a)   What a Lawyer Must Not Do

A lawyer must not:

- neglect a legal matter;
- handle a legal matter without adequate preparation; or
- handle a legal matter that the lawyer is not competent to handle, without associating with a lawyer who is competent to handle it.

MRPC 1.1.

(1)   Definition of Prohibited Neglect of Legal Matter

Neglect involves indifference and either a conscious disregard for the lawyer's responsibility to the client or the lawyer's consistent failure to carry out the obligations assumed to the client. ABA Informal Ethics Opinion 1273 (1973).

★★   2)   SCOPE OF THE REPRESENTATION

Both lawyer and client have authority and responsibility in the objectives and means of representation. The client has ultimate authority to determine the objectives to be served by legal representation (i.e., whether to accept settlement proposal). On the other hand, the lawyer may make decisions regarding legal strategy. A lawyer must provide a client with sufficient information to make informed decisions about their representation, including who will be their counsel. MRPC 1.4.

a)   Limiting the Representation's Objectives

If a client consents after consultation, then a lawyer may limit the objectives of the representation, provided that the representation is in accordance with the MRPC and the law. MRPC 1.2(b) and cmt.

★★   3)   DUTY OF DILIGENCE

A lawyer must act with reasonable diligence and promptness in representing a client. MRPC 1.3. Common exam questions involve attorneys procrastinating in different aspects of their practice. The duty of diligent representation of the lawyer's clients does not include lying on their behalf.

★★   4)   DUTY TO COMMUNICATE

A lawyer must keep a client reasonably informed about significant developments relating to the representation, including promptly complying with reasonable requests for information and copies of significant documents when necessary to keep the client so informed. The lawyer must also explain a matter to the extent reasonably necessary to enable the client to make an informed decision.

★★   a)   Settlement Offers

(1)   Required Communication

A lawyer must promptly convey the terms of any settlement offer to the client before the client considers agreeing to the settlement offer. MRPC 1.4. Also, a lawyer is obligated to advise a client of the pitfalls of accepting and rejecting a case evaluation award. MRPC 1.2(a), 1.4(a)-(b).

(2)   No Restriction Upon Lawyer's Right to Practice

★   (a)   Settlement Agreement

A lawyer may not offer or make an agreement restricting the lawyer's "right to practice" as a condition of settlement. MRPC 5.6(b). Accordingly, any lawyer who offers (e.g., proposes or negotiates), drafts, and/or enters into the agreement by signing it violates the foregoing rule. *Id.*

An example of such a prohibited settlement agreement is one with a term that makes a plaintiff's counsel a consultant for a defendant, the effect of which is to make the plaintiff's counsel a lawyer for the defendant in any subsequent case similar to the plaintiff's case against the defendant. This term would unethically restrict the plaintiff's counsel from taking certain types of cases in the future. Additionally, if this term is made part of the settlement agreement, the plaintiff's counsel's own interest in getting the consulting arrangement is in conflict with this counsel's duties to the plaintiff, triggering the conflict of interest provision of MRPC 1.7(b). This counsel could not possibly exercise independent professional judgment on behalf of the plaintiff with respect to the settlement agreement while also trying to make a consulting arrangement deal with the defendant. Such an agreement would be improper under both MRPC 5.6(b) and MRPC 1.7(b).

★   (b)   Employment or Partnership Agreement

A lawyer may not offer or make an employment or partnership agreement restricting the lawyer's "right to practice after termination of the relationship," unless the restriction is limited to retirement benefits. MRPC 5.6(a).

(i)   Limit on Solicitation of Clients

A limitation on solicitation of clients is considered a "restriction on right to practice," such that this type of provision in an employment agreement is improper. Michigan Ethics Opinion RI-86 (1991).

(ii)   Non-Compete Agreement

Although section 445.774a of the Michigan Compiled Laws allows covenants not to compete provided they are "reasonable as to its duration, geographical area, and the type of employment or line of business," the Michigan Supreme Court's adoption of MRPC 5.6 postdates the statute and is promulgated in furtherance of the Court's supervisory power over the bar. Non-compete agreements are not permitted for lawyers.

★★★★   5)   DUTY OF CONFIDENTIALITY

                   a)   General Rule and Exceptions

A lawyer must never knowingly reveal a confidence or secret relating to the representation of a client unless: 1) the client gives informed consent after full disclosure by the lawyer; 2) the disclosure is permitted or required by the MRPC (e.g., MRPC 3.3(a)(2) discussed below); 3) to rectify a client fraud in which the lawyer's services were used; 4) to prevent a crime; and 5) to collect a fee (e.g., a claim between the lawyer and the client). MRPC 1.6(c).

★★★   b)   Confidences and Secrets

MRPC 1.6 protects confidences and secrets. "Confidences" refer to information protected by the attorney-client privilege. If, for example, the terms of a proposed settlement agreement were negotiated with opposing counsel, they cannot be privileged. "Secrets," however, include anything related to the representation that would be embarrassing or detrimental to the client or that the client has requested be protected. For example, settlement agreements with potentially invalid terms could be held void, which would be detrimental to the clients.

★   (1)   Identity of Clients

Although the identity of the clients is not always privileged, i.e., "confidences" under the foregoing rule, it can be a "secret," i.e., "information gained in the professional relationship that the client has requested be held inviolate or the disclosure of which would be embarrassing or would likely to be detrimental to the client." MRPC 1.6(a).

★   (2)   Prohibited Use

A lawyer may not use a confidence or secret for the advantage of the lawyer unless the client consents after full disclosure. MRPC 1.6(b)(3).

★★★   6)   DUTY TO SAFEKEEP CLIENT'S PROPERTY

                   a)   General Considerations

A lawyer should hold property of others with the care required of a professional fiduciary. Securities should be kept in a safe deposit box, except when some other form of safekeeping is warranted by special circumstances. All property, which is the property of clients or third persons, should be kept separate from the lawyer's business and personal property. Separate trust accounts may be warranted when administering estates or acting in similar fiduciary capacities, such as in a transaction involving escrow funds.

★★   b)   Lawyer Trust Accounts

                              (1)   MRPC Amendment

Prior to the 2005 amendments to MRPC 1.15, the rule only required advance fees to be deposited into a trust account. With the amendment, however, MRPC 1.15(d) states: "A lawyer shall hold property of clients or third persons in connection with a representation separate from the lawyer's own property. All client or third person funds shall be deposited in an IOLTA or non-IOLTA account." *Id.* The acronym IOLTA stands for the words Interest on Lawyers Trust Account.

(a)   IOLTA Account

As a practical matter, an IOLTA account is a type of trust account for holding funds provided from a client or third person to a lawyer. An IOLTA account with an eligible financial institution bears interest or dividends and must only contain client or third-person funds that can be withdrawn upon request when permitted by law. MRPC 1.15(a). One purpose of an IOLTA account is to separate client or third-person funds from a lawyer's funds in order to avoid commingling of those funds that should be maintained in separate accounts.

(2)   Trust Account Overdraft Notification Rule

The acronym TAON stands for the words Trust Account Overdraft Notification. Pursuant to the TAON rule, a Michigan lawyer must maintain their client and third person trust accounts in financial institutions that the State Bar of Michigan has approved to serve as a depository for lawyer trust accounts (IOLTA and non-IOLTA accounts). MRPC 1.15A. The name of a non-IOLTA account must include the word "escrow" or "trust." *Id.* The approved financial institutions must provide overdraft reports containing certain information to the State Bar of Michigan. *Id.* The TAON rule does not apply to lawyers' personal and general business accounts.

★   c)   Retainer Fee

Sometimes, a lawyer and a client will enter into a written agreement pursuant to which the client provides a certain amount of money as a retainer from which the lawyer may be paid for legal services rendered to the client. There is nothing unethical about such an agreement requiring the client to replenish a retainer when it is depleted, as long as the client has been told about and understands the obligation. A lawyer must provide the client with all information necessary to make informed decisions about the representation. MRPC 1.4. One way to satisfy this requirement is for the lawyer to place the cost/expense retainer balance on the client's billing statements (if billing statements are regularly sent), so the client will have advance warning of when replenishment is required. If these precautions are taken, there is nothing improper about the lawyer requesting a replenishing retainer to cover costs.

★   d)   Escrow Funds in Interest Bearing Account

A lawyer may not deposit a client's escrow funds into a non-interest bearing account, even if the parties so stipulate. A lawyer must place all client funds held by the lawyer into interest-bearing accounts. These funds include, for example, escrow funds. MRPC 1.15(d). If the parties want an account containing escrow funds to be in a non-interest bearing account, then a lawyer cannot serve as their escrow agent.

(1)   Closing Escrow Funds

Suppose, for example, that a client gives funds to a lawyer for a specific purpose such as closing escrow. As a general rule, the lawyer is required to preserve the asset for that purpose and may not take the lawyer's fees from those funds. If, for example, the engagement language in a fee agreement allowing the lawyer a retainer does not specifically say the retainer may be taken from the closing escrow, then the lawyer's use of the closing escrow for the lawyer's own purposes is misappropriation.

(a)   Fiduciary Duties to Non-Client

When agreeing to hold the closing escrow, a lawyer takes on fiduciary duties to the other party to the transaction (e.g., non-client) in addition to the lawyer-client duties the lawyer has to the client. The lawyer may not unilaterally distribute the escrow funds to either party when the lawyer knows the funds are in dispute. MRPC 1.15(c). Suppose, for example, that there is a lawsuit involving the lawyer's client and the other party involving the disposition of the closing escrow. In the event of a settlement of this lawsuit for an equal amount between those parties, the lawyer must disburse half the closing escrow to the client and half to the other party. The lawyer could then bill the client for any outstanding fees.

e)   Money from Third Parties

Attorneys often receive money from third parties from which the attorney's fee will ultimately be paid. If there is risk that the client may divert funds without paying the fee, then the lawyer is not required to remit the portion from which the fee is to be paid. However, a lawyer may not hold funds to coerce a client into accepting the lawyer's contention. Additionally, any undisputed portion of the funds must be promptly distributed.

★   (1)   Settlement Escrow Funds

A lawyer may, for example, hold settlement escrow funds from non-parties to a lawsuit who are not the lawyer's clients even though only one party to the lawsuit is the lawyer's client. But the lawyer undertakes fiduciary duties to both non-parties/non-clients when agreeing to hold the funds for them. MRPC 1.15(a). If the lawyer has consent from the non-clients/non-parties and the client to settle the lawsuit, the lawyer has sufficient authority to settle even when one of the non-parties/non-clients has not paid the agreed upon amount of settlement escrow funds. MRPC 1.8(g).

In such a situation, although the non-party/non-client has not deposited funds into the settlement escrow, all funds in the escrow were intended to pay for a settlement of the lawsuit, and the lawyer has a duty to promptly disburse the funds once the settlement has been accepted. MRPC 1.15(b).

In the event of a settlement of this lawsuit for an equal amount between the two parties, the settlement escrow and any accrued interests should be divided and returned to the lawyer's client and the non-party/non-client who deposited the funds. The lawyer could then bill the client for any legal fees, and cannot take them from the settlement escrow.

★★★★   7)   DUTY OF LOYALTY

A lawyer owes a duty to act in the utmost good faith and in the client's best interests. This duty prohibits a lawyer from accepting representation that will result in a conflict of interest with another client. Consent is virtually never reasonable if each client's interest is directly opposed to one another.

Additionally, the lawyer owes a duty of loyalty to the client, not another party who pays the client's bills. The lawyer should disclose this duty to the paying party.

★★★   a)   Direct Conflicts

            (1)   General Rule (Client v. Client)

The attorney may pursue such representation that will be directly adverse to another client or be materially limited by the attorney's duties to another client or a third person if: 1) the attorney reasonably believed the representation will not adversely affect the relationship with the other client; and 2) each client consents after consultation. MRPC 1.7.

For example, arguably a client's consent cannot waive a conflict of interest when a lawyer's representation of an organization as a client is adverse to the lawyer's concurrent representation of a constituent of the organization in dissolving the organization. MRPC 1.7; MRPC 1.13(e).

In one case, the court found that since a law firm took no affirmative steps to terminate its responsibilities under a settlement provision previously entered into by the law firm's client, the law firm should be deemed to have a current client-lawyer relationship with the client. *Jones v. Rabanco Ltd.*, 2006 U.S. Dist LEXIS 53766 (W.D. Wash. 2006).

            (a)   Imputed Conflict

Imputed conflicts of interest may arise in the context of a corporate family, such as when one corporation owns other separately incorporated subsidiaries. A split of authority exists about conflicts of interest in this context, with some courts requiring disqualification and other courts denying disqualification when counsel for a corporate party files suit against a corporate affiliate. In determining whether representation is permitted, the following factors can be considered:

- whether legal work for one entity is intended to benefit all affiliates or entails collecting confidential information from all of them, such as stock issues or financing;
- whether counsel was engaged by or reports to officers of the other affiliate;
- whether the affiliate shared protected information with the lawyer with the expectation that the lawyer would use it in representing the affiliate, or for the purpose of furthering the representation; and

- whether one affiliate is the alter ego of the other.

ABA Ethics Opinion 95-390 (discussing ABA Rule similar to MRPC 1.7).

A comment indicates that for conflict of interest purposes, the client is the corporation that retains the lawyer, not other companies in which the corporation has an ownership interest or that hold an ownership interest in the corporation. *Restatement Lawyers*, § 121, cmt. d (2000). The comment advises, however, that the lawyer's obligations extend to an affiliated entity where financial loss or benefit to the non-client entity will have a direct, adverse impact on the client. Also, the comment states that a client's significant control of an affiliated entity may suffice to require the lawyer to treat the affiliated entity as a client for the purpose of determining whether a lawyer's representation of another client with interests adverse to the affiliated entity entails a conflict of interest.

★★★   (2)   Former Client (Client v. Former Client)

                                        (a)   Materially Adverse Interests

An attorney who represented a client must not represent a new client if the new client's interests in the subject matter of the new representation are materially adverse to the former client's interests in it, which are the same as, or substantially related to, the subject matter of the prior representation, unless the former client consents after consultation. MRPC 1.9(a).

                                                (i)   Substantially Related Representation

A subsequent representation is substantially related to a prior representation when:

- the subsequent representation's subject matter is the same as that of the prior representation;
- these representations' legal or factual issues overlap; or
- a likelihood exists that confidential information received in the prior representation will pertain to the subsequent representation. *Id.*

                                                (ii)   Confidential Information

An attorney may not reveal to the new client any secrets or confidences received by the attorney in the professional relationship with the former client. MRPC 1.6(b)(1). The attorney may not use such secrets or confidences, or "any information relating to the representation," to the former client's disadvantage (unless the former client consents after consultation). MRPC 1.6(b)(2); MRPC 1.8(b); MRPC 1.9(c).

                                        (b)   Lawyer in a Firm

Unless the former client consents after consultation, an attorney must not represent a different client in the same or substantially related matter in which the firm with which the attorney formerly was associated has previously represented the former client: 1) whose interests are materially adverse to the different client; and 2) about whom the attorney had acquired information confidential and protected by MRPC 1.6 that is material to the matter. MRPC 1.9(b).

★★   (i)   Imputed Disqualification

Under the general rule for imputed disqualification, if one lawyer in the firm is disqualified from representing a client in a matter, then all other members of the firm are also disqualified. MRPC 1.10(a).

However, a law firm may avoid imputed disqualification in some instances when a lawyer joins the firm, by screening the transferring lawyer from the matter and the fee, and by giving written notice to the appropriate tribunal. MRPC 1.10(b). However, the foregoing rule would permit a law firm to avoid imputed disqualification only for an attorney's disqualification under MRPC 1.9(b), which this outline addresses earlier. The foregoing rule does not permit the law firm to represent a client when the attorney is disqualified under MRPC 1.9(a), as addressed earlier.

★   (ii)   Restrictions on Firm that Lawyer Left

After a lawyer has left a firm, the firm is disqualified from representation of a client having interests materially adverse to the lawyer's client, if both these criteria exist: 1) the representation is substantially related to the lawyer's former representation; and 2) lawyers in the firm have information protected by the rule of confidentiality that is material to the matter. MRPC 1.10(c).

★   (iii)   Lateral Moves and Conflict Check

The foregoing rules both address lateral moves by a lawyer between different law firms. MRPC 1.9-1.10. If a "lateral lawyer" is adequately screened by the new employer for conflicts, then the new employer can avoid imputed disqualification caused by the participation of the lateral lawyer at the former law firm. A screen is not adequate unless it is established promptly.

★   (iv)   Confidentiality of Conflict Lists

Generally, a lawyer must maintain confidences and secrets of clients, and under certain circumstances the mere identity of a client may be protected from disclosure. MRPC 1.6. The fact that an opposing counsel represents a party-opponent in a matter for which the lawyer represents a client, and therefore the matter is in dispute, does not mean the matter is public, and that information about the representation may be disclosed, even for the purpose of checking for a conflict of interest of the lawyer's prospective subsequent employer. Further, such conflict lists usually contain more information than just client names and opposing counsel: conflict lists could contain addresses, witnesses, information about payment of fees, account numbers, timekeepers working on the file, etc. This type of proprietary information of a law firm that presently employs the lawyer may not be disclosed by the lawyer to a third party such as the lawyer's prospective subsequent employer without the law firm's permission, and in some cases, permission from the law firm's clients.

★★   b)   Potential Conflict

A potential conflict exists when the representation, although not directly adverse to another client or interest, may become directly adverse at some time in the future. The attorney may pursue such representation if: 1) the attorney reasonably believes the representation will not adversely affect the relationship with the other client; and 2) the client to be represented consents after consultation (some states require written consent).

                    c)   Business Transaction with or Adverse to Client

The attorney may pursue such a transaction only if:

- The transaction is fair and reasonable to the client, fully disclosed, and transmitted in writing to the client; and

- The client is given a reasonable opportunity to seek the advice of independent counsel in the transaction; and

- The client consents in writing to the transaction.

                    d)   Special Considerations for Government Attorneys

Under the ABA Model Rules, an attorney who was previously employed by the government must avoid working on any of the same matters in private practice unless there is informed consent from the client and agency.

★★   **B.   Attorney's Fees**

Fees for legal services are set by agreement between the lawyer and client. Generally, the agreement must be in writing and clearly set forth the terms of the representation.

            1)   <u>REASONABLE FEE REQUIREMENT</u>

★

The fee must be reasonable under a totality of the circumstances based on an analysis of various factors, which include the time, skill, and labor required. Using those factors to enhance a fee otherwise subject to straightforward calculation may transform the arrangement into a contingent fee. That could occur when, for example, an attorney wants to have a fee agreement in which a client agrees to pay, in addition to the attorney's standard hourly rate, an additional sum based upon the amount involved, results obtained by the attorney, and value added to the representation by the attorney's expertise, ability, and reputation. The fee cannot be illegal or clearly excessive (i.e., unreasonable).

                    a)   Communication to Client

If an attorney has not regularly represented a client, then the attorney is obligated to communicate the fee's rate or basis to the client, preferably in writing, at the time of commencement of the representation or shortly thereafter. MRPC 1.5(b).

★   2)   <u>CONTINGENCY FEES</u>

Such fees are permissible, except in criminal or domestic relations cases. Contingency fee agreements must be in writing and describe how "the fee is to be determined." MRPC 1.5(c).

★   3)   <u>FEE SPLITTING WITH OTHER LAWYERS</u>

              a)   ABA

The division of reasonable legal fees is permitted under the ABA Model Rules if: 1) the fee is reasonable; 2) the client consents upon disclosure to the client, and 3) the fee is proportionally based upon work done or both attorneys must take responsibility for the representation.

              4)   <u>LIMITING LIABILITY FOR MALPRACTICE</u>

A lawyer may not attempt to contract with the client to limit her malpractice liability. Additionally, a lawyer cannot attempt to settle a claim with a client for malpractice liability unless the client is informed, in writing, of the ability to obtain independent counsel.

II.   LAWYER AS ADVOCATE

★   **A.   Meritorious Claims and Contentions**

A lawyer must not bring or defend a case or issue unless there is a basis for doing so that is not frivolous. However, a lawyer may make a good faith argument for an extension, modification, or reversal of existing law.

★   **B.   Expedite Litigation**

A lawyer must make all reasonable efforts to expedite litigation consistent with the interests of the client. This goes hand-in-hand with the lawyer's duty of diligence.

C.   Candor Toward Tribunal

★★   1)   <u>GENERAL PROHIBITIONS</u>

A lawyer cannot knowingly:

- false statements: make a false statement of material fact or law to a tribunal, or fail to correct such a false statement that the lawyer made;

- binding legal authority: fail to disclose to the tribunal legal authority in the controlling jurisdiction known to the lawyer to be directly adverse to the position of the client and not disclosed by opposing counsel; or
- false evidence: offer evidence that the lawyer knows to be false. If a lawyer has offered material evidence and comes to know of its falsity, the lawyer must take reasonable remedial measures.

2)   FRAUDULENT OR CRIMINAL CONDUCT

"If a lawyer knows that the lawyer's client or other person intends to engage, is engaging, or has engaged in" fraudulent or criminal conduct related to an adjudicative proceeding involving the client, then the lawyer must take reasonable remedial measures, which may include disclosure to a tribunal, if necessary. MRPC 3.3(b).

3)   DURATION OF APPLICABILITY

The foregoing types of duties continue until the proceeding's conclusion. MRPC 3.3(c).

4)   REASONABLE REMEDIAL MEASURES FOR FALSE EVIDENCE

Upon determining that material evidence is false, a lawyer should try to convince a client either to not offer the evidence or to disclose its false character. If the lawyer cannot convince the client to do that, then the lawyer must take subsequent remedial measures. The lawyer should try to withdraw if that will rectify the situation. If withdrawal is not allowed or will not rectify the effect of false evidence, then the lawyer must make such disclosure to the tribunal as is reasonably necessary to rectify the situation, even if doing that requires the lawyer to reveal information that otherwise would be protected by the rule of confidentiality. MRPC 3.3(e).

5)   SCOPE OF APPLICABILITY

Generally, discovery proceedings and depositions occur "before the court" (i.e., tribunal) and implicate the foregoing types of duties. MRPC 3.3 cmt.

★   ### 6)   UNBUNDLED LEGAL SERVICES

Basically, unbundled legal services means that a lawyer performs only specific, restricted tasks, instead of handling every facet of a matter. Michigan Ethics Opinion RI-347 (April 23, 2010). According to the circumstances, the availability of unbundled legal services permits clients to restrict their legal costs by seeing a lawyer for particular advice and paying for only that, without having to pay the lawyer for other additional expenses, such as drafting a legal document. *Id.*

Suppose, for example, that a client hires a Michigan attorney to just work "as needed" on her new lawsuit, and in the background, at least for a while. In particular, the client asks whether or not the attorney could simply draft the complaint, a motion and brief, and related documents, without putting the attorney's name on the pleadings or filing an appearance. This situation could involve a couple of potential conclusions as to its ethical permissibility.

a)   Possibly Permissible

Under one conclusion, presuming compliance with the MRPC and other law, an attorney can, without appearing or otherwise disclosing the attorney's assistance, aid a *pro se* litigant by providing advice on the content of documents to be filed in court, including pleadings, by drafting these documents and providing advice about what to do in court. *Id.*; ABA Formal Opinion 07-446 (May 5, 2007); Arizona Ethics Opinion 05-06 (July 2005).

b)   Possibly Impermissible

Another conclusion could provide that, because a court considers that a party -- who files a pleading under the party's own name -- is not represented, an attorney who ghostwrites a client's pleading is assisting the client in misleading a court. Courts may hold unrepresented litigants' pleadings to less stringent standards. *Kircher v. Ypsilanti Twp.*, 2007 US Dist. LEXIS 93690 (Dec. 21, 2007). Therefore, a client unjustly obtains a benefit when an attorney aids a client by drafting a pleading for the client without revealing that to the court. *Grievance Administrator v. Miller*, 06-125-Rd (HP. 2/7/2009).

★★★   D.   Fairness to Third Parties and Opposing Counsel

1)   GENERAL CONSIDERATIONS

A lawyer may not obstruct an opponent's access to evidence, unlawfully conceal or destroy evidence, make a frivolous discovery request, or fail to make a reasonably diligent effort to comply with a legally proper discovery request. At trial, a lawyer may not allude to any matter that is not supported by admissible evidence or assert personal knowledge of facts in issue.

A lawyer may not ask a witness not to be "available" to provide testimony since that would "unlawfully obstruct another party's access to evidence." MRPC 3.4(a).

A lawyer may not request that a person other than a client refrain from voluntarily providing information to another party, unless: 1) the person is "an employee or other agent" of the client for purposes of the relevant Michigan Rule of Evidence regarding admissions by a party-opponent; and 2) "the lawyer reasonably believes that the person's interests will not be adversely affected by refraining from giving such information." MRPC 3.4(f).

★★   2)   INDUCEMENT FOR TESTIMONY

Under the common law of most jurisdictions, a fact witness may be paid for time and expenses incurred as a witness, as long as the payment is not an inducement to testify in a particular way.

A lawyer may not offer an improper inducement for testimony that is prohibited by law. MRPC 3.4(b). Moreover, "it is not improper to pay a witness' expenses or to compensate an expert witness on terms permitted by law. It is improper to pay an occurrence witness any fee for testifying beyond that authorized by law, and it is improper to pay an expert witness a contingent fee." *Id.* at cmt.

For example, offering a prospective witness $2,500 in anticipation of testimony, when there is no proceeding pending in which testimony would be taken, smacks of improper inducement.

E.   Improper Contact with Court or Jurors

1)   GENERAL PROHIBITIONS

An attorney may not seek to influence by means prohibited by law, or make unauthorized *ex-parte* communication with: jurors, prospective jurors, or other judicial officers (e.g., judges). MRPC 3.5(a)-(b).

2)   COMMUNICATIONS AFTER DISCHARGE OF JURY

An attorney may not communicate with a juror after discharge of the jury if:

- law or a court order prohibits the communication;
- the juror has informed the attorney of a desire not to communicate; or
- the communication involves misrepresentation, duress, coercion, or harassment.

MRPC 3.5(c).

F.   Trial Publicity

"A lawyer who is participating or has participated in the investigation or litigation of a matter" must not "make an extrajudicial statement that the lawyer knows or reasonably should know will be disseminated by means of public communication and will have a substantial likelihood of materially prejudicing" a proceeding in the matter. MPRC 3.6(a).

★   G.   Lawyer as a Witness

A lawyer cannot represent a client in a matter in which he will testify unless the testimony relates to an uncontested issue or disqualification of the lawyer would be a substantial hardship on the client. The lawyer cannot represent the client when he is a necessary witness in the matter.

★★ H.   Organization as Client

1)   GENERAL CONSIDERATIONS

When a lawyer represents an organization (i.e., entity), the lawyer represents (and owes a fiduciary duty to) the organization itself. MRPC 1.13(a). Such a duty is distinct from (and paramount to) any duty to the individual officers, directors, shareholders, or other constituents (e.g., employees) of the organization. *Id.*

★   a)   Lawyer's Duty to Identify Who is Client

                             (1)   Business Attorneys' Professional Corporation

In Michigan, a common situation for business attorneys when setting up their law firm as a professional corporation ("P.C.") is whether another lawyer who prepares their formation documents (e.g., incorporation papers and bylaws) represents the P.C. as an organization, all of them as shareholders, or just some of them. In this situation, it is the responsibility of the lawyer who prepares the P.C.'s formation documents to identify who the client is when the lawyer believes that this explanation is needed to avoid any misunderstanding by the shareholders. MRPC 1.2(c), 1.4(b), 1.13(d). Otherwise, the issue could arise as to who the client is when each shareholder separately contacts the lawyer regarding their separate complaints about each other's conduct relative to the P.C.

★   b)   Consent to Representation

A lawyer for an organization may also represent an officer, director, shareholder, or other constituent of the organization personally, subject to the MRPC regarding direct conflicts of interest. MRPC 1.13(e), 1.7.

★   I.   **Dealing with Unrepresented People**

When dealing on behalf of a client with a person who is not represented by an attorney, a lawyer must not imply that the lawyer is disinterested. The attorney must not appear "disinterested" and should not give any advice other than advice for the person to seek legal counsel. MRPC 4.3.

★★   J.   **Dealing with Represented People**

The prohibition against contacting persons represented by counsel does not apply when no action has been filed and the person is not "represented by counsel in the matter." MRPC 4.2.

Unless an attorney has consent from the counsel of a represented opposing party that is an organization, the attorney is prohibited from contacting the opposing party's managers and supervisors whose statements may constitute admissions or whose acts may be imputed to the opposing party. MRPC 4.2, cmt. A split of authority exists among the states as to whether this prohibition applies to former managers of this type of opposing party. Former managers are not covered by the prohibition. ABA Opinion 91-359; *Valassis v. Samuelson*, 143 FRD 118 (E.D. Mich. 1992).

The rule does not prohibit paying a fact witness for expenses or for loss of time due to the testimony or preparation for testifying, including research. ABA Opinion 96-402. The key is that the witness compensation not be related to the substance of testimony, i.e., a witness should not be paid for telling the truth, that the compensation be "reasonable" to avoid tainting the testimony, and that the compensation not be a secret arrangement.

K.   False Statements or Fraud

★★
1)   FALSE STATEMENTS

A lawyer may not knowingly making a false statement of material fact to another person. MRPC 4.1. A lawyer has a duty to correct a statement if the lawyer learns that it was false. To remain silent would be equivalent to making a false statement, and could expose the lawyer to liability for conduct involving dishonesty, fraud, deceit, or misrepresentation. MRPC 8.4(b).

★
2)   NON-DISCLOSURES

The duty of diligent representation of the lawyer's clients does not include lying on their behalf. But the lawyer does not have a duty to volunteer answers to questions that opposing counsel should have asked the lawyer. Regarding undisclosed principals represented by the lawyer, the lawyer's nondisclosure of them to opposing counsel is not improper as long as nondisclosure does not constitute fraud. MRPC 4.1, cmt.

★
3)   DISCLOSURES

A lawyer may not allow the lawyer's services to be used to assist the clients in fraud. MRPC 1.2(c). The lawyer has a duty to provide the clients with all information necessary to make an informed decision regarding the representation. MRPC 1.4(b). Part of that information and counseling includes telling the clients that the lawyer has discretion, although not a duty, to disclose confidences and secrets to rectify the consequences of a client's illegal or fraudulent act, in furtherance of which the lawyer's services have been used. MRPC 1.6(c)(3).

a)   Withdrawal

A lawyer's withdrawal is only required if the lawyer's continued representation would violate the MRPC. MRPC 1.16. If a client cannot be persuaded to allow the lawyer to make the appropriate disclosures, then the lawyer must withdraw from representation. MRPC 1.16(a).

★
4)   BAR APPLICATION OR DISCIPLINARY MATTER

"An applicant for admission to the bar, or a lawyer in connection with a bar admission application or in connection with a disciplinary matter," must not knowingly:

- "make a false statement of material fact; or

- fail to disclose a fact necessary to correct a misapprehension known by the person to have arisen in the matter; or

- fail to respond to a lawful demand for information from an admissions or disciplinary authority";

except that disclosure of information protected by the rule of confidentiality is not required.

MRPC 8.1(a).

★★   **L.   Conduct Prejudicial to the Administration of Justice**

A lawyer may not engage in conduct prejudicial to the administration of justice. MRPC 8.4(c). Arguably, a lawyer could violate this rule by failing to appear for a hearing as required by a court rule.

III.   PROFESSIONAL INTEGRITY IN GENERAL

   A.   **Unauthorized Practice of Law**

      1)   WHEN PRACTICE OF LAW IS AUTHORIZED

A lawyer may only practice law in a jurisdiction where the lawyer is authorized to practice law. MRPC 5.5, cmt. A lawyer must neither practice law in a jurisdiction in violation of the jurisdiction's regulation of the legal profession, nor aid any person or entity in such unauthorized practice of law. MRPC 5.5(a).

      2)   MULTIJURISDICTIONAL PRACTICE OF LAW

An attorney who is not admitted to practice law in Michigan may not: 1) except as authorized by the MPRC or law, establish an office or other continuous and systematic presence in Michigan for the practice of law; or 2) hold out to the public or otherwise represent that the attorney is admitted to practice law in Michigan. MRPC 5.5(b). Under certain circumstances, an attorney admitted to practice law in another jurisdiction may provide legal services in Michigan. MRPC 5.5(c)-(d).

   B.   **Business Relationships with Non-Lawyer**

      1)   FORMING PARTNERSHIP WITH NON-LAWYER

A lawyer cannot form a partnership with a non-lawyer if any activity of the partnership can be considered the practice of law. MRPC 5.4(b).

★   2)   FEE SHARING WITH NON-LAWYER

Generally, a lawyer may not share legal fees with any non-lawyer. MRPC 5.4(a). Also, a lawyer may not provide a gift to a person who recommended the lawyer's services unless the "gift" is not given as consideration for any promise that the gift would be forthcoming or that referrals would be made in the future.

★★   **C.   Financial Assistance to Client**

Lawyers are not required to advance costs and expenses of a representation matter. When the matter is litigation, MRPC 1.8(e) applies. Unlike the ABA Model Rule, which permits the lawyer to forego collection of costs and expenses from the client if the litigation is unsuccessful,

MRPC 1.8(e) requires that the client remain ultimately responsible for payment of the costs and expenses.

Specifically, a lawyer must not provide financial assistance to a client in connection with pending or contemplated litigation, except that a lawyer may advance court costs and expenses of litigation for which the client remains responsible and a lawyer representing an indigent client may pay court costs and expenses of litigation on behalf of the client. MRPC 1.8(e).

★★ **D.   Withdrawal**

★★   1)   DISCHARGE BY ATTORNEY

The lawyer must withdraw if continued representation will result in a violation of the MRPC or a conflict. MRPC 1.16. Additionally, the lawyer must withdraw if she knows or should know that the client is advancing a position or litigation without probable cause.

★★   2)   DISCHARGE BY CLIENT

The relationship can be terminated at the will of client. However, an attorney may be entitled to quasi-contract damages. The client's position should not be jeopardized by withdrawal. The attorney possesses a duty to promptly provide files for continued representation.

E.   Sexual Relations with Client

The lawyer may not coerce, intimidate, or take advantage of any client in an attempt to have sexual relations. The rule is intended to prohibit sexual exploitation by a lawyer in the course of a professional representation.

★★ **F.   Reporting Professional Misconduct**

A lawyer must inform Michigan's Attorney Grievance Commission if the lawyer has knowledge of a violation of the MRPC which substantially bears upon another lawyer's trustworthiness, honesty, and fitness to act as a lawyer. Specifically, such reporting is required when the lawyer (a) has knowledge, (b) of another lawyer's significant ethics violation, (c) that raises substantial questions about this other lawyer's honesty, trustworthiness, or fitness. MRPC 8.3. Here, the word "substantial" refers to the violation's seriousness, rather than the amount of evidence of the violation known to the reporting lawyer. If a Professional Conduct essay question tests the issue of reporting professional misconduct, then you should fully analyze the facts using each element of this MRPC to maximize your potential for success in answering the question.

This reporting rule is not triggered, however, when information is protected by the rule of confidentiality. In other words, without a client's permission to report such information that is subject to the lawyer's duty of confidentiality, a lawyer has no duty to report it.

★ **G.   Types of Professional Misconduct**

Of course, a lawyer generally commits professional misconduct when the lawyer violates a MRPC. For example, a lawyer specifically commits professional misconduct when the lawyer engages in conduct "involving dishonesty, fraud, deceit, misrepresentation, or violation of the criminal law, where such conduct   reflects adversely on the lawyer's honesty, trustworthiness, or fitness as a lawyer." MRPC 8.4(c)

★★ IV.   ADVERTISING AND SOLICITATION

Historically, ethical rules prohibited attorneys from advertising their services. Today, lawyers are permitted to conduct limited advertisements. Regulation of advertising and solicitation is subject to constitutional limitations.

A.   Advertising

1)   MUST BE TRUTHFUL

A lawyer cannot make false or misleading statements about the lawyer's services. The statement may neither contain a material misrepresentation of law or fact nor omit a fact required "to make the statement considered as a whole not materially misleading." MRPC 7.1.

a)   Unjustified Expectations

A lawyer may not include statements of fact or opinion that would create unjustified expectation (i.e., "opposing counsel shivers when they hear I represent the plaintiff.").

b)   Unfair Comparisons

A lawyer may not include unfair comparisons to other lawyers that cannot be substantiated. *Id.*

2)   "SPECIALTIES"

An attorney may state the attorney's field of practice, even claiming a specialty. However, a lawyer may not claim that the lawyer is a "certified" specialist unless certified as a specialist by an organization approved by an appropriate state authority or accredited by the American Bar Association and the name of the certifying organization is clearly identified in the communication.

3)   JURISDICTION ADMISSIONS

A law firm with offices in more than one jurisdiction may use the same name or other professional designation in each jurisdiction, but identification of the lawyers in an office of the firm must indicate the jurisdictional limitations on those not licensed to practice in the jurisdiction where the office is located.

4)   CONTENTS OF ADVERTISEMENTS

Under the ABA Model Rules, advertisements must contain the name and address of an attorney or law firm responsible for its contents. Additionally, an advertisement may not mention other clients unless the client is regularly represented by that lawyer or firm and the client consents in advance. The MRPC do not require the name of a lawyer in an ad or an "advertising" label.

5)   KEEPING COPIES OF ADVERTISEMENTS

Many states now require lawyers to keep copies of written or electronic advertisements for two years. The copies must be produced on demand from the state regulatory authorities.

6)   PLACE OF ADVERTISEMENTS

A court may inquire as to where the advertisement is located. For example, an advertisement located in a hospital will generally not be permitted because of the potentially vulnerable nature of the patients.

★★   B.   Solicitation

As a general rule, solicitation is prohibited. However, only in person, by telephone or telegraph, by letter or other writing, or by other "real-time" contact directed to a particular recipient is considered impermissible solicitation. MRPC 7.3(a). Consequently, written communications can be considered solicitation.

1)   EXCEPTION TO PROHIBITION

The prohibition is not applicable if the person solicited 1) is a lawyer; or 2) has a family, close personal, or prior professional relationship with the lawyer.

The word "solicit" does not include letters addressed or advertising circulars distributed generally to persons not known to need legal services of the kind provided by the lawyer in a particular matter, but who are so situated that they might, in general, find such services useful, nor does the term "solicit" include "sending truthful and non-deceptive letters to potential clients known to face particular legal problems." *Shapero v. Kentucky Bar Ass'n*, 486 U.S. 466 (1988).

a)   Example

A hospital visit is in-person solicitation, which is prohibited under MRPC 7.3, if a lawyer has no family or prior professional relationship with the person solicited in person in the hospital. *Id.*

2)   REGULATION OF WRITTEN SOLICITATIONS

a)   Desire not to be Contacted

A lawyer cannot solicit business from a person if the person has made it known that she is not interested in the lawyer's services.

        b)   Coercion

A lawyer may not solicit business using coercion, duress, or harassment.

★★   c)   "Advertising Material"

        (1)   ABA Model Rule – Other States

Every written, recorded, or electronic communication from a lawyer soliciting professional employment from a prospective client known to be in need of legal services in a particular matter must include the words "Advertising Material" on the outside envelope and at the beginning and ending of any such recorded or electronic communication.

        (2)   MRPC -- Michigan

The MRPC do not require the name of a lawyer in an ad or an "advertising" label. One testable issue is whether a preprinted notice (to call a law firm about participating in a class action lawsuit) that would be handed out by a person to strangers on a street (A) is mere "advertising," restricted only by requirements of MRPC 7.1 that a public communication about a lawyer's services not be false, fraudulent, deceptive, or misleading, or whether (B) it is an improper in-person "solicitation" to people not known to need the legal services being offered under MRPC 7.3. The resolution of an issue such as whether or not the hand-out is proper could depend upon the text of the notice, the pitch used by the person handing out the flyers to the people on the street, and if the situation taken as a whole is more solicitation than advertising.

In some circumstances, merely handing out a flyer, without any verbal communication, could be considered impermissible advertising. For example, a hand-out like the foregoing one without verbal communication could be improper as deceptive by omission if it does not reveal that the phone number on the flyer is for calling the law firm.

★   d)   Source of List of People Solicited

Possession of a list of people to solicit is not improperly obtained if it is from a public source.

★   e)   E-mail Solicitation

An e-mail communication could be considered akin to direct-mail letter-writing, or akin to a phone call, since it is sent in real time. "Real-time electronic contact" amounts to forbidden solicitation. ABA Model Rule 7.3. Michigan has no MRPC on e-mail communication. However, e-mail directed to a specific addressee or group of addressees is permitted as direct-mail solicitation. Michigan Ethics Opinion RI-276. Interactive e-mail communication is governed by rules on in-person solicitation. *Id.*

More and more businesses are using e-mail in the regular course of business as a substitute of

U.S. Mail, i.e. as letter substitutes. If Michigan people solicited by e-mail could be considered persons "so situated that they might in general find such services useful," then an e-mail could fall into the solicitation exception for prohibited mail solicitation. If a communication's content clearly shows it is from a lawyer, and leaves it up to the prospective client to respond if interested, then such a communication by e-mail could possibly not be considered a violation of the MRPC.

★   **C.**   **Solicitation by Third Parties**

If the solicitation is carried about by a third party, then it will be attributed to an attorney if the elements of solicitation are otherwise present and the communication was directed by the attorney.

V.   MISCELLANEOUS CONCEPTS

★   **A.**   **Public Officials**

Generally, it is illegal for public officials to receive favors from vendors of the government, or to accept personal favors in exchange for government contracts.

★   **B.**   **Using Threats of Criminal Charges in Exchange for Settling a Civil Matter**

A question may arise as to whether a lawyer's raising of a person's misconduct is improperly using threats of criminal charges in exchange for settling a civil matter. The MRPC do not have a specific rule that addresses such threats, but several existing rules may apply in a particular case. With respect to that omission:

> No specific ethical rule prohibits a lawyer, when acting in good faith and without purpose of harassment, to call to the attention of an opposing party the possible applicability of a penal statute or make reference to specific criminal sanctions, or to warn of the possibility of criminal prosecution, even if done in order to assist in the enforcement of a valid right or legitimate claim of a client.

Michigan Ethics Opinion RI-78.

Whether a lawyer violates the underlying concept greatly depends upon how the lawyer raises the matter with the opposing party. If withholding criminal charges is discussed as a constructive means, then mentioning it in the context of resolving the lawyer's client's matter would not be improper. If the criminal charges are raised to coerce or intimidate the opposing party, then it would be improper.

★   **C.**   **Supervisory and Subordinate Lawyers**

A subordinate lawyer may follow a supervisory lawyer's decision regarding an arguable question of professional ethics. MRPC 5.2(b).

★   **D.**   **Lawyer's Responsibility for Another Lawyer's Ethical Violation**

A lawyer is responsible for another lawyer's violation of the MRPC if the lawyer is a partner in the law firm in which the other lawyer practices and knows of the conduct at a time when its consequences can be mitigated or avoided, but does not take responsible remedial action. MRPC 5.1(c)(2).

MICHIGAN

AMERIBAR BAR REVIEW

Michigan Bar Review

No-Fault

TABLE OF CONTENTS

NO-FAULT

Issues regarding no-fault insurance may be tested in the context of a Torts essay question on the Michigan Bar Exam.

Prior to 1973, an individual injured in an accident involving a motor vehicle usually brought an action for damages pursuant to the common law. *Kreiner v. Fischer,* 471 Mich. 109 (2004), overruled on other grounds by *McCormick v. Carrier,* 487 Mich. 108 (2010). In 1973, the Michigan Legislature enacted a no-fault act that generally abolished tort liability in cases regarding motor vehicle accidents and replaced it with a statutory scheme entitling an individual injured in a motor vehicle accident to specified economic loss benefits from the individual's vehicle insurance company (i.e., insurer) irrespective of fault for the accident. *Id.* In exchange for receiving these benefits, the individual can only sue a negligent owner, operator, or maintainer of a motor vehicle for non-economic damages if the individual suffered "death, serious impairment of bodily function, or permanent serious disfigurement." *Id.*; Mich. Comp. Laws § 500.3135(1). The individual may sue such an owner for economic damages only in certain situations. Mich. Comp. Laws § 500.3135(3)(a), (c). Otherwise, a Michigan no-fault insurance policy can afford basic coverage for accidental harms to people and property.

I.   NO-FAULT ACT

Michigan statutory law contains the Insurance Code of 1956, which includes Chapter 31 regarding Motor Vehicle Personal and Property Protection. Mich. Comp. Laws §§ 500.3101-500.3179. Michigan's no-fault act is within these statutes and requires every auto owner to obtain certain minimum no-fault insurance coverage in order to obtain valid Michigan license plates and to legally drive the auto, or legally allow it to be driven, in Michigan. Office of Financial and Insurance Services, Insurance Counselor, Insurance Consumer Information Sheet, *Brief Explanation of Michigan No-Fault Insurance,* FIS-PUB 0202, 10/07, p. 1, at http://www.michigan.gov/documents/cis_ofis_ip202_25083_7.pdf (hereafter "FIS-PUB").

Michigan law imposes criminal penalties for operating a motor vehicle when no valid automobile insurance coverage is in effect for the motor vehicle. *Id.* An individual who operates a motor vehicle when it lacks valid automobile insurance coverage is sometimes referred to as an "uninsured motorist." An uninsured motorist generally is exposed to greater personal liability than an insured motorist for any harm to people or property that results from the motorist's operation of the uninsured motor vehicle. An uninsured motorist generally lacks any of the no-fault insurance coverage described later. Uninsured motorist auto insurance coverage is an optional type of coverage that may be purchased to receive certain compensation in the event that covered harm is done by an uninsured motorist or a hit and run vehicle.

★   A.   **Definitions**

   1)   <u>BODILY INJURY</u>

The definition of bodily injury includes death resulting from that injury. Mich. Comp. Laws § 500.3105(3).

2)   ACCIDENTAL BODILY INJURY

Generally, a bodily injury is accidental as to an individual claiming PPI benefits, unless the bodily injury is (a) intentionally suffered by the injured individual or (b) intentionally caused by the claimant. Mich. Comp. Laws § 500.3105(4). Even if an individual knows that the individual's act or omission is substantially certain to cause bodily injury, the individual does not cause or suffer injury intentionally if the individual acts or refrains from acting in order to avoid injury to any people or any property. *Id.*

★   ### 3)   SERIOUS IMPAIRMENT OF BODILY FUNCTION

Michigan law defines "serious impairment of body function" as "an objectively manifested impairment of an important body function that affects the person's general ability to lead his or her normal life." Mich. Comp. Laws § 500.3135(7).

B.   Types of No-Fault Insurance Coverage

1)   BASIC NO-FAULT INSURANCE COVERAGE

Generally, regardless of who caused an automobile accident, no fault insurance will pay for wage loss and medical expenses and the damages done to other people's property. FIS-PUB. The minimal level of legally required no-fault auto insurance, however, generally does not cover:

- repairs of your insured auto after an accident, regardless of who is at fault, unless it was properly parked and hit by another vehicle (in which case the other driver's no-fault coverage will pay for the repair);
- repairs of another individual's insured auto after an accident, regardless of who is at fault, unless it was properly parked (in which event the no-fault coverage of the driver that accidentally hit the properly parked auto will pay for this repair); or
- replacement of the auto that is totally wrecked or stolen. *Id.*

a)   Optional Collision Coverage

Additional and optional coverage beyond the legally required minimum no-fault coverage obtained for the purpose of paying for repairs of autos damaged in an accidental crash is available and known as collision coverage. *Id.* Collision coverage basically pays for the cost of an insured owner's auto repair or replacement as a result of an auto accident involving another motor vehicle. *Id.* The three main types of collision coverage are limited, standard, and broad form. *Id.* These coverages include a deductible amount that the insured agrees to pay for the auto repair cost before the insurer pays for the balance. *Id.*

b)   Optional Comprehensive Coverage

Comprehensive coverage essentially pays for the cost of an insured owner's auto repair or replacement resulting from an auto accident involving an animal, or from other specified types of casualty losses such as vandalism, falling objects, fire, theft, flood, etc. *Id.*

c)   Required Coverage

Michigan's no-fault act does not require either collision coverage or comprehensive coverage. Michigan's no-fault act, however, requires the owner or registrant of a motor vehicle required to be registered in Michigan to maintain an automobile insurance policy as a type of security for payment of the following types of benefits: 1) personal protection insurance; 2) property protection insurance; and 3) residual liability insurance. Mich. Comp. Laws § 500.3101(1).

2)   PERSONAL INJURY PROTECTION ("PIP")

PIP insurance benefits are available pursuant to Michigan law. Under PIP, an insurer is liable to pay benefits for accidental bodily injury to an individual arising from the "ownership, operation, maintenance or use of a motor vehicle." Mich. Comp. Laws § 500.3105(1). PIP benefits are due without regard to fault under Michigan's no-fault act. Mich. Comp. Laws § 500.3105(2). In other words, PIP benefits are a type of "no-fault" benefit available with respect to accidents involving an insured motor vehicle and an injured individual.

★   a)   Medical Costs as Allowable Expenses

PIP benefits pay for medical costs of an individual injured in, for example, an auto accident. *Id.* Medical costs include the allowable expenses of the injured individual's "care, recovery, or rehabilitation." Mich. Comp. Laws § 300.3107(1)(a). Benefits are also payable for funeral and burial expenses between $1,750 and $5,000. Mich. Comp. Laws § 300.3107(1)(a).

★   b)   Wage-Loss

Another PIP benefit pays for wage loss (i.e., work loss), for the first three years from the accident date and up to 85% of the income the injured individual would have earned if he had not sustained the bodily harm in the auto accident. FIS-PUB and Mich. Comp. Laws § 300.3107(1)(b). During most of 2007, this wage-loss benefit was approximately $4,400 per month. Effective for one year starting October 1, 2007, the maximum amount of this benefit is $4,713 per month. FIS-PUB. The amount of this benefit is annually adjusted for the cost of living. Mich. Comp. Laws § 300.3107(1)(b).

c)   Survivor's Loss

The survivor's loss is a PIP benefit payable to the dependents of an individual who dies as a result of a bodily injury from, for example, an unintentional auto accident. Mich. Comp. Laws § 300.3108(1). The benefit is measured by the amount of loss of the individual's contributions of tangible things of economic value, excluding services. *Id.* The amount of expenses incurred for services in lieu of those that the individual had provided may not exceed $20.00 per day. *Id.* The survivor's loss "is not payable beyond the first three years" from the accident date. *Id.*

d)   Replacement Services

Another PIP benefit from the insurer is a payment of $20 each day to cover the cost of "ordinary and necessary" replacement services that an injured individual is unable to perform for the individual or the individual's family during the first three years from the accident date. FIS-PUB and Mich. Comp. Laws § 300.3107(1)(c). These types of services include, for example, maintaining a home and its yard.

3)   PROPERTY PROTECTION INSURANCE ("PPI")

a)   When PPI Benefits are Payable

If an insured's auto accidentally (i.e., unintentionally) harms the property of other people, like fences or buildings, then that harm may be paid for with no-fault coverage of PPI benefits up to one million dollars. FIS-PUB and Mich. Comp. Laws § 300.3121(5). This type of no-fault coverage also applies to pay for accidental harm that an insured person's auto inflicts upon another person's motorized vehicle that is properly parked, but not other types of damage to vehicles. *Id.* and Mich. Comp. Laws § 300.3123(1)(a).

(1)   PPI Benefits Exclusions

This type of no-fault coverage will not be available, however, when certain exclusions apply. Thus, the following types of property are excluded from no-fault PPI benefits.

(a)   Motorized Vehicles unless Properly Parked

Vehicles and their contents, as well as trailers, designed for operation upon or operated on a public highway (e.g., cars and trucks, but not go-carts, etc.), unless the vehicle is parked so as not to cause unreasonable risk of the property damage that occurred. *Id.*

(b)   PPI Policy

Another type of property excluded from no-fault PPI benefits coverage is property owned by (1) an individual named in a PPI policy, (2) the individual's spouse, or (3) a relative of either of them domiciled in the same household with them, if any of them was the (a) owner, (b) registrant, or (c) operator of "a vehicle involved in the motor vehicle accident out of which the property damage arose." Mich. Comp. Laws § 300.3123(1)(b).

(c)   Accident Outside of Michigan

One exclusion applies when property damage arises from a motor vehicle accident that occurs outside of Michigan (e.g., in another state). Mich. Comp. Laws § 300.3123(2).

(d)   Certain Utility Transmission Property

PPI benefits are not payable for property damage to utility transmission lines, wires, or cables arising from the failure to comply with Michigan law by a municipality, utility company, or cable television company. Mich. Comp. Laws § 300.3123(3).

4)   RESIDUAL LIABILITY INSURANCE

a)   Required Coverage

Residual liability insurance must cover bodily injury and property damage that occurs in the United States or in Canada. Mich. Comp. Laws § 500.3131(1). This insurance must provide coverage for tort liability for non-economic loss caused by an individual's ownership maintenance, or use of a motor vehicle if an injured individual "has suffered death, serious impairment of bodily function, or permanent serious disfigurement." *Id.* and Mich. Comp. Laws § 500.3135(1). This coverage is further described later.

b)   When Insured may be Sued

Insureds are generally protected by Michigan's no-fault insurance law from being sued as a consequence of an auto accident, unless one the following four situations exist:

- if the insured is sued for up to $500 and the insured is at least 50% at fault in an auto accident that causes damages to another individual's car that are not covered by insurance;

★★
- if the insured causes an auto accident within Michigan as a result of which an individual is "killed, seriously injured, or permanently disfigured" for which tort liability exists for non-economic damages (as further discussed below);

- if the insured is involved in an auto accident in a state other than Michigan; or

- if the insured is involved in an auto accident within Michigan involving a non-resident of Michigan "who is an occupant of a motor vehicle not registered in Michigan."

FIS-PUB.

c)   Required Insurance Coverage Amounts

(1)   What Amounts Insurance Policy Covers

An insured's no-fault auto insurance policy will cover up to the amounts specified in the residual liability portion of the policy if the insured is held legally responsible in a lawsuit arising from an accident in one of the aforementioned four situations. *Id.*

Michigan law requires certain minimum amounts of insurance coverage from which an adverse judgment against the insured would be paid. *Id.* Of course, an insurer may offer, and an insured can purchase, more than the mandatory minimum coverage amounts to increase the insured's protection. *Id.*

(2)   Minimum Required Insurance Coverage Amounts

The minimum required residual liability coverage limits of a no-fault insurance policy are:

- $20,000 for an individual's bodily injury or death in an accident,

- $40,000 for bodily injury to or death of at least 2 individuals in each accident, and

- $10,000 because of injury to or destruction of property of others in any accident, even if the accident occurred in a state other than Michigan.

Mich. Comp. Laws §§ 500.3131(2), 500.3009(1), and FIS-PUB.

d)   Purpose of Residual Liability Insurance Coverage

Residual liability insurance serves to pay the costs of defending an insured and any damages for which the insured is held legally responsible as the result of an auto accident, up to the amounts of the policy's limits. FIS-PUB. Accordingly, if an insured is sued as a consequence of an auto accident under one of the four situations described earlier, the insured is covered by the residual liability insurance up to the amounts of the policy's limits. *Id.* In the event that a judgment is entered against the insured for more than those amounts, the insured would be personally liable for any additional amount of the judgment above and beyond those amounts. *Id.* In other words, the insurer must pay for damages assessed against the insured pursuant to the policy and up to the policy limits and the insured is personally liable to pay any amount of damages above and beyond the policy limits.

C.   **Recovery of No-Fault Benefits**

★   1)   PRIORITY OF RECOVERY OF NO FAULT BENEFITS

Under the Michigan no-fault insurance system, an insured individual suffering a bodily injury arising out of an automobile accident must look to his insurer first for first-party no-fault benefits. Mich. Comp. Laws § 500.3114(1). If the person does not have no-fault insurance, the person would look to the policy of an insured relative with whom he shares a domicile. *Id.* If the person has no such relative, then the person would look to the insurer of the owner or registrant of the vehicle, then to the vehicle operator's insurer. Mich. Comp. Laws § 500.3114(4). If none of those parties is insured, then the person would look to the assigned claims plan. Mich. Comp. Laws § 500.3172(1).

D.   **Recovery of Damages**

★★   1)   TORT LIABILITY FOR DAMAGES

Notwithstanding other provisions of law, generally "tort liability arising from the ownership, maintenance, or use" in Michigan of a motor vehicle is abolished except for:

- "intentionally caused harm to persons or property" (i.e., non-accidental harm).

- non-economic damages (e.g., pain and suffering) only if an injured individual has suffered death, serious impairment of body function, or permanent serious disfigurement.

- economic damages for medical costs as allowable expenses, wage loss (i.e., work loss), survivor's loss, and replacement services, that exceed the statutory limits upon those types of PIP benefits reimbursed as first-party benefits (described earlier in this outline).

Mich. Comp. Laws § 500.3135(3)(a)-(c).

a)   Economic Damages

Economic damages generally include allowable medical costs, wage loss (i.e., work loss), survivor's loss, and replacement services (described earlier in this outline). *Id.*

For example, a passenger injured when the driver hit a tree may seek to recover certain economic damages such as the passenger's wage-loss in excess of those benefits that the passenger received from the passenger's insurer.

★★★   b)   Non-economic Damages

An injured individual can recover in a tort action non-economic damages (e.g., pain and suffering) from a motor vehicle operator only if the individual has suffered death, serious impairment of body function, or permanent serious disfigurement.   Mich. Comp. Laws § 500.3135(1).

(1)   Determining Threshold for Non-economic Damages

Generally, the no-fault act bars tort remedies unless a plaintiff pleads and proves that the plaintiff has met the statutory threshold for non-economic tort damages.

★★   (a)   Serious Impairment of Body Function

The Michigan Supreme Court has articulated a multi-step process for determining whether a plaintiff (e.g., injured individual) has reached the "serious impairment of body function" threshold ("serious impairment threshold" herein) in order to maintain an action for non-economic damages based on the plaintiff's injuries. *McCormick v. Carrier*, 487 Mich. 180 (2010).

(i)   Nature and Extent of Injuries

The court must initially determine if there is a material factual dispute concerning the nature and extent of the plaintiff's injuries. *Id.* If a material factual dispute exists regarding the nature and extent of the plaintiff's injuries, then the court should not determine whether the plaintiff has suffered a serious impairment of body function as a matter of law. *Id.* If no material factual dispute exists regarding the nature and extent of the plaintiff's injuries, then the court should determine whether the plaintiff has suffered a serious impairment of body function as a matter of law. *Id.*; Mich. Comp. Laws § 500.3135(2)(a)(i). In the latter type of cases, when the court should determine whether the serious impairment threshold is met as a matter of law, the court can move on to the next step.

Next, the court must determine whether a plaintiff has a "serious impairment of body function" under the following three prongs: "(1) an objectively manifested impairment (2) of an important body function that (3) affects" the plaintiff's general ability to lead the plaintiff's normal life. *Id.*

(ii)   Objectively Manifested Impairment

Commonly, an "objectively manifested" impairment is understood as one perceivable or observable by a third party from a plaintiff's actual symptoms or conditions. *Id.* The "proper inquiry is whether the impairment is objectively manifested, not the injury or its symptoms." *Id.* When considering an impairment, the court should focus on how the injuries affect a specific body function, not on the injuries themselves. *Id.*

A person does not satisfy the serious impairment threshold only with evidence of the plaintiff's pain and suffering. *Id.* The plaintiff must present evidence of "objectively manifested injuries," which mean injuries that affect functioning of the plaintiff's body. *Id.* The plaintiff must "introduce evidence establishing that there is a physical basis for their subjective complaints of pain and suffering" *Id.* quoting *DiFranco v. Pickard*, 427 Mich. 32 (1986).

(iii)   Impairment of Important Body Function

If an objectively manifested impairment of body function exists, then the next question is whether the impaired body function is important. A body function is important when it has great value, significance, or consequence. *Id.* This factor involves a subjective inquiry on a case-specific basis because it will hinge upon whether a body function has great value, significance, or consequence to the plaintiff. *Id.*

(iv)   Impairment's Effect Upon Normal Life

If a plaintiff's important body function has suffered an objectively manifested impairment, then the next inquiry involves determining whether the impairment affects the plaintiff's general ability to conduct a normal life. *Id.* This factor involves a subjective inquiry on a case-specific basis as to the extent of the impairment's influence on the plaintiff's ability to live in the plaintiff's normal way after the injuries occurred. *Id.* This inquiry involves a comparison of the plaintiff's life before and after the injuries occurred. *Id.*

A plaintiff's ability to conduct the plaintiff's normal life only has to be affected, not destroyed. *Id.*

Although the extent that a plaintiff's ability to conduct the plaintiff's normal life is affected by an impairment is related to what the plaintiff's normal way of living is, no minimum metric exists as to the extent that the plaintiff's normal way of living must be affected. *Id.*

An impairment need not exist for any specific duration in order for the impairment to have an effect on the plaintiff's general ability to conduct the plaintiff's normal life. *Id.*

★   (b)   Permanent Serious Disfigurement

Whether a personal injury constitutes a permanent serious disfigurement of a person depends on the injury's physical characteristics instead of its effect on the person's ability to lead a normal life. *Kosack v. Moore*, 144 Mich. App. 485 (1985). One must answer the issue of whether an injury such as a scar is serious by using common knowledge and experience. *Nelson v. Myers*, 146 Mich. App. 444 (1985). A hardly discernable scar is not a permanent serious disfigurement. *Petaja v. Guck*, 178 Mich. App. 577 (1989). The scar must be readily noticeable. *Id.*

                    (2)   Non-economic Damages Procedural Considerations

The following rules apply in a tort case filed on or after July 26, 1996, seeking non-economic damages (e.g., pain and suffering) of an injured individual who suffered serious impairment of body function or permanent serious disfigurement. Mich. Comp. Laws § 500.3135(2)(a).

                              (a)   Questions of Law for the Court

The issues of whether an injured individual has suffered those types of harm are questions of law for the court if the court finds either that: 1) no factual dispute exists regarding the extent and nature of the individual's injuries; or 2) a factual dispute exists regarding the extent and nature of the individual's injuries, but the dispute is not material to determining if the person suffered those types of harm. *Id.*

                              (b)   Assessment of Damages

Damages must be assessed on the basis of comparative fault, except that damages must not be assessed for a party over 50% at fault. Mich. Comp. Laws § 500.3135(2)(b).

                              (c)   No Damages for Uninsured Party

Damages must not be assessed for a party that was operating the party's own vehicle when the injury occurred and did not have vehicle insurance coverage in effect for that motor vehicle when the injury occurred (e.g., an "uninsured motorist"). Mich. Comp. Laws § 500.3135(2)(c).

AMERIBAR BAR REVIEW

Michigan Bar Review

PERSONAL PROPERTY

TABLE OF CONTENTS

PERSONAL PROPERTY

Personal property issues are testable within Real & Personal Property essay questions on the Michigan Bar Exam. Traditionally, one of these questions has appeared on each exam or every other exam, although this frequency of testing in the past may not be the same going forward. Certain past Real & Personal Property questions have tended to test personal property issues separately from real property issues, although some overlap or combination of these issues could occur. Traditionally, the most frequently tested personal property issue in some past questions was bailments. Various facets of the main rules regarding bailments were examined, including but not limited to their formation, the bailee's duties, and exceptions. A less frequently tested issue in those past questions was gifts. Some previous questions have tested issues of lost or abandoned personal property.

I.   WILD ANIMALS (POSSESSION AND CAPTURE)

Generally, as a practical matter, possession is most of what proves ownership with wild animals and most personal property. Some pieces of personal property require more than possession (i.e., title) because they are so valuable.

A.   Possession

Possession or "occupancy" requires a person to:

    (1)   have the intention to appropriate the thing and
    (2)   to deprive it of its natural liberty.

B.   Constructive Possession

Constructive possession includes mortal wounding or trapping. However, pursuit alone does not constitute possession.

C.   First in Time – First in Right

As a general rule, the first person to capture the animal has rightful possession.

★   D.   The People of Michigan Own Its Wild Animals

In Michigan, wild animals (*ferae naturae*) are the property of the people of Michigan. Mich. Comp. Laws § 324.40105. Therefore, someone can acquire only such qualified or limited property interest in wild animals as the State of Michigan permits. *People v. Zimberg*, 321 Mich. 655 (1948). For example, someone who hunts deer in Michigan without having a valid Michigan hunting license lacks the State's permission to take these deer, which belong to the State. This example applies even when this hunter takes the deer on a private tract of land that he owns. While the land belongs to the hunter, the deer do not. The State may regulate the hunting and use of the deer as it sees fit. *People v. Van Pelt*, 130 Mich. 621 (1902). The hunter may face misdemeanor criminal charges for taking deer without a hunting license. Mich. Comp. Laws § 324.40118(3). Also, the hunter may have to reimburse the State for the value of each deer that he takes. Mich. Comp. Laws § 324.40119(1)(b).

II.   REAL VS. PERSONAL PROPERTY

Personal property includes chattels and movable items (e.g., goods). Real property is land and things attached to it in some way. Fixtures are attached to the land, and therefore pass with the land even though, before they are affixed, they may be personal property. Questions may raise the issue of whether an object is a fixture or personal property.

A.   Fixtures

When classifying personal property as a fixture, the following factors may be examined:

- annexation: Whether the property is attached to the real property;
- adaptation: Whether the property is used as a part of a larger function of the real property;
- trade fixture: Whether the property is used for business purpose. If so, it is likely to be a fixture.

III.   ABANDONED PROPERTY

A.   General Considerations

As a general rule, the owner of a personal property who manifests an intent to abandon and actually abandons the property, loses her rights to the personal property. When an object is abandoned, it goes to the finder. The finder will be deemed in possession when she 1) exercises power over the personal property and 2) manifests the intent to control the personal property.

1)   WHETHER PERSON INTENDED TO ABANDON OBJECT

The issue that often arises involves whether the person intended to abandon the object. Answering requires a thorough analysis of all the facts that makes for a great exam question.

B.   Michigan's Uniform Unclaimed Property Act

★   1)   WHEN CERTAIN PROPERTY IS PRESUMED ABANDONED

Michigan's Uniform Unclaimed Property Act can apply, for example, to property contained in a safe deposit box under certain circumstances. Mich. Comp. Laws § 567.221 *et seq.* In particular, if such property goes unclaimed by the property owner for over five years after the safe deposit box lease period has expired, then the property is presumed abandoned. Mich. Comp. Laws § 567.237. Abandoned property is turned over to the State of Michigan. If the owner fails to claim the property within three years, then the property is sold. This sale's proceeds revert to the State's general fund. Mich. Comp. Laws §§ 567.243(1), 567.244.

IV.   FINDER'S RIGHTS ABSENT ABANDONMENT

A prior finder has rights above anyone but the true owner though some exceptions exist.

A.   Equitable Considerations

If a possessor wrongfully obtained possession of the property, he may be estopped from asserting ownership. For example, a trespasser who finds personal property on another's land cannot assert ownership of the personal property against the landowner.

★   **B.   Rights versus Owner of Land upon which Property Found**

1)   LOST PROPERTY

a)   Definition

Lost property is property that the owner accidentally and casually lost (e.g. a ring slips through a hole in a pocket).

b)   General Rule

Lost property goes to the finder, rather than the owner of the premises.

★   c)   Effect of Reward

In Michigan, one who finds lost property for which a reward has been offered (i.e., finder) may retain the property until such time as the reward is paid. *Wood v. Pierson,* 45 Mich. 313 (1881). The finder's failure to permit an inspection of the "found" property by its owner (i.e., offeror of the reward) does not waive a claim to the reward. *Id.* Rather, it is incumbent upon the owner to prove ownership and at that time to pay the reward. If the finder maintains the property due to a legitimate doubt as to the owner, it does not affect a waiver of the reward nor does it give rise to a conversion claim. *Id.*

2)   MISLAID PROPERTY

Mislaid property is property that is intentionally placed somewhere, and then forgotten. As a general rule, mislaid property goes to the owner of the premises.

★   **C.   Michigan's Lost and Unclaimed Property Act**

1)   LOST OR MISLAID PROPERTY IS SUBJECT TO STATUTE

Michigan's Lost and Unclaimed Property Act governs certain types of found property. Mich. Comp. Laws § 434.21 *et seq.* This finder's statute applies whether the property was mislaid or lost. *Willsmore v. Oceola Twp.*, 106 Mich. App. 671 (1981), superseded by statute per *People v. $27,490*, unpublished opinion per curiam of the Court of Appeals, issued 11/26/1996 (Docket No. 173507). This statute applies, for example when a landowner finds someone else's case containing money on the landowner's property. In this event, the landowner must either deliver the money to local law enforcement or report this finding of the money. If the landowner wants to receive the money if it is not claimed, then the landowner must give her name and address to the law enforcement agency. The money is returned to its owner if the owner can be identified. If its owner is not identified within six months, then the money goes to the landowner. Mich. Comp. Laws §§ 434.24(7), 434.26(1)(a).

Now, suppose that the case found by the landowner contained a key to a safe deposit box and a list of the box's contents. In this event, the landowner could not make any claim to the box's contents under the Lost and Unclaimed Property Act. At most, the landowner could only receive the key. The earlier discussion of Michigan's Uniform Unclaimed Property Act pertains to this situation.

V.   BAILMENTS

A bailment exists when an item is delivered to the bailee and limited rights of possession are given to the bailee. A bailment, therefore, is the rightful possession of goods by one who is not their owner. A bailment does not change their title. *Dunlap v. Gleason*, 16 Mich. 158 (1867).

★★   A.   Common Law Rules

Ordinarily, a bailment cannot arise without the bailee's consent. The bailee generally must accept care and custody of the bailed goods. *Generally,* 5 Mich. L. & Prac. 2d, Bailment § 4 (2000).

A bailment is defined as the "delivery of goods, without the passing of title, whereby the goods are to be returned when the purpose of the delivery has been fulfilled." 4 Mich. L. & Prac. 2d, Bailment, § 1 (2003). "The term bailment imports the delivery of personal property by one person to another . . . for a specific purpose, with a contract, express or implied, that . . . the property [be] returned or duly accounted for when the special purpose is accomplished or the bailor claims it." *Nat'l Ben Franklin Ins. Co. v. Bakhaus Contractors, Inc.,* 124 Mich. App. 510, 512, n.2 (1983). In other words, the personal property is to be disposed of pursuant to the wishes of the bailor at the end of the bailment. The contract further provides that the goods will be properly cared for while out of the possession of the title owner.

The title owner is the bailor and the party taking possession of the goods is the bailee. At common law, a bailee did not have title to bailed goods and could not convey title to a third person. *Ball-Barnhart-Putnum Co. v. Lane,* 135 Mich. 275 (1903); *generally*, 4 Mich. L. & Prac. 2d, Bailment, § 13 (2003). This rule is subject to an exception for buyers in the ordinary course of business, which is discussed later in the Bona Fide Purchasers section of this Personal Property Outline.

B.   Delivery to Bailee

Delivery must be actual, constructive (key to safe), or symbolic (deed) delivery. The bailee must have control and the intent to possess (like a regular possession). Whether a bailment exists is often judged by conduct of the parties.

★★   **C.   Bailee's Duty during Custody**

Generally, once a bailment occurs, a bailee has a duty to use a proper degree of care in exercising custody over bailed goods. Of course, the duty does not arise if there is no bailment. During the time that the bailee has the object in his possession, he is not an insurer of it. The bailee is liable only for lack of care, but the precise standard depends on who is benefited. Bailments are generally classified as to whether the relation benefits the bailor, the bailee or both. *Generally*, 5 Mich. L. & Prac. 2d, Bailment § 3 (2000). Traditionally, the following classifications have been used to define the bailee's duty of care in exercising custody over the bailed goods.

1)   MUTUAL BENEFIT

a)   General Rule

If the bailment is beneficial to both parties (e.g., paying rent), then the bailee must use ordinary diligence/reasonable care to protect the bailor's bailed object from damage or loss.

(1)   Liability of Bailee and Wrong Bailor

Under a bailee's duty to exercise ordinary care, the bailee must surrender bailed property only to the correct bailor. *Gen. Exch. Ins. Co. v. Serv. Parking Grounds*, 254 Mich. 1 (1931). A bailee who violates this duty may have liability to the correct bailor for damages resulting from surrendering bailed property to the wrong bailor. In that event, if the correct bailor recovers the bailed property from the wrong bailor, then this recovery will offset all or some of the damages to which the correct bailor is entitled from the bailee. If the correct bailor recovers the bailed property from the wrong bailor, then the bailee may have liability to the wrong bailor for damages resulting from surrendering bailed property to the wrong bailor. The wrong bailor may recover the amount of the wrong bailor's actual loss, or "his bargain which he would have realized but for defendant's breach." *Demirjian v. Kurtis*, 353 Mich. 619 (1958).

(2)   Rebuttable Presumption of Bailee's Negligence

Evidence that personal property was destroyed or damaged when in the bailee's possession creates a rebuttable presumption of negligence. *Columbus Jack Corp. v. Swedish Crucible Steel Corp.*, 393 Mich. 478 (1975). In the event of such damage or destruction resulting from a fire or theft, the bailee must "produce evidence of the actual circumstances of the fire or theft including the precautions taken to prevent the loss." *Id.* For example, the bailee could present the following types of evidence to rebut the presumption:

- the bailee's premises are in a low-crime area;
- the premises has a burglar alarm system;
- the premises has a fire alarm and suppression system;
- the bailee did not have flammable materials on the premises;
- the bailee kept the premises in good repair; or
- the fire seems to be the work of an arsonist. *Id.*

b) When Mutual Benefit Bailment

A bailment for the mutual benefit of both parties exists when the bailor gives the bailee temporary possession of some personal property other than money, in which the bailee agrees to return the property to the bailor at some future time, and the bailor agrees to pay a fee or some form of compensation for the bailee's service.

(1) Bailment for Hire

Bailments for hire exist where the bailee accepts the property with the understanding that the bailee is to perform a service that relates to the property. These bailments are also bailments for the mutual benefit of the parties.

2) BAILOR ALONE BENEFITS

a) General Rule

If the benefit is solely for the bailor's benefit, the bailee is liable only for gross negligence. Such a "gratuitous bailment" involving a "gratuitous bailee" entails this lower standard of care. *Generally,* 5 Mich. L. & Prac. 2d, Bailment § 6 (2000). In other words, a gratuitous bailee is only liable for gross neglect if the bailed goods were damaged while in the bailee's possession. *Cadwell v. Peninsular State Bank,* 195 Mich. 407 (1917).

b) When Bailor Alone Benefits

A bailment for the sole benefit of the bailor exists when the bailor's goods are cared for by the bailee without a surcharge or fee and as a mere accommodation to the bailor. Under such bailment, the bailee is required only to act in good faith and, as aforementioned, is liable only for gross negligence. *Gerrish v. Muskegon Savs. Bank,* 138 Mich. 46 (1904).

3) BAILEE ALONE BENEFITS

If the bailment is solely for the benefit of the bailee (i.e., the bailor lends the object to the bailee for the bailee's use at no cost), the bailee is required to use extraordinary care (i.e., the highest degree of care) in protecting the goods from loss or damage. However, the bailee is still not an insurer, and is liable only if some degree of fault is shown. For example, the bailee is responsible for loss or damage that arises from even slight negligence. *Beller v. Shultz,* 44 Mich. 529 (1880).

4) PRIMA FACIE CASE / REBUTTABLE PRESUMPTION

Showing that the personal property in question was damaged or destroyed while in the possession of the bailee may make a *prima facie* case against a bailee. Thus, when it is established that the personal property that is the subject of the bailment has been damaged or lost, the bailee has the burden of rebutting the presumption that the loss is the fault of the bailee. The bailee may overcome the presumption by showing evidence that the loss is not the fault of the bailee--whatever level of fault may apply to the bailee pursuant to the type of bailment.

5) MODERN CRITIQUE

Michigan law follows the foregoing three category traditional classification scheme that some commentators have criticized. They generally have proposed a single standard of care for all bailments, often stated as a duty of reasonable care under the circumstances. *E.g., Kurt Phillip Autor, Bailment Liability: Toward a Standard of Reasonable Care,* 61 So. 2d Cal. L. Rev. 2117 (1988).

6) CONTRACTUAL LIMITATION

The modern trend permits parties to change these rules by contractual provisions. But even by contract, the bailee generally may not relieve himself from liability for gross negligence. However, for such a provision to be binding, the bailor must know of the contractual provision and "accept" it.

7) ADDITIONAL ITEMS

Under some circumstances, the bailor may leave additional items with the item delivered for the bailee. The bailee will be responsible for items that could reasonably be expected to be with the personal property. Therefore, a bailee of a car at a garage will not be liable for the suitcase full of money in the trunk, but a bailee of a coat at a coat check may be responsible for the handkerchief in the jacket pocket.

★ **D.   Duty to Redeliver**

A bailee possesses a strict duty to return the item back to the owner, regardless of the type of benefit the bailee has been provided. This is a strict duty unless the bailee is an involuntary bailee. If involuntary, the bailee is only liable if she is negligent.

VI.   GIFTS
★
A gift is a present transfer of property by one person to another without any consideration or compensation. A gift is generally not revocable once made. Accordingly, the donor cannot "take back" the gift except for gifts made in contemplation of death, which are revocable if the donor escapes from the peril of death, which prompted the gift.

A.   Three Requirements

There are three requirements for the making of a valid gift: (1) there must be a delivery from the donor to the donee (unless the gift is already in the donee's possession); (2) the donor must possess an intent to gratuitously make a present gift; and (3) the donee must accept the gift. *Comerica Bank v. Goldman (In re Handelsman),* 266 Mich. App. 433, 437-438 (2005), quoting *Davidson v. Bugbee,* 227 Mich. App. 264, 268 (1997).

1)   DELIVERY

Control of the property must pass from donor to donee. Therefore, a mere oral statement that a gift is being made is insufficient.

a)   Symbolic and Constructive Delivery

"Symbolic" or "constructive" delivery is sufficient if the property cannot be physically delivered (intangibles), or which would be very inconvenient to deliver (large items). Delivery of something representing the gift, or of something that gives the donee a means of obtaining the gift, is enough.

b)   Written Instrument

Generally, a written instrument is a valid substitute for physical delivery of the property. For example, if Don writes a letter to Dee saying, "I hereby give you my 100 shares of IBM stock," the delivery requirement would be satisfied.

c)   Gifts *Causa Mortis*

Courts disfavor gifts *causa mortis* (in contemplation of death) because they effectively work to avoid testamentary formalities. Therefore, they frequently impose stricter requirements for delivery in such cases than where the gift is made *inter vivos* with no expectation of death. See the Wills & Estates outline for further discussion of gifts *causa mortis*.

2)   INTENT

Donor must possess the intent to make the gift. The intent must be to make a present, not future, gift.

3)   ACCEPTANCE

The acceptance requirement is usually not an issue. Acceptance is generally presumed if it is beneficial to the donee. *Id.* However, if the donee expressly rejects the gift, then the acceptance requirement will not be satisfied.

VII.   BONA FIDE PURCHASERS

Typically, the problem of the *bona-fide* purchaser ("BFP") arises when a person who is in wrongful possession of goods (a thief or defrauder), sells them to one who buys the item for fair value and without notice that the seller has no title.

A.   General Rule

The general rule regarding BFPs is that a seller may not convey better title than that which he possesses. Therefore, a thief conveys void title, as does a bailee.

1)   EXCEPTIONS

Where the goods are acquired from the original owner by less than outright theft, the BFP may be protected.

a)   Voidable Title

If the original rightful owner intended to transfer any sort of ownership interest to the original buyer, then the title is voidable, not void. A BFP who takes property from a person who has a "voidable" title is protected. Therefore, if S obtains goods by misrepresentation (bad check) from O, S will obtain voidable title. If S immediately resells the property to B, a BFP, A cannot get them back from B.

★★   b)   Entrustment

                   (1)   General Rule

Additionally, the owner may lose to the BFP by virtue of estoppel. One who entrusts goods to a merchant who deals in goods of that type gives the merchant power to transfer full ownership rights to a BFP. This is viewed from the BFP's perspective. The inquiry is whether it appears as if the seller has the right to sell. If so, the BFP is protected. The merchant is liable to the original owner for the amount paid by the BFP.

★   (a)   UCC / Buyer in Ordinary Course

The Uniform Commercial Code ("UCC"), created an exception to the common law rule that a bailee (e.g., merchant) lacked title to a bailor's (i.e., owner's) bailed goods and could not convey title to a third person (e.g., BFP). Under the UCC, a person who entrusts goods to a merchant who deals in goods of that kind empowers the merchant to transfer all the entruster's rights to a buyer in the ordinary course of business. UCC § 2-403(2); Mich. Comp. Laws § 440.2403(2). A person who buys at retail from such a merchant will generally be held to be a buyer in the ordinary course if the person purchases the goods in good faith and without notice that the sale contravenes another's rights. Mich. Comp. Laws § 440.1201(9) (defining the term "buyer in the ordinary course"). A person who buys in bulk, however, does not have the rights of a buyer in the ordinary course. *Id.*

★   c)   Michigan's Self-Service Storage Facility Act

Suppose, for example, that a tenant of a Michigan self-service storage facility signs a lease on a self-storage lot to keep certain personal property there. The tenant fails to make a rental payment to the facility's owner. The owner gives the tenant written notice of a demand for a missing rent payment. The notice states that the owner will take the property in the tenant's storage space and sell it if the tenant fails to pay this past due rent. After the tenant fails to respond to the notice, the owner sells the property to a third-party purchaser to recover this unpaid rent.

In this situation, if the purchaser is a BFP, then Michigan's Self-Service Storage Facility Act (Act) could protect the purchaser by precluding the tenant's recovery of this property from the purchaser in a replevin action. Mich. Comp. Laws § 570.521 *et seq.*

(1)   Knowledge that Sale Violates Act Prevents BFP Status

A BFP is an "innocent purchaser of the property for value." *Bellows v. Goodfellow*, 276 Mich. 471 (1936). However, a purchaser who has knowledge (actual or constructive) that an owner's sale violated the Act is not a BFP. In that event, the purchaser would lack an interest in the property superior to the tenant, who could recover the property from the purchaser by a replevin action.

(a)   When Recovery of Property is Available

Michigan's replevin statute permits a property owner to recover personal property that was unlawfully taken or unlawfully detained. Mich. Comp. Laws § 600.2920. Under the common law, even a BFP of property unlawfully taken or detained lacked title to that property as against the owner whose property has been converted. *Ward v. Carey*, 200 Mich. 217 (1918). Therefore, if no statute precludes an action under Michigan's replevin statute, then the tenant could recover the property from the purchaser if the owner unlawfully detained or took the tenant's property. This outline addresses Michigan's replevin statute later.

(b)   When Recovery of Property is Unavailable

The Act can preclude recovery of the property when, in a situation like this example, the purchaser is a BFP. The Act provides a BFP with a property right in the property sold by the owner to enforce a lien created under the Act, despite the owner's noncompliance with the Act's requirements for notice of sale of the property. Mich. Comp. Laws § 570.525(12). This property right is free of any right of someone against whom the lien is valid. *Id.* Therefore, in our example, if the purchaser is a BFP, then the BFP owns the property free and clear of any claim by the tenant.

(2)   Michigan's Definition of Lien

Under the common law, a lien is "a right or claim against some interest in property created by law as an incident of [a] contract." *Cheff v. Haan*, 269 Mich. 593 (1934). A lien provides the right of enforcement by sale of the encumbered property. *McClintic-Marshall Co. v. Ford Motor Co.*, 254 Mich. 305 (1931). However, this sale only occurs when approved by a court order or permitted by a statute. *Aldine Mfg. Co. v. Phillips*, 118 Mich. 162 (1898).

(3)   Act Authorizes Enforcement of Lien by Sale

Accordingly, in our example, the common law only would allow the owner to detain the property until the debt is paid. Thus, the owner lacks authority to sell the property under the common law, absent a court order, and would be liable to the tenant for conversion in the absence of statutory authority to sell the property. The Act authorizes an owner to sell a tenant's property in specific circumstances. The Act provides a statutory lien to the owner on all personal property held at a self-storage facility. Mich. Comp. Laws § 570.523(1). The Act provides a means of enforcing the lien by a sale of the property. The sale is the owner's only way to enforce the lien. Mich. Comp. Laws § 570.525(1). The owner has to take certain steps before enforcing the lien by a sale.

(4)   Certain Steps Required for Enforcement of Lien

Generally, the owner must provide a written notice delivered to the tenant in person, by first-class mail, or by e-mail. The notice must state the owner's claim, the amount due, a demand for payment, and allow the tenant at least 14 days to pay the rent owed to the owner. Mich. Comp. Laws § 570.525(2)(b)-(c). Also, the owner must publish an advertisement of the sale of the property once a week for two consecutive weeks in a newspaper of general circulation in the area of the facility's location. Mich. Comp. Laws § 570.525(5). After taking these steps, the owner may enforce the lien by selling the property.

(5)   Tenant's Remedy for Noncompliance with Act

The tenant may bring an action to recover for the owner's violation of the Act's enforcement provisions. Such a violation could involve, for example, the owner's noncompliance with the Act's requirement of proper notice. The tenant may recover the greater of $250.00 or the actual amount of the damages, plus reasonable attorney fees. Mich. Comp. Laws § 570.526(1). The tenant can recover the value of the property, subject to a deduction of unpaid rent owed by the tenant to the owner, plus attorney fees.

For example, the tenant could recover such damages if the tenant can show that he would have paid the rent but for the owner's sale of the tenant's property in violation of the Act's notice requirements. Even if the tenant cannot show that he would have paid the rent before a lawful sale of the property, the tenant is entitled to any proceeds of the sale after satisfying the owner's lien and any other "outstanding balances owed to prior perfected lienholders." Mich. Comp. Laws § 570.525(13).

VIII. REPLEVIN

★★   A.   **Claim and Delivery Action to Recover Personal Property**

1)   PROPERTY UNLAWFULLY TAKEN OR DETAINED

The common law action of replevin has been codified in Michigan. There, it is commonly

AMERIBAR BAR REVIEW   PERSONAL PROPERTY

referred to as a claim and delivery action. If a party has a right to possess the goods or chattels, then the party may bring such an action "to recover possession of any goods or chattels which have been unlawfully taken or unlawfully detained and to recover damages sustained by the unlawful taking or unlawful detention." Mich. Comp. Laws §§ 600.2920(1), 600.2929(c).

        a)   Exceptions when Claim and Delivery Action Not Available

This provision is subject to exceptions. An action for replevin may not be brought:

- "to recover possession of or damages for goods or chattels taken by virtue of a warrant for the collection of a tax, assessment, or fine in pursuance" of a Michigan statute;

- "to recover possession of or damages for goods or chattels seized by virtue of an execution or attachment" unless they "are exempted by law from execution or attachment";

- by any person who "does not have a right to possession of the goods or chattels taken or detained." *Id.*

        (1)   Procedural Considerations

Also, "a writ, order, or process for delivery of goods or chattels before judgment may not be issued: 1) unless the court," following (a) notice and a (b) hearing and (c) pursuant to proper procedures, finds that the claim for recovery by replevin is probably valid; and 2) "unless the party claiming a right to recover possession of the goods or chattels files a sufficient bond" (i.e., security). *Id.*

        b)   When Good Faith Recipient of Property Lacks Title

Pursuant to the common law, in a replevin action, even a good faith recipient of property lacks title to that property as against its true owner. *Ward v. Carey*, 200 Mich. 217 (1918).

MICHIGAN BAR REVIEW   12   PERSONAL PROPERTY

AMERIBAR BAR REVIEW

Michigan Bar Review

TRUSTS, WILLS & ESTATES

TRUSTS

TRUSTS

Past administrations of the essay portion of the Michigan Bar Exam usually have included one or two questions regarding Trusts & Wills. The majority of these past Trusts and Wills questions have focused upon issues regarding wills, which is the subject of the separate Wills & Estates Outline later in this book. The minority of those questions have focused upon trusts. This Trusts Outline includes law pertaining to those questions as well as other general legal principles regarding trusts.

The sample answers provided for Trusts & Wills questions on the Michigan Bar Exam describe and cite to modern Michigan law. These controlling rules governing trusts and wills are generally derived from either common law or the statutory Michigan Estates and Protected Individuals Code ("EPIC"), when applicable. Sometimes, the sample answers for these questions are based on the version of these rules, or the proper construction of them, provided in decisions of the Michigan Court of Appeals and/or the Michigan Supreme Court.

Some of the previously tested trusts issues in prior Trusts & Wills questions have involved a testamentary charitable trust, the *Cy Pres* doctrine, an irrevocable inter vivos trust, and interpretation of the residuary clause of that trust in terms of *per stirpes* distribution, future interests, and substitute gifts.

EPIC includes the Michigan Trust Code, effective April 1, 2010. Mich. Comp. Laws §§ 700.7101, 700.8204. Generally, the Michigan Trust Code applies to most trusts that were made prior to, upon, or following its effective date. Mich. Comp. Laws §§ 700.7102, 700.8206(1)(a). Basically, among other things, the Michigan Trust Code: 1) codifies and maintains state trust law; 2) provides default rules from which a trust's provisions may vary; and 3) fills some gaps in state trusts law. Mark K. Harder, *Introducing the Michigan Trust Code*, Michigan Bar Journal, May 2010, 24, 24-25.

I.   TRUSTS

A trust is a fiduciary relationship between a trustee(s) and the trust beneficiaries. When a trust is created, title to property is divided. The trustee holds legal title to the property. That is, the trustee becomes owner of record for the property. A beneficiary holds equitable title to the property. As such, the beneficiary is entitled to the financial benefits of the property.

- Common Definitions

Settlor: The settlor is the person who creates the trust. The settlor is usually the person who transfers or places the original assets into the trust.

Trustee: The trustee is a person or entity who holds the assets of the trust for the benefit of the beneficiaries and manages the trust and its assets under the terms of the trust.

When a trustee possesses title to property, the trustee holds title only for the benefit of the trust and its beneficiaries.

Beneficiary: The beneficiary is a person or entity who is to receive assets or profits from the trust. The beneficiary is the holder of equitable title of the trust.

Res: The term res, refers to the property making up the trust as a whole. The res can be money, land, stocks, bonds, or just about anything which can be owned and transferred.

A.   Classification of Trusts

Trusts can be loosely categorized as either express or implied trusts.

1)   EXPRESS TRUST

An express trust is created because a person (1) expresses intent to create a trust and (2) satisfies requisite formalities. For example, suppose A, owner of Blackacre, properly executes a writing, which declares himself trustee of Blackacre for the benefit of B. A has created an express trust.

2)   IMPLIED TRUST

Sometimes a trust is created even if a trustee expresses no intent to create one. Implied trusts are either constructive or resulting trusts.

a)   Resulting Trust

If a court infers from certain facts that the parties intended to create a trust, although they never expresses such an intent in writing or otherwise, the court may determine that a resulting trust was created.

(1)   Presumption is Rebuttable

The presumption may be rebutted by contrary evidence.

(2)   Examples of Resulting Trusts

(a)   Purchase Money Resulting Trust

If someone purchases property in another's name, a presumption of a resulting trust exists. The new owner is presumed to be holding the property in trust for the purchaser. If A pays $100,000 to B for a home but requests that the title be made out to C, the law presumes that C holds the property in trust for A.

(b)   Failure of Express Trust

If an express trust fails for lack of intent, a trustee may still hold the property in a resulting trust for a settlor, to whom the property will revert.

b)   Constructive Trust

A constructive trust is often called an "involuntary trust." It is not, in any way, concerned with the intent, either express or presumed, of the parties. Instead, a constructive trust is imposed by law on the owner(s) of property to accomplish justice or to avoid unjust enrichment.

Example: A is B's fiduciary. A fraudulently obtains B's property by abusing his position of trust. A court may declare A the constructive trustee of the property for the benefit of B.

★★   B.   Creation of Express Trusts

In order to create an express trust, the following elements must be present:

1.   Intent: A settlor must have intended to create the trust;
2.   Formalities: The parties must comply with the requisite formalities;
3.   Res: There must be a trust res (property);
4.   Ascertainable Beneficiaries: One or more beneficiaries must exist;
5.   Trustee: A trust must possess a trustee. However, if none was named by the settlor, a court may appoint a trustee. In other words, although a trust must have a trustee, a trust will not fail for lack of a trustee.

★★   1)   INTENT TO CREATE TRUST

a)   General Intent Must Be Expressed

The settlor must express the intent to create a trust.

(1)   Written and Spoken Words

Usually, a court will examine written and spoken words.

(2)   Court May Examine Conduct

Additionally, the conduct of the settlor may be examined when determining intent.

(3)   No Specific Words Required

There are no specific words that must be used to create a trust. However, it must be clear that a settlor intended to create the legal relationships and duties of a trust. Keep in mind that, under this test, the settlor need not even know what a trust is.

b)   Precatory Words

In the classic example of a trust, a settlor directs a person to hold property "in trust for" another. Sometimes, however, the creation of the trustee relationship will not be so clear. For example, A conveys Blackacre to B "with the hope that B will use it for the benefit of C." Is a trust created under these circumstances? The answer is generally no. If a trust merely uses words of recommendation or wishes, a court will not infer that the grantor intended to create a trust. Nonetheless, when confronted with precatory language, a court will examine all facts and circumstances in order to determine whether the grantor intended to create a trust, or mere recommendations.

★★   c)   Judicial Interpretation – Michigan Law

The primary goal in construing a testamentary instrument is to determine and give effect to the intent of the settlor. *In re Woodworth Trust,* 196 Mich. App. 326, 327 (1992). The first step in determining the intent of the settlor is to review the language of the testamentary document. "Where there is no ambiguity, that intention is to be gleaned from the four corners of the instrument." *Id.* Testamentary documents must also be interpreted in a way that gives effect to every word in the document. *Detroit Bank & Trust Co v. Grout,* 95 Mich. App. 253, 268-269 (1980). Where the plain and ordinary meaning of the instrument gives rise to only one reasonable interpretation, the court must ignore extrinsic evidence of the drafter's intent and derive the intent of the drafter from the four corners of the instrument. *Woodworth, supra.*

                       (1)   Ambiguity

Where the instrument is ambiguous, a court can consider extrinsic evidence to determine the drafter's intent. However, "[t]he fact that the parties dispute the meaning of [a provision] . . . does not, in itself, establish an ambiguity." *Cole v. Ladbroke Racing Michigan, Inc.,* 241 Mich. App. 1, 14 (2000).

                       (a)   Latent Ambiguity

Seemingly clear trust language may still evidence a latent ambiguity. A "latent ambiguity exists where the language and its meaning is [sic] clear, but some extrinsic fact creates the possibility of more than one meaning." *Woodworth, supra.* Thus, a court may consider facts extrinsic to the trust instrument for the purpose of considering the existence of a latent ambiguity. *In re McPeak Estate,* 210 Mich. App. 410, 412 (1995).

              d)   Capacity

The laws of capacity with regard to property transfer apply equally to trusts. If a person possesses the capacity to convey title to property, she also possesses the capacity to create a trust.

              e)   Savings Account Trusts

If a person opens a bank account and directs that the account be held "in trust for" someone else, a trust is not automatically created. Courts have determined that the person depositing the funds may have intended to create one of several other relationships. For example, such an arrangement may be evidence of the promise to create a future trust or a trust upon the depositor's death. Under these circumstances, a court will examine all facts and circumstances surrounding the creation of the account to determine whether the depositor intended to create a trust. The court may examine evidence of the relationship and nature of the account, as well as the account documents themselves.

★★   2)   FORMALITIES REQUIRED TO CREATE TRUST

The formalities required to create a trust depend upon two factors – the trust property and when the trust is executed.

              a)   Trust Property – Statute of Frauds

The creation of a trust must comport with the Statute of Frauds.

                     (1)   Real Property

Specifically, if a trust involves real property, it must be created or proved (occurs subsequent to creation) in writing. The writing does not need be comprehensive. However, it must describe all essential express terms of the trust.

                     (2)   Personal Property

A trust involving personal property need not comply with the Statute of Frauds.

              b)   Timing – Statute of Wills

                     (1)   Testamentary Trusts

Testamentary trusts, which are to enter into existence upon the death of a person and dispose of the person's property, must comport with the Statute of Wills. Therefore, they must be executed with the same formalities of a will. Sometimes, these trusts are executed along with the will.

                     (2)   Inter-Vivos Trusts Disposing of Property at Death

If a trust created during the lifetime of a person purports to dispose of the person's property upon his death, such a trust must also comply with the Statute of Wills.

              c)   Delivery

Generally, a settlor must deliver the trust instrument to the trustee before the trust will come into existence. In a trust consisting of personal property, the settlor must deliver the personal property. The mechanics of the delivery of this type of trust are the same as that for a gift.

Courts have generally recognized that constructive or symbolic delivery is appropriate if the subject matter cannot be physically delivered at the time the settlor wishes to complete the delivery.

        d)   Consideration

             (1)   Present Trust - No Consideration

No consideration is required to create a present express trust. An express trust is generally irrevocable and not amendable unless that power is expressly reserved.

             (2)   Promise to Create Trust - Requires Consideration

A promise to create a trust in the future is unenforceable unless the promise is supported by consideration sufficient for the formation of a contract. *Generally, Scott on Trusts* § 30 (4th ed.); Bogert, *Trusts* § 24 (6th ed. 1987).

        e)   Common Methods of Trust Creation

There are a few common methods of creating a trust including:

             (1)   Declaration Regarding Owned Property

For example, suppose A owns Blackacre and declares, in writing, that she owns Blackacre "in trust for B."

             (2)   Transfer of Legal Title by Property Owner

For example, suppose B owns Blackacre. C negotiates to purchase Blackacre from B. B conveys Blackacre "to A in trust for C."

             (3)   Contract in Favor of Trustee

For example, suppose that A contracts to buy a car. A executes a promissory note payable "to B in trust for C."

★★   3)   <u>REQUIREMENT OF TRUST *RES*</u>

The *res* of a trust is the property or subject matter of the trust.

        a)   Trust Property Required

A trust must have some property as its *res* or it will fail. A trustee's obligation to manage funds must be over a specific subject matter. Otherwise, it would be a false obligation.

        b)   Settlor Must Identify *Res* with Certainty

The *res* must be described with such certainty and definiteness that a court and all involved parties can be assured that the intended trust is being carried on. Failure to adequately describe the trust *res* is as fatal as having none. The *res* must either be 1) specifically described or 2) a method for ascertaining it must be described. A settlor, thus, may create a trust consisting of "one third of my net estate at death." However, compare a trust providing for "the support of B with any remaining property to be held in trust for C." The trust is invalid with regard to C because the property interest, if one were to exist, is not sufficiently certain.

★★   4)   <u>REQUIREMENT OF BENEFICIARY</u>

A beneficiary is the person who possesses equitable title to the *res* of a trust.

                   a)   Who May be a Beneficiary

A beneficiary must be able to possess title. A beneficiary need not possess the capacity to manage the funds. The settlor can be a beneficiary. Moreover, the trustee can be a beneficiary. However, the sole trustee cannot be the sole beneficiary.

★★   b)   Beneficiary Must be Identified or Ascertainable

In order to create a valid trust, a settlor must identify a beneficiary or the beneficiaries must be ascertainable. If a settlor does not adequately describe a beneficiary, the trust will fail.

A settlor is not required to specifically name a beneficiary of the trust at the time of trust creation. A trust document may merely describe how a beneficiary may be identified when the trust is to enter into existence. Nonetheless, it is best to describe a beneficiary by name if possible.

                   c)   Classes of Beneficiaries are Allowed if Described

A settlor may create a trust for the benefit of a class of people that may change before the trust enters into existence (i.e., my children). The class must be reasonably described. For example, a settlor may create a trust for the benefit of his nephews. Nonetheless, the class must be ascertainable. Therefore, a settlor may not create a trust for the benefit of "some of my siblings," or "a few of my grandchildren," or "my friends." These terms do not allow for the identification of the intended beneficiaries.

                   d)   Trustee's Limited Discretion to Select Beneficiaries

A trust that provides a trustee with some discretion to choose beneficiaries from a select group may be valid. For example, a trustee may select beneficiaries of a scholarship from the class of the settlor's children. A settlor may provide the trustee with guidelines for such a selection or may provide the trustee with absolute discretion. However, the trust document cannot permit a trustee to select beneficiaries from "anybody in the world he finds deserving." The trust must provide some guidance for the trustee's selection.

e)   Honorary Trust

A trust that provides for the care of a pet is a classic honorary trust. Generally, these trusts are not valid. A trust requires a beneficiary capable of holding title. A trustee of an honorary trust may, if she chooses, honor the trust. A person may be able to provide for a pet by creating a trust for the benefit of a person, and condition payment upon the person caring for the animal.

f)   Disclaimer

A beneficiary may disclaim an interest in the trust. However, acceptance is presumed. Therefore, a beneficiary must take affirmative action to disclaim an interest as a beneficiary. Disclaimer must occur before accepting any benefits of the trust. Disclaimer cannot be conditional. However, a person may disclaim part of the interest in the trust.

(1)   Effect – Proceed as if Beneficiary Pre-deceased

The disclaimed property passes as if the disclaimant predeceased the trust coming into existence.

★★   5)   REQUIREMENT OF TRUSTEE

a)   A Trust Must Have a Trustee

Although a trustee is needed to create a trust, the trust will not fail for want of a trustee. *Generally,* Bogert, *Trusts* § 30 (6th ed. 1987). A court may appoint a trustee if the settlor did not name a trustee. Additionally, even if the sole individual acting as trustee dies, the trust does not terminate if the grantor intended the trust to continue beyond the death of the trustee. *Id.* Rather, the court of equity having jurisdiction over the trust can appoint another to act as a successor trustee. *Id.*

(1)   Exception: Creation Conditioned on Trustee Accepting

On very rare occasions, the settlor may provide that a trust should fail if a named trustee does not accept the position, is deceased, or is otherwise unable to serve. Under these circumstances, the trust will fail.

b)   Mechanics of Trustee Position

(1)   Entity Capable of Holding Title May Be Trustee

Any individual or legal entity capable of holding title to property may be named as a trustee. If, however, the appointed individual possesses a legal disability like incapacity that would prevent her from administering the trust, a court may remove the trustee and appoint another.

(2)   A Trust May Have More Than One Trustee

A trust may have several trustees. As a practical matter, it is a good idea to have an odd number of trustees to avoid deadlocks.

        (3)   Majority Vote Required to Authorize Action

In most jurisdictions, a majority vote of the trustees is required to authorize action. Some jurisdictions, however, require a unanimous vote of the trustees.

        (4)   Trustee Compensation

At common law, the trustee received no compensation unless the trust instrument provided otherwise. Today, the trustee is entitled to reasonable fee for her services. Generally, with regard to professional corporate trustees, the fee may be a percentage of the value of the principal. Other trustee fees are examined on a case-by-case basis taking into account all relevant factors. If a special family relationship exists, a court may require a trustee to serve without compensation.

C.   **Types of Trusts**

There are several different types of trusts. A trust can be created *inter-vivos*, which means during the life of the settlor. The settlor can also create a testamentary trust which enters into exists at the death of the settlor. A trust may be revocable by the settlor or irrevocable. A trust may be for the benefit of a societal purpose, as opposed to an individual. Each of these types of trusts carries some specific rules with it.

★★   1)   <u>REVOCABLE TRUSTS</u>

A revocable trust is an *inter-vivos* (created during the life of the settlor) trust. When a settlor creates a trust, she may expressly reserve the right to revoke or amend the trust at any time. One of the main benefits of establishing this kind of trust is avoiding probate. It permits the settlor to control if and when to amend or revoke the trust. In effect, the settlor may create the trust and keep full control of it during her lifetime or for the time set forth in the trust instrument. The settlor may serve as or select the trustee and may also serve as the primary beneficiary (with a separate remainder beneficiary).

        a)   The Michigan Trust Code Presumes a Trust Revocable

A trust created in Michigan after March 31, 2010, is presumed revocable unless the trust provides that it is irrevocable. Mich. Comp. Laws § 700.7602(1).

        b)   The Michigan Trust Code Imposes a Statute of Limitations

As of April 1, 2010, a statute of limitation of up to two years duration applies to when a person may bring a judicial proceeding to contest the validity of a revocable trust in Michigan. Mich. Comp. Laws § 700.7604(1).

        2)   <u>IRREVOCABLE TRUSTS</u>

An irrevocable trust is an *inter-vivos* trust. In most jurisdictions, a trust is irrevocable unless the settlor expressly retains the right to revoke or amend the trust. In a few jurisdictions, the opposite rule provides that a trust is revocable unless the trust expressly provides otherwise. If a trust is irrevocable, it may provide tax benefits that a revocable trust cannot by reducing the estate's overall tax liability. Once the trust comes into existence, however, it generally can never be altered or revoked by the settlor.

★   3)   TESTAMENTARY TRUSTS

A testamentary trust is an express trust that is set out in a testator's will. It does not exist during the settlor's life. It enters into existence when the testator dies and the will is executed. By contrast, an *inter-vivos* trust is one that comes into existence when the settlor is still alive. Because it is executed as part of a will, it is executed with the same formalities.

        4)   POUR OVER TRUSTS

A pour over provision in a will is a clause that leaves property to a previously existing inter-vivos trust. As such, property of the decedent may "pour" into the trust. The property, therefore, would pass by terms created while the settlor was alive. Rather than creating a testamentary trust or placing all property in her estate, the testator/settlor would have a better ability to see how the trust works and make any necessary changes while she is still living.

★   5)   CHARITABLE TRUSTS

        a)   General

A charitable trust is a trust with the purpose of accomplishing a substantial amount of social benefit to the public at large or to a reasonably large class. For example, striving to achieve world peace is a charitable purpose.

        b)   Charitable Purpose

Courts employ several different approaches when determining whether a given purpose is charitable.

            (1)   General Acceptance Test

If the general public accepts a particular purpose as charitable, then the trust may be classified as a charitable trust. This test, although seemingly fair, completely discourages the exploration of new ideas. For example, at one time, a trust to fund research to determine whether the sun was the center of the solar system would have been rejected.

            (2)   Advancement of Ideas and Concepts

Some courts are likely to classify trusts as charitable if they advance ideas or concepts. For example, a trust that furthers a political viewpoint may be upheld.

(3)   Religious Purpose

Some courts give deference to charitable trusts that have a religious purpose. If a trust furthering religious beliefs is not criminal in nature or against public policy, it will be classified as charitable.

(a)   Purpose Must Be Selfless

The purpose of the settlor must be selfless. For example, a trust providing for scholarships for the relatives of the settlor would not be charitable. However, trusts created to provide scholarships for deserving residents of an entire town would be charitable.

c)   Rule Against Perpetuities Does Not Apply

The Rule Against Perpetuities does not apply to charitable trusts.

D.   Alienability of Trust Interests

Trust interests are alienable, devisable, and descendible unless the terms of a trust expressly or impliedly provide otherwise. However, a spendthrift clause may prevent transfer. Additionally, if the trust provides only a life interest, the interest is not descendible.

E.   Protective Trusts

Trusts for support can be divided into two broad categories: a pure support trust and a discretionary support trust. Classification of support trusts can be made only after a careful review of the governing instrument in order to determine the grantor's intent.

1)   <u>DISCRETIONARY TRUSTS</u>

a)   Trustee Possesses Discretion to Withhold Support

In a discretionary support trust, the trustee possesses discretion to withhold payments of trust property from a beneficiary who has a support need. *Generally*, McGovern, Kurtz & Rein, *Wills, Trusts and Estates,* § 8.2. The point to keep in mind is that the trustee is entrusted with the discretion of whether to pay all, part, or none of the income to the beneficiary. Some discretionary trusts provide guidelines that a trustee should use in making the determination. In others, the trustee possesses absolute discretion. The term "absolute," however, is a bit misleading because the trustee will be liable for actions taken in bad faith or fraudulently.

In some discretionary trusts, a trustee may provide for more than a beneficiary's support needs. Under this type of trust, a trustee might have discretion to pay expenses incurred by a beneficiary for more than mere support items, such as luxuries.

2)   <u>SUPPORT TRUSTS</u>

a)   Pure Support Trust Limited to Education and Maintenance

A pure support trust is a trust under which payments are limited for a beneficiary's support. The trustee is obligated to spend only so much of the income as is necessary for the education and maintenance of the beneficiary. Accordingly, if the beneficiary has a support need, the trustee must pay the beneficiary trust property (income or principal, depending upon the terms of the trust) to the extent of available funds. In some jurisdictions, this rule may be tempered by another rule that would require the trustee to consider the beneficiary's non-trust financial resources before using trust property for the beneficiary's support. *E.g., Loar v. Massey*, 164 W.Va. 155, 261 S.E.2d 83 (1979).

b)   Trustee Possesses No Discretion to Withhold Support

If it is determined that the trustee has no discretion or duty to assess "necessity," and therefore a support trust exists, one would also have to conclude that the trustee has *no* discretion to withhold support payments. A beneficiary of a support trust has an enforceable legal right to trust property that, under the terms of the trust, must be distributed in satisfaction of the beneficiary's support need when that need arises. Waggoner, Wellman, Alexander & Fellows, *Family Property Law,* 689 (1992). Conversely, a trustee's refusal to distribute amounts that must be paid to the beneficiary for support is a breach of trust for which a trustee can be held accountable.

c)   Trust Interest Not Assignable or Reachable by Creditors

Because of the nature of the trust, a beneficiary cannot assign her interest in a support trust. Moreover, a creditor of the beneficiary cannot reach the trust assets. Interestingly, the fact that a creditor may be seeking reimbursement for the provision of past support or educational services to beneficiary is of no consequence.

3)   SPENDTHRIFT TRUSTS

A spendthrift trust is a trust that contains a "spendthrift" provision. In a typical spendthrift provision, 1) the beneficiary is not permitted to transfer his beneficial interest; and 2) the beneficiary's creditors cannot reach the beneficiary's beneficial interest. Spendthrift trusts are designed to protect a beneficiary from his own carelessness.

a)   Rights of Creditors

(1)   General

The creditors of the beneficiary of a trust have no greater rights in the trust property than the beneficiary has. If a trust instrument prevents a beneficiary from receiving trust principal, his creditors have no right to reach trust principal either. If a beneficiary's creditors could reach trust principal under these circumstances, they would infringe on the property rights of the remainder beneficiaries of the trust.

(2)   Creditor's Right to Income Interest

Absent a spendthrift clause in an instrument, a beneficiary's creditors would be able to attach to the income interest.   However, if the governing instrument contains a spendthrift clause prohibiting a beneficiary's creditors from attaching the beneficiary's interest, the beneficiary's creditors usually cannot reach the beneficiary's trust interest in satisfaction of their claims. Most courts uphold spendthrift clauses, at least when applied against the claims of most creditors of a beneficiary.   A minority of states hold that spendthrift clauses are unenforceable. *Generally* George Bogert, *Trusts* § 40 (6th ed. 1987).

In the minority of states that bar the enforcement of spendthrift clauses, a potential creditor may compel a trustee to pay its claim against a beneficiary from trust income. However, in the large majority of states that uphold spendthrift clauses, a creditor could not compel payment of the claim from trust income while in the hands of the trustee.

(3)   Creditor Can Reach Interest Once Distributed

Spendthrift clauses in a trust do not operate to bar a trust beneficiary's creditors from reaching the distributed income or principal once it has actually been paid to the beneficiary. Bogert, *supra* § 40 at 150. If the grantor attempts to restrain the beneficiary's ability to alienate the trust income once distributed to the beneficiary, it would be an invalid restraint on alienation. Thus, once trust income is actually paid to the beneficiary, a potential creditor may reach that income in satisfaction of a claim by resorting to the customary legal processes for the enforcement of judgments.   The reason that this is critical is because a trustee may pay the beneficiary's expenses directly from the beneficiary's interest in the trust. Accordingly, the funds may never be possessed by the beneficiary himself.   Additionally, if the funds are directly paid to the beneficiary, he may be able to "hide" the money before the creditor can attach to the funds.

b)   Restrictions on Spendthrift Trusts

(1)   Alimony and Child Support

Even in the large majority of states that uphold spendthrift clauses, if the particular creditor's claim is for unpaid alimony or child support, the policy of effectuating the settlor's intent by generally upholding spendthrift clauses runs afoul of a stronger public policy favoring the payment of alimony and child support. *E.g., Bacardi v. White,* 463 So. 2d 218 (Fla. 1985). Today, most state courts hold that the policy favoring the payment of alimony and child support trumps the policy of generally supporting spendthrift clauses. In those states a trust beneficiary is not permitted to enjoy trust income while failing to support his children and former spouse. *Generally Restatement (Second) of Trusts* § 157.

In a small minority of states, spendthrift clauses continue to be valid even as against unpaid alimony. *E.g., Erickson v. Erickson,* 266 N.W. 161 (Minn. 1936).

(2)   Settlor Cannot Be Beneficiary

A settlor cannot create a spendthrift trust that makes himself its beneficiary.

(3)   Claims for Necessaries Are Exempt

A creditor seeking reimbursement for the provision of "necessaries" is not subject to the spendthrift provision. A contrary result would discourage creditors from providing necessaries to spendthrifts.

F.   Powers of Invasion

In general, unless a trust instrument authorizes the trustee to invade trust principal, an income beneficiary is only entitled to trust income. *Restatement (Second) of Trusts* § 128 comment i.

1)   ONE BENEFICIARY

If one beneficiary exists, a trustee may invade the principal. However, when the income beneficiary will ultimately receive the trust principal, a court may permit the trustee to invade the principal to assist the income beneficiary, unless an invasion of trust principal would be inconsistent with the testator's express directions in creating the trust. *Restatement (Second) of Trusts* § 168. If there was only one trust beneficiary, a court might authorize a trustee to invade the principal to permit the beneficiary to make specific purchase under some circumstances.

2)   SIGNIFICANT CHANGE IN CIRCUMSTANCES

A major change of circumstances may justify an invasion of the trust's principal. A court might also permit an invasion due to a significant change in circumstances after the trust's creation. For example, a testator executes a will creating a testamentary trust believing that the trust income will be adequate to meet the income beneficiary's needs until the beneficiary reaches 40 years of age. However, after the will is executed, the testator's business misfortunes significantly reduced the amount of income that the beneficiary would receive. Under those circumstances, the trustee may be permitted to invade the trust principal in order to provide extra income for the income beneficiary.

3)   EXPRESS DISCRETION

The trust may provide a trustee with discretion to invade the principal. A settlor may confer on the trustee absolute or qualified discretion to invade the principal to provide for the income beneficiary.

a)   Court Will Not Act Absent Abuse of Discretion

When a testator confers discretion (or absolute discretion) on a trustee to make or withhold distributions, courts do not compel trustees to exercise that discretion unless the trustee's failure constitutes an abuse of discretion. *Restatement (Second) of Trusts* § 187; Bogert, *Trusts and Trustees* § 560; *also Gulf Nat'l Bank v. Sturtevant*, 511 So. 2d 936 (Miss. 1987); *Restatement (Second) of Trusts* § 187; *Dunkley v. Peoples Bank & Trust Co.*, 728 F. Supp. 547 (W.D. Ark

1989). Likewise, courts do not enjoin trustees from exercising such power unless an exercise of the power would be an abuse of discretion. *Restatement (Second) of Trusts* § 187; *Dunkley*, 728 F. Supp. 547.

(1)   Trustee Must Act with Reasonable Judgment

If the trust instrument provides a standard by which a trustee's conduct may be judged, a court will control the trustee in the exercise of a power where he acts beyond the bounds of a reasonable judgment.

G.   Modification of Trusts

A trust may be modified or altered by a court or by the parties.

1)   JUDICIAL MODIFICATION TO REFLECT SETTLOR'S WISHES

Modification of a trust instrument by a court may be necessary in order to amend the trust to conform to the wishes of the settlor. There are two methods to modify the trust by judicial action – deviation and the *Cy Pres* doctrine.

a)   Deviation

A trustee or beneficiary may apply to the court and request that the court permit "deviation" from the terms of the trust with regard to administrative provisions of the trust instrument. Generally, there a four circumstances when a court will permit deviation:

- The purposes of the trust have been fulfilled;
- The purposes of the trust have become illegal;
- The purposes of the trust are impossible; and
- Compliance with the terms of the trust may defeat or impair the purposes of the trust.

If a court agrees to the deviation, the court must modify the trust to reflect the settlor's interests at the time the trust document was executed.

★   ### b)   Cy Pres

(1)   Court May Substitute Beneficiary

(a)   General Considerations

The *Cy Pres* doctrine is applicable when 1) property is placed in trust for a charitable purpose that has become impossible to effectuate, and 2) where a testator has manifested a *general* intention to devote the property to charitable purposes. *Restatement of Trusts, Second*, § 399. A testator may exhibit a general charitable intention by giving reasons for limiting the share of the estate to others (non-charitable bequests), and by omitting any reverter clause to take effect if the charitable bequest were to fail. *Compare, e.g. Trammell v. Elliott,* 230 Ga. 841, 199 S.E.2d 194 (1973) (*Cy Pres* applied; no reverter clause in will) with *Simmons v. Parsons Coll.,* 256 N.W.2d 225 (Iowa 1977) (*Cy Pres* not applied because will included a reverter clause).

For example, suppose that a settlor created a trust with a beneficiary organization whose purpose was finding a cure for a certain disease. Sometime later, the disease is cured. What happens to the trust? The answer depends upon what the intent of the settlor was when he created the trust. If the settlor included a clause providing that the funds would revert to his heirs if a cure was found, then the funds would revert to his heirs. On the other hand, if the settlor expressed the intent to combat illness throughout the world staring with this disease, then the court would likely substitute a new beneficiary.

(b)   Michigan Law

(i)   Common Law

At common law, the *Cy Pres* doctrine was used as a saving device when the specific purpose of the settlor could not be carried out then the charitable intention could be fulfilled as nearly as possible. The Michigan Court of Appeals adopted three requirements for application of *Cy Pres*: (1) the court must determine whether a valid charitable trust has been created, (2) it must be shown that it is impossible or impracticable to carry out the specific purpose of the trust, and (3) the court must determine whether the testator had a general charitable intent. *In re Rood Estate,* 41 Mich. App. 405, 416-417 (1972); *In re Karp Estate,* 108 Mich. App. 129, 131-132 (1981).

(ii)   Statutory Law

In 1976, the Michigan Legislature adopted Michigan Compiled Laws § 451.1201 *et seq.,* stating in the preamble that its purpose was "to establish guidelines for the management and use of investments held by eleemosynary institutions and funds," but this statute did not limit the application of the doctrine of *Cy Pres*. While the statute uses the terms "obsolete, inappropriate or impracticable," the Michigan Court of Appeals has found that as a practical matter, there is no significant distinction between these terms and the language of *Cy Pres*.

(iii)   Reverter

As a general rule, the trust fund will revert to a settlor's estate or heirs at law even in the absence of an express reservation clause if the settler did not have a general charitable purpose, but instead contemplated one or more specific purposes that cannot be fulfilled because of impossibility or impracticability.

(iv)   Accumulation Provision

An accumulation provision in a charitable trust is neither invalid nor inappropriate merely because its duration is indefinite or perpetual.

c)   Selection of Beneficiary Must Effectuate Settlor's Wishes

In determining which charity should receive the bequest, a court will seek to effectuate a testator's wishes as closely as possible. Bogert, *Trusts* (6th ed.), § 147, at 521,526.

★   2)   MODIFICATION BY THE PARTIES

On some occasions, the parties may modify the trust instrument.

a)   Settlor Lacks Power to Modify Unless Settlor Reserved It

Generally, a trust is irrevocable and cannot be modified unless the settlor retained the right in the trust instrument. Interestingly, a few jurisdictions provide that a trust is presumed revocable unless expressly made irrevocable.

(1)   Power to Modify by Two Settlors

"If the power to amend is reserved to two settlors, it must be exercised by both, and the survivor cannot use the power." Bogert, *Trusts and Trustees* (2d ed.), § 993, p. 241-242.

b)   Modification of a Trust by Settlor

2 *Restatement Trusts, 3d*, § 63, discusses a settlor's power to modify a trust, and provides:

"(1)   The settlor of an inter vivos trust has power to revoke or modify the trust to the extent the terms of the trust so provide.

"(2)   If the settlor has failed expressly to provide whether the trust is subject to a retained power of revocation or amendment, the question is one of interpretation . . .

"(3)   Absent contrary provision in the terms of the trust, the settlor's power to revoke or modify the trust can be exercised in any way that provides clear and convincing evidence of the settlor's intention to do so."

(1)   Terms of the Trust

Under foregoing subparagraph (1), a settlor's power to modify a trust is determined by the terms of the trust. "The phrase 'terms of the trust' means 'the manifestation of intention of the settlor with respect to the trust provisions expressed in a manner that admits of its proof in judicial proceeding." 2 *Restatement Trusts 3d*, § 4.

H.   **Termination of Trusts**

1)   BY AGREEMENT

A trust may be revoked with the unanimous agreement of the settlor and *all* of the trust's beneficiaries. If there are unborn beneficiaries or incompetent beneficiaries, the trust cannot be terminated since their consent to terminate cannot be obtained.

a)   All Beneficiaries May Sometimes Terminate Trust

If all beneficiaries of the trust agree and no material purposes remain, the court may terminate a trust. However, courts are reluctant to find that no material purpose remains. A court will almost never terminate a protective trust by agreement of all beneficiaries.

2)   BY ITS TERMS

If, by the terms of a trust, the trust is to terminate upon the happening of a specified event, then the trust will terminate on the occurrence of that event unless the termination provision is invalid. Upon termination, unless the trust instrument provides otherwise, the trust principal reverts to the settlor or his heirs.

3)   DOCTRINE OF ACCELERATION

Under the doctrine of acceleration, if the income beneficiary of a trust disclaims this beneficiary's interest, the trust principal becomes immediately distributable to the presumptive remainder beneficiaries of the trust, provided no one would be harmed by making a distribution to them earlier than it would have been made had the income beneficiary not disclaimed. *Generally Ohio Nat'l Bank of Columbus v. Adair,* 54 Ohio St. 2d 26, 374 N.E.2d 415 (1978). *See also* Simes, *The Law of Future Interests* § 110. For example, a remainder might not accelerate if to do so would result in the class gift to the remainder beneficiaries closing earlier than it otherwise would.

★★   I.   Powers and Duties of Trustees

A trustee is a fiduciary holding legal title to the trust assets. The trustee must manage trust assets exclusively for the benefit of all the trust's beneficiaries. If a trustee violates her fiduciary duties, she may be personally liable to the beneficiaries, and she may be enjoined or removed and replaced with a court appointed trustee. P. Haskell, *Preface to Wills, Trusts, and Administration* 77 (1987).

The powers of a trustee can be derived from:

- a trust instrument;
- a statute - usually very extensive;
- implied powers - all powers settlor must have intended for trustee to exercise duties; or
- court ordered powers.

The trustee owes several duties to the beneficiaries, including the following.

★★   1)   PRUDENT PERSON RULE AND DUTY OF CARE

The trustee has a continuing duty to administer the trust in a prudent manner. Unif. Probate Code § 705. The trustee has an overall duty to exercise reasonable care and skill in managing trust property to make it profitable.

    a)   General

        (1)   Duty of Skill of Person Dealing with Own Property

A trustee possesses a duty to exercise such care and skill as a person of ordinary prudence would exercise in dealing with the trustee's own property. A trustee is not permitted to speculate regarding the trust investments.

Some jurisdictions provide for an elevated standard of care with regard to the duties of the trustee. In those jurisdictions, a trustee is required to exercise such care and skill as a person of ordinary prudence would exercise in dealing with the property of another. The rationale behind the rule is that a person should exercise greater prudence over someone else's property.

        (2)   Focus is on Conduct not Results

When conducting any analysis regarding the duty of care owed by a trustee, a court will examine the conduct of the trustee rather than the ultimate results. Although the results of the trustee's conduct may have been terrible, if the conduct itself was reasonable at the time it occurred, a trustee will not be liable.

    b)   Exculpatory Clauses-Generally Valid

        (1)   Settlor may Limit Liability of Trustee

In a majority of jurisdictions, a settlor may limit the potential liability of a trustee by including an "exculpatory" clause in the trust document.

            (a)   Exception – Bad Faith or Gross Negligence

A trustee will never be excused from exercising bad faith or acting with gross negligence. Enforcing an exculpatory clause to this extent would violate public policy.

★★   2)   <u>DUTY OF LOYALTY</u>

    a)   Trustee Owes Beneficiary Undivided Loyalty

The trustee has a duty of loyalty to the beneficiaries. The trustee may not obtain any personal gain from administering the trust, except for fees.

        (1)   Self-Dealing Breaches the Duty of Loyalty *Per Se*

Self--dealing is a breach *per se*. It is a breach of trust for the trustee to sell trust property to himself individually, or as trustee to buy property from himself individually. It is immaterial that the price is the fair market price and that the purchase or sale is in all other respects proper and in the best interest of the trust.

(a)   Exception- Settlor Can Permit Self-Dealings

The settlor may expressly waive the trustee's duty of loyalty under certain circumstances in the trust instrument. However, the trustee will not be excused from acting in bad faith or fraudulently.

(2)   Beneficiary is Entitled to Recover Profit of Breach

A beneficiary is entitled to recover any profit made by a trustee as a result of the trustee's breach, even if the beneficiary itself benefited from the transaction. Additionally, a trustee's good faith is no defense.

(3)   Trustee Owes Duty Outside Context of the Trust

A trustee's duty of loyalty to a beneficiary is not limited to the actions trustee takes with regard to the trust. If a trustee is involved with the beneficiary in a potential transaction not involving trust funds, the trustee still owes the beneficiary a duty of loyalty. It is not reasonable for a beneficiary to expect loyalty from the trustee in some contexts but not all.

★★   3)   DUTY TO ACT IMPARTIALLY

a)   Conflicting Interests of Beneficiaries

Some trusts have two different types of beneficiaries – income beneficiaries and remainder beneficiaries. For example, assume a trustee holds legal title to a $100,000 bank account "in trust for the benefit of A during the life of A, then to B." The interests of A (the income beneficiary) and B (the remainder beneficiary), are in direct conflict. In this trust, A would want the trust funds to be distributed as often as possible while B would want the account to retain earnings and accumulate in value over time. Often, a conflict will arise regarding whether an investment is likely to accumulate income or preserve the trust account.

b)   Trustee Owes Duty of Impartiality

The trustee possesses a duty to be impartial with respect to all beneficiaries, including present and remainder beneficiaries, whose interests in maximizing income and preserving or increasing principal are often in conflict. A trustee must act with proper motives and without partiality or vindictiveness. A trustee may only make an investment affecting the remainder beneficiary's interest if she had adopted "accounting, investment, or other administrative practices reasonably designed to protect" the trust property's purchasing power, assuming the investment is otherwise proper. *Restatement of Trusts, Third*, §§ 239(a), 232, general comment c. A remainder beneficiary is entitled to recover the amounts the remainder beneficiary would have received had a trustee made appropriate provision for protecting the remainderman.

4) PRINCIPAL AND INCOME ALLOCATIONS

As was examined above with regard to a trustee's duty to treat all beneficiaries impartially, the income and remainder beneficiaries have an inherent conflict of interests. Income beneficiaries seek high yield from high income assets of the trust. Remainder beneficiaries seek high growth of, and the preservation of, trust assets. Two general questions often arise in this context. First, are trust expenses to be paid from the trust income or the trust principal? Second, are newly acquired assets to be treated as trust income or principal?

a) Common Allocations

(1) Assets Treated as Principal

A trust instrument may specify what assets a trustee should consider principal. It may also indicate if newly acquired assets should be apportioned as trust income or principal. The Uniform Principal and Income Act, where adopted by a state, mandates the proper allocation of such assets.

(a) Funds Received from Sale of Trust Asset

The Revised Uniform Principal and Income Act provides in part that: "A trustee shall allocate to principal…money or other property received from the sale, exchange, liquidation, or change in form of a principal asset, including realized profit." Rev. Unif. Prin. Inc. Act § 404(2).

(b) Repayment of Loan Principal

"A trustee shall allocate to principal an amount received from the sale, redemption, or other disposition of an obligation to pay money to the trustee more than one year after it is purchased or acquired by the trustee, including an obligation whose purchase price or value when it is acquired is less than its value at maturity. If the obligation matures within one year after it is purchased or acquired by the trustee, an amount received in excess of its purchase price or its value when acquired by the trust must be allocated to income." Rev. Unif. Prin. Inc. Act § 404(6)(b).

(2) Common Assets Treated as Income

(a) Rent Received by Trustee for Trust Property

A trustee is authorized to invest trust property. The trustee has correlative obligations to make the trust's property productive and exercise reasonable skill and care in selecting and administering the trust's investments. "To the extent that a trustee accounts for receipts from rental property pursuant to this section, the trustee shall allocate to income an amount received as rent of real or personal property, including an amount received for cancellation or renewal of a lease. An amount received as a refundable deposit, including a security deposit or a deposit that is to be applied as rent for future periods, must be added to principal and held subject to the terms of the lease and is not available for distribution to a beneficiary until the trustee's contractual obligations have been satisfied with respect to that amount." Rev. Unif. Prin. Inc. Act § 403.

(b)   Repayment of Loan Interest

"An amount received as interest, whether determined at a fixed, variable, or floating rate, on an obligation to pay money to the trustee, including an amount received as consideration for prepaying principal, must be allocated to income without any provision for amortization of premium." Rev. Unif. Prin. Inc. Act § 406(a).

b)   Corporate Distributions

(1)   Stock Splits and Stock Dividends

In the absence of a provision that determines how a trustee should apportion corporate dividends, stock dividends should be deemed additions to principal.

The Uniform Principal and Income Act treats distributions of stock, whether characterized as a stock dividend or as a stock split, as principal. Unif. Prin. Inc. Act § 6(a). The Revised Act adopts the same position. Rev. Unif. Prin. Inc. Act § 401(c)(1).

The Revised Act gives a trustee limited power to allocate a stock dividend between income and principal in cases where the distributing corporation had made no distributions to shareholders except in the form of dividends paid in stock. In such cases, a trustee might be justified in allocating some of the stock dividend to income to effectuate a grantor's intent to provide a beneficiary with trust income if applicable.

(2)   Cash Dividends

In the absence of a rule that establishes how a trustee should apportion corporate dividends, cash dividends should be treated as income.

c)   "Wasting" Assets

Wasting assets are assets that go down in value over time. Some examples include patents, copyrights, and some natural resources. A trustee may apportion a part of the income to be treated as principal in order to protect the interest of the remainder beneficiaries. Some states have statutes governing the distribution. If not, the trustee must comport his actions to the duty to act impartially.

d)   Trust Expenses

(1)   Everyday Expenses are Charged to Income

As a general rule, day-to-day expenses of the trust will be allocated against income. Ask yourself who the expense is being used to benefit? If the trust asset is an apartment complex providing rent for the income beneficiary and appreciation in value to the remainder beneficiary, a salary paid to an office manager would come from the trust income. On the other hand, payment of capital gains tax from the sale of the complex would come from the principal.

II.   FUTURE INTERESTS

A future interest is a present interest in land that may become a possessory interest in the land at some time in the future.

★ In Michigan, a future interest can be created under the terms of a trust. A "future interest under the terms of a trust" means a future interest that is created by a transfer creating a trust or to an existing trust or by an exercise of a power of appointment to an existing trust, directing the continuance of an existing trust, designating a beneficiary of an existing trust, or creating a trust." Mich. Comp. Laws § 700.2713(f).

★ Michigan law further provides that "if a governing instrument creates an alternative future interest with respect to a future interest for which a substitute gift is created[,] . . . the substitute gift is superseded by the alternative future interest only if an expressly designated beneficiary of the alternative future interest is entitled to take in possession or enjoyment." Mich. Comp. Laws § 700.2714(d).

A.   Classification of Reversions, Remainders, and Executory Interests

1)   POSSIBILITY OF REVERTER – INTEREST IN GRANTOR

A possibility of reverter is a future interest that the grantor retains when the grantor conveys a fee simple determinable. A fee simple determinable is an interest that is subject to potential reversion to the grantor if a certain event occurs.

For example, O conveys Blackacre to A for so long as the premises are not used as a brothel. A's interest in the land is conditioned on the premises not being used in a certain way. There is no additional event, which needs to occur before the grantor retakes possession other than the failure of the stated condition. Therefore, O retains a possibility of reverter.

The Rule Against Perpetuities is not applicable to a possibility of reverter.

2)   RIGHT OF RE-ENTRY – INTEREST IN GRANTOR

A right of re-entry is similar to the possibility of reverter. However, with a right of re-entry, the grantor must take affirmative action in order for the estate to revert back to the grantor (as opposed to the automatic conversion upon the happening of the condition with the possibility of reverter). The right of re-entry always follows a fee simple subject to condition subsequent.

For example, O conveys Blackacre to A, but if Blackacre is ever used as a brothel, O reserves the right to re-enter and terminate the estate of A. O retains a right of re-entry because there is an additional event that must occur (O reentering) for O to retake.

The Rule Against Perpetuities is not applicable to a right of re-entry.

3)   REVERSION – INTEREST IN GRANTOR

A reversion interest is created when the grantor conveys something less than a fee simple. For example, if a grantor conveys a life estate or a term for years, the grantor reserves a reversion interest in the property.

The Rule Against Perpetuities is not applicable to a reversion.

4)   REMAINDER – INTEREST IN THIRD PARTY

A remainder is similar to a reversion interest that is in a third party. The remainder interest generally follows a life estate or a term for years. A remainder will never follow a fee interest in land. It only comes into existence at the natural expiration of the prior estate.

For example, O conveys Blackacre to A for A's life, then to B. B possesses a remainder interest in the property.

5)   EXECUTORY INTEREST – INTEREST IN THIRD PARTY

An executory interest is an interest in a third party that always follows a fee interest. For example, O conveys Blackacre to A for so long as the premises are not used as a brothel, then to B. A possesses a fee simple determinable because upon the happening of the event, A's estate is eliminated. B possesses an executory interest because it cuts off a fee simple interest by means of a fee simple determinable.

a)   Springing Executory Interest

A springing executory interest is an interest that becomes possessory directly from the grantor to the interest holder grantee. For example, O conveys Blackacre to A when and if A reaches the age of 30. A possesses a springing executory interest because title passes from the grantor (O) to the grantee (A).

In another example, O conveys Blackacre to A for A's life, then 10 years after A's death, to B. In this example, title passes from O to A as a life estate holder, back to O for ten years, then to B. B possesses a springing executory interest because he obtains title from O.

b)   Shifting Executory Interest

A shifting executory interest is an interest that becomes possessory by directly shifting from one grantee to another. For example, O conveys Blackacre to A for so long as the premises are not used as a brothel, then to B. B possesses a shifting executory interest because title passes from grantee A to another grantee B.

B.   Life Estates and Terms of Years

1)   LIFE ESTATE

a)   General

A life estate is a possessory interest in land that lasts for the life of some person (usually the grantee). O conveys Blackacre to A for A's life.

b)   Life Estate *pur Autre Vie*

A life estate *pur autre vie* is a life estate measured by the life of someone other than the life tenant. For example, O conveys Blackacre to A for the life of B. A possesses a life estate *pur autre vie*.

A life estate *pur autre vie* can also be created by the transfer of a life estate interest. For example, O conveys Blackacre to A for A's life. Ten years later, A conveys her interest to B. B possesses a life estate *pur autre vie* (for the life of A).

c)   Duties of Life Estate Holders

A holder of a life estate interest possesses a duty not to commit waste that would unreasonable impair the value of the property when the future interest holder takes possession (i.e., destruction of the property).

2)   ESTATE FOR A TERM OF YEARS

An estate for a term of years is a possessory estate held by the grantee for the time set forth in the conveyance. For example, O conveys Blackacre to A for five years. A possesses an estate for a term of years (five years).

C.   Vested and Contingent Interests

The distinction between vested and contingent remainders is important because vested remainders are not subject to the Rule Against Perpetuities, but contingent remainders are subject to the Rule.

1)   CLASSIFICATION OF REMAINDER

A remainder is a vested remainder if: 1) it exists in an ascertainable person or persons; and 2) it is not subject to an express condition precedent.

For example, O conveys Blackacre to A for life, then to B. B possesses a vested remainder because B is ascertainable and there is no contingency. A dying is not a contingency, but rather the natural expiration of A's estate.

All other remainders are contingent.

a)   Condition Precedent (Contingent)

If the remainder is subject to an express condition that must be met before the interest becomes possessory, then it is subject to a condition precedent. For example, O conveys Blackacre to A for A life's, then if B is alive and has two children at the time of his death, to B and his heirs. B possesses a contingent remainder because the condition must be met before B takes possession.

b)   Condition Subsequent (Vested)

It is critical to distinguish a condition precedent from a condition subsequent because a condition subsequent results in a vested remainder. If the express condition is directly incorporated into the clause providing the remainder interest, then the remainder is contingent. For example, O conveys Blackacre to A for A's life, then to B if he is alive at the time of A's death. But if one clause in the conveyance creates the remainder interest and a separate and subsequent clause provides the condition which may eliminate the interest, the remainder is subject to a condition subsequent and hence vested.

For example, O conveys Blackacre to A for A's life, then to B and his heirs, but if B is not employed as an attorney at the time of A's death, then to C and his heirs. A possesses a life estate. B possesses a vested remainder because the provision creating the property interest comes before a separate (separated by a comma) and subsequent clause which provides for the potential elimination of the interest. C possesses a contingent remainder (contingent upon B's failure to satisfy the condition subsequent).

c)   Unascertainable People

Generally, if a person is named and alive, the person is ascertainable.

(1)   Heirs are not Ascertainable until Death

A person's heirs are not identifiable until a person's death. Therefore, a gift to A's heirs is contingent until A dies.

(2)   Remainders to Unborn People

If a person is not identifiable or not yet born, the person is not ascertainable.

Assume O conveys Blackacre to A for A's life, then to B's children. If B has one child who is living, C, then C is ascertainable and possesses a vested remainder subject to open. If B is alive, B's unborn children possess contingent remainders, which are contingent upon them being born.

2)   DESTRUCTIBILITY OF CONTINGENT REMAINDERS

At common law, a contingent remainder was destroyed unless it vested at or before the expiration of the prior estate. Assume O conveys Blackacre to A for life, then to A's children who reach the age of 30. If, at A's death, A's only child B was 29, B's remainder was destroyed and the property reverted to the grantor.

This harsh rule has been abolished in a great majority of jurisdictions by statute or case law. Today, as a general rule, a remainderman who subsequently meets the condition will be entitled to the present interest in the property. For example, O conveys Blackacre to A for life, then to A's children who reach the age of 30. If A's only child B is 29 at A's death, he will be entitled to the property when and if he turns 30. In the interim, O would be entitled to possession of the property.

D.   Powers of Appointment

A power of appointment gives the holder of the power (usually the trustee of a trust) the right to appoint or give away property, usually the property held by a trust. The power is usually conveyed by will or trust from one person, a donor, to another, a donee.

1)   GENERAL POWER OF APPOINTMENT

The donee of a general power receives all rights to appoint the property to herself, her creditors, or any others. Therefore, if a power is exercisable in favor of the holder, it is a general power of appointment. A power of appointment is general unless limited by the terms of its creation.

2)   SPECIAL POWER OF APPOINTMENT

A special power of appointment is a power that is not exercisable in favor of the donee, his estate, his creditors, or the creditors of his estate. With a special power of appointment, the power holder cannot appropriate the property into the power holder's own hands. The power must be limited by the terms of its creation in order for it to be a special power of appointment.

3)   EXERCISE OF POWER OF APPOINTMENT

A power of appointment will be properly exercised if the holder intends to exercise the power. A common question involves whether a power of appointment can be exercised in a general residuary clause of a will. For example, the decedent in his will gives "the rest of the property in my estate or over which I possess a power of appointment over, to A and his heirs." In the absence of a requirement in the power itself, that the power of appointment be exercised by specific reference to the power, a general residuary clause may effectively exercise the power only if 1) the power is a general power or 2) the testator's will manifests an intention to include the property subject to the power.

4)   POWERS ARE SUBJECT TO RULE AGAINST PERPETUITIES

A power of appointment is subject to the Rule Against Perpetuities. It must become exercisable within the perpetuities period. Additionally, any interest created by the exercise of a special power of appointment is valid only if the interest will in all events vest, or fail to vest, no later than 21 years after the death of a life in being at the time the power was executed.

E.   Acceleration of Future Interests

If a life estate or other future interest is disclaimed, the problem of whether succeeding interests or estates accelerate in possession or enjoyment or whether the disclaimed interest must be marshaled to await the actual happening of the contingency, may be raised. For example, assume O conveys Blackacre to A for A's life, then to B. If A disclaims, must B await A's death to take possession? Generally, under these circumstances, remainder interests are accelerated and the "future interest" takes effect as if the disclaimant had predeceased and the contingent event has been satisfied. A conveyance may be drafted to avoid acceleration if desired.

F.   Rule Against Perpetuities

The Rule Against Perpetuities is a clear expression of the common law's abhorrence of things uncertain. The rule limits the duration of legal interests which suspend property rights in perpetuity. The common law prefers that property be fully owned by just one person. The common law will tolerate temporary contingent interests for a certain time only. That limitation is no longer than 21 years after the death of a life in being at the time of the initial conveyance.

1)   COMMON LAW

An interest must vest, if at all, within 21 years of the death of a life in being. If there is any possibility, no matter how remote, that the interest will not vest within the time period, the future interest will fail. The rule is applicable to contingent remainders (not vested remainders as they are already vested), executory interests, powers of appointment, and option to purchase land. The rule does not apply to interests the grantor retains.

2)   WAIT-AND-SEE

Many states have reformed the harsh common law rule and have taken a "wait and see" approach. Under these statutes, a court will actually wait out the perpetuities period to determine whether the interest actually vests or fails within the period. That is the opposite of the harsh common law standard invalidating an interest if it is merely possible that the interest may vest or fail after the period.

3)   CY PRES

In some jurisdictions, under the *Cy Pres* Doctrine, a court may reform a non-vested interest to assure that it will vest within the permissible period. In exercising this reformation power, courts are directed to fashion a reform to most closely approximate the intention of the creator of the interest in order that the non-vested interest will vest within the period of the perpetuities period.

4)   OTHER REFORMS

There has been a modern trend to reform the rigid common law Rule Against Perpetuities. In addition to the wait and see and *Cy Pres* approaches, some courts have rewritten age requirements exceeding 21 years in some conveyances to validate them.

For example, assume O conveys Blackacre to A for life, then to A's children who attain the age of 35. Such an interest would violate the common law rule because A's children could reach 35 more than 21 years after A's death. Some courts would rewrite the requirement to state "to A for life, then to A's children who attain the age of 21."

Other courts would save a disposition from being void for remoteness by excluding a person from a class if the person's inclusion would invalidate the gift.

G.   Construction Problems

1)   GIFTS TO CLASSES

A settlor may expressly exclude an heir or anyone from receiving a gift in trust. A settlor may transfer property in trust to a class of individuals. For example, the settlor's trust instrument might require that $20,000 be divided equally among the children of Bob. This is a class gift and the class may increase or decrease in number until the settlor's death. The implication of a class gift is that if a member of the class predeceases the settlor, her share goes to the remaining members of the class.

a)   Definite Class

A trust may have beneficiaries who are members of a definite class. *Restatement (Second) of Trusts*, sec. 120. Those members are not entitled to equal treatment. A trustee may be empowered to decide which class members will receive benefits and in what amount. A trust instrument needs to specify the standards by which the trustee will operate.

b)   Indefinite Class

If the identity of any member is not ascertainable, then the class of beneficiaries is indefinite. No trust is created by a transfer in trust to members of an indefinite class because no beneficiary will exist to enforce it. If no class members are ascertainable, then the trust will fail. A trust instrument may empower a trustee to select the class members that will receive the trust property once a member becomes ascertainable.

The Rule Against Perpetuities applies to class gifts in trust. Thus, if the beneficiaries of such a gift cannot be ascertained within the period of the Rule, then the gift will fail. If the members will only be ascertained when a transferee selects them, then that authority to select is limited to the period of the Rule.

2)   GIFTS TO HEIRS

A settlor may make a gift in trust to heirs or family members. The scope of inclusion under the terms of "heirs" or "family" will depend upon the trust instrument and the factual circumstances.

Restatement (Second) of Trusts, sec. 120, cmt. b. A trust for the benefit of relatives of a family member may enable a trustee to select which members receive a transfer of property and in what amount. *Restatement (Second) of Trusts*, sec. 121. If a trustee does not exercise that authority of selection, then the property must be equally divided among the next of kin. Their identity will depend on which relatives would inherit under a state's intestate succession statute. When a settlor leaves property in trust for an indefinite class of relatives but a trustee lacks authority to select which of them will receive property, that lack of ascertainable beneficiaries will cause the trust to fail.

3)   RULE IN SHELLEY'S CASE

The Rule concerns conveyances, which provide: "From a settlor to a beneficiary for life, then to the beneficiary's heirs." The rule operates to merge a life estate in a person with a remainder interest in the person's heirs. The rule only operates when an equivalent quality of (legal or equitable) title exists in a beneficiary and the beneficiary's heirs. Most jurisdictions have abolished the rule. *Restatement (Second) of Trusts*, sec. 127. Where applicable, the rule is disfavored and narrowly interpreted.

4)   DOCTRINE OF WORTHIER TITLE

The Doctrine applies to conveyances stating that: "From a settlor to a beneficiary for life and then to the settlor's heirs." With respect to such an *inter vivos* transfer, the Doctrine provides that the settlor receives a reversion and the settlor's heirs do not take a remainder. The Uniform Probate Code and several states have abolished the Doctrine. Unif. Probate Code § 2-710. The doctrine provides a rebuttable presumption that a settlor did not intend to establish an interest in her heirs, but rather intended to retain a reversionary interest. A clear demonstration of the settlor's intent to create an interest in the settlor's heirs will defeat the rule's operation.

5)   GIFTS TO CHILDREN AND ISSUE

Children and issue are not ascertainable if they are neither born nor identifiable. A settlor's children and issue are not completely ascertainable until the settlor's death. In that respect a settlor's gift in trust to the children remains contingent until the settlor dies.

Without any opposite proof of intent, a settlor's gift in trust to a certain person's children will only include the first generation descendants of that person. *Restatement (Second) of Property*, Donative Transfers, sec. 25.1.

If a class is described as issue, descendants, grandchildren, siblings, nephews and nieces, cousins, or another similar relationship, the preferred method of ascertaining which persons are included in the class is to replace the word "children" for the actual class that was described. *Restatement (Second) of Property*, Donative Transfers, sec. 25.8-9.

If a settlor makes a gift in trust to an individual's "family" as a class, then at a minimum the class includes the individual's spouse and minor children. *Restatement (Second) of Property*, Donative Transfers, sec. 25.10.

a)   Adopted Children

A settlor may adopt children into her family. Generally, adopted children are considered as included in a settlor's gift to his children. *Restatement (Second) of Property*, Donative Transfers, sec. 25.4; Unif. Probate Code § 2-705. The same treatment is afforded to adopted children of someone other than the settlor who have lived with the settlor as a minor. Adopted adults are not so included unless they also lived in the settlor's household as a minor.

A settlor may adopt children out of her family. Unless a settlor makes a contrary provision in a trust instrument, a gift in trust to a beneficiary's children does not include a child that was adopted out of the beneficiary's family. *Restatement (Second) of Property*, Donative Transfers, sec. 25.5. An exception applies if a stepparent adopted the child after the death of a natural parent. In that event, the child may inherit from both of the natural parent's families and the stepparent's family.

A child who was adopted out of a family will not be considered a natural parent's child for purposes of inheritance if the relationship of natural parent and child terminated before the adoption occurred.

b)   Child Born Out of Wedlock

The common law prohibited a child born out of wedlock from inheriting any part of an estate on the basis that the child belonged to nobody. Generally, such a formerly "illegitimate" child, and the child's descendants may receive class gifts in trust. *Restatement (Second) of Property*, Donative Transfers, sec. 25.2; Unif. Probate Code § 2-705(a). The Uniform Probate Code, however, excludes any gift that is not from the child's parent if the child did not, as a minor, live "as a regular member of the household of that natural parent or of that parent's parent, spouse or surviving spouse." Unif. Probate Code § 2-705(b). A settlor may, by making a clear showing of intent, exclude a child born out of wedlock from a class gift or a residuary clause.

Inheritance from and through the mother of a child born out of wedlock is permitted in all states. The Uniform Probate Code provides that proof of paternity is required for a child born out of wedlock to inherit through or from a putative father. Unif. Probate Code § 2-611.

Pursuant to the Uniform Parentage Act, the father-child relationship is established between a man and a child by 1) an effective acknowledgment of paternity by the man unless the acknowledgment has been rescinded or successfully challenged; or 2) an adjudication of the man's paternity; or 3) adoption of the child by the man.

6)   DEATH WITHOUT ISSUE

This question arises when a settlor makes a gift in trust to a specific beneficiary, which provides that: If the beneficiary dies without issue, then the gift will go to a third person. Section 25.9 of *Restatement (Second) of Property*, Donative Transfers, covers that situation. It provides that if the beneficiary dies without issue, the gift will be considered to have created an interest in the third person after the beneficiary dies.

If a beneficiary dies intestate and without any heirs, then the beneficiary's estate will "escheat" to the government under both the common law and the Uniform Probate Code. Unif. Prob. Code § 2-105.

7)   GIFTS BY IMPLICATION

      a)   Resulting Trusts

Resulting trusts are implied in law from the presumed intent of parties to specific types of transactions. Particular situations give rise to an intent to establish a trust to return property to a settlor or the settlor's heirs. That presumption of intent is rebuttable by evidence of a settlor's intent that no resulting trust exists. A resulting trust may arise in at least three situations.

The first situation occurs when an express trust is defective or improperly formed. In that event, the trustee will hold the trust property for the settlor, the settlor's heirs, or the settlor's successors.

The second situation occurs when the property of a trust is greater than the amount that is needed for the trust's purposes. In that case the excess property will be maintained in a resulting trust for the settlor, the settlor's heirs, or the settlor's successors.

The third situation occurs when a first person pays for a purchase of property for a second person who receives possession of, and is named on the title to, the property. A presumption exists that the first person will receive the beneficial use of the property. A contrary presumption exists if the first person purchased the property under an obligation to support the second person.

      b)   Constructive Trusts

Even if at least two parties do not intend to create a trust, a court may find that a constructive trust exists. The purpose of that equitable remedy is to prevent a first party from being unjustly enriched at a second party's expense when the property's legal title was improperly obtained. The *Restatement (Second) of Trusts* describes three ways in which that property could have been wrongfully gained: (1) by fraud, (2) in violation of a confidential or fiduciary relationship; (3) by a testamentary devise or intestate succession in exchange for a promise to keep the property in trust. *Restatement (Second) of Trusts*, sec. 45.

A constructive trust is neither an active nor a long-term entity. The single duty of its trustee is to convey the possession of and title to property back to its proper owner. That owner could either be an intended beneficiary or a settlor.

WILLS & ESTATES

WILLS & ESTATES

Past administrations of the essay portion of the Michigan Bar Examination usually have included one or two questions regarding Trusts & Wills. The majority of these past Trusts and Wills questions have focused upon issues regarding wills. The minority of those questions have focused upon trusts, which are discussed in the Trusts Outline *supra*. This Wills & Estates Outline includes law pertaining to those questions as well as other general legal principles regarding wills and estates.

The sample answers provided for Trusts & Wills questions on the Michigan Bar Exam describe and cite to modern Michigan law. These controlling rules governing trusts and wills are generally derived from either common law or the statutory Michigan Estates and Protected Individuals Code ("EPIC"), when applicable. Sometimes the sample answers for these questions are based on the version of these rules, or the proper construction of them, provided in decisions of the Michigan Court of Appeals and/or the Michigan Supreme Court.

Traditionally, some past exams usually have tested certain issues regarding wills with some frequency. Sometimes, however, questions have tested different issues. Of those past questions regarding wills rather than trusts, most of them have examined testate succession issues involving wills. Some of those questions have tested both issues of testate succession and intestate succession. A few of the questions mainly have tested intestate succession.

Some of the most frequently tested wills issues in certain past Trusts & Wills questions of the Michigan Bar Exam include execution requirements, holographic documents, interested witnesses, and revocation by divorce. Some other often tested issues in former wills questions are inter vivos gifts, gifts *causa mortis*, anti-lapse, and interlineation or alteration of wills. Other previously tested wills issues include codicils, will interpretation, testamentary capacity, undue influence, class gift, and abatement. Some more infrequently tested wills issues involving some degree of intestacy or the application of statutory provisions include omitted child, spouse's elective share, and pretermitted spouse. Sometimes former questions tested intestate succession issues of distribution among a surviving spouse and/or descendants, including the determination and calculation of proper shares of distribution, and advancement. One past wills question tested making a claim against a decedent's estate and another one tested distinguishing a will from a deed.

I.   INTESTATE SUCCESSION

Most people die without a will. Consequently, the property of a person who dies without a will is, by default, distributed in accordance with a relevant jurisdiction's intestate succession statute. That statute may be based on or similar to sections of the model example provided in the Uniform Probate Code ("UPC"). In Michigan, the statute is the Estates and Protected Individuals Code ("EPIC"). Mich. Comp. Laws § 700.1101 *et seq*. The laws of intestacy, based in part on the UPC, also have significant applicability to the following situations.

- If a decedent executes a will that is invalid, then the decedent's estate's property will be distributed according to the intestate succession statute.
- If a decedent executes a will that disposes of only part of his property, the remainder of it must be distributed according to the intestate succession statute.
- If a person leaving a will merely references the person's "heirs," the rules of intestate succession may be utilized to determine the identity of the person's heirs.

★★ **A.   Share of the Surviving Spouse**

The dollar amounts stated in the following provisions for a surviving spouse's share are adjusted annually for inflation for decedents who died in 2001 or after. Mich. Comp. Laws § 700.1210.

1)   DECEDENT NOT SURVIVED BY DESCENDANTS OR PARENTS

If a decedent is not survived by any descendants or parents, a surviving spouse inherits a decedent's entire estate. Mich. Comp. Laws § 700.2102(1)(a).

2)   DECEDENT SURVIVED BY DESCENDANTS OF DECEDENT AND SURVIVING SPOUSE

A surviving spouse inherits the first $150,000 plus one-half of a decedent's estate if all of a decedent's surviving descendants are also descendants of the surviving spouse and no other descendant of that spouse survives the decedent. Mich. Comp. Laws § 700.2102(1)(b).

3)   DECEDENT SURVIVED BY PARENT(S)

A surviving spouse inherits the first $150,000 plus three-quarters of a decedent's estate if no descendant of the decedent survives the decedent, but a parent of the decedent survives the decedent. Mich. Comp. Laws § 700.2102(1)(c).

4)   DECEDENT SURVIVED BY DESCENDANTS OF DECEDENT AND SURVIVING SPOUSE AND SURVIVING SPOUSE'S DESCENDANTS WHO ARE NOT DECEDENT'S DESCENDANTS

A surviving spouse inherits the first $150,000 plus one half of a decedent's estate if all surviving descendants of the decedent also are the surviving spouse's descendants and the surviving spouse has at least one surviving descendant that is not the decedent's descendant. Mich. Comp. Laws § 700.2102(1)(d).

5)   DECEDENT SURVIVED BY DESCENDANTS SOME OF WHO ARE NOT DESCENDANTS OF SURVIVING SPOUSE

A surviving spouse inherits the first $150,000 plus one-half of a decedent's estate if at least one, but not all, surviving descendants of the decedent are not the surviving spouse's descendants. Mich. Comp. Laws § 700.2102(1)(e).

6)   NONE OF DECEDENT'S SURVIVING DESCENDANTS ARE
      SURVIVING SPOUSE'S DESCENDANTS

A surviving spouse inherits the first $100,000 plus one-half of a decedent's estate if none of the surviving descendants of the decedent are the surviving spouse's descendants. Mich. Comp. Laws § 700.2102(1)(f).

B.   Share of Children and Remote Descendants

For purposes of intestate succession under EPIC, the definition of a parent's child does not include a stepchild, a foster child, or a grandchild or more remote descendant. Mich. Comp. Laws § 700.1103(f).

1)   SURVIVING SPOUSE

If a decedent has a surviving spouse, descendents of the decedent will take the portion of the estate that remains after the surviving spouse takes his or her share.

★   2)   NO SURVIVING SPOUSE

A decedent's estate is distributable solely to the decedent's surviving descendants when the decedent dies without a surviving spouse. Mich. Comp. Laws § 700.2103(a). If all of the decedent's children are alive, each shares equally in the estate by representation. *Id.* and Mich. Comp. Laws § 700.2106(1). If not all of the decedent's children are alive, the estate is divided into (1) as many equal shares as the total of surviving descendants in the nearest generation containing a surviving descendant and (2) the number of deceased descendants in that generation with surviving descendants. *Id.* Each surviving descendant in the nearest generation receives one share. *Id.* The remaining shares are combined and divided the same way among the surviving descendants of the deceased descendants. *Id.* This approach is also described later under the heading titled "*Per Capita* at Each Generation."

★   3)   CHILD PREDECEASED INTESTATE DECEDENT

A complicated issue arises if a child has predeceased a parent who is an intestate decedent. Three rules address how to distribute an intestate estate under these circumstances. They are as follows:

a)   Strict *Per Stirpes*

Strict *per stirpes* is the common law approach that is recognized in a minority of states. Under a strict *per stirpes* distribution, the estate is divided at the generation of children that is closest to a decedent, whether or not any of the children were actually living at the decedent's death. Remember that each child fills the shoes of his or her parent. Accordingly, strict *per stirpes* distribution gives descendants the same shares they would have received if the order of deaths in the family were more "traditional" (parent before child). Take the following illustration as an example.

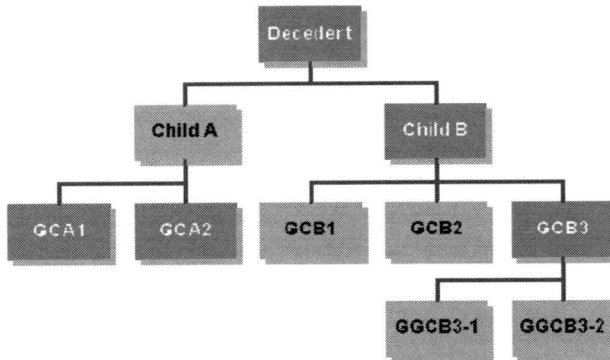

Child B and grandchild GCB3 have passed away before the decedent. If the statute in effect follows a strict *per stirpes* approach, then Child A gets one-half, and the grandchildren through Child A (GCA1 and GCA2) get nothing. Child B gets nothing because he is dead. If two grandchildren through Child B are living (GCB1 and GCB2) and one is dead (GCB3), each of the two living grandchildren receive one-third of what their parent Child B would have gotten if he had lived (one-third of one-half or one-sixth). The two great-grandchildren (GGCB3-1 and GGCB3-2) of the deceased grandchild (GCB3) split one-sixth and take one-twelfth each.

A serious problem with strict *per stirpes* arises if all of the decedent's children are dead and the estate passes only to the grandchildren. Assume in the above example that GCB3 has not died, but that Child A and Child B are deceased. Under strict *per stirpes*, GCA1 and GCA2 would each be entitled to one quarter of the estate because they fill the shoes of Child A. GCB1, GCB2, and GCB3 would only be entitled to one sixth each, however, because they must split Child B's one-half interest in half. Accordingly, the grandchildren were not treated equally under the strict *per stirpes* approach under those circumstances.

b)   *Per Capita* – Michigan Law

The modern *per stirpes* approach splits an estate equally among the living and deceased members of the first generation with one living member. For example, in the example above in which Child A and Child B died and GCB3 survived, the estate would pass a one fifth share to each grandchild. If any of the grandchildren are deceased, then their one-fifth share would be split among their own descendants.

In Michigan:

> If a governing instrument calls for property to be distributed 'per stirpes', the property is divided into as many equal shares as there are surviving children of the designated ancestor and deceased children who left surviving descendants. Each surviving child, if any, is allocated 1 share. The share of each deceased child with surviving descendants is divided in the same manner, with subdivision repeating

at each succeeding generation until the property is fully allocated among surviving descendants.

Mich. Comp. Laws § 700.2718(2).

        c)   *Per Capita* at Each Generation – Michigan Law

Under the UPC and EPIC approach, the decedent's estate is divided at the closest generation to the decedent in which one or more of the descendants are alive. Mich. Comp. Laws § 700.2106(1) (intestate succession when no surviving spouse); Mich. Comp. Laws § 700.2718(1) (statute or governing instruments). That approach is just like the modern *per stirpes* approach. However, shares of the deceased descendants on each level are added together and divided equally among all representatives of the deceased descendants in the next generation level. *Id.*

        4)   ADOPTED CHILDREN

        a)   General

Today, adopted children are entitled to receive the same share as biological children.

        b)   Equitable Adoption

What about the situation in which a child was never formally adopted, but treated like a child? If such a surviving child can establish an adoption by estoppel, the child could inherit from the decedent as if that survivor was a legally adopted child. The essential requirement is that the "adopting" parent must have treated the "adopted" child in the same manner as a parent generally would treat a child. Relevant factors that establish a relationship that warrants an adoption by estoppel might include: (1) the "adopting" parent's bestowal of love and affection on the child, (2) the "adopting" parent's performance of parental duties toward the child, (3) the child's obedience to and companionship toward the "adopting" parent, (4) the child's reliance on an adoptive relationship, and (5) the "adopting" parent's holding out the child as his child.

Many courts also require the child to prove that the "adopting parent" had promised, agreed, or attempted to adopt the child formally. *E.g., Cavanaugh* v. *Davis,* 149 Tex. 573, 235 S.W.2d 972 (1951). Generally, such a promise to adopt is not likely to be implied. Courts have rarely implied a contract to adopt even when a stepparent raises a stepchild. *Matter of Van Cleave's Estate,* 610 S.W.2d 620 (Mo. 1980).

Michigan case law recognizes the doctrine of equitable adoption. *E.g., Van v. Zahorik*, No. 111254 (Mich. 07/07/1999). "In Michigan, this doctrine has been 'used to create a right of intestate succession in children where there was an effort to adopt which was ineffective due to a failure to meet statutory requirements or where there was an agreement to adopt which the parent failed to perform." *Crossman v. Attorney Gen. of Michigan,* 145 Mich. App. 154 (1985).

        c)   Right to Inherit from Biological Parents Terminated

Adoption, whether it occurs in fact or by estoppel, generally severs the natural parent-child relationship. Consequently, an adopted child's right to inherit from biological parents is terminated. Accordingly, the adopted child cannot inherit via intestacy from her biological parents or another biological family member, such as a grandparent, uncle, etc. However, a child adopted by his stepparent may usually inherit from the child's biological parents as well. *E.g.*, Mich. Comp. Laws § 700.2114(2).

A minority of states permit an adopted child to inherit from both adoptive and biological parents.

5) CHILD BORN OUT OF WEDLOCK

The common law prohibited a child born out of wedlock from inheriting any part of an estate. Today, however, a so-called "illegitimate" child may inherit from either parent provided that the facts establish a parent-child relationship under a relevant jurisdiction's statute. States differ, however, regarding the burden of proof that a child born out of wedlock must meet to establish paternity, ranging from "preponderance of evidence" in some states to evidence that is "clear and convincing" in other states. Some states may also impose additional requirements such as recognition of paternity in writing or by some other act; some may require a judicial order of paternity. Under the UPC and EPIC, generally a person is a child of the person's biological parents without regard to the parents' marital status. UPC § 2-114(a) and Mich. Comp. Laws § 700.2114(1).

★   a)   Father-Child Relationship

Pursuant to the Uniform Parentage Act ("UPA") and EPIC, if a child is born out of wedlock or if a child is born or conceived in a marriage but not the issue of the marriage, the father-child relationship is established between a man and a child by:

- an effective acknowledgment of paternity by the man unless the acknowledgment has been revoked or successfully challenged (Mich. Comp. Laws §§ 700.2114(1)(b)(i), 700.1011);

- an adjudication of the man's paternity (Mich. Comp. Laws §§ 700.2114(1)(b)(iv)-(v), 700.714);

- adoption of the child by the man (Mich. Comp. Laws § 700.2114(2));

- under EPIC, the child's birth certificate is corrected upon the written request of the man and the child's mother (Mich. Comp. Laws § 700.2114(1)(b)(ii)); or

- under EPIC, a mutually acknowledged relationship of parent and child is established by the man and child, which begins before the child becomes 18 years old and continues until either of them dies (Mich. Comp. Laws § 700.2114(1)(b)(iii)).

Moreover, a man is presumed to be the father of a child if:

- under the UPA and EPIC, the man and the mother of the child are married to each other and the child is born during the marriage (Mich. Comp. Laws § 700.2114(1)(a));

- only under the UPA, the man and the mother of the child were married to each other and the child is born within 300 days after the marriage is terminated;

- under the UPA and EPIC, before the birth of the child the man and the mother of the child married each other in apparent compliance with law, even if the attempted marriage is or could be declared invalid (UPA) or void (EPIC). Mich. Comp. Laws § 700.2114(1)(a). The UPA further qualifies this rule by adding that the child is born during this marriage or within 300 days after its termination.

6)   HALF BLOOD CHILDREN

Half-blood children or kindred are two people who share one parent, but not the other. In almost every state, including Michigan, half-blood children are treated equally as whole-blood children. Mich. Comp. Laws § 700.2107. In a minority of jurisdictions, other than Michigan, they are treated less favorably (sometimes even excluded if whole blood kin exist).

★   7)   CHILD CONCEIVED OR BORN DURING MARRIAGE

For purposes of intestate succession under EPIC, both spouses are presumed the biological parents of a child conceived or born during their marriage. Mich. Comp. Laws § 700.2114(1)(a).

a)   Child Conceived Using Reproductive Technology

Also, a child conceived by a married woman with her husband's consent using reproductive technology is considered as this couple's child for the purposes of intestate succession. *Id.* The husband's consent is presumed unless clear and convincing evidence shows that he did not consent. *Id.*

★   8)   AFTERBORN HEIRS

Generally, under an afterborn heir provision, a parent's child conceived prior to the parent's death, but born after the parent's death, inherits as if the child was born before the parent's death. In Michigan, a child who is in gestation at a specific time is treated as living at that time if the child lives at least 120 hours after birth. Mich. Comp. Laws § 700.2108. Thus, a child in gestation before a parent's death who is born after the parent's death is treated -- for the purposes of intestate succession – as though the child was living when the parent died if the child survives for 120 hours after the child's birth.

C.   Share of Ancestors and Collaterals

1)   WHEN DESCENDANTS OR SURVIVING SPOUSE EXIST

If an intestate decedent has surviving descendants, ancestors and collaterals take nothing. If an intestate decedent has no descendants, but leaves a surviving spouse and parent(s), then the parent(s) take the share of estate not going to the surviving spouse.

2) DECEDENT LEAVES PARENTS, SIBLINGS, OR DESCENDANTS OF SIBLINGS

If there are neither descendants nor a surviving spouse of an intestate decedent, parents take in equal shares if they both survive the decedent. Mich. Comp. Laws § 700.2103(b). If only one parent survives, the surviving parent takes the entire share. *Id.* If there are no descendants and neither a surviving spouse nor parent, the decedent's siblings take in equal shares. Mich. Comp. Laws § 700.2103(c). Descendants of deceased siblings take the deceased siblings' share by representation. *Id.*

3) DESCENDANTS OF GRANDPARENTS

If there are no surviving descendants, parents, or descendants of parents of an intestate decedent, but the decedent is survived by at least one grandparent or descendants of grandparents, descendants of grandparents take to the exclusion of descendants of more remote ancestors. Half of the estate passes to the paternal grandparents or the surviving paternal grandparent or to the descendants of them both or either of them if both are deceased. Mich. Comp. Laws § 700.2103(d). The other half goes to the maternal grandparents in the same way. *Id.* If one "side" has no descendants living, the other side takes the entire estate. *Id.* The descendants of grandparents take by representation. *Id.*

4) DESCENDANTS OF GREAT-GRANDPARENTS

Many states, including Michigan, cut off the right of intestacy to descendants of grandparents only. However, a minority of jurisdictions permit descendants of great-grandparents to take via intestacy if there are no descendants of grandparents.

5) ESCHEAT

If an intestate decedent dies intestate and without any heirs, the decedent's estate "escheats" to the government under both the common law and Unif. Prob. Code § 2-105.

★ **D. Advancements**

1) DEFINITION

Historically, a lifetime transfer to a transferee who was a transferor's heir was treated as a down payment (also known as an advancement) of the transferee's share of the transferor's estate. Today, in Michigan a transfer will be classified an advancement only if (1) the decedent declared the decedent's intent to make an advancement in a contemporaneous writing, or (2) the heir acknowledged the transfer to be an advancement in writing. Mich. Comp. Laws §

700.2109(1)(a).

2)   ESTATE DIVISION

If the court finds a lifetime gift to be an advancement, the value of the gift is added to the probate estate. The estate is then divided among the heirs, with the lifetime gift deducted from the intestate share of the heir who received it. This process, sometimes called the "hotchpot" method, is not spelled out in Michigan's statute. It is the method used at common law, however, and is specified by the comment to Uniform Probate Code § 2-109, which served as a model for the Michigan statute. Uniform Probate Code § 2-109, comment (amended 2002), 8 ULA 27-28 (Supp. 2003); *generally,* William M. McGovern, Jr. & Sheldon F. Kurtz, *Wills, Trusts and Estates,* 65 (2d ed. 2001).

E.   Simultaneous Death

1)   ORIGINAL STATUTE

The initial version of the Uniform Simultaneous Death Act (USDA) provides that:

> Where the title to property or the devolution thereof depends upon priority of death and there is no sufficient evidence that the persons have died otherwise than simultaneously, the property of each person shall be disposed of as if he had survived.

Under the original USDA, evidence of survivorship, no matter how brief in duration, is sufficient to establish a sequence of death.

2)   REVISED USDA

Under the Revised Act, adopted in some jurisdictions, even if there is sufficient evidence to establish that a beneficiary named in a will in fact survived a testator, a beneficiary is only treated as having survived the testator if there is clear and convincing evidence that the beneficiary survived the testator by 120 hours. Revised Uniform Simultaneous Death Act, § 2 (1993).

3)   UPC – MICHIGAN LAW

Section 2-104 of the Uniform Probate Code and Michigan law requires proof by clear and convincing evidence that a person who would otherwise be a decedent's heir must survive a decedent by 120 hours. Mich. Comp. Laws § 700.2104. The UPC follows the Revised USDA approach.

II.   WILLS

In Michigan, a will is any testamentary instrument that, at a minimum, "excludes or limits the right of an individual or class to succeed to the decedent's property." Mich. Comp. Laws §

700.1108(b). The right to make a will is favored in the law and every effort is made to carry out a testator's or a testatrix's intent. (For purposes of convenience, herein that person will be referred to as a testator.) The testator makes and executes his last will and testament. The testator is always presumed competent to make and execute his will. The burden is upon those contesting the will to prove that the testator suffered from an unsound mind or was subjected to undue influence when making the will. The rules of will interpretation and construction must be must be carefully if not rigidly applied because a deceased testator cannot communicate that intent. A will speaks only from the moment of death. 23 *Mich. L & Prac.* 2d, Wills § 176 (2003).

★★★★ **A.   Execution Requirements (Signature and Witnesses)**

A testator must sign his will. If the testator is incapable of signing the will, then he must have another sign his name in his presence and by his direction. Any mark intended to validate the document is a valid signature. The will must be signed by at least two individuals as witnesses. Each of them must sign within a reasonable time after witnessing either the signing of the will, the testator's acknowledgment of that signature, or his acknowledgment of the will, in the testator's presence. Mich. Comp. Laws § 700.2502(1).

★   1)   <u>WRITINGS INTENDED AS WILLS</u>

In Michigan, a will lacking the necessary execution formalities is treated as if this testamentary document complies with EPIC's execution requirements if the will's proponent establishes by clear and convincing evidence that the deceased testator intended the document to constitute his will. Mich. Comp. Laws § 700.2503(a).

In other words, and more specifically, although a testamentary document or writing added upon a document was not executed in compliance with EPIC's execution requirements, the testamentary document or writing is considered as if it had been executed in compliance with those requirements if the proponent of the testamentary document or writing proves by clear and convincing evidence that the decedent intended the testamentary document or writing to constitute the decedent's will. *Id.*

2)   <u>GOVERNING LAW</u>

The law of a decedent's domicile at death usually governs the disposition of the decedent's personal property. However, the law of the jurisdiction in which the real property is located governs the disposition of that real property.

3)   <u>COMPLYING WITH LAW OF DOMICILE & FOREIGN WILLS</u>

A written will is valid if (1) it was executed in compliance with formalities set forth above (signature and two witnesses), or (2) its execution complies with the law at the time of execution of the place where the will was executed, or (3) its execution complies with the law of the place where, at the time of execution, or at the time of death, the testator was domiciled if it was his place of abode or a nation.

★★★   4)   HOLOGRAPHIC WILLS

a)   General Considerations

Most states do not recognize holographic wills. A holographic will is an unwitnessed will, which is handwritten and signed by the testator. In Michigan, which recognizes holographic wills, in addition to EPIC's requirement that such a will be signed and dated, all material portions of it must be in a testator's handwriting. Mich. Comp. Laws § 700.2502(2).

b)   Signature

For a holographic will to be valid, the testator must sign holographic will personally. Unlike general wills, no proxy signatures are permitted. Additionally, signatures should be at the end of the document.

c)   Verbiage

No precise words are required to create a will, but every will must contain operative words legally sufficient to validly devise the property. In fact, even letters can be holographic wills if they properly devise property.

★★   5)   INTERLINEATION OR ALTERATION

An interlineation (i.e., the addition of words to a will), even if they are in the testator's handwriting, is generally deemed insufficient to amend a will. Such additions lack the testator's signature and proper attestation. *E.g., In re Houghten's Estate*, 310 Mich. 613 (1945). However, Michigan law allows an alteration to take effect even if it fails to meet the formal requirements of a will if the testator's intention to make the change is established by clear and convincing evidence. Mich. Comp. Laws § 700.2503(c). An interlineation to a will in the testator's own handwriting that is signed and dated may, however, be valid as a holograph. Mich. Comp. Laws § 700.2502(2).

★   6)   CONSTRUING WILLS AND EXTRINSIC EVIDENCE

Michigan law permits a court to consider printed language in addition to handwritten terms when the court is construing a will or holographic will. Mich. Comp. Laws § 700.2502(3). "Intent that the document constitutes a testator's will can be established by extrinsic evidence, including, for a holographic will, portions of the document that are not in the testator's handwriting." *Id.*

★★★   7)   INTERESTED WITNESSES

a)   Common Law

(1)   Jurisdictions other than Michigan

At common law, if a witness who received a benefit under a will witnessed the will, the will was invalid unless two disinterested witnesses also witnessed the will. The will was invalid because the interested witness was not competent to testify about the validity of the will in court. Thus, its validity could not be judicially established.

(2)   Former Michigan Law

Michigan requires two witnesses to a will for the will to be valid. Under Michigan common law, any person who was to receive a gift under the terms of the will was unable to serve as a witness to the signing. However, if an interested person served as a witness to the will, the will was still valid but the specific bequest to the witness was void. *In Re Fay's Estate,* 353 Mich. 83 (1958); Michigan Compiled Laws §§ 617.63, 702.5, and 702.7, all repealed.

b)   Modern Trend – Current Michigan Law

In virtually every state including Michigan, the common-law rule has been abolished and the witnessing of a will by an interested witness does not affect the validity of the will. *E.g.,* Unif. Probate Code § 2-505 and Mich. Comp. Laws § 700.2505(2). Thus, pursuant to EPIC, interest no longer disqualifies a person as a witness nor invalidates any gift under a will. In other words, a testator's bequest of property to the witnesses of his will would not render them incompetent to witness his will. Moreover, current Michigan law would not require them to forfeit the bequest of property. If the will is otherwise valid, the witnesses would receive the property in the distribution of the testator's estate.

In a minority of states, unless two additional disinterested witnesses serve to witness the will, the interested witness forfeits his bequest. Some states temper this result, however, by permitting the interested witness to take up to what he would have received, had the testator died intestate.

B.   Integration of Wills

The integration doctrine provides that all papers intended to be part of a will that are present at the time of its execution are integrated into the will. The doctrine applies when pages or portions of a will become separated. A party may bring multiple pages into court in order to prove that they were meant to be treated as one document. Factors that tend to demonstrate that pages were meant to be taken together include:

- A testator's signature or initials appear on each page.
- Handwriting appears in the same non-black ink.
- There is a uniform font and ink.
- There is a uniform paper (size and color).
- Sentences carry over from page to page.

If an individual can demonstrate that the separate pages were meant to be taken together, then a court will consider the pages integrated back into original will.

★   **C.   Codicils**

1)   GENERAL CONSIDERATIONS

A codicil is a separate written document that amends a will. It must be dated, signed, and witnessed in the same manner as a will. Mich. Comp. Laws §§ 700.2502, 700.1108(b). In other words, a codicil must satisfy all the requirements of a will under EPIC. A codicil must make some reference to the will that it amends. A codicil can add to, subtract from, or modify the terms of an original will. When a testator dies, both the original will and the codicil are submitted for approval by a court. They provide a basis and authority for administration of the testator's estate and the distribution of his belongings.

2)   REPUBLICATION

At the time a person makes a codicil, the original will is treated as republished. However, there must be a valid will or codicil has nothing to attach. But note that under certain circumstances, a holographic codicil, if holographic wills are recognized in the jurisdiction, may validate a will that was not originally valid because it did not meet statutory requirements. The holographic codicil could be deemed a holographic will that incorporates the invalid will by reference. Conversely, a holographic codicil could effectively partially revoke a prior will (to the extent it is inconsistent).

★   ## 3)   INTERPRETATION

Formerly in Michigan, if a testator intended that a letter be a holographic codicil to his will, he needed to express his testamentary intent within the four corners of the letter. Traditionally, the intent of a putative codicil had to be gleaned from the instrument itself. *In re Henry's Estate,* 259 Mich. 499 (1932) rev'd on other grounds, 324 Mich. 568 (1949). Today, under EPIC, the intent of the testator in the execution of a testamentary document may be ascertained from extrinsic evidence. Mich. Comp. Laws § 700.2502(3); also, *In re Smith,* 252 Mich. App. 120 (2002).

In Michigan, the probate court must make a threshold determination whether the codicil satisfies all the requirements of a holographic will. Mich. Comp. Laws § 700.2502(2). If the probate court determines that a putative holographic codicil fails to satisfy those requirements, it may nonetheless be admitted into probate. However, the proponent of the codicil must establish by clear and convincing evidence that the decedent intended the writing to constitute a codicil to the will. Mich. Comp. Laws § 700.2503(c). *Also In re Smith,* 252 Mich. App. 120 (2002).

★★   **D.   Incorporation by Reference**

Under the doctrine of incorporation by reference, a will may incorporate into the will another document that is extrinsic to the will. The dispositive terms in that extrinsic document may be given testamentary effect even if the extrinsic document was not executed in accordance with the formalities that the Statute of Wills requires. In order for the doctrine to apply, the extrinsic document: 1) must have been in existence when the will was executed; and 2) the will's language (A) manifests the intent to incorporate the writing and (B) sufficiently describes the writing in order to identify it. Mich. Comp. Laws § 700.2510.

E.   Facts of Independent Significance

Under one condition, a court may give effect to events or acts that would change the disposition of a testator's estate after the testator has executed his will. The condition is that those events must have significance apart from a change in the testator's testamentary scheme. Mich. Comp. Laws § 700.2512. These facts of independent significance can occur after or before either the will is executed or the testator's death. *Id.* One such event is the revocation or execution of another individual's will. *Id.*

Generally, a disposition is invalid when the facts from which it can be ascertained have no significance apart from the disposition. This doctrine is relevant under two circumstances: 1) when a testator's will makes reference to facts or events of independent significance to the determination of the beneficiaries of the will; or 2) when the testator's will makes references to facts or events of independent significance to determining what property an ascertained beneficiary will receive.

For example, devises to persons named in an unattested memorandum not properly incorporated in a will by reference are invalid on the basis that the memorandum has no significance apart from the will. Thus, the following devise of personal property would not be valid under the doctrine of fact of independent significance: "to those persons designated in a memorandum which I shall prepare and leave in my safe-deposit box." However, one could make a valid bequest of "all the money in my bank account," since that is a fact of independent legal significance.

F.   Revocation

A will may be revoked in one of several different manners. It can be revoked by physical act. For example, a testator may cancel a will or create a subsequent will tearing up the earlier will. Additionally, a will may be revoked by operation of law. For example, a testator obtained a divorce after the will's execution.

The common law rules were very rigid. A testator was required to perform certain acts or the revocation would not be effective. Today, a testator's intent is a key factor. As such, the rigid common law rules have been somewhat relaxed.

1)   DEPENDENT RELATIVE REVOCATION

Under the doctrine of dependent relative revocation (DRR), a revocation can be deemed conditional on the validity of a subsequently executed will or codicil if that would accomplish the testator's intent. W. McGovern, S. Kurtz, and J. Rein, *Wills, Trusts and Estates* § 5.3 (1988). Under this doctrine, if the subsequently executed will is invalid, then the revocation that was dependent upon it is ignored. *Id.* Typically, however, courts apply that doctrine only when there is a sufficiently close identity between the bequest that was revoked and the bequest that was expressed in the invalid subsequent will.

The revocation of a will may be ignored under DRR if a valid will is revoked by a physical act under a testator's mistaken belief that in doing so the testator could revive an earlier will. Because the DRR is an intent-effectuating doctrine, it applies only when a court determines that a testator would prefer the disposition in the revoked will to that resulting from a determination that the testator died intestate. *Generally Estate of Alburn* 18 Wis. 2d 340, 118 N.W.2d 919 (1963). Courts are more likely to apply DRR if the distribution of the estate using DRR approximates more closely the distribution that the testator actually intended than the distribution that would occur if DRR did not apply. When that is not the case, courts are more likely to reject using DRR.

2) REVOCATION DUE TO CHANGED CIRCUMSTANCES

In certain circumstances, dispositions made under a will may be revoked by operation of law. Traditionally, two circumstances affected a revocation – homicide and divorce. If a beneficiary under a will or intestacy is found guilty of the felonious homicide of the testator, the beneficiary forfeits any bequest under the will.

★★★   ### 3) DIVORCE

At common law, divorce did not revoke a testator's devise to a former spouse by operation of law. Today, a divorce revokes a provision in a will for the testator's former spouse unless the will or a court order expressly provides otherwise. *E.g.,* Mich. Comp. Laws § 700.2807. Where a provision in favor of the former spouse is revoked by operation of law, the bequest passes as if the former spouse predeceased the testator. It could, for example, pass under the will's residuary clause. The gift is revived if the spouses remarry. *Id.*

4) REVOCATION BY PHYSICAL ACT

A will can be revoked by a number of physical acts.

a) Subsequent Written Instrument

A will may be revoked in two ways: (1) by a subsequent will that is executed solely for that purpose; or (2) by a subsequent will containing a revocation clause or provisions that are inconsistent with those of the previous will. Mich. Comp. Laws § 700.2507(1)(a), (2). The fact that a second will was made does not necessarily create a presumption that it revokes the prior will.

(1) Writing Intended as a Will that Revokes a Will

In Michigan, a will lacking the necessary execution formalities is treated as if this testamentary document complies with EPIC's execution requirements if the will's proponent establishes by clear and convincing evidence that the deceased testator intended the document to constitute a revocation of his will. Mich. Comp. Laws § 700.2503(b).

b) Revocatory Acts of Cancellation

A will is revoked if a testator, or another person in his presence and at his direction, burns, tears, cancels, obliterates, or destroys the will with the intent and for the purpose of revoking it. Mich. Comp. Laws § 700.2507(1)(b). Under EPIC, these types of revocatory acts to the will do not need to touch any words of the will. *Id.* Under the UPC and EPIC, words of cancellation need not touch any of the words of the will, but they must be somewhere on the will.

Pursuant to the common law rule, however, the words of cancellation must "touch" the words of the will.

          c)   Partial Revocation

Most jurisdictions, including Michigan, recognize "partial revocation by physical act." UPC § 2-507(a). In Michigan, the testator's execution of a later will can revoke part of a prior will, expressly or by inconsistency. Mich. Comp. Laws § 700.2507(a).

Generally, when marks of cancellation are found on a will known to last have been in the testator's possession, a presumption arises that such marks were made by the testator with the intent to revoke. William McGovern, Sheldon F. Kurtz & Jan Rein, *Wills, Trusts and Estates,* § 5.2. The presumption of revocation is rebuttable. The burden to overcome this presumption is on the party claiming that the bequest has not been revoked.

If a bequest is revoked, then it passes as part of the residuary estate. Some jurisdictions other than Michigan do not permit partial revocations.

G.   Revival

Under the common law, the revocation of a later will revives a prior will. That rule flowed from the principle that wills only speak at the time of death. Thus, when the later will was revoked and therefore became a nullity, only the prior will had legal effect. Because of the belief that the common-law rule frustrated the intent of testators who revoked the later will with the intent of dying intestate, many states adopted statutes rejecting the common-law revival rule.

The state statutes, which reject that rule, can take at least two forms. One in states other than Michigan is that the revocation of the later will does not revive the prior will. The other form, as provided in EPIC, is that the revocation of the later will does not revive the prior will unless the prior will (or the revoked part of it) is revived to the extent that the later will's terms indicate the testator's intent that the prior will take effect. Mich. Comp. Laws § 700.2509(3). Also, in Michigan, a will lacking the necessary execution formalities is treated as if this testamentary document complies with EPIC's execution requirements if the will's proponent establishes by clear and convincing evidence that the deceased testator intended the document to constitute a revival of part or all of the testator's revoked will or a revoked part of his will. Mich. Comp. Laws § 700.2503(d).

H.   Contractual Wills

        1)   <u>WRITING REQUIRED</u>

a)   Majority Rule

Ordinarily, contracts to make a will must be in writing. In the absence of a writing, such contracts are unenforceable. Jurisdictions that do not expressly address this matter in their probate codes may reach the same result by applying a statute of frauds.

b)   Michigan Law

The following types of written contracts executed after July 1, 1979 – "to make a will or devise, not to revoke a will or devise, or to die intestate" can be established only by at least one of the following items:

- A will's provisions stating the contract's material provisions.

- A will's express reference a contract and extrinsic evidence proving the contract's terms.

- A writing that the decedent signed evidencing the contract.

Mich. Comp. Laws § 700.2514(1).

"The execution of a joint will or mutual wills does not create a presumption of a contract not to revoke the will or wills." Mich. Comp. Laws § 700.2514(2).

2)   NO WRITING REQUIRED

a)   Minority Rule

If a jurisdiction does not require a writing (significant minority) to establish a contract to make a will, a party may be able to recover the amount of their damages.

b)   Unjust Enrichment

A party may also be able to recover damages in an amount equal to the reasonable value of their services in reliance upon a purported contract to make a will under an unjust enrichment theory. Under such circumstances, a court may impose a constructive trust for such amount on the successor of the testator's estate.

I.   Construction Problems

★★   1)   LAPSED LEGACIES

If a devisee named in the will predeceases a testator, then the devise lapses into the estate's residue unless the jurisdiction's anti-lapse statute preserves the devise for the devisee's descendants. In Michigan, a devise to a deceased person (i.e., devisee) who is a grandparent, a grandparent's descendant, or the testator's stepchild, does not lapse if the deceased person's descendants survive the testator. Rather, a substituted gift is created in the deceased person's (i.e., the deceased devisee's) surviving descendants. Mich. Comp. Laws § 700.2603(b). They "take by representation the share to which the deceased devisee would have been entitled had the deceased devisee survived the testator." *Id.* The theory behind anti-lapse statutes is that when a testator leaves property to a sufficiently close relative, the testator would want the issue of that devisee to take the property if the devisee predeceases the testator.

★   2)   ADEMPTION

        a)   General Common Law Approach

Under the doctrine of ademption, if the subject matter of a specific devise is not in the probate estate at the time of a testator's death, the bequest to the devisee adeems or fails. *Generally* William H. McGovern, Jr. & Sheldon F. Kurtz, *Wills, Trusts and Estates* 295 (2d ed. 2001). The doctrine of ademption by extinction applies only to specific devises. It does not apply to general or demonstrative devises. For example, assume that a testator leaves "my ABC Motorcycle to Able." Before the testator's death, he sells the motorcycle to a third party for $5,000. Under the general rule, Able receives nothing because the gift adeems by extinction.

Some courts will temper this result and implement an intent theory to determine whether a testator intended for the gift to adeem. If a beneficiary can prove that the testator lacked that intent, then the beneficiary will be entitled to a gift of equal value.

        b)   Michigan Approach Presumes Non-Ademption

Traditionally, in Michigan, ademption would operate to cause a devise to fail. *Hankey v. French*, 281 Mich. 454 (1937). Today, Michigan's EPIC statute provides a presumption of non-ademption. Mich. Comp. Laws § 700.2606(1)(f). If no other statutory provision compensates a devisee for the replacement or value of specifically devised property, then the devisee has a right to the property's value, unless the circumstances and facts show that the testator intended the ademption or it was within the testator's manifested distribution plan. *Id.*

                (1)   Insurance Proceeds or Replacement Property

Potentially, a devisee is entitled to: 1) any insurance proceeds for harm to the specifically devised property that is unpaid upon the testator's death; or 2) property obtained by the testator as a replacement for the specifically devised property. Mich. Comp. Laws § 700.2606(1)(c), (e).

        3)   SLAYER STATUTES

Generally, a person who feloniously and intentionally kills a decedent is barred from claiming a share of the decedent's estate as either an heir or a beneficiary under the decedent's will. Mich. Comp. Laws § 700.2803(1). If the decedent died intestate, the decedent's estate is then disposed of as if the killer had disclaimed the killer's intestate share of it. *Id.* It the decedent died testate, all provisions of the decedent's will that dispose of property to the killer are revoked and given effect as if the killer disclaimed them. Mich. Comp. Laws § 700.2803(2)(a)(i), (4).

A conviction of felonious and intentional homicide conclusively establishes that the killer feloniously and intentionally killed the decedent, for purposes of the probate proceedings. Unif. Prob. Code § 2-803(g); Mich. Comp. Laws § 700.2803(6). In some states other than Michigan, inheritance is barred only if there has been a conviction. In most states including Michigan, if there has been no conviction, the court having jurisdiction over the decedent's estate must determine whether a preponderance of evidence supports the conclusion that the alleged killer feloniously and intentionally took the life of the decedent. *Id.* Some states other than Michigan, however, use a clear and convincing standard, rather than a preponderance of the evidence standard. *E.g., Estate of Safran,* 102 Wis.2d 79, 306 N.W.2d 27 (1981).

In some states other than Michigan where there is no slayer statute, courts apply the equitable principle that a wrongdoer cannot profit from his own wrong to prevent the killer from inheriting. In such states, a court is likely to hold that a killer succeeds to the property of the deceased victim but holds it as constructive trustee for others. *E.g., Estate of Mahoney,* 126 Vt. 31, 220 A.2d 475 (1966).

4)   DISCLAIMER

A beneficiary under a will can "disclaim" (i.e., renounce) the beneficiary's interest under a testator's will. Mich. Comp. Laws § 700.2902. This right to disclaim the interest is barred if certain events occur between when the right arises upon the testator's death and the disclaimer is made. Mich. Comp. Laws §§ 700.2904, 700.2910. Generally, if the disclaimer is not barred, the disclaimed property interest passes as if the disclaimant predeceased the testator. Mich. Comp. Laws § 700.2907.

5)   CLASSIFICATION OF LEGACIES AND DEVISES

a)   Specific Bequests

A bequest is specific if the subject matter of the bequest is specific property. *Generally* W. McGovern, S. Kurtz & J. Rein, *Wills, Trusts and Estates § 10.1 at 398.* For example, a gift of a specific automobile or table would be considered specific.

b)   General Bequests

A bequest is general if it can be satisfied with any estate assets. Typically, a bequest of a specific dollar amount is general since it can be funded with cash or other property having a value equal to the amount of the bequest.

c)   Demonstrative Bequests

A bequest of a specific dollar amount that is payable from a designated fund is a demonstrative bequest. To the extent of the designated fund, a demonstrative bequest is specific since it is the designated fund from which the bequest is to be paid. A demonstrative bequest is general, however, to the extent the fund is insufficient to pay the dollar amount of the bequest in full.

6) ABATEMENT

Beneficiaries under wills are entitled only to the net value of estate assets. The net value represents what remains of the decedent's assets owned at death after the payment of debts, expenses, and taxes. All states have abatement statutes that determine how debts, expenses, and taxes should be allocated among the beneficiaries of residuary, specific, and general legacies. The statutes provide that, unless the will otherwise provides, legacies abate in the following order to pay debts, expenses, and taxes:

    (1)   property not disposed of by will;
    (2)   residuary devises;
    (3)   general devises; and then
    (4)   specific devises.

The gifts of each class are abated on a pro-rata basis.

For example, assume that a testator's estate consists of $100,000, a $5,000 car and ABC stock worth $10,000. Assume the testator's valid will disposes of his property as follows:

    (1) $15,000 of my ABC Stock to Able;
    (2)   My car to Bob;
    (3) $15,000 to Charles;
    (4)   The residue of my estate to XYZ Charity.

Before dying, the testator was involved in litigation that rendered him liable to a creditor for $90,000. As a result, the creditor receives $90,000 from the testator's estate in a judgment and the testator's cash is reduced to $10,000. In accordance with the rule set forth above, the gifts to the beneficiaries will be abated as follows:

    (1)   Property not Disposed of by Will;

There is no property not disposed of by will.

    (2)   Residuary Devises;

XYZ charities will receive nothing because its entire gift will abate.

    (3)   General Devises; and then

Charles is a general devisee of $15,000 in cash.

Able is a general devisee of $5,000 in cash and a specific devisee of the $10,000 of ABC stock. Able's gift is a demonstrative devise. As set forth above, a bequest of a specific dollar amount that is payable from a designated fund is a demonstrative bequest. To the extent of the designated fund, a demonstrative bequest is specific since it is the designated fund from which the bequest is to be paid. A demonstrative bequest is general, however, to the extent the fund is insufficient to pay the dollar amount of the bequest in full. Therefore, Able is a general devisee of $5,000 and a specific devisee of the $10,000 of ABC stock.

Only $10,000 of cash is available in the testator's estate. Therefore, the two general devises will abate on a pro-rate basis. Able's general devise ($5,000) is one-fourth of the total general devises ($15,000 + $5,000). Therefore, Able will receive one-fourth of the cash left in the estate or $2,500. Charles will receive three-fourths or $7,500.

(4) Specific Devises

Bob will receive the car. Able will also receive $10,000 worth of ABC stock because the gift is specific.

★★   7)   GIFTS TO CLASSES

A testator may devise property to a class of individuals. For example, he may devise $20,000 to be divided equally among the children of Bob. This is a class gift and the class may increase or decrease in number until the testator's death. The implication of a class gift is that if a member of the class predeceases the testator, her share goes to the remaining members of the class. It does not lapse to the residue. Mich. Comp. Laws § 2604. An issue often arises as to whether a devise is a class gift under the circumstances. An examinee should analyze the wording of the gift and make a logical conclusion. For example, a testator may leave "$15,000, to be divided among A, C, and D, who are Bob's children." That provision can be argued as being either a class gift to the children or as three individual devises of $5,000. It is likely that a court would deem that a class gift as it calls for a division of funds among the children of Bob. Nonetheless, a compelling argument can be made to the contrary because A, C, and D, are individually named.

In Michigan, individuals born out of wedlock share in class gifts defined by a relationship to the decedent if they stand in that relationship. Mich. Comp. Laws § 700.2707.

a)   Effect of Anti-Lapse Statutes

A gift to a class member who qualifies under an anti-lapse statute would pass to the class member's descendents. Mich. Comp. Laws § 700.2709(b).

8)   EXONERATION

Under the common-law doctrine of exoneration, the specific devisee of encumbered real property was entitled to have the mortgage on the property paid from the estate as a debt of the decedent unless there was evidence of a contrary intent on the part of the testator.

Today, most states including Michigan, have adopted statutes contrary to this common-law rule of exoneration. Specifically, the Uniform Probate Code and EPIC provide that "a specific devise . . . passes subject to any mortgage interest existing at the date of death, without right of exoneration, regardless of a general directive in the will to pay debts." Unif. Probate Code § 2-607; Mich. Comp. Laws § 700.2607. In states like Michigan with statutes of this type, the specific devisee of encumbered property takes subject to the mortgage notwithstanding the fact that the will contained a clause directing the executor to pay the decedent's debts.

Courts have also held that a general directive to pay debts is insufficient to evidence an intent to exonerate the devisee of specifically devised property. *E.g.*, *Griffin v. Gould,* 72 Ill. App. 3d 747, 391 N.E.2d 124 (1979).

      9)   SATISFACTION

          a)   Common Law

Under the common law, if, subsequent to the execution of a will, a testator gives property to a person who is named as a general legatee (i.e., money recipient) in a will that is executed by the testator prior to the making of the gift, a rebuttable presumption arises that the testator intended the gift to be in satisfaction of the general legacy. This is known as the doctrine of "satisfaction" or "ademption by satisfaction." *Generally* W. McGovern, S. Kurtz & J. Rein, *Wills, Trusts and Estates* 30 (1988).

          b)   UPC / EPIC

The common-law rule is often abrogated or modified by statute. For example, under Unif. Probate Code § 2-609(a)(ii) a gift to a legatee is not in satisfaction of the legacy unless the testator declared in a contemporaneous writing that he intended the gift to be in satisfaction of the bequest. Similarly, under EPIC, a testator's gift to a devisee during the testator's lifetime is a satisfaction of a devise only in any of these events:

- "The testator declared in a contemporaneous writing that the gift is in satisfaction of the devise or that its value be deducted from" the devise's value.

- The devisee acknowledges in writing either that the gift is in satisfaction of the devise or that the gift's value is to be deducted from the devise's value.

- "The will provides for a deduction of the gift."

Mich. Comp. Laws § 700.2608(1).

      10)   ACCRETIONS

          a)   General Considerations

An accretion is the change in value of a gifted property between the time of will execution and the time of a testator's death. An accretion is not considered when distributing the testator's property. Generally, the beneficiaries of a will bear the burden of depreciation and reap the benefit of appreciation. In some cases, the form of a gift changes before a testator's dies. If such a change is only in form, then the beneficiary will receive the property as transformed. If, however, the change is substantive, the beneficiary will receive the value of the gift that existed before the change. In order to answer a question regarding an accretion, one must ask what the nature of the change is. Is it form or substance?

> b)   Increases in Securities; Accessions

EPIC provides that when a testator executes a will which devises securities and at that time the testator owns securities as described in the will, the devise will include additional securities that the testator owns upon his death to the extent that he acquired the additional securities after the will's execution as a result of his ownership of them and the securities are of one of these types:

- Securities of the same organization acquired by reason of action initiated by the organization or any successor, related, or acquiring organization, excluding any acquired by exercise of purchase options.

- Securities of another organization acquired as a result of a merger, consolidation, reorganization, or other distribution by the organization or any successor, related, or acquiring organization.

- Securities of the same organization acquired as a result of a plan of reinvestment.

Mich. Comp. Laws § 700.2605(1).

An example of accession by an increase in securities is a stock that splits over time. For example, suppose that a testator executes a will devising 100 shares of ABC stock to Able. Thereafter, the ABC corporation splits its stock 3 for 1 so that the testator owns 300 shares at his death. In that situation, does Able take 100 shares or 300 shares? Pursuant to EPIC, Able as the devisee of this ABC stock is entitled to the additional shares received by the testator as a result of the stock split.

★   11)   GIFTS TO CHILDREN AND ISSUE

A testator may also devise a gift to the testator's "children" or "heirs" or "issue." Under these circumstances, a court would likely look to the jurisdiction's intestacy statute to determine how the gift should be distributed if members of the class are no longer living (i.e., *per stirpes, per capita*, etc.)

> a)   Adoption, Children Born out of Wedlock, and Half-Blood

In most jurisdictions like Michigan, adopted children, children born out of wedlock, and half-blood children are included in the class.

> (1)   Gift from Grandparents to Grandchildren

What about when grandparents leave a gift to their "grandchildren"? Would adopted, half-blood, or children out of wedlock be included? It depends. Most statutes only apply to children not grandchildren. Therefore, under such statutes, the answer would be no. However, under common law principles, if one could demonstrate that the testator intended to include the child, then a court may give effect to that intent.

★★ J.   Will Contests

In will contests, a contestant challenges the validity of a will that a proponent submits to a probate court to administer. The contestant has the burden of proving that a will should be judicially invalidated. Ordinarily, a finding of lack of testamentary capacity will invalidate the entire will, while a finding of undue influence, fraud, or mistake might only invalidate those provisions that relate to the specific problem.

★   1)   AGE REQUIREMENT

An individual 18 years old or older may make a will in Michigan. Mich. Comp. Laws § 700.2501.

★   2)   MENTAL CAPACITY

In Michigan, a person of sound mind can make a will. *Id.* There is a presumption of mental capacity. A will is invalid if a testator lacked mental capacity to execute the will. In order to prevail in a will contest on this ground, a contestant must prove that the testator did not know either: (1) the nature and extent of his property; (2) the persons who are the natural objects of his bounty; or (3) the disposition he was making of his property. *E.g., In re Sprenger's Estate,* 337 Mich. 514 (1953).

★   3)   UNDUE INFLUENCE

a)   General Considerations

A will is invalid if a testator executed the will while under undue influence. In order to prevail in a will contest on this ground, a contestant must prove that "such control was exercised over the mind of the testator as to overcome his or her free agency and free will and to substitute the will of another so as to cause the testator to do what he would not otherwise have done but for such control." *Lipper v. Weslow,* 369 S.W. 2d 698 (Tex. Ct. App. 1963).

b)   Some Analytical Factors of Undue Influence

Other courts have noted that to be successful a contestant must prove that:

- A testator was susceptible to undue influence;
- An alleged influencer had the opportunity to exercise undue influence over the testator;

- The alleged influencer was disposed to influence the testator to obtain an improper favor; and
- The will evidenced a result that appears to be the effect of undue influence.

        c)   Evidence Needed for Presumption of Undue Influence

In Michigan, a party who introduces evidence that establishes the following three elements is entitled to a presumption of undue influence:

- the existence of a fiduciary or confidential relationship between a fiduciary and the grantor;

- an interest represented by the fiduciary benefits from a transaction; and

- the fiduciary possessed an obligation to influence the grantor's decision as to the transaction.

Kar v. Hogan, 399 Mich. 529 (1976).

Michigan law provides that the weaker the degree of the testator's strength or intellect, the easier it is to infer that this influence is undue. *In re Shepard's Estate*, 161 Mich. 441 (1910); *Schneider v. Vosburgh*, 143 Mich. 476 (1906).

        4)   FRAUD

Courts can set aside wills whose provisions reflect a testator's belief in false information arising from fraudulent misrepresentations that were made to him by a beneficiary. In order to invalidate a will on these grounds, a contestant must prove:

- That a misrepresentation of a material fact was made to a testator; and
- The testator relied on and was influenced by that misrepresentation in disposing of his property by will.

The contestant has the burden of proving that the making of the will involved fraud.

        5)   MISTAKE

On rare occasions, a will can be successfully contested on the grounds of mistake. For example, if a testator leaves his estate to only one son based on a mistaken belief that the other son is wealthy, a court may reform the will to provide for the son who was left out. A court may reform the will if a testator mistakenly leaves out an intended clause or the will mistakenly includes an unintended clause or typographical error.

★   6)   NO-CONTEST CLAUSES

No-contest (i.e., *in terrorem*) clauses are commonly called forfeiture clauses. The purpose of a no-contest clause is to discourage potential will contestants by forcing them to choose either the bequest in the will if no contest action is filed, or nothing if their contest action fails. A minority of jurisdictions flatly enforce no-contest clauses. Others find them invalid as a matter of public policy. Most jurisdictions including Michigan follow an intermediate rule that such a clause that purports to penalize a contestant is unenforceable "if probable cause exists for" instituting a will contest. Mich. Comp. Laws § 700.2518.

           a)   Probable Cause Based on Evidence of Successful Challenge

Probable cause is generally defined objectively. "Probable cause exists when, at the time of instituting the proceeding there was evidence that would lead a reasonable person, properly informed and advised, to conclude that there was a substantial likelihood that the challenge would be successful." 2 *Restatement Property, 3d*, Wills and Other Donative transfers, § 8.5, Cmt. c, p 195.

      7)   STANDING TO CONTEST

For the most part, only those who have a potential pecuniary interest in an estate have standing to contest it.

Standing to contest a will mostly depends on statute. Usually, a will is admitted to probate upon proof of due execution which raises a presumption of validity. Then, within the period allowed by statute, challengers may petition to revoke probate upon any grounds they may have. Once the period for contests has passed, the probate court no longer has jurisdiction to hear an action

    K.   **Non-Probate Transfers**

★★   1)   INTER-VIVOS GIFTS

A gift *inter-vivos* means that the gift is given by a living person to a living person. A question may arise as to whether property was properly disposed of as an *inter-vivos* gift. For example, assume that a testator's entire estate is devised "to mother." However, one week before the testator's death, he purchased a ring for his girlfriend. Whether the ring is given to the testator's girlfriend or mother will depend on if the ring was given to the girlfriend as a complete and valid *inter-vivos* gift. If so, then the girlfriend may keep the ring. If not, the ring becomes a part of the estate and the mother will ultimately receive it.

           a)   Elements of Inter Vivos Gifts

An *inter-vivos* gift requires 1) intent, 2) delivery, and 3) acceptance. 18 *Mich. L & Prac. Encyclopedia*, 2d Ed. (Gifts) § 1 (2002). Generally, for a gift to be valid, three elements must be satisfied: (1) the donor must possess the intent to transfer title gratuitously to the donee, (2) there must be actual or constructive delivery of the subject matter to the donee, unless it is already in the donee's possession, and (3) the donee must accept the gift. *Davidson v. Bugbee,* 227 Mich. App. 264, 268 (1997).

(1)   Acceptance

Acceptance of a gift *inter-vivos* is generally presumed, particularly when the subject matter of the gift is something of value.   Ordinarily, the law will presume acceptance if the gift is beneficial to the donee. *E.g.*, *Buell v. Orion State Bank*, 327 Mich. 43 (1950). Acceptance is not an issue when it can be presumed because the gift is beneficial to the donee. *In re Handelsman,* 266 Mich. App. 433, 437-438 (2005), quoting *Davidson, supra.*

(2)   Intent

In some instances, the issue is if a donor intended to immediately vest a donee with an interest in property or to do that only at some future time. In the latter event, then the donor has not made a gift. In the former event, the gift is completed only if the delivery is appropriate under the facts and circumstances.

Instances in which the transfer of physical possession of the subject-matter of a gift is deferred until sometime in the future, present a difficult issue. The deferral of the transfer until the future might suggest the absence of an intent to make an immediate gift. That deferral might suggest an intent to make an immediate gift of a "future interest" in the property because the donor wants to retain possession of the item for life. The common law recognizes both present and future interests in property as distinct property interests. Thus, there is no reason why one cannot make an immediate gift of a future interest. In one case, the court held that a donor had made a gift to his son of a future interest in a painting where the donor wished to defer transferring possession of the painting to his son so that the donor could retain possession of the painting for the rest of his life. *Gruen v. Gruen*, 68 N.Y.2d 48, 505 N.Y.S.2d 849, 496 N.E.2d 869 (1986). *Also, Innes v. Potter,* 130 Minn. 320, 153 N.W. 604 (1915).

(3)   Delivery

(a)   Actual Delivery

Actual delivery of the property qualifies as valid delivery. Delivery is not presumed. Generally, a donee must show that the donor parted with dominion and control of the given property. 18 *Mich. L & Prac. Encyclopedia*, 2d Ed. (Gifts) § 4 (2002). It is usually ruled that a donor does not make a sufficient delivery of items left in a safe deposit box held jointly with the donee. *E.g.*, *Taylor v. Taylor*, 292 Mich. 95 (1940). In such cases, the donor retains the ability to remove the items from the box and, therefore, has not fully parted with dominion and control. *Id.*

(b)   Constructive or Symbolic Delivery

In addition to actual delivery, courts have generally recognized that constructive or symbolic delivery of a gift is appropriate if the subject matter of the gift cannot be physically delivered to the donee at the time a donor wishes to complete the gift. *In re Cohn,* 187 App. Div. 392, 176 N.Y.S. 225 (1919). If the subject matter of the gift is a future interest in property rather than the property itself, then the gift can only be evidenced by a constructive or symbolic delivery, since the subject matter of the gift has no physical shape. In such a case the best delivery would be a writing evidencing the gift that is signed and delivered to the donee. *Gruen v. Gruen, supra.*

(c)   Delivery Through Third Person

Delivery may be accomplished through a third person. However, if the third person is an agent of the donor, the courts often hold that the gift is not made until the property is actually delivered to the donee. The donor is deemed to retain control of the property so long as it remains in the agent's possession. As the principal, the donor has the power to recall the gift in the agent's hands. 18 *Mich. L & Prac. Encyclopedia,* 2d Ed. (Gifts) § 5 (2002).

b)   Challenging Inter Vivos Gifts

A person who attacks the validity of a gift has the burden of proving that no gift was made. *Vander Honing v. Taylor,* 344 Mich. 24, 29-30 (1955).

2)   GIFTS *CAUSA MORTIS*

★★

a)   General Considerations

A gift *causa mortis* is a gift that is made under an immediate apprehension of death, usually from a known peril, which is revocable if a donor does not die. In other words, a gift causa mortis is a gift of personal property made by the donor in view of his impending death from a present condition, accompanied by appropriate delivery under the circumstances. *In re Reh's Estate,* 196 Mich. 210 (1917). The donor of a gift *causa mortis* must believe he is facing death from a condition, and he then predeceases the donee as a result of the condition. *In re Van Wormer's Estate,* 255 Mich. 399 (1931).

b)   Elements

Like an *inter vivos* gift, a gift *causa mortis* must be evidenced by intent, delivery, and acceptance.

The donor must possess the intent to gratuitously pass title to the donor. *Chamberlin v. Eddy,* 154 Mich. 593 (1908).

Delivery, actual or constructive, must be made. *In re Van Wormer's Estate, supra.* And the donee must accept it. If there is no delivery, then there is no gift *causa mortis. Lumbers v. Commonwealth Bank,* 295 Mich. 566 (1940). Manual delivery is not required but can be accomplished constructively. The donor's motivation is irrelevant. *Jackman v. Jackman,* 271 Mich. 585 (1935).

A donee is presumed to accept a gift that is beneficial to him. *Holmes v. McDonald,* 119 Mich. 563 (1899).

Some courts appear to require a greater degree of proof of intent, delivery, and acceptance in the case of a *causa mortis* gift because of a concern that such gifts are inconsistent with policies underlying statutes of wills in that they are often unwitnessed transfers. *E.g., Foster v. Reiss*, 18 N.J. 41, 112 A.2d 553 (1955). A gift *causa mortis* may be used to avoid the claims of creditors because the creditors generally cannot obtain property that is properly gifted.

★   c)   No Real Property – Only Personal Property

Real property cannot be the subject of a gift *causa mortis. E.g., In re Reh's Estate*, 196 Mich. 210 (1917). Such gifts may be made of personal property only. 18 *Mich. L & Prac. Encyclopedia*, 2d Ed. (Gifts) § 32 (2002). Under Michigan law, a lessor's interest under a lease has been held to be real property that could not be given *causa mortis. In re Reh's Estate, supra*, at 219-20.

            3)   JOINT TENANCY

                  a)   Common Law

Under common law, property interests that are held as joint tenants with the right of survivorship generally provide a surviving joint tenant with a right to all of the remaining property. For example, assume that A and B own a bank account as joint tenants pursuant to the following verbiage: "A and B as joint tenants with right of survivorship." If A dies, B takes sole title of the bank account. As a result of the common law rules, A and B could effectively avoid the claims of their estate creditors by holding the property as joint tenants with the right of survivorship. Generally, the surviving joint tenant of a joint bank account ordinarily is entitled to the money in the account at the death of the first joint tenant. The deceased depositor's creditors have no claim to the money in that account. In some states the survivorship feature is conclusive. *In re Estate of Gainer*, 466 So.2d 1055 (Fla. 1985). In other states, the survivorship feature can be avoided if fraud, duress, undue influence, or mental incapacity is shown. Annot. 43 A.L.R.3d 971 (1972).

                  b)   Modern Statutes

In Michigan, deposits in a statutory joint account are subject to the rights of creditors of the account owners to the extent of their ownership, except that the funds are subject to laws applicable to transfers in fraud of creditors. Mich. Comp. Laws § 487.718.

Under the UPC, if a decedent's probate estate is insufficient to pay the claims of creditors, the creditors' claim to funds in a joint account is superior to the rights of a surviving joint tenant to the extent that the decedent deposited money into the joint bank account. Similarly, in Michigan, if a decedent's estate is insolvent, the estate can recover from the surviving joint owner the extent of the decedent's deposits that are required to satisfy claims against the estate of the decedent's creditors. *Id.*

            4)   TENTATIVE TRUSTS AND PAY-ON-DEATH ACCOUNTS

a)   Tentative or Totten Trusts

A person may deposit funds in a bank in the form "A in trust for B" and create a so-called tentative trust account, bank account trust, or Totten trust. The latter name is derived from the famous New York case that upheld a bank account trust against a challenge that it violated the policies underlying the Statute of Wills. *In re Totten*, 179 N.Y. 112, 71 N.E. 748 (1904). These types of accounts are also recognized by statutes in many states.

Absent clear and convincing evidence of a different intent, a depositor is the sole owner of an account throughout his lifetime. Upon the owner's death, the remaining sums on deposit belong to a designated beneficiary. However, courts and statutes provide that if the depositor's probate estate is insufficient to pay claims against the estate, then the money on deposit in the trust account is available for the payment of claims. The right of creditors to reach the bank account trust assets is justified on the ground that up until the moment of a decedent's death, the decedent has the unrestricted right to the use and enjoyment of the bank account funds in the same manner as the decedent has with respect to other assets that were in the decedent's probate estate.

b)   Pay on Death Account

A pay on death account is an account in which a depositor directs a bank to pay the funds in the account to a third party upon the depositor's death. Sometimes, a joint tenancy account will be judicially declared as a pay on death account. If a depositor intends only that a non-depositor will be entitled to the funds in the account at the depositor's death, but that the non-depositor will have no right of withdrawal in the depositor's lifetime, then a true joint tenancy is not created. That account would instead be a pay-on-death account.

Pay on death accounts are generally utilized to avoid the probate process. However, courts would likely conclude that if a depositor's probate estate is insufficient to pay the claims against the estate, then the money on deposit in the pay on death account is available for the payment of claims.

5)   LIFE INSURANCE

Life insurance is a contract made between an insured and an insurance company. Life insurance is generally a non-probate distribution. In most jurisdictions including Michigan, life insurance proceeds are payable to the beneficiary named with the insurance company even if the insured subsequently names a different beneficiary.

However, a minority of states permit an insured to change a beneficiary designation by will if his insurance company does not object. *E.g.*, *Burkett v. Mott*, 733 P.2d 673 (Ariz. 1986).

★   6)   CONVEYANCE OF A PROPERTY INTEREST

An issue can arise as to whether a conveyance of a property interest is a deed or a will.

a)   Distinguishing Deeds from Wills

Whether a legal document is a deed (e.g., a gift deed) or a will turns on whether it conveys a present interest, in which case it is deemed a deed, or an interest on the death of the person who executed it, in which case it is a will. *Benton Harbor Federation of Women's Clubs v. Nelson,* 301 Mich. 465, 470 (1942).

(1)   Intent is Key

That determination of whether the document is a deed or a will turns on the intent of the person who executed the document. However, for wills and deeds alike, the intent of the drafter is gleaned from the instrument itself, from the circumstances surrounding its creation, and from the manner in which the parties subsequently dealt with it. *Id.* at 471.

b)   Presumption of Undue Influence

The circumstances surrounding the creation of a document that could be a deed or a will can give rise to a presumption of undue influence. A presumption of undue influence exists upon a showing of: "(1) the existence of a confidential or fiduciary relationship between the grantor and a fiduciary, (2) the fiduciary or an interest which he represents benefits from a transaction, and (3) the fiduciary had an opportunity to influence the grantor's decision in that transaction." *In re Estate of Karmey,* 468 Mich. 68 (2003).

(1)   Confidential Relationship

A confidential relationship is one in which dominion may be exercised by one person over another. *Id.* To establish undue influence, it must be shown that the grantor was subjected to threats, misrepresentation, undue flattery, fraud, or physical or moral coercion sufficient to destroy free agency and impel the grantor to act against his inclination and free will. *Id.*

L.   **Powers and Duties of Personal Representatives**

1)   LETTERS TESTAMENTARY

Any personal representative or beneficiary named in a testator's will, or any other person interested in the testator's estate, may at any time after the death of a decedent, petition a court for the purpose of proving the validity of a will. When petitioning the court for probate, a request must also be made for the named personal representative to have the court's authorization to act on behalf of the estate. That authorization takes the form of documents that are referred to as "Letters Testamentary."

2)   POWERS OF PERSONAL REPRESENTATIVES

Generally, until Letters Testamentary are issued, a testator's personal representative only has the power to pay funeral charges and to take the steps necessary to preserve the testator's estate. However, once the Letters Testamentary are issued, the personal representative has the authority to marshal the assets of the estate, receive service of process, pay creditor's claims, wind up the business, and perform contracts of the decedent, and to take all other steps necessary to prepare the testator's estate for final distribution.

During administration, the personal representative has the right to possess all of the real and personal property of the testator, which is subject to probate. While in possession, the personal representative is charged with keeping all such property in good repair. Also, the personal representative must collect all of the debts owed to the testator at the testator's date of death. The personal representative must take all action necessary to bring suits to quiet title or to partition the estate.

3)   DUTIES OF PERSONAL REPRESENTATIVES

While managing a testator's estate, a personal representative acts in a fiduciary capacity. Therefore, the personal representative is held to an ethical standard of trust, honesty, and loyalty in winding up the affairs of the decedent. The personal representative must use reasonable diligence in performing all duties and in administrating the estate.

★   M.   Claims against Decedents' Estates

1)   ALLOWANCE AND DISALLOWANCE OF CLAIMS

Generally, a claimant (e.g., a creditor or purported beneficiary) can make a claim against a decedent's estate asserting an interest in the property it contains. The estate's personal representative can allow or disallow the claim. If the personal representative disallows it, the claimant only possesses the option of filing a lawsuit against the estate. This lawsuit must be filed within 63 days of notice of disallowance. Mich. Comp. Laws § 700.3806(2). However, an untimely claim may be allowed by the judge to "avoid injustice," in which case the court may grant an extension of time as long as the applicable statute of limitations has not expired. *Id.* The decision to grant an extension of time is within the discretion of the court. *In re Estate of Charles A. Weber,* 257 Mich. App. 558 (2003).

2)   PROMISE TO TRANSFER ASSET UPON DEATH

A promise to transfer an asset upon death is unenforceable absent a will or any other written document evidencing such intent on the part of the decedent. *Estate of Weber, supra,* citing *In re McKim Estate,* 238 Mich. App. 453 (1999). Further, the Michigan Court of Appeals has held that a claim to a home that a decedent allegedly promised to transfer to the claimant upon death based on the claimant's contribution towards the home is also without merit. *Estate of Weber, supra,* citing *In re Lewis Estate,* 168 Mich. App. 70 (1988).

III.   FAMILY PROTECTION

Generally speaking, when a person dies testate, spouses and children who are not provided for in the deceased's will may still be entitled to a share of the estate. In limited instances, EPIC provides a person with statutory rights to claim from an estate when the person may not be provided for in a will.

★★ **A.   Spouse's Forced or Elective Shares**

Most states create a statutory forced share of a decedent's estate for the benefit of a surviving spouse. The forced share is a reflection of a public policy that it is, to some extent, inappropriate to disinherit a spouse who contributed toward the accumulation of the deceased spouse's wealth during the marriage. A surviving spouse may possess and exercise a statutory right to either elect to receive that share or to waive it.

1)   WAIVER OF ELECTIVE SHARE RIGHTS

Voluntary waiver of an elective share is permitted after a fair disclosure or waiver of disclosure of all the facts has occurred. Fair disclosure mandates that each spouse should be given information concerning each other's net worth.

2)   SIZE OF ELECTIVE SHARE

a)   Determining Amount of Elective Share

(1)   UPC and Some States

Pursuant to a schedule, the UPC determines the elective share amount of an augmented estate based on the number of years that the spouses were married. The size of the share may vary among each state's statute, but a typical share in states other than Michigan is one third of a testator's entire estate.

(2)   Michigan Law

In Michigan, the surviving spouse of a decedent who is domiciled in Michigan and who dies testate may elect to either abide by the terms of the will, take one-half of the sum or share that would have passed to the surviving spouse if the decedent had died intestate, reduced by one-half of the value of all property derived by the spouse from the decedent by any means other than testate or intestate succession upon the decedent's death, or "take her dower right" under statute. Mich. Comp. Laws § 700.2202(2)(a)-(c). "Unless the testator's will plainly shows a contrary intent, the surviving spouse electing . . . is limited" to one of those choices. Mich. Comp. Laws § 700.2202(3). In Michigan, the right to take under the statutory election cannot be barred by a provision in the will, such as one that expressly disinherits the surviving spouse. *In re Povey's Estate*, 271 Mich. 627 (1935).

(a)   Types of Property Derived by Other Means

"Property derived by the spouse from the decedent" by any means other than intestate or testate or succession upon the decedent's death includes life insurance proceeds, jointly held bank accounts, and large transfers made within two years before the decedent's death. Mich. Comp. Laws § 700.2202(2)(b), (7)(a), (c).

(b)   Michigan's Statutory Dower Right

Generally, a widow may claim a life estate in one-third of any land in which her husband held an inheritable interest during marriage. Mich. Comp. Laws § 558.1.

(3)   Calculation of the Elective Share

The precise calculation of the elective share can vary depending on the elective share laws of the jurisdiction. It is typical, however, that the spouse's elective share will be charged first against the residuary estate and then against specific bequests. In Michigan, the surviving spouse's intestate share is determined according to the intestacy provisions described earlier under "Intestate Succession" and "Share of the Surviving Spouse."

b)   Other Considerations

Under elective share statutes like the one in EPIC, the surviving spouse must elect between the elective share amount and the amount the surviving spouse would have received under the will. *Id.* The surviving spouse is not entitled to receive both amounts. Mich. Comp. Laws § 700.2202(3). Also, the right of election is personal. Therefore, if the surviving spouse dies before an election is made, the estate may not make an election on behalf of the surviving spouse. *Id.* In some states other than Michigan, the election must be made within six to seven months of the will's probate. In Michigan, EPIC provides that the election must be made the later of "within 63 days after the date for presentment of claims or within 63 days after service of the inventory upon the surviving spouse." *Id.*

★   B.   Share of Pretermitted Spouse

Michigan's pretermitted spouse statute generally provides for a surviving spouse of the decedent spouse whose premarital will omits the surviving spouse. A "pretermitted spouse," i.e., a surviving spouse who married the testator after the will was executed, is entitled to receive an intestate share of a specified portion of the estate. Mich. Comp. Laws § 700.2301(1). The surviving spouse's share is calculated by deducting that which is granted to a child of the decedent, so long as the child is not also the child of the surviving spouse.

1)   ELECTIVE SHARE AND PRETERMITTED SPOUSE

The Michigan Court of Appeals has held that a surviving spouse who married the testator after the will was executed is not barred from claiming an elective share under the terms of the elective share statute, if that provision yields a larger amount, and that the amount to which the surviving spouse was entitled under the pretermitted spouse statute will then be considered a part of the elective share. *In re Estate of Sprenkle-Hill,* 265 Mich. App. 254 (2005), lv. den., 474 Mich. (January 5, 2006). The Court also has held that if the share available to a surviving spouse under the pretermitted spouse statute is greater than the elective share under the elective share statute, the surviving spouse will receive the full share under the pretermitted spouse statute by electing to abide by the terms of the will. *Id.* In addition, in that case of *Sprenkle-Hill*, the Court found that the Michigan Legislature's intent was to insulate all spouses from disinheritance while allowing the decedent's testamentary intent to be honored to the extent possible. *Id.*

After *Sprenkle-Hill* was released, the Michigan Legislature added a subsection to the pretermitted spouse statute. Mich. Comp. Laws § 700.2301(4). That subsection addresses the surviving spouse's right of election under the elective share statute. Specifically, the amended pretermitted spouse statute (i.e., an intestate statute) provides: "A spouse who receives an intestate share under this section may also exercise the right of election under section 2202 [elective share statute], but the intestate share received by the spouse under this section reduces the sum available to the spouse under section 2202(2)(b) [elective share statute]." *Id.*

The surviving spouse takes her intestate share, which is determined according to the intestacy provisions described earlier under "Intestate Succession" and "Share of the Surviving Spouse," from the remainder of the estate after devises to children (not stepchildren) are subtracted. Mich. Comp. Laws § 700.2301(3); *In Re Estate of Bennett*, 255 Mich. App. 545 (2003). Stepchildren do not meet the statutory definition of "child." *Id.*

★★★   **C.   Share of After-Born or Pretermitted Child**

1)   OMITTED CHILDREN BORN AFTER WILL EXECUTION

A pretermitted heir provision may apply when a child is not mentioned in a testator's will. For example, Michigan's omitted child statute would apply if a child of the testator was born or adopted after the testator executed a will that does not provide for the child. Mich. Comp. Laws § 700.2302(1). Alternatively, pretermitted heir provisions may apply when a testator's child, once believed dead, is found to be alive.

a)   No Children Alive at Will Execution

If applicable, Michigan's omitted child statute provides that an omitted child, if the testator had no living children when the testator executed the will, is entitled to the share that the child would have received had the testator died intestate, "unless the will devised all or substantially all of the estate to the other parent of the omitted child." Mich. Comp. Laws § 700.2302(1)(a).

b)   Testator's Intent

A court must determine the intent of a testator from his will. If the testator's intent cannot be determined from the will, a court may examine extrinsic evidence. Some exam questions may indicate that the testator expressed that he did not believe that children should inherit. Other questions might present a minor child who would be taken care of under a bequest to her surviving parent. The ultimate question that must be resolved is: Did a testator intentionally not provide for the after-born child? If that intent can be established, then the court may not provide for the after-born child.

2)   OMITTED CHILDREN ALIVE AT TIME OF WILL EXECUTION

    a)   General Rule

Generally, children born to a testator in advance of his will's execution are not protected. Accordingly, children who are born to the testator before a will is executed are not entitled to take a pretermitted child's share of the testator's estate.

    b)   Unintentional versus Intentional Omission -- Michigan

In Michigan, unless a contrary intention appears, if the testator had one or more children alive when he executed the will and the will devised property to at least one of these children, the after-born child is entitled to share in the property distributed under the will to the same extent as the children included in the instrument. Mich. Comp. Laws § 700.2302(1)(b), (2)(a). Any gift to the children included in the will is ratably abated to allow the omitted child to share in the estate. Mich. Comp. Laws § 700.2302(1)(b)(iv). If it appears from the will that the testator intentionally omitted the child, Michigan's omitted child statute would not apply. Mich. Comp. Laws § 700.2302(2).

3)   DISINHERITED CHILDREN

Michigan's omitted child statute, section 700.2302 of the Michigan Compiled Laws, is silent on the appropriate share to a child born after the execution of a will in which the child is not provided for when the testator has one or more children who were living at the time he executed his will but the testator expressly disinherited the then living children. While in that event, the child alive when the testator executed the will, may claim under section 700.1201 of the Michigan Compiled Laws that the father, by not expressly disinheriting that child, intended that this child receive a statutory share, it appears that the child will get nothing except, perhaps, a family allowance pursuant to section 700.2403 of the Michigan Compiled Laws.

    a)   Express Disinheritance

Where the testator expressly disinherits a child, that child receives nothing. Mich. Comp. Laws § 700.2302(3) (entitling a child who is living at the time a will is executed but who is not provided for in the will a share of the estate only if the failure to provide for the child is "solely because the [testator] believes the child to be dead"). *Also, Brown v. Blesch*, 270 Mich. 576 (1935) (reason for disinheriting an heir at law need not be disclosed in the will).

★   **D.   Homestead Allowance and Exempt Property**

In addition to an elective share, in Michigan a surviving spouse can claim the Homestead Allowance, Exempt Property, and Family Allowance. Mich. Comp. Laws §§ 700.2402-700.2404. Generally, these provisions have priority over claims against the estate except for administration costs and reasonable funeral and burial expenses. Mich. Comp. Laws §§ 2402, 2403(2), 2404(2). The dollar amounts of these provisions are adjusted annually for inflation for decedents who died in 2001 or after. Mich. Comp. Laws § 700.1210.

1)   HOMESTEAD ALLOWANCE

In an effort to protect the family of a testator, many jurisdictions including Michigan, permit homestead allowances. In these jurisdictions, the property subject to the allowance is set aside and not subject to the creditors' claims. In some states other than Michigan, the surviving spouse is entitled to keep $10,000 plus $5,000 for each dependent minor child. In Michigan, the surviving spouse generally is entitled to keep $15,000. Mich. Comp. Laws § 700.2402. EPIC also provides that if there is no surviving spouse, then each surviving minor child or dependent child generally is entitled to an amount based on the total of $15,000, as divided by the number of such children. *Id.* "A homestead allowance is in addition to any share passing to the surviving spouse or minor or dependent child by the will of the decedent, unless otherwise provided, by intestate succession, or by elective share." *Id.*

2)   EXEMPT PROPERTY

Above and beyond their provision for homestead property, the UPC and EPIC also grant a decedent's surviving spouse an exemption of other estate property. In Michigan, the value of the exempted property cannot exceed $10,000 beyond the amount of security interests in that property, inclusive of "household furniture, automobiles, furnishings, appliances, and personal effects." Unif. Probate Code § 2-403; Mich. Comp. Laws § 700.2404.

3)   FAMILY ALLOWANCE

EPIC provides a reasonable family allowance to maintain a decedent's surviving spouse and children during the administration of the decedent's estate. Mich. Comp. Laws § 700.2403. The family allowance of $18,000 is payable as a lump sum. Mich. Comp. Laws § 700.2405(2).

E.   Limitations on Charitable Bequests

Traditionally, states limited the amount (as a percentage of the estate) that a testator could leave to charity in order to protect the family. Additionally, states did not recognize bequests made to charity within a certain time of death. It was believed that they were made under fear of going to hell. These laws were called Mortmain laws. They have been abolished in almost every state.

IV.   LIVING WILLS AND DURABLE HEALTH CARE POWERS

Living wills and durable powers of attorney are called advance health care directives.

A living will is a document in which one specifies which life-prolonging measures one does, and does not, want to be taken if one becomes terminally ill or incapacitated.

A durable power of attorney is a document that enables an individual to designate another person, called the attorney-in-fact, to act on the individual's behalf, even in the event the individual becomes disabled or incapacitated. Generally, an agent of a principal is immunized from civil liability for health care decisions made in good faith including the decision to withhold or withdraw life-sustaining treatment, including food and hydration. Unif. Health Care Decisions Act § 1(6).

A.   Execution Requirements

1)   DURABLE POWER OF ATTORNEY

An adult or emancipated minor may create a durable power of attorney for healthcare, which may authorize an agent to make any health care decision the principal could have made while having capacity. The power must be in writing and signed by the principal. The power should comport with the same formalities that are required for the execution of a will. Although sometimes permissible, the power should generally not be witnessed by the designated agent. At least one witness to the execution of the durable power of attorney for health care must not be a health care provider providing direct care to the principal.

2)   LIVING WILL

An adult or emancipated minor may create a living will. The living will must generally be in writing and signed by the person and two witnesses.

B.   Revocation

1)   REVOKING HEALTH-CARE DIRECTIVES

An individual may revoke any portion of an advance health-care directive at any time and in any manner that communicates the intent to revoke the directive.

2)   REVOKING DESIGNATION OF AGENT UNDER HEALTH-CARE DIRECTIVES

A restrictive standard applies to the revocation of the portion of a power of attorney for health care relating to the designation of the agent. A principal may revoke the designation of an agent only by a signed writing or by personally informing the supervising healthcare provider of that revocation. This high standard is justified to avoid the risk of a false revocation of an agent's designation. Another justification for it is to avoid a misinterpretation or miscommunication of a principal's statement that is communicated through a third party. For example, without this higher standard, an individual motivated by a desire to gain control over a patient might be able to assume authority to act as agent by falsely informing a health-care provider that the principal no longer wishes the previously designated agent to act but instead wishes to appoint the individual.

3)   DUTY TO INFORM SUPERVISING HEALTH CARE PROVIDER OF REVOCATION

A health-care provider or agent who is informed of a revocation of the designation of an agent must promptly communicate that fact to the supervising health-care provider and to any health-care institution at which the patient is receiving care.

C.   Individuals Eligible to be Agent or Attorney-in-Fact

Unless related to a principal, an agent may not be affiliated with the health care institution at which the principal is receiving care.

D.   Authority of Agent or Attorney-in-Fact

1)   EXECUTED HEALTH CARE POWER OF ATTORNEY

Agents act within the scope of state law when they conduct themselves in accordance with a properly executed durable health care power of attorney. State laws vary, however, on whether the person designated as the agent can be a witness to the execution of the durable health care power of attorney. For example, under the Uniform Health Care Decisions Act, the designated agent is not prohibited from being a witness to that execution. In fact, no witnessing of the power is required under that Act. On the other hand, in many states, the person designated as the agent cannot be a witness to the power.

2)   FAMILY CONSENT LAWS

Authority can also be established under so-called "family consent" laws. These laws permit close family members, typically in the order listed in the statute, to act as a surrogate decision maker for a patient where there is no properly authorized agent acting under a durable power.

3)   EFFECTIVE PERIOD

Unless otherwise specified, the authority of an agent becomes effective only upon a determination that a principal lacks capacity. The agent's power ceases to be effective upon a determination that the principal has recovered capacity.

MICHIGAN

AMERIBAR BAR REVIEW

Michigan Bar Review

UNIFORM COMMERCIAL CODE
COMMERCIAL PAPER & SECURED TRANSACTIONS

UCC – COMMERCIAL PAPER

COMMERCIAL PAPER
UCC ARTICLE 3

Traditionally, one UCC question usually has appeared in the essay portion of one of the two Michigan Bar Exams ("Exam") administered each year. Many of those questions have focused upon UCC Article 2 regarding sales, except for a question regarding accord and satisfaction with respect to a check, rather than a contract, to which UCC Article 3 applies. Nonetheless, issues related to UCC Article 3 remain subject to being tested on the Exam.

Facts and rules derived from cases decided by the Michigan Court of Appeals and/or the Michigan Supreme Court have provided the basis for past UCC questions and answers. The Michigan Compiled Laws is another source for tested rules as well. Although the sample answers for past questions indicate that Michigan statutes and court cases should be the basis for answering questions, they could be answered using controlling general legal principles contained in this outline.

I.   GENERAL UCC PRINCIPLES

A.   Rules of Construction and Application

The Uniform Commercial Code ("UCC" or "Code") must be liberally construed and applied to promote its underlying purposes and policies which are: 1) to simplify, clarify, and modernize the law governing commercial transactions; 2) to permit the continued expansion of commercial practices through custom, usage, and agreement of the parties; and 3) to make uniform the law among the various jurisdictions.

Unless displaced by particular provisions of the Code, the principles of law and equity, including the law relative to capacity, principal and agent, estoppel, fraud, misrepresentation, duress, coercion, mistake, bankruptcy supplement the Code's provisions.

II.   GENERAL PROVISIONS AND DEFINITIONS

A.   Definitions

1)   NEGOTIABLE INSTRUMENT

A negotiable instrument is a written and signed unconditional promise ("note") or order ("draft") to pay a fixed amount of money to bearer or order, on demand or at a definite time. Under the Code, the terms "instrument" and "negotiable instrument" are interchangeable. There are two types of instruments: 1) notes, and 2) orders.

2)   NOTE

A note is a promise to pay. The "maker" promises to pay the "payee" or "bearer." Assignment of the note by the payee to a third party ("indorsee") for value creates a "holder" of the instrument.

> a)   Maker

A maker is a person who signs or is identified in a note as a person undertaking to pay.

> b)   Promise

A promise is a written undertaking to pay money signed by the person undertaking to pay. An acknowledgment of an obligation (e.g., "IOU") by the obligor is not a promise unless the obligor also undertakes to pay the obligation.

> c)   Certificates of Deposit ("CD")

A CD is a note issued by a bank to acknowledge the receipt of money; in doing so, the bank acts as a maker and thus, makes a promise of repayment to the holder (with interest). A note is payable to the holder.

> 3)   DRAFT

A draft is an order to pay something to a third party.

> a)   Order

An order is a written instruction (usually to a bank) to pay money to another person. It is signed by the person giving the instruction. An authorization to pay is not an order, unless the person authorized to pay is also instructed to pay (i.e. "pay to the order of"). The following are examples of common types of orders:

> (1)   Personal Check

A check is an order or instruction by the drawer (person writing the check) to the drawee (the person's bank) to pay to payee (the person to whom the check is made out) on demand. If the payee indorses the check to another party, that third party then becomes a holder of the instrument.

A check may be payable to "bearer" or "cash" as payee.

> (2)   Cashier's and Certified Checks

For these checks, a bank draws the check on itself or guarantees acceptance by writing across the face of the check.

> (3)   Teller's Check

A teller's check is a check drawn by a bank (the drawer) on its own account with another issuing bank (the drawee).

> (4)   Traveler's Check

A traveler's check is a negotiable instrument which requires, as a condition to payment, a countersignature by a person whose specimen signature appears on the instrument.

> b)   Drawer and Drawee

A drawer is a person who signs or is identified in a draft as a person ordering payment (i.e., check writer). A drawee is a person ordered in a draft to make payment (i.e., bank).

B.   Negotiable Instrument, Issue, Unconditional Promise or Order

As set forth above, a negotiable instrument is an unconditional promise or order to pay a fixed amount of money to bearer or order, on demand or at a definite time. Negotiable instruments permit parties to transfer large sums of money without ever touching cash or bank accounts. In fact, they were developed centuries ago by merchants who were reluctant to carry large sums of gold and currency. One document could effectively pass from party to party for substantial amounts of time without any hard currency changing hands.

Since negotiable instruments are required to act as a substitute for currency, parties that must pay under the document cannot generally claim contract defenses for obligations underlying the negotiable instruments. If a document is deemed a negotiable instrument, then a "holder in due course" of the instrument possesses special rights not possessed by a party to a contract. Therefore, in most commercial paper questions, it is imperative to first determine whether a document is a negotiable instrument.

★★   1)   ESSENTIAL ELEMENTS OF NEGOTIABILITY

Examiners are known to leave out one of these elements that determine whether a document is negotiable.

> a)   Unconditional

The promise or order must be unconditional. It must not state "any other undertaking or instruction by the person promising or ordering payment to do any act in addition to the payment of money."

> b)   Promise or Order

The instrument must be a promise (note) or order (draft) to pay money.

> (1)   Promise

There must be an unconditional promise. For example, an "IOU" or other document merely acknowledging a debt is inadequate.

(2)   Order

The instrument must unambiguously order some party to pay money to the payee. A mere authorization to pay is inadequate. Therefore, the word "pay" or something similar must be used.

c)   Money

There must be a promise or order to pay a fixed amount of money.

(1)   Amount

The amount of money to be paid is a "fixed amount." This can include interest.

(2)   Currency

Any generally accepted medium of exchange, including foreign currencies, is acceptable, but no other local barter satisfies the condition.

d)   Writing and Signed

The instrument must be in writing. As a general rule, a tape-recorded promise to pay is not a negotiable instrument. A bright examinee will realize that it may be a contract. The instrument must also be signed. The intent to authenticate the document is critical.

e)   Payable on Demand or at Definite Time

A negotiable instrument must be payable on demand or at a definite time. A promise or order is "payable on demand" if it: 1) states that it is payable on demand or at sight, or otherwise indicates that it is payable at the will of the holder; or 2) does not state any time of payment. A promise or order is "payable at a definite time" if it is payable upon the lapse of a definite period of time after sight or acceptance, at a fixed date, or at a time readily ascertainable at the time the promise or order is issued.

f)   Payable to Order or Bearer; Identification of Payee

A negotiable instrument must be payable to bearer or order. A document satisfies the order requirement if it is payable to the order of a specific payee. A document satisfies the alternative requirement that it is payable to bearer when the instrument states that it is payable to:

- bearer;
- the order of bearer;

- cash;
- the order of cash; or
- some similar designation that is not a person or entity.

C.   Other Terms

1)   PLACE OF PAYMENT

An instrument is payable at the place of payment stated in the instrument. If no place of payment is stated, an instrument is payable at the address of the drawee or maker stated in the instrument. If no address is stated, the place of payment is any place of business of the drawee or maker. If the drawee or maker has no place of business, the place of payment is the residence of the drawee or maker.

2)   INTEREST

As a default, if not specified on the instrument, an instrument is not payable with interest. If interest is provided for, it is payable from the date of the instrument.

a)   Default Rate

If an instrument provides for interest, but the amount payable cannot be ascertained from the description, interest is payable at the judgment rate in effect at the place of payment and at the time interest first accrues.

3)   DATE OF INSTRUMENT

An instrument may be antedated or postdated. The date stated determines the time of payment if the instrument is payable at a fixed period. As a general rule, an instrument payable on demand is not payable before the date of the instrument. If an instrument is undated, its date is the date of its issue or, in the case of an unissued instrument, the date it first comes into the possession of a holder.

D.   Contradictory Terms; Incomplete Terms

1)   CONTRADICTORY TERMS

When the terms of a note contradict, typewritten terms prevail over mechanically printed terms, handwritten terms prevail over both, and words prevail over numbers (i.e., a check made out for "one hundred dollars" prevails over "$140" written on same check).

2)   INCOMPLETE TERMS

An incomplete instrument is a signed writing that is incomplete at the time of signing, but the signer intended it to be completed at a later time by the addition of words or numbers. The UCC indicates that an instrument that is not negotiable because of omissions is still enforceable "according to its terms as augmented by the completion." If the words or numbers were added to the incomplete instrument without the authority of the signer, the instrument is treated as an altered instrument and special rules apply.

E.   Joint and Several Liability and Contribution

Co-makers of a note possess joint and several liability to any holder in a position to enforce the note. One co-maker has a right of contribution against another co-maker in the absence of language in the note to the contrary.

F.   Other Agreements Affecting Instrument

The obligation of a party to an instrument may be modified, supplemented, or nullified by a separate agreement of the obligor and a person entitled to enforce the instrument. To the extent an obligation is modified, supplemented, or nullified by an agreement, the agreement is a defense to the obligation. The UCC effectively provides that the separate agreement modifies the terms of the note by stating a condition to the obligation [of the obligor] to pay the note. If the condition is not met, the obligor is not obligated to pay the note to the original creditor or to any subsequent holder who is not a holder in due course.

For example, suppose that, as a maker, Carl signs a note payable to Bank. However, the parties agree that, as a condition to Carl signing, the Bank must obtain the signature of Davis as a co-maker of the note. The terms of the additional agreement impose a condition that will be incorporated into the note, at least with regard to the Bank. However, the defense cannot be enforced against a holder in due course (HDC) because the HDC possesses no knowledge of the condition.

G.   Statute of Limitations; Notice of Right to Defend

1)   STATUTE OF LIMITATIONS

In general, an action to enforce the obligation of a party to pay a note payable at a definite time must be commenced within six years after the due date or dates stated in the note or, if a due date is accelerated, within six years after the accelerated due date. In general, an action to enforce the obligation of a party to pay a note payable on demand must be commenced within six years after the date of demand. However, if no demand for payment is made to the maker, an action to enforce the note is barred if neither principal nor interest on the note has been paid for a continuous period of 10 years.

2)   NOTICE OF RIGHT TO DEFEND

In an action for breach of an obligation for which a third person is answerable (i.e., guarantor or surety), the defendant may give the third person notice of the litigation in a record, and the person notified may then give similar notice to any other person who is answerable. If the notice states: 1) that the person notified may come in and defend, and 2) that failure to do so will bind the notified person in a later action by the person giving the notice as to any determination of fact common to the two litigations. The person notified is so bound unless after receipt of the notice, the person notified does come in and defend.

III.   NEGOTIATION, TRANSFER, AND INDORSEMENT

A.   Negotiation, Rescission, and Transfer

1)   NEGOTIATION

A negotiation is a transfer of possession of an instrument, whether voluntary or involuntary, by a person other than the issuer, to a person who thereby becomes its holder. Generally, if an instrument is payable to an identified person, negotiation requires transfer of possession of the instrument and its indorsement by the holder. If an instrument is payable to bearer, it may be negotiated by transfer of possession alone. The significance of the difference between bearer and order paper cannot be understated. A thief may come across a bearer paper and become a holder (entitled to enforce) by possession alone. A thief cannot become a holder of order paper without proper indorsement.

2)   NEGOTIATION SUBJECT TO RESCISSION

Negotiation is effective even if obtained: 1) from an infant, a corporation exceeding its powers, or a person without capacity; 2) by fraud, duress, or mistake; or 3) in breach of duty or as part of an illegal transaction. To the extent permitted by other (notably contract) laws, negotiation may be rescinded. However, such rescission may not be asserted against a subsequent holder in due course or a person paying for the instrument in good faith and without knowledge of facts that are the bases for rescission.

3)   TRANSFER OF INSTRUMENT; RIGHTS ACQUIRED BY TRANSFER

a)   Shelter Rule

Under the UCC, when a document is delivered by a person other than its issuer for the purpose of giving to the person receiving delivery the right to enforce the instrument (theft would not be a "transfer for the purpose of giving to the person receiving delivery the right to enforce the instrument" under the Code but a mere "transfer of possession"), special rights are created in the transferee. Delivery vests any right of the transferor to enforce the instrument in the transferee, including any right as a holder in due course. This is known as the "shelter rule." This can be significant when the instrument is given as a gift. The transferee would not be a holder in due course because no value was given. However, if the transferor was an HDC, the transferee would obtain the rights of the transferor (rights of an HDC) under the shelter rule. However, if the transferee engaged in fraud or illegality affecting the instrument, he will not acquire the rights of a holder in due course even if the transfer to him was made by a holder in due course.

b)   Transfer of Less than Entire Instrument

If a transferor purports to transfer less than the entire instrument, negotiation of the instrument does not occur. The transferee obtains no rights under Article 3 and has only the rights of a partial assignee.

B.   Indorsements (§§ 3-204 through 3-206)

An indorsement is the act of writing a name on a negotiable instrument. Generally, a party indorses a note to transfer the note. An indorsement must be written on the instrument (or on a paper firmly affixed to it so as to become a part of it, not just clipped to it) by or on behalf of the holder. By transferring an instrument, a person warrants that he is a person entitled to enforce the instrument. For breach of warranty, a person who took the instrument in good faith may recover damages from the warrantor in an amount equal to the loss suffered as a result of the breach. As an indorser, a person has a potential right of recourse with respect to the maker(s).

1)   SPECIAL INDORSEMENT

A special indorsement specifies to whom (or to whose order) the instrument is payable (e.g., "to the order of Jack Brown"). Only the special indorsee may further negotiate the instrument.

2)   BLANK INDORSEMENT

In a blank indorsement, no particular indorsee is specified. A blank indorsement shows only the signature of the last indorsee or holder; no other directions are found on the instrument. It is negotiable by delivery only and makes the instrument payable to bearer.

3)   CONVERSION OF BLANK INDORSEMENT

A holder can convert a blank indorsement into a special indorsement.

4)   QUALIFIED INDORSEMENTS

Indorsers are liable to one another in the order of their indorsements. However, an indorser may limit liability by marking an indorsement "without recourse." If those words are not used, an indorsement is made with recourse.

5)   RESTRICTIVE INDORSEMENTS

A holder may restrict further negotiation by providing a restrictive indorsement. For example, a holder may write "For Deposit Only" or "Pay to X in trust for Y." If a party disobeys such an indorsement, it may be liable for conversion.

6)   UNENDORSED ORDER

If an order document (made to the order of a specific party) is not indorsed, but only delivered, it is not properly negotiated. As a consequence, the transferee is not a holder in due course.

Remember, however, delivery of possession of a bearer instrument is sufficient negotiation if the transferee is a *bona fide* purchaser for value without notice.

7)   INSTRUMENT PAYABLE TO MULTIPLE PARTIES

If an instrument is payable to two or more persons not alternatively, for example, it is not payable to A or B but rather to A *and* B, it may be negotiated only by all of them. If it is payable to A *or* B, it may be negotiated by either of them.

C.   Reacquisition (§ 3-207)

Reacquisition of an instrument occurs if it is transferred to a former holder, by negotiation or otherwise. A former holder who reacquires the instrument may cancel indorsements made after the re-acquirer first became a holder of the instrument. If the cancellation causes the instrument to be payable to the re-acquirer or to bearer, the re-acquirer may negotiate the instrument. An indorser whose indorsement is canceled is discharged, and the discharge is effective against any subsequent holder.

IV.   ENFORCEMENT OF INSTRUMENTS

A.   Person Entitled to Enforce; Holder in Due Course

A holder of a note is a person entitled to enforce the instrument. However, the ability of the holder to avoid certain defenses will depend upon whether the holder is a holder in due course. First, one must determine whether a person is a holder. Then, one must examine whether the holder is a holder in due course.

★   1)   HOLDER

To qualify as a holder of the instrument, the instrument must be taken by negotiation. The test to determine whether a party is a holder depends upon whether the instrument is bearer or order paper.

a)   Bearer Paper

An instrument that is payable to the bearer is negotiated by transfer of possession only. The transfer of possession of the instrument completes delivery. The person in possession is a holder.

b)   Order Paper

An instrument that is payable to the order of some party is negotiated by delivery plus proper indorsement. An order instrument that contains the forged signature of a payee is not properly indorsed by that payee. Therefore, a person in possession of that forged instrument cannot be a holder. However, the legal effect is different when an instrument is stolen after it has acquired the authentic indorsement of the payee: here, the person in possession of the instrument can be a holder, assuming all indorsements are proper.

★★
   2) HOLDER IN DUE COURSE

★★
     a) Significance

A holder in due course takes the instrument free from any defects in the underlying obligation that the instrument may represent. The holder in due course is not subject to any of the defenses that would normally exist with a contractual obligation.

For example, if a thief steals a negotiable instrument from A and sells it to B, who does not know that such instrument is a stolen one, A is not entitled to the instrument back if B qualifies as a holder in due course.

★★
     b) Elements

A person possessing an instrument is a holder in due course if he is: 1) a holder; 2) for value; 3) in good faith; and 4) without notice.

      (1) Holder

A person is a holder if he possesses the instrument as a result of a proper negotiation as set forth above.

      (2) For Value

A person must have given some consideration. However, a promise for a future act not yet performed is not acceptable.

      (3) In Good Faith

The good faith requirement focuses on whether the holder knew that there may have been some defect under the circumstances. It requires honesty in fact.

      (4) Without Notice

The holder must take the instrument without notice that that it is overdue, contains defects (e.g., forgery), or is subject to defenses.

     c) Rights of a Holder in Due Course

A holder in due course:

- may enforce the instrument in one's own name;
- may transfer or negotiate the instrument;

- may obtain a judgment on instrument;
- takes the note free from all defenses except "real defenses."

B.   Overdue Instrument (§ 3-304)

1)   GENERAL RULES

A negotiable instrument payable on demand becomes overdue at the earliest of the following times:

- the day after demand for payment is duly made;
- if a check, 90 days after its date; or
- if not a check, when the instrument has been outstanding for a period of time after its date which is unreasonably long under the circumstances.

2)   NOTES PAYABLE ON DEMAND

a)   Installments

With respect to an instrument payable at a definite time, the instrument becomes overdue upon default under the instrument for nonpayment of an installment, and the instrument remains overdue until the default is cured.

b)   No Installments

If the principal is not payable in installments and the due date has not been accelerated, the instrument becomes overdue on the day after the due date.

C.   Defenses

★★   ### 1)   GENERAL RULE

The holder in due course of a negotiable instrument takes it free from all "personal defenses" of the maker.

a)   Failure or Lack of Consideration

Failure or lack of consideration is not a valid defense to an instrument held by a holder in due course.

b)   Other Personal Defenses

A holder in due course takes the instrument free from other personal defenses listed in the UCC including: breach of contract; mistake; duress; unconscionability; waiver; and impossibility of performance. These are defenses to contract actions but are not available against the holder in due course of an instrument. Personal defenses may be used against a holder, but not a holder in due course.

(1)   Personal to Party

Personal defenses are personal to each party. Therefore, one party may not assert against the person entitled to enforce the instrument, a defense of another person.

★★   2)   <u>REAL DEFENSES</u>

Real defenses may be asserted against a holder and a holder in due course. Real defenses include:

- infancy of the obligor;
- duress, lack of legal capacity, or illegality of the transaction which nullifies the obligation of the obligor;
- fraud that induced the obligor to sign the instrument; and
- discharge of the obligor in insolvency proceedings.

D.   Notice of Breach of Fiduciary Duty (§ 3-307)

A special analysis is used when an instrument is made payable to a person through his agent. For example, suppose Maker creates a note payable "to Agent, as agent for Principal." Under the UCC, Agent is a "fiduciary," and Principal is a "Represented Person." If a person or entity (e.g., a bank) takes an instrument from a fiduciary: 1) for value; and 2) the taker has knowledge of the fiduciary relationship; and 3) the "represented person" makes a claim to the instrument on the basis that the transaction of the fiduciary is a breach of fiduciary duty, special rules apply. If the taker has notice of the breach of fiduciary duty, the taker will not be a holder in due course.

If the instrument is payable to the represented person or the fiduciary as such a fiduciary of the represented person, the taker is presumed to have notice of the breach of fiduciary duty if the instrument is: 1) taken in a transaction known by the taker to be for the personal benefit of the fiduciary; or 2) deposited to an account other than an account of the fiduciary as fiduciary or of the represented person.

E.   Proof of Signatures

In a legal action with respect to an instrument, the authenticity of each signature on the instrument is admitted unless specifically denied in the pleadings. If the validity of a signature is denied in the pleadings, the burden of establishing validity is on the person claiming validity.

F.   Enforcement of Lost, Destroyed or Stolen Instrument

If a holder sues on a note without producing it, he can obtain a judgment only if it meets the conditions set out in the Code. UCC § 3-309. In order to qualify, the holder must show that: 1) it was in possession of the instrument and entitled to enforce it at the time of its loss; 2) the loss was not the result of a transfer; and 3) the instrument's whereabouts cannot be determined. The holder must also prove the terms of the instrument. A court may require the holder to post a bond.

G.   Effect of Instrument on Obligation; Accord and Satisfaction

1)   CERTIFIED, CASHIER'S, OR TELLER'S CHECKS

If a certified, cashier's, or teller's check is taken for an obligation, the obligation is discharged just as if an amount of money equal to the instrument were taken in payment of the obligation. A certified check is an obligation of the bank upon which it is drawn. The law presumes that the holder of a certified check takes or holds the check in reliance on the certifying bank's obligation rather than on the drawer's obligation. UCC § 3-414, comment 3. The certified check is treated as the equivalent of cash. Acceptance of the certified check fully discharges the underlying obligation. However, discharge does not affect any liability that the obligor may have as an indorser of the instrument.

2)   REGULAR CHECKS AND NOTES

If an uncertified (i.e., personal) check or note is taken for an obligation, the obligation is suspended and the following rules apply:

a)   Checks

Suspension of the obligation continues until dishonor or payment. Payment results in discharge of the obligation.

b)   Notes

Suspension of the obligation continues until dishonor or payment. Payment of the note results in discharge.

★
3)   ACCORD AND SATISFACTION

If a person against whom a claim is asserted demonstrates that a person in good faith tendered an instrument to the claimant as full satisfaction of the claim, the claim was either subject to a *bona fide* dispute or unliquidated, and the claimant obtained payment of the instrument, the following provisions apply.

a)   Notation on Instrument

The claim is discharged if the person against whom the claim is asserted proves that the instrument contained a conspicuous statement to the effect that the instrument was tendered as full satisfaction of the claim.

b)   Proof of Knowledge of Full Tender

A claim is discharged if the person proves that the claimant knew that the instrument was tendered in full satisfaction of the claim.

        c)   Potential Defense

Organizational creditors, such as a department store, can require a debtor to mail an accord and satisfaction check to some address besides their address for receiving routine payments, in order to avoid inadvertent accord and satisfaction by the debtor. UCC § 3-311(c).

V.   LIABILITY OF PARTIES

The maker of a note and the drawee (usually the bank) of a draft are primary parties and bear unconditional liability on the instruments (no conditions precedent).

A.   Signatures and Other General Provisions

1)   INTENT TO AUTHENTICATE IS KEY

Lithographs, thumbprint, initials, mechanical reproductions, etc., are all adequate if the party possesses the intent to authenticate the writing.

2)   LOCATION OF SIGNATURE IS IRRELEVANT

The signature may appear anywhere on the instrument.

3)   SIGNATURE BY REPRESENTATIVE

        a)   Distinguished from Signature by Forgery

Generally, a first person will not be liable on a negotiable instrument unless either the person executed the instrument or authorized a second person to execute it for her or him. UCC § 3-401(a). Absent evidence that the first person authorized the second person to execute the instrument (e.g., a check) for him, the second person's signature will be effective only as the second person's signature, not as that of the first person. UCC § 3-403. Thus, if the second person steals the check from the first person and signs it, the first person will not be liable on the check unless she or he cannot establish that the second person forged the first person's signature.

        b)   Liability of Represented Person

The signature of a representative may bind him to an instrument. A represented person is bound by an agent's signature on the check if he would be bound by the agent's signature on a simple contract. General authorization to sign checks creates apparent authority adequate to make the agent's signature binding on the represented person. Therefore, one must be extremely careful in determining the permitted signing authority on an account.

c)   Liability of Representative

If the form of the signature does not show unambiguously that the signature is made in a representative capacity or the represented person is not identified in the instrument, the representative is liable on the instrument to a holder in due course that took the instrument without notice that the representative was not intended to be liable on the instrument.

4)   FICTITIOUS PAYEE RULE

The Fictitious Payee Rule is an exception to the general rule that the drawer is not liable for unauthorized instruments. For example, if an employer's accountant writes checks for the employer to an employee or service provider that does not exist and then forges the fictitious payee's name, the employer is still liable. Alternatively, an indorsement in the name of a fictitious payee is also effective. If a person whose intent determines to whom an instrument is payable does not intend the person identified as payee to have any interest in the instrument, then an indorsement by any person in the name of the payee stated in the instrument is effective as the indorsement of the payee.

★   5)   IMPOSTOR RULE

The Impostor Rule is also an exception to the general rule that the drawer is not liable for forged instruments. If a drawer makes a check payable to an impostor or person claiming to be an agent of a respectable person, the drawer is liable even though the impostor/payee forges someone else's signature, because the drawer is in a better position than the drawee (e.g., bank) to detect the impostor.

B.   **Employer's Responsibility for Employee Fraud**

Usually, negotiation of an instrument will not occur as a result of an unauthorized signature (i.e., indorsement). UCC § 3-403(a). This general rule is subject to an exception when, for example, an employer authorizes an employee to process a check for "deposit to an account" and the employee fraudulently indorses the check. UCC § 3-405(a)(3)(ii). Under certain circumstances, an employer will be held liable for the fraudulent acts of an employee. If an employer entrusted an employee with responsibility with respect to an instrument, and the employee or a person acting in concert with the employee fraudulently indorses the instrument, the indorsement is effective as the indorsement of the person to whom the instrument is payable who takes the instrument in good faith and for value. UCC § 3-405(b).

However, if the person paying the instrument, taking it for value, or taking it for collection fails to exercise ordinary care in paying or taking the instrument and that failure substantially contributes to loss resulting from the fraud, the person bearing the loss (i.e., employer) may recover from the person who fails to exercise ordinary care to the extent that the failure to exercise ordinary care contributed to the loss. The rule favors placing the risk of loss on the employer who is in a better position to avoid the fraud and who placed the employee in a role that enabled the fraud.

C.   Alteration

1)   DEFINITION

An alteration is defined as either 1) an unauthorized change to the terms of an instrument modifying the obligation of the obligor, or 2) an unauthorized completion of an incomplete instrument.

2)   GENERAL RULE REGARDING CHANGES

The Code sets out a general rule that fraudulent alterations serve to discharge the party whose obligation is affected by the alteration. UCC § 3-407(b). This defense is subject to the applicable doctrines set forth herein regarding fictitious payees, impostors, and employer liability. However, a holder in due course or paying bank may enforce the obligation according to its original terms.

★   #### 3)   COMPLETION OF INCOMPLETE DOCUMENTS

A person who takes a note for value, in good faith, and without notice of the addition, is allowed to enforce the note against the original obligor according to its terms as completed. "If blanks are filled or an incomplete instrument is otherwise completed, subsection (c) places the loss upon the party who left the instrument incomplete by permitting enforcement in its completed form." This is consistent with the idea that good-faith purchasers for value should not be adversely affected by the original obligor's omissions, and that the loss in cases like this should be placed on the party who left the instrument incomplete. UCC § 3-407 comment 2.

4)   NEGLIGENCE CONTRIBUTING TO FORGERY OR ALTERATION

A first person, whose failure to exercise ordinary care substantially contributes to an alteration of an instrument or to a forgery on the instrument by a second person, is precluded from asserting the alteration or the forgery against a third person who pays the instrument or takes it for value in good faith. UCC § 3-406.

D.   Drawee not Liable on Unaccepted Draft (§ 3-408)

A drawee is a person ordered in a draft to make payment (e.g., a bank). A check or draft does not automatically operate as an assignment of funds into the hands of the drawee. The drawee is not liable on the instrument until the drawee accepts it.

E.   Acceptance of Draft

1)   GENERAL

An "acceptance" is a drawee's (e.g., bank's) signed agreement to pay a draft (e.g., check) as presented. It must be written on the draft and may consist of the drawee's signature alone. A draft may be accepted even if it is not signed by the drawer, is otherwise incomplete, is overdue, or has been dishonored.

2)   VARYING TERMS

If the terms of a drawee's (bank's) acceptance vary from the terms of the draft or check as presented, the holder may refuse the acceptance and treat the draft as dishonored. However, if the holder (person cashing the check) agrees to an acceptance varying the terms of a draft, the obligation of each drawer and indorser that does not expressly assent to the acceptance is discharged.

F.   Refusal to Pay Cashier's, Teller's, and Certified Checks

If the obligated bank wrongfully refuses to pay a cashier's, certified, or teller's check, the person asserting the right to enforce the check is entitled to compensation for expenses and loss of interest resulting from the nonpayment and may recover consequential damages if the obligated bank refuses to pay after receiving notice of particular circumstances giving rise to the damages.

G.   Obligations of Issuer, Acceptor, Drawer, Indorser

1)   OBLIGATIONS OF ISSUER

The issuer of a note or draft is obligated to pay the instrument according to its terms at the time it was issued, or, if the issuer signed an incomplete instrument, according to its terms when completed. The obligation is owed to a person entitled to enforce the instrument or to an indorser who paid the instrument.

2)   OBLIGATIONS OF ACCEPTOR

The acceptor (e.g., bank cashing check for holder) is obliged to pay the draft according to its terms at the time it was accepted or if the acceptance is of a draft that is incomplete, according to its terms when completed. The obligation is owed to a person entitled to enforce the instrument or to an indorser who paid the instrument.

3)   OBLIGATIONS OF DRAWER

With the exception of cashier's, certified, and teller's checks, if an unaccepted draft is dishonored, the drawer is obliged to pay the draft according to its terms at the time it was issued or, if the drawer signed an incomplete instrument, according to its terms when completed. The obligation is owed to a person entitled to enforce the instrument or to an indorser who paid the instrument.

a)   Discharge by Acceptance

If a draft is accepted by a bank, the drawer is discharged, regardless of when or by whom acceptance was obtained. If a draft is accepted and the acceptor is not a bank, the obligation of the drawer to pay the draft if the draft is dishonored by the acceptor is the same as the obligation of an indorser.

4) OBLIGATIONS OF INDORSER

If an instrument is dishonored, an indorser is obligated to pay the amount due on the instrument according to the terms of the instrument at the time it was indorsed, or if the indorser indorsed an incomplete instrument, according to its terms when completed. The obligation of the indorser is owed to a person entitled to enforce the instrument or to a subsequent indorser who paid the instrument.

a) Indorsement Without Recourse

If an indorsement states that it is made "without recourse" or otherwise disclaims liability of the indorser, the indorser is not liable to pay the instrument.

b) Notice of Dishonor

If notice of dishonor is required but not provided, the liability of the indorser is discharged.

c) Acceptance by Bank Discharges Obligation

If a draft is accepted by a bank, the liability of the prior indorser is discharged.

H.   Transfer and Presentment Warranties

There are two types of warranties that exist in the law of commercial paper. First, a person transferring an instrument makes certain transfer warranties. Second, a person presenting an instrument for payment makes certain presentment warranties.

1) TRANSFER WARRANTIES

A person who transfers an instrument for consideration warrants to the transferee and subsequent transferees that:

- The warrantor is entitled to enforce the instrument;
- All signatures are authorized;
- The instrument has not been altered;
- The instrument is not subject to a defense which can be asserted against the warrantor; and
- The warrantor has no knowledge of the maker's insolvency proceedings.

a) Remedies for Breach

A person who took the instrument in good faith may recover damages from the warrantor in an amount equal to the loss suffered as a result of the breach.

b)   Transfer Warranties Cannot be Disclaimed

The indorsement "without recourse," although it may be effective in other respects, is not effective to disclaim warranties.

2)   PRESENTMENT WARRANTIES

When a draft is presented to the drawee (e.g., bank) for payment and the drawee accepts the draft, the person obtaining payment at the time of presentment, and a previous transferor of the draft, at the time of transfer, warrant to the drawee making payment in good faith that:

- The warrantor is a person entitled to enforce the draft;
- The draft has not been altered; and
- The warrantor has no knowledge that the signature of the drawer is unauthorized.

a)   Presentment to Drawer or Indorser

Any party (including a bank) that presents to a drawer or indorser a check for payment warrants to the person making payment that the person obtaining payment is entitled to enforce the instrument or is acting on behalf of someone entitled to enforce the instrument. The amount recoverable for this breach of warranty is the amount paid on the check plus expenses and loss of interest resulting from the breach. UCC § 3-417(d)(2).

b)   Damages

A bank or drawee making payment may recover from any warrantor damages for breach of warranty equal to the amount paid by the drawee. In addition, the drawee is entitled to compensation for expenses and loss of interest resulting from the breach. The right of the drawee to recover damages is not affected by any failure of the drawee to exercise ordinary care in making payment.

c)   Presentment Warranties Cannot be Disclaimed

The indorsement "without recourse," although it may be effective in other respects, is not effective to disclaim warranties.

I.   **Payment or Acceptance by Mistake**

The Code generally applies to payments over a stop order or to payments where the drawer's signature was unauthorized. UCC § 3-418.

If the drawee of a draft pays or accepts the draft on the mistaken belief that payment of the draft had not been stopped or the signature of the drawer of the draft was authorized, the drawee may recover the amount of the draft from the person to whom payment was made. Rights of the drawee under this subsection are not affected by failure of the drawee to exercise ordinary care in paying or accepting the draft. However, the drawee may not seek return of payment from a holder in due course or a person who in good faith changed position in reliance on the payment.

★   **J.   Instruments Signed for Accommodation**

An accommodation party is a person who signs commercial paper in any capacity for the purpose of lending his name (i.e. credit) to another party to the instrument. An accommodation party who pays the instrument is entitled to reimbursement from the accommodated party to the extent of payment and is entitled to enforce the instrument against the accommodated party. UCC § 3-419(e). An accommodation party, such as a guarantor, can sign the instrument simply in order to incur liability for it without being a beneficiary of the value provided for in the instrument.

>   1)   LIABILITY OF ACCOMMODATION PARTY

>>   a)   Accommodation Party as Guarantor

An accommodation party may be, for example, a guarantor of a promissory note between a creditor and a principal obligor. For example, when an accommodation party signs a note as a guarantor, this party signs his name as "a guarantor" below the word "guaranteed" in order to provide notice that he is signing the note in this capacity. UCC § 3-419(a), (c).

>>   b)   Guarantor as Maker

An accommodation party must "pay the instrument in the capacity in which the accommodation party signs." UCC § 3-419(b). A person who signs an instrument on the front of it in the area where any other parties sign it is a person undertaking to pay the instrument in the capacity of a maker. UCC § 3-103(a)(7). The maker must pay the instrument to a holder. UCC § 3-412. This duty to pay generally applies although the person seeking to enforce that instrument possesses notice of the maker's capacity of accommodation party. UCC § 3-419(c). Absent any valid defense to payment by this person, his or her signing the instrument for accommodation does not relieve the person of the requirement to pay the instrument by its terms to another person entitled to enforce it. *Id.* Potential defenses to payment include, for example, unauthorized negotiation or a separate contract altering an obligation of a note. UCC § 3-117.

>>   c)   Guarantor as Secondary Obligor

If a person entitled to enforce a note allows for an intentional voluntary discharge of the principal obligor on a negotiable instrument, this does not discharge the accommodation party's obligation on the instrument. UCC § 3-605(b). An accommodation party qualifies as a "secondary obligor" on a negotiable instrument. UCC § 3-103(a)(17). A secondary obligor possesses defenses. UCC § 3-605 (revised).

>>   d)   Discharge by Release

If the duty of the principal obligor to pay on a negotiable instrument is released by the person entitled to enforce the instrument, then "the secondary obligor is discharged to the same extent as the principal obligor from any unperformed portion of its obligation on the instrument." UCC § 3-605(a)(2) (revised). Unless the release specifically retains rights of the person entitled to enforce the instrument against the secondary obligor, the secondary obligor will be discharged.

For example, the guarantor as secondary obligor will be liable to a creditor on the note's unpaid balance due after the creditor discharges the principal obligor, such as by means of a proper release. UCC § 3-605. In that situation, the guarantor's liability to the creditor on the note can be decreased by any previous payment on the debt by the principal obligor to the creditor. UCC § 3-419(e).

2)   ANOMALOUS SIGNATURES PRESUMED AS ACCOMMODATION

A person signing an instrument in a random place or order is presumed to be an accommodation party. If the signature is anomalous (not in the chain of indorsement), then the signing party is presumed to be an accommodation party.

★   K.   Conversion of Instrument

A person who takes (e.g., receives) an instrument "is subject to a claim of a property or possessory right in the instrument." UCC § 3-306. Thus, a payee of an instrument generally has a property and possessory right in the instrument because the payee owns it. Usually, this payee can assert its rights in the instrument to recover it from either a thief of the instrument or another person who received the instrument from the thief. But the payee cannot successfully assert this claim against a person with the rights to enforce the instrument as its holder in due course. *Id.* For example, a holder in due course would not be subject to such a claim asserted by an entity from which someone embezzled an instrument. *American Parkinson Disease Ass'n, Inc. v. First Nat. Bank of Northfield,* 584 N.W.2d 437 (Minn. 1998).

The law applicable to conversion of personal property applies to instruments as well. An instrument is converted if: 1) it is taken by transfer from a person not entitled to enforce the instrument; or 2) a bank makes or obtains payment with respect to the instrument for a person not entitled to enforce the instrument or receive payment. The liability runs in favor of the true owner or the person entitled to enforce the instrument, and is presumed to be the amount payable on the instrument. UCC § 3-420(b).

VI.   DISHONOR

A.   Presentment

A presentment is a timely demand for payment or acceptance upon the maker of a note or drawee (usually the bank) of a draft who may require exhibition of the instrument and identification of the party making presentment.

B.   Dishonor

Dishonor occurs when a proper presentment is made and payment is refused.

C.   Notice of Dishonor to Indorser/Drawer (30 Days)

The indorsers or drawer are liable as secondary parties. Such liability on the instrument is conditioned upon presentment for payment, notice of dishonor, and formal protest. In order to hold an indorser liable, a holder must give them notice that the maker or drawee (usually the bank) has dishonored the instrument. Timely notice of dishonor is defined by statute. Notice must be given within 30 days of the dishonor. Failure to give timely notice of dishonor discharges indorser liability, not drawer liability.

D.   Excused Presentment and Notice of Dishonor

1)   PRESENTMENT

Presentment for payment is excused if: 1) the person entitled to present the instrument cannot with reasonable diligence make presentment; or 2) the maker or acceptor has repudiated an obligation to pay the instrument or is dead or in insolvency proceedings; or 3) the drawer or indorser whose obligation is being enforced has waived presentment.

2)   NOTICE OF DISHONOR

Notice of dishonor is excused if by the terms of the instrument, notice of dishonor is not necessary to enforce the obligation of a party to pay the instrument or the party whose obligation is being enforced waived notice of dishonor. A waiver of presentment acts as a waiver of notice of dishonor.

a)   Delay

Delay in giving notice of dishonor is excused if the delay was caused by circumstances beyond the control of the person giving the notice, and the person giving the notice exercised reasonable diligence after the cause of the delay ceased to operate.

E.   Evidence of Dishonor

The following are admissible as evidence and create a presumption of dishonor and of any notice of dishonor stated:

- a protest document;
- a writing of the drawee stating that acceptance has been refused;
- a record of the drawee which demonstrates dishonor.

1)   PROTEST DOCUMENT

A protest is a document made by the person entitled to enforce the instrument. It must be in writing and made under oath. The protest must identify the instrument and certify either that presentment has been made or, if not made, the reason why it was not made, and that the instrument has been dishonored by non-acceptance or nonpayment.

VII.   DISCHARGE AND PAYMENT

A.   Discharge and Effect of Discharge

The obligations of a party obligated to pay an instrument may be discharged in several ways as set forth below. However, discharge of a party is not effective against a person acquiring the rights of a holder in due course of the instrument who has no notice of the discharge.

★★★   B.   Payment; Tender of Payment

1)   PAYMENT

A party obligated to pay the instrument is discharged on the instrument when it makes payment to a person entitled to enforce the instrument. The discharge of liability is valid to the extent of the payment to the holder of the instrument. Remember however, that discharge is not effective against a person acquiring the rights of a holder in due course of the instrument who has no notice of the discharge.

2)   TENDER OF PAYMENT

a)   Indorsers Discharged upon Refusal of Tender

If tender of payment of an instrument is made to a person entitled to enforce the instrument and the tender is refused, there is discharge, to the extent of the amount of the tender, of the obligation of an indorser or accommodation party having a right of recourse with respect to the obligation to which the tender relates. For example, assume a maker tenders payment to a holder and the holder refuses payment. The maker will remain liable; however, any indorser who possesses a right of recourse (all indorsers) against the maker will be discharged if maker subsequently dishonors.

b)   Interest Obligation Discharged upon Refusal of Tender

If tender of payment on an instrument is made to a person entitled to enforce the instrument, the obligation of the obligor to pay interest after the due date on the amount tendered is discharged.

c)   Adequacy of Tender

If presentment is required and the obligor is able and ready to pay on the due date at every place of payment stated in the instrument, the obligor is deemed to have made tender of payment on the due date to the person entitled to enforce the instrument.

C.   Discharge by Cancellation, Renunciation (§ 3-604)

A person entitled to enforce an instrument may discharge the obligation of a party to pay the instrument by: 1) an intentional voluntary act, such as surrender of the instrument to the party, destruction, mutilation, or cancellation of the instrument, cancellation or striking out of the party's signature, or the addition of words to the instrument indicating discharge; or 2) agreeing not to sue or otherwise renouncing rights against the party by a signed record.

D.   Discharge by Impairment of Collateral

If a person entitled to enforce the instrument impairs the value of the collateral that secures the instrument's obligation, then an accommodation party or indorser having a right of recourse against the obligor is discharged to the extent of the impairment.

SECURED TRANSACTIONS

SECURED TRANSACTIONS
UCC ARTICLE 9

INTRODUCTION

Because of the perceived complexity and intimidating nature of Article 9 of the UCC, a brief introduction is in order. The good news is that Article 9 not tested on every exam. Additional good news is that, when tested, generally only key concepts are tested.

Traditionally, one UCC question usually has appeared in the essay portion of one of the two Michigan Bar Exams ("Exam") administered each year. Several of those questions have focused upon UCC Article 2 regarding sales, although questions to which UCC Article 3 applies may be asked. Issues related to Article 9 also are subject to being tested on the Exam.

Facts and rules derived from cases decided by the Michigan Court of Appeals and/or the Michigan Supreme Court have provided the basis for some past UCC questions and answers. The Michigan Compiled Laws is another source for tested rules as well. Although the sample answers for certain past questions indicate that Michigan statutes and court cases should be the basis for answering questions, future questions could be answerable using controlling general legal principles and UCC provisions contained in this outline.

Article 9 concerns the transfer of a personal property interest to secure an obligation. A security interest gives a creditor the right to sell a debtor's property to satisfy a debt. The most common example of a security interest is a mortgage on real property, which is an interest in real estate that secures obligations, such as the obligation to purchase that real estate. Article 9 does not govern mortgages on real property. It governs personal property security interests. Article 9 focuses only on the security interest, and not the rights of the parties to the underlying obligations. For example, Article 9 addresses how a security interest is created and what a creditor's rights are to that security interest, while other applicable bodies of substantive law, such as UCC Article 2 and general contract law, govern rights to the underlying obligations.

I.   APPLICABILITY AND DEFINITIONS

A.   Subject Matter of Article 9

1)   GENERAL

a)   Security Interests

Article 9 applies to any transaction intended to create a security interest in personal property or fixtures. Article 9 governs if the security interest qualifies under this rule regardless of the form of the transaction. For example, if an acquisition is structured as an extremely long-term lease in order to take advantage of tax benefits, the corresponding security interest would be governed by Article 9.

b)   Consignments

Article 9 also covers consignments of non-consumer goods over $1000 in value. A consignment is an arrangement for a consignee to sell property on behalf of the consignor.

c)   2001 Revisions

In 2001, the scope of Article 9 was broadened. As a result of the revisions, more transactions are now subject to the terms of Article 9.

(1)   Broadened Scope

Some examples of transactions now subject to Article 9 include sale of depository accounts (in commercial settings), sale of promissory notes, sale of health care receivables, and sale of commercial tort claims. These transactions may now be the subject of lien creation transactions and the priority competing rights are governed by Article 9.

(2)   Agricultural Liens

Article 9 now also governs some statutory liens on agricultural commodities.

2)   MECHANICS OF TRANSACTION

In an Article 9 transaction, personal property or fixtures secure the payment of debt(s) or insure performance of a contract obligation. Additionally, lease-purchase agreements and consignments are covered by Article 9. A creditor/debtor relationship is created with property serving as "collateral." A vendor/vendee relationship may support a purchase money security interest in property if collateral is the property being purchased.

3)   WHAT PROCESSES ARE GOVERNED BY ARTICLE 9

Article 9 governs how security interests are 1) created, 2) perfected, and 3) enforced. Additionally, Article 9 governs how priority is determined among competing security interests.

B.   Perfection of Security Interests in Multiple State Transactions

A security interest must be properly created and perfected for a creditor to enforce a security interest against other creditors. "Perfection" is the process of "putting the world on notice" of the security interest in order to make the secured parties' rights fully enforceable. For example, filing a certificate of title in a car perfects a security interest and makes the lender's rights in the car enforceable against other creditors.

1)   PERFECTION AND FILING

As a general matter, the law of the state in which the debtor is located governs perfection and filing. UCC § 9-301. A "registered organization," such as a corporation or limited liability company, is located in the state where the debtor is organized (i.e., state of incorporation). An individual is located at the individual's principal residence.

2) PRIORITY IN COLLATERAL

For tangible collateral, the law of the jurisdiction where the collateral is located governs priority and perfection. For intangible collateral, the jurisdiction in which the debtor is located governs.

C. Excluded Transactions

Generally, Article 9 expressly excludes coverage of the following transactions:

- landlord's lien;
- statutory lien; and
- assignment of a claim for wages, salary, or other compensation of an employee.

D. General Definitions

1) SECURED PARTY

The secured party is the creditor who possesses the benefit of the security interest.

2) DEBTOR

The debtor is the party who has the possessory or other interest in the personal property securing the obligation.

3) OBLIGOR

The party who owes the underlying obligation is the obligor. Usually, the debtor is also the obligor. However, in some cases, they are different parties. For example, assume A is a shareholder of ABC Corp. ABC Corp. seeks a loan from Bank. If shareholder A permits ABC Corp. to use his personal property as collateral for a loan from Bank, A becomes the debtor. ABC Corp., however, is the obligor.

Article 9 is concerned more with the debtor than the obligor. Substantive contract law will govern whether an obligor must perform.

4) COLLATERAL

Collateral refers to the property in which a security interest is created.

5) ACCOUNT OBLIGATIONS

A security interest in a debtor's "accounts" covers any "right to payment of a monetary obligation, whether or not earned by performance, for property that has been or is to be sold . . ." UCC § 9-102(a)(2). A secured party can collect directly from the account debtor (the person who owes the debtor) if the debtor defaults. A deposit account includes demand accounts (e.g., checking accounts). UCC § 9-102(a)(29).

6)   GOODS

Goods are all things that are movable when a security interest attaches. UCC § 9-102(a)(44).

7)   CONSUMER GOODS

"Consumer goods" are goods used mainly for personal, family, or household purposes. UCC § 9-102(a)(23).

8)   INVENTORY

Inventory means goods that are kept by a person for sale. UCC § 9-102(a)(48).

II.   ATTACHMENT OF SECURITY INTEREST

★★   **A.   General**

"Attachment" is essentially how a security interest is created. Once a security interest attaches, it becomes enforceable.

B.   Three Elements Required for Attachment

The three elements required for attachment are: 1) a valid security agreement, 2) the debtor possesses rights in collateral, and 3) value.

1)   SECURITY AGREEMENT

a)   Definition

For the purposes of Article 9, a security agreement is any agreement that gives a secured party a security interest in collateral.

b)   Elements of Valid Agreement

Although called an agreement, only the debtor must agree to create the security agreement. Generally, the debtor must 1) authenticate the agreement, and 2) describe the collateral.

(1)   Authentication of Agreement by Debtor

To obtain a security interest in a debtor's assets, a creditor must receive the debtor's agreement to grant such an interest. In general, a security interest will not attach to the collateral unless "the debtor has authenticated a security agreement that provides a description of the collateral." UCC § 9-203(b)(3)(A). Lithographed, thumbprint, initials, mechanical reproductions, etc., are all adequate proof of authentication so long as the debtor possessed the intent to authenticate the writing.

> (a) Possession or Control of Collateral by Secured Party May Eliminate Authentication Requirement

Sometimes, the Code will not require a debtor to authenticate an agreement in order for it to be enforceable. Authentication is unnecessary if:

- the collateral is not a certificated security and is in the possession of the secured party pursuant to the debtor's security agreement;
- the collateral is a certificated security and the security certificate has been delivered to the secured party pursuant to the debtor's security agreement; or
- the collateral is a deposit account (e.g., bank account or demand account), investment property, or letter of credit right, or other electronic document, and the secured party has control of it pursuant to the debtor's security agreement.

UCC § 9-203(b)(3)(B-D).

> (2) Collateral Description

The collateral must be reasonably described.

★ 2) RIGHTS IN COLLATERAL

The debtor must have rights in the collateral beyond mere possession. However, the debtor need not possess good title to the property. For example, the debtor may have voidable title or be a lessee of the property. The debtor cannot transfer any interest greater than what she possesses in the collateral. Additionally, title may be held in either the debtor or the secured party. UCC § 9-202.

3) VALUE

The giving of value is almost never an issue. For the most part, any consideration will do. If, for example, a secured party opens a line of credit for the obligor, opening the line of credit alone is sufficient value.

4) ATTACHMENT IN CONSIGNMENTS

a) General Considerations

Typically, a creditor's security interest only attaches to collateral in which a debtor possesses rights, and this interest is only effective to the degree of the debtor's rights. UCC § 9-203(b)(2). Generally, in a consignment arrangement, a consignee is the debtor and does not own a consignor's collateral because the consignor retains title. Thus, the consignee typically does not own collateral for attachment purposes. However, Article 9 provides that in order to determine the rights of a consignee's creditor, the consignee has "rights and title to the goods identical to those [of] the consignor." UCC § 9-319(a). Under such a consignment, the consignee possesses the full ownership interest of the consignor in the goods, such that as the security interest of the consignee's creditor will attach to them.

    b)   Article 9 Consignment

A consignment exists under Article 9 when:

- for the purpose of sale, goods are delivered by a consignor to a merchant that is not an auctioneer;
- the merchant deals in such goods using a different name than that of the consignor;
- immediately prior to delivery of goods to the merchant, they are not consumer goods;
- the goods' value is or exceeds $1,000 upon delivery; and
- a security interest is not otherwise created by this transaction.

Mich. Comp. Laws § 440.9102(1)(t).

    c)   Consignor's Interest in Consigned Goods

While a consignor owns consigned goods outright, the consignor's interest in the goods during consignment is that of a Purchase Money Security Interest ("PMSI") in inventory. UCC §§ 9-102(a)(72)(c), 9-103(d). A PMSI is 1) a security interest held by the seller of collateral to secure payment of all or part of the price, or 2) a security interest of a person that gives value to a debtor so that the debtor may acquire rights in or the use of collateral.

C.   **Miscellaneous Security Agreement Issues**

    1)   FUTURE ADVANCES

Article 9 permits security agreements to cover future advances only if the security agreement explicitly includes a future advances clause. For example, assume S loans A $50,000 secured by A's Yacht. In one year, S may provide A with an additional $20,000 also secured by A's Yacht if the security agreement contains a future advance clause.

    2)   AFTER-ACQUIRED PROPERTY

    a)   Generally Enforceable

After-acquired property may be secured in favor of the secured party if included in the security agreement. For example, assume S loans A $50,000 secured by A's Yacht. The security agreement provides that it is also secured by property that the debtor acquires in the future. S will also possess an interest in the property that the debtor acquires after the parties enter into the security agreement.

b)   Exception

A security agreement containing an after-acquired property clause will not apply to 1) consumer goods unless the debtor acquires rights in them within 10 days after the secured party gives value, or 2) a commercial tort claim.

3)   DEFAULT

The parties can specifically define what constitutes a default. If not defined, generally non-payment constitutes a default.

4)   ACCELERATION

The parties may provide for the acceleration of payments upon the happening of a specified event. For example, the parties may agree that the full balance becomes due if any payment is 10 days late.

5)   COVENANTS

The parties may covenant certain things to each other regarding the collateral. For example, a secured party may require that the debtor maintain insurance covering the collateral in case of loss, theft, or damage (common in automotive transactions).

6)   USE OR DISPOSITION OF COLLATERAL BY DEBTOR

A security agreement will not be invalid because the debtor possesses a right to use or even dispose of the collateral.

7)   COLLATERAL IN SECURED PARTY'S POSSESSION

A secured party must use reasonable care in the custody and preservation of collateral in the secured party's possession.

8)   REQUESTS FOR ACCOUNTING

Article 9 provides a procedure for a debtor to obtain information from the secured party about the secured obligation and the collateral in which the secured party may claim a security interest. A debtor can ask the secured party to prepare and send an "accounting" of the debt secured by the collateral. A secured party must respond to a request within 14 days following receipt of the request.

The debtor's right to an accounting may not be waived or varied. The debtor is entitled to receive one "free" response to a request every six months.

      9)   ACCESSIONS AND COMMINGLED GOODS

            a)   Accessions

An accession is collateral that is incorporated into another good but the identity of the collateral is not changed. A security interest may be created in an accession and continues in collateral that becomes an accession. For example, assume A possesses a security interest in an automobile engine. If the engine is installed in a vehicle, the interest will not become invalid. It will continue in the engine even as installed in the automobile.

            b)   Commingled Goods

A "commingled good" is collateral that loses its identity when physically united with other goods. For example, 200 pounds of flour may change into 1000 cakes. The flour in the cakes loses its identity as flour and becomes a commingled good. If collateral becomes commingled goods, a security interest attaches to the product or mass that results (e.g., the cake). If the interest in the original goods is perfected, the interest in the resulting product or mass is perfected. If two commingled goods that are perfected make the same resulting product, they are deemed perfected at the same time (not when originally perfected). For example, assume A possesses a perfected security interest in eggs. Assume B has a perfected security interest in flour. Assume A's interest has priority over B's interest. Assume that the eggs and flour are subsequently combined to create 1000 cakes. The interests of A and B will be deemed equal in time. Consequently, A will lose its priority.

III.   PERFECTION OF SECURITY INTEREST

★★   **A.**   **Introduction**

Once the security interest attaches, it is enforceable. Perfection of the interest only enhances the secured party's right to the collateral. As we will see, perfection of the interest will generally (but not always) protect the secured party from other third party claims. Most importantly, a perfected interest will obtain priority over a trustee's claim made in a bankruptcy proceeding.

However, if the security interest does not attach, then it cannot be perfected no matter what the creditor does. Filing a financing statement without attachment carries no legal significance because such a financing statement is effective "only to the extent that it was filed by a person that may file it." UCC § 9-510.

★★   **B.**   **Perfection Methods**

Depending upon the circumstances and the nature of the security interest, there are several different methods by which a security interest may be perfected including filing, taking possession, or automatically. The method to use will generally depend upon the type of collateral and the circumstances.

      1)   FILING

Filing is the primary method for perfection of security interests. Notice is given to potential third parties through filing of a "financing statement" or the security agreement with the state.

      a)   Required Contents of Filing

A filing must contain:

- the debtor's name;
- the secured party's name;
- an adequate description of collateral; and
- the filing fee.

The debtor's signature is not required under revised Article 9. Under the old version of Article 9, financing statements required the signature of the debtor. Under revised Article 9, the debtor's signature is not necessary. UCC § 9-502(a) and comment 3. Although filings must still be authorized by the debtor, UCC § 9-509(a), the debtor's authentication of a security agreement covering particular collateral is an authorization for the secured party to file a financing statement covering that collateral. UCC § 9-509(b)(1) and comment 4.

      b)   Exceptions to Filing as Method of Perfection

There are two main exceptions to filing as a method of perfection. They are:

- money and deposit accounts (perfected by possession or control) and
- goods governed by other laws such as certain aviation materials.

      (1)   Deposit Accounts Distinguished from Accounts

An account differs from a deposit account under Article 9. An account means a right to payment of a monetary obligation. A security interest in an account is only perfected by filing a financial statement in the proper official office. A security interest in a deposit account generally may only be perfected by control. UCC § 9-310(a).

      (2)   Assignments of Accounts

Besides perfection by filing, Article 9 allows for automatic perfection by attachment for an assignment of accounts where an assignor does not "transfer a significant part of the assignor's outstanding accounts" to the secured party. UCC § 9-309(2). Although Article 9 does not describe what constitutes a "significant part" of assigned accounts, this provision can protect "casual or isolated assignments . . . which no one would think of filing," and provides that those who "regularly" receive assignments of accounts should perfect their security interest by filing them. *Id.* at comment.

> c)   Time Limitation

>> (1)   Five Years

Generally, a filing lapses after five years. However, manufactured home interests last for 30 years.

>> (2)   Extensions

Filings may be extended for five years by filing proper continuation forms.

>> (3)   Termination Statements

Because filings lapse after five years, a secured party is not generally required to file a termination statement when the obligation has been satisfied or otherwise discharged.

>>> (a)   Consumer Goods Exception

However, a duty to file a termination statement exists for a secured party if the collateral consists of consumer goods and 1) there is no obligation secured by the collateral, or 2) the interest is not authorized. A secured party will have 30 days from the time when the obligation ceases to exist, or 20 days from when a debtor properly requests termination, to comport with the request.

>>> (b)   Unauthorized Filings

If a debtor sends an authenticated request to the secured party to file a termination statement of an unauthorized or otherwise discharged interest, the secured party must send a termination statement to the debtor or file a termination statement. A secured party has 20 days after a debtor properly requests termination to comply.

> d)   Authorization to File is Required

A party may file a financing statement only if authorized. UCC § 9-509(a). Authorization is presumed by the debtor's authentication of a security agreement. However, the secured party may not file an overbroad financing statement. By filing an overbroad financing statement, a party violates its "duty to refrain from filing [an] unauthorized financing statement." UCC § 9-625, comment 2. Moreover, a secured party has a duty to terminate an unauthorized filing when termination is requested by the debtor. UCC § 9-513(c)(4). A party is liable to the debtor for any damages caused by a violation of this duty.

> e)   Financing Statement Error

>> (1)   Registered Organizations

Generally, Article 9 refers to debtors that are certain types of entities which the law requires to file documents with a state office in order to be officially formed as "registered organizations" (e.g., corporations or limited liability companies). Creditors may obtain a security interest in collateral by filing a financing statement with respect to a debtor that is a registered organization, rather than an individual person.

(2)   Registered Name versus Trade Name

An effective financing statement must sufficiently set forth the debtor's name. UCC § 9-502(a)(1). The financing statement must set forth a debtor's official registered name when the debtor is a registered organization. UCC § 9-503(a)(1). If the financing statement instead sets forth the debtor's trade name, rather than its registered name, the financing statement is not effective. UCC § 9-503(c).

(3)   Seriously Misleading Financing Statement

A minor error does not make a financing statement ineffective unless the error makes it "seriously misleading." UCC § 9-506(a).

(a)   Failure to State Name Is Seriously
Misleading

In order for a financing statement to adequately identify a registered organization, the financing statement must set forth the registered organization's name as stated "on the public record" which "shows the debtor to have been organized." UCC § 9-503(a)(1). A financing statement that does not sufficiently provide the debtor's name is seriously misleading. UCC § 9-506(b).

(b)   Safe Harbor

Under the safe harbor provision, a financing statement that incorrectly states the debtor's name is not seriously misleading when "a search of the records of the filing office under the debtor's correct name, using the filing office's standard search logic, if any, would disclose a financing statement that [otherwise] fails . . . to provide the name of the debtor . . . the name provided does not make the financing statement seriously misleading." UCC § 9-506(c). Note that the filing office of certain states allows for informal searches of their records that do not involve standard search logic.

2)   <u>POSSESSION</u>

a)   General

Security interests in certain types of collateral may be perfected by mere possession of the item. A secured party may perfect a security interest in negotiable documents, goods, instruments, or money just by taking possession of them. For example, assume a secured party fails to timely file a financing statement to perfect a PMSI. The secured party will subsequently perfect the interest if the secured party peaceably repossesses the goods.

b)   Goods with Certificate of Title Issued by State

A secured party may perfect a security interest in certificated securities by taking delivery (not possession) of the certificated securities. Delivery is defined by statute and requires an authentic indorsement on the title to the secured party.

3)   CONTROL

A "security interest in a deposit account may be perfected only by control." UCC § 9-312. A secured party possesses control of a deposit account when:

- "the secured party is the bank with which the deposit account is maintained";
- the bank maintaining the deposit account provides a written agreement to abide by the secured party's instructions; or
- the secured party is the bank's customer relative to this deposit account.

UCC § 9-104.

4)   AUTOMATIC PERFECTION

a)   General

Under certain circumstances, perfection occurs automatically upon creation or attachment of the security interest. For example, a PMSI in consumer goods is automatic upon attachment. However, such attachment does not protect a secured party if the item has a certificate of title. Also, it does not protect from purchases made by subsequent consumers.

Some questions require examinees to determine whether goods are consumer goods or business equipment. Generally, if the goods are consumer goods, a PMSI is perfected upon attachment. If the goods are business equipment, filing is required.

b)   Classification of Goods – Intent vs. Actual Use

To classify goods either as business or consumer goods, one must examine 1) the expressed intent at the time of purchase, and 2) the actual use of the collateral in the hands of the debtor. One approach is that the debtor's intended use at the time of the sale should govern the classification. This approach is justified on the policy ground that the secured party should be able to rely on what the debtor represents as the intended use and should not be encouraged to police the collateral and keep the debtor under surveillance. J. White and R. Summers, *Uniform Commercial Code* 78-3-84 (4th ed. 1995). There is, however, authority for the proposition that the ultimate use controls. T. Crandall, R. Hagedorn, and F. Smith, *The Law of Debtors and Creditors* § 7.06[3][e] (1991). Therefore, when answering a question, an examinee should acknowledge the two approaches and analyze it with regard to both potential conclusions.

c)   Promissory Notes and Payment Intangibles

Promissory notes and payment intangibles are now within the scope of Article 9 (due to 2001 revisions). These security interests are automatically perfected.

IV.   PRIORITIES
★★

When a third party makes a claim to the collateral of a secured party, one must determine who has "priority" to the collateral. It is imperative to first determine what type of interest each competing party has to the collateral and when each party attached, perfected, and/or filed its security interest.

A.   Status Determines Test

Depending upon the status of the competing parties, different rules will apply to determine priority.

★★   1)   FIRST TO ATTACH

If neither party has perfected its security interest, then the first interest to attach will prevail. As a practical matter, however, this rule is rarely, if ever, utilized because one of the parties may defeat the other by perfecting immediately upon determining that both parties have not perfected.

      2)   FIRST TO FILE OR PERFECT
★★

      a)   Two Secured Parties

As between two secured creditors, the general priority rule is found in the UCC -- the first to file or perfect has priority. UCC § 9-322 (2000).

This is an important concept to elaborate on and understand because a party may file before they perfect. Take the time to fully understand the following example:

> Example: Assume Bank A is considering extending credit to ABC Corp. which is to be secured by ABC Corp.'s inventory. Bank A, however, has not made a final determination on whether to extend the credit. Bank A may file a financing statement before actually approving and extending credit (and in effect perfecting or attaching) to give notice of the possible creation of the security interest. Assume Bank A files on January 1. Assume that Bank A actually perfects and extends the credit on January 15. Now assume another bank, Bank B, also extends credit to ABC Corp. which is secured by the same inventory. Assume Bank B extends the credit and files on January 6. Bank A will have priority over Bank B because it filed before Bank B, even though Bank A's security interest

was perfected later than the perfection of Bank B's security interest. Accordingly, a party may "pre-file" (before perfection) for priority.

b) Lien Creditors (such as Bankruptcy Trustees)

Lien creditors possess almost the same status as perfected secured creditors. Accordingly, if a party becomes a lien creditor before a secured party perfects or files, the lien creditor will enjoy priority over that party. Conversely, a secured party who perfects or files early will be protected from a subsequent lien creditor such as a bankruptcy trustee. Note, however, that a secured party who fails to perfect will not have priority over a bankruptcy trustee.

c) Effect of Knowledge of Prior Unperfected Interest

As a general rule, even if a potential secured party has knowledge of the existence of a prior unsecured interest, it will not be prevented from filing first to obtain priority over that other unperfected interest. Good faith is required, however, if the party is somehow affiliated with the debtor.

d) Future Advances between Lien Creditors and Secured Creditors

Lien creditors are subordinate to perfected security interests only to the extent that the interest secures advances made (1) before the lien arose; (2) within 45 days of the lien; (3) without knowledge of the lien; or (4) pursuant to a commitment entered into without knowledge of the lien.

> Example: Bank loaned Debtor $5,000 and took a proper security interest in Debtor's "equipment now owned or hereafter acquired." The security agreement contained a proper future advance clause. Bank promptly filed the financing statement. One month later, a sheriff lawfully seized Debtor's computer pursuant to a writ of execution obtained by a judgment creditor of Debtor. One week later, Bank advanced Debtor $12,000 pursuant to the future advance clause. Bank will be protected with regard to the $12,000 advance because it was made within 45 days of the lien.

3) FIRST TO PERFECT

Some collateral is not subject to the state filing system or cannot otherwise be filed. In these cases, the first to perfect obtains priority. For example, an unperfected interest in inventory will be subject to priority in a perfected interest in that inventory. UCC § 9-322(a)(2). This priority applies to any proceeds from this inventory. UCC § 9-322(b)(1).

★★ 4) CUTOFFS (EXCEPTIONS TO PRIORITY RULES)

Some purchasers are protected even though their interest in the property is created *after* the attachment or perfection of a security interest. Essentially, these types of buyers are exceptions to the general rules regarding priority. They include buyers in the ordinary course of business, consumers buying from other consumers, and PMSIs.

★★   a)   Sale Made in the Ordinary Course of Business

A buyer in the ordinary course is a person who, 1) in good faith and without knowledge that the sale to him is in violation of the security interest of a third party, 2) buys in the ordinary course from a person in the business of selling goods of that kind. A buyer in the ordinary course of business takes free of a security interest created by a seller even if the security interest is perfected and even if the buyer knows of the security interest.

                                 b)   Consumers Buying from Consumers

A buyer of goods from a person who used or bought the goods for use primarily for personal, family, or household purposes takes free of a security interest, even if perfected, if the buyer buys:

- without knowledge of the security interest;
- for value;
- primarily for the buyer's personal, family, or household purposes; and
- before the filing of a financing statement covering the goods.

★★   c)   Purchase Money Security Interest ("PMSI")

A PMSI is 1) a security interest held by the seller of collateral to secure payment of all or part of the price, or 2) a security interest of a person that gives value to a debtor so that the debtor may acquire rights in or the use of collateral. For example, if A purchases an automobile from Dealership on credit with Dealership, Dealership may create a PMSI using the automobile as collateral.

Essentially, the PMSI is to personal property what a mortgage is to real property. The question that must be asked is whether the debt obligation was used to purchase the property serving as collateral. If yes, then a PMSI has likely been created. PMSIs possess priority over prior perfected security interests if the PMSI is properly executed.

                                 (1)   Inventory

A PMSI in inventory has priority over a conflicting security interest in the same collateral if the PMSI is perfected (i.e., filed) at the time the debtor receives possession and notice is provided to prior creditors. UCC § 9-324(b) (2000). But an unperfected PMSI in inventory will be subject to priority of a perfected security interest in the same collateral. UCC § 9-322(a)(2).

                                 (2)   Non-Inventory

A PMSI in collateral other than inventory has priority over a conflicting security interest in the same collateral if the PMSI is perfected (i.e., filed) at the time the debtor receives possession of the collateral or within 20 days thereafter. UCC § 9-324(a) (2000). So if perfection of this PMSI does not occur when the debtor receives possession and does happen within the next 20 days, it will be effective retroactively to its attachment date.

> (3)   Consumer Goods

A PMSI in consumer goods perfects automatically upon attachment. Generally, no filing is required.

> (4)   PMSI versus Lien Creditor (20 Day Grace Period)

Only if a creditor becomes a judgment "lien creditor" before the perfection of a conflicting security interest will this creditor possess priority over the security interest. UCC § 9-317. A secured party who files with respect to a PMSI within 20 days after the debtor receives possession (i.e., receives delivery) of the collateral takes priority over the rights of a lien creditor that arise between the time the security interest attaches and the time of filing. In other words, a PMSI secured creditor has a 20-day grace period within which to protect itself from a lien that is filed after the PMSI goods are delivered, but before the PMSI is perfected.

B.   Subordination by Agreement

A party with priority may agree to subordinate its interest to the interest of another party.

V.   DEFAULT

★   **A.   Introduction**

Upon a default of the underlying obligation, a secured party may attempt to realize its interest in the collateral. There are three different sources of rights that provide a secured party with different available options. They include 1) the provisions of Article 9, 2) the provisions of the security agreement, and 3) judicial remedies.

> 1)   DEFAULT

>> a)   Definition

Events constituting a default should be provided in the security agreement. If the parties do not define the default, it is presumed upon nonpayment of the obligation.

>> b)   Acceleration

The parties may elect to have all payments accelerated upon nonpayment or default of the obligation. If there is no express acceleration clause, the payments will not be accelerated and the secured party will only be able to obtain the current interest due in the collateral.

c)   Effect of Attachment

Remember, a security agreement is enforceable once it attaches. Therefore, perfection and priority only come into play when a third party asserts rights to the collateral.

2)   GENERAL OPTIONS

★★   a)   Self-Help (Repossession)

The secured party may attempt to take possession without committing a "breach of the peace." This "self-help repossession" is a significant right accruing to the secured party under Article 9's default provisions, and it may be exercised without giving prior notice to a defaulted debtor.

Article 9 does not provide a clear definition of what actions constitute a "breach of the peace." One approach suggests that claims of breach of the peace be analyzed with a "crude two-factor formula of creditor entry and debtor response . . . refined by a consideration of third-party response, the type of premises entered and possible creditor deceit in procuring consent." White and Summers, *Uniform Commercial Code*, § 25-7 at 219 (5th ed. 2000).

White and Summers also state that: "An opposition to the entry or seizure, however slight and even though merely verbal, normally results in a breach of the peace. The law should not make a debtor physically confront a repossessor in order to sustain a claim of breach of the peace." White and Summers, § 25-7 at 221 (5th ed.). On the other hand, some courts have held that oral protest alone does not unequivocally preclude self-help repossession.

An exam question involving whether an action constitutes a breach of the peace is an excellent opportunity for thorough case-by-case factual analysis. Be prepared to thoroughly analyze the facts.

b)   Replevin

Replevin is a judicial action to take possession of the property.

c)   Sale (Non-Judicial Foreclosure)

Upon default, a secured party may dispose of collateral properly in its possession by way of a commercially reasonable sale. This remedy may be used in conjunction with others. For example, a secured party may repossesses property and then sell it. Additionally, reasonable notice of a proposed resale must be sent to the debtor, and any resale must be commercially reasonable as to "method, manner, time, place, and terms." A public sale pursuant to notice is commercially reasonable and often includes competitive bidding. White and Summers, 1217 (3d ed. 1988).

(1)   Notice

Article 9 requires the secured party to send reasonable notification of the time and place of any public sale to 1) the debtor, 2) any secondary obligor (i.e., guarantor), and 3) a person who provides the secured creditor with notice that it claims an interest in the property. The notification must be sent in such time that persons entitled to receive it have sufficient time to take appropriate steps to protect their interests (e.g., by taking part in the sale). The purpose of notice is to provide the debtor with an opportunity to redeem the collateral or to maximize the number of bidders at the sale and thereby reduce any deficiency.

(2)   Advance Publicity

Advance publicity is important to increase the likelihood that a public sale will realize the market value of the collateral. B. Clark, *The Law of Secured Transactions Under the Uniform Commercial Code* § 4.08[5][d] (1988).

(3)   Fair Market Price as Evidence of Unreasonableness

While Article 9 specifies that a low price received at the sale does not always establish a lack of commercial reasonableness, most courts assume that a low price is a factor in deciding on commercial reasonableness. T. Crandall, R. Hagedorn, and F. Smith, *The Law of Debtors and Creditors* § 7.05[7][d][ii]; White and Summers, § 25-15. When accompanied with procedural irregularities, a low resale price is the "paradigm commercially unreasonable resale." White and Summers, 1234-35.

d)   Strict Foreclosure

Under certain circumstances, the secured party may purchase the collateral itself instead of selling it to a third party. This process is called "strict foreclosure." A secured party may purchase the collateral at any public disposition or at some private dispositions. A private disposition is only permissible if the collateral is of a kind that is customarily sold on a recognized market (i.e., stock market) or the subject of widely distributed standard price quotations.

e)   Right of Redemption

(1)   General

Generally, a debtor or secondary obligor possesses the right of redemption until the sale is completed unless otherwise agreed to by the debtor *after* the default occurs. To exercise this right, the debtor or secondary obligor must satisfy the obligation plus any reasonable fees of the secured party including attorney fees. The right of redemption is usually extinguished when collateral is properly disposed of by the creditor in compliance with the Code. UCC § 9-623.

(2)   No Waiver Before Default

The right to redeem collateral is a mandatory right that may not be waived in the security agreement. UCC § 9-602(11). A waiver of a debtor's right to redeem is effective only if it is done "by an agreement to that effect entered into and authenticated after default." UCC § 9-624(c).

      3)   RIGHT OF SECURED PARTY SEEKING DEBT OF ACCOUNT DEBTOR

          a)   General

A security interest in a debtor's "accounts" covers any "right to payment of a monetary obligation, whether or not earned by performance, for services rendered or to be rendered. . . for property that has been or is to be sold." UCC § 9-102(a)(2). Article 9 provides a secured party the right to collect directly from the account debtor (the person who owes the debtor on the account) in the event of a default by the debtor.

          b)   Notice

To exercise the right to collect from the account debtor effectively, the secured party must send an authenticated notification to the account debtor informing the account debtor that the amount due has been assigned and that payment is to be made to the assignee. Once an account debtor receives proper notification to make future payments directly to an assignee, the account debtor may discharge its payment obligation only by payment to the assignee. Payments made to the assignor (i.e., debtor) do not result in discharge. UCC § 9-406(a).

          c)   Subject to Underlying Defenses

The rights of a secured party enforcing an account obligation are subject to "any defense or claim in recoupment arising from the transaction that gave rise to the [underlying] contract." UCC § 9-404(a)(1). The account debtor may assert contract claims against the secured party to reduce the amount the account debtor owes. UCC § 9-404(b).

> Example: Securo, a secured party, possesses a security interest in Debtor's accounts receivable. AccoDebto is an account debtor and owes Debtor $5000 for a tractor. Securo may seek collection of the debt directly from AccoDebto if it provides AccoDebto with adequate notice. AccoDebto may assert, against Securo, any defenses it possesses directly against Debtor.

      4)   SURPLUS AND DEFICIENCY

          a)   General Rule

When a secured party sells or disposes of collateral, the amount collected typically varies from the amount of the obligation. If the sale brings more than the underlying obligation, the secured party must account to and pay the debtor for any surplus. On the other hand, when the sale brings less than the underlying obligation, the obligor is liable for any deficiency.

b)   Exception – Certain Intangibles

If the underlying transaction is a sale of accounts, chattel paper, payment intangibles, or promissory notes, the debtor is not entitled to any surplus and the obligor is not liable for any deficiency.

c)   Deficiency Judgment Sometimes Not Available

If it can be established that a secured party is not proceeding with a sale in accordance with Article 9, the sale may be ordered or restrained on appropriate terms and conditions. If the disposition has occurred, then any person entitled to notification has a right to recover from the secured party any loss caused by a failure to comply with the provisions of Article 9 (i.e., to conduct a reasonable sale).

Article 9 does not expressly address the right of a creditor to recover a deficiency judgment after violating the rules contained in Article 9 in the case of consumer goods (but for business goods, the rebuttable presumption rule applies). However, many courts have addressed the effect of the secured party's violation of such debtor protection provisions. Courts have taken three approaches, none of which are clearly identified as the majority.

(1)   Absolute Defense

The first approach is to deny the secured creditor any deficiency if Article 9 has been violated. For example, a security holder who sells without notice may not look to the debtor for any loss. Thus, under this approach, the debtor has an absolute defense to a secured creditor's deficiency judgment, such that the creditor is barred from recovering any deficiency. Additionally, the debtor possesses a general right to recover damages for the secured creditor's violation of Article 9.

(2)   Rebuttable Presumption Rule

A second approach applies the "rebuttable presumption" rule. Under this rule, a debtor who is not notified of a sale has the benefit of a presumption that the value of the collateral was equal to the debt. Accordingly, the secured creditor carries a burden of demonstrating that even at a complying sale, the collateral is worth less than the amount owed by the debtor.

Remember, under Article 9, the rebuttable presumption rule expressly applies in the case of non-consumer good transactions (i.e., business purposes).

(3)   Set-Off

While a majority of courts would follow one of the two above approaches, some courts permit only a set-off for the loss proven by the debtor to have been caused by the secured party's failure to provide notice.

5)   SALE INVOLVING MULTIPLE SECURED CREDITORS

In some circumstances, a junior secured party may seek to enforce a security agreement subject to the interest of a senior secured party.

> Example: A and B possess valid perfected security agreements with debtor secured by the same property. Assume that A's interest has priority. Upon default to B, B may attempt to repossess the property and dispose of it to satisfy B's interest. However, A may intervene in any judicial foreclosure action and, as the prior in time secured party, may conduct the foreclosure sale. Any proceeds from the sale would be applied first to the expenses of conducting the sale, including reasonable attorney's fees, then to satisfy the debt of A. Any remaining balance may satisfy the claims of subordinate secured parties, including B.

> If A either elects not to intervene in the conduct of the foreclosure sale, or simply is unaware of it, the collateral would be sold subject to A's security interest and A's recourse would be to repossess the collateral from the buyer at the foreclosure sale and sell it to satisfy its security interest.

★

6)   GOODS VERSUS FIXTURES

A secured party ordinarily has the right to repossess collateral that secures an obligation when the debtor is in default on the obligation. However, the presence of collateral located on real property adds a wrinkle to the general rule. If goods are not classified as fixtures, then Article 9 provisions will apply. Any real property encumbrances are irrelevant and the priority rules of Article 9 will govern. If, however, the goods are classified as "fixtures," then any real property encumbrances are considered in determining priority and rights upon default.

a)   Classification as Fixtures

Article 9 provides that goods are "fixtures" when they become so related to particular real estate that an interest in them arises under real estate law. In other words, fixtures are so intertwined with the real property that they become a part of the real property. Article 9 generally leaves the determination of the status of goods as fixtures to the local real property law of the jurisdiction concerned.

b)   Perfection of Security Interests In Fixtures

A security interest in fixtures may be perfected by an Article 9 filing as to goods or by a fixture filing under local real estate law.

c)   Priority of Fixtures Against Real Estate Interests

Generally, a security interest in a fixture will be subject to "a conflicting interest of an encumbrancer or owner of the related real property other than the debtor." UCC § 9-334(c). Certain exceptions to this rule apply, for example, with respect to PMSIs in fixtures (discussed later in this outline) or when the debtor possesses an interest of record in the real estate where the fixture is located. UCC § 9-334(d), (e)(1).

(1)   Prior Perfected Fixture Interests Generally Prevail

A fixture filing made before an interest of a competing real estate claimant is recorded generally enables the secured party claiming a security interest in the fixtures to prevail over the real estate claimant if the secured party prevailed over the real estate claimant's predecessor in interest.

(2)   PMSI in Fixtures

A purchase-money security interest in goods that become fixtures generally prevails over an existing interest of record of a competing real estate claimant if a fixture filing is made as to the goods within 20 days after the goods become fixtures. In other words, perfection of this PMSI is effective retroactively to its attachment date.

(3)   Construction Mortgages

A fixture security interest is generally subordinate to the construction mortgage of a construction mortgagee where the goods become fixtures before completion of construction. Nonetheless, a security interest perfected before the goods become fixtures has priority over a competing real estate claimant in the goods, including a construction mortgagee.

d)   Remedies Available to Secured Party in Interest in Fixtures

In some ways, the protection provided by Article 9 to encumbrancers of real estate over holders of security interests in fixtures operates to limit the secured party's repossession rights. First, the secured party must have priority over all real property encumbrancers. A secured party who has priority over all owners and encumbrancers of the real estate is entitled, upon default, to remove the collateral from the real estate. Moreover, even if the secured party has priority over all real estate interests, the secured party must reimburse the real estate interests for any physical injury caused by removal of the fixtures.

B.   **Debtor's Remedies when Creditor Violates Article 9**

1)   GENERAL CONSIDERATIONS

If a secured party fails to comply with Article 9, a court may order disposition of the collateral. Further, a secured party is liable for damages in the amount of any loss caused by a failure to comply with Article 9. Damages may be recovered by a person who is a debtor at the time of the failure of compliance with Article 9. UCC § 9-625(c).

For example, suppose a secured party files an overbroad financing statement (secured by more goods than agreed) naming Donald as the debtor. Donald may recover damages including losses resulting from his inability to obtain alternative financing. Damages should be limited to an amount reasonably calculated to put the debtor in the position that he would have occupied had no violation occurred.

2)   NON-COMPLYING DISPOSITION OF COLLATERAL

When a creditor makes a non-complying disposition of collateral (i.e., sells the collateral in a manner unauthorized by Article 9), the debtor can 1) recover minimum statutory damages, 2) recover actual damages, or 3) be subject to judicially mandated disposition of the collateral.

a)   Statutory Damages

The amount of "statutory damages" will not be lower than the credit service charge (i.e., credit loan interest) plus 10% of the loan's principal amount. UCC § 9-625(c)(2). Statutory damages serve to "ensure that every noncompliance [with Code provisions that govern disposing of collateral] in a consumer goods transaction results in liability, regardless of any injury that may have resulted." *Id.* at comment 4.

b)   Actual Damages

Actual damages are "those reasonably calculated to put an eligible claimant in the position that it would have occupied had no violation occurred." UCC § 9-625(b), comment 3.

c)   Judicially Ordered Disposition of Collateral

When a creditor possesses collateral obtained from a debtor by non-judicial foreclosure and the creditor is improperly disposing of it, a judge "may order or restrain . . . disposition on appropriate terms and conditions." UCC § 625(a). For example, the judge could order the creditor to allow the debtor to redeem the collateral or conduct a public sale of it.

3)   DOUBLE RECOVERY

Under a strict interpretation of the law, a debtor could have a deficiency removed, either under the rebuttable presumption rule or the absolute defense rule, as well as recover statutory damages. In the context of secured transactions not involving consumer goods, such over-compensation or double recovery is forbidden. Article 9 "is silent as to whether a double recovery or other over-compensation is possible in a consumer transaction." UCC § 9-625, comment 3. Accordingly, some courts have decided that a consumer may recover statutory damages despite a denial of deficiency. *Coxall v. Clover Commercial Corp.,* 781 N.Y.S.2d 567 (N.Y. City Civ. Ct. 2004).

AMERIBAR BAR REVIEW

Michigan Bar Review

WORKER'S COMPENSATION

TABLE OF CONTENTS

WORKER'S COMPENSATION

In Michigan, worker's compensation is a statutory scheme that basically provides that an employee who suffers an accidental injury while working for an employer can receive certain benefits. This system obligates the employer to furnish the benefits for an accidental injury to the employee without regard to the negligence. Thus, this is a type of no-fault system. Unless an employer is exempt from the system, the employer must participate in it and comply with the statutory scheme by obtaining the appropriate worker's compensation insurance coverage against which injured employees can make claims and receive benefits for covered workplace injuries, occupational disease, or death.

An example of a compensable injury might be when part of an employee's body gets caught and harmed in a machine on an assembly line. Even though this might, at first glance, seem like simply a tort law issue, worker's compensation law provides a statutory basis for furnishing a remedy for this injury. Worker's compensation is generally the exclusive remedy for workplace injuries. Thus, when worker's compensation applies, an employee cannot bring a negligence action against the employer. Worker's compensation coverage will not, however, protect the employer from a suit based on an intentional tort. The rationale of this exclusive remedy is that an employer which agrees to "assume automatic responsibility for all" covered injuries pursuant to the worker's compensation statutes "protects itself from potentially excessive damage awards rendered against it and that the employee is assured of receiving payment for" these injuries. *Farrell v. Dearborn Mfg. Co.*, 416 Mich. 267 (1982).

Although the Worker's Disability Compensation Act of 1969 (WDCA) exists in the state where the "big three" American automakers are headquartered, the application of the WDCA is not limited to any particular industry. Rather the WDCA, subject to exception, generally applies to employers and employees involved in various types of work, as indicated by certain past Worker's Compensation essay questions on the Michigan Bar Exam and the WDCA. Mich. Comp. Laws §§ 418.111, 418.115, 418.118-.119.

Some past Worker's Compensation questions frequently tested specific provisions of the WDCA as well as certain Michigan appellate court decisions discussing them. This outline highlights certain key WDCA provisions that should be memorized and applied in a fact specific way when answering a question. Thorough factual analysis will enable you to earn valuable points and demonstrate your knowledge of the law when responding to a worker's compensation question. These provisions were identified and used in the sample answers to past questions for which illustrative analyses were provided.

According to some past exams, some frequently tested issues and core concepts that you need to know include what constitutes an injury arising out of and in the course of employment (physical and mental), when an employee is "disabled," the meaning of disability in terms of wage earning capacity, and what diminished maximum wage earning ability is. Some other less frequently tested issues consist of mental disabilities and conditions of the aging process (physical and mental), the exclusive remedy rule with its exception for intentional torts, the exception to benefits for a social or recreational injury, and the recovery of medical expenses. Some other tested issues include partial disability and distinguishing an "employee" from a self-employed subcontractor.

I.   ELEMENTS REQUIRED FOR COVERAGE

If a Worker's Compensation question involves an injury to an employee, generally your approach to it should include analysis of whether the following elements required for worker's compensation coverage exist:

- Covered Employer

Traditionally, past questions did not test whether the employer was subject the WDCA.

★   • Covered Employee

Most past questions did not examine whether the employee was subject to the WDCA. However, a question tested whether an individual was an employee subject to the WDCA or an independent contractor not subject to the WDCA.

★★★★   • Accidental Injury or Occupational Disease

Past questions described an individual's accidental injury. Analysis is needed to answer these questions in terms of whether the individual's harm is a work-related injury or occupational disease to which the WDCA applies.

★★★★   • Scope of Employment

The determination of whether an employee's injury occurred in the course of employment is consistently tested and should be thoroughly analyzed based on the law and the facts.

★★★★   • Disability or Death

Previous questions have involved issues of employee disability rather than death. An important issue for analysis is determining the extent of the disability and how it affects the employee's capacity to return to work and what type of work the employee can do.

★★★★   • Causation

The determination of whether an employee's injury arose out of employment is consistently tested and should be thoroughly analyzed based on the law and the facts.

A.   Covered Employer

1)   GENERAL RULE

Unless the WDCA expressly provides otherwise, all employers and employees are subject to and bound by its provisions. Mich. Comp. Laws § 418.111.

2)   PUBLIC EMPLOYERS

Regardless of the number of employees, all public employers are subject to the WDCA. Mich. Comp. Laws § 418.115(c).

3)   PRIVATE EMPLOYERS

a)   General Employers

A private employer, other than agricultural employers, is bound by the WDCA if the employer regularly possesses:

- three or more regular employees. Mich. Comp. Laws § 418.115(a).
- less than 3 employees if at least 1 employee was employed for at least 35 hours a week for at least 13 consecutive weeks during the previous 52 weeks. Mich. Comp. Laws § 418.115(b).

b)   Agricultural Employers

An agricultural employer is bound by the WDCA if the employer regularly possesses:

- 3 or more regular employees paid salary or wages that were employed for at least 35 hours a week for at least 13 consecutive weeks during the previous 52 weeks. Mich. Comp. Laws § 418.115(d).
- 1 or more employees employed for at least 35 hours a week for at least 5 consecutive weeks, who must be provided hospital and medical coverage. Mich. Comp. Laws § 418.115(e).

Any other agricultural employers are exempt from the WDCA.

B.   Covered Employee

★   1)   INDEPENDENT CONTRACTOR

Generally, employees are covered by the WDCA, but independent contractors are not covered. A two-part analysis applies to determine if an individual is an employee or an independent contractor.

★ The first part of the analysis involves two steps. Factors indicating that an individual is an employee are that the individual is engaged 1) "in the service of another, [i.e., a contractual relationship] 2) under any contract of hire, express or implied" for substantial compensation (e.g., wages) -- and that other person is an employer. Mich. Comp. Laws § 418.161(1)(l) and *Reed v. Yackell*, 473 Mich. 520 (2005).

When an individual is an employee because the individual performed services pursuant to a contract of hire for substantial compensation, then the next inquiry is if the individual is excluded from this "employee category" by the following WDCA provision. *Id.*

The second part of the analysis involves three considerations. Generally, an individual who has previously worked for other third parties as an independent subcontractor will not be excluded from the "employee" category or status (described earlier) if the circumstances of this individual's employment satisfy the terms of Mich. Comp. Laws § 418.161(1)(n), which provides:

> "Every person performing service in the course of the trade, business, profession, or occupation of an employer at the time of the injury, if the person in relation to this service [1] does not maintain a separate business, [2] does not hold himself or herself out to and render service to the public, and [3] is not an employer subject to this act."

All three of those numbered factors of the foregoing provision must be fulfilled to establish that an individual is an employee rather than an independent contractor. *Id.* and *Blanzy v. Brigadier,* 240 Mich. App. 632 (2000). "Conversely, a person is not an employee if any one or more of the following applies: (1) the person maintains a separate business in relation to the service; (2) the person holds himself or herself out to and renders service to the public in relation to the service; or (3) the person is an employer subject to the workers' compensation statute in relation to the service." *Id.*

For example, an individual who has previously held himself out to render service to the public as an independent subcontractor (and perhaps maintained a separate business as well), can abandon that line of work when hired and by "the time of the injury" when working for an employer could have become an employee of the employer. Such things as hourly pay, fringe benefits, and union membership are hallmarks differentiating employees from independent contractors.

In Michigan, however, the "common-law 'economic realities test' for determining whether a worker is an employee or an independent contractor was superseded to the extent that it was inconsistent with" the foregoing WDCA provision. *Reed v. Yackell,* 473 Mich. 520 (2005).

2)   STATUTORY EMPLOYEE

As a practical matter, a general contractor should ensure that all employees of its subcontractors are covered by worker's compensation insurance. The general contractor may cover them itself or require the subcontractor to obtain this insurance for them. Either way, the general contractor is considered to be the statutory employer of the subcontractor's employees (i.e., statutory employees). The statutory employer gets the usual employer protections against being liable for more than the amount of worker's compensation benefits set out in the WDCA.

Specifically, an employer subject to the WDCA (herein the "principal") that contracts with a contractor (e.g., general contractor or subcontractor), which is not subject to the WDCA or has failed to comply with the WDCA before a statutory employee's injury or death occurs, is liable to pay the statutory employee any compensation under the WDCA that the principal would be liable for if this statutory employee directly worked for the principal. A principal is liable for the benefits when the statutory employee is injured while performing work for the principal. Mich. Comp. Laws § 418.171(1).

If the principal is liable to pay compensation under the foregoing provision, then the principal is entitled to be indemnified by the contractor in an action against the contractor. Mich. Comp. Laws § 418.171(2).

"Under the WDCA, the liability of the statutory employer (i.e., the principal) stems from its contractual relationship with the direct employer of the disabled person" (i.e., the statutory employee). *Viele v. D.C.M.A.*, 167 Mich. App. 571 (1988).

3)   DOMESTIC SERVANTS

A household domestic servant is not an employee if this individual is a member of the employer's family residing in the house (e.g., child or wife). Mich. Comp. Laws § 418.118(1).

A private employer is not liable under the WDCA to an individual employed as a domestic servant for less than 35 hours each week for at least 13 weeks during the previous 52 weeks, unless this employer voluntarily assumes coverage. Mich. Comp. Laws § 418.118(2).

4)   REAL ESTATE SALESPERSON OR ASSOCIATE BROKER

A Michigan licensed real estate salesperson or associate real estate broker ("person") is not an employee under the WDCA if both:

- not less than 75% of the person's remuneration is directly related to the volume of real estate sold rather than the amount of hours worked; and

- the person has a written agreement with the real estate broker who employs the person stating that the person is not an employee for tax purposes.

Mich. Comp. Laws § 418.119.

C.   Causation (Injury must Arise out of Employment)

There must be a causal connection between the work and the injury. The burden of proof is on the employee to demonstrate the injury and "that the injury occurred in connection with his employment, arising out of and in the course of that employment." *Eversman v. Concrete Cutting & Breaking*, 463 Mich. 86 (2000).

★★★★
1)   GENERAL CONSIDERATIONS

Under the WDCA, an employee is entitled to receive compensation benefits if the employee "receives a personal injury arising out of and in the course of employment" by an employer who is subject to the WDCA. Mich. Comp. Laws § 418.301(l). This rule should be committed to memory to recite and apply when answering a Worker's Compensation essay question.

An employee who suffers an injury arising out of and in the course of employment is eligible for compensation benefits regardless whether the employer was at fault for the injury. *Id.* In return, the employer is immunized from tort liability, except in narrow circumstances. Mich. Comp. Laws § 418.131.

★★　　　a)　　Pre-existing Problem

The fact that an employee had a pre-existing sports-related knee injury, for example, would not preclude a claim that the employee's most recent problem is compensable under the worker's compensation system because employers take their employees as they are with their pre-existing problems (i.e., condition). *E.g., Sheppard v. Michigan Nat'l Bank*, 348 Mich. 577 (1957). Therefore, the mere fact that the employee had a pre-existing problem would not bar a worker's compensation claim.

★★　　　(1)　　Aggravation of Pre-existing Problem

However, where an employee brings to the workplace a pre-existing problem and alleges work aggravated that problem, the employee must demonstrate that the work event caused a problem "medically distinguishable" from the pre-existing problem. *Rakestraw v. Gen. Dynamics Land Sys., Inc.*, 469 Mich. 220 (2003). If the work event merely aggravates the symptoms of the pre-existing problem, no "medically distinguishable" personal injury has occurred. *Rakestraw, supra* at 226-230; *Fahr v. Gen. Motors Corp.*, 478 Mich. 922 (2007). In this event, the employee would need to demonstrate a change in the underlying pathology of his pre-existing condition in order to meet the "personal injury" requirement. *Fahr, supra.* When work does aggravate a pre-existing condition in a compensable way, the consequent problem is considered entirely work related for purposes of Worker's Compensation. *E.g., Smith v. Lawrence Banking Co.*, 370 Mich. 169 (1963).

★　　　(2)　　Condition of the Aging Process

If the pre-existing problem constitutes a "condition of the aging process," (i.e., a problem which naturally develops while time passes), then a claimant must show that work contributed toward the pre-existing problem "in a significant manner," instead of merely in an insignificant way. Mich. Comp. Laws §§ 418.301(2), 418.401(2)(b).

　　　2)　　DEFINITIONS AND RULE

　　　a)　　Definitions

★　　　(1)　　Personal Injury

The WDCA defines "personal injury" to include a disease or disability that is due to a cause or condition that is "characteristic of and peculiar to the business of the employer and which arises out of and in the course of the employment. An ordinary disease of life to which the public is generally exposed outside of the employment is not compensable." Mich. Comp. Laws § 418.401(2)(b).

(2)   Mental Disabilities/Conditions of Aging Process

"Mental disabilities and conditions of the aging process, including but not limited to heart and cardiovascular conditions, shall be compensable if contributed to or aggravated or accelerated by the employment in a significant manner. Mental disabilities shall be compensable when arising out of actual events of employment, not unfounded perceptions thereof." *Id.*

(3)   Hernia

"A hernia to be compensable must be clearly recent in origin and result from a strain arising out of and in the course of the employment and be promptly reported to the employer." *Id.*

★★   b)   Controlling Rule

Mental disabilities and conditions of the aging process, including but not limited to heart and cardiovascular conditions, are compensable if the employment contributes to, aggravates, or accelerates the condition "in a significant manner." Mich. Comp. Laws § 418.301(2). This rule should be committed to memory to recite and apply when answering a Worker's Compensation essay question.

3)   SPECIFIC INJURIES

★   a)   Heart Attack

A Worker's Compensation question involving an employee's heart attack may include an issue of fact as to the existence of a work related physical or mental stress beyond normal life stresses. The issue would be whether work related stress from working at a desk contributes to, aggravates, or accelerates a heart condition "in a significant manner." If such a work related connection to the heart attack exists, recovery could be permitted depending upon a factual analysis of the surrounding circumstances pursuant to the foregoing rule, even if a pre-existing heart disease exists. *Id.*

For example, an employee's weight, smoking and dietary habits are factors that may contribute to the employee suffering a heart attack during the course of employment. However, if the employee's work aggravated or contributed to this heart attack "in a significant manner," then the employee can collect benefits, these lifestyle choices notwithstanding.

It is certainly possible that the stress of work could aggravate or accelerate the employee's heart attack. If, however, it is unclear from the facts that the employment contributed to the employee's heart attack "in a significant manner," this will be a question of fact for the magistrate to decide in a worker's compensation claim dispute.

★★   b)   Mental Illness or Injury without Physical Trauma

This type of injury generally requires something more than just ordinary stress incident to the employment. Pursuant to section 418.301(2), for mental disabilities to be compensable there needs to be evidence that the employment contributes to, aggravates, or accelerates these types of mental conditions "in a significant manner."

(1)   Significant Manner

Accordingly, an employee who finds work too demanding and stressful as a result of increased workload, such that the employee stops reporting to work pursuant to his family doctor's advice, must prove that this work stress contributed "in a significant manner" toward the employee's psychological problems.

The determination of whether work's contribution to these problems is "significant" or not is made by comparing the potential non-work-related explanations for the problems (e.g., family history, childhood difficulties, etc.) to work's contribution. *Holden v. Ford Motor Co.* (After Remand, On Second Remand), 226 Mich. App. 138 (1997); *Lombardi v. William Beaumont Hosp.* (On Remand), 199 Mich. App. 428 (1993); compare also, *Farrington v. Total Petroleum, Inc.*, 442 Mich. 201 (1993).

(2)   Unfounded Perceptions

For example, an employee could seek to prove that his or her employment contributed to the employee's debilitating depression "in a significant manner." In addition, mental disabilities are compensable only when they arise "out of actual events of employment, not unfounded perceptions thereof." *Id.*

★★ The Michigan Supreme Court has held that, in order to satisfy the mental disability requirements of section 418.301(2), a claimant must demonstrate that: 1) an actual employment event led to the claimed mental disability; and 2) the claimant's perception of the employment event was grounded in fact or reality, not delusion or imagination. In analyzing the claimant's perception, the magistrate must apply an objective standard to the employment event and determine how a reasonable person would have perceived the event under like circumstances. *Robertson v. Daimler Chrysler*, 465 Mich. 732 (2002).

(3)   Examples

An employee could suffer a mental injury or psychological injury from, for example, seeing a co-employee die in an accident involving them both and arising out of and in the course of their employment. The employee could suffer from this kind of psychiatric injury even though the employee suffered no physical injury from the accident.

Other possible examples of employment events that could be subject to this type of analysis include, for example, termination (e.g., discharge, layoffs), a supervisor lying about a promised promotion, or prolonged overtime with extra duties.

★★   c)   Exclusion for Injury from Employee's Misconduct

Under certain circumstances, an employer may invoke the following WDCA provision in opposition to an employee's claim for worker's compensation: No worker's compensation will be received if an employee's injury resulted "by reason of" the employee's "intentional and willful misconduct." Mich. Comp. Laws § 418.305.

(1)   Connection of Misconduct to Injury

It is not necessary that the injury arise contemporaneously with the misconduct. If the injury flowed directly and predictably from misconduct, then the injury is deemed to have occurred "by reason of" the misconduct. *Daniel v. Dep't of Corrections*, 468 Mich. 34 (2003).

(2)   Horseplay

For example, an employee's playful tossing of a work glove towards a co-employee is not likely to be determined "intentional and willful misconduct," as opposed to mere "horseplay" at work. Injuries resulting from "horseplay" at work can be compensable because "horseplay" is viewed as a natural consequence of employees working together. *E.g.*, *Crilly v. Ballow*, 353 Mich. 303 (1958).

(3)   Violation of Employer's Rule

The employee may not receive worker's compensation if the employee's injury resulted from violating a rule that the employer clearly announced and regularly enforced. A rule could, for example, prohibit an employee from getting intoxicated during lunch break and/or working while intoxicated.

D.   **Scope of Employment (Injury must Occur in the Course of Employment)**

The injury must occur in the scope of the employment. As a practical matter, the time, place, and duties being done must possess a connection with work.

★★★★

Under the WDCA, an employee is entitled to receive compensation benefits if the employee "receives a personal injury arising out of and in the course of employment" by an employer who is subject to the WDCA. Mich. Comp. Laws § 418.301(l). This rule should be committed to memory to recite and apply when answering a Worker's Compensation essay question.

An employee who suffers an injury arising out of and in the course of employment is eligible for compensation benefits regardless of whether the employer was at fault for the injury. In return, the employer is immunized from tort liability, except in narrow circumstances. Mich. Comp. Laws § 418.131.

1)   TRAVEL

If an employer furnishes the transportation, then the employee's injury can be covered if it arises out of and in the course of employment and is not subject to any other exception.

★★   a)   Going and Coming Rule

Workers are presumed to be in the course of employment in many circumstances, including traveling to and from work. Mich. Comp. Laws § 418.301(3). Generally, "[a]n employee going to or from his or her work, while on the premises where the employee's work is to be performed, and within a reasonable time before and after his or her working hours, is presumed to be in the course of his or her employment." *Id.* When analyzing an injury during a mealtime, look to see if the facts indicate a work-related mission to the meal or if employer required meals on premises.

For example, although a company's supervisors were driving in a non-company car and although their car's accident occurred after regular work hours, injury to the supervisors resulting from this accident while driving to a work-related event should be deemed to arise out of and in the course of employment largely because the owner of the company definitely urged the supervisors to attend the event and because their attendance would benefit the company as their employer. Contrast, *James v. Auto Lab Diagnostics*, 474 Mich. 1061 (2006); *Camburn v. Northwest Sch. Dist.*, 459 Mich. 471 (1999).

b)   Traveling Employees

As a general rule, when traveling is a large part of the job, a traveling employee usually remains in the scope of the employment from the time he leaves home on a business trip until he returns. Generally, scope of employment covers both time and place of travel as well as business activities along the route. However, a traveling employee who suffers an injury during a distinct departure for a personal errand or a social or recreational activity may not recover worker's compensation. *Bowman v. R.L. Coolsaet Constr. Co.*, 272 Mich. App. 27 (2006).

2)   DEPARTURE OR DEVIATION

An injury will be deemed not in the scope of employment if it occurs during a distinct departure from employment purposes for purely personal reasons. *Id.* Generally, a brief deviation does not take an employee's injury out of the course and scope of employment. However, even with a major deviation, coverage returns when employee returns to engaging in the employer's business.

★★   3)   SOCIAL OR RECREATIONAL ACTIVITY

a)   General Presumption

Workers are presumed to be in the course of employment in many circumstances, including traveling to and from work. Mich. Comp. Laws § 418.301(3). However, when the injury occurs "in the pursuit of an activity the major purpose of which is social or recreational," the injury is not covered under the WDCA. *Id.* An injury occurring at a company picnic is usually not covered, although under certain circumstances it may be covered. For example, an injury sustained while entertaining potential business associates at the employer's picnic could be covered under the WDCA.

(1)   Inquiry Focused on Purpose

In considering whether section 301(3) is applicable and precludes benefits, the focus is on the major purpose of the activity the injured worker was engaged in at the time of the injury. If the major purpose was social or recreational, benefits are precluded (i.e., not permitted). However, even when an event at which an employee was injured was in some respects social, because the major purpose of the employee's activities was work related rather than social or recreational, the employee is not precluded from collecting benefits under the WDCA. *Eversman v. Concrete Cutting & Breaking*, 463 Mich. 86 (2000).

(a)   Example

Suppose, for example, that an employee was unable to work for a few hours during a storm and took shelter in a tavern for that period. The employee chose not to resume working after the storm passed and instead spent several hours playing darts, shooting pool, and drinking beer at a tavern. As the employee left the tavern to go home, he tripped, fell, and suffered a concussion and fractured ankle. Because the major purpose of the employee's activities was social or recreational, the employee will be unable to collect benefits under the WDCA.

II.   DEFENSES

Some general defenses to an employee's claim for worker's compensation discussed elsewhere in this outline include, for example, that the injury neither arose out of employment nor occurred in the course of employment.

A.   Unavailable Defenses

1)   NEGLIGENCE

The negligence (e.g., contributory fault) of an employee is no defense unless the employee's negligence was willful. Mich. Comp. Laws § 418.141(a). That a fellow employee's negligence caused the employee's injury is no defense. Mich. Comp. Laws § 418.141(b).

2)   ASSUMPTION OF RISK

Assumption of risk of an employee is no defense. Mich. Comp. Laws § 418.141(c).

3)   EMPLOYER CONDUCT

Lack of employer negligence is no defense.

B.   Agreement

Generally, an agreement of an employee to waive rights to worker's compensation will be invalid. Mich. Comp. Laws § 418.815.

III.   EXCLUSIVITY OF REMEDY

When a work-related injury, occupational disease, or death is covered by worker's compensation, certain claims against tortfeasors may be lost because worker's compensation is an exclusive remedy. This exclusivity does not, however, limit claims unrelated to such injury, disease, or death of an employee, such as claims based on contracts, civil rights statutes, and other employment laws.

A.   Employer/Co-employee

1)   NEGLIGENCE VERSUS INTENTIONAL TORT CLAIMS

If an injury or occupational disease is covered, the injured or diseased employee's claim for negligence against an employer, statutory employer, or co-employee, is barred. Tort claims for intentional or willful acts of an employer or co-employee are not barred. In other words, one employee can sue another employee for the commission of an intentional tort. *Travis v. Dreis & Krump Mfg. Co.*, 453 Mich. 149 (1996).

★★   2)   INTENTIONAL TORT CLAIMS AGAINST EMPLOYER

The WDCA provides that the right to the recovery of worker's compensation benefits is the employee's "exclusive remedy against the employer" for a work-related personal injury or occupational disease. Mich. Comp. Laws § 418.131(1). This rule and the following exception to it should be committed to memory to recite and apply when answering a Worker's Compensation essay question.

a)   Exception to Exclusive Remedy Rule

The only exception to this exclusive remedy is an intentional tort. However, this exception is exceedingly narrow because the WDCA defines an intentional tort as follows: An intentional tort exists only when an employee is injured as a result of a deliberate act of the employer and the employer specifically intended an injury. *Id.* An employer is deemed to have intended the injury if the employer had actual knowledge that an injury was certain to occur and willfully disregarded that knowledge. *Id.*

Thus, under section 131(1), a plaintiff must show that the employer deliberately acted or failed to act while possessing either of the following states of mind: 1) the employer acted with the purpose of inflicting injury upon the employee; or 2) the employer had actual knowledge that injury was certain to occur and willfully disregarded that knowledge. *Gray v. Morley*, 460 Mich. 738 (1999); *Palazzola v. Karmazin Prods. Corp.*, 223 Mich. App. 141 (1997). An inherently dangerous condition and "substantial certainty" of injury are not enough to bring the case within the exception. *Gray v. Morley* (after remand), 460 Mich. 738 (1999); *Travis v. Dreis & Krump Mfg. Co.*, 453 Mich. 149 (1996).

B.   Third Party

There is no tort bar against third parties as plaintiffs or defendants. Therefore, third parties, including customers, can sue or be sued on any tort including negligence.

1)   TORT CLAIMS AGAINST THIRD PARTY

An employer or its worker's compensation insurer can recoup workers compensation benefits paid to an employee from an award of damages to an employee recovered in the employee's action against a third party.

IV.   DISABILITY

★★★★   ### A.   What Disability Means

1)   WDCA DEFINITION OF DISABILITY

Disability is statutorily defined as:

> a limitation of an employee's wage earning capacity in work suitable to his or her qualifications and training resulting from a personal injury or work related disease. The establishment of disability does not create a presumption of wage loss.

Mich. Comp. Laws §§ 418.301(4), 418.401(1). This definition should be committed to memory to recite and apply when answering a Worker's Compensation essay question.

In other words, an employee is disabled only if the employee has suffered a limitation in the employee's wage earning capacity in work suitable to the employee's qualifications and training due to the work-related injury or occupational disease.

2)   LIMITATION OF WAGE EARNING CAPACITY

Disability is not the physical or psychological impairment itself, but, by statute, is a limitation of one's maximum wage-earning capacity in work suitable to one's qualifications and training. And, the limitation of the ability to work is not the inability to resume the same job for the same employer when injured. The fact that an employee will not or cannot work for an employer due to a mental injury or psychological injury does not, in itself, demonstrate disability. If the employee can perform such equally well-paying work elsewhere, then the employee is not disabled. *Sington v. Daimler Chrysler Corp.*, 467 Mich. 144 (2002).

a)   Wage Earning Capacity

In *Sington*, the Michigan Supreme Court held that "capacity" meant "maximum output or producing ability." *Id.* Therefore, an employee would suffer a compensable disability if the employee's injury resulted in a reduction of the employee's maximum wage earning ability in work suitable to the employee's qualifications and training.

★★★★ **B.   Whether Disability Exists**

1)   WHEN EMPLOYEE IS NOT DISABLED

An employee is not "disabled" for the purposes of the WDCA when the individual has suffered no limitation in the employee's wage earning capacity as a result of a work-related injury or occupational disease. An employee who is not disabled is not entitled to weekly wage loss benefits.

For example, if an employee's injuries from working as a rodeo clown do not prevent the employee from working as a commodities broker (at least one of the jobs within the employee's qualifications and training), and if the employee's wages as a commodities broker would be at least as much as he would earn working as a rodeo clown, the employee would not be considered disabled and would not be entitled to weekly wage loss benefits.

★★ **2)   WHEN EMPLOYEE IS DISABLED**

Presuming there are no other jobs within an employee's qualifications and training that pay as much as the position that the employee had with the employer, the employee would be "disabled" and would be entitled to wage-loss benefits under the WDCA. Mich. Comp. Laws § 418.301(4). Thus, an employee suffers a compensable disability if the employee can no longer earn the employee's maximum wages in work suitable to the employee's qualifications and training as a result of the employee's injuries.

a)   Diminished Maximum Wage Earning Ability

In order to determine whether an employee has suffered a diminished maximum wage earning ability, it must be ascertained what types of jobs are within the employee's qualifications and training, and whether those jobs pay as much as the employee earned working a specific position such as, for example, a crane operator. Even if the employee was determined to be completely disabled as a crane operator, the employee would not be considered disabled for the purposes of the WDCA if the employee were able to perform a different, equally well-paying job suitable to the employee's qualifications and training.

b)   Legal Standard of Disability

For example, while as the result of a work injury an employee can no longer do the elevated work necessitated at times by construction workers, that inability does not necessarily render the employee disabled under Michigan law. Mich. Comp. Laws § 418.301(4); *Sington v. Chrysler Corp.*, 467 Mich. 144 (2002). This employee would need to demonstrate that "all" equally well-paying jobs suitable to his qualifications and training are precluded by this work injury. If the employee could perform work other than tasks that he cannot perform due to his physical injury, the employee's chances of prevailing on the disability issue are not good.

c)   Elements of Prima Facie Case of Disability

In order for an employee (i.e., claimant) to prove that the employee is "disabled" and so has a right to worker's compensation of weekly wage loss benefits, the employee must prove four elements. *Stokes v. Chrysler LLC*, 481 Mich. 266 (2008). These elements are:

- The employee's full disclosure all of training and qualifications, including skills, experience, training, and education, "whether or not they are relevant to the" work that the employee was performing when the injury occurred. *Id.*

- The employee needs to give a reasonable way to assess employment opportunities at any suitable work positions (i.e., jobs) within a common salary range, including those work positions to which the employee's training and qualifications might "translate." *Id.* The employee cannot restrict consideration to only those work positions that the employee has in fact performed during the employee's work history. *Id.* The employee must prove that the work injury prevents the employee from performing a few or every one of those work positions. *Id.*

- If there are any work positions suitable to the employee's training and qualifications that the employee has the ability to perform post-injury, then the employee must prove that the employee has exerted a good faith effort to obtain "post-injury employment" when work positions exist at the same or a higher salary. *Id.*

An employee should consider producing a "transferable skills analysis" and vocational testimony in order to prove how the employee's training and qualifications might translate to other work positions besides those previously performed by the employee. *Id.*

d)   Partial Disability

If the employee is only able to earn less post-injury than the employee did pre-injury, then the employee is disabled but only partially disabled.

V.   BENEFITS

The WDCA provides that an employee who is injured on the job can receive certain types of benefits: medical benefits, rehabilitation benefits, wage loss benefits, and death benefits. Upon the employee's rehabilitation, the employee may resume the same job position with same employer or take another job position with either that employer or some other employer.

As a general matter, when a covered employee is unable to work as a result of a covered incident, the employee's amount of benefits will depend upon the duration and severity of the injury.

★★   **A.   Medical Benefits**

An injured worker is entitled to all reasonable and necessary medical services required to treat the injury. Mich. Comp. Laws § 418.315(1). The duration of the obligation to furnish medical services continues until the need for them ends.

An employee can recover medical expenses under the WDCA regardless of whether the employee obtains wage loss benefits. *Id.* Besides wage loss benefits, the WDCA provides for payment of reasonable and necessary medical treatment for work-related injuries. *Id.* For example, the physical health care costs of an employee who suffered a physical injury would be recoverable. Likewise, the mental health care costs of an employee who suffered a mental injury or psychological injury would be recoverable.

B.   Rehabilitation Benefits

An employee may receive rehabilitation benefits in the form of altering the employee's job position to one that the employee can perform or assisting the employee in locating another job position the employee can perform with a different employer.

C.   Wage Loss Benefits

★★   1)   <u>GENERAL CONSIDERATIONS</u>

Wage loss benefits are weekly income payments that replace the employee's wages. The weekly loss in wages is the percentage of the employee's average weekly earnings based on the extent of the impairment of the employee's earning capacity in the job the employee was working when the injury occurred. Mich. Comp. Laws § 418.371(1). The weekly loss in wages must be fixed as of the time of the injury, and determined considering the nature and extent of the injury, and may not exceed the employee's average weekly earnings when the injury occurred. *Id.*

★★   2)   <u>ENTITLEMENT TO WAGE LOSS BENEFITS</u>

    a)   Job Offer to Disabled Employee

        (1)   When not Entitled to Weekly Wage Loss Benefits

Generally, a disabled employee otherwise entitled to weekly wage loss benefits under the WDCA will be considered to have voluntarily removed herself or himself from the work force and will not be entitled to those benefits for the duration of the employee's refusal of: 1) a *bona fide* (i.e., good faith) offer of "reasonable employment" from the employee's previous employer, another employer, or through the Michigan Employment Security Commission (Michigan's Unemployment Insurance Agency); and 2) the employee lacks "good and reasonable cause" for this refusal. Mich. Comp. Laws § 418.301(5)(a).

(2)   Reasonable Employment

The WDCA offers liberal protections to employees disabled by work injuries who resume work after injury at what the WDCA calls "reasonable employment." Mich. Comp. Laws § 418.301(5)-(9); *McJunkin v. Cellasto Plastic Corp.*, 461 Mich. 590 (2000).

(a)   Definition of Reasonable Employment

The WDCA defines "reasonable employment," as work: 1) "that is within the employee's capacity to perform that poses no clear and proximate threat to that employee's health and safety"; and 2) that "is within a reasonable distance from that employee's residence." Mich. Comp. Laws § 418.301(9).

"Reasonable employment" is a statutory term of art that includes work tailored to accommodate restrictions resulting from a work injury. *Id.; McJunkin v. Cellasto Plastic Corp.*, 461 Mich. 590 (2000). "Reasonable employment" is post-injury work that a "disabled" employee can perform.

(3)   Bona Fide Offer

In summary, an employee is not entitled to weekly wage loss benefits if the employee refuses a *bona fide* offer of reasonable employment "without good and reasonable cause." Mich. Comp. Laws § 418.301(5)(a).

(a)   Reasonable Distance

But, to be "*bona fide*," the offer of reasonable employment must be an offer of work "within a reasonable distance from that employee's residence." Mich. Comp. Laws § 418.301(9). For example, an employer's offer to an employee of work in another state than Michigan would not be considered "within a reasonable distance" of the employee's residence in Michigan while working for the employer in Michigan. In that event, the offer would not be *bona fide* and the employee can refuse it without any legal repercussions, such as forfeiting weekly wage loss benefits.

(4)   Compensation Based on Wage at Date of Injury

An employee who labors at post-injury reasonable employment for less than 100 weeks and who loses his job will receive compensation based upon his wage at the injury's original date. Mich. Comp. Laws § 418.301(5)(e); *Russell v. Whirlpool Fin. Corp.*, 461 Mich. 579 (2000). For example, although an employee's cessation of work results from his employer's plant closing, Michigan law protects his right to weekly compensation when he loses this job after having performed less than 100 weeks of "reasonable employment" for the employer.

D.   Death Benefits

If the covered injury causes death, then certain surviving dependents of the deceased may be eligible for benefits. Mich. Comp. Laws § 418.301(1).

E.   Unemployment Compensation Benefits

Basically, an employee who is laid off due to no fault of his own may qualify to receive unemployment compensation benefits pursuant to the Michigan Employment Security Act (Act). The Michigan Employment Security Commission (Commission) administers the Act.

Unemployment compensation is an insurance benefit. Unemployment compensation benefits are distinct and separate from worker's compensation benefits. Generally, unemployment compensation benefit law is not directly testable and beyond this outline's scope. However, a past essay question examined the issue of whether an employee may simultaneously receive both unemployment compensation benefits and worker's compensation benefits.

1)   UNEMPLOYMENT AND WORKER'S COMPENSATION BENEFITS

a)   Employee May Receive Both Benefits Concurrently

Generally, an employee's receipt of unemployment compensation benefits does not preclude receipt of weekly worker's compensation benefits. The employee may receive both. Mich. Comp. Laws § 418.358; *Paschke v. Retool Indus.*, 445 Mich. 502 (1994). However, when an employee receives both benefits, the employee's weekly worker's compensation benefits are reduced dollar-for-dollar by the unemployment compensation benefits. Mich. Comp. Laws § 418.358.

b)   These Benefits are of Different Amounts and Durations

Usually, unemployment compensation benefits are much less than weekly worker's compensation benefits. Unemployment compensation benefits are limited in duration. In contrast, weekly worker's compensation benefits can continue for their recipient's lifetime.

c)   Effect of Refusal of Bona Fide Offer of Reasonable Employment

An insurance carrier must notify the Michigan Employment Security Commission (Commission), Michigan's Unemployment Insurance Agency, of any injured employee who is unemployed and to which the carrier is paying benefits under the WDCA. Mich. Comp. Laws § 418.301(6). The Commission must give priority to finding employment for unemployed, injured employees. Mich. Comp. Laws § 418.301(7). The Commission must provide the Bureau of Worker's Compensation (Bureau), which administers the WDCA, with written notice of any unemployed, injured employee who refuses any *bona fide* offer of reasonable employment, as addressed earlier. The Bureau must notify the carrier of this refusal. The carrier must terminate such employee's benefits under the WDCA. Mich. Comp. Laws § 418.301(8).

VI.   PROCEDURE

A.   Notice

An injured employee must give notice of an injury to the employer within 90 days of the occurrence of injury, "or within 90 days after the employee knew, or should have known, of the injury." Mich. Comp. Laws § 418.381(1).

The employee should notify his or her employer of the employee's injury or illness either verbally or in writing. *Id.* If the employer fails to report the injury to the Bureau of Worker's Compensation, the employee can file a written claim with the Bureau on the prescribed form. *Id.* If the employer disputes the claim for benefits, the claimant may seek a determination of the claim pursuant to an administrative hearing before a magistrate.

★   **B.   Statute of Limitations**

A claim must be initially brought within two years from the date of injury or of death. Mich. Comp. Laws § 418.381(1).

C.   Burden of Proof

The burden of proof is on the employee to establish the employee's entitlement to worker's compensation and benefits by a preponderance of the evidence. Mich. Comp. Laws § 418.851.

D.   Appeals

The determination made after an administrative hearing before a magistrate can be appealed to the Worker's Compensation Appellate Commission. The Commission's decision can be appealed to the Michigan Court of Appeals. That court's decision can be appealed to the Michigan Supreme Court.

AMERIBAR BAR REVIEW

Michigan Bar Review

MBE Subject Distinctions & Common Issues

CONSTITUTIONAL LAW

Commonly Tested Issues

★★★

- 1st Amendment – Freedom of Speech
- 14th Amendment – Equal Protection Clause
- 14th Amendment – Incorporation Doctrine
- 1st Amendment – Content Regulation

★★

- 1st Amendment – Public Forum
- 1st Amendment – Vagueness/Overbreadth

★

- Article I – Commerce Clause
- Article I – *Ex Post Facto* Laws
- Article II – Presidential Authority
- Article III – Standing
- 1st Amendment – Non-public Forum
- 1st Amendment – Prior Restraint
- 1st Amendment – Obscene, Profane, or Indecent Speech
- 4th Amendment – Sobriety Checkpoints
- 14th Amendment – Right to Vote
- 14th Amendment – Right to Travel

TABLE OF CONTENTS

CONSTITUTIONAL LAW

Michigan Common Issues and Distinctions

The following outline is based on analysis of questions on the essay portion of the Michigan Bar Exam. The outline may address general legal principles and Michigan-specific rules. The general rules may be identical to those covered in your outlines for the Multistate Bar Exam ("MBE"). To the extent that this outline repeats identical rules covered in your MBE outline, such repetition is provided for the beneficial purposes of 1) learning how the rules are construed, applied, and tested in Michigan, and 2) learning which rules are tested most often on the essay portion of the examination (most topics appearing in this outline have appeared on a recent administration of the essay portion of the exam). Moreover, these general rules are sometimes stated in different ways by Michigan's courts. The general rules, along with any unique provisions of Michigan law (Michigan distinctions), are presented in the manner that Michigan's bar examiners view them with respect to analyzing essay questions on previously tested issues of law.

THIS OUTLINE IS NOT A COMPLETE OUTLINE OF CONSTITUTIONAL LAW FOR THE ESSAY PORTION OF THE MICHIGAN BAR EXAMINATION. It is designed to be used conjunction with your MBE outline. Any essay questions testing topics of MBE subjects that are not covered in this outline should be answered according to the law you have learned for the MBE.

The essay portion of the Michigan Bar Exam includes Constitutional Law as a separately testable subject. Traditionally, one of these questions has appeared on each exam or every other exam, although the frequency of testing in the past may not be the same going forward. Previously, somewhat frequently tested issues include freedom of speech and equal protection.

Facts and rules derived from cases decided by the Michigan appellate courts and federal appellate courts have provided the basis for some of the facts and/or rules for certain past Constitutional Law questions and answers. The Federal Constitution and Michigan Constitution are other sources for tested rules as well. Although the sample answers for certain past questions indicate that some Michigan law and court cases should be the basis for answering questions, future questions could be answerable using controlling general legal principles covered in the MBE outline for Constitutional Law.

I.   FIRST AMENDMENT

The First Amendment to the United States Constitution provides for freedom of speech and expression. Part of the First Amendment provides, "Congress shall make no law . . . abridging the freedom of speech." U.S. Const. amend. I. The analogous provision in the Michigan Constitution provides that "[e]very person may freely speak, write, express and publish his views on all subjects, being responsible for the abuse of such right; and no law shall be enacted to restrain or abridge the liberty of speech or of the press." Mich. Const. art. I, § 5.

A.   Regulation of Content

The First Amendment (as under the Fourteenth Amendment applied to the states) restricts most forms of "content control" for speech. Unless speech is "less protected" because it is commercial (intermediate) or unprotected (fighting words, incitement to violence), content controls are presumed invalid.

1)   PUBLIC FORUM

Even in public forums though, time, place and manner ("TPM") restrictions are allowed, as long as they are content and viewpoint neutral, leave alternative opportunities for the speech to take place and are narrowly tailored to serve a significant state interest. Public forums are those public areas traditionally set aside for exercise of First Amendment rights. As a public forum, no content or viewpoint restrictions are allowed.

a)   Speech in Courtroom

Speech or expression that is restricted because of the content of the message it conveys is subject to the most exacting scrutiny. The content of speech in a courtroom may only be restricted if it constitutes an imminent threat to the administration of justice. The danger must not be remote or even probable; it must immediately imperil the administration of justice. *In re Contempt of Dudzinski,* 257 Mich. App. 96 (2003).

2)   NON-PUBLIC FORUM

Non-public forums may regulate by content, but not viewpoint.

3)   COMMERCIAL SPEECH

Commercial speech does not receive the same scope of protection as expressive speech or political speech. *Rochester Hills v. Schultz,* 459 Mich. 486 (1999). Still, commercial speech receives constitutional protection from unwarranted governmental regulation. *Id.*

a)   Analytical Test of Constitutionality of Regulation

Four factors are considered when determining whether commercial speech is unconstitutionally regulated:

- the speech is not misleading and concerns lawful activity;
- a substantial governmental interest justifies the government's restriction;
- the governmental interest is directly advanced by the regulation; and
- the regulation is wider than necessary to serve the governmental interest. *Id.*

b)   Open Communication Channels Serve to Inform People

The protection afforded speech by the First Amendment to the United States Constitution is based on the notion that "people will perceive their own best interests if only they are well enough informed, and that the best means to that end is to open the channels of communication rather than to close them." *Id.* quoting *Virginia Pharmacy Bd. v. Virginia Citizens Consumer Council*, 425 U.S. 748 (1976).

B.   Vagueness

Statutes are presumed constitutional, and "courts have a duty to construe a statute as constitutional unless unconstitutionality is clearly apparent. A statute may be unconstitutionally vague and in violation of the Due Process Clause of the Fourteenth Amendment if: (1) it does not provide fair notice of the conduct proscribed; (2) it confers on the trier of fact unstructured and unlimited discretion to determine whether an offense has been committed; and (3) its coverage is overly broad and impinges on First Amendment freedoms." Vagueness challenges not involving First Amendment freedoms are analyzed in light of the facts of the particular case. *In re Gosnell*, 234 Mich. App. 326 (1999).

1)   ADEQUATE NOTICE

The State of Michigan has a statute that provides that a Michigan district court judge, in order to preserve the public peace, could, after a hearing, require a person to post a bond to conserve the peace as required by the laws of the state. The statute provided that the court could require security for up to two years, incarcerate an individual for that period for failure to provide the ordered security or for violation of the provisions of the bond. Provisions were made for a hearing to determine if the individual could afford to post security and provided various criteria for the court to follow concerning this issue. The statute further provided that upon receipt of a complaint under oath that a person has threatened to commit an offense against the person or property of another, the court was to examine the complainant under oath and any witnesses before ordering any bond be posted.

The Michigan Court of Appeals has held that the portion of that statute, which provides "to commit an offense against the person or property of another" gives adequate notice of the prohibited conduct. The Court interpreted this verbiage to involve some threat of personal violence and that a person of ordinary intelligence is provided a reasonable opportunity to know what is prohibited.

The Michigan Court of Appeals has approved a sentence imposed in a criminal matter in excess of the Michigan district courts' jurisdictional limit of one year on the basis that the duty to keep the peace is separate and distinct from the performance of ordinary judicial functions. The Michigan Constitution provides and requires such judges to be conservators of the peace and, based upon this authority, Michigan district courts can sentence under such a statute beyond the one-year period.

2) MICHIGAN ANTI-TERRORISM ACT

The Michigan Anti-Terrorism Act (Act) criminalizes communicating to any other person a serious expression of intent to commit an act of terrorism. Particularly, the Act criminalizes communicating to any other person a serious expression of an intent to commit a "willful and deliberate act" constituting "a violent felony" under Michigan law, which the communicator "has reason to know is dangerous to human life," and is "intended to intimidate or coerce a civilian population or influence or affect the conduct of government." Mich. Comp. Laws § 750.543a *et seq.*

a) General Constitutionality

The Michigan Court of Appeals sustained the Anti-Terrorism Act of Michigan as constitutional as against challenges based on freedom of speech, vagueness, and lack of notice of what constitutes criminal conduct. *People v. Osantowski*, 274 Mich. App. 593, 736 N.W.2d 289 (2007), reversed in part on other grounds, *People v. Osantowski*, No. 134244 (Mich. 05/07/2008) (reinstating trial court's sentencing points score and judgment of sentence).

The Court opined that true threats need not include an intent for direct intimidation of a specific victim, finding that fear of violence to others can engender disruption similar to the disruption engendered by fear of violence to oneself. The Court held that true threats of violence fall outside First Amendment protections even in the absence of direct victim intimidation.

The Court found that because the Act requires the existence of an intent to "intimidate or coerce," it extends beyond the type of speech or expressive conduct afforded protection by the First Amendment. The Act, by its terms, does not sweep within its ambit other activities that in ordinary circumstances constitute an exercise of freedom of speech.

b) Due Process of Law

The *Osantowski* court held that the Michigan Anti-Terrorism Act was constitutional: the Act did not violate the right to due process of law. The Court held that the meaning of the Act is readily ascertainable. Specifically, the Act criminalizes communicating a serious expression of an intent to commit a "willful and deliberate act" constituting "a serious felony" under Michigan law, which the communicator "has reason to know is dangerous to human life," and is "intended to intimidate or coerce a civilian population or influence or affect the government." The *Osantowski* court determined that based on this language and the definitions of the terms used, the Act affords a person of ordinary intelligence a reasonable opportunity to know what conduct or behavior is prohibited.

II.   FOURTH AMENDMENT

A.   Constitutionality of Sobriety Checkpoints

1)   MICHIGAN CONSTITUTIONAL LAW PROHIBITS SOBRIETY
CHECKPOINTS

a)   Unreasonable Searches and Seizures Prohibited

The Michigan Constitution of 1963 prohibits unreasonable searches and seizures. It states that:

> The person, houses, papers and possessions of every person shall be secure from
> unreasonable searches and seizures. No warrant to search any place or to seize
> any person or things shall issue without describing them, nor without probable
> cause, supported by oath or affirmation.

Mich. Const. 1963, art I, § 11.

b)   Interpretation of Federal and Michigan Constitutions

Although that provision resembles text of the Fourth Amendment of the United States
Constitution, they are not identical. Michigan courts must interpret the Michigan Constitution
independent of the protections and rights provided in the United States Constitution. In the event
of a conflict of competing rights under the Michigan and federal constitutions, the Supremacy
Clause of the United States Constitution dictates that the federal right prevails. *Sitz v. Dept. of
State Police*, 443 Mich. 744 (1993) (*Sitz II*) citing U.S. Const. art. VI, cl. 2.

When the United States Constitution provides a right, it does not necessarily follow that a state
constitution must be construed as providing the same right. *Id.* Because these respective
constitutions were written by different people at different times, the protections afforded under
each constitution may be greater, lesser, or the same. *Id.* Michigan courts are not required to
accept what is considered a major contradiction of citizen protections under the Michigan
Constitution simply because the United States Supreme Court has done that in its construction of
the United States Constitution. *Id.*

The prohibition against unreasonable searches and seizures found in the Michigan Constitution
should "be construed to provide the same protection as that secured by the Fourth Amendment,
absent 'compelling reason' to impose a different interpretation." *People v. Collins*, 438 Mich. 8
(1991).   A compelling reason exists where there is a "principled basis in this history of
[Michigan] jurisprudence for the creation of new rights." *Sitz II, supra.*

c)   Michigan Constitution's Protection from Sobriety Checkpoints

Compelling reasons exist to interpret the Michigan Constitution to provide greater protection
than that afforded under the Fourth Amendment to the United States Constitution with respect to
sobriety checkpoints.   *Id.*   Historically, Michigan courts have interpreted the Michigan

Constitution to: 1) provide the people traveling on public roadways the fullest legal protection available; and 2) distinguish between searches and seizures made for regulatory or administrative purposes from searches and seizures involving criminal investigations. *Id.*, at 775, citing *Pinkerton v. Verberg*, 78 Mich. 573 (1889). In Michigan, "seizures with the primary goal of enforcing criminal law have generally required some level of suspicion." *Id.*

(1)   Reasonable Cause Required; Limits on Stops and Searches

Generally, an officer must have reasonable cause to stop or search cars operated on Michigan's public roadways. *E.g., People ex rel Attorney Gen. v. Lansing Mun. Judge*, 327 Mich. 410 (1950) (finding unconstitutional a statute that allowed certain warrantless searches, including some involving automobiles); *People v. Stein*, 265 Mich. 610 (1933) ("[i]f conditions demand a special rule of search on highways, the remedy is by amendment of the [Michigan] Constitution"); *People v. Roache*, 237 Mich. 215 (1927) ("[n]o one will contend that an officer may promiscuously stop automobiles upon the public highway and demand the driver's license merely as a subterfuge to invade the constitutional right of the traveler to be secure against unreasonable search and seizure."); *People v. Kamhout*, 227 Mich. 172 (1924) (officers "have no right to stop and search an automobile . . . for the purpose of ascertaining whether it is being used [to further illegal activity] unless they have . . . reasonable grounds of suspicion . . . as would induce in any prudent man, an honest belief that the law is being violated").

d)   Michigan's Constitution Protects More than Federal Constitution

Michigan's jurisprudence and constitutional history gives a compelling reason to construe the prohibition against unreasonable searches and seizures contained in the Michigan Constitution more broadly than the protection afforded under the Fourth Amendment to the United States Constitution. Thus, sobriety checkpoints violate the Michigan Constitution. *Spitz II, supra.*

2)   FEDERAL CONSTITUTIONAL LAW ALLOWS SOBRIETY CHECKPOINTS

a)   Unreasonable Searches and Seizures Prohibited

The Fourth Amendment to the United States Constitution prohibits unreasonable searches and seizures made without a warrant issued upon probable cause. An exception to the warrant requirement applies to permit searches or seizures of cars when probable cause exists to believe that a lawfully stopped vehicle contains evidence of a crime or contraband. *Florida v. White*, 526 U.S. 559 (1999). The Fourteenth Amendment to the United States Constitution extends to the various states the protections afforded by the Fourth Amendment.

b)   Reasonableness of Warrantless Seizure without Probable Cause

A state can plan to stop every vehicle at a designated place and time in order to investigate whether the driver is intoxicated and operating the vehicle. Such stops at a sobriety checkpoint, regardless of duration, constitute seizures under the Fourth Amendment. *United States v. Martinez-Fuerte*, 428 U.S. 543 (1976) (Fourth Amendment "seizure" happens when a vehicle is stopped at an illegal alien checkpoint). If no warrant is issued allowing such seizures and probable cause does not exist to justify that police action, then the key issue about the constitutionality of such a sobriety checkpoint under the Fourth Amendment is the warrantless activity's reasonableness. *Michigan State Police v. Sitz*, 496 U.S. 444 (1990).

(1)   Balancing Test Applies to Determine Reasonableness

When determining a warrantless seizure's reasonableness under the Fourth Amendment, courts apply a three-part balancing test:

- the state's interest in preventing accidents caused by drunk drivers;
- the level of delay and intrusion imposed upon motorists going through the checkpoint; and
- the effectiveness of sobriety checkpoints in accomplishing the state's goal.

Brown v. Texas, 443 U.S. 47 (1979).

After applying these three factors in a Michigan sobriety checkpoint case, the United States Supreme Court determined that roadside sobriety testing does not offend the Fourth Amendment to the United States Constitution. The Court analyzed the facts using those three factors as follows.

First, states possess a "grave and legitimate" interest in controlling drunk driving because of all the highway deaths caused by intoxicated drivers. *Sitz, supra.*

Second, the level of delay and intrusion imposed upon motorists passing through the checkpoint was reasonable. The Supreme Court stated, "the circumstances surrounding a checkpoint stop and search are far less intrusive than those attending a roving patrol stop. Roving patrols often operate at night on seldom-traveled roads, and their approach may frighten motorists. At traffic checkpoints, the motorist can see that other vehicles are being stopped, he can see visible signs of the officers' authority, and he is much less likely to be frightened or annoyed by the intrusion." *Sitz, supra*, quoting *People v. Ortiz*, 422 U.S. 891 (1975).

Third, sobriety checkpoints provide an effective means of advancing the state's interests to diminish drunk driving. Local "governmental officials are entitled to deference because of their "unique understanding of, and a responsibility for, limited public resources, including a finite number of police officers." *Id.*

III.   FOURTEENTH AMENDMENT

A.   Equal Protection Clause

Under the Equal Protection Clause of the Fourteenth Amendment to the United States Constitution, no state shall "deny to any person . . . the equal protection of the law." U.S. Const. amend. XIV. Applied to the states pursuant to the incorporation doctrine, the Fourteenth Amendment is the "vehicle" for extending constitutional safeguards.

1)   STRICT SCRUTINY

For fundamental rights and protections, the state is subject to a higher burden to justify any regulations. This burden is known as "strict scrutiny" and requires regulation to be narrowly tailored and necessary for a compelling government interest. The government must prove that the law is necessary to achieve a compelling interest.

        a)   Right to Vote

The United States Constitution and courts seek to protect the right to vote, that is, the right to "influence elections."

        b)   Right to Travel

Individuals have the right to move from one state to another, and state laws that have the effect of hindering this right will require a strong government justification.

2)   RATIONAL BASIS

The Equal Protection Clause is implicated when the state decides to treat people differently. For most types of regulation--economic, business and general regulatory--differences are tested under the rational basis test, requiring "any rational reason" from the state. Under the rational basis test, the petitioner must prove that the law lacks a rational basis and is unrelated to any legitimate objective.

        a)   Classification by Age

The Michigan Constitution contains a provision that "no person shall be elected or appointed to a judicial office after reaching the age of 70 years." Mich. Const. art 6, § 19. This provision is similar to a mandatory retirement provision that the United States Supreme Court held did not violate the Equal Protection Clause. *Gregory v. Ashcroft,* 501 U.S. 452; 111 S. Ct. 2395; 115 L. Ed. 2d 410 (1991). The *Gregory v. Ashcroft* case addressed a provision of the Missouri Constitution, which states that "all judges other than municipal judges shall retire at the age of 70 years." *Id.*

Such a classification based on age is not a suspect classification under the Equal Protection Clause. Therefore, the appropriate standard of review is the "rational basis test." *Id.*

In cases where the classification burdens neither a suspect class nor a fundamental interest, courts are reluctant to overturn government action on the grounds that it denies equal protection of the laws. The government action can be a constitutional provision like the one requiring that judges retire, which reflects the judgment of the Michigan Legislature that proposed it as well as that of the Michigan citizens who voted for it.

Under the rational basis test, the provision challenged will not be overturned "unless the varying treatment of different groups or persons is so unrelated to the achievement of legitimate purposes that we can only conclude that the [people's] actions were irrational." *Id.* In *Gregory*, the Supreme Court found that the state of Missouri had a legitimate--compelling--interest in maintaining a judiciary capable of performing the demanding tasks that judges must perform. The court found the mandatory retirement provision to be rationally related to that interest, noting that physical and mental capacity can diminish with age.

The fact that a judge who challenges such a law is physically and mentally fit is not sufficient to nullify the provision. A state does not violate the Equal Protection Clause merely because the classifications made by its laws are flawed. The person challenging the provision must show that the facts on which the classification is based could not reasonably be construed as legitimate by the decision maker.

IV.   ARTICLE ONE

A.   Commerce Clause

The Commerce Clause of Article I of the United States Constitution provides in part that Congress has the power: "To regulate Commerce . . . among the several States." U.S. Const. art. I, § 8, para. 3.

1)   DISCRIMINATORY REGULATION

The Commerce Clause precludes any state from imposing laws that pose an undue burden on interstate commerce or prevent the free flow of interstate commerce. In *Granholm v. Heald*, the United States Supreme Court stated:

> [I]n all but the narrowest circumstances, state laws violate the Commerce Clause if they mandate 'differential treatment of in-state and out-of-state economic interests that benefits the former and burdens the latter.' *Oregon Waste Systems, Inc v. Department of Environmental Quality of Ore*, 511 U.S. 93, 99 (1994). *See also New Energy Co of Ind v. Limbach*, 486 U.S. 269, 274 (1988) . . . The mere fact of non-residence should not foreclose a producer in one State from access to markets in other States. *HP Hood & Sons, Inc. v. Du Mond*, 336 U.S. 525, 539 (1949).

Granholm v. Heald, 544 U.S. 460, 472 (2005).

The Court also stated: "State laws that discriminate against interstate commerce face 'a virtually *per se* rule of invalidity.'" *Heald*, p. 476, quoting *Philadelphia v. New Jersey*, 437 U.S. 617, 624 (1978). Further, the Court stated "we still must consider whether either State regime 'advances a legitimate local purpose that cannot be adequately served by reasonable nondiscriminatory alternatives. The burden is on the state." *Heald*, p. 489.

> Our Commerce Clause cases demand more than mere speculation to support discrimination against out-of-state goods. The 'burden is on the State to show that

"the discrimination is demonstrably justified,'" *Chemical Waste Management, Inc v. Hunt,* 504 U.S. 334, 344 (1992) (emphasis in original). The Court has upheld state regulations that discriminate against interstate commerce only after finding, based on concrete record evidence, that a State's nondiscriminatory alternatives will prove unworkable. *See, e.g., Maine v. Taylor,* 477 U.S. 131, 141-144 (1986).

Heald, p. 492.

B.   Ex Post Facto Laws

The prohibition of the enactment of *ex post facto* laws by a state is found in the United States Constitution, art. 1, § 10, cl. 1. The prohibition of the enactment of *ex post facto* laws by the Michigan Legislature is found in the Michigan Constitution, art 1, § 10. An *ex post facto* law has been defined as:

> "Every law that makes an action done before the passing of the law, and which was innocent when done, criminal; and punishes such action. Every law that aggravates a crime, or makes it greater than it was, when committed. Every law that changes the punishment, and inflicts a greater punishment, than the law annexed to the crime, when committed. Every law that alters the legal rules of evidence, and receives less, or different, testimony, than the law required at the time of the commission of the offense (sic) in order to convict the offender."

Carmell v. Texas, 529 U.S. 513; 146 L. Ed. 2d 577; 120 S. Ct. 1620 (2000), citing *Calder v. Bull,* 3 U.S. 386, 390.

For example, a law that reduces the quantum of evidence required to convict an individual of a criminal offense is *ex post facto.* Also, a law that retroactively eliminates an element of the offense increases the punishment for an existing offense, or lowers the burden of proof is an *ex post facto* law. *People v. Dolph-Hostettler,* Lawyers Weekly 07-48860.

V.   ARTICLE TWO

A.   Presidential Authority

Generally, either the United States Constitution or an act of Congress may authorize the President of the United States to take certain types of action.

1)   LIMITED ROLE IN LAWMAKING PROCESS

The Constitution limits a President's role in the lawmaking process to: 1) the recommending of laws that the President thinks wise; and 2) the vetoing of laws that the President thinks bad. *Youngstown Sheet & Tube Co. v. Sawyer,* 343 U.S. 579 (1952). The President may request that Congress enact laws. *Id.* The President may not direct that Congress execute a presidential policy in a way that the President prescribes. *Id.*

2) EMERGENCY POWERS

The President has some residual emergency powers not explicitly stated in the Constitution. Such powers can allow the President to, for example, order the Secretary of Agriculture to divert the federal funds appropriated for one food-related industry to another comparable industry. *U.S. v. Bishop*, 555 F.2d 771 (Ct. App. 10, 1977). When presidential emergency powers are recognized, however, the emergency is much more urgent than dietary concerns. *CJS*, War Powers of the President, § 54.

VI. ARTICLE THREE

A. Standing

Article III of the United States Constitution provides for the adjudication of "cases or controversies" only. U.S. Const. art. III, § 2. This is a jurisdictional requirement that either a court or the parties in a case may raise at any time during the proceedings. Standing is a threshold question that the federal courts consider before adjudicating a civil legal proceeding.

Standing is found when: 1) the plaintiff suffers an injury in fact, that is concrete and specific to the plaintiff; 2) the harm is "fairly traceable" to the government's action; and 3) the court has power to redress (i.e., remedy) the injury.

CONTRACTS

Commonly Tested Issues

★★★★

- ⬇ Breach of Contract

★★★

- ⬇ UCC – Sales of Goods
- ⬇ UCC – Statute of Frauds
- ⬇ Defenses – Statute of Frauds

★★

- ⬇ Formation – Consideration
- ⬇ Defenses – Waiver
- ⬇ UCC – Express Warranty
- ⬇ UCC – Implied Warranties
- ⬇ UCC – Installment Contract
- ⬇ UCC – Perfect Tender Rule
- ⬇ UCC – Revocation of Acceptance
- ⬇ UCC – Delegation and Assignment
- ⬇ Missing Price Term
- ⬇ Impracticability
- ⬇ Frustration of Purpose
- ⬇ Anticipatory Repudiation
- ⬇ Specific Performance
- ⬇ Condition Precedent
- ⬇ Damages
- ⬇ Cancellation
- ⬇ Rescission and Reformation

★

- ⬇ Intended Third-Party Beneficiary
- ⬇ Pre-existing Duty Rule
- ⬇ Accord and Satisfaction
- ⬇ Employment Contract
- ⬇ Noncompetition Agreement
- ⬇ Substituted Agreement
- ⬇ Adhesion Contract
- ⬇ UCC – Requirements Contract
- ⬇ UCC – Exclusive Dealings Contract
- ⬇ UCC – Rejection for Substantial Nonconformity

TABLE OF CONTENTS

CONTRACTS

Michigan Common Issues and Distinctions

The following outline is based on analysis of questions on the essay portion of the Michigan Bar Exam. The outline may address general legal principles and Michigan-specific rules. The general rules may be identical to those covered in your outlines for the Multistate Bar Exam ("MBE"). To the extent that this outline repeats identical rules covered in your MBE outline, such repetition is provided for the beneficial purposes of 1) learning how the rules are construed, applied, and tested in Michigan, and 2) learning which rules are tested most often on the essay portion of the examination (most topics appearing in this outline have appeared on a recent administration of the essay portion of the exam). Moreover, these general rules are sometimes stated in different ways by Michigan's courts. The general rules, along with any unique provisions of Michigan law (Michigan distinctions), are presented in the manner that Michigan's bar examiners view them with respect to analyzing essay questions on previously tested issues of law.

THIS OUTLINE IS NOT A COMPLETE OUTLINE OF CONTRACTS LAW FOR THE ESSAY PORTION OF THE MICHIGAN BAR EXAMINATION. It is designed to be used conjunction with your MBE outline. Any essay questions testing topics of MBE subjects that are not covered in this outline should be answered according to the law you have learned for the MBE.

The essay portion of the Michigan Bar Exam includes Contracts as a separately testable subject. Traditionally, at least one and sometimes two Contracts questions has appeared on each exam, although this frequency of testing in the past may not be the same going forward. As with the corresponding MBE Contracts outline, this outline includes some of both general legal principles of contract law as well as rules from Article 2 of the Uniform Commercial Code ("UCC" or Code) regarding sales. These Article 2 rules are typically testable in both Contracts questions and UCC questions. Some of these rules also have been examined in Real & Personal Property questions.

Traditionally, one UCC question usually has appeared in the essay portion of one of the two Michigan Bar Exams administered each year. Previously, several of those questions have focused upon UCC Article 2 regarding sales, although questions to which UCC Article 3 applies may be asked. Issues related to Article 9 also are subject to being tested on the Exam.

Facts and rules derived from cases decided by the Michigan appellate courts and certain federal courts have provided the basis for some past Contracts and UCC questions and answers. The Michigan Compiled Laws is another source for tested rules as well. Although the sample answers for certain past questions indicate that Michigan statutes and court cases should be the basis for answering questions, future questions could be answerable using controlling general legal principles and UCC provisions contained in the outlines.

According to some past exams, some types of frequently tested issues include breach of contract and sales of goods. Some other less frequently tested issues include warranties, installment contracts, anticipatory repudiation, and missing price term. Some infrequently tested issues include the statute of frauds, impracticability, frustration of purpose, custom goods, anticipatory repudiation, damages, specific performance, and cancellation. Some occasionally tested issues involve formation, rescission, accord and satisfaction, certain types of contracts (both generally and under the UCC), contractual limitation of remedies, battle of the forms, liquidated damages, "lost volume" seller, lost profits, good faith, modification, and waiver.

I.   GENERAL CONTRACT LAW

A.   Consideration

The enforceability of a contract depends upon consideration and not mutuality of obligation. Consideration for a contract can consist of a benefit conferred upon third parties pursuant to a request by one of the contracting parties. *Plastray Corp. v. Cole*, 324 Mich. 433 (1949). Moreover, when one of the types of consideration fails, but another one survives, the surviving consideration will usually sustain the parties' agreement. *Nichols v. Seaks*, 296 Mich. 154 (1941).

B.   Statute of Frauds

1)   GENERAL RULE

The statute of frauds generally provides that an agreement, contract, or promise is void unless that agreement, contract, or promise or a note or memorandum of the agreement contract, or promise is in writing and signed with an authorized signature by the party to be charged with the agreement, contract, or promise which from its terms is not to be performed within one year from the making of the agreement.

One federal court, for example, decided that under Michigan law, an endorsed check was a sufficient writing to satisfy the statute of frauds. *Adell Broadcasting Corp. v. Cablevision Indus.*, 854 F. Supp. 1280 (E.D. Mich. 1994) (decided when no published Michigan cases existed on this issue).

2)   EQUITABLE ESTOPPEL

The doctrine of equitable estoppel has been used by the Michigan Supreme Court as an exception to the statute of frauds. *Kelly Stehney & Assocs., Inc. v. MacDonald's Indus. Prods., Inc.*, 254 Mich. App. 608 (2002) recognizing *Opdyke Inv. Co. v. Norris Grain Co.*, 413 Mich. 354 (1982). Equitable estoppel may arise where (1) a party, by representations, admissions, or silence intentionally or negligently induces another party to believe facts, (2) the other party justifiably relies and acts on that belief, and (3) the other party is prejudiced if the first party is allowed to deny the existence of those facts.

3)   MODIFICATION OF AGREEMENT

Generally, where an original contract was required to be made in writing, under the statute of frauds, any modification of the agreement should also be in writing.

a)   Waiver

Courts have concluded, however, that a clause in a contract stating that it cannot be orally modified is not necessarily binding. Parties to a contract are free to mutually waive or modify their contract, notwithstanding a written modification or anti-waiver clause. A waiver of this provision in the contract is proven through clear and convincing evidence of a written agreement, oral agreement or affirmative conduct establishing mutual agreement to modify or waive the provisions in the original contract. A party may not unilaterally alter the original contract. To establish a waiver, mere silence is not enough and the party claiming the waiver must produce clear and convincing evidence that the parties mutually agreed to modify or waive their contract. Even if there is no written modification, as a practical matter affirmative conduct may be considered as evidence tending to establish a mutual agreement to modify the original contract.

(1)   Failure

"A party's failure to object to the terms of a modification of an agreement within a reasonable time is an indication that the parties agreed to the modification." *Evans v. F. J. Boutell Driveway Co., Inc.,* 48 Mich. App. 411 (1973).

C.   Conditions

1)   CONDITIONS PRECEDENT

A condition precedent is a condition that must be met by one party before the other party is obligated to perform. When a contract is subject to the occurrence of a future event, there is an implied agreement that the promisor will place no obstacle in the way of the happening of such event.

A condition precedent consists of "a fact or event that the parties intend must take place before there is a right of performance." *Mikonczyk v. Detroit Newspapers,* 238 Mich. App. 347 (1999). No cause of action results from a failure to perform due to the non-fulfillment of a condition precedent. *Berkel & Co. v. Christman Co.,* 210 Mich. App. 416 (1995). A condition precedent contains an implied agreement "that the promisor will place no obstacle in the way of the happening of such event." *Mehling v. Evening News Assn.,* 374 Mich. 349 (1965). This type of obstacle generally involves a refusal to take action pursuant to the contract or some affirmative conduct. The condition will be discharged or excused when a party's conduct prevents occurrence of the condition. *Id.* at 352.

2)   CONDITIONS SUBSEQUENT

A condition subsequent is a condition that, if not met by one party, abrogates the other party's obligation to perform.

D.   Parol Evidence Rule and Exception

Usually, parol evidence of contemporaneous or prior negotiations or agreements is not admissible to contradict or vary the terms of an unambiguous written contract. The main exceptions to the parol evidence rule permit parol evidence to be admitted to prove that: 1) the parties did not intend the document to be a final and complete expression of their contract (a "fully integrated" agreement), or 2) the contract was not fully integrated because essential elements were not put in writing, or 3) the contract lacks legal effect due to illegality, fraud, or mistake. *NAG Enters., Inc. v. Allstate Indus., Inc.*, 407 Mich. 407 (1979).

Under Michigan law, extrinsic evidence is not permitted on the threshold question of whether the contract is integrated when the parties' contract contains an express merger clause stating that the written contract is the entire agreement. *UAW-GM Recreation Ctr. v. KSL Recreation Corp.*, 228 Mich. App. 486, 493 497 (1998). This goes along with the basic principle, underscored by Michigan courts, of honoring unambiguous contracts written by the parties for themselves and not making new agreements for them.

E.   Waiver of Breach of Contract

In Michigan, a party to a contract may waive the other party's breach thereof. A waiver is voluntary and intentional abandonment of a known right. *Roberts v. Mecosta Co. Hosp.*, 466 Mich. 57, 64 n. 4 (2002). A "waiver implies an intention to overlook a deficiency, or to forego a right to have the defect remedied or to have compensation therefore, and necessarily implies knowledge of the defect that is waived, or acquiescence under circumstances reasonably implying unconditional acceptance of the work as full performance." *Eaton v. Bladwell*, 108 Mich. 678, 680-681 (1896). However, a party may not unilaterally modify a contract by waiver. "This principle follows from the contract formation requirement that is elementary to the exercise of one's freedom to contract: mutual assent." *Quality Prods. and Concepts Co. v. Nagel Precision, Inc.*, 469 Mich. 362, 372 (2003). The mutuality requirement may be met by affirmative conduct establishing mutual agreement to waive the terms of the original contract. *Quality Prods., supra* at 374.

F.   Types of Agreements

1)   EMPLOYMENT CONTRACT

In Michigan, the terms of an employment application have been recognized as being a part of the employment contract between employer and employee and the fact this was found in the application for employment would not be a basis to avoid the application of the statute of limitations provision.

2)   NON-COMPETITION AGREEMENT

a)   Common Law

The common law of Michigan upheld non-competition agreements under what has been referred to as the rule of reason. This was defined in various ways but originally it was said that "if, considered with reference to the situation, business and objects of the parties, and in the light of all the surrounding circumstances with reference to which the contract was made, the restraint contracted for appears to have been for a just and honest purpose, for the protection of the legitimate interests of the party in whose favor it is imposed, reasonable as between them and not specifically injurious to the public, the restraint will be held valid." *Hubbard v. Miller,* 27 Mich. 15 (1873).

b)   Prior Statutory Law

There have been several changes in the common law, the first being a statute prohibiting non-competition agreements, irrespective of their reasonableness and declaring such agreements to be against public policy, illegal and void. This statute, however, has now been repudiated in the employment context by a statute that permits reasonable non-competition agreements, while subjecting any unreasonable terms to a "blue pencil" process by which the court endeavors to make the agreement reasonable in light of the circumstances in which it was made.

c)   Reasonable Approach

An argument has been made that the current statute only permits non-competition agreements between employer and employee, thereby invalidating other non-competition agreements. Such agreements are again to be considered void and illegal. The Court of Appeals in Michigan has rejected this argument and has essentially returned to the common law rule of reasonable approach to non-competition agreements that fall outside of the employment arena. The court, by statute, is authorized to limit the agreement to render it reasonable in light of the circumstances in which it was made.

d)   Duration

While there is no definitive period of time that a non-competition agreement can remain in effect, it is possible that a three-year period would be invalidated. The courts have upheld one-year periods as being reasonable. *Robert Half Int'l, Inc. v. Van Steenis,* 784 F. Supp. 1263 (1991).

e)   Geographic Range

A radius of 100 miles from the closest location could be upheld by the court. Anything beyond this distance would be questionable. A distance of 50 miles was held to be unreasonable in one case, but the reasonableness of both the time and distance is dependent on the facts of each case.

3)   ADHESION CONTRACT

The Michigan Supreme Court has dealt with the definition and application of law of an adhesive contract. *Rory v. Cont'l Ins.,* 473 Mich. 457 (2005). The term "adhesion contract" may be used to describe a contract for goods or services offered on a take-it-or-leave-it basis. But it may not be used as a justification for creating any adverse presumptions or for failing to enforce a contract as written.

The Court stated that it is of no legal relevance that a contract is or is not described as "adhesive." In either case, the contract is to be enforced according to its plain language. Regardless of whether a contract is adhesive, a court may not revise or void the unambiguous language of the agreement to achieve a result that it views as fairer or more reasonable.

Even before the Supreme Court limited the impact of a contract of adhesion, it had determined that a shortened statute of limitations to 180 days by agreement was not inherently unreasonable. Generally, the courts will not invalidate contracts as adhesion contracts where the challenged provision is not unreasonable.

4)   SUBSTITUTED AGREEMENT

Parties are free to execute a substituted agreement, which supersedes the terms of the original agreement.

G.   Defenses

1)   FRUSTRATION OF PURPOSE

The doctrines of frustration of purpose and supervening impossibility/ impracticability are related excuses for nonperformance of contractual obligations and are governed by similar principles.

There is Michigan case law to the effect that the frustration of purpose doctrine does not apply to errors in prediction as to future occurrences or non-occurrence. However, Michigan courts have shown a willingness to apply this doctrine under certain circumstances. To apply this doctrine: (1) a contract must be at least partially executory; (2) both parties must have known of the frustrated party's purpose in making the contract when they entered into it; and (3) an event must have thoroughly frustrated the contract's purpose that was foreseeable when the contract was made, and the event is not due to the frustrated party's fault, and the risk of which the party did not assume. *Liggett v. City of Pontiac*, 260 Mich. App. 127, 134-35 (2003).

2)   ACCORD AND SATISFACTION

a)   General Considerations

An accord and satisfaction can be used to discharge a contract. An "accord" is an agreement, which is substituted for the underlying contract. A "satisfaction" is the execution or performance of such new agreement. For there to be an accord and satisfaction, the tender must be accompanied by an explicit and clear condition indicating that, if the money is accepted, it is accepted in discharge of the whole claim. For example, placing on the check the statement "paid in full" does not, standing alone, affect an accord and satisfaction.

b)   Severance of Condition

If the creditor is fully informed of the condition accompanying acceptance, the creditor cannot sever from the acceptance the condition and claim the acceptance is not in full satisfaction of the debt.

c)   Burden of Proof

The burden of proving that there was an accord and satisfaction is on defendant.

3)   REMEDIES

a)   Liquidated Damages

(1)   General Considerations

Concerning liquidated damages, a court would begin by reviewing the contract, looking to the language used in its plan and ordinary meaning, avoiding constrained and technical interpretations. *UAW-GM Human Res. Ctr. v. KSL Recreation Corp.,* 228 Mich. App. 486, 491-492 (1998). Generally, parties to a contract may agree to the amount of damages that will be owed in the event of a breach. A contractual provision for liquidated damages is nothing more than agreement by the parties fixing the amount of damages. *Papo v. Aglo Restaurants of San Jose, Inc.,* 149 Mich. App. 285, 294 (1986). "The distinction between a valid liquidated damages clause and an illegal penalty depends on the relationship between the amount stipulated to in the liquidated damages clause and the subject matter of the cause of action." *Papo, supra* at 294.

(2)   Reasonableness

Courts are to sustain a provision for liquidated damages if the amount is reasonable in relation to the potential injury suffered and not unconscionable or excessive. *UAW-GM, supra* at 508. Parties are not permitted to stipulate unreasonable sums as damages. *Moore v. St. Clair Co.,* 120 Mich. App. 335, 340 (1982). The fact that the parties used the term "liquidated damages" as the title of the provision, and that the provision stated the payment was not a penalty, does not establish that the provision was valid. *Id.*

b)   Benefit of the Bargain

Benefit of the bargain damages for breach of land sale contract are measured by the difference between the agreed price and the land's value at the time of breach.

c)   Specific Performance

No specific performance of a land sale contract may occur when the property has been sold and conveyed to a good faith purchaser.

II.   UCC ARTICLE 2

A.   Exclusive Dealing Sales Contract

The UCC provides that in an exclusive dealing sales contract, the seller is obligated to use its "best efforts" to sell--a more demanding standard than just good faith. The UCC states that "[a] lawful agreement by either the seller or the buyer for exclusive dealing in the kind of goods concerned imposes unless otherwise agreed an obligation by the seller to use best efforts to supply the goods and by the buyer to use best efforts to promote their sale." UCC § 2-306(2); Mich. Comp. Laws § 440.2306.

B.   Sales Contract

1)   BATTLE OF THE FORMS

As a practical matter, when each of the parties' two writings regarding their sales transaction, such as a buyer's purchase order and a seller's acknowledgement, contain an inconsistent and essential term such as price, no contract will be formed by these writings in the absence of any other definite and seasonable expression of acceptance. However, depending on the circumstances, there could be a contract by performance. If a court were to find that such a contract exists, then the price would be set by the UCC's "gap-filler," which provides for a reasonable price at the time of delivery.

The liberalized view of the UCC is that offer and acceptance should not be determined by formalities or who had the "last shot." Mich. Comp. Laws §§ 440.2204, .2207, .2305. Thus, most courts applying the Michigan Compiled Laws reject the idea that acceptance of delivered goods operates as acceptance of whatever writing was last put on the table because that is unlikely to reflect intent. Mich. Comp. Laws § 440.2207.

2)   PRICE TERM

a)   General Considerations

The failure to fix a price at the conclusion of the negotiations does not automatically render the contract unenforceable. Section 440.2305 of the Michigan Compiled Laws provides in pertinent part:

(1)   The parties if they so intend can conclude a contract for sale even though the price is not settled. In such a case the price is a reasonable price at the time for delivery if (a) nothing is said as to price; or (b) the price is left to be agreed by the parties and they fail to agree; or (c) the price is to be fixed in terms of some agreed market or other standard as set or recorded by third person or agency and it is not so set or recorded.

(2)   A price to be fixed by the seller or by the buyer means a price for him to fix in good faith.

(3)   When a price left to be fixed otherwise than by agreement of the parties fails to be fixed through fault of one party the other may at his option treat the contract as cancelled or himself fix a reasonable price."'(4)   Where, however, the parties intend not to be bound unless the price be fixed or agreed and it is not fixed or agreed there is no contract. In such a case the buyer must return any goods already received or if unable so to do must pay their reasonable value at the time of delivery and the seller must return any portion of the price paid on account.

The inability to use a market index due to its closing, for example, does not render an agreement unenforceable, but calls into place the Michigan Compiled Laws, which would require that the price be set at a "reasonable price." Mich. Comp. Laws § 440.2305(1)(c).

b)   Gap Filler

The Michigan Compiled Laws state that an implied contract is to be enforced using the Code's gap-fillers. Mich. Comp. Laws § 440.2207(3). A gap-filler in the Michigan Compiled Laws states that when the parties intend to contract but have not agreed to a price, the price is a reasonable price at the time and place of delivery. Mich. Comp. Laws § 440.2305. However, it is possible to say that no contract was intended when both of the parties had inconsistent views about the price, and neither was unreasonable in its beliefs. But then the Michigan Compiled Laws state that a buyer, unable to return the goods, must pay the reasonable value at the time of delivery. Mich. Comp. Laws § 440.2305(4). Although a price and value are different words, they probably mean the same thing here.

3)   TERMINATION

The UCC provides that a sales contract of indefinite duration--though terminable at will by either party--requires reasonable notification prior to termination. UCC § 2-309. The UCC states that in the absence of a specified duration in a sales contract the contract last for a reasonable time but "may be terminated at any time by either party." Mich. Comp. Laws § 440.2309. Note that the "[t]ermination of a contract by one party . . . requires that reasonable notification be received by the other party." Official Comment eight states that normal practice and good faith mean that notification should be effective so as to "give the other party reasonable time to seek a substitute arrangement."

4)   PERFECT TENDER RULE

a)   Rejection and Cancellation

Under the UCC, a buyer who has not yet "accepted" the goods has a right to reject delivery and cancel if the goods fail in any respect to conform to the contract. Hence, the first question with respect to this remedy is whether acceptance has occurred. Under the UCC, acceptance occurs when, after reasonable opportunity to inspect the goods, the buyer indicates that he will take or retain them or otherwise fails to make an effective rejection. If, for example, a court finds a buyer's discovery of the defect occurring a day after the good's delivery to constitute a timely initial inspection, then the buyer would have the right to reject and cancel.

If a court were to find that the buyer accepted the goods because the buyer discovered the defect too late, then the buyer would have to revoke that acceptance in order to get the buyer's money back. As further addressed later, a buyer can revoke an acceptance if the defect substantially impairs its value to the buyer and the acceptance was reasonably induced by the difficulty of discovering the defect.

The UCC's so-called "perfect tender" rule creates a broad right of rejection prior to acceptance, subject only to limited "right to cure" as stated in the UCC. UCC §§ 2-508, 2-601; Mich. Comp. Laws § 440.2601.

The UCC defines acceptance in a number of ways, including failure "to make an effective rejection . . . but such opportunity does not occur until the buyer has had reasonable opportunity to inspect" the goods. UCC § 2-606; Mich. Comp. Laws § 440.2606.

b)   Revocation of Acceptance

Under the UCC, a buyer may prove a claim of revocation of an acceptance of goods (and seek cancellation and damages) by showing that:

- the buyer accepted goods "whose nonconformity substantially impairs" their value to the buyer;
- the buyer accepted them based on: 1) a reasonable assumption that the seller would cure the nonconformity; or 2) without discovering such nonconformity if the buyer's "acceptance was reasonably induced either by the difficulty of discovery before acceptance or the seller's assurances";
- the buyer's revocation of acceptance occurred within a reasonable time after the buyer discovered, or should have discovered, the grounds for revocation; and
- the buyer revoked before the occurrence of a substantial change in the condition of the goods, except as due to the nonconformity.

Mich. Comp. Laws § 440.2608.

(1)   Substantial Impairment

In certain circumstances, a buyer can make an effective revocation of acceptance for goods although their nonconformity does not substantially impair their monetary value. In that situation, "a buyer must show the nonconformity has a special devaluing effect on him and that the buyer's assessment of it is factually correct." *Colonial Dodge, Inc. v. Miller,* 420 Mich. 452 (1984). For example, a buyer could make a effective revocation of acceptance of a car that he purchased from a dealer, provided that: 1) the dealer failed to include a spare tire with the car; and 2) that failure had a special devaluing effect on the buyer because the buyer purchased special tires for the car and extensively used it. *Id.*

(2)   Reasonable Time

"The seller's attempts to repair are likewise a factor in determining whether the buyer notified the seller of revocation within a 'reasonable time' after discovering the defect." *Head v. Phillips Camper Sales & Rentals*, 234 Mich. App. 94 (1999) (buyer duly revoked acceptance of camper almost one year since purchase and after three attempted repairs).

(3)   Seller's Right to Cure

Most courts state that a seller lacks a right to cure when acceptance is properly revoked. *Id.*

c) Remedies

The UCC permits a buyer who rightfully rejects the goods or revokes acceptance to cancel the contract and seek a return of the purchase price (i.e., refund), among other things. UCC § 2-711; Mich. Comp. Laws § 440.2711.

5) DELEGATION, ASSIGNMENT, AND ETC.

The obligations under a contract for the sale of goods can be delegated to a third party without the consent of the other party unless the other party has a "substantial interest" in having the original party perform. A delegation does not relieve the delegating party of its obligations under the contract unless the other party to the contract agrees to release that party and substitute a new one (a novation). Merely consenting to a delegation does not create a novation.

a) Contract Rights and Obligations in the Sale of a Business

The status of contract rights and obligations in the sale of a business (or a part thereof) is an important business law issue. The UCC sets forth the basic applicable rules, which were summarized in the paragraph earlier in the outline and are further described in the following paragraphs. UCC § 2-210; Mich. Comp. Laws § 440.2210.

(1) Substantial Interest

First, under subsection one, obligations are presumptively delegable "unless the other party has a substantial interest in having his original promisor perform or control the acts required by the contract." Mich. Comp. Laws § 440.2210(1). Absent the existence of a substantial interest, courts are usually willing to facilitate the sale of a business by allowing the contractual obligations to be transferred to the buyer without the need for the other party's consent.

(2) Delegation

Subsection one then goes on to say that "[n]o delegation of performance relieves the party delegating of any duty to perform to any liability for breach." *Plastech Eng. Prod. v. Grand Haven Plastics*, 2005 WL 736519 (Mich. Ct. App. 2005).

(3) Novation

A party can seek the consent of the original party to a release and substitution--called a novation--but this requires express assent to the novation. Consenting to the delegation is not enough.

(4) Assignment

Subsection five states that a contractual assignment is typically treated as both an assignment of rights and a delegation of duties, "and its acceptance by the assignee constitutes a promise by him to perform those duties. This promise is enforceable by either the assignor or the other party to the original contract." Mich. Comp. Laws § 440.2210(5). In essence, the Code treats the other party as a third party beneficiary of the assignment and delegation.

C.   Installment Contracts

1)   REJECTION FOR SUBSTANTIAL NON-CONFORMITY

a)   An Installment

Article 2 of the UCC creates a special rule for installment contracts for goods. In contrast to the perfect tender rule that exists for single lot sales, the buyer's ability to reject a nonconforming delivery arises only when the nonconformity substantially impairs the value of that installment and cannot be cured.

b)   Entire Contract

As to the contract as a whole, the UCC is even more demanding. The defects in one installment must substantially impair the value of the whole contract for there to be grounds to cancel.

c)   Distinguished from Perfect Tender Rule

A section of the UCC and its official commentary make clear that, whatever the standards are for rejection in sales contracts generally (and the "perfect tender" rule normally does apply), installment contracts are treated differently. UCC § 2-612; Mich. Comp. Laws § 440.2612. A case demonstrating this is *Midwest Mobile Diagnostics v. Dynamics Corp. of Am.,* 965 F. Supp. 1003 (W.D. Mich. 1997). "The buyer may reject any installment which is non-conforming if the non-conformity substantially impairs the value of that installment and cannot be cured . . . but if the non-conformity does not fall within subsection (3) and the seller gives adequate assurances of its cure, the buyer must accept that installment." In turn, subsection (3) states that cancellation of the contract in its entirety is justifiable only if the non-conformity "substantially impairs the value of the whole contract." Case law has been relatively strict in applying the substantial performance standards when goods are to be delivered in installments.

d)   Good Faith

Note that using a minor defect as an excuse for escaping a bad bargain may itself operate as a violation of the UCC's good faith requirement.

D.   Statute of Frauds

1)   GENERAL RULE

Pursuant to the UCC's "statute of frauds," a contract for the sale of goods valued at more than $1,000 is *prima facie* unenforceable unless a sufficient written memorandum exists. Mich. Comp. Laws § 440.2201. Note that the "old" UCC statute of frauds used $500 as the cut off for what has to be in writing. Michigan and some other states have revised that figure. In Michigan's case, the amount is $1,000. *Id.*

a)   Exceptions

The UCC generally insists on a writing signed by the party to be charged. *Id.* However, the UCC does provide for a number of exceptions:

- If, within a reasonable time, a merchant sends a confirmation of the contract sufficient against the sender and the recipient has reason to know of its contents, but does not object to the confirmation within 10 days, then the sender can enforce it. Mich. Comp. Laws § 440.2201(2).

- The goods have been accepted and paid for by the buyer. Mich. Comp. Laws § 440.2201(3)(c).

- The buyer made an admission of the contract's existence. Mich. Comp. Laws § 440.2201(3)(b).

- The goods are to be specially manufactured for the buyer and not suitable for sale to others, and the seller has at least made a substantial beginning to their manufacture. Mich. Comp. Laws § 440.2201(3)(a).

The foregoing exception permits enforcement "if the goods are to be specially manufactured for the buyer and are not suitable for sale to others in the ordinary course of the seller's business and the seller, before notice of repudiation is received and under circumstances which reasonably indicate that the goods are for the buyer, has made either a substantial beginning to their manufacture or commitments for their procurement." *Webcor Packaging Corp. v. Autozone Inc.,* 158 F.2d 354 (CA 6, 1998); *SC Gray Inc. v. Ford Motor Co.,* 92 Mich. App. 789 (1979).

2)   PROMISSORY ESTOPPEL

There has been much litigation over whether, assuming the UCC denies enforceability of a particular contract, the aggrieved party can sue in equity--invoking the doctrine of promissory estoppel--to nonetheless recover. Michigan appears to fall into the category of jurisdictions that allow this. *Fairway Mach. Sales v. Cont'l Motors,* 40 Mich. App. 270 (1972).

3)   NO ORAL MODIFICATION CLAUSE

a)   Enforceability

No oral modification clauses are valid and enforceable. However, the UCC clearly provides that an attempt at modification may operate as a waiver. The UCC provides that a party who has made a waiver may retract it by reasonable notification, unless the retraction would be unjust in light of detrimental reliance on the waiver. Were the non-retracting party's reliance on the waiver severe enough, for example, there might even be an argument that the waiver is unretractable.

b)   Specific Provisions

The UCC states that a "signed agreement that excludes modification or rescission except by a signed writing cannot be otherwise modified or rescinded." UCC § 2-209(2); Mich. Comp. Laws § 440.2209. That changed the older common-law approach. *West Cent. Pack Corp. v. A. F. Murch Co.,* 109 Mich. App. 493 (1981).

The UCC states that "although an attempt at modification or rescission does not satisfy (subsection [2 above]) it can operate as a waiver." UCC § 2-209(4). The UCC states that a "party who has made a waiver affecting an executory portion of the contract may retract the waiver by reasonable notification received by the other party that strict performance will be required of any term waived, unless retraction would be unjust in view of a material change of position in reliance on the waiver." UCC § 2-209(5). Waiver is an equitable doctrine, and hence not subject to rule-like application.

E.   **Anticipatory Repudiation**

One of the hardest issues in the law of sales (and contracts generally) is knowing how to respond when the other party appears unable or unwilling to perform the contract, but does not say so explicitly. The UCC provides a useful tool in this situation. UCC § 2-609; Mich. Comp. Laws § 440.2609.

1)   BREACH OF CONTRACT

A buyer's cancellation of its agreement with a seller may be a present breach of contract, even though time for performance had not yet come, under the law of anticipatory repudiation. UCC § 2-610; Mich. Comp. Laws § 440.2610. When a party engages in anticipatory repudiation, the other party can exercise the right to cancel its performance of their contract and seek an appropriate remedy. UCC § 2-703; Mich. Comp. Laws § 440.2703.

2)   UNEQUIVOCAL

Courts tend to hold that a party repudiates only by words or actions that demonstrate an unequivocal, rather than equivocal, unwillingness or inability to perform. As under common law, pursuant to the UCC, a party does not commit an anticipatory repudiation except by unequivocal words or actions. Indeed, a premature termination can make the terminating party the first material breacher. *Harlow & Jones v. Advance Steel Co.,* 424 F. Supp. 770 (E.D. Mich. 1976).

3)   ASSURANCES

However, the UCC does provide a mechanism for when one party has reasonable grounds for insecurity as to whether it will receive the promised performance. In this situation, it can, in writing, demand adequate assurances of due performance. If the other party fails to provide adequate assurances within a reasonable time not exceeding 30 days, then it is deemed to have repudiated the contract--and the demanding party is free to cancel because that failure to respond to such a demand constitutes grounds for termination. As commentators have indicated, even under this process, the insecure party faces significant uncertainty--what kinds of assurances can be demanded, for example? J.J. White, *Eight Cases and Section 251*, 67 Cornell L. Rev. 841 (1982).

F.   Defenses

    1)   UNCONSCIONABILITY

Unconscionability would apply if the court thought that the inequality of bargaining power between the parties and their "take it or leave it" form of negotiation resulted in the imposition of a commercially unreasonable term.

    2)   IMPRACTICABILITY AND FRUSTRATION OF PURPOSE

        a)   General Considerations

As a general matter, impracticability and frustration of purpose rarely give a buyer the right to avoid responsibility under a sales contract simply because of a change in a third party's plans, especially if the buyer made no effort to protect itself from that risk.

In the absence of a term in a contract for the sales of goods making the purchase contingent on obtaining satisfactory financing, a buyer generally bears the risk of not obtaining the needed financing. When the risk of not obtaining financing is perfectly foreseeable, in the absence of other circumstances the buyer generally may possess little basis for raising the defenses of "frustration of purpose" or impracticability.

        b)   Impracticability for Sellers

The UCC creates only a defense of impracticability for sellers. UCC § 2-615; Mich. Comp. Laws § 440.2615. However, courts in jurisdictions other than Michigan acknowledge that the same concept can be read to protect buyers as well, but only if a stringent test is satisfied; performance must be rendered prohibitively expensive by an unforeseen occurrence for which the party seeking avoidance bears no blame.

    3)   MISTAKE

        a)   Two-Part Inquiry

A Michigan trial court may, in its sound discretion, grant rescission of a contract on account of the parties' mutual mistake. The trial court needs to determine (a) if one or both parties held a mistaken belief, and, if yes, (b) the mistaken belief's legal significance.

        b)   Definition of Mistake

Michigan law defines a mistake in a contract as: "a belief that is not in accord with the facts. The erroneous belief of one or both of the parties must relate to a fact in existence at the time the contract is executed. That is to say, the belief which is found to be in error may not be, in substance, a prediction as to a future occurrence or non-occurrence." *Dingeman v. Reffitt,* 152 Mich. App. 350 (1986); citing *Lenawee Co. Bd. of Health v. Messerly*, 417 Mich. 17 (1982).

   c) Remedies

    (1) Rescission

An appropriate equitable remedy for mutual mistake involves rescission of the contract, unless one party assumed the risk of loss. That may occur, for example, by means of an "as is" clause. "The 'as is' clause incorporated into the contract is a persuasive indication that the parties intended the [seller] would bear both the risks and the benefits of the present condition of the property." *Dingeman v. Reffitt, supra.*

Michigan courts must decide which innocent party will assume the loss attributable to their common mistake when both parties are blameless.

    (2) Reformation

A written contract will not be judicially reformed based on a mistake unless the mistake was mutual and common to both parties to the contract. *Id. citing Stevenson v. Aalto*, 333 Mich. 582 (1952). "If the asserted mutual mistake is with respect to an extrinsic fact, reformation is not allowed, even though the fact is one which would have caused the parties to make a different contract, because courts cannot make a new contract for the parties." *Id., citing E. R. Brenner Co. v. Brooker Eng'g Co.*, 301 Mich. 719 (1942).

G. Mitigation of Damages

Like the common law of contracts, the UCC effectively imposes a duty to mitigate damages. UCC § 2-704[2].

   1) UNCOMPLETED GOODS

A seller that commenced performance under a contract for manufacturing goods for which a buyer engaged in anticipatory repudiation may "stop work and salvage." The UCC gives the seller the alternative option of completing production of the goods when this would be a reasonable means of mitigating damages. Depending upon the circumstances, that could be wasteful unless the custom goods are readily marketable to someone else, which could be unlikely if the goods are customized for the breaching buyer's needs. If stopping work is the more reasonable course of action, then the seller could be made whole by being awarded the "sunk" costs associated with its performance plus its lost profit.

    a) Continuing Production

As to goods that are uncompleted at the time of breach, the seller may continue production, only if doing so is a "reasonable commercial judgment" - which could be the case, for example, if the goods would have substantial value to other potential buyers in the marketplace. Mich. Comp. Laws § 440.2704[2].

> b)   Stopping Production

If, however, the seller's stopping of work is the more reasonable course of action, then the UCC affords an acceptable remedy. UCC § 2-708(2); Mich. Comp. Laws § 440.2708(2). Essentially, this remedy is the sum of sunk costs plus (net) lost profit, which includes reasonable overhead. Another way of expressing this is the contract price less costs saved by not having to complete performance and less any residual value to what remains.

> **H.**   **Damages**

> 1)   "LOST VOLUME" SELLER

To assert the status of a "lost volume" seller, the seller must show that even had a first customer purchased the goods as per the contract, the seller would have been able to make a second sale of goods as well – by selling substantially similar goods to a second customer a few days later. If so, the seller is entitled to its lost profit on the contract with the first customer; the seller is not made whole just because of the resale of the goods to the second customer that the first customer failed to purchase as agreed.

> a)   Determining Damages

Normally, reselling the goods at the same price would mean that there are no damages (putting aside the possibility of incidental costs associated with the resale). However, courts have constructed the UCC to allow recovery by the lost volume seller who can show that it was selling essentially "fungible" goods so that had there been no breach because the subsequent sale would have occurred anyway--giving the seller profits on two transactions, not just one. Mich. Code Ann. 440.2708; UCC § 2-708; *e.g.*, Calamari & Perillo, *Contracts,* sec. 14.23. This applies most clearly where the seller has an essentially unlimited supply of goods. But at least one case has recognized the possibility with respect to pleasure boats (*Nerd v. Retail Marine Corp.,* 285 N.E.2d 311 [NY 1972]).

> **I.**   **Remedies**

> 1)   CONTRACTUALLY LIMITED REMEDY

A contract provision that limits the available remedy to "repair or replace" a defective item could be struck down on one of two possible grounds: 1) unconscionability (discussed earlier); or 2) failure of essential purpose.

> a)   Failure of Essential Purpose

Under the UCC, a contractual provision for a limited remedy of either repairing or replacing a defective item can be disregarded when the remedy has "failed of its essential purpose." In that event, an aggrieved party can resort to other remedies made available to it by the law. Courts have often found such failure of a limited remedy when an item's defect is undetectable until such time when repair or replacement of the item is not an effective cure of the defect.

(1)   Exclusions of Consequential Damages

Many courts have struck down exclusions of consequential damages on the basis that these exclusions are one of the terms of the contract that fail as a "failure of essential purpose" and thus can also be disregarded. It should be recognized, however, that other courts have treated such exclusions as separate and distinct limitations to be upheld unless they are unconscionable.

2)   SPECIFIC PERFORMANCE

The Uniform Commercial Code expanded the right to a buyer of goods to specific performance of the contract of sale. Under the UCC, a buyer of consumer goods has a specifically enforceable right to the goods as soon as they have been identified to the contract. UCC § 2-716(3), official cmt. 3 (2003). Goods are identified to a contract when they have been marked for shipment. UCC § 2-501(1)(b) (2003).

CRIMINAL LAW & PROCEDURE

Commonly Tested Issues

★★★★

★★★

- Motion to Suppress

★★

- 4th Amendment – Vehicle Search
- 4th Amendment – "Knock and Announce"
- 4th Amendment – Search Warrant and Exceptions
- 4th Amendment – Dwelling Search
- 5th Amendment – Double Jeopardy
- 5th Amendment – Voluntariness of Confession
- 14th Amendment – Incorporation
- Offenses – Armed Robbery
- Offenses – Weapon Offenses
- Defenses – Self-Defense
- Motion to Dismiss
- Exclusionary Rule

★

- 4th Amendment – Warrantless Arrest
- 4th Amendment – Person Search
- 4th Amendment – Inevitable Discovery Rule
- 5th Amendment – Miranda Warnings and Waiver
- 6th Amendment – Right to Counsel
- Right to Self-Representation
- 14th Amendment – Due Process at Lineup
- Arraignment
- Offenses – First-Degree Premeditated Murder
- Offenses – First-Degree Felony Murder
- Offenses – Aiding and Abetting Felony Murder
- Offenses – Second-Degree Murder
- Offenses – Aiding and Abetting Felony Firearm
- Offenses – Necessarily Lesser Included Offenses

TABLE OF CONTENTS

CRIMINAL LAW & PROCEDURE

Michigan Common Issues & Distinctions

The following outline is based on analysis of questions on the essay portion of the Michigan Bar Exam. The outline may address general legal principles and Michigan-specific rules. The general rules may be identical to those covered in your outlines for the Multistate Bar Exam ("MBE"). To the extent that this outline repeats identical rules covered in your MBE outline, such repetition is provided for the beneficial purposes of 1) learning how the rules are construed, applied, and tested in Michigan, and 2) learning which rules are tested most often on the essay portion of the examination (most topics appearing in this outline have appeared on a recent administration of the essay portion of the exam). Moreover, these general rules are sometimes stated in different ways by Michigan's courts. The general rules, along with any unique provisions of Michigan law (Michigan distinctions), are presented in the manner that Michigan's bar examiners view them with respect to analyzing essay questions on previously tested issues of law.

THIS OUTLINE IS NOT A COMPLETE OUTLINE OF CRIMINAL LAW & PROCEDURE FOR THE ESSAY PORTION OF THE MICHIGAN BAR EXAMINATION. It is designed to be used conjunction with your MBE outline. Any essay questions testing topics of MBE subjects that are not covered in this outline, should be answered according to the law you have learned for the MBE.

Facts and rules derived from cases decided by the Michigan appellate courts and certain federal courts have provided the basis for some past Criminal Law & Procedure questions and answers. The Michigan Compiled Laws is another source for tested rules as well. Although the sample answers for certain past questions indicate that Michigan statutes and court cases should be the basis for answering questions, future questions could be answerable using controlling general legal principles contained in the MBE outlines for Criminal Law and Criminal Procedure.

Traditionally, at least one and as many as three Criminal Law & Procedure questions have appeared on each exam, although this frequency of testing in the past may not be the same going forward.

According to some past exams, some frequently tested issues include motions to suppress and searches and seizures. Some less frequently tested issues include vehicle searches, double jeopardy, confessions, armed robbery, self-defense, and motion to dismiss. Some occasionally tested issues include warrantless arrest, "knock and announce," Miranda warnings and waiver, right to counsel, arraignment, First-Degree Felony Murder, Aiding and Abetting Felony Murder, Second-Degree Murder, Aiding and Abetting Felony Firearm, Necessarily Lesser Included

Offenses, Cognate Lesser Included Offenses, Motion for Directed Verdict, Motion for New Trial, and prosecutor's *res gestae* witnesses.

I.   FOURTH AMENDMENT

The Fourth Amendment to the United States Constitution is applicable to the states under the Fourteenth Amendment to the United States Constitution. U.S. Const. amend. IV and U.S. Const. amend. XIV.

A.   Search Warrant

The Fourth Amendment protects against unreasonable searches and seizures of persons or property and generally requires that a warrant be obtained to conduct certain searches, subject to exception. For a search warrant to be valid, it must (1) be based on probable cause; (2) particularly describe the place to be searched and the items to be seized; and (3) be signed by a neutral and detached magistrate. If the officers acted in reasonable reliance on the search warrant issued by a neutral and detached magistrate, the Fourth Amendment exclusionary rule should not be applied. *United States v. Leon*, 468 U.S. 897 (1984).

1)   PROBABLE CAUSE REQUIREMENT

Probable cause is found to exist "when acts and circumstances warrant a reasonably prudent person to believe that a crime has been committed and that the evidence sought will be found in a stated place." *People v. Brzezinski*, 243 Mich. App. 431 (2000).

a)   Confidential Informant

When a warrant is based upon information received from a confidential informant, the judge looks at the totality of the circumstances to determine whether the informant is credible and reliable. *Illinois v. Gates*, 462 U.S. 213 (1983); *People v. Keller*, 479 Mich. 467 (2007). Further, the officer has a duty to present corroborating facts to support a finding of probable cause.

2)   DESCRIPTION REQUIREMENT

A search warrant is required to designate and describe the house, building, location or place to be searched and the property to be seized. Mich. Comp. Laws § 780.654. Generally speaking, the description in a search warrant is sufficient to satisfy the particularity requirement if the description is such that the officers can, with reasonable effort, ascertain and identify the place intended to be searched. *People v. Hampton*, 237 Mich. App. 143 (1999).

a)   What Premises Include

A search of the "premises" has been held to include permission to search the entire area where the object of the search may be found including closets, furniture, drawers and containers whether specified in the warrant or not. *United States v. Ross*, 456 U.S. 798 (1982). The appellate courts have increasingly held that a car found on the premises should be viewed in the same way as any other personal effects. It is considered as no less fixed than a purse or container found on the premises. *People v. Jones*, 249 Mich. App. 131 (2002).

3)   "KNOCK AND ANNOUNCE" STATUTE

a)   General Considerations

Michigan's knock and announce statute has its basis in the Fourth Amendment and, if the statute is violated, evidence seized during a search as a result of this violation would be properly excluded. The statute provides that:

> The officer to whom a warrant is directed, or any person assisting him, may break any outer or inner door or window of a house or building, or anything therein, in order to execute the warrant, if, after notice of his authority and purpose, he is refused admittance, or when necessary to liberate himself or any person assisting him in execution of the warrant.

One of the purposes of the statute is to allow the occupants the "brief opportunity" to order their personal affairs before the officers enter. However, the purpose of the statute is not meant to allow the occupant the time to destroy evidence.

Assuming that there is a violation of the statute, which does not necessarily require a finding with respect to a motion to suppress that the evidence should be suppressed. The knock and announce statute does not control the execution of a valid warrant, it merely delays entry.

b)   Inevitable Discovery Doctrine

There is some disagreement among federal courts on the use of the "inevitable discovery" doctrine. However, the Michigan Supreme Court has approved of the application of this doctrine in knock and announce cases. In considering this doctrine, the Michigan Supreme Court has approved the following statement: "[I]t is hard to understand how the discovery of evidence inside a house could be anything but 'inevitable' once the police arrive with a warrant." *People v. Stephens,* 460 Mich. 626 (1999). As a general matter, the occupant or defendant of a house that was searched after the police knocked and announced their presence before entering the house would not be allowed to contend that, had the officers announced their presence and waited longer to enter, the defendant would have had time to destroy the evidence they seized as a result of their search.

4)   WARRANT REQUIREMENT EXCEPTIONS

A couple of the exceptions to the general requirement of a search warrant to conduct a search are known as "plain smell" and "plain feel."

a)   "Plain Smell" Exception

The Michigan Supreme Court has held that the smell of marijuana by a person qualified to recognize the smell as contraband is sufficient to justify the search of a motor vehicle without the need for a search warrant. *People v. Kazmierczak,* 461 Mich. 411 (2000). The Supreme Court also stated that the smell of marijuana alone by a person qualified to know the odor is sufficient in and of itself to justify a warrantless search of a motor vehicle and there need be no other probable cause. *Id.*

                b)   "Plain Feel" Exception

The "plain feel" exception to the search warrant requirement was set forth by the United States Supreme Court in *Minnesota v. Dickerson*. *Minnesota v. Dickerson*, 508 U.S. 366 (1993). The Michigan Supreme Court adopted this exception in *People v. Champion*. *People v. Champion*, 452 Mich. 92 (1996). Pursuant to *Champion*, an object felt during an authorized pat-down search may be seized without a warrant if the item's incriminating character is immediately apparent, that is, if the officer develops probable cause to believe that the item felt is contraband before going beyond the legitimate scope of the pat-down search.

The *Champion* court articulated the degree of certainty required that an object felt during a pat-down search is contraband before a police officer may remove that object from the person being searched. The court held that the "immediately apparent" qualification in *Dickerson* does not require a higher degree of certainty. Rather, the degree of certainty required for plain feel seizures is probable cause. The *Champion* court "emphasized that courts applying the plain feel exception must appreciate the totality of the circumstances in the given case." *Champion*, p. 112.

    B.   **Vehicle Search**

        1)   CONSENT

When a person is the driver and owner of a vehicle, the person's consent is sufficient to permit a valid search of the vehicle and any containers found therein. *Florida v. Jimeno*, 500 U.S. 248 (1991); *People v. Dagwan*, 269 Mich. App. 338 (2005). Thus, the claimed lack of consent on the part of a passenger in the vehicle searched would lack merit and would not affect the validity of the search of the vehicle to which its driver and owner provided proper consent.

        2)   SEARCH INCIDENT TO ARREST

                a)   General Rule

The United State Supreme Court has held that where a police officer makes a valid arrest of a passenger in a vehicle, the officer is permitted to search the interior of the vehicle as well as any containers located therein. *New York v. Belton*, 453 U.S. 454 (1981). That holding in *New York v. Belton* was applied to Michigan by the Court of Appeals in *People v. Catanzarite*. *People v. Catanzarite*, 211 Mich. App. 573 (1995).

                    (1)   Example A

In *Catanzarite*, the defendant's vehicle was stopped as he was towing a trailer that did not have a license plate. The officer asked the defendant and his passenger for identification, and ran computer checks on each person. A computer check showed the passenger had an outstanding arrest warrant for disorderly person, and the passenger was arrested on the warrant. After the arrest, the officer searched the vehicle and found cocaine in a small bag being held by the defendant. The defendant challenged the search of the bag and subsequent seizure of the cocaine.

The Court of Appeals, relying upon *Belton*, held the search was proper. The Court of Appeals held law enforcement officers may search the interior of a vehicle after arresting a passenger.

(2)   Example B

In another Michigan case, a traffic stop was made of defendant's vehicle. A computer check of defendant's passenger revealed outstanding warrants and he was arrested. Defendant's vehicle was searched and a handgun was found under the defendant's seat. Defendant was then arrested and charged with carrying a concealed weapon. Defendant moved to suppress evidence of the gun. The Court of Appeals held under *Belton* that the search was permissible, noting that a full search of the vehicle was allowable even though the passenger had already been removed from the vehicle, handcuffed and placed in a secure area. *People v. Mungo*, 277 Mich. App. 577 (2008).

C.   Arrest

1)   ARRAIGNMENT AFTER WARRANTLESS ARREST

a)   Prompt Arraignment Required

By statute in Michigan, a person arrested without a warrant must be brought before a magistrate for arraignment without unnecessary delay. Mich. Comp. Laws §§ 764.13, 764.26. The statute providing for the prompt arraignment is not a constitutional right. As discussed later, unnecessary delay in arraignment is only one of the factors that is to be considered in evaluating the voluntariness of a confession (i.e., a defendant's statement).

(1)   Presumptively Unreasonable Delay

The United States Supreme Court in *Riverside Co. v. McLaughlin,* has indicated that the arraignment must take place no later than 48 hours after the arrest, and beyond that time period the delay is presumptively unreasonable and violative of the Fourth Amendment. *Riverside Co. v. McLaughlin,* 500 U.S. 44 (1991).

II.   FIFTH AMENDMENT

The Fifth Amendment to the United States Constitution is applicable to the states under the Fourteenth Amendment to the United States Constitution. U.S. Const. amend. V and U.S. Const. amend. XIV. The Fifth Amendment includes the right against self-incrimination.

A.   Admissibility of Defendant's Statement

When a defendant challenges the admissibility of a statement made by the defendant, the admissibility is to be determined by the court prior to trial, as a matter of law. *People v. Walker,* 374 Mich. 331 (1965). However, where law enforcement alleges a defendant has made an incriminating statement, and the defendant denies having made the statement, the defendant is not entitled to an evidentiary hearing. *People v. Weatherspoon,* 171 Mich. App. 549 (1988).

1)   WALKER HEARING

The Michigan Court of Appeals has since held that a defendant may be entitled to a *Walker* hearing where the defendant claims he signed a fabricated statement under duress. *People v. Neal,* 182 Mich. App. 368 (1990). In *People v. Neal,* the Court of Appeals held:

> At the hearing the trial court must determine, assuming the defendant made the statement, whether he did so voluntarily. If it is found that the defendant voluntarily made the statement, the defendant is free to argue to the jury that the police fabricated it. However, if the trial court at the hearing finds that the statement was involuntarily made, the statement is inadmissible, regardless of the defendant's claim that he never actually made it. [*Neal, supra,* p. 372.]

This has been clarified by the Court of Appeals in *People v. Bell. People v. Bell,* unpublished opinion per curiam of the Court of Appeals, issued August 5, 1997 (Docket No. 187997). In *Bell,* the Court of Appeals held once a defendant denies making a statement, he is no longer entitled to an evidentiary hearing challenging the admissibility of the statement. This is an issue for the jury to determine. Logically, this is the only conclusion because if the defendant denies making a statement, he cannot assert he made the statement involuntarily, under coercion, or unknowingly. Conversely, a defendant who acknowledges making the statement can challenge it by making such assertions.

a)   Burden of Proof

When a defendant challenges a confession, the burden rests squarely on the prosecution to demonstrate the admissibility by a preponderance of the evidence. *People v. Daoud,* 462 Mich. 621 (2000).

b)   Admissibility of a Confession

(1)   Totality of Circumstances

In Michigan, in determining the admissibility of a confession, the court must review the totality of the circumstances surrounding the making of the statement. *People v. Cipriano,* 431 Mich. 315 (1988).

(2)   Voluntariness of Confession

The test to determine whether a confession is voluntary is "in considering the totality of all the surrounding circumstances, the confession is the product of an essentially free and unconstrained choice by its maker, or whether the accused's will has been overborne and his capacity for self-determination critically impaired." *Id.*

There are a number of factors that are to be considered in making this decision. One factor is the length of delay between the arrest and the interrogation. Another is whether the police intended to cause a delay between the arrest and arraignment of defendant so they could obtain a confession. The focus on reaching a determination is not necessarily the length of the delay, but what occurred during the delay. *Id.* An additional factor is whether the accused requested an attorney. Some more factors include the defendant's age, education or intelligence level, prior experience with police, whether the defendant was informed of his rights, the length of questioning, the defendant's physical and mental condition, or whether the defendant was under the influence of drugs or alcohol. *Id.* The court must also consider whether the defendant was threatened with abuse, abused in any way, or deprived of medication, sleep, food or drink. *Id.*

B.   Double Jeopardy Clause

Double Jeopardy Clause provides that no "person shall be subject for the same offense to be twice put in jeopardy of life or limb." U.S. Const. amend. V. This Clause applies to the states through the Fourteenth Amendment. U.S. Const. amend. XIV. The Michigan Constitution has essentially the same prohibition. Mich. Const. art I, § 15.

1)   PURPOSES OF PROTECTION

The Double Jeopardy Clause protects against the successive punishments and successive prosecutions for the same criminal offense. The purposes of double jeopardy protections against successive prosecutions for the same offense are to preserve the finality of judgments in criminal prosecutions and to protect the defendant from prosecutorial overreaching. The purpose of the double jeopardy protection against multiple punishments for the same offense is to protect the defendant from having more punishment imposed than the Michigan Legislature intended.

2)   APPLICATION TO NONSUMMARY PROCEEDINGS

Criminal contempt that is enforced through non-summary proceedings is considered a crime in the ordinary sense and the Double Jeopardy Clause applies to such proceedings.

3)   SAME ELEMENTS TEST

The test to determine if the two charges can survive a double jeopardy challenge is the "same element" test. This test looks at whether each offense contains an element not contained in the other, and if not, they are the same offense within the meaning of the Double Jeopardy Clause. Even though the same conduct is the subject of the charge, the United States Supreme Court has overruled the "same conduct" test as a consideration in deciding double jeopardy issues. *United States v. Dixon*, 509 U.S. 688.

a)   Separate Types of Robbery Offenses

Parts of the Michigan statute regarding armed robbery and the Michigan statute regarding bank, safe and vault robbery were determined separate offenses, so sentencing the defendant on both of these convictions did not violate the double jeopardy rights of the defendant. *People v. Ford,* 262 Mich. App. 443 (2004). Compare, for example, relevant parts of the statutes for these two offenses.

Michigan's armed robbery statute provides in pertinent part that: "a person who in the course of committing a larceny of any money or other property and in the course of engaging in that conduct, possesses a dangerous weapon is guilty of a felony punishable by imprisonment for life or for any term of years."

Michigan's bank, safe and vault robbery statute provides in pertinent part that: "Any person who, with intent to commit the crime of larceny, or any felony shall threaten to kill or shall put in fear any person for the purpose of stealing from any . . . safe or other depository of money or other valuables shall be guilty of a felony punishable by imprisonment in the state prison for life or any term of years."

b)   Social Norms Test

In Michigan, the "social norms" test requires the court to identify the type of harm the legislature was intending to prevent, and where two statutes prohibit violations of the same social norm generally the legislature did not intend separate punishments. *People v. Robideau,* 419 Mich. 458 (1984).

III.   SIXTH AMENDMENT

A.   Introduction

The Sixth Amendment to the United States Constitution is applicable to the states under the Fourteenth Amendment to the United States Constitution. U.S. Const. amend. VI and U.S. Const. amend. XIV. The Sixth Amendment includes the right to counsel.

B.   Right to Counsel

1)   WHEN CONSTITUTIONAL RIGHT TO COUNSEL APPLIES

a)   Incarceration from a Conviction

The Sixth Amendment only requires an attorney for a charge where incarceration results from a conviction.

(1)   Waiver

However, an individual can waive his right to an attorney and if that occurs, there is no violation of the right to counsel. The waiver must be knowingly and intelligently made.

(2)   Misdemeanor Case without Jail Time

When there is no jail time imposed in a misdemeanor case, the courts have held that there was no right to an attorney in that case.

b)   Subsequent Offense

When sentencing a defendant for a subsequent offense, a Michigan state circuit court judge may not consider a prior misdemeanor conviction that was obtained without benefit of counsel or a valid waiver of the right to counsel. The judge, however, may consider a prior conviction when no right to counsel existed for that offense because no incarceration could have been imposed for it.

c)   Sentencing Enhancement

When a defendant has counsel in the defendant's felony trial and a sentence is imposed for the conviction of this felony, additional months can be added as a sentencing enhancement of the punishment for the conviction. *Nichols v. United States*, 511 U.S. 738 (1994); *Argersinger v. Hamlin*, 407 U.S. 25 (1972); *Alabama v. Shelton*, 535 U.S. 654 (2002).

C.   Right to Self-Representation

The Sixth Amendment implies the right to self-representation. Michigan law expressly guarantees the right to self-representation. Mich. Comp. Laws § 763.1; Mich. Const. 1963, art. I, § 13.

1)   <u>WAIVER OF COUNSEL PROCEDURES</u>

A trial court must measure the right to self-representation against the right to counsel. Therefore, the court must comply with certain waiver of counsel procedures before allowing a defendant to represent himself.

a)   Court Must Ask Defendant Certain Questions

In particular, the trial court must:

- make sure the defendant's waiver request is unequivocal;
- make sure the defendant's waiver is knowingly, intelligently, and voluntarily made; and
- find that the defendant will not unduly inconvenience, disrupt, and burden the court.

People v. Anderson, 398 Mich. 361 (1976).

b)   Court Must Tell Defendant Certain Information

Also, the court must inform a prospective self-representing (i.e., in *pro per*) defendant of the charges and the maximum or mandatory minimum sentences. MCR 6.005(D). The court must advise the defendant of the risks of self-representation. *Id.* For example, the court should tell a defendant that a criminal trial is governed by rules of evidence and procedure and that it is very difficult for someone untrained in the law to comply with them. The court must give the defendant the opportunity to consult with counsel before deciding to proceed without counsel.

Id.

         c)   Court Must Substantially Comply with Procedures

The court must substantially comply, rather than strictly comply, with the required waiver of counsel procedures. *People v. Russell*, 471 Mich. 182 (2004). In order to substantially comply with them, the court must tell the defendant about them in a short colloquy with the defendant, and make an express finding that the defendant fully recognizes, understands, and agrees to waive them. *Id.*

         d)   Presumption Against Waiver of Right to Counsel

The court must indulge every reasonable presumption against the defendant's waiver of the right to counsel. *Id.*

IV.   FOURTEENTH AMENDMENT

A.   Due Process

         1)   IDENTIFICATION OF DEFENDANT IN LINEUP

As a practical matter, a victim of a crime and/or a witness to the crime may report it to the police. If the assailant who perpetrated the crime is not apprehended when the crime occurred, then victim and/or witness may describe this culprit to the police to help them apprehend him. If the police apprehend someone that they consider a suspect in the crime's commission, then they may conduct a lineup. Basically, to do that the police place some people, including the suspect, in a row and allow the victim and/or the witness to view them in order to identify which one of these people is the culprit to charge with the crime. One issue that can arise from this means of identification of a culprit is whether the lineup was unduly suggestive because, for example, most of the people in the lineup differed in their physical appearance from the accused. However, the fact that the police told the victim and/or witness that the culprit is one of the people in the lineup is not unduly suggestive as a matter of law. *People v. McElhaney*, 215 Mich. App. 269 (1996).

         a)   Challenge to Identification in Lineup as Unduly Suggestive

A lineup that is suggestive of who committed the crime and susceptible to misidentification may deny a criminal defendant due process of law. *Stovall v. Denno*, 388 U.S. 293 (1967); *People v. Hickman*, 470 Mich. 602 (2004).

A defendant who challenges an identification based on a lack of due process must prove that the pre-trial identification procedure was so suggestive under the totality of circumstances that it led to a "substantial likelihood of misidentification." *People v. Kurylczyk*, 443 Mich. 289 (1993); *People v. Williams*, 244 Mich. App. 533 (2001). If a defendant makes a credible contention that the lineup procedure is constitutionally suspect, then a Michigan trial court should have an evidentiary hearing to determine the issue.

(1)   Court Considers Fairness of Identification Procedure

The court evaluates the fairness of an identification procedure under the total circumstances. *Kurylczyk, supra*; *People v. Murphy* (On Remand), 282 Mich. App. 571 (2009). Discrepancies between the physical characteristics of an accused, the witness' description of the assailant, and the people who participated in the lineup do not necessarily make the lineup procedure defective. *Id.*; *People v. Hornsby*, 251 Mich. App. 462 (2002). The lineup participants are not required to resemble the witness' description of the assailant. The lineup participants must resemble the description of the culprit. *Id.*; *People v. Holmes*, 132 Mich. App. 730 (1984).

(a)   Differences in the Appearances of Participants

Differences in the appearances of lineup participants usually relate to the weight of an identification and not to its admissibility. *Hornsby, supra*. Differences matter only to the degree that they are evident to the identifying witness and substantially differentiate the defendant from the other lineup participants. *Kurylczyk, supra*; *Hornsby, supra*. For example, minor variations in height of lineup participants will not make a lineup unduly suggestive. *People v. Rivera*, 61 Mich. App. 427 (1975). Likewise, differences in the clothing worn by lineup participants usually will not make the lineup procedure defective. The police may present a suspect in the lineup who is wearing the same clothing that the suspect wore when he was arrested. *People v. Gunter*, 76 Mich. App. 483 (1977).

(b)   Considerations in Evaluating Fairness of Lineup

Also, a court reviewing a lineup's fairness will consider:

- the witness' opportunity to view the culprit when the alleged crime occurred;
- the accuracy of the witness' prior description of the culprit;
- the witness' degree of attention;
- the level of certainty demonstrated by witness at the identification, and
- the amount of time elapsed between the crime and the identification.

Neil v. Biggers, 409 U.S. 188 (1972); *People v. Solomon*, 391 Mich. 767 (1974).

V.   OFFENSES AGAINST PERSONS

As a general matter, a criminal defendant who commits an offense against a person takes the victim as found, for example, either in good health or in poor health.

A.   Murder

1)   FIRST-DEGREE MURDER

a)   Premeditated Murder

In Michigan, the elements of first-degree premeditated murder are:

- Defendant caused the decedent's death;
- Defendant intended to kill the decedent;
- Defendant had premeditated intent to kill;
- The killing was deliberate; and
- The killing was not excused or justified under the law.

CJI2d 16.1; Mich. Comp. Laws § 750.316(1)(a).

Premeditated murder includes murder perpetrated by means of poison. Mich. Comp. Laws § 750.316(1)(a).

(1)   *Corpus Delicti* Rule in Criminal Homicide of Murder

Basically, the Latin phrase *corpus delicti* means "body of crime." Under Michigan's *corpus delicti* rule, a prosecutor cannot introduce in evidence an accused's inculpatory statements without evidence of the *corpus delicti*. *People v. McMahan*, 451 Mich. 543 (1996). This rule protects against erroneous convictions for criminal homicides that did not happen. The rule decreases the weight attributed to confessions of defendants by requiring collateral evidence to support a conviction. *Id.*; *People v. Konrad*, 449 Mich. 263 (1995).

(a)   Other Evidence is Required to Admit Confession

The rule "provides that a defendant's confession may not be admitted unless there is direct or circumstantial evidence independent of the confession establishing (1) the occurrence of the specific injury (for example, death in cases of homicide) and (2) some criminal agency as the source of the injury." *Konrad, supra*, citing *People v. Cotto*n, 191 Mich. App. 377 (1991); *see also McMahan, supra*.

(b)   Preponderance of Evidence of Elements is Required

The prosecutor need not prove every element of the charged crime before the confession is admissible. *People v. Ish*, 252 Mich. App. 115 (2001). Moreover, the prosecutor does not have to prove the elements of murder beyond a reasonable doubt. It is enough if the trial court finds that a preponderance of the evidence establishes the elements. *People v. King*, 271 Mich. App. 235 (2006). By doing that, courts may weigh the probabilities and draw reasonable inferences. *People v. Mumford*, 171 Mich. App. 514 (1988).

b)   Felony Murder

The intent to commit the underlying felony, standing alone, is not sufficient to establish the necessary *mens rea* for murder.

First-degree felony murder does not require a specific intent to kill. First-degree felony murder requires a showing of malice. Malice is defined as the intention to kill, the intent to do great bodily harm, or the wanton and willful disregard of the likelihood that the natural tendency of defendant's behavior is to cause death or great bodily harm.

(1)   Aiding and Abetting Felony Murder

The elements necessary to support a finding of aiding and abetting a felony murder are:

- Felony murder was committed by the defendant or some other person;

- The defendant performed acts or gave encouragement that assisted the commission of felony murder;

- The defendant intended the commission of felony murder or had knowledge that the principal intended its commission at the time he gave aid and encouragement.

People v. Carines, 460 Mich. 750 (1999).

(2)   Arson

Arson is an offense included in the felony murder statute. Mich. Comp. Laws § 750.316. Arson is defined as the willful or malicious burning of any dwelling house, either occupied or unoccupied.

2)   SECOND-DEGREE MURDER

Second-degree murder requires that the defendant caused the death of the victim and that the killing was done with malice and without justification. Malice is the intent to kill, the intent to do great bodily harm, or the intent to create a high risk of death or great bodily harm with knowledge that death or great bodily harm will be the probable result. Malice may be inferred from the facts and circumstances of the killing. *People v. Harris,* 190 Mich. App. 652 (1991).

B.   Armed Robbery

1)   STATUTE

The armed robbery statute provides that "any person who shall assault another and shall feloniously rob, steal and take from his person, or in his presence . . . property which may be the subject of a larceny, such robber being armed with a dangerous weapon or any article used or fashioned in a manner to lead the person so assaulted to reasonably believe it to be . . . shall be guilty of a felony." Mich. Comp. Laws § 750.529.

2)   ELEMENTS

The elements of armed robbery are: 1) an assault, 2) a felonious taking of property from the victim's presence or person, 3) while the defendant is armed with a dangerous weapon. *People v.*

Carines, 460 Mich. 750 (1990).

3)   TRANSACTIONAL APPROACH

The "transactional approach" that has found some favor in the law looks at the robbery as not being complete until the robber has escaped with the stolen merchandise. Under this approach, the robber can turn a larceny into an armed or unarmed robbery if he employs the requisite degree of force to affect his escape or retain the property. The Michigan Court of Appeals has determined that the armed robbery and unarmed robbery statute require a taking from the person accompanied by contemporaneous application or threat of force or violence. If the force and/or threat is used later to retain the property, no armed or unarmed robbery has occurred. *People v. Scruggs,* 256 Mich. App. 303 (2003).

VI.   OTHER OFFENSES

A.   Larceny

In Michigan, larceny involves stealing another person's money, goods, or chattels. Mich. Comp. Laws § 750.356(1)(a). Larceny is a misdemeanor when the value of the goods stolen is under $200. Mich. Comp. Laws § 750.356(5).

B.   Weapons Offenses

1)   FIREARM OFFENSES

A defendant may be charged with the offense of a felon in possession of a firearm. Mich. Comp. Laws § 750.224f(1). A defendant may be charged with the offense of possession of a firearm in the commission of a felony. Mich. Comp. Laws § 750.227b. The statute defines a firearm as "a weapon from which a dangerous projectile may be propelled by an explosive, or by gas or air." Mich. Comp. Laws § 750.222(d).

a)   Example

The Michigan Supreme Court addressed the issue of whether a defendant may be convicted of those firearm-related offenses when the defendant was apprehended in possession of a handgun rendered inoperable because several of its pieces were missing. The Court held that the handgun fit the statutory definition of a firearm and affirmed the defendant's conviction. *People v. Peals,* 476 Mich. 636 (2006). The Court focused on the term "may" as found in the definition of "firearm." *Id.* The Court also noted the legislature failed to use the terms "operable" or "inoperable." *Id.*

To hold that pieces of a firearm, or that a firearm that is missing a piece, does not meet the statutory definition of "firearm" would be to permit a felon to avoid prosecution merely by hiding a minor piece. *Id.*

The Court determined that operability is not a requirement, and thus as the firearm was missing pieces which made it inoperable, it remained a firearm. *Id.* The Supreme Court noted the Court of Appeals had held operability was not a factor in felony firearm cases, the purpose of the statute being to protect the public. As the Supreme Court quoted with approval, "The victim is no less frightened if the gun (most likely unknown to him) just happens to be inoperable." *Id.*, quoting *People v. Pierce*, 119 Mich. App. 780 (1982).

Thus, operability is not an element within the statutory definition of "firearm." The key to the issue is the statute's use of the term "may," which permits even an inoperable gun to fall within the definition. The Court noted that it was possible that a firearm could be so substantially redesigned or altered that it would cease to be a firearm under the statutory definition. Operability would still not be the test. The question would be whether the weapon was so substantially redesigned or altered that it no longer falls within the category of weapons described in a Michigan statute. Mich. Comp. Laws § 750.222(d). The Court gave an example of a cannon plugged with cement and displayed in a park.

2) CARRYING A CONCEALED WEAPON

The prosecution must prove the following elements beyond a reasonable doubt when a defendant is charged with carrying a concealed weapon in a vehicle:

- The instrument or item was indeed a dangerous weapon (e.g., a gun).
- The dangerous weapon was in a vehicle that defendant was in.
- The defendant knew the instrument was in the vehicle. And,
- The defendant took part in carrying or keeping the dangerous weapon in the vehicle.

CJI 2d, 11.2.

a) Certain Defenses Not Available

A person's brief, innocent possession of a concealed weapon does not afford a defense to a charge of carrying a concealed weapon. *People v. Hernandez-Garcia*, 477 Mich. 1039 (2007). The defense of self-defense is not available in response to the charge of carrying a concealed weapon. *People v. Townsel*, 13 Mich. App. 600 (1968).

C. Arson

In Michigan, people commit arson by willfully or maliciously burning a dwelling house (a 20-year felony) or insured property (a 10-year felony). Mich. Comp. Laws §§ 750.72, 750.75.

1) ARSON OF A DWELLING

To find a person guilty of arson of a dwelling, the prosecutor must prove beyond a reasonable doubt that the person intentionally set on fire either a home (occupied or unoccupied) or a building within the home's curtilage. Mich. Comp. Laws § 750.72.

2)   ARSON OF INSURED PROPERTY

To find a person guilty of arson of an insured property, the prosecutor must prove beyond a reasonable doubt that a person intentionally set on fire an insured property for the purpose of making an insurance claim with the insurer. Mich. Comp. Laws § 750.75.

3)   NO DOUBLE JEOPARDY VIOLATION

Convictions of one person for both arson of a dwelling house and for arson of an insured property do not violate federal and state constitutional guarantees against double jeopardy. *People v. Ayers*, 213 Mich. App. 708 (1995). These two arson statutes protect against different harms, require different proof, and impose different and escalating penalties. The statute that criminalizes arson of a dwelling protects those endangered by dwelling fires. The statute that criminalizes arson of an insured property protects insurers. *Id.*

D.   Home Invasion

1)   IN THE FIRST DEGREE

In Michigan, first-degree home invasion includes these elements:

- a person broke and entered a dwelling or entered the dwelling without permission;
- when the person did that, she intended to commit a felony, assault, or larceny, or she committed a felony, assault, or larceny while entering, being present in, or leaving the dwelling; and
- the defendant was armed with a dangerous weapon or another person was lawfully present in the dwelling.

People v. Sands, 261 Mich. App. 158 (2004), Mich. Comp. Laws § 750.110a(2).

a)   Compared to Common Law Burglary

First-degree home invasion has similar elements to those of common law burglary, except that: 1) a person must commit common law burglary at night; and 2) there is no requirement that a person legally be inside the dwelling or that defendant be armed with a dangerous weapon. *People v. Saxton*, 118 Mich. App. 681 (1982), citing LaFave and Scott, *Handbook of Criminal Law*, § 96, p. 708.

(1)   Dwelling

At common law, the word dwelling included any structure inside the home's curtilage. A Michigan statute defines a "dwelling" as "a structure or shelter that is used permanently or temporarily as a place of abode, including an appurtenant structure attached to that structure or shelter." Mich. Comp. Laws § 750.110a(1)(a).

E.   Attempt and Controlled Substances Offenses

1)   ATTEMPT AND IMPOSSIBILITY

The words of Michigan's attempt statute do not show any legislative intent that the concept of "impossibility" provide any obstacle to charging a person with, or convicting him of, an attempted crime." *People v. Thousand*, 465 Mich. 149 (2001).

2)   ATTEMPT AND DELIVERY OF CONTROLLED SUBSTANCES

Arguably, under certain circumstances, Michigan's attempt statute may not apply when the attempt is subsumed under the crime of delivery of controlled substances. *People v. Alexander*, 188 Mich. App. 96 (1991).

a)   When Delivery is Prohibited

Michigan's controlled substance statute provides, in part that "a person shall not . . . deliver or possess with intent to . . . deliver a controlled substance." Mich. Comp. Laws § 333.7401. These words make the person's intent to deliver equivalent to actual delivery. Therefore, an attempt to deliver controlled substances is equivalent to the principal charge of delivery. In addition, Michigan's controlled substance statute requires the possession of a controlled substance.

(1)   Supported by Certain Criminal Standard Jury Instructions

One of Michigan's criminal standard jury instructions support the foregoing concepts. These instructions set forth the elements for the unlawful possession of a controlled substance with the intent to deliver. The initial three of these elements relate to the foregoing issue:

- the defendant knowingly had a controlled substance;

- the defendant intended to deliver the substance to someone else; and

- the defendant had a controlled substance and defendant knew it.

3)   POSSESSION WITH INTENT TO DELIVER IMITATION CONTROLLED SUBSTANCES

a)   Definition

"Imitation controlled substance" consists of "a substance that is not a controlled substance . . . [which] by representation . . . would lead a reasonable person to believe that the substance is a controlled substance." Mich. Comp. Laws § 333.7341(8).

b)   Felony Offense

Possession with intent to deliver an imitation controlled substance is a felony punishable by imprisonment of up to two years. *Id.*; Mich. Comp. Laws § 333.7341(3).

VII.   MISCELLANEOUS CONCEPTS

A.   Aiding and Abetting

Aiding and abetting is not a separate crime. Instead, it is a statutorily defined basis for prosecution that imposes vicarious criminal liability upon a person for a defendant's crime. Mich. Comp. Laws § 767.39; *People v. Robinson*, 475 Mich. 1 (2006). The person's mere presence at the crime, despite knowledge that the defendant is about to commit the crime, is not enough to make the person an aider and abettor. *People v. Norris*, 236 Mich. App. 411 (1999).

1)   GENERAL CONSIDERATIONS

In Michigan, a defendant is subject to conviction of a crime whether the defendant directly commits the crime or procures, counsels, aids, or abets in its commission. Aiding and abetting means to assist the crime's perpetrator. An aider and abettor is someone who is present at the crime scene and by deed or word gives active encouragement to the perpetrator, or by her conduct makes clear that she is ready to assist the perpetrator if such assistance is needed.

2)   PRINCIPAL'S GUILT

A defendant cannot be convicted of aiding and abetting if the guilt of the principal has not been shown. Although the guilt of the principal needs to be established, the principal does not have to be convicted in order for a defendant to be charged and convicted of aiding and abetting. The identity of the principal is not necessary to convict as long as there is sufficient evidence of the principal's guilt. *People v. Wilson*, 196 Mich. App. 604 (1992); *People v. Brown*, 120 Mich. App. 765 (1982).

3)   ELEMENTS

To support a finding that the defendant aided and abetted a crime, the prosecution must show: "(1) the crime charged was committed by the defendant or some other person, (2) the defendant performed acts or gave encouragement that assisted the commission of the crime, and (3) the defendant intended the commission of the crime or had knowledge that the principal intended its commission at the time [the defendant] gave aid and encouragement." *People v. Moore*, 470 Mich. 56, cert. den. sub. nom *Harris v. Mich*, 543 U.S. 947 (2004).

4)   STATE OF MIND

An aider and abettor's state of mind may be inferred from all the facts and circumstances. Factors that may be considered include "a close association between the defendant and the principal, the defendant's participation in the planning or execution of the crime, and evidence of flight after the crime." *People v. Carines*, 460 Mich. 750 (1999). It does not matter how much help, advice, or encouragement that the defendant actually gave, although mere presence is insufficient.

5)   FELONY-FIREARM OFFENSE

At one point in Michigan, it was necessary for a conviction of aiding and abetting the possession of a firearm to establish that the defendant procured, counseled, aided or abetted the principal in obtaining or retaining possession of the firearm. The Michigan Supreme Court has subsequently decided that what is required to be proven is that defendant aided and abetted another in carrying or having in his possession a firearm while that other commits or attempts to commit a felony. It is still necessary to establish that the defendant performed acts or gave encouragement that assisted in the commission of the felony-firearm violation. The amount of advice, aid, or encouragement is not material if it had the effect of inducing the commission of the crime. *People v. Moore,* 470 Mich. 56 (2004).

B.   Lesser Included Offenses

A distinction exists between necessarily lesser included offenses and cognate lesser included offenses.

1)   NECESSARILY LESSER INCLUDED OFFENSES

Necessarily included lesser offenses encompass situations in which it is impossible to commit the greater offense without first having committed the lesser offense.

2)   COGNATE LESSER INCLUDED OFFENSES

"Cognate" lesser included offenses are those that share some common elements, and are of the same class or category as the greater offense, but have some additional elements not found in the greater offense.

3)   INFERIOR OFFENSE INSTRUCTIONS

Michigan law provides that a jury may convict a defendant of an offense inferior to that charged in the indictment or an attempt to commit that offense. Mich. Comp. Laws § 768.32. In *People v. Cornell,* the Supreme Court concluded that the statute only permitted consideration of necessarily included lesser offenses. *People v. Cornell,* 466 Mich. 335 (2002). Under *Cornell,* a lesser-included offense instruction is only proper where the charged greater offense requires the jury to find a disputed factual element that is not required for a conviction of the lesser-included offense. *Cornell* further provides that the inferior-offense instruction is only appropriate where a "rational view of the evidence" would support such an instruction. Prior to *Cornell,* a jury could also be instructed on cognate offenses if the greater offense and the lesser offense were of the same class or category, and if the evidence adduced at trial would support a conviction of the lesser offense. *People v. Mendoza,* 468 Mich. 527 (2003).

VIII. DEFENSES

A.   **Self-Defense**

        1)   DEFENDANT AS AGGRESSOR

Self-defense is not available when the defendant is the aggressor, unless he withdraws from any further encounter with the victim and communicates that withdrawal to the victim.

        2)   USE OF DEADLY FORCE

Self-defense normally requires that the actor try to avoid the use of deadly force if he can safely and reasonably do so, for example, by applying non-deadly force or by utilizing an obvious and safe avenue of retreat. However, a defendant is not "required to retreat from a sudden, fierce, and violent attack" or "from an attacker who he reasonably believes is about to use a deadly weapon." Under such circumstances, as long as the defendant honestly and reasonably believes that it is necessary to exercise deadly force in self-defense, "he may stand his ground and meet force with force."

                a)   Retreat

Regardless of the circumstances, if the defendant is attacked in his own home, he "is never required to retreat where it is otherwise necessary to exercise deadly force in self-defense."

        3)   JUSTIFIABLE HOMICIDE

A killing in self-defense "is justifiable homicide if the defendant honestly and reasonably believes that his life is in imminent danger or that there is a threat of serious bodily harm." When a defendant uses deadly force, the test for determining whether he acted in lawful self-defense has three parts: 1) defendant honestly and reasonably believed that he was in danger, 2) the danger which he feared was serious bodily harm or death, and 3) the action taken by the defendant appeared at the time to be immediately necessary, i.e., defendant is only entitled to use the amount of force necessary to defend himself.

        4)   BURDEN OF PROOF

Once evidence of self-defense is introduced, the prosecutor bears the burden of disproving it beyond a reasonable doubt.

        5)   USING FORCE OR VIOLENCE OR ASSAULT

                a)   During Larceny

Michigan Compiled Laws section 750.530 provides in part that:

        (1)   A person who, in the course of committing a larceny of any money or other property that may be the subject of larceny, uses force or violence against any person who is present, or who assaults or puts the person in

fear, is guilty of a felony punishable by imprisonment for not more than 15 years."

(2)   As used in this section, 'in the course of committing a larceny' includes acts that occur in an attempt to commit the larceny, or during commission of the larceny, or in flight or attempted flight after the commission of the larceny, or in an attempt to retain possession of the property.

b)   Judicial Interpretation

One case found that a defendant's argument -- that he was merely trying to evade capture by wrestling himself free, and not that he was directing any force or violence at any person -- lacked merit, holding that the statute's clear and unambiguous language punishes a defendant for using force or violence, committing an assault, or placing a person in fear during flight or attempted flight after the larceny was committed. *People v. Passage*, 277 Mich. App. 175 (2007).

(1)   Seeking to Evade Capture

The statute makes no distinction between using force to evade capture as part of a physical struggle against pursuers in an effort to break free from their grasp or attempts at restraint and force used affirmatively and not within that context. Rather, the use of any force against a person during the course of committing a larceny, which includes the period of flight, is sufficient under the statute.

(2)   Use of Force

(a)   Definition

"Force" is nothing more than the exertion of strength and physical power. *Random House Webster's College Dictionary* (2001). Exerting strength and physical power to free oneself from another's grasp constitutes "force." Mich. Comp. Laws § 750.530.

(b)   Example

In *Passage*, there was evidence that the defendant engaged in the use of force during flight, or attempted flight, by physically struggling with the department store's personnel and attempting to kick them. Therefore, there was sufficient evidence to support the robbery conviction, given that there was no dispute that the defendant committed a larceny.

IX.   MOTIONS

A.   Motion to Suppress

One highly testable issue is the use of a motion to suppress, which generally seeks to exclude improperly obtained evidence from being admitted in a criminal proceeding. This motion may be used to challenge the validity of a search conducted pursuant to a warrant or without a warrant. This motion may assert that evidence seized as a result of the search is inadmissible because the search unlawfully occurred or was improperly conducted.

B.   Motion for a New Trial

1)   TIMING OF MOTION

A defendant may make a motion for new trial at any time prior to filing of a claim of appeal. MCR 6.431(A).

2)   GROUNDS FOR MOTION

A Michigan trial court can grant a motion for new trial "on any ground that would support appellate reversal of the conviction or because it believes that the verdict has resulted in a miscarriage of justice." MCR 6.431(B). Similarly, the court "may grant a new trial to the defendant, for any cause for which by law a new trial may be granted, or when it appears to the court that justice has not been done." Mich. Comp. Laws § 770.1.

3)   NEWLY DISCOVERED EVIDENCE

a)   Elements to Prove

In seeking new trial for newly discovered evidence, the defendant must show that (1) the evidence itself, not merely its materiality, is newly discovered; (2) the evidence is not merely cumulative; (3) the evidence would render a different result probable on retrial; and (4) the defendant could not with reasonable diligence have produced it at trial.

b)   Polygraph Exam Results

The court in its discretion may consider the result of a polygraph exam in a post-conviction hearing on a motion for new trial based on newly discovered evidence if: (1) it is offered on behalf of the defendant; (2) the test was taken voluntarily; (3) the professional qualifications and the quality of the polygraph equipment meet with the approval of the court; (4) either the prosecutor or the court is able to obtain an independent examination of the subject or of the test result by an operator of the court's choice, and (5) the result is considered only with regard to the general credibility of the subject. *People v. Cress,* 468 Mich. 678 (2003).

c)   Miscellaneous Concepts

The decision to grant a new trial is within the trial court's discretion. *Id.*

A confession that does not coincide with established facts does not warrant a new trial. *Id.*

C.   Motion for Directed Verdict

A defendant may make a motion for directed verdict of not guilty alleging that the evidence is insufficient to convict the defendant of the offense charged.

D.   Motion to Set Aside Plea

Basically, a party can make a motion to set aside a defendant's plea. When a defendant pleads *nolo contendere* or guilty to the charged offense, this cannot infringe upon the prosecutor's charging authority. A defendant's entry of such a plea does not limit the prosecutor's right to present more facts at proper times points in the case's remaining pendency, "such as during allocution at sentencing." *People v. Cobbs*, 443 Mich. 276 (1993).

E.   Motion to Reassign Case

1)   DE NOVO REVIEW

Essentially, a motion to reassign a case (from one judge to another) constitutes a motion to disqualify the trial court judge because of some ground such as bias. A Michigan circuit's chief judge conducts a *de novo* review of the trial court's decision on a motion to reassign a case. MCR 2.003(D)(3)(a). The State Court Administrator's Office assigns the chief judge. *Id.*

2)   EFFECT ON SENTENCING

After a trial court rules on a defendant's motion to reassign the case, the trial court should decline from sentencing the defendant or taking any further steps in the case until the occurrence of a *de novo* review of the motion to reassign the case to another judge.

X.   TRIAL COURT PROCEDURE

A.   Bail and Bond

1)   BAIL

Generally, a court may require a defendant to provide bail to ensure that the defendant will appear before the court to answer the prosecutor's charges. Typically, a court sets bail in an initial proceeding at which the prosecutor presents its charges against the defendant. As a practical matter, bail can involve a posting a bond as a form of security.

2)   BOND

a)   Release Bond

Generally, a criminal defendant not charged with treason or murder may have a reasonable release bond established pending trial. Mich. Const. 1963, art. I, §§ 15-16; Mich. Comp. Laws §§ 765.5, 765.6. A court can revoke the release bond, for example, upon the defendant's conviction of a crime. The defendant can make a motion for reinstatement of the release bond in the event that the court grants his motion for a new trial that was duly made after his conviction.

B.   Discovery

1)   RES GESTAE WITNESSES

In 1986, the Michigan statute requiring the prosecutor to list and produce at trial all *res gestae* witnesses was amended. When the prosecutor does not satisfy the statutory obligation, the missing witness instruction is available to address the situation. As amended, the pertinent portion of the statute states:

> (1)   The prosecuting attorney shall attach to the filed information a list of all witnesses known to the prosecuting attorney who might be called at trial and all *res gestae* witnesses known to the prosecuting attorney or investigating law enforcement officers.

> (3)   Not less than 30 days before trial, the prosecuting attorney shall send to the defendant or his or her attorney a list of the witnesses the prosecuting attorney intends to produce at trial.

> (4)   The prosecuting attorney may add or delete from the list of witnesses he or she intends to call at trial at any time upon leave of the court and for good cause shown or by stipulation of the parties.

> (5)   The prosecuting attorney or investigative law enforcement agency shall provide to the defendant, or defense counsel, upon request, reasonable assistance, including investigative assistance, as may be necessary to locate and serve process upon a witness. The request for assistance shall be made in writing by defendant or defense counsel not less than 10 days before the trial of the case or at such other time as the court directs.

Under the amended statute, the prosecutor is required to subpoena a witness. The defendant may rely on the appearance of a witness on the prosecutor's list with no further need to subpoena that witness himself. However, the particular statute imposes no penalty on the prosecutor for a witness' failure to honor a subpoena.

C.   Sentencing

1)   PROSECUTOR'S ROLE

The prosecutor possesses broad discretion to charge, but after a decision to charge is made, the prosecutor is not entitled to dictate the sentence. The trial court has the exclusive right and duty to impose the sentence. In sentencing, the prosecutor has the limited role of informing the trial court.

2)   JUDICIAL INVOLVEMENT IN SENTENCE BARGAINING

Generally, a Michigan trial court should only have limited participation in the bargaining of a sentence between the parties to a criminal prosecution. *People v. Killebrew*, 419 Mich. 189 (1982). This restriction on judicial involvement is necessary "to minimize the potential coercive effect on the defendant, to retain the function of the judge as a neutral arbiter, and to preserve the public perception of the judge as an impartial dispenser of justice." *Id*. However, as a matter of law, the trial court is not prevented from intervening in pre-conviction negotiations about a sentence. *Id*. This is because the trial court has sentencing discretion and authority, which the trial court "may not abdicate . . . by allowing sentence agreements to control the sentencing process." *People v. Cobbs*, 443 Mich. 276 (1993).

a)   When Trial Court May Reveal its Sentencing Considerations

Under certain circumstances, a trial court can disclose its thoughts on sentencing before its acceptance of a plea. "At the request of a party, and not on the judge's own initiative, a judge may state on the record the length of sentence that, on the basis of the information then available to the judge, appears to be appropriate for the charged offense." *Id*.

(1)   When Trial Court May Answer Question

The trial court's coercive position is decreased when the trial court does not start the sentencing discussion, but is simply responding to a question about sentencing. Moreover, the trial court must avoid indicating alternative sentencing possibilities, such as sentencing variations that can arise from a trial by jury. *Id*. In addition, this is required to avoid the potential of coercion. *Id*. "The judge's neutral and impartial role is enhanced when a judge provides a clear statement of information that is helpful to the parties." *Id*.

(2)   Effect of Preliminary Evaluation on Sentencing Discretion

"The judge's preliminary evaluation of the case does not bind the judge's sentencing discretion." *Id*. While a case proceeds, probably more facts will become known to the court that affect sentencing determinations. When the trial court states its inability to abide by the preliminary sentence evaluation, a defendant who entered a plea in reliance on this evaluation has the "absolute right to withdraw the plea." *Id*.

3)   JUDICIAL DISQUALIFICATION RULES MAY APPLY

To the extent that a defendant wants to withdraw a plea and go to trial, a trial court that has stated opinions about sentencing the defendant is subject to the judicial disqualification rules. MCR 2.003.

a)   Judicial Recusal

It is not a *per se* ground for recusal that the trial court's decides not to sentence the defendant according to a preliminary sentencing evaluation. "A judge's candid statement of how a case appears at an early stage of the proceedings does not prevent the judge from deciding the case in a fair and evenhanded manner later, when additional facts become known." *Id*.

XI.   APPEAL

A.   Right to Appellate Review

1)   FORMER RIGHT TO APPEAL ELIMINATED

Formerly, a right to appeal to the Michigan Court of Appeals existed for all criminal convictions. Then, the right to appeal applied to appeals to those that resulted from a *nolo contendere* plea and a guilty plea. In 1994, however, the Michigan Constitution was amended to eliminate the right to appeal criminal convictions that result from *nolo contendere* pleas and guilty pleas. Mich. Const., art. I, § 20 (1963).

2)   LEAVE TO APPEAL REQUIRED FROM CERTAIN PLEAS

Specifically, "an appeal by an accused who pleads guilty or *nolo contendere* shall be by leave of the court." *Id.* (italics added). The appellate remedies of an accused who pleads *nolo contendere* or guilty are restricted to the filing of an application for leave to appeal.

In contrast to an appeal by right, from which the Michigan Court of Appeals must afford plenary review of the merits of all timely filed claim of appeal, the decision of whether to afford plenary review of the merits of claims raised in an application for leave to appeal is left to the Michigan Court of Appeals' discretion.

a)   Twenty-One Day Limit for Applying for Leave to Appeal

The time requirements for filing an application for leave to appeal in the Michigan Court of Appeals is described as follows: "An application for leave to appeal must be filed within 21 days after entry of the judgment or order to be appealed from or within other time as allowed by law or rule." MCR 7.205(A).

b)   Delayed Application for Leave to Appeal

Additionally, a person may file a delayed application for leave to appeal. MCR 7.205(F).

(1)   Required Information

A party who makes a delayed application for leave to appeal must provide the Court of Appeals with a statement of the party's allegations of error and the relief sought. Also, the party must explain the delay for not timely filing an application for leave to appeal. MCR 7.205(F)(1).

(2)   Delay in Filing Considered by Court of Appeals

The Court of Appeals may consider the basis for the delay in filing when assessing whether to deny or grant the application. As with a timely application for leave to appeal, the Court of Appeals has discretion when deciding whether to grant plenary review of the delayed application for leave to appeal.

c)   Request for Leave to Appeal to Michigan Supreme Court

An applicant who is denied leave to appeal in the Court of Appeals may request a leave to appeal in the Michigan Supreme Court. MCR 7.302. However, these applications are rarely granted. The Supreme Court has discretion over whether to grant an application for leave to appeal. *Id.*

B.   Appellate Counsel

The Sixth Amendment to the United States Constitution states that "[I]n all criminal prosecutions, the accused shall enjoy the right . . . to have the assistance of counsel for his defense."

1)   STATES MUST PROVIDE APPOINTED COUNSEL

The United States Supreme Court held that the Sixth Amendment right to counsel provides a fundamental right and that the Fourteenth Amendment obligates states to provide appointed counsel to indigent criminal defendants at state expense to assist criminal defendants at trial. *Gideon v. Wainwright*, 372 U.S. 335 (1963). The Fourteenth Amendment provides the right to appointed counsel for indigent defendants in their first appeals as of right after a criminal conviction. *Douglas v. California*, 372 U.S. 353 (1963).

        a)   Appointed Counsel Not Required for Discretionary Appeal

In contrast, the federal constitution does not require states to appoint counsel to help an indigent convict to assist in discretionary appeals to either the United States Supreme Court or to the state's highest court. *Ross v. Moffitt*, 417 U.S. 600 (1974).

        b)   Michigan Must Appoint Counsel for Appeals from Pleas

The United States Supreme Court determined that with respect to the appointment of counsel, Michigan's constitutionally mandated review system for plea-based convictions is governed by the above case of *Douglas versus California*. *Halbert v. Michigan*, 545 U.S. 605 (2005). Thus, the State of Michigan must appoint counsel to indigent defendants who plead *nolo contendere* or guilty to assist them in getting initial leave discretionary review before the Michigan Court of Appeals.

                (1)   Grounds for Requiring Appointed Counsel

The United States Supreme Court based its holding in that case on two features of Michigan's criminal appellate process. One, when deciding applications for leave to appeal, the Michigan Court of Appeals considers the merits of any claims raised by the defendant. *Id.* at 617. Thus, the Court of Appeals' ruling is the initial and likely the sole direct review of the merits of the conviction and sentence of defendant. Two, indigent defendants requesting review by the Michigan Court of Appeals are not qualified to represent themselves *pro se*. *Id.* People without legal skills are unable to help the appellate court in determining their claims' legal merits.

                (2)   Time for Requesting Appellate Counsel

The Michigan Court Rules were amended pursuant to the United States Supreme Court's case law. Consequently, in Michigan indigent defendants have 42 days to request appellate counsel. MCR 6.425(G)(1)(c). A Michigan trial court has to grant a timely filed request for the appointment of appellate counsel. *Id.*

EVIDENCE

Commonly Tested Issues

★★★★

- Hearsay Evidence – General
- Relevance

★★★

- Hearsay Exceptions – Witness Unavailable
- Hearsay Exceptions – Witness Availability Immaterial
- Hearsay Exceptions – Admission of Party Opponent
- Character – Prior Bad Acts

★★

- Impeachment – Prior Convictions
- Impeachment – Prior Inconsistent Statements
- Impeachment – Specific Conduct
- Offer to Pay Medical Expenses
- Subsequent Remedial Measures
- Witnesses – Expert Testimony
- Witnesses – Competency
- Liability Insurance
- Statements in Plea Negotiations
- Settlement Offers and Statements
- Motion in *Limine*
- Best Evidence Rule
- Authentication

★

- Character – Opinion or Reputation
- Routine Practice of Organization
- Habit of Individual
- Impeachment – Impeaching Own Witness
- Impeachment – Religious Beliefs
- Witnesses – Layperson Testimony
- Witnesses – Judge as Witness
- Self-Authentication
- Rule of Completeness
- Hearsay Exceptions – Statement of Agent or Servant
- Interview Notes
- Interpreters
- Statements
- Refreshing Recollection
- Work Product

⬧ Improper Argument

TABLE OF CONTENTS

EVIDENCE

Michigan Common Issues & Distinctions

The following outline is based on analysis of questions on the essay portion of the Michigan Bar Exam. The outline may address general legal principles and Michigan-specific rules. The general rules may be identical to those covered in your outlines for the Multistate Bar Exam ("MBE"). To the extent that this outline repeats identical rules covered in your MBE outline, such repetition is provided for the beneficial purposes of 1) learning how the rules are construed, applied, and tested in Michigan, and 2) learning which rules are tested most often on the essay portion of the examination (most topics appearing in this outline have appeared on a recent administration of the essay portion of the exam). Moreover, these general rules are sometimes stated in different ways by Michigan's courts. The general rules, along with any unique provisions of Michigan law (Michigan distinctions), are presented in the manner that Michigan's bar examiners view them with respect to analyzing essay questions on previously tested issues of law.

THIS OUTLINE IS NOT A COMPLETE OUTLINE OF EVIDENCE LAW FOR THE ESSAY PORTION OF THE MICHIGAN BAR EXAMINATION. It is designed to be used conjunction with your MBE outline. Any essay questions testing topics of MBE subjects that are not covered in this outline, should be answered according to the law you have learned for the MBE.

Traditionally, one or two Evidence questions have appeared on each exam, although this frequency of testing in the past may not be the same going forward.

Generally, the Michigan Rules of Evidence ("MRE") is the main source of previously tested legal principles. The MRE, as well as facts and rules derived from cases decided by the Michigan appellate courts, have provided the basis for some past Evidence questions and answers. Although the sample answers for certain past questions indicate that Michigan law should be the basis for answering questions, future questions could be answerable using controlling general legal principles contained in the MBE outline for Evidence. This may be the case to the extent that the MRE are similar to the Federal Rules of Evidence ("FRE"), which are described in the MBE outline for Evidence. Both the MRE and FRE are similarly numbered and include comparable rules as well as distinctions. Of course, when answering an Evidence question that tests a rule that is comparable under both the MRE and FRE, ideally an answer would discuss the MRE, particularly if the controlling MRE contains a distinction from the FRE. The following supplemental outline discusses some of these distinctions that pertain to certain previously tested issues, along with some other tested rules.

According to some past exams, some frequently tested issues include the hearsay rule and its exceptions and methods of impeachment. Some less frequently tested issues involve character evidence, insurance coverage, expert testimony, guilty pleas, and motions in *limine*. Some occasionally tested issues are witness competency, offers to pay medical expenses, subsequent remedial measures, routine practice of an organization, a statement made in plea negotiations, impeaching a party's own witness, layperson opinion testimony, authentication, self-authentication, the best evidence rule, witness interview notes, refreshing recollection, work product, and improper argument.

I.   CHARACTER EVIDENCE

A.   Generally

Both FRE 404(a) and MRE 404(a) provide certain exceptions to their general rule excluding evidence of an individual's character to prove the individual's conduct in conformity with this character on a specific occasion.

1)   CHARACTER OF AN ACCUSED

Both FRE 404(a)(1) and MRE 404(a)(1) provide similar exceptions for evidence of an accused's character.

2)   CHARACTER OF AN ALLEGED VICTIM

Although both FRE 404(a)(2) and MRE 404(a)(2) provide exceptions regarding evidence of an alleged victim's character, this entire Michigan provision only applies with respect to charge of homicide, while only the second part of the federal provision -- regarding evidence of the victim's character for peaceableness – expressly applies in homicide cases. The verbiage of the first part of this federal provision, however, concerning the evidence of a crime victim's character offered by the accused, does not limit its application to prosecution in any particular types of criminal cases.

a)   Alleged Victim of Homicide

Michigan Evidence Rule 404(a)(2) provides the following exception to the general rule of character evidence, which applies to homicide charges:

> When self-defense is an issue in a charge of homicide, evidence of a trait of character for aggression of the alleged victim of the crime offered by an accused, or evidence offered by the prosecution to rebut the same, or evidence of a character trait of peacefulness of the alleged victim offered by the prosecution in a charge of homicide to rebut evidence that the alleged victim was the first aggressor.

Mich. R. Evid. 404(a)(2).

b)   Alleged Victim of a Sexual Conduct Crime

Another Michigan Rule of Evidence also includes a provision absent from the comparable Federal Rule of Evidence regarding the character of an alleged victim of a sexual conduct crime. Some Federal Rules of Evidence pertain to certain evidence involving sex offenses, sexual assault, and child molestation. Fed. Rs. Evid. 412-415.

Michigan Evidence Rule 404(a)(3) provides the following exception to the general rule of character evidence, which applies to criminal sexual conduct charges:

In a prosecution for criminal sexual conduct, evidence of the alleged victim's past sexual conduct with the defendant and evidence of specific instances of sexual activity showing the source or origin of semen, pregnancy, or disease.

Mich. R. Evid. 404(a)(3).

B.   Prior Bad Acts

As a general proposition, character evidence, including prior bad acts, is inadmissible to prove conformity with that character. MRE 404(b). However, prior bad acts evidence is admissible to prove motive, opportunity, plan, etc. MRE 404(b)(1).

1)   MRE DISTINCTIONS

a)   MRE 404(b)(1)

MRE 404(b)(1) and FRE 404(b) are basically similar. MRE 404(b)(1), however, contains some additional phrases. Specifically, one other purpose for which prior bad acts evidence may be admitted under MRE 404(b)(1) is to show a "system in doing an act." MRE 404(b)(1) also provides that the permissible types of prior bad acts evidence are admissible "when the same is material, whether such other crimes, wrongs, or acts are contemporaneous with, or prior or subsequent to the conduct at issue in the case."

b)   MRE 404(b)(2)

MRE 404(b)(2) is similar to FRE 404(b). MRE includes the italicized additional phrases.

The prosecution in a criminal case shall provide reasonable notice in advance of trial, or during trial if the court excuses pretrial notice on good cause shown, of the general nature of any such evidence it intends to introduce at trial and the rationale, whether or not mentioned in subparagraph [404](b)(1), for admitting the evidence. If necessary to a determination of the admissibility of the evidence under this rule, the defendant shall be required to state the theory or theories of defense, limited only by the defendant's privilege against self-incrimination.

2)   FACTORS OF ADMISSIBILITY

The Michigan Supreme Court has established factors for the admissibility of prior bad acts evidence under MRE 404(b). *People v. Vandervliet,* 444 Mich. 52 (1993). In order to be admissible, the proponent of the evidence must show: (1) that the evidence is offered for a proper purpose (i.e., something other than propensity); (2) that the evidence is relevant under MRE 402, and that the unfair prejudice does not substantially outweigh the probative value of the evidence. *Id.*; *People v. Khox,* 469 Mich. 502 (2004). In addition, the trial court may, upon request, provide a limiting jury instruction regarding the evidence.

3)   LOGICAL RELEVANCE

When the issue in a case is whether the evidence of an uncharged act is being offered for a proper purpose under MRE 404(b), one potential theory of its logical relevance (to a charged act) that can be proffered by the prosecutor is one of scheme, plan, or system. In *People v. Sabin,* the Michigan Supreme Court clarified this theory of logical relevance. *People v. Sabin,* 463 Mich. 43 (2000). Logical relevance involves a consideration of whether the prior bad act is sufficiently similar to the subject matter of the instant lawsuit to show any proper purpose for it to be admitted as evidence. *Id.*

a)   Scheme, Plan, or System

Scheme or plan can happen in one of two circumstances: (1) where the charged and uncharged acts are each a piece of a larger plan; or (2) where a scheme is used repeatedly to perpetuate separate but similar crimes.

Generally similarity is insufficient to establish a plan, scheme, or system. There must be a "concurrence of common features." The common features must indicate the existence of a plan rather than a series of spontaneous acts, but the plan need not be distinctive or unusual. When, for example, there are no common features between the charged and uncharged acts, the evidence is not properly admissible to show a scheme, plan, or system.

4)   DOMESTIC VIOLENCE PROSECUTION

a)   Propensity Evidence Admissible

In 2006, the Michigan Legislature enacted Michigan Compiled Law section 768.27b, which permits the admission into evidence a defendant's other acts of domestic violence "for any purpose for which it is relevant." Thus, in contrast to the general evidentiary rule of MRE 404(b), prior acts of domestic violence are now admissible in a domestic violence prosecution for propensity purposes. Mich. Comp. Laws § 768.27b.

(1)   Exception

This modern statute specifically provides, however, that the defendant's other acts of domestic violence occurring more than 10 years before the charged domestic violence offense are inadmissible unless the admission of the evidence "is in the interest of justice." Mich. Comp. Laws § 768.27b(4).

II.   PLEAS AND PLEA DISCUSSIONS

A.   Plea of Nolo Contendere

1)   GENERAL RULE

Generally, under MRE 410(2) and FRE 410(2), evidence of a *nolo contendere* plea is not, in any civil or criminal proceeding, admissible against the defendant who made the plea or was a participant in the plea discussions.

a) Exception

The foregoing general rule is subject to an exception in MRE 410(2) that, to the extent that evidence of a guilty plea would be admissible, evidence of a plea of *nolo contendere* to a criminal charge can be admitted in a civil proceeding to support a defense against a claim asserted by the person who entered the plea. FRE 410(2) lacks such an exception for the admissibility of a plea of *nolo contendere*.

III. IMPEACHMENT

A. Impeachment with Hearsay Testimony

Although under MRE 607 and FRE 607, any party can impeach the credibility of a witness including its own witness, if the witness denies that a declarant made a statement to the witness, the witness cannot be impeached by hearsay testimony from a third party that asserts the truth of the matter -- that the declarant's alleged statement that the witness denied was made to the witness had been made to the witness.

B. Impeachment by Prior Conviction

1) MRE 609

a) General Rule

Pursuant to MRE 609(a), for the purpose of attacking the credibility of a witness, evidence that the witness has been convicted of a crime is admissible if the evidence has been elicited from the witness or established by public record during cross-examination, and (1) the crime contained an element of dishonesty or false statement, or (2) the crime contained an element of theft, and (a) the crime was punishable by imprisonment in excess of one year or death under the law under which the witness was convicted, and (b) the court determines that the evidence has significant probative value on the issue of credibility and, if the witness is the defendant in a criminal trial, the court further determines that the probative value of the evidence outweighs its prejudicial effect.

(1) Probative Value Determination

Under MRE 609(b), for purposes of determining probative value under MRE 609(a)(2)(B), the court may consider only the age of the conviction and the degree to which a conviction of the crime is indicative of veracity; additionally, for purposes of determining prejudicial effect, the court must consider only the conviction's similarity to the charged offense and the possible effects on the decisional process if admitting the evidence causes the defendant to elect not to testify.

(a)   Articulation of Analysis

Under MRE 609(b), a trial judge is required to articulate, on the record, the judge's analysis of the probative value and prejudicial effect of the evidence.

(2)   Ten Year Limitation

Under MRE 609(c), evidence of a conviction under the rule is not admissible if a period of more than ten years has elapsed since the date of the conviction or of the release of the witness from the confinement imposed for that conviction, whichever is the later date.

2)   MRE DISTINCTIONS

a)   General Comparisons

Neither MRE 609(a)(1) nor FRE 609(a)(2) require that a crime involving an element of dishonesty or false statement be punishable by imprisonment in excess of one year or death. Only MRE 609(a)(2), but not FRE 609, specifically provides for admissibility of evidence of a prior conviction of a crime involving an element of theft that is punishable by imprisonment for over one year or death. However, FRE 609(a)(1) provides for the admissibility of evidence of a prior conviction of a crime (not involving an element of dishonesty or false statement) if it was punishable by imprisonment for over one year or death.

b)   Witness is not the Defendant/Accused

If the witness is not the defendant, to be admissible under MRE 609(a)(2) evidence of a prior crime involving an element of theft must have significant probative value regarding the witness's credibility.

If the witness is not the accused, to be admissible under FRE 609(a)(1), evidence of a prior crime (not involving an element of dishonesty or false statement) "may be excluded if its probative value is substantially outweighed by the danger of unfair prejudice, confusion of the issues, or misleading the jury, or by considerations of undue delay, waste of time, or needless presentation of cumulative evidence." FRE 403.

c)   Witness is the Defendant/Accused

If the witness is the defendant, to be admissible under MRE 609(a)(2) evidence of a prior crime involving an element of theft must have significant probative value regarding the witness' credibility and the probative value must exceed its prejudicial effect.

If the witness is the accused, to be admissible under FRE 609(a)(1) evidence of a prior crime (not involving an element of dishonesty or false statement) generally must have probative value that outweighs it prejudicial affect to the accused.

C.   Witness' Religious Opinions or Beliefs

1)   EVIDENCE OF OPINIONS OR BELIEFS INADMISSIBLE

Evidence about the opinions or beliefs of a witness regarding matters of religion is not admissible to prove that the witness' credibility is enhanced or impaired by reason of those opinions or beliefs. MRE 610; FRE 610.

IV.   WITNESSES

A.   Competency of Witnesses

In addition to the general principle that all people are competent to serve as witnesses except as otherwise provided by the rules of evidence, a Michigan court may find that a person lacks the physical or mental capacity or sense of obligation to testify understandably and truthfully. MRE 601.

B.   Layperson Witnesses

Under MRE 701, a layperson can provide opinion testimony if the opinion is within the general competence of a layperson, is rationally based on the perception of the witness, and if the testimony is helpful to the determination of a fact in issue. For example, an individual who witnessed a vehicle incident involving a plaintiff and a defendant may be able to give opinion testimony regarding the incident in their lawsuit in which the defendant's fault for the incident is at issue, provided the proper foundation is laid establishing that the witness is competent to estimate vehicle speed. If the witness is an experienced driver, and has experience estimating car speed, this should be sufficient to qualify the witness to give this lay opinion testimony. *People v. Oliver,* 170 Mich. App. 38 (1988).

C.   Expert Witnesses

MRE 702 provides that expert testimony is admissible only if the trial court initially finds that "scientific, technical, or other specialized knowledge will assist the trier of fact to understand the evidence or to determine a fact in issue."

1)   MOTION TO EXCLUDE TESTIMONY OF EXPERT WITNESS

A party can make a motion to exclude the testimony of an expert witness and request a hearing on the motion. Under MRE 104(a), preliminary issues of witness qualification must be determined by the court. In *Gilbert v. Daimler Chrysler,* the Michigan Supreme Court held that this rule imposes a duty on the trial court to act as a gatekeeper during all stages of expert testimony. *Gilbert v. Daimler Chrysler,* 470 Mich. 749 (2004). Therefore, as a precondition to admitting testimony by an expert, the trial court is required to determine that the expert testimony will assist the trier of fact and meet the additional conditions noted below.

a)   Hearing on Motion

Neither MRE 702 nor *Gilbert* specially require a hearing, but, depending upon the nature of the expert's testimony and the clear requirement that the trial court vet proffered expert testimony before allowing a jury to hear it, a hearing may be the most prudent course of action.

b)   Burden of Proof

A party seeking to introduce the expert testimony bears the burden of proving that the testimony is admissible under MRE 702. *Gilbert, supra,* at 781. The testimony of an individual expert is admissible only if the subject matter of the testimony will "assist" the trier of fact, and the expert witness is "qualified as an expert by knowledge, skill, experience, training, or education." MRE 702. "An expert who lacks 'knowledge' in the field at issue cannot 'assist the trier of fact.'" *Gilbert, supra,* at 789.

c)   Purpose of Hearing

Conducting a hearing could ensure both that the expert's testimony will assist the jury to understand some issue in the case and that the expert is "qualified" as defined in MRE 702 to speak on the subject of that testimony. At the hearing, a party introducing an expert witness should be required to demonstrate to the trial court's satisfaction that an expert's training is fundamentally related to the subject matter of the expert's proposed testimony.

V.   HEARSAY AND EXCEPTIONS

A.   Statements Not Hearsay

1)   ADMISSION BY PARTY-OPPONENT

Generally, a party's own statement made in an individual or representative capacity is not hearsay when offered as evidence against the party. MRE 801(d)(2)(A).

a)   Motor Vehicle Exceptions

However, one exception applies to a statement "made in connection with a guilty plea to a misdemeanor motor vehicle violation." *Id.* Another exception applies to an admission of responsibility for a motor vehicle civil infraction. *Id.*

B.   Availability of Declarant Immaterial

1)   PUBLIC RECORDS AND REPORTS

Under MRE 803(8), the hearsay rule does not exclude records setting forth (a) the activities of a public office or agency or (b) matters observed pursuant to duty imposed by law as to which matters there was a duty to report, "excluding, however, in criminal cases matters observed by police officers and other law enforcement personnel." A lab report prepared by a police officer regarding evidence of crime by a defendant is adversarial. If, for example, the report was specifically prepared to establish the identity of a controlled substance as an element of a crime and by use of hearsay observations made by the officer, the report cannot be admitted. *People v. McDaniel,* 469 Mich. 409 (2003).

2)   RECORDS OF REGULARLY CONDUCTED ACTIVITY

Such a report would also not be admissible under MRE 803(6), which provides that records kept in the course of a regularly conducted business activity are not excluded by the hearsay rule "unless the source of information or the method or circumstances of preparation indicate lack of trustworthiness." When the lab report was prepared in anticipation of litigation, it would be inadmissible hearsay because the circumstances of its preparation indicated lack of truth worthiness. *McDaniel, supra.*

3)   JUDGMENT OF PRIOR CONVICTION

Under MRE 803(22), evidence of a final judgment of conviction entered upon a plea of guilty (or upon a plea of *nolo contendere* if evidence of the plea is not excluded by MRE 410) is not excluded by the hearsay rule, but only if the crime is "punishable by death or imprisonment in excess of one year." FRE 803(22) lacks such an exception for the admissibility of a judgment of previous conviction upon a plea of *nolo contendere*.

C.   Declarant Unavailable

1)   STATEMENT AGAINST PENAL INTEREST

A statement that is hearsay is admissible under MRE 804(b)(3), which permits the admission of statements against penal interest. A statement is "against penal interest" when, at the time of its making, it subjects the declarant to criminal liability such that a reasonable person would not have made the statement unless he believed it to be true.

Additionally, where the statement exposes the declarant to criminal liability and is offered to exculpate the accused, the statement is not admissible unless corroborating circumstances clearly indicate the trustworthiness of the statement. For example, the evidence would not be offered to exculpate an accused in the context of a civil claim (e.g., false imprisonment) rather than a criminal case (e.g., kidnapping).

2)   MRE DISTINCTIONS

MRE 804 contains two hearsay exceptions that apply when a declarant is unavailable and which are not expressly contained in FRE 804. One concerns the use of deposition testimony and the other applies to a statement made by a declarant that an opponent makes unavailable.

a)   Deposition Testimony

MRE 804(b)(5) allows for deposition testimony to be admitted when the declarant is unavailable and the person whom it is admitted against had an opportunity to cross-examine the witness with a similar motive to develop testimony.

                b)   Wrongdoing Procuring Unavailability

MRE 804(b)(6) allows for a statement by a declarant that is made unavailable by an opponent to be admitted when "the statement is offered against a party that has engaged in or encouraged wrongdoing that was intended to, and did, procure the unavailability of the declarant as a witness."

VI.   MISCELLANEOUS CONCEPTS

A.   Interview Notes

1)   DEFINITION OF STATEMENT

The Michigan Court Rules define a statement as being "a written statement signed or otherwise adopted or approved by the person making it or a stenographic, mechanical, electrical or other recording or transcription of a statement." A prosecutor's notes of an interview with a witness to an alleged crime that occurred before an accused was charged with the alleged crime would probably not fall under that definition of a statement.

2)   REFRESHING RECOLLECTION

Such notes could be admissible if they were used to refresh the witness's memory under MRE 612, rather than by the prosecutor to remind the witness of what the witness said earlier. *Id.*

3)   WORK PRODUCT

These notes would probably not be considered admissible as evidence is that they would be considered part of the work product as defined by MCR 6.210(C). Typically, interview notes constitute paraphrasing of statements, and highlights of the witnesses' comments that are filtered through the attorney's own subjective impressions of the witnesses. These notes likely contain a mental impression, conclusion, and opinion of the attorney and as such constitute work product, and are protected from discovery. *People v. Holtzman,* 234 Mich. App. 166 (1999).

B.   Improper Argument

A prosecutor may not argue the effect of testimony that was not entered into evidence at trial. *People v. Stanaway,* 446 Mich. 643 (1994). If, for example, records are inadmissible because of a statutory privilege, it is error for the prosecutor to argue to the jury what was allegedly in these records. *Id.* Also, a prosecutor also cannot vouch for the credibility of facts and evidence not in the case. *Id.* Suppose, for example, an objection to such an argument is properly made but overruled by the court. *Id.* Without a curative instruction the argument is error and would, standing alone, probably constitute grounds to reverse a defendant's conviction. *Id.*

C.   Motion in Limine

A party may make a pretrial motion in *limine* seeking to exclude evidence. This motion is usually made before voir dire (e.g., jury trial) or trial (e.g., bench trial) to receive a preliminary ruling regarding the admissibility of certain evidence.

REAL PROPERTY

Commonly Tested Issues

★★★★

★★★

+ Quitclaim Deed
+ Tenancy by the Entirety

★★

+ Doctrine of Acquiescence
+ Adverse Possession
+ Contract of Sale
+ Action to Quiet Title
+ Concurrent Interests
+ Easements – Express
+ Easements – By Necessity
+ Easements – Prescriptive
+ Easements – Scope
+ Public Trust Doctrine
+ Recording Statutes – Lien Priority
+ Good Faith Purchaser – Notice
+ Landlord and Tenant – Eviction by Summary Proceedings

★

+ Marketable Title
+ Warranty Deed – General Warranty
+ Doctrine of Merger by Deed
+ Statute of Frauds
+ Possibility of Reverter
+ Dower
+ Tenancy in Common
+ Joint Tenancy
+ Future Advance Mortgage
+ Easements – Termination
+ Landlord and Tenant – Term and Termination
+ Landlord and Tenant – Discrimination (Michigan Civil Right Act)
+ Landlord and Tenant – Successor Landlord & Existing Tenant
+ Landlord and Tenant – Pet Ownership
+ Seller Disclosure Act
+ Dedication of Property
+ Riparian Owner's Rights
+ Littoral Property
+ Trespass

TABLE OF CONTENTS

REAL PROPERTY

Michigan Common Issues & Distinctions

The following outline is based on analysis of questions on the essay portion of the Michigan Bar Exam. The outline may address general legal principles and Michigan-specific rules. The general rules may be identical to those covered in your outlines for the Multistate Bar Exam ("MBE"). To the extent that this outline repeats identical rules covered in your MBE outline, such repetition is provided for the beneficial purposes of 1) learning how the rules are construed, applied, and tested in Michigan, and 2) learning which rules are tested most often on the essay portion of the examination (most topics appearing in this outline have appeared on a recent administration of the essay portion of the exam). Moreover, these general rules are sometimes stated in different ways by Michigan's courts. The general rules, along with any unique provisions of Michigan law (Michigan distinctions), are presented in the manner that Michigan's bar examiners view them with respect to analyzing essay questions on previously tested issues of law.

THIS OUTLINE IS NOT A COMPLETE OUTLINE OF PROPERTY LAW FOR THE ESSAY PORTION OF THE MICHIGAN BAR EXAMINATION. It is designed to be used conjunction with your MBE outline. Any essay questions testing topics of MBE subjects that are not covered in this outline, should be answered according to the law you have learned for the MBE.

Facts and rules derived from cases decided by the Michigan appellate courts have provided the basis for some of the facts and/or rules for certain past Real & Personal Property questions and answers. The Michigan Compiled Laws and common law are other sources for tested rules as well. Although the sample answers for certain past questions indicate that some Michigan law and court cases should be the basis for answering questions, future questions could be answerable using controlling general legal principles contained in the MBE outline for Property.

Real & Personal Property essay questions on the Michigan Bar Exam have tended to test real property issues separately from personal property issues, although some overlap or combination of these issues could occur. Personal Property rules are discussed in the separate Personal Property outline. The following Real Property outline supplements the MBE outline for Property. Traditionally, one Real & Personal Property essay question has appeared on each exam or every other exam, although this frequency of testing in the past may not be the same going forward. According to some past exams, some previously tested issues include contracts of sale, actions to quiet title, the doctrine of acquiescence, adverse possession, easements, concurrent interests, and future interests. Some other occasionally tested issues involve marketable title, quitclaim deed, warranty deed, the doctrine of merger by deed, the Public Trust Doctrine, the statute of frauds, possibility of reverter, dower, recording statutes, future advance mortgage, as well as lease term and termination.

I.   EASEMENTS

A.   General Considerations

An easement is an interest in real estate that gives one person the right to use another person's land for a specific purpose. An easement displaces the rights of the landowner only to the extent necessary to allow the holder of the easement to enjoy the rights conveyed under the easement. An easement is inherently limited and is generally confined to a specific purpose. Once created, easements pass with the land unless otherwise modified or extinguished.

1)   CREATION OF EASEMENT

An easement may be created by express grant or by operation of law. *Forge v. Smith*, 458 Mich. 198 (1998). An express easement must be very clear in its intent, and it must be in writing. *Id.*; *Myers v. Spencer*, 318 Mich. 155 (1947). An easement by necessity is one type of easement that may be created by operation of law. *Schmidt v. Eger*, 94 Mich. App. 728 (1980); *also Chapdelaine v. Sochocki*, 247 Mich. App. 167 (2001). An easement will also be implied in law by prescription.

2)   SCOPE OF EASEMENT

Easements have traditionally been strictly construed in Michigan. "Once granted, an easement cannot be modified by either party or unilaterally. The owner of the easement cannot materially increase the burden of it on the servient estate or impose thereon a new and additional burden." *Schadewald v. Brul*, 225 Mich. App. 26, 36 (1997). Further, the Michigan Supreme Court has rejected a party's attempt to expand the scope of an easement beyond the express language granting the easement. *DNR v. Cardmody-Lahti Real Estate,* 472 Mich. 359, 378-379 (2005).

3)   TERMINATION

An easement may be terminated when the titles to the dominant and servient estates are merged. *Von Meding v. Strahl,* 319 Mich. 598 (1948). A person cannot hold an easement over the person's own property. *Bricault v. Cavanaugh,* 261 Mich. 70 (1932).

B.   Types of Easements

1)   EASEMENT BY NECESSITY

Though older Michigan cases spoke of a requirement of strict or absolute necessity, a "grant of an easement by necessity requires (in the least) a showing of reasonable necessity." *Waubun Beach Ass'n v. Wilson*, 274 Mich. 598, 609 (1936); *Tomecek v. Bavas*, 276 Mich. App. 252, 256 (2007). "The scope of an easement by necessity is that which is reasonably necessary for proper enjoyment of the property, with minimum burden on the servient estate." *Schumacher v. Dep't of Natural Res.*, 256 Mich. App. 103, 106 (2003).

a)   Landlocked

Michigan law recognizes that an easement may be granted out of necessity where a landowner has subdivided his property and left one of the parcels landlocked. *Chapdelaine v. Sochacki*, 247 Mich. App. 167, 172-173 (2001).

        b)   Not Landlocked

Michigan has joined a growing number of jurisdictions that recognize easements by necessity where the landowner is not physically landlocked from his property. *Tomecek v. Bavas,* 276 Mich. App. 252 (2007). In *Tomecek v. Bavas*, the Court of Appeals concluded that the common-law doctrine of easement by necessity includes a "right to access utilities for properties landlocked from utility services unless, consistent with the traditional principles of easement by necessity, the parties to the conveyance that left the property without such access 'clearly indicate[d] that they intended a contrary result.'" *Id.* quoting *Chapdelaine, supra.* As noted in the *Restatement of Property 3d*, § 2.15, cmt. D:

> [T]he increasing dependence in recent years on electricity and telephone service, delivered through overland cables, justify the conclusion that implied servitudes by necessity will be recognized for those purposes. Whether access for other utilities and services has also become necessary to reasonable enjoyment of property depends on the nature and location of the property and normal land uses in the community.

      2)   <u>PRESCRIPTIVE EASEMENT</u>

A prescriptive easement is akin to fee title that passed by adverse possession. One who prevails in a claim of prescriptive easement gains the right to use the easement, not ownership of the land subject to the prescriptive easement. In comparison, one who prevails in a claim of adverse possession action will own the disputed land.

        a)   Elements

        (1)   General

In order to claim a prescriptive easement, one must use without permission the land of another for a particular purpose and without interruption for a minimum period of 15 years. Mich. Comp. Laws § 600.5801(4). Although case law presents several varying elements of an easement by prescription, Michigan courts have consistently identified that an easement by prescription requires elements similar to adverse possession except exclusivity. *Id.*, citing *Plymouth Canton Community Crier, Inc. v. Prose*, 242 Mich. App. 676, 679 (2000). Thus, the following elements have been noted: actual use, visible use, open use, notorious use, hostile use, use under cover of claim or right, and continuous use for 15 years.

        (2)   Modern Trend

In some more modern cases, however, Michigan courts have only required that a prescriptive easement result from use of another's property that is open, notorious, adverse, and continuous for a period of 15 years. *Higgins Lake Prop. Owners Assn. v. Gerrish Twp.*, 255 Mich. App. 83, 118 (2003). (Citations omitted), citing *Plymouth Canton Community Crier, Inc., supra* at 676; *Goodall v. Whitefish Hunting Club*, 208 Mich. App. 642, 645 (1995); Mich. Comp. Laws § 600.5801(4); *also Marr v. Hemenny*, 297 Mich. 311 (1941); *Mumrow v. Riddle*, 67 Mich. App. 693, 698 (1976); *Dyer v. Thurston*, 32 Mich. App. 341, 343 (1971).

(a)   Burden of Proof

The burden of proving the existence of a prescriptive easement rests on the party claiming the easement. *Stewart v. Hunt*, 303 Mich. 161 (1942).

(3)   Qualified Possession

The prescriptive easement does not displace the true owner of the property, but rather grants the holder of the easement "qualified possession only to the extent necessary for enjoyment of the rights conferred by the easement." *Day v. Molitor,* unpublished opinion per curiam of the Court of Appeals, decided December 27, 2005 (Docket No. 256489), citing *Schadewald v. Brul,* 225 Mich. App. 26, 35 (1997).

(4)   Scope

A prescriptive easement is generally limited in scope by the manner in which it was acquired and the previous enjoyment. *Heydon v. Media One of Southeast Michigan, Inc.*, 275 Mich. App. 267, 270-271 (2007), citing 25 Am. Jur. 2d, Easements and Licenses, § 81, p 579. "One who holds a prescriptive easement is allowed to do such acts as are necessary to make effective the enjoyment of the easement unless the burden on the servient estate is unreasonably increased; the scope of the privilege is determined largely by what is reasonable under the circumstances." *Id.* citing *Mumrow, supra* at 699-700.

(5)   Hostile or Adverse

The term "hostile," as used in the law of adverse possession, is a term of art and does not imply ill will. *Plymouth Canton Community Crier, Inc., supra* at 681. Adverse or hostile use is use that is inconsistent with the right of the owner, without permission asked or given, that would entitle the owner to a cause of action against the intruder for trespassing. *Id.*

(6)   Frequency of Use

In regard to continuous use, "a use is continuous when it is regular, even if not constant." *Dyer, supra.*

The Michigan Supreme Court has held that use need not be continuous, or daily, but only on an as-needed basis. Specifically, the Supreme Court held as follows:

An omission to use when not needed does not disprove a continuity of use, shown by using it when needed, for it is not required that a person shall use the easement every day for the prescriptive period. It simply means that he shall exercise the right more or less frequently, according to the nature of the use to which its enjoyment may be applied.

Von Meding v. Strahl, 319 Mich. 598, 613-614 (1948), quoting *St. Cecilia Society v. Universal Car & Serv. Co.,* 213 Mich. 569, 577 (1921).

II.   PROPERTY DISPUTES

A.   Adverse Possession

1)   ELEMENTS

To prove a claim of adverse possession of a defendant's land, a plaintiff must show clear and cogent "proof of possession that is actual, visible, open, notorious, exclusive, continuous, and uninterrupted for the statutory period of 15 years, hostile, and under cover of a claim of right." *McQueen v. Black,* 168 Mich. App. 641 (1988).   Clear and convincing evidence of adverse possession is required because the theory of adverse possession is not favored.

a)   Whether Possession is Hostile

Where "a landowner takes possession of land of an adjacent owner, with the intent to hold to the true line, the possession is not hostile and adverse possession cannot be established." *Warner v. Noble,* 286 Mich. 654 (1938), cited in *McQueen, supra.* In contrast, a plaintiff may engage in hostile possession of a defendant's land by erection of a fence on the land without regard for the boundary line. *Werner v. Noble*, 286 Mich. 654 (1938); *DeGroot v. Barber*, 198 Mich. App. 48 (1993).

2)   TACKING

Tacking is a plaintiff's ability to assume the plaintiff's predecessor's adverse possession. *Connelly v. Buckingham*, 136 Mich. App. 462 (1984). For example, if the predecessor engages in adverse possession for 5 years and its successor, the plaintiff, continues in adverse possession for another 10 years, then the 15 year statutory period is satisfied by tacking together both periods of adverse possession if they are all without any interruption.

B.   Doctrine of Acquiescence

Acquiescence is a theory by which a plaintiff could acquire title to land. A 15-year statute of limitations applies to the law of acquiescence when adjoining property owners are mutually mistaken about the location of their properties' common boundary line. They may consider this boundary line, such as a fence, their property line. However, when the property line of record is different from this boundary line, one property owner possesses some of the other property owner's land.

Until the 15-year statute of limitations expires, the other property owner may bring a lawsuit against the one property owner to enforce his title and recover possession of the land. After the expiration of the 15-year statute of limitations, the other property owner cannot bring an action to enforce his title. In that event, the one property owner acquires title to that portion of the land on account of this acquiescence in possession of the land. *Jackson v. Deemer*, 373 Mich. 22 (1964). The theory of acquiescence rests upon an implied agreement among adjoining property owners.

1) CLAIM OF ACQUIESCENCE

To prove a claim of acquiescence, a plaintiff need only prove the parties (or their predecessors in interest) had agreed to a boundary line for the statutory period of 15 years. *Sackett v. Atyeo,* 217 Mich. App. 676 (1996).

2) LEGAL BOUNDARY

Under Michigan law, if adjoining property owners acquiesce to a boundary line for more than 15 years, the courts will treat that line as the legal boundary between the owners' lots.

3) DISTINGUISHED FROM ADVERSE POSSESSION

Unlike a claim based upon adverse possession, the doctrine of acquiescence does not require a showing that the possession of the land in dispute was "hostile" or without permission. *Killips v. Mannisto*, 244 Mich. App. 256, 260 (2001); *Walters v. Snyder*, 239 Mich. App. 453, 456 (2000).

C.   Action to Quiet Title

1) EQUITABLE REMEDY

Actions to quiet title brought under the Revised Judicature Act of Michigan are "equitable in nature." (i.e., an action in equity) Mich. Comp. Laws § 600.2932(5).

a)   Limited Equitable Power

However, a court may not use its equity powers to avoid the application of a statute. *Stokes v. Millen Roofing Co.,* 466 Mich. 660, 671 (2002). Moreover, equity follows the law, including the law of recording statutes.

III.   RECORDING STATUTES

A.   Race-Notice

1) EFFECT OF RECORDING

Michigan law includes a race-notice type of recording statute. Once the holder of a property interest (e.g., mortgagee) records the instrument for that interest, (A) generally the instrument will be notice to all persons "of the liens, rights, and interests" acquired or involved" and (B) "[a]ll subsequent owners or encumbrances shall take subject to the perfected liens, rights, or interests." Mich. Comp. Laws § 565.25(4). For example, a recorded mortgage provides notice and any subsequent interests or encumbrances take subject to it. Accordingly, a mortgagee that is first in time to record its mortgage may be first in right over subsequent owners or encumbrancers of the real property subject to the mortgage.

2)   EFFECT OF NOT RECORDING

Also, a conveyance of real property that is not properly recorded will be void as against any subsequent good faith purchaser who pays valuable consideration for the same real property and who records the later conveyance first, even if that conveyance is by a quit claim deed -- which of itself is not notice of any unrecorded conveyance of the same real property. Mich. Comp. Laws § 565.29. In other words, a subsequent interest holder can obtain priority over a prior conveyed interest only when the subsequent interest holder takes its interest "in good faith" and records it before any other interest holder.

a)   Notice to Good Faith Purchaser of Third Party's Interest

Another aspect of a good faith purchaser besides acquiring an interest in real property for valuable consideration is that this purchaser take the interest without notice of a third party's claimed interest in the same property. The purchaser can receive either actual or constructive notice of the third party's interest. *Richards v. Tibaldi*, 272 Mich. App. 522 (2006).

(1)   Actual Notice

A purchaser could receive actual notice of the third party's interest by, for example, a letter stating that interest.

(2)   Constructive Notice

In Michigan, a purchaser has constructive notice when the purchaser knows of facts that would lead an honest person, of ordinary caution, to make further inquiries about another's possible rights in property, and the purchaser fails to make such inquiries. *Kastle v. Clemons*, 330 Mich. 28 (1951). Issues that may arise about constructive notice is whether sufficient facts give rise to the purchaser's need to make further inquiry and, if yes, whether the purchaser used due diligence in making the inquiry. *Am. Fed. S & L Ass'n v. Orenstein*, 81 Mich. App. 249 (1978).

B.   Future Advance Mortgages

1)   DEFINITIONS

A future advance is an obligation or indebtedness that a mortgage secures and which is incurred after the mortgage has been recorded. Mich. Comp. Laws § 565.901(a). A future advance mortgage is a mortgage that secures a future advance and is recorded. Mich. Comp. Laws § 565.901(b).

2) PRIORITY

A future advance mortgage reserves priority for later advanced loans "as if the future advance was made at the time the future advance was recorded." Mich. Comp. Laws § 565.902.

C. Contractual Relationship

When a financial institution creates a contractual relationship with a client, an unauthorized third party cannot modify or direct that the contract be altered.

IV. CONVEYANCES

A. Statute of Frauds

1) REQUIRED ELEMENTS

Like most common law jurisdictions, Michigan requires contracts for the sale of land to be in writing signed by the person to be charged. Mich. Comp. Laws § 566.108. To satisfy the statute, the writing must set forth the contract's essential terms. The writing must identify the parties, state the price and describe the property. *Generally,* 17 Mich. L. & Prac. 2d, Statute of Frauds, § 72, at 478 (2003).

a) Example

Suppose, for example, that a Buyer handwrites the following notation on a page of note pad paper during a verbal discussion with a Seller resulting in a meeting of the minds regarding the purchase of a residence: "Terms of Sale--1313 Collingwood Ave.--$150,000--Buyer to pay all closing costs." Buyer then hands the pad to Seller and Seller initials the page just beneath the quoted terms.

(1) Identification

The terms of that writing, including Seller's initials, describe the parties in such a manner that they may be identified. *Generally,* 17 Mich. L. & Prac. 2d, Statute of Frauds, § 73 at 478-79 (2003).

(2) Signature

Under Michigan's statute of frauds, the seller of the land or the seller's agent must sign the writing. Mich. Comp. Laws § 566.108. No particular form of signature is required however. The seller's initials are sufficient if made by the seller with the present intention to authenticate the writing. *Archhold v. Indus. Land Co.,* 264 Mich. 289 (1933).

(3) Description

The memorandum on that page of paper initialed by Seller and prepared by Buyer also describes the property by a city street address, which is generally sufficient under Michigan's statute of frauds. *Wozniak v. Kuzinski,* 352 Mich. 431 (1958).

(4)   Price and Payment or Closing

Finally, the purchase price agreed to by the parties is stated in the memorandum from the note pad. The failure to state the time of payment or closing is not fatal. The law will imply that closing must occur within a reasonable time. *Duke v. Miller,* 355 Mich. 540 (1959).

B.   Marketable Title

Ordinarily, a land vendor breaches a promise to deliver marketable title if the vendor cannot deliver a title reasonably free from doubt to the land described in the contract. *E.g., Madhaven v. Sucher,* 105 Mich. App. 284, 288 (1981). A quitclaim deed, on the other hand, makes no promise with regard to title quality. It simply conveys whatever title the vendor had at the time it is tendered. 13 Mich. L. & Prac. Encyclopedia, 2d Ed. (Deeds) § 152 (2002).

C.   Doctrine of Merger by Deed

Generally, all promises in a contract to sell land that relate to title quality are held to merge into the deed which is accepted at closing on the sale. *Crane v. Smith,* 243 Mich. 447, 450 (1928). Thus, under the doctrine of merger by deed, a vendee who accepts a quitclaim deed at closing loses any right to sue on a promise to deliver marketable title set forth in the contract for sale.

D.   Deed Covenant of General Warranty

The covenant of general warranty in a deed warrants that the title conveyed is not subject to any lawful claim of superior title. *McCausey v. Oliver,* 253 Mich. App. 703 (2002); *also, Simons v. Diamond Match Co.,* 159 Mich. 241 (1909); Mich. Comp. Laws § 565.151. The covenant of general warranty, like the related covenant of quiet enjoyment, is a future covenant, meaning it is breached at the time a paramount title is established. "[T]he covenant is prospective in character, and, until breach occurs, passes with the estate by descent or purchase." *Simons v. Diamond Match Co., supra,* 248-249. In other words, the covenant runs with the land to benefit remote grantees of the warrantor. William B. Stoebuck & Dale A. Whitman, *The Law of Property,* § 11.13 p. 911 (3rd ed. 2000). A remote grantee should provide a remote grantor notice of a quiet title action to afford that grantor an opportunity to maintain the title that the grantor warranted in a warranty deed. 10 Mich. L. & Prac. Encyclopedia, 2d Ed. (Covenants) § 54 (2002).

E.   Quitclaim Deed

"A deed of quitclaim and release . . . shall be sufficient to pass all the estate which the grantor could lawfully convey by a deed of bargain and sale." Mich. Comp. Laws § 565.3. A quitclaim deed does not carry any warranty of title with it.

F.   Seller Disclosure Act

1)   WRITTEN DISCLOSURE STATEMENT REQUIRED

Michigan's Seller Disclosure Act requires a transferor of property to provide a written disclosure statement to the purchaser. Mich. Comp. Laws § 565.954(1). This statement must mirror a statutory disclosure form, on which the transferor has to disclose any history of infestation of the property, including termites. Mich. Comp. Laws § 565.957(1).

a)   Transferor Must Make Disclosure in Good Faith

The transferor must make each disclosure in "good faith." Good faith is "honesty in fact in the conduct of the transaction." Mich. Comp. Laws § 565.960.

2)   WHEN TRANSFEROR IS NOT LIABLE

a)   Information Other Than Personal Knowledge

The transferor is not liable for errors or inaccuracies in the disclosure statement when its information was not within the transferor's personal knowledge, "or was based entirely on information provided by . . . [an expert], and ordinary care was exercised in transmitting the information." Mich. Comp. Laws § 565.955(1).

b)   Information about Inaccessible Areas or Discoverable by Experts

The transferor also cannot be held liable if the failure to disclose related to information "that could be obtained only through inspection or observation of inaccessible portions of real estate or could be discovered only" by an expert. Mich. Comp. Laws § 565.955(1), (3).

3)   WHEN TRANSFEROR IS LIABLE

A transferor of property to a purchaser may have liability under the Seller Disclosure Act to a purchaser when, for example, the transferor had personal knowledge of structural damage to property from a prior infestation by termites and failed to act honestly by not revealing that information in the Seller's Disclosure Statement.

a)   Fraudulent Misrepresentation Claim

In that event, consistent with the Seller Disclosure Act, a purchaser can pursue a claim against a transferor for fraudulent misrepresentation. The purchaser's claim may allege:

- that the transferor made a material representation;
- the material misrepresentation was false;
- the transferor knew it was false then or recklessly made the statement as an assertion without knowledge;
- the transferor intended that the purchaser act on the statement;

- the purchaser did act in reliance on it; and
- the purchaser was injured as a result.

Roberts v. Saffell, 280 Mich. App. 397 (2008), *aff'd*, 483 Mich. 1089 (2009).

        b)   Innocent Misrepresentation Claim

The purchaser's claim will fail if the purchaser cannot prove that the transferor actually knew about the prior infestation. The Seller Disclosure Act precludes a claim for "innocent misrepresentation" because the claim does not require proof of knowledge. *Id.*

V.   FUTURE INTERESTS

A.   Possibility of Reverter

A possibility of reverter may be created in a deed's *habendum* clause (i.e., granting clause). The clause can provide, for example, that real property must be "used as a single family residence only" and that the grantee would lose his right to possession of the property automatically if either he or his successors should ever use it for any commercial purpose.

1)   RECORDING REQUIREMENT

Under Michigan law, the holder of a possibility of reverter must record a notice to preserve the future interest which lapses every thirty years unless re-recorded. Mich. Comp. Laws § 554.65. A holder that has never recorded any such notice would thus lose its right to enforce its possibility of reverter. *Ditmore v. Michalik*, 244 Mich. App. 569 (2001).

2)   STATUTE OF LIMITATION

Under Michigan law, an action to recover possession of real property must be brought within 15 years. Mich. Comp. Laws § 600.5821. The statute of limitations begins to run on the holder of a possibility of reverter as soon as the condition ending the determinable fee occurs. Moynihan & Kurtz, *Introduction to the Law of Real Property*, 138-139 (2002).

For example, when a grantor's possibility of reverter became possessory 40 years ago, the grantor's failure to record or pursue it within that span of time would make it unenforceable in an action forty years later, which would be time-barred.

B.   Right of Dower

Michigan has codified the right of dower. Generally, a widow may claim a life estate in one third of any land in which her husband held an inheritable interest during marriage. Mich. Comp. Laws § 558.1. Without his wife's consent, a husband cannot convey property free of dower. *E.g., Slater Mgmt. Corp. v. Nash*, 212 Mich. App. 30, 32 (1995) ("A husband may not bargain away his wife's dower interest.").

VI.   JOINT TENANCY

A.   Tenancy in Common

In Michigan, the modern presumption for resolving an ambiguous grant of concurrent interests to at least two people is that the grant created a tenancy in common, unless the grant is "expressly declared to be in joint tenancy." Mich. Comp. Laws § 554.44. A tenant in common may devise the tenant's interest. Moynihan & Kurtz, *Introduction to the Law of Real Property,* 268 (2002).

B.   Joint Tenancy

Two types of joint tenancies are recognized by Michigan law: 1) an ordinary joint tenancy; and 2) a joint tenancy with full rights of survivorship. *Albro v. Allen,* 434 Mich. 271 (1990).

1)   ORDINARY JOINT TENANCY

In most American jurisdictions, a grant of property to two persons as "joint tenants with right of survivorship" creates a joint tenancy. William B. Stoebuck & Dale A. Whitman, *The Law of Property,* 185-186 (3d ed. 2000). As such, either of the joint tenants can sever the relationship by an inter vivos conveyance. Upon severance, the remaining tenant and the transferee would be treated as tenants in common. *Id.,* at 189.

2)   JOINT TENANCY WITH FULL RIGHTS OF SURVIVORSHIP

The Michigan courts construe a grant to two persons as "joint tenants with right of survivorship" as a joint life estate with a remainder in the survivor. *E.g., Albro v. Allen,* 434 Mich. 271 (1990); *Butler v. Butler,* 122 Mich. App. 361, 364 (1983). In other words, a grant to two people in a "joint tenancy with full rights of survivorship" consists of a "joint life estate with dual contingent remainders." *Albro, supra.* This construction preserves the survivorship feature of the conveyance. Neither of the joint owners can eliminate the other's remainder by some act, which renders their remainders indestructible. *Albro, supra,* 434 Mich. at 284-86; and *generally,* Byron D. Cooper. *Continuing Problems with Michigan's Joint Tenancy "with Right of Survivorship,"* 78 Mich. Bar. J. 966 (Sept. 1999).

C.   Tenancy by the Entirety

1)   PRESUMPTION

When property is conveyed to a husband and wife the presumption in favor of a tenancy in common does not apply. Mich. Comp. Laws § 554.45. Michigan continues to follow the common law presumption that a grant of property to a married couple creates a tenancy by the entirety. *E.g., Butler v. Butler,* 122 Mich. App. 361 (1983). For example, when a grantor's deed conveys real property to a husband and his wife, it creates a tenancy by the entirety, not a tenancy in common or joint tenancy. Tenancy by the entireties is created by operation of common law rather than by the act of the parties through their deed. *Michigan Real Property Law,* p. 324 (ICLE 3rd Ed. 2005).

a)   No Conveyance or Encumbrance by One Spouse

Neither a husband nor a wife may act alone to convey any part of real property that is held by
both of them as tenants by the entireties. Mich. Comp. Laws §§ 557.101-102; *Hearns v. Hearns*,
333 Mich. 423 (1952). When a married couple owns their marital home as tenants by the
entireties, one spouse lacks any legal power to unilaterally convey or encumber this marital
property. Both spouses must act together in order to convey or encumber this marital property.
Berman v. State Land Office Bd., 308 Mich. 143 (1944). Moreover, "land held by husband and
wife as tenants by [the] entirety is not subject to levy under execution on judgment rendered
against either husband or wife alone." *Sanford v. Bertrau*, 204 Mich. 244 (1918).

b)   Other Considerations

The common law provides that a tenancy in the entirety is created when a properly married
couple obtain property as joint tenants and share the unities of title, time, interest, and
possession. *Budwit v. Herr*, 339 Mich. 265 (1954). A Michigan statute eliminates the unities of
title and time. Mich. Comp. Laws § 565.49. A deed of conveyance to a married couple must
expressly indicate whether the parties intend to have some other estate instead of a tenancy in the
entirety. *DeYoung v. Mesler*, 373 Mich. 499 (1964). For example, if a deed states only that the
property is conveyed to a married couple "jointly as husband and wife," then the property
constitutes a tenancy in the entirety. Each spouse possesses an indivisible interest in the entire
property. *Rogers v. Rogers*, 136 Mich. App. 125 (1984). Termination of a tenancy in the
entirety can occur by death of either spouse, the spouses' divorce, mutual agreement, or
execution on a security lien by both of the spouses' joint creditor.

2)   RIGHT OF SURVIVORSHIP

Unlike tenants in common, tenants by the entirety enjoy a right of survivorship. The share of a
deceased spouse in property held by the entirety immediately passes to the other spouse outside
probate. No interest in such property passes under the will of the deceased spouse. *Generally,*
18 Mich. L. & Prac. 2d, Husband and Wife, § 23 (2003).

VII.   LANDLORD AND TENANT

A.   Lease Term and Termination

1)   GENERAL CONSIDERATIONS

A lease creates a term of years when the lease specifies an ending date for the term with no
provision for renewal. 20 Mich. L. & Prac. 2d, Landlord and Tenant, § 51 (2003). When a
tenant remains in possession beyond that term without a landlord's objection after the term
expires, the parties' lease is not renewed. Instead, under Michigan law, a new lease arises.
When the rent under the original lease was payable monthly, a tenancy from month to month
commences. A tenancy from month to month can be terminated on one month's notice. *Cox v.
McGregor*, 330 Mich. 260 (1951); *Marks v. Corliss' Estate,* 256 Mich. 460 (1932); *also*, Mich.

Comp. Laws § 554.134(1) (providing the same result for a holdover tenant).

2)   LATE PAYMENTS

A landlord may not terminate a tenant's tenancy solely on account of the tenant's habitually late payments unless the parties' lease agreement expressly provides for this.

B.   Eviction

1)   SUMMARY PROCEEDINGS

A landlord may exercise legal recourse to evict a tenant by means of summary proceedings to recover possession of premises. Mich. Comp. Laws § 600.5701 *et seq.*

a)   Demand for Non-Payment of Rent

A landlord may serve a tenant currently behind in rent payments a seven-day written demand for non-payment of rent, which requires payment of rent or possession of the premises within seven days after the date of delivery of the notice. After the expiration time on the service of the seven-day notice, if the landlord has not received the past due rent and the tenant has not vacated the premises, the landlord may file in the landlord tenant division of a Michigan state district court a complaint for eviction. The seven-day notice and a copy of the lease must accompany the complaint.

b)   Hearing

No earlier than seven days after the complaint has been filed, the district court may set the matter for a hearing known as a summary proceeding, which should be limited to the issue of the tenant's non-payment of rent. If the tenant appears at the hearing but the tenant is unable to pay the past due rent, then the court will issue a judgment for rent and possession. If the tenant appears at the hearing and expresses an unwillingness to pay the rent due to a problem with the premises, then the landlord should ask the court to require the tenant to pay the rent in an escrow account while the merit of the tenant's complaint is investigated. In either instance, a judgment requiring payment of the rent should issue.

c)   Appeal Period

The tenant will then be afforded a 10-day appeal period during which time a Writ of Restitution may not issue. If the tenant pays the past due rent at any time during the court proceedings or within the 10-day period, the landlord must accept the rent and cannot evict the tenant.

d)   Writ of Restitution

However, if the tenant fails to pay the past due rent and does not evacuate the premises within the appeal period, the landlord may obtain from the court a Writ of Restitution that will enable a court officer to physically remove the tenant and her belongings from the premises. If an appeal from the judgment is filed, the landlord should move for an appeal bond and payment of the past due rent in an escrow account.

C.   Discrimination

1)   MICHIGAN CIVIL RIGHTS ACT

The Michigan Civil Rights Act (CRA), which applies to real estate transactions, including residential landlord tenant transactions, expressly precludes a landlord from making a public housing determination on the basis of a tenant's family and marital status. Mich. Comp. Laws § 37.2101 *et seq*. Specifically, the CRA prohibits discrimination on the basis of religion, race, color, national origin, age, sex, height, weight, or marital or familial status. *Id.*

a)   Exception for Owner-Occupied Residential Property

The CRA carves out an exception to this rule as it relates to rental of owner-occupied residential property. Specifically, in pertinent part, the CRA does not apply to the rental of "a housing accommodation in a building that contains housing accommodations for not more than 2 families living independently of each other if the owner or a member of the owner's immediate family resides in 1 of the housing accommodations." Mich. Comp. Laws § 37.2503(1)(a).

D.   Successor Landlord and Existing Tenant

Upon conveyance of title for a leased property by a transferor to a transferee, the latter receives the property subject to the rights of the tenant (i.e., tenant). Thus, the new landlord (i.e., landlord) takes the place of the former landlord. The duties, rights, and obligations of the former landlord and tenant go to the new landlord and tenant. *Plaza Inv. Co. v. Abel*, 8 Mich. App. 19 (1967).

E.   Pet Ownership

Michigan law does not preclude a landlord from using pet ownership as grounds for discriminating among tenants.

VI.   OTHER PROPERTY RIGHTS

A.   Riparian Owner Rights

1)   DETERMINATION OF RIGHTS

Whether an owner of a back lot (i.e., a non-waterfront lot) of a subdivided plat containing both waterfront lots and back lots is deemed to be a riparian owner and whether the owner possesses riparian rights is determined by the plat dedication. *Thies v. Howland*, 424 Mich. 282 (1985). The permissible use of lots will be determined by the intent of the plattors. *Id.* "The intent of the plattors [those who created the plat of real property] must be determined from the language they used [in the plat] and the surrounding circumstances." *Id.*, at 293.

a)   Case Law

For example, the plat may dedicate a waterfront lot of the subdivision to joint use of all owners of the subdivision to provide access to a body of water, such as a lake. Also, a walkway could be put in place that is dedicated to the "joint use" of all the owners of the plat to provide access to the waterfront lot and the lake along part of its border. In this event, the term "joint use" suggests that the owner of a back lot is not a riparian owner.

In *Thies v. Howland*, the Michigan Supreme Court considered the rights of back lot owners who were provided lake access by way of a walk that was dedicated in the plat. In *Thies*, the back lot owners in a waterfront subdivision constructed a dock at the end of their easement that granted them lake access. The Supreme Court looked to the plat dedication, which dedicated the walk to the "joint use of all the owners of the plat" and concluded that the use of the term "joint use" in the dedication did not support the conclusion that a fee interest passed in the land that would afford the back lot owners riparian rights to construct a dock. Note that in *Thies*, unlike the foregoing example, the plat did not dedicate a waterfront lot for the use of the subdivision owners.

In one case, the Michigan Court of Appeals held that the dedication of a waterfront lot in a plat to "the use of the owners of the lots in this plat which have no lake frontage" established an easement in favor of all back lot subdivision owners. *Dobie v. Morrison*, 227 Mich. App. 536, 537 (1998). However, the Court held that the dedication did not create a passing of a fee interest that would include riparian rights.

b)   No Unreasonable Interference with Rights

Non-riparian land owners who are granted lake access through an easement may not unreasonably interfere with the riparian owners' use and enjoyment of riparian property. *Park Trustees for Cass County v. Wendt*, 361 Mich. 247 (1960).

2)   CONSTRUCTION OF A DOCK

The right to construct a dock for the purpose of using and enjoying a lake is a well-recognized right of riparian owners. *McCardel v. Smolen*, 404 Mich. 89 (1978); *Blain v. Craigie*, 294 Mich. 545 (1940).

3)   CONSTRUCTION OF A FENCE

Note that the same legal standards would apply to the construction of fences by the back lot owner along the property lines of the waterfront lot dedicated in the plat to the use of the back lot owners.

a)   Public Trust Doctrine

The Public Trust Doctrine applies with respect to real property located on the shore of a public body of water like Lake Michigan. In that situation, a private property owner's installation of a fence from his waterfront property "to the water" and perpendicular to the shoreline would violate the public's right to walk the beaches up to the high water mark pursuant to this Doctrine. *Glass v. Goeckel*, 473 Mich. 667 (2005). Some of these concepts are further described below.

B.   Littoral Property

Generally, an owner of Great Lakes' beachfront property in Michigan cannot prevent people from walking along land held by the State of Michigan in public trust. The State holds this land that way for the public benefit. *Id.*

1)   CONVEYANCE SUBJECT TO PUBLIC TRUST

The State may convey land abutting the Great Lakes ("littoral" property) to private citizens, but only subject to the public trust. The Public Trust Doctrine provides that the State holds land between the water's edge and the "ordinary high water mark" in trust for all its citizens' use. *Id.*

2)   ORDINARY HIGH WATER MARK

The Great Lakes' water levels, which change over time, create the "ordinary high water mark." This mark is the point where "the presence and action of the water is so continuous as to leave a distinct mark either by erosion, destruction of terrestrial vegetation, or other easily recognized characteristic." *Id.*

a)   Fee Simple Overlaps with Ordinary High Water Mark

In Michigan, a Great Lakes' beachfront property owner has fee simple title to the water's edge. This fee simple overlaps with the public trust between the "ordinary high water mark" and the water's edge. Such a property owner can prevent the public from trespassing onto his private property above the "ordinary high water mark." However, the owner lacks any recourse to prevent the public from walking the shore between the water's edge and the "ordinary high water mark." *Id.*

TORTS

Commonly Tested Issues

★★★★

★★★

- Negligence – Elements
- Negligence – Standards of Care
- Negligence – Causation
- Intentional Torts – Battery
- No Fault Act – Non-economic Damages
- Comparative Fault Statute
- Premises Liability – Private
- Open and Obvious Danger
- Vicarious Liability
- Defenses
- Damages

★★

- Negligent Operation of a Motor Vehicle
- Negligence – Limited Duty Rule
- Negligence – Medical Malpractice
- Negligence – Wrongful Death
- Government Tort Liability Act and Exceptions
- Intentional Torts – Assault
- Statutory Conversion
- Release

★

- Joint and Several Liability – Non-economic Damages
- Transferred Intent
- Negligence – Violation of Safety Statute
- Negligent Parental Supervision
- Negligent Infliction of Emotional Distress
- "Eggshell-Skull" Rule
- Premises Liability – Public
- Attractive Nuisance
- Products Liability
- Several Liability
- Dramshop Act

TABLE OF CONTENTS

TORTS

Michigan Common Issues & Distinctions

The following outline is based on analysis of questions on the essay portion of the Michigan Bar Exam. The outline may address general legal principles and Michigan-specific rules. The general rules may be identical to those covered in your outlines for the Multistate Bar Exam ("MBE"). To the extent that this outline repeats identical rules covered in your MBE outline, such repetition is provided for the beneficial purposes of 1) learning how the rules are construed, applied, and tested in Michigan, and 2) learning which rules are tested most often on the essay portion of the examination (most topics appearing in this outline have appeared on a recent administration of the essay portion of the exam). Moreover, these general rules are sometimes stated in different ways by Michigan's courts. The general rules, along with any unique provisions of Michigan law (Michigan distinctions), are presented in the manner that Michigan's bar examiners view them with respect to analyzing essay questions on previously tested issues of law.

THIS OUTLINE IS NOT A COMPLETE OUTLINE OF TORTS LAW FOR THE ESSAY PORTION OF THE MICHIGAN BAR EXAMINATION. It is designed to be used conjunction with your MBE outline. Any essay questions testing topics of MBE subjects that are not covered in this outline, should be answered according to the law you have learned for the MBE.

Facts and rules derived from cases decided by the Michigan appellate courts have provided the basis for some of the facts and/or rules for certain past Torts questions and answers. The Michigan Compiled Laws and common law are other sources for tested rules as well. Although the sample answers for certain past questions indicate that some Michigan law and court cases should be the basis for answering questions, future questions could be answerable using controlling general legal principles contained in the MBE outline for Torts.

Traditionally, one (and sometimes two) Torts essay question has appeared on each exam, although this frequency of testing in the past may not be the same going forward.

According to some past exams, some frequently tested Torts issues include negligence generally, its standards of care, causation, and damages. Some other less frequently tested issues involve comparative fault, the limited duty rule, premises liability, open and obvious danger, statutory conversion, release, wrongful death, and medical malpractice. Some occasionally tested issues include intentional torts such as assault or battery, violation of a safety statute, negligent parental supervision, negligent infliction of emotional distress, the "eggshell-skull" rule, vicarious liability, products liability, public premises liability, governmental immunity, and several liability.

I.   INTENTIONAL TORTS

A.   Assault or Battery

In Michigan:

> An assault is defined as any intentional unlawful offer of corporal injury to another person by force, or force unlawfully directed toward the person of another, under circumstances which create a well-founded apprehension of imminent contact, coupled with the apparent present ability to accomplish the contact. *Tinkler v. Richter,* 295 Mich. 396, 401; 295 N.W. 201 (1940); *Prosser & Keeton,* Torts (5th ed.), § 9, p. 39. A battery is the willful and harmful or offensive touching of another person which results from an act intended to cause such a contact. *Tinkler, supra; Prosser & Keeton, supra.*

Espinoza v. Thomas, 189 Mich. App. 110 (1991).

Liability for either tort would extend to physical harms caused by the defendant's conduct.

To prove battery, the plaintiff must show that that defendant had the intent to cause a harmful or offensive contact, or knew, with substantial certainty, that such contact would result. *Boumelhem v. BIC Corp.,* 211 Mich. App. 175 (1995).

B.   Transferred Intent Doctrine

This transferred intent doctrine generally applies to certain intentional torts. For example, one who intends to commit the tort of false imprisonment against a particular individual will be liable for that tort even if a different individual suffers the harm. *Adams v. Nat'l Bank of Detroit,* 444 Mich. 329 (1993). This principle applies to assault or battery as well.

II.   NEGLIGENCE CONCEPTS

A.   Standards of Care

The basic elements of a negligence tort include duty, breach, causation and damages. The standard of care refers to the type of duty owed by a defendant to plaintiff. The type of defendant may be determinative of which type of standard of care is applicable.

1)   REASONABLE PERSON

Ordinarily, the standard of care applicable to a defendant is the reasonable person standard.

a)   Industry Custom

One type of proof of unreasonable conduct is a defendant's failure to comply with industry custom. This failure is relevant but not conclusive on the question of the defendant's negligence. *Marietta v. Cliffs Ridge, Inc.,* 385 Mich. 364 (1971): "The standard by which the negligent or non-negligent character of the defendant's conduct is to be determined is that of a reasonably prudent man under the same or similar circumstances. *McKinney v. Yelavich* (1958), 352 Mich. 687 (1958). The customary usage and practice of the industry is relevant evidence to be used in determining whether or not this standard has been met. Such usage cannot, however, be determinative of the standard. As stated by Justice Holmes:

"'What usually is done may be evidence of what ought to be done, but what ought to be done is fixed by a standard of reasonable prudence, whether it usually is complied with or not.' *Texas and Pacific R. Co. v. Behymer* (1903), 189 U.S. 468, 470, 23 S.Ct. 622, 47 L. Ed. 905.'"

b)   Impairment

The psychological disability category of impairment does not preclude application of the usual tort standard of reasonable care to the conduct of a defendant. A jury would be permitted to reach a conclusion about the conduct of a defendant who suffers from psychological disability based on its own common knowledge.

2)   CHILD

The child's standard of care applies to minors. Minors are required to exercise "that degree of care which a reasonably careful minor of the age, mental capacity and experience" of other similarly situated minors would exercise under the circumstances. *MCJI 2d* 10.06. *Also, Fire Ins. Exch. v. Diehl,* 450 Mich. 678, 688 (1996), overruled in part on other grounds, *Wilkie v. Auto-Owners Ins. Co.,* 469 Mich. 41 (2003); *Stevens v. Veenstra,* 226 Mich. App. 441, 443 (1997).

3)   GENERAL PRACTITIONER

The standard of care applicable to a general practitioner is the "recognized standard of acceptable professional practice of care in the community in which the defendant practices or in a similar community" Mich. Comp. Laws § 600.2912a.

a)   Expert Testimony

Testimony from an expert with knowledge of that same or similar locality standard of care for general practitioners would be required to establish whether general practitioners would ordinarily take particular steps in treating certain symptoms. Some rules regarding expert testimony are described later.

4)   SPECIALIST

The standard of care applicable to a specialist is "the recognized standard of practice or care within that specialty." Mich. Comp. Laws § 600.2912a.

a)   Expert Testimony

Testimony from an expert with knowledge of a national standard for the specialty would be required to establish whether, for example, the dosage administered by the specialist was appropriate. Some rules regarding expert testimony are described later.

(1)   Common Knowledge Exception

There is a slight possibility that a specialist's alleged negligence of administering an excessive dosage would fit within the common knowledge exception to the requirement of expert testimony in medical malpractice cases, since lay jurors could understand the issues associated with weights and measures. *Dorris v. Detroit Osteopathic Hosp.*, 460 Mich. 26, 44-46 (1999) (while issues of ordinary negligence can be judged by common knowledge and experience of a jury, allegations about hospital staffing decisions require expert testimony). *Id.* However, expert testimony would likely be required to determine what dosage should have been given, even if jurors could then understand a deviation from that proper dosage without the help of an expert.

5)   EXPERT WITNESS TESTIMONY

Regarding expert witness testimony, Mich. Comp. Laws § 600.2169 provides in part:

(1)   in an action alleging medical malpractice, a person shall not give expert testimony on the appropriate standard of practice or care unless the person is licensed as a health professional in this state or another state and meets the following criteria:

(a)   If the party against whom or on whose behalf the testimony is offered is a specialist, specializes at the time of the occurrence that is the basis for the action in the same specialty as the party against whom or on whose behalf the testimony is offered. However, if the party against whom or on whose behalf the testimony is offered is a specialist who is board certified, the expert witness must be a specialist who is board certified in that specialty.

(b)   Subject to subdivision (c), during the year immediately preceding the date of the occurrence that is the basis for the claim or action, devoted a majority of his or her professional time to either or both of the following:

(i)   The active clinical practice of the same health profession in which the party against whom or on whose behalf the testimony is offered is licensed and, if that party is a specialist, the active clinical practice of that specialty.

(ii)   The instruction of students in an accredited health professional school or accredited residency or clinical research program in the same health profession in which the party against whom or on whose behalf the testimony is offered is licensed and, if that party is a specialist, an accredited health professional school or accredited residency or clinical research program in the same specialty.

(2)   In determining the qualifications of an expert witness in an action alleging medical malpractice, the court shall, at a minimum, evaluate all of the following:

    (a)   The educational and professional training of the expert witness

    (b)   The area of specialization of the expert witness.

    (c)   The length of time the expert witness has been engaged in the active clinical practice or instruction of the health profession or the specialty.

6)   LIMITED DUTY RULE

Pursuant to the limited duty rule, a participant in a recreational sport such as baseball can be liable to another participant for an injury only if the injury was inflicted recklessly or intentionally. In other words, when a plaintiff and defendant are participating in a recreational sport, a plaintiff's only duty towards a defendant is to refrain from injuring the defendant recklessly or intentionally. In *Ritchie-Gamester v. City of Berkley,* the plaintiff was injured while ice skating during an open skating session by another skater skating backwards, who ran into her causing her to fall and allegedly sustain injuries. *Ritchie-Gamester v. City of Berkley,* 461 Mich. 73, 89 (1999). The Supreme Court affirmed the trial court's dismissal of the plaintiff's negligence claim, holding that "co-participants in a recreational activity owe each other a duty not to act recklessly." *Id.* (skating injury case would be governed by recklessness standard).

a)   Recklessness

The Supreme Court has defined recklessness as follows:

One who is properly charged with recklessness or wantonness is not simply more careless than one who is only guilty of negligence. His conduct must be such as to put him in the class with the willful doer of wrong.

The only respect in which is attitude is less blameworthy than that of the intentional wrongdoer is that, instead of affirmatively wishing to injure another, he is merely willing to do so. The difference is that between him who casts a missile intending that it shall strike another and him who casts it where he has reason to believe it will strike another, being indifferent whether it does so or not.

Gibbard v. Cursan, 225 Mich. 311, 321 (1923), quoting *Atchison, T. & SF. R. Co. v. Baker,* 79 Kan. 183, 189-190; 98 P. 804 (1908).

(1)   Example

Suppose, for example, an upset baseball player throws a bat into the infield while other players were in position there and without regard for the specific direction in which the bat was thrown. This conduct cannot be characterized as part of the game of baseball; furthermore there is a high probability of serious injury inherent in the act. If this conduct – which results in another player's personal injury from being hit by the bat that was thrown -- is found to have been reckless, that other player would be entitled to recover damages. If the conduct was found to have been careless or unreasonable, but not reckless, then the other player's claim would fail.

7)   VIOLATION OF SAFETY STATUTE

Violation of a relevant safety statute is *prima facie* evidence of negligence (subject to a jury's consideration of excuses for violation). *Zeni v. Anderson,* 397 Mich. 117 (1976). However, to be applicable, a statute must have been enacted to protect against the type of harm the plaintiff suffered. *Beals v. Walker,* 416 Mich. 469 (1982).

B.   Causation

A plaintiff must prove that the defendant's conduct was both a cause in fact and a legal, or proximate cause of his damages. *Skinner v. Square D. Co.,* 445 Mich. 153, 162-163 (1994).

1)   CAUSE IN FACT

The defendant's conduct will be considered a cause in fact of damages if the damages, more than likely, would not have occurred but for the at-fault conduct. *Haliw v. City of Sterling Heights,* 464 Mich. 297, 310 (2001).

A causation theory must have a basis in established fact. Additionally:

> [a] basis in only slight evidence is not enough. Nor is it sufficient to submit a causation theory that, while factually supported, is, at best, just as possible as another theory. Rather, the plaintiff must present substantial evidence from which a jury may conclude that more likely than not, but for the defendant's conduct, the plaintiff's injuries would not have occurred.

Skinner v. Square D. Co., 445 Mich. 153, 164-165 (1994) (cause-in-fact cannot be satisfied by a theory that is a mere possibility or suggests a course of events that is, at most, equally as probable as other courses of events).

2)   PROXIMATE CAUSE

A proximate cause is one that in a natural and continuous sequence, unbroken by any new, independent cause, produces the injury, without which such injury would not have occurred. *Weissert v. Escanaba*, 298 Mich. 443, 452 (1941).

a) Jury Issue

Proximate cause is usually a factual issue for the jury to determine. *Schutte v. Celotex Corp.,* 196 Mich. App. 135, 138 (1992).

3) INTERVENING CAUSE

An intervening cause breaks the chain of causation and constitutes a superseding cause which relieves the original actor of liability, unless it is found that the intervening act was "reasonably foreseeable." *E.g., Moning v. Alfono*, 400 Mich. 425, 442 (1977).

a) Medical Malpractice

A jury would be justified in concluding that negligent conduct by a patient in his interaction with another doctor was foreseeable. Similarly, a jury would be justified in concluding that a foreseeable consequence of conduct that leads a plaintiff to seek medical treatment would be negligent medical treatment. *Reed v. City of Detroit*, 108 Mich. 224 (1896) (defendant who negligently injures plaintiff is also liable for further injuries done to plaintiff by the malpractice of a seemingly competent physician engaged to treat the injury); *Stahl v. Southern M. R. Co.,* 211 Mich. 350, 355 (1920) ("If a person receives an injury through the negligent act of another, and the injury is afterwards aggravated, and a recovery retarded through some accident not the result of want of ordinary care on the part of the injured person, he may recover for the entire injury sustained, as the law regards the probability of such aggravation as a consequent and natural result likely to follow from the original injury"); *Gulick v. Kentucky Fried Chicken Mfg. Corp.*, 73 Mich. App. 746, 750 (1977) ("appellants faced potential liability on the principle that they are liable for all foreseeable consequences including that a doctor may act negligently in treating the plaintiff's original injury").

C. Damages

1) CONTRIBUTORY FAULT

Subject to the Michigan's comparative fault (i.e., negligence) statute, in tort actions and other actions seeking damages for personal injury, property damage, or wrongful death, a plaintiff's contributory fault (i.e., negligence) "does not bar that plaintiff's recovery of damages." Mich. Comp. Laws § 600.2958.

2) COMPARATIVE FAULT

Michigan's comparative fault (i.e., negligence) statute generally covers all fault including even intentional conduct as well as any other breach of a legal duty. This statute applies to tort actions and other actions seeking damages for personal injury, property damage, or wrongful death. Mich. Comp. Laws § 600.2959.

a)   Fifty-One Percent Rule

This statute provides that if a plaintiff is at least 51 percent at fault for the plaintiff's injury, then his economic damages are reduced by the percentage of his fault and he cannot recover non-economic damages. *Id.*

(1)   Example

For example, if a jury assigned the plaintiff 55 percent of responsibility for his injury, the comparative fault statute would allow him to recover 45 percent of his economic damages, but would preclude him from recovering any part of his non-economic damages. The remaining 45 percent responsibility for economic damages could be allocated among any other defendants.

b)   Intentional Conduct

In *Lamp v. Reynolds,* the court noted that Michigan's comparative fault statutes define the term "fault" to include intentional conduct. *Lamp v. Reynolds,* 249 Mich. App. 591 (2002); Mich. Comp. Laws § 600.6304(8). It recognized that a Michigan Supreme Court decision rendered prior to the adoption of the current statute had rejected application of comparative fault doctrines where an actor's conduct was intentionally tortious. *Hickey v. Zezulka* (On Resubmission), 439 Mich. 408, 442 (1992). However, the court concluded that "distinguishing types of at-fault conduct is no longer a proper consideration when determining the viability of a comparative fault defense pursuant to the statutes at issue here (MCL 600.2957, 600.2959 and 600.6304)."

3)   TYPES OF DAMAGES

a)   Economic Damages

Economic damages include the expenses of "medical care, rehabilitation services, custodial care, loss of wages, loss of future earnings, burial costs, loss of use of property, costs of repair or replacement of property, costs of obtaining substitute domestic services, loss of employment," and other monetary loss. Mich. Comp. Laws § 600.2945(c).

(1)   Economic Losses -- Physical Injury Requirement

In Michigan, "a plaintiff must demonstrate a present physical injury to person or property *in addition* to economic losses that result from that injury in order to recover under a negligence theory [for economic losses]." *Henry v. Dow Chem. Co.,* 473 Mich. 63 (2005) (emphasis added). The comparative fault statute's definition of economic losses includes certain types of economic damages. Mich. Comp. Laws § 600.2945(c).

b)   Noneconomic Damages

Noneconomic damages include pain, suffering, inconvenience, physical impairment, disfigurement, mental anguish, emotional distress, loss of society and companionship, loss of consortium, injury to reputation, humiliation, or other non-pecuniary damages." Mich. Comp. Laws § 600.2945(f).

4)   SEVERAL LIABILITY

Subject to exceptions for joint and several liability, generally in tort actions and other actions seeking damages for personal injury, property damage, or wrongful death, each defendant's liability for damages is several only and is not joint. Mich. Comp. Laws § 600.2956. This provisions does not, however, abolish the vicarious liability of an employer for an employee's act or omission. *Id.*

5)   JOINT AND SEVERAL LIABILITY

As a result of tort reform in Michigan, joint and several liability generally is barred for the recovery of damages except in cases (1) of medical malpractice when the plaintiff lacks any percentage of fault or (2) when the defendant's act or omission constitutes certain criminal offenses for which the defendant is convicted. Mich. Comp. Laws §§ 600.6304(4), (6)(a), and 600.6312. In the latter case, a "defendant that is found liable for an act or omission that causes personal injury, property damage, or wrongful death is jointly and severally liable if the defendant's act or omission is any of the following: [1)] A crime, an element of which is gross negligence, for which the defendant is convicted. [2)] A crime involving the use of alcohol or a controlled substance for which the defendant is convicted and that is a violation of 1 or more of" certain subject-matter specific statutes. Mich. Comp. Laws § 600.6312.

Although Michigan has abolished joint and several liability for most torts, the statute abolishing joint and several liability does not apply to negligent operation of a motor vehicle under a Michigan Compiled Law. Mich. Comp. Laws § 257.401(1) (discussed later); *Kaiser v. Allen*, 480 Mich. 31 (2008).

III.   NEGLIGENCE ACTIONS

A.   Premises Liability

1)   PRIVATE PREMISES

Michigan law recognizes the three common-law classifications of visitors who enter upon a landowner's premises or land: licensee, invitee, or trespasser. *Stitt v. Holland Abundant Life*, 462 Mich. 591 (2000). The visitor's classification determines the landowner's duty to the visitor. *Id.*

a)   Duty of Care

(1)   Trespasser

(a)   Undiscovered Trespasser

As for an undiscovered trespasser, a landowner must refrain from injuring the undiscovered trespasser by willful and wanton misconduct. *Id.* This misconduct requires either an intent to harm or indifference to whether harm will result that is equivalent of the landowner's willingness that the harm result. *Burnett v. City of Adrian*, 414 Mich. 448 (1982); *James v. Leco Corp.*, 170 Mich. App. 184 (1988).

(2)   Invitee

With regard to premises liability, the duty a property owner owes an invitee is to exercise reasonable care to protect the invitee from an unreasonable risk of harm caused by a dangerous condition on the land. *Bertrand v. Alan Ford, Inc.*, 449 Mich. 606 (1995).

(a)   Open and Obvious Danger

This duty does not require the property owner to protect the invitee from an open and obvious danger that the invitee might reasonably be expected to discover unless that danger has "special aspects" that make the risk unreasonable. *Lugo v. Ameritech Corp., Inc.*, 464 Mich. 512 (2001) (invitor had no duty to protect invitee from pothole in parking lot). A pothole, for example, is likely an open and obvious danger.

(i)   Special Aspects

Special aspects would be characteristics that make the danger extremely difficult to avoid, like a puddle of water located in a position that required an invitee to traverse it to leave a building. "Only those special aspects that give rise to a uniquely high likelihood of harm or severity of harm if the risk is not avoided will serve to remove that condition from the open and obvious danger doctrine." *Lugo, supra.* For example, a puddle in a large bathroom would not be such a hazard since it did not pose an extraordinarily high risk and since it could be avoided by an individual who encountered it.

(b)   Analytical Factors

The open and obvious doctrine attacks the duty element of negligence. *Lugo, supra.* The trial court must determine (1) whether there was an open and obvious condition, and (2) whether there were special aspects of the condition that made it unreasonably dangerous despite being open and obvious. *Lugo, supra.*

(i)   Objective Standard

The determination of whether a condition is open and obvious is governed by an objective standard: "Would an average user with ordinary intelligence have been able to discover the danger and the risk presented upon casual inspection?" *Novotney v. Burger King Corp. (On Remand),* 198 Mich. App. 470 (1993). A danger, however, might be "not discoverable" to people who are not experienced with respect to the circumstances in which it arose.

b)   Third-Party Criminal Conduct

With regard to criminal conduct by a patron, the duty a business operator owes to an invitee is "to respond reasonably to situations occurring on the premises that pose a risk of imminent and foreseeable harm to identifiable invitees." *MacDonald v. PKT, Inc.,* 464 Mich. 322 (2001). The business operator is required to respond by "reasonably expediting the involvement of the police." *MacDonald,* at 326. Past events at the location, even if criminal, do not alter or increase this duty.

2)   PUBLIC PREMISES

When a plaintiff brings a negligence claim arising out of an alleged building defect against a governmental entity, a two-question analysis is warranted. *Johnson v. Detroit,* 457 Mich. 695 (1998).

a)   Public Building Exception to Governmental Immunity

The first question involves whether plaintiff's claim invokes the public building exception to governmental immunity. A governmental agency is generally immune from tort liability if it is engaged in the exercise or discharge of a governmental function. Mich. Comp. Laws § 691.1407(1); *Swell v. Southfield Pub. Schs.,* 456 Mich. 670, 674 (1998). The public building exception to governmental immunity provides:

> Governmental agencies have the obligation to repair and maintain public buildings under their control when open for use by members of the public. Governmental agencies are liable for bodily injury and property damage resulting from a dangerous or defective condition of a public building if the governmental agency had actual or constructive knowledge of the defect and, for a reasonable time after acquiring knowledge, failed to remedy the condition or to take action reasonably necessary to protect the public against the condition.

Mich. Comp. Laws § 691.1406.

(1)   Elements

In order for the public building exception to apply, plaintiff must establish the following:

- a governmental agency is involved;
- the public building in question is open for use by members of the public;
- a dangerous or defective condition of the public building itself exists;
- the governmental agency had actual or constructive knowledge of the alleged

defect, and;

● the governmental agency failed to remedy the alleged defective condition after a reasonable period.

Sewell, supra, at 675.

> b)   Other Considerations

The public building exception can apply to buildings to which the building has limited access and to areas within those buildings that are not open for use by the general public. *Kerberski v. Northern Michigan Univ.*, 458 Mich. 525 (1998).

Invoking the public building exception does not negate traditional tort law principles. *Johnson, supra,* at 710; *Kerbinski, supra,* at 525, n 5. A conclusion that the public building exception applies merely establishes that the government defendant undertook a duty to maintain its public building in good repair. This duty is only a general duty owed to the general public. A plaintiff must still demonstrate the elements of the negligence claim, including the duty owed to the plaintiff under the circumstances. Thus, the second question involves whether plaintiff's can demonstrate the negligence claim elements.

> 3)   ATTRACTIVE NUISANCE DOCTRINE

The Attractive Nuisance Doctrine places liability on landowners for harm sustained by trespassing children. Michigan law follows the five-prong test described in the Torts Outline for the Multistate Bar Exam. 2 *Restatement Torts, 2d*, § 339, p. 197.

> a)   Hazardous Condition Need Not Cause Children's Trespass

"The term 'attractive nuisance' is a misnomer (or historical leftover) because it is not necessary, in order to maintain such an action, that the hazardous condition be the reason that the children came onto the property." *Pippin v. Atallah*, 245 Mich. App. 136, fn. 3 (2001).

B.   Negligent Parental Supervision

In *American States Insurance Company v. Albin,* the court explained the liability for a parent under a negligent parental supervision theory:

> The law in Michigan is that a parent is under a duty to exercise reasonable care so to control his minor children as to prevent them from intentionally harming others or from so conducting themselves as to create an unreasonable risk of bodily harm to them if the parent knows or has reason to know that he has the ability to control his children and knows or should know of the necessity and opportunity for exercising such control.

Am. States Ins. Co. v. Albin, 118 Mich. App. 201, 206 (1982), citing *Dortman v. Lester,* 380 Mich. 80, 84; 155 N.W. 2d 846 (1968), citing *May v. Goulding,* 365 Mich. 143; 111 N.W. 2d

862 (1961); *Muma v. Brown,* 378 Mich. 637; 148 N.W. 2d 760 (1967).

C.   Negligent Infliction of Emotional Distress

1)   GENERAL RULE

To succeed on a claim of negligent infliction of emotional distress, a plaintiff parent would have to show (among other factors) that a defendant acted tortiously towards the parent's child and that the parent suffered physical manifestations of emotional distress caused by seeing the defendant's conduct.

2)   ELEMENTS

In Michigan, to establish a claim for negligent infliction of emotional distress, a plaintiff must establish:

> (1) 'the injury threatened or inflicted on the third person must be a serious one, of a nature to cause severe mental disturbance to the plaintiff'; (2) the shock must result in actual physical harm; (3) the plaintiff must be a member of the immediate family, or at least a parent, child, husband or wife; and (4) the plaintiff must actually be present at the time of the accident or at least suffer shock 'fairly contemporaneous' with the accident.

Wargelin v. Sisters of Mercy Health Corp., 149 Mich. App. 75, 81 (1986), quoting *Gustafson v. Faris,* 67 Mich. App. 363, 368-369 (1976).

a)   Physical Injury Requirement

To recover for negligent infliction of emotional distress, a plaintiff must establish that he suffered "a definite and objective physical injury." *Daley v. LaCroix,* 384 Mich. 4, 12-13 (1970).

D.   Negligent Operation of a Motor Vehicle

Under Michigan law, both the owner and operator of a motor vehicle are liable for "an injury caused by the negligent operation of [a] motor vehicle" if the owner expressly or impliedly consents or knows about the use of the vehicle. Mich. Comp. Laws § 257.401(1).

1)   NON-ECONOMIC DAMAGES

However, as further discussed in the No-Fault Outline, a plaintiff may only recover non-economic damages from the owner or operator of the motor vehicle if the plaintiff has suffered death, serious impairment of body function, or permanent serious disfigurement. Mich. Comp. Laws § 500. 3135(1).

E.   Medical Malpractice

1)   LOSS OF CHANCE OF SURVIVAL

When a plaintiff's action seeks recovery for medical malpractice that caused loss of a chance of survival, "the plaintiff cannot recover for loss of an opportunity to survive or an opportunity to achieve a better result unless the opportunity was greater than 50" percent. Mich. Comp. Laws § 600.2912a(2).

The estate must show that the opportunity to survive was reduced by greater than 50 percent because of the alleged malpractice. *Fulton v. Pontiac Gen. Hosp.,* 253 Mich. App. 70 (2002). In other words, a decedent's estate must show the decedent's chances of survival fell more than 50 percentage points between the time of the alleged malpractice and the discovery of the fatal health condition. Mich. Comp. Laws § 600.2912a(2).

IV.   OTHER TORT ACTIONS

A.   Statutory Conversion

1)   GENERAL RULES

A statutory conversion claim may allow recovery for a plaintiff damaged as a result of another person's buying, receiving, or aiding in the concealment of any stolen, embezzled, or converted property when the person buying, receiving, or aiding in the concealment of any stolen, embezzled, or converted property knew that the property was stolen, embezzled, or converted. Mich. Comp. Laws § 600.2919a. A plaintiff may "recover three times the amount of actual damages, plus costs and reasonable attorney's fees." *Id.* However, there is no provision to compel the return of the stolen items. *Id.*

a)   Limitations on Recovery

A plaintiff may recover only against a person who receives the property with knowledge the property has been stolen, embezzled, or converted. The conversion statute does not, however, allow recovery against the individual who has actually stolen, embezzled, or converted the property (i.e., the actual thief). *Campbell v. Sullins,* 257 Mich. App. 179 (2003). That individual could be subject to criminal liability.

B.   Products Liability

1)   MICHIGAN STATUTES

Products liability is governed by statutes in Michigan. Mich. Comp. Laws § 600.2945 *et seq.* There are two possible causes of action under the statutes. A plaintiff can sue for harm caused by a defective product, Mich. Comp. Laws § 600.2946(2), or harm caused by the manufacturer or seller's failure to warn of a material risk, Mich. Comp. Laws § 600.2948. Two entities that could be liable under the statutes are the seller and the manufacturer of a product by which a plaintiff suffers harm.

a)   Seller Other Than the Manufacturer

Under the statute, a seller other than a manufacturer is only liable if one of the following conditions is met: 1) "[t]he seller failed to exercise reasonable care, including breach of any implied warranty, with respect to the product and that failure was a proximate cause of the person's injuries"; or 2) "[t]he seller made an express warranty as to the product, the product failed to conform to the warranty, and the failure to conform to the warranty was a proximate cause of the person's harm." Mich. Comp. Laws § 600.2947(6).

(1)   Warranty of Merchantability

To be merchantable, among other things, goods must be: 1) fit for the ordinary purpose for which they are used; and 2) of fair average quality within the contract's description of them. Mich. Comp. Laws § 440.2314(2)(b)-(c). Pursuant to the warranty of merchantability, the goods must be of average quality within the industry. *Computer Network, Inc. v. AM Gen. Corp.*, 265 Mich. App. 309 (2005). Merchantable does not mean perfect. *Id.* Generally, other implied warranties may arise from usage of trade or course of dealing. Mich. Comp. Laws § 440.2314(3). Usually, a seller can disclaim (i.e., modify or exclude) the warranty of merchantability. Mich. Comp. Laws § 440.2316(2).

(2)   Warranty for Fitness for a Particular Purpose

Generally, an implied warranty for the goods' fitness for a particular purpose may exist when the seller knows, at the time of sale: 1) the particular purpose for which the buyer requires the goods; and 2) that the buyer is relying on the seller's skill or judgment to select or furnish goods suitable for the purpose. Mich. Comp. Laws § 440.2315. Usually, a seller can disclaim (i.e., modify or exclude) the warranty of fitness for a particular purpose. Mich. Comp. Laws § 440.2316(2).

b)   Manufacturer

Michigan law provides that "[a] manufacturer or seller is not liable in a product liability action for harm caused by misuse of a product unless the misuse was reasonably foreseeable. Whether there was a misuse of a product and whether misuse was reasonably foreseeable are legal issues to be resolved by the court." Mich. Comp. Laws § 600.2947(2). This standard makes such claims more amenable to dismissal on motions because the foreseeability issue is a legal one.

2)   MISUSE OF PRODUCT

A "misuse" is statutorily defined as "use of a product in a materially different manner than the product's intended use. Misuse includes uses inconsistent with the specifications and standards applicable to the product, uses contrary to a warning or instruction provided by the manufacturer, seller, or another person possessing knowledge or training regarding the use or maintenance of the product, and uses other than those for which the product would be considered suitable by a reasonably prudent person in the same or similar circumstances." Mich. Comp. Laws § 600.2945(e).

a)   Example

For example, using a bagel slicer as a general chopping blade for non-food items is unlikely to "be considered suitable by a reasonably prudent person in the same or similar circumstances." Because a Michigan statute is an absolute bar to liability, if it applies in the event of misuse of a product, it would preclude both a failure to warn and a defective product claim by a plaintiff. Mich. Comp. Laws § 600.2947(2).

3)   FAILURE TO WARN

Under Michigan law, "[a] defendant is not liable for failure to warn of a material risk that is or should be obvious to a reasonably prudent product user or a material risk that is or should be a matter of common knowledge to persons in the same or similar position as the person upon whose injury or death the claim is based in a product liability action." Mich. Comp. Laws § 600.2948(2).

a)   Objective Standard

The foregoing statute employs an objective standard and does not require manufacturers to warn of obvious material risks. *Greene v. AP Products,* 475 Mich. 502, 509-510 (2006). In the bagel slicer example, the material risk of breaking the bagel slicer cutting blade while cutting hard non-food items and injuring oneself in the process "should be obvious to a reasonably prudent product user." Thus, there is no duty to warn of that risk.

C.   Michigan's Dramshop Act

1)   LIABILITY FOR SELLING ALCOHOL TO INTOXICATED PERSON

Michigan's Dramshop Act allows a plaintiff injured by a visibly intoxicated person to sue a retail establishment (e.g., tavern, bar) that unlawfully sells alcohol to the visibly intoxicated person, if the unlawful sale is a proximate cause of the plaintiff's injury. Mich. Comp. Laws § 436.1801(3); *Reed v. Breton*, 475 Mich. 531 (2006).

a)   Objective Manifestations of Visible Intoxication Required

Proof of the person's "visible intoxication" requires objective manifestations of the person's intoxication. *Reed, supra; Miller v. Ochampaugh,* 191 Mich. App. 48 (1991). Some common examples of objective manifestations of intoxication include slurring of speech, lack of balance, or change in mood. Circumstantial evidence like the person's blood alcohol content taken after an accident involving the person cannot alone demonstrate that the person was visibly intoxicated. *Reed, supra.*

V.   MISCELLANEOUS CONCEPTS

A.   Vicarious Liability

1)   HOSPITAL AND PHYSICIAN

In general, a hospital is not vicariously liable for the negligence of a physician who is an independent contractor and simply uses the hospital's facilities to provide treatment to his own patients.

a)   Agency by Estoppel

However, if the patient looked to the hospital to provide medical treatment, and the hospital made a representation that medical treatment would be afforded by physicians working at the hospital, an agency by estoppel may be found.

b)   Ostensible Agency

An agency is ostensible when the principal intentionally, or by want of ordinary care, causes a third person to believe him to be the principal's agent when he is not actually employed by the principal.

(1)   Elements

There are three elements necessary to establish the creation of an ostensible agency: 1) the person dealing with the agent must do so with belief in the agent's authority and this belief must be a reasonable one; 2) the belief must be generated by some act or neglect on the part of the principal sought to be charged; and 3) the person relying on the agent's authority must not himself be guilty of negligence.

(a)   Example

In the case of a hospital, as the putative principal it must have done something that would create in a patient's mind the reasonable belief that a doctor who was an independent contractor was acting on behalf of the hospital. The most critical question is whether the patient "looked to" the hospital for treatment.

The fact that a doctor used a hospital's facilities to treat a patient is not sufficient to give the patient a reasonable belief that the doctor was an agent of the hospital. Also, the fact that a doctor has staff privileges at a hospital, by itself, is insufficient to establish an agency relationship.

B.   Release

1)   GENERAL CONSIDERATIONS

A release of liability for negligence is valid if it is fairly and knowingly made. *Wyrembelski v. St. Clair Shores,* 281 Mich. App. 125 (1996). A release that is fairly made will be enforced even if it excuses an actor from liability for negligence. *Xu v. Gay,* 257 Mich. App. 263 (2003). However, if it is obtained by fraudulent or overreaching conduct, it will be void. *Skotak v. Vic*

Tanny Int'l, Inc., 203 Mich. App. 616 (1994).

2)   ENFORCEABILITY

In *Cudnik v. William Beaumont Hospital,* the Michigan Court of Appeals held that, on public policy grounds, a signed release purporting to release a hospital from negligence liability was unenforceable. *Cudnik v. William Beaumont Hosp.,* 207 Mich. App. 378 (1994). This position is held by the overwhelming majority of states that have addressed the question. The Court noted that medical services are of great public importance, are a practical necessity, and that the release was a standardized contract offered by an actor with an advantage in bargaining strength over any member of the public who sought medical services.

In *Paul v. Lee,* the Michigan Supreme Court stated that the holding in *Cudnik* was *not* applicable to its case, but that "we view the language in *Cudnik* suggesting that all covenants not to sue or releases from liability in the context of medical treatment are invalid and unenforceable, even those involving nonessential, nonlife threatening medical treatment, as dicta." *Paul v. Lee,* 455 Mich. 204 (1997). This suggests that the Court would likely apply the factors the *Cudnik* Court specified on a case-by-case basis; the facts of a case could involve treatment for a serious health problem, not the kind of "nonessential nonlife threatening" medical situation covered by the dicta in *Cudnik.*

C.   "Eggshell Skull" Rule

A defendant's unusual weakness does not preclude recognition of the full effect of a plaintiff's tortious conduct on the defendant. The "eggshell skull" rule requires a defendant to take the plaintiff as he finds him. *Wilkinson v. Lee,* 463 Mich. 388 (2000).

D.   Governmental Immunity

1)   THE GOVERNMENT TORT LIABILITY ACT

a)   General Rule

Subject to exception, the Government Tort Liability Act (GTLA) generally protects the State of Michigan, its agencies, their employees, and some other types of related parties from liability for torts that occur while performing certain governmental functions. Mich. Comp. Laws § 691.1401 *et seq.* When suing a defendant covered by the GTLA, a plaintiff must plead in avoidance of governmental immunity.

(1)   Motor Vehicle Exception

One exception to government immunity under the GTLA is the "motor vehicle exception." Mich. Comp. Laws § 691.1405. This provision imposes liability upon a governmental agency for property damage and bodily injury resulting from the negligent operation of a motor vehicle owned by the agency and operated by the agency's agent, officer, or employee. *Id.*

(a)   Pursuing Police Vehicle

The Michigan Supreme Court held that an innocent passenger of a fleeing vehicle could not maintain a claim against the government where "the pursuing police vehicle did not hit the fleeing car or otherwise physically force it off the road or into another vehicle or object." *Robinson v. City of Detroit*, 462 Mich. 439, 457 (2000). The Court also held "that the decision to pursue a fleeing motorist, which is separate from the operation of the vehicle itself, is not encompassed within a narrow construction of the phrase 'operation of a motor vehicle." *Id.*

b)   Requirements for Governmental Immunity and Avoiding It

Also, the Court discussed the requirements for avoiding governmental immunity under the GTLA when suing an individual employee of governmental agency for personal injury or property damage. A government employee and others must meet the following requirements in order to avoid liability for such harm under governmental immunity:

- the employee must be acting, or reasonably believe that he is acting, within the scope of his authority;

- the agency must be engaged in the exercise or discharge of a governmental function; and

- the employee's conduct cannot "amount to gross negligence that is the proximate cause of the injury or damage."

Mich. Comp. Laws § 691.1407(2).

Note that the foregoing requirements also apply to officers of a governmental agency, members of boards, councils, commissions, or statutorily created task forces of a governmental agency who caused such harm during the course of employment or service or a volunteer of such an agency who did so while acting on behalf of the agency. *Id.*

(1)   Gross Negligence

The Court has held that governmental immunity applies "unless the employee's conduct amounts to gross negligence that is the one most immediate, efficient, and direct cause of the injury or damage." *Robinson v. City of Detroit*, 462 Mich. 439, 462 (2000). "Gross negligence" consists of "conduct so reckless as to demonstrate a substantial lack of concern for whether an injury results." Mich. Comp. Laws § 691.1407(7)(a).

(a)   Question of Fact

A question of fact may arise as to whether the government employee was negligent for purposes of the agency's liability and grossly negligent for purposes of his liability. Mich. Comp. Laws §§ 691.1405, 1407(2)(c). For example, a police officer, a governmental employee, is grossly negligent when the police officer uses excessive force to subdue a suspect. Conversely, if the police officer is immune from tort liability, then the police officer's employer is immune.

(b)   Excessive Force

When subduing a suspect, a police officer can use a substantial amount of force that can even result in injury to the suspect, provided that the use of that force was necessary. *Sudul v. Hamtramck*, 221 Mich. App. 485 (1997) citing *Burns v. Malak*, 897 F. Supp. 985 (E.D. Mich. 1995). In order to determine whether or not the amount of force used by a police officer is justified, a court must determine whether or not the force was "objectively reasonable under the circumstances." *VanVorous v. Burmeister*, 262 Mich. App. 467 (2004) citing *Brewer v. Perrin*, 132 Mich. App. 520 (1984). "Police officers . . . must be given a wide degree of discretion in determining what type of action will best ensure the safety of the individuals involved . . . the general public . . . and the apprehension of wrongdoers." *Brown v. Shavers*, 210 Mich. App. 272 (1995) quoting *Ross v. Consumers Power Co.* (on rehearing), 420 Mich. 567 (1984). Therefore, if the court determines that excessive force was used, then the governmental employee has tort liability for the plaintiff's injuries.

c)   Respondent Superior Doctrine

The doctrine of *respondent superior* provides the basis for a municipality's vicarious liability for its employees' torts. Generally, a court can impose vicarious liability only when the individual tortfeasor acted in the course of the individual's employment and within the scope of the individual's authority. *Meadows v. City of Detroit*, 164 Mich. App. 418 (1987), citing *Ross v. Consumers Power Co.* (on rehearing), 420 Mich. 567 (1984).

Made in the USA
Charleston, SC
01 June 2011